"Frail children of dust and feeble as frail,
In thee do we trust, nor find thee to fail;
Thy mercies how tender, how firm to the end,
Our maker, defender, redeemer, and friend."

"O Worship the King, All Glorious Above,"
Robert Grant (1779-1838)

Dust Bound for Heaven

Explorations in the Theology of Thomas Aquinas

Reinhard Hütter

WILLIAM B. EERDMANS PUBLISHING COMPANY
GRAND RAPIDS, MICHIGAN / CAMBRIDGE, U.K.

Published 2012 by
Wm. B. Eerdmans Publishing Co.
2140 Oak Industrial Drive N.E., Grand Rapids, Michigan 49505 /
P.O. Box 163, Cambridge CB3 9PU U.K.

Printed in the United States of America

18 17 16 15 14 13 12   7 6 5 4 3 2 1

Library of Congress Cataloging-in-Publication Data

Hütter, Reinhard, 1958-
     Dust bound for heaven: explorations in the theology
     of Thomas Aquinas / Reinhard Hütter.
          p.   cm.
     Includes bibliographical references (P.   ).
     ISBN 978-0-8028-6741-4 (cloth: alk. paper)
     1. Thomas Aquinas, Saint, 1225?-1274.   I. Title.

B765.T54H88   2012
230′.2092 — dc23
                                                  2012002499

www.eerdmans.com

To

The Thomistic Institute

at

The Pontifical Faculty of the Immaculate Conception
The Dominican House of Studies
Washington, D.C.

Contents

Acknowledgments

This book has grown over the course of the last seven years. After a ten-year pilgrimage of theological searching and probing, my wife and I were received into the full communion of the Catholic Church on the Feast of the Holy Innocents, December 28, 2004. Between then and now, between 2004 and 2011, I became again a student of theology, this time of Catholic theology. On the — to date — seven-year-long journey of becoming a Catholic theologian, I discovered that Thomas Aquinas is still the Common Doctor of the Catholic Church, the Dumb Ox, whose teaching bellows through the ages: "He who has ears to hear, let him hear" (Mt 11:15; RSV). (A brief account of my theological journey into the Catholic Church can be found in *Nova et Vetera: The English Edition of the International Theological Journal* 9/4 [Fall 2011].)

A book like this, which has grown over many years, would be inconceivable without the innumerable conversations that have shaped me and the thoughts that have informed this book. For their various ways of helping me in becoming a better student of Thomas Aquinas, a better Dominican Tertiary, a better Catholic theologian, and last but not least a more faithful Christian, my heartfelt thanks go to Sr. Maria of the Angels, O.P., John F. Boyle, James Brent, O.P., Stephen L. Brock, Romanus Cessario, O.P., †W. Norris Clarke, S.J., Edgardo Colón-Emeric, Archbishop J. Augustine DiNoia, O.P., Gilles Emery, O.P., Josef Freitag, Paul J. Griffiths, Russell Hittinger, Warren Kinghorn, Gregory LaNave, Matthew L. Lamb, Emma Louise Law, Matthew Levering, Steven A. Long, †Edward P. Mahoney, Guy Mansini, O.S.B., Bruce D. Marshall, †Ralph McInerny, Gabriel O'Donnell, O.P., Philip Rolnick, Miguel Romero, Michael Root, Richard Schenk, O.P.,

ACKNOWLEDGMENTS

John O'Callaghan, Michael Sherwin, O.P., Henry Stachyra, Holly Taylor Coolman, Craig Steven Titus, Jörgen Vijgen, Michael Waldstein, Joseph P. Wawrykow, Thomas Joseph White, O.P., Ian C. Willeford, Msgr. John Joseph Williams, and Msgr. John Wippel. I am especially grateful for the wisdom, patience, and good humor of my wife and best friend Nancy Heitzenrater Hütter, without whose unfailing love and support I would not have been able to write this book nor would I be who I am.

I am indebted to the constructive and critical feed-back I received from the academicians of the Pontifical Academy of St. Thomas in regard to earlier versions of two of the following chapters. I am equally indebted to the instructive questions and comments that the faculty and the students at the Dominican House of Studies raised in response to earlier versions of two other chapters that I presented as lectures at the first "Thomistic Circles" conferences. Last but not least, I am indebted to Thomas Joseph White, O.P., who gave me important feedback at the last stage of this project.

I am also grateful to Jon Pott, editor-in-chief at the William B. Eerdmans Publishing Company, for his ongoing interest in my work. Special thanks go to Judith Heyhoe, Colin McGuigan, and Matthew Whelan, without whose constructive comments and criticisms, patient editorial assistance, and able compilation of indices the book would be the poorer.

Some of the chapters in this book have appeared, in earlier forms, in *Nova et Vetera: The English Edition of the International Theological Journal* and *The Thomist*. I thank these journals, as well as T&T Clark International and Eerdmans Publishing Company for granting me permission to reprint material that is included here. For further publication details the reader is directed to the credits at the end of the volume.

I dedicate this book in gratitude to The Thomistic Institute at The Pontifical Faculty of the Immaculate Conception, The Dominican House of Studies, Washington, D.C.

REINHARD HÜTTER
Feast of St. Thomas Aquinas
January 28, 2012

CHAPTER 1

By Way of an Introduction: Thomas Aquinas and Us; or, "Waiting for Thomas"

I. Ressourcement in Thomas Aquinas

This book is an invitation to rediscover the perennial relevance of the theology of Thomas Aquinas, the Common Doctor of the Church. Such an invitation might be met with two objections I want to name up front. There is, first, the objection that after the Enlightenment critique Thomas's thought is irretrievably passé, philosophically as well as theologically, and that any investigation into his thought belongs exclusively to the discipline of historical studies. There is, second, the objection that it is virtually impossible to recover a sense of Thomas's culture and wherewithal in order to reclaim him as the Common Doctor.

The first is a modern secular objection. It goes roughly like this: At the beginning of the twenty-first century, what could be more irrelevant, inconsequential, unpromising, and, in short, hopeless than returning to the theology of Thomas Aquinas? Has Thomas's theology not been put decisively to the side by Protestant theologians since the Reformation and by Catholic theologians since the Second Vatican Council? Has Thomas's philosophy not died the death of a thousand qualifications since the dawning of modernity — that is, since the days of Bacon, Hume, Kant — and especially since the more recent ascendancy of postmodernity — under the aegis of Nietzsche, Heidegger, Derrida, and Wittgenstein? My answer will clearly be to affirm Thomas's thought, and this I do at length in the prelude, "Faith and Reason."

The second objection voices a kind of MacIntyrean reservation, a reservation that is not infrequently held by those who hold Thomas Aquinas in high esteem. I would like to flesh this objection out by giving voice to an author who deserves to be remembered and read again more broadly. In his recently republished *The Restoration of Christian Culture*,[1] John Senior forcefully points out what he regards to be the practical difficulty, indeed, impossibility of a full recovery of Thomas Aquinas as the Common Doctor.

First, he asks where the kind of students who would be the "beginners" whom Thomas intends to teach, especially with his masterwork, the *Summa theologiae*, are to be found.[2] Being attuned since elementary school to multitasking on a laptop while listening to their iPods, contemporary "beginners" in theology are increasingly unaccustomed to and unfit for the practices of silence, prayer, and meditation, the art of reading slowly and attentively, and the training of the memory — skills and practices indispensable for rigorous philosophical and theological contemplation. Also, it does not help that college, seminary, and university curricula that would foster these skills and practices in the context of a coherent, teleologically ordered philosophical and theological education belong largely to the past.

Second, and worse, it seems that the kind of culture that once made possible a Thomas Aquinas, a Fra Angelico, and a Dante Alighieri has irreversibly disappeared. Senior puts it as drastically as precisely:

> St. Thomas is still the Common Doctor of the Church but there aren't many common Catholics. The whole of Christian Culture, the seedbed of scholastic art and science, is depleted. We are in a dustbowl, as the Kansans used to say, and if you plant wheat, though it may sprout up, it will almost instantly wither in the drought. There are many times in

---

1. John Senior, *The Restoration of Christian Culture* (Norfolk, VA: IHS Press, 2008 [1983]). John Senior (1923-1999) was a Classics professor and well-known Catholic writer of international reputation. From 1969 to 1979 he taught in the Integrated Humanities Program of the University of Kansas. His books include *The Way Down and Out* (1959), *The Death of Christian Culture* (1978), *The Restoration of Christian Culture* (1983), *Pale Horse, Easy Rider* (1992), and *The Idea of a School* (1994).

2. "A few uncommon and relatively unknown, and old, theologians still study and teach St. Thomas, but he is no longer received as the Common Doctor of the Church. The *Summa Theologiae*, St. Thomas himself says in the Prologue, is a book 'for beginners'; but we have few real beginners anymore. Our schools and colleges turn out advanced technicians in what are called the arts and sciences, but none has the ordinary prerequisites to traditional philosophical and theological study, none with the famous *mens sana in corpore sano* of the ancients, that is, disciplined in the perception, memory, and imagination of reality" (Senior, *Restoration of Christian Culture*, p. 73).

history, as in life, when the most difficult virtue of patience must be practiced with a cheerful heart; we must even, as Chaucer says, "counterfeite cheer," sure as we are in the knowledge that, as Milton put it, in the sonnet on his blindness, "They also serve who only stand and wait."[3]

Acknowledging the truth of Senior's diagnosis, I do submit the following explorations into the theology of the Common Doctor as simply a mode of patiently and actively "waiting for Thomas." This waiting occurs in the context of Western Civilization in its late modern state, a state in which Christians and especially theologians find themselves not infrequently in the role of Kierkegaard's clown in the village. In his 1968 *Introduction to Christianity*, Joseph Ratzinger offers a pithy summary of what Kierkegaard intends to be a parable:

> According to this story a travelling circus in Denmark had caught fire. The manager thereupon sent the clown, who was already dressed and made-up for the performance, into the neighbouring village to fetch help, especially as there was a danger that the fire would spread across the fields of dry stubble and engulf the village itself. The clown hurried into the village and requested the inhabitants to come as quickly as possible to the blazing circus to help put the fire out. But the villagers took the clown's shouts simply for an excellent piece of advertising, meant to attract as many people as possible to the performance; they applauded the clown and laughed till they cried. The clown felt more like weeping than laughing; he tried in vain to get people to be serious, to make it clear to them that it was not a trick but bitter earnest, that there really was a fire. His supplications only increased the laughter; people thought he was playing his part splendidly — until finally the fire did engulf the village, it was too late for help and both circus and village were burned to the ground.[4]

Joseph Ratzinger — now Pope Benedict XVI — rightly emphasizes that despite this tragic-comic miscommunication, there is a deep, hidden connection between the clown and the villagers as well as between believers and unbelievers. While the modern unbeliever is inevitably looking for

---

3. Senior, *Restoration of Christian Culture*, p. 75.

4. Joseph Ratzinger, *Introduction to Christianity*, trans. J. R. Foster (London: Search Press, 1969), pp. 15f. The German original, *Einführung in das Christentum*, appeared in 1968.

something in which to have ultimate faith, the modern believer is always threatened by "the insecurity of his own faith, the oppressive power of unbelief in the midst of his own will to believe."[5] In short, in the middle of tragic-comic misunderstandings, the modern believer and the modern unbeliever often understand each other better than it might at first appear. To put it differently, the very indetermination of the late modern supermarket of ideas opens the opportunity for moments of a fresh receptivity for insights the Common Doctor has to offer to those who are in search of perspectives that are trustworthy and well-framed. The late modern deconstruction of all objective standards of judgment leaves the human mind tangibly unsatisfied. While many simply drift, for a growing number this dissatisfaction turns into the hungry search for the real possibility of a perennial wisdom. This book is written in the confidence that Thomas is still today able to guide this search and lead the seekers of a sapiential perspective up-stream to the source of all wisdom.

My explorations into the theology of Thomas Aquinas are an invitation to catch a glimpse of what makes his theology "original" in the classical sense, that is, what makes his teaching a conduit to the origin, to the source of all wisdom and goodness itself, and what makes him, consequently, the Common Doctor. My hope is that such a "ressourcement" in Thomas's theology will eventually allow theology to reclaim the dignity of its proper origin, a theology that would again be worthy of its surpassingly excellent and noble subject matter — and hence of its name. Such a ressourcement in Thomas can be nothing but a "waiting for Thomas." And while we wait as patiently and actively as we can, we do not miss any opportunity for formation that offers itself. And the opportunities for such a formation have greatly increased in the last two decades, because help has come from a direction that neither Joseph Ratzinger was able to foresee in 1968 nor even John Senior in 1983 — the most remarkable revival of academic Aquinas scholarship in the course of the last twenty years.

II. How a Ressourcement in Thomas Differs from a Revival of Aquinas Scholarship

Over the last two decades, there has occurred a most remarkable and unexpected revival of scholarly interest in Thomas's philosophy and theology.

5. Ratzinger, *Introduction to Christianity*, p. 17.

For the most part the historical, interpretive, and reconstructive work done on virtually all aspects of Thomas's thought has been rigorous scholarship at the highest level of academic standards. At a first glance, this revival of Aquinas scholarship seems to immaterialize the concern that the present spiritual, intellectual, and cultural conditions are fundamentally adverse to any serious reception of Thomas's teaching. At a second and more considered glance, however, it becomes quickly obvious that a revival of rigorous Aquinas scholarship does not necessarily translate into a genuine, substantive, and normative turning to Thomas's philosophical and theological vision. There is no causal relationship between a revival of scholarly attention to Aquinas and a ressourcement in the philosophy and theology of the Common Doctor. On the contrary, the way the modern academy tends to function, the revival of Aquinas scholarship might — unwittingly — bury even deeper Thomas's teaching as that of the *doctor communis*. It all depends on whether the end of the inquiry is Thomas as an eminent figure of thought, or what eminently preoccupied Thomas's thought and what is found in his teaching. The latter and only the latter is a true ressourcement.

While I gratefully draw upon the currently burgeoning Aquinas scholarship (see the fourth section of this introduction), I understand this book as an exercise in ressourcement in which I explore Thomas's theology as a path to the source of perennial wisdom, a path that if traveled again more frequently will lead to an overdue theological renewal after a dire period of pervasive theological fragmentation and disorientation.[6] The contemporary theological eye has grown accustomed to the spiritual dusk and even darkness cast by the modern secular culture and hence can hardly stand in the spiritual noon-day light of thirteenth-century Christian intellectual contemplation. A ressourcement in Thomas's theology should, I would hope, contribute to recovering the vision of a theology strong-eyed, high-spirited, and disciplined enough in the practices of prayer and meditation to gaze again at the dazzling light of divine truth: "In lumine tuo videbimus lumen" (Ps 36:9[10]).

John Senior aptly names the substantive reasons why a ressourcement in Thomas's theology is categorically different from even the best Aquinas scholarship, why the former claims the theologian qua theologian while the latter lures the theologian qua scholar:

---

6. See my article "The Ruins of Discontinuity," *First Things* 209 (January 2011): 37-41.

[R]epeatedly affirmed by successive popes over so long a time, with no dissent, as an infallible teaching of the Ordinary Magisterium, the *Summa Theologiae* is the norm and measure of all Catholic theology before and since. Catholics must believe Thomas Aquinas to be the Common Doctor of the Church with the same degree of certainty that he is a saint. Saints Augustine, Gregory, Bernard, Bonaventure, John of the Cross and others are Doctors also, precious, good, beloved, indispensable and intensely personal to many, but all are measured by the ordinary rule of St. Thomas and read by his light. I don't say *in*, because they have lights of their own, but *by* his light. St. Thomas holds a special place among theologians analogous to that of the Blessed Virgin among saints: he holds the mean between dogma and opinion, what we might call hyper-doxy, as Mary by hyperdulia holds the mean between veneration and worship. Unlike the Mother of God, St. Thomas is theoretically surpassable; and, of course, the Church has never taught that every syllable of the *Summa* is *de fide* like the Creed.[7]

It is the designation "Common Doctor" that makes the small but important difference between Aquinas scholarship and a ressourcement in Thomas. The following explorations are an invitation to rediscover Thomas as the *doctor communis.* They are written in service of a ressourcement that in turn stands in service of the Faith.

However, I am only too keenly aware of the fact that in order to sustain such a ressourcement over a longer period, some other things are needed — a coherent philosophical and theological curriculum *ad mentem S. Thomae,* a body of teachers competent and dedicated to implement such a curriculum, gifted students dedicated to the arduous task of being "beginners" under the tutelage of Thomas Aquinas, a way of apostolic life and witness of which study and contemplation are integral components, and last but not least an institution that enables, coordinates, and fosters such an ambitious and complex intellectual endeavor. It is for this very reason that I have dedicated this volume to the Thomistic Institute of the Pontifical Faculty of the Immaculate Conception at the Dominican House of Studies in Washington, D.C. In Dominican life, there is an aspiration toward the unity of proclamation and contemplation, of prayer and study, to which this volume aspires as well.

Let me now turn to the substance of the explorations themselves.

---

7. Senior, *Restoration of Christian Culture,* p. 80.

The main body of the book is dedicated to the topic announced in the title: "Dust bound for heaven": Thomas's philosophical and theological doctrine of the human being — the constitution of the human as a hylemorphic body-soul unity and the ordination of the human being to eternal communion with God — forms a currently most pertinent portal into the depths of Thomas's theology. However, these primarily anthropological concerns are framed by a prelude in which I attend to what I regard to be the intellectual urgency that makes a "waiting for Thomas" imperative, and a postlude that brings into focus the Christological heart of the matter, the core of Thomas's theology.

III. The Course the Explorations Take; or, Dust Bound For Heaven

My prelude, "Faith and Reason," comprises one single chapter, "Is There a Cure for Reason's Presumption and Despair? — Why Thomas Matters Today." Here I pursue a twofold purpose: first, I offer a more extensive account of why Thomas matters today, both philosophically and theologically. And while the philosophical and theological reasons for Thomas's ongoing relevance are clearly distinct, they are still two sides of the same coin. We, that is, Christians in what has come to be called the "West," are currently experiencing a dramatic crisis of reason and an equally dramatic crisis of faith. That these two crises coincide is far from accidental, and, according to Thomas, the coincidence of such crises is actually to be expected. The modern self-enclosure of reason into the realm of the empirical, the mechanical, the quantifiable, and the instrumental has not only debased reason but dehumanized the human being. At the same time, the equally modern banishment of reason from the center of the faith has made a mockery of God, while rendering his Word as transrational or, even worse, irrational. If the Reformation theologians had the tendency to banish the natural light of reason as much as possible from the enterprise of Christian theology, with the Enlightenment, this tendency was not only reversed. Rather, the type of reason the Enlightenment thinkers brought back was also changed. Called back from its exile, reason took an unprecedented revenge. Significant strands of Protestant (and even Catholic) theology became rationalistic in a way and to a degree absolutely foreign to the medieval scholastics. One defining characteristic of human life under the conditions of post-Enlightenment modernity is that faith and reason are divorced from and at war with each other: here Hegel, there Kierkegaard. The crisis of the one is the crisis of the other, wherefore they can overcome their respective crises only together. And it is precisely for this reason that Thomas matters today. For he arguably remains the surpassing teacher of two lessons late modernity is in urgent need to re-learn: First, the lesson of faith's centrality for reason's best exercise. Successful discursive reasoning presupposes the proper interplay of intellect and will. Because the will is profoundly affected by the reality of sin, reason's best exercise depends on the will's healing and restoration. Second, the lesson of reason's importance for faith's full flourishing. Contemplating the mysteries of the faith in order to seek understanding is greatly aided by the exercise of reason in its inherent openness to transcendence. For it is this metaphysical and contemplative exercise of reason in the service of the faith that protects the faith from suffering two perennial distortions that arise from the legitimate opposition to the sovereignty of Enlightenment rationality — fideism and traditionalism: Fideism conceives faith as an essentially pre-linguistic and pre-rational personal experience that yearns for ever new and ever changing authentic symbolic expression, while traditionalism regards faith as an always already cultural-linguistic "given" that is mediated by a doctrinal-liturgical structure embracing a comprehensive way of life.

In order to operate at its full metaphysical range, reason cannot afford to ignore the mysteries of the faith. For, while they transcend reason, they do not contradict reason, but rather offer reason the most eminent subject-matter to turn to and thereby discover both its full range as well as its limit. Thus, while reason protects the exercise of faith from falling into fideism and traditionalism, faith protects the exercise of reason from submitting to the two perennial excesses to which reason is prone under the condition of modernity — the pride of hyperrationalism and the despair of irrationalism.

The prelude suggests that there is no better place to recover from the twofold crisis of faith and the twofold crisis of reason than by entering the school of the Common Doctor and by reconsidering the full vision of the human nature and destiny that underlies Thomas's theology: the anthropological call to glory. What has fallen apart notoriously and to our great loss in modern theological and philosophical anthropology is held in a surpassing balance and synthesis in Thomas's thought. The human being is neither animal nor angel; neither a unique configuration of cosmic dust destined to return just to that, dust; nor a spirit or mind that in its essence, the *res cogitans,* never really left the community of angelic spirits and is only accidentally and therefore tragically embodied. The human being is indeed made of dust, but divinely informed and configured by a rational soul that ordains this piece of dust for heaven, for the eternal communion with God. How to hold these utter extremes together without losing, repressing, or even ever so slightly neglecting the specificity of each of these co-constitutive principles of human nature is an urgent lesson for which Thomas serves as a most helpful guide and mentor.

The first section of the main part of the book, "Human Nature, Wounded but Not Destroyed," comprises two chapters that consider the resourcefulness of Thomas's thought in light of two realities central to human flourishing but in a state of crisis in late modernity: the constructive role of human affectivity in "body politics" and the indispensable role of the natural love of God for a flourishing of the common good in democratic politics.

In chapter 3, "Body Politics beyond Angelism and Animalism," I consider an aspect of human reality that profoundly shapes human life and is a major cause for its success and failure, for happiness and misery — the complex and elusive reality of human affectivity, what Thomas together with the premodern tradition called "passions." Reducing human affectivity to the results of bodily bio-chemical processes or rethinking human affectivity as irreducible experiences in the life of the mind are the pitfalls of a modern anthropology that vacillates uneasily between materialism and idealism. Thomas's astute and expansive theological adaptation of Aristotelian hylemorphism into a subtle and balanced account of the indispensable role of human affectivity for full human flourishing points the way forward. Instead of being perilous to the operations of faith and reason, Thomas regards human affectivity as an indispensable component of full human flourishing. The effective exercise of reason and the life of faith indeed rely on the proper functioning of human affectivity. This proper functioning itself, however, is the result of reason exercising an indispensable political rule over the passions and of the virtues, acquired or infused, schooling the passions in a way that they become increasingly amenable to reason's political rule over them. Far from repressing and neutralizing the passions, the end of reason's political rule over them is their proper flourishing as ordered to the human ordination to communion with God. Without the strong sound-board of human affectivity, the operations of faith and reason would remain fragile and feeble. Like violin strings without the body of the instrument, faith and reason would lack the vibrancy and strength that only human affectivity can provide. Simultaneously, in light of human destiny, human affectivity must be formed, indeed transformed, for the passions have the power to undermine as well as underscore the human ordination to communion with God. In short, only when the irreducible spiritual dimension of human affectivity is fully recovered, will theological anthropology become invulnerable to the equally pernicious tendencies of early modernity to reduce the human to the mind and of late modernity to reduce the human to the body.

Chapter 4, "Democracy after Christendom," is a small exercise in Thomist political theology. Aristotle teaches and Thomas agrees that the human being is an irreducibly social and political animal. Hence, a contemporary consideration of "dust bound for heaven" along Thomas's lines would go seriously amiss if it were lacking any reflection on the political implications of human nature and destiny. One of the questions that has haunted modern political theory and politics since the Enlightenment and with increased intensity since the mutual destruction of the modern European colonial empires during the cataclysmic First World War, is what constitutional democracies are to be like after the demise of Christendom as the dominant religious, cultural, and political source that assured the fundamental moral consensus of European and American societies. Current instantiations of such post-Christendom democratic societies vacillate uneasily between an aggressively anti-religious, laicist, sovereign secularism, a religiously indifferent, mere liberalism, and fledgling attempts at a theologically enlightened, genuine liberalism. Reflecting on his recent visit to Great Britain, arguably one of the most secular societies of contemporary Europe, Pope Benedict XVI offered some pertinent remarks that hit the very heart of a problem for which Thomas's thought remains a vital resource:

> Alexis de Tocqueville, in his day, observed that democracy in America had become possible and had worked because there existed a fundamental moral consensus which, transcending individual denominations, united everyone. Only if there is such a consensus on the essentials can constitutions and law function. This fundamental consensus derived from the Christian heritage is at risk wherever its place, the place of moral reasoning, is taken by the purely instrumental rationality of which I spoke earlier. In reality, this makes reason blind to what is essential. To resist this eclipse of reason and to preserve its capacity for seeing the essential, for seeing God and man, for seeing what is good and what is true, is the common interest that must unite all people of good will. The very future of the world is at stake.[8]

8. *Address of His Holiness Benedict XVI on the Occasion of Christmas Greetings to the Roman Curia,* December 20, 2010; Vatican website.

Can all people of good will be truly united without the Christian faith somehow informing and instructing them in the shape of some democratic neo-Christendom? Or is the consensus of all people of good will best secured by a liberal state that protects its citizens as much as possible from the intrusion of religion into the privacy of their lives while some public vestiges of religious presence might be tolerated — mere liberalism? Or can all people of good will only be united in a political configuration "after religion," in a post-religious, truly enlightened polity in which political engineering guided by applied natural and social sciences creates a brave new world unencumbered by the prejudices and inhibitions of outmoded religious worldviews — sovereign secularism? Post-Christendom sovereign secularism (an anti-religious and at bottom atheistic form of "laicism") and mere liberalism (paternalistically tolerant of Judaism and domesticated versions of Islam), in short, the two faces of the Janus-like Enlightenment daydream of the inherent goodness of the natural, pre-political man, struggle over the soul and heart of Europe and, indeed, the whole western world. The vision lost in-between (due to its inherent fragility) is a theologically enlightened, genuine liberalism — a liberalism characterized by a keen awareness of two truths about human beings that when unattended wreak havoc and eventually undermine free societies. These two truths are, first, an understanding of the inherent moral and political fragility of the human being and the need for resources and practices essential for the sort of character formation necessary for any genuine democracy; and second, an understanding that such resources and practices need to be of a religious, familial, and cultural nature that a constitutional, democratic state can neither produce nor prescribe. Inspired and guided by Vatican II's vision of the Church's role in the modern world, Popes Paul VI, John Paul II, and Benedict XVI have outlined in theory and in practice how the Church's proximate political vocation consists in encouraging, fostering, and defending such a theologically enlightened, genuine liberalism. However, it is Thomas who offers the philosophical and theological resources that allow us to understand why democracy after Christendom requires for its own survival, let alone flourishing, nothing less than such a theologically enlightened, genuine liberalism. Thomas's astute anthropology gives us reasons to see why mere liberalism — theologically unenlightened as it is — will always eventually decline into sovereign secularism, an anti-religious framework that is bent upon occluding those religious, familial, and cultural sources upon which a genuinely free society relies for its flourishing. The modern political vacillation between the false optimism of a puerile, revolutionary utopianism and the equally false pessimism of a cynically refined, quietist fatalism reflects modernity's philosophical and theological failure properly to understand the human condition and call to glory. The aim of chapter 4, then, is to point to the resources Thomas's theological anthropology offers to account for the unique human condition that requires us to hold together in one vision the notion of "all people of good will" with the recognition that human nature is seriously wounded in intellect, will, and affectivity such that the "zoon politikon," the "political animal," stands in need of profound healing, a healing that is intrinsically linked to the practice of "religio." Thomas's profound reflections on the natural love for God and the wounds of human nature consequent upon sin afford a theological reading, and indeed critique, of modern liberalism and secularism. The critical as well as constructive perspective that Thomas's theological anthropology affords, offers last but not least a distinct and salutary perspective on the Church's proximate political vocation in the wake of "democracy after Christendom."

"Created for Happiness — Bound for Heaven" comprises chapters 5 and 6. Here I address the very heart of the matter at stake in human nature's ordination to glory. It is the question of the natural desire for the vision of God, a question that with the distinct but closely related topics of "nature and grace," "nature and the supernatural," and "creation and redemption" has preoccupied much, if not all of Catholic theology since the Reformation, and has — most often unbeknownst to its protagonists — haunted much of Protestant theology. While it may be argued that there are two distinct strands discernible in the history of theology, each strand understands the human call to glory in marked difference from the other. The first strand holds that there is an insatiable thirst in humanity for God, a thirst that sends all humans onto an irrepressible religious quest and that can only be quenched by the vision of God, and a thirst for transcendence that sits at the root of every religion and that, when met by the universal grace that effuses from Christ's atoning death for all humanity, will lead humanity sooner or later, but infallibly, to its final destination — the vision of God. (Jesuit theologians like Molina et al. and eventually Henri de Lubac, Hans Urs von Balthasar, and in a radicalized version the sophiology of Sergius Bulgakov have their place here; a sophisticated Anglican version of it can be found in the work of John Milbank.) The second strand claims that the human dust, ensouled but mortally wounded after the fall, must be soteriologically re-created and become a "new creation" all the way down ontologically to be readied for heaven. For if the original ordination toward God is lost, corrupt human nature is bereft of any trace of a tangible desire for the vision of God. Only the elect, those for whom Christ died on the Cross in a limited atonement, will be restored by an irresistible act of grace. Once healed by that efficacious and irresistible grace, the elect — and only they — will display an elicited, active desire for the vision of God. Because of their status as elect and because of the irresistibility of grace, this desire will eventually terminate in its fulfillment, the eternal communion with God. (Jansenism and the traditional forms of Lutheranism, Calvinism, and all versions of Calvinistically inspired Evangelicalism have their home here.)

Both these construals of the natural desire for the vision of God are commonly encountered, but both have significant shortcomings. Attending to Thomas's profound and complex philosophical and theological synthesis allows us to come to understand why they fall short of the mark and why Thomas's own solution, as astute as it is subtle, could be claimed and, in consequence, misunderstood by each of the above strands. While in chapter 5 I attend primarily to the task of adumbrating the two strands, in chapter 6 I advance a reading of Thomas that accounts for the superiority of his position over against both strands.

Chapter 5, "Palaeothomism? — The Continuing Debate over the Natural Desire for the Vision of God," takes stock of a remarkable turn in the debate between the two strands. For more than forty years Henri de Lubac's position enjoyed the status of the received *opinio communis* of most theologians and seemed to have settled the matter once and for all. In recent years, however, critics of Henri de Lubac's teaching on the natural desire for the vision of God have raised substantive objections to his construal of the history of the question, as well as to the philosophical coherence and theological validity of his position. The single most important intervention that effectively unsettled the status quo is a scholarly study as massive as meticulous by Lawrence Feingold. In a spirited attack the Anglican theologian John Milbank dismissed Feingold's critique of Henri de Lubac as an ill-conceived exercise in "palaeothomism." Mapping this recent debate onto the richer and wider theological and doctrinal canvas of Catholic theology sets the stage for chapter 6, "Thomist Ressourcement — A Rereading of Thomas on the Natural Desire for the Vision of God." Here I attend to the task of demonstrating two things. First, that it is impossible to read Thomas as a straightforward representative of the first or the second strand and, second, that Thomas's own approach is rather a subtle way of weaving versions of both strands together without fusing them or reducing one to the other, the first strand serving a primarily metaphysical, the second a primarily theological purpose. At the end of the day, when closely read and carefully considered, Thomas comes out far ahead of the alternatives that are predominantly considered in contemporary theology. In light of Thomas's superior solution, contemporary theologians can begin to reflect on the respective merits and demerits of the two dominant strands presently in operation. For the human call to glory can come into view without distortion, inflation, or reduction only if viewed in light of considering simultaneously these two constitutive principles, nature and destiny — or constitution and ordination — that remain irreducible to each other.

In my third section, "Bound to Be Free, Suffering Divine Things — Grace and the Theological Virtues," the insights gained in the first two sections begin to pay off. Given Thomas's insistence upon the ordination of humanity to an end and fulfillment that infinitely transcends human nature, the question arises as to how God leads human beings to this end without frustrating God's will and without destroying human freedom. Chapter 7, "Thomas the Augustinian — Recovering a Surpassing Synthesis of Grace and Free Will," is dedicated to this topic. Considering the order of salvation, what is the relationship between divine and human causality (or in more recent parlance, agency)? Or differently put, the relationship between divine grace and human freedom? This question has haunted Christian theology at least since Augustine's argument with Pelagius and the monks of Cassiacum, a question that after having been put to rest by Augustine's arguments and authority for about a millennium (save for minor rumblings) erupted with wild force during the Reformation and has never fully quieted down since.

Thomas offers a surpassing synthesis of the various concerns that typically divide the contending parties of this question — the honor of divine sovereignty and integrity of human freedom — such that the dead ends they produce, versions of determinism and fatalism on the one side, and versions of divine dependency on human causality/agency on the other side are effectively overcome. I argue that the way Thomas correlates divine grace and human freedom in the act of conversion remains a surpassing criterion, that is, an indispensable "golden thread" if one wants to find an exit from the maze of the early modern discussion on "grace and free will" since the Dominican-Jesuit controversy "De auxiliis" at the turn of the sixteenth to the seventeenth century, and the roughly contemporaneous debate between Calvinists and Arminians.

Thomas employs two important concepts in his surpassing Augustinian synthesis: first, the concept of transcendent causality/agency (the notion of the non-competition of divine and human causality/agency in the general outlines of the metaphysics of being adumbrated already in chapter 2); second — and one of utmost importance to grasp — the difference between the call to glory being an orientation of all human beings inscribed into their created constitution (in other words, being in potency to its fulfillment) and the call to glory being an event in motion (a potency reduced to act). According to Thomas, the efficacious actualization of this orientation belongs exclusively to the causality of grace, operative and habitual.

But does Thomas's teaching on grace, and especially on sanctifying grace as a reality not only in, but of the faithful, stand a chance in light of the biblical witness and of contemporary Catholic teaching? Is it still possible and indeed desirable to conceive faith, hope, and charity as infused habits, as supernatural dispositions effected by sanctifying grace? Is the true theological life coming from above taking a hold of the believer like a second nature that eventually cleanses, heals, and perfects whatever has been wounded, diminished, and distorted in the believer — or is the Christian life, the life of faith, hope, and charity, essentially nothing but the redemption and rectification of the natural moral life wounded by sin? In chapter 8, "In Hope He Believed Against Hope — The Unity of Faith and Hope in Paul, Thomas, and Benedict XVI," I demonstrate how Thomas's account of faith and hope as supernatural, infused virtues does indeed unlock the central thrust of the most recent magisterial teaching on faith and hope as found in Pope Benedict XVI's encyclical letter *Spe salvi*. Moreover and more importantly, Thomas's account of faith and hope as theological virtues opens a particular theological avenue to reading the Apostle Paul on faith and hope that avoids some of the modern exegetical tendencies of reducing faith and hope to mere existential attitudes, tendencies against which *Spe salvi* most explicitly turns. Thomas's understanding of faith and hope as virtues given from above by way of sanctifying grace affords a much deeper theological appreciation of faith and hope, as they arguably command the center of the teaching of the Apostle Paul as well as that of *Spe salvi*: while being fiducial and existential, in faith and hope the Christian already participates inchoately in the very divine object of faith and hope. And it is the inchoate participation in the divine reality that faith and hope convey that offers a uniquely pertinent message of hope to modernity in crisis, an offer that accounts for and gives perspective to human existence *in statu viatoris,* as wayfarers, "dust bound for heaven."

In chapter 9, "A Forgotten Truth? — Theological Faith, Source and Guarantee of Theology's Inner Unity," I continue to explore the implications of a full recovery of faith as an infused theological virtue by way of which the believer, guided by the light of faith and under the impulse of grace, assents to the divine truth and thereby inchoately participates in the object of faith. If Thomas is right about the nature of faith as ultimately divine faith, that is, divinely caused and inchoately participating in the divine truth, faith must have a profound impact on theology — on what it is in categorical distinction from philosophy, from religious studies, and for that matter, from any contemporaneous academic instantiation of what "humanities" are — and on how theology operates as a coherent but internally differentiated whole. By way of comparing two recent ways of conceiving the task of theology — each holding paradigmatically the place for a comprehensive and normative vision — I argue that a robust account of theological faith along the lines conceived by Thomas is indispensable in order to overcome the present deplorable fragmentation and dissipation of theology and to recover its inherent unity, which is first and foremost sapiential. In light of the pervasive contemporary balkanization of theology into a host of largely heterogeneous inquiries that are at best extrinsically brought into proximity for the pragmatic purpose of "training for ministry," I recommend Thomas's vision of sacred teaching, informed by theological faith, as a relevant resource for recovering that unity of theology that is to be realized *in* each of its integral parts. The metaphysical concept of the potential whole proves to be of surprising pertinence in addressing the current typical but detrimental ways in which the unity of theology is misconceived; that is, either as a mixed bag of essentially pre-theological inquiries that are eventually brought together as a "theological" training-program for ministry, or as a conglomeration of discrete "theologies" or sub-disciplines that claim "to do theology" on their own. In contrast to these reductive ways of conceiving the unity of theology, theology as a potential whole means that all disciplines are essentially theological but not in the same way and to the same degree of perfection. Without an appreciation of the indispensable role of theological faith for the proper ordering of the theological disciplines, even the concept of the potential whole will remain without much usefulness. The problem strikes me as going deep, and the only remedy I see to recover the proper unity of theology in all its parts (that is, as a potential whole) is by way of recovering the central role of theological faith that makes theology first and foremost sapiential, faith seeking understanding, and thereby achieving an inchoate intellectual participation in the mystery to which we give assent in faith.

Following right on the heels of the treatment of the sapiential nature of theology, the fourth and final section, "Seeking Truth — Wisdom and Contemplation," comprises two chapters in which I expand my appeal to *sapientia* in two directions.

First, in chapter 10, "The Wisdom of Analogy Defended — From Effect to Cause, from Creation to God," I attend to the complex and often misunderstood way in which the pursuit of philosophical wisdom plays an auxiliary, though indispensable, role in Thomas's theology. The best way to understand this complex role of philosophical contemplation in service of sapiential theology is by attending to Thomas's doctrine of analogy. And the best way of giving an accessible account of this admittedly difficult and controversial aspect of his thought seems to be to defend and illuminate it in light of the most important criticism against it proffered by Protestant theologians in the twentieth century — Wolfhart Pannenberg and Eberhard Jüngel. By way of this approach it becomes clear how and why Thomas's doctrine can be misunderstood and become open to attack. At the same time, this contrastive approach brings to the fore the theological, metaphysical, and logical principles and arguments available in Thomas's thought to counter these prominent criticisms. It is philosophical *sapientia* in service of a sapiential theology that allows Thomas to plumb the depths the way he does and that opens paths to address the difficulties raised by the criticisms of Pannenberg and Jüngel. Rightly understood, the analogy of being is not an invention of the Anti-Christ (Karl Barth), but indeed reflective of the kind of wisdom the metaphysics of being affords.

Second, in chapter 11, "Seeking Truth on Dry Soil and under Thornbushes — God, the University, and the Missing Link: Wisdom," I turn from asking what the role of philosophical contemplation plays in service of theology, sapientially conceived, to the role philosophical contemplation plays in the service of all other pursuits of knowledge as undertaken in the modern research university. By engaging the thought of two eminent Thomist philosophers, Alasdair MacIntyre and Benedict Ashley, O.P., as they reflect on the role of philosophy in giving coherence to the university as "universitas," the fruitfulness of a contemporary reconstruction of Thomist philosophy becomes clear. For not only do MacIntyre and Ashley attempt to recover the contemporary university's coherence and intelligibility, they also fully reveal its disconcerting state of disorientation and disintegration. John Henry Newman's claim, expressed forcefully in his still eminently relevant *The Idea of a University,* that without a natural theology (as part and parcel of metaphysical contemplation) the university will become unintelligible as a coherent whole of scientific inquiry, turns out to be uncannily prescient. While Newman was, of course, not a Thomist, MacIntyre and Ashley show that Thomism has rich if not singular resources not only to heed Newman's warning but to address it constructively. MacIntyre's and Ashley's Thomist reflections on the nature and task of the university form a sobering reminder that the pursuit of a unifying, architectonic wisdom might be more essential to the future life of the university as such than is currently realized in most of the late modern research universities. Such a realization itself would be an intellectual achievement integral to the pursuit of a unifying wisdom.

The Postlude, chapter 12, "This Is My Body — Eucharistic Adoration and Metaphysical Contemplation," holds the place of a summary. It offers a concluding shortcut into the hidden Christological center that arguably drives all of Thomas's theological thought and, derivatively, also the chapters of this volume. Instead of offering some conventional gesture of closure or synthesis that would be premature and would most likely claim more than an exploration into Thomas's theology could reasonably yield, the postlude brings into play all the central theological and philosophical motives of Thomas's thought explored in the previous chapters. By focusing on one specific liturgical practice, Eucharistic adoration, I return once more to the book's central theme, human nature's ordination to glory. For few if any other practices of the Catholic faith that Thomas held, illuminated, and defended, condense with such utter clarity the human ordination to communion with God. And so the book's implicit Christological center does at last become explicit: Christ, the way, the truth, and the life, in and through whom humanity's primordial ordination to communion with God is realized. As Christ is the heart of the divine faith and the impetus of all of Thomas's thought, so he is the key to the intelligibility, actuality, and final realization of human nature and destiny. Instead of treating "Christology" as a separate and distinct subject of Thomas's thought, the postlude goes about it as a postlude tends to do: it shows how all the aspects of Thomas's theology and philosophy are needed in order to contemplate properly the utterly Christ-constituted and Christ-centered liturgical practice of Eucharistic adoration and the theological truth entailed therein — Eucharistic transubstantiation.

Unfortunately, I was not able to include in this volume, next to the treatment of faith and hope, a separate treatment of Thomas's profound teaching on charity. However, the postlude serves as an, admittedly somewhat unusual, entry into this arguably deepest aspect of Thomas's theology. For Thomas, quite innovatively, understands the divine love of charity as a form of friendship, indeed, the highest form of friendship, the friendship of virtue. God, by way of the mission of the Son (the incarnation, the life, death, and resurrection of Christ) and of the Spirit (whose created effects are sanctifying grace and the infused theological and moral virtues and the gifts and fruits), befriends humanity and in and through charity begins to conform the believer more and more to the Triune life of charity. For "God is charity" (1 John 4:8; Douay-Rheims). And because friends want to share and delight in each other's presence, Christ's greatest gift of friendship to those whom he has called his friends (John 15:15) but who are still in the state of pilgrimage *(in statu viatoris)* is the gift of his personal Eucharistic presence. Rightly understood, therefore, Eucharistic adoration is nothing but a practice that is reflective of that form of friendship that the divine love of charity is — to remain and delight in the presence of the one who has befriended us while we were still sinners. It is in the presence of the divine friend where delight, adoration, praise, supplication, and lament are inseparably part of a single effusion of mutual charity.

In his Eucharistic theology, the Christological heartbeat of Thomas's faith, piety, and theology is at its strongest. It is a heartbeat that is so easily missed when one looks at Thomas's theology through the lenses that are shaped by the tacit antecedent presuppositions of a modern postmetaphysical theology, Catholic or Protestant, a theology bereft of its essential link to divine faith and contemptuous of the indispensable service that the metaphysics of being affords for a theology that has fallen into profound amnesia about its own sapiential task. One need only turn to Thomas's commentary on the Gospel of John to realize that in the West (with Maximus Confessor as an equal in the East) there is no theologian who surpassed the all-encompassing and all-penetrating Christological synthesis Thomas advanced. And contrary to the conventional modern prejudices du jour, philosophical contemplation drawn into the service of sapiential theology in no way diminishes, distorts, or distracts from the proper theological task and its Christological center. On the contrary, as compellingly displayed in the synthesis of Thomas Aquinas, philosophical contemplation, rightly undertaken along metaphysical lines, serves as an indispensable instrument for theology to realize its sapiential vocation and indeed receive the mystery of Christ in all its fullness.

IV. An Invitation to Further Explorations

These explorations in the theology of Thomas Aquinas might elicit in the reader the distinct desire to delve deeper into the thought of the *doctor communis*. Following this desire is commendable, especially for the beginner, for as Alexander Pope rendered it unforgettably in his 1704 *Essay on Criticism:*

> A little learning is a dangerous thing;
> drink deep, or taste not the Pierian spring:
> there shallow draughts intoxicate the brain,
> and drinking largely sobers us again.

For those readers who come as neophytes to the thought of Thomas, the following invitation to further explorations should serve as a beginner's guide to his philosophy and theology, a beginner's guide that gradually progresses to some more substantive and demanding interpretations of Thomas that are most helpful. For those readers already more advanced in their encounter with Thomas's teaching and for those who would call themselves Thomists, the more demanding among the following list of studies simply indicate among a much larger body of Aquinas scholarship those works to which I am most gratefully indebted.

The best popular introduction to Thomas's life and work remains G. K. Chesterton, *Saint Thomas Aquinas* (2009) and the best recent scholarly introduction is Jean-Pierre Torrell, O.P., *Saint Thomas Aquinas,* Volume 1: *The Person and His Work* (2005). For a lovely, accessible, yet still profound paraphrase of the *Summa theologiae* in pocket size, the reader might turn to Walter Farrell, O.P., and Martin J. Healy, *My Way of Life: Pocket Edition of St. Thomas: The Summa Simplified for Everyone* (1952).

The most accessible and concise introduction to Thomas's philosophy is Edward Feser, *Aquinas: A Beginner's Guide* (2009), to Thomas's theology is Michael Dauphinais and Matthew Levering, *Knowing the Love of Christ: An Introduction to the Theology of St. Thomas Aquinas* (2002), to Thomas's ethics is Paul Wadell, *The Primacy of Love: An Introduction to the Ethics of Thomas Aquinas* (1992), and to Thomas's masterwork, the *Summa theologiae,* is Jean-Pierre Torrell, O.P., *Aquinas's Summa: Background, Structure, and Reception* (2005). An exceedingly helpful resource to Thomas's theology for beginners is Joseph P. Wawrykow, *The Westminster*

Handbook to Thomas Aquinas (2005). Those readers who want to get an exposure to Thomas's theology under the guidance of leading contemporary Aquinas scholars should turn to *The Theology of Thomas Aquinas,* edited by Rik Van Nieuwenhove and Joseph Wawrykow (2005). For a brief, concise, and lucid account of the remarkable history of reception, interpretation, defense, and application of Thomas's thought in the course of the more than seven centuries since his death, students of Thomas should turn to Romanus Cessario, O.P., *A Short History of Thomism* (2005). For a useful guide into various aspects of Thomas's philosophical thought that organizes his theology, the beginner might turn to *The Cambridge Companion to Aquinas,* edited by Norman Kretzmann and Eleonore Stump (1993). For a first introduction into Thomas's metaphysics that is as accessible as it is lucid, one can hardly do better than to avail oneself of W. Norris Clarke, S.J., *The One and the Many: A Contemporary Thomistic Metaphysics* (2001).

For a balanced and lucid overview of and solid introduction to all topics treated in the *Summa theologiae,* the student of Thomas's thought might first want to consult Brian Davies, O.P., *The Thought of Thomas Aquinas* (1992). However, the reader who is looking for guides to the most central treatises of Thomas's masterpiece will find excellent guidance from the following studies, which are not listed alphabetically but along the lines of the order of teaching *(ordo disciplinae)* the *Summa theologiae* unfolds.

On the First Part of the Summa:

The Hackett Aquinas: The Treatise on the Divine Nature. Summa Theologiae I, 1-13 (2006); Rudi te Velde, *Aquinas on God: The "Divine Science" of the* Summa Theologiae (2006); Reginald Garrigou-Lagrange, O.P., *The One God: A Commentary on the First Part of St. Thomas' Theological Summa* (1943); Matthew Levering, *Scripture and Metaphysics: Aquinas and the Renewal of Trinitarian Theology* (2004); Gilles Emery, O.P., *The Trinitarian Theology of St. Thomas Aquinas* (2010); Reginald Garrigou-Lagrange, O.P., *The Trinity and God the Creator: Commentary on St. Thomas' Theological Summa I, 27-119* (1952); Robert E. Brennan, O.P., *Thomistic Psychology: A Philosophic Analysis of the Nature of Man* (1941); Pia Francesca de Solenni, *A Hermeneutic of Aquinas's* Mens *through a Sexually Differentiated Epistemology: Toward the Understanding of Woman as Imago Dei* (2000); Bernard Lonergan, S.J., *Grace and Freedom: Operative Grace in the Thought of St.*

Thomas Aquinas (2000); Jacques Maritain, *God and the Permission of Evil* (1966); and Herbert McCabe, O.P., *God and Evil in the Theology of St. Thomas Aquinas* (2010).

On the First of the Second Part of the Summa:

Servais Pinckaers, O.P., *The Sources of Christian Ethics* (1995); Denis J. M. Bradley, *Aquinas on the Twofold Human Good: Reason and Human Happiness in Aquinas's Moral Science* (1997); Reginald Garrigou-Lagrange, O.P., *Beatitude: A Commentary on Thomas' Theological Summa I-II, 1-54* (1956); Ralph McInerny, *Ethica Thomistica: The Moral Philosophy of Thomas Aquinas* (1982); Steven A. Long, *The Teleological Grammar of the Moral Act* (2007); Stephen L. Brock, *Action and Conduct: Thomas Aquinas and the Theory of Action* (1998); Nicholas E. Lombardo, O.P., *The Logic of Desire: Aquinas on Emotion* (2010); George P. Klubertanz, S.J., *Habits and Virtues: A Philosophical Analysis* (1965); Josef Pieper, *The Four Cardinal Virtues: Prudence, Justice, Fortitude, Temperance* (1965); Romanus Cessario, O.P., *The Moral Virtues and Theological Ethics* (2008); Fulvio di Blasi, *God and the Natural Law: A Rereading of Thomas Aquinas* (2006); Jean Porter, *Nature as Reason: A Thomistic Theory of the Natural Law* (2005); Charles Journet, *The Meaning of Grace* (1960); Reginald Garrigou-Lagrange, O.P., *Grace: Commentary on the Summa Theologica of St. Thomas, I-II, 109-114* (2010); and Joseph P. Wawrykow, *God's Grace and Human Action: "Merit" in the Theology of Thomas Aquinas* (1995).

On the Second of the Second Part of the Summa:

Stephen J. Pope (ed.), *The Ethics of Aquinas* (2002); Lawrence Dewan, O.P., *Wisdom, Law, and Virtue: Essays in Thomistic Ethics* (2008); Romanus Cessario, O.P., *Christian Faith and the Theological Life* (1996) and *The Virtues, Or, the Examined Life* (2002); Reginald Garrigou-Lagrange, O.P., *The Theological Virtues*, Volume 1: *On Faith* (1965); Michael Sherwin, O.P., *By Knowledge and by Love: Charity and Knowledge in the Moral Theology of St. Thomas Aquinas* (2004); Josef Pieper, *Faith, Hope, Love* (1997); and Hans Urs von Balthasar, *Thomas und die Charismatik: Kommentar zu Thomas von Aquin, Summa Theologica II-II 171-182, besondere Gnadengaben und die zwei Wege menschlichen Lebens* (1996).

On the Third Part of the Summa:

Romanus Cessario, O.P., *Christian Satisfaction in Aquinas* (1982); Paul Gondreau, *The Passions of Christ's Soul in the Theology of St. Thomas Aquinas* (2009); Matthew Levering, *Christ's Fulfillment of Torah and Temple: Salvation according to Thomas Aquinas* (2002); Reginald Garrigou-Lagrange, O.P., *Christ the Saviour: A Commentary on the Third Part of the Theological Summa of St. Thomas* (1950); Matthew Levering and Michael Dauphinais (eds.), *Rediscovering Aquinas and the Sacraments: Studies in Sacramental Theology* (2009); Coleman E. O'Neill, O.P., *Meeting Christ in the Sacraments* (2002); Abbot Vonier, O.S.B., *A Key to the Doctrine of the Eucharist* (2003-2004); and Charles Journet, *The Mass: The Presence of the Sacrifice of the Cross* (2008).

Thomas's theology cannot be adequately understood, let alone appreciated without a mature grasp of his profound, but demanding philosophy. Fortunately, there are several outstanding guides available for those who are ready to immerse themselves into the depths of Thomas's philosophy. The most thorough historical-genetic treatment of Thomas's philosophy is John F. Wippel, *The Metaphysical Thought of Thomas Aquinas: From Finite Being to Uncreated Being* (2000). The best account to see Thomas' metaphysics concretely at work in a conceptual reconstruction of its main moves would be Lawrence Dewan, O.P., *Form and Being* (2006). Eleonore Stump, *Aquinas* (2003), offers an excellent treatment of Thomas's thought, primarily his philosophy, but also aspects of his theology, that is directed to a readership influenced by analytic philosophy and the natural sciences. Inspired by an Aristotelian-Thomist integration of natural philosophy and metaphysics, Benedict M. Ashley, O.P., in his *opus magnum, The Way toward Wisdom: An Interdisciplinary and Intercultural Introduction to Metaphysics* (2006), offers an impressive demonstration of how the pursuit of philosophical wisdom along the lines of Thomas — metaphysics as meta-science — allows a comprehensive vision of all human sciences in a coherent and expansive framework. Jacques Maritain's earlier and in many ways unsurpassed classic, *Distinguish to Unite or The Degrees of Knowledge* (1995), offers an even more expansive framework of Thomist epistemology: from the knowledge conveyed by the senses to natural philosophy and natural science, from there to metaphysical knowledge and theological knowledge, and finally to mystical knowledge. And in order to find out why indeed Thomism as a coherent intellectual tradition of philosophical discourse and inquiry proves superior to modern and postmodern modes of such discourse and inquiry, one cannot do better than turn to think through the argument advanced in what has become a classic in a very brief time: Alasdair MacIntyre's Gifford Lectures, *Three Rival Versions of Moral Inquiry: Tradition, Encyclopaedia, Genealogy* (1990). Another set of expanded Gifford Lectures offers a brilliant and spirited defense of Thomas's understanding of philosophical wisdom. No other recent work will help the interested reader better to understand why natural theology was absolutely indispensable to Thomas's overall theological project than Ralph McInerny, *Praeambula Fidei: Thomism and the God of the Philosophers* (2006). For a contemporary restatement of Thomas's natural theology that addresses and rebuts the criticisms against natural theology raised by Kant and Heidegger, one best turns to the lucidly argued book by Thomas Joseph White, O.P., *Wisdom in the Face of Modernity: A Study in Thomistic Natural Theology* (2009).

Those who want to find out — contrary to recent rumors — why Thomas's philosophy is far from dead but intensely engaged by contemporary analytic philosophers might want to consult John Haldane (ed.), *Mind, Metaphysics, and Value in Thomistic and Analytic Traditions* (2002), John P. O'Callaghan, *Thomist Realism and the Linguistic Turn: Toward a More Perfect Form of Existence* (2003), Craig Paterson and Matthew Pugh, *Analytical Thomism* (2006), and David S. Oderberg, *Real Essentialism* (2007). For an instructive and very broad-minded Thomist engagement of philosophy as presently practiced in America, one might turn to Thomas Hibbs, *Aquinas, Ethics, and Philosophy of Religion: Metaphysics and Practice* (2007), and for learning to appreciate the ongoing relevance of Thomas's doctrine of natural law for contemporary political and legal theory and for the practice of law-making, the reader will profit immensely from Russell Hittinger, *The First Grace: Rediscovering the Natural Law in a Post-Christian World* (2003) and from J. Budziszewski, *The Line Through the Heart: Natural Law as Fact, Theory, and Sign of Contradiction* (2009).

For those readers who are interested to find out how Thomas's theology inspires and informs the work of contemporary theologians, they might want to turn to *Ressourcement Thomism: Sacred Doctrine, the Sacraments, and the Moral Life*, edited by Reinhard Hütter and Matthew Levering (2010) and to *The Analogy of Being: Invention of the Antichrist or the Wisdom of God?*, edited by Thomas Joseph White, O.P. (2011).

By the time the reader has reached this point of the introduction it might have dawned upon him or her that this kind of invitation to a deeper exploration of Thomas's philosophical and theological thought might presuppose a more encompassing intellectual reorientation and re-education. Such a reader is well advised to take advantage of two rather unique books, one as precious as the other: A. G. Sertillanges, O.P., *The Intellectual Life: Its Spirit, Conditions, Methods* (1980), and Josef Pieper, *Leisure — The Basis of Culture* (1998).

Prelude — Faith and Reason

"Is There a Cure for Reason's Presumption and Despair?" — Why Thomas Matters Today

I. The Directedness of Reason and the Crisis of Metaphysics — Why It Matters Theologically

It is hard to imagine a gulf deeper than the one that currently exists between those who regard human reason[1] in terms of utmost triumph and those who regard it in terms of utmost despair. Mathematically disciplined and technologically executed, human reason has transformed the globe in unprecedented ways. The academic disciplines based on reason's mathematical and technological acumen hold a robust trust — if not faith — in reason's capacity to grasp reality and, precisely because of this grasp, successfully to conform the world to human interests and needs.

Ironically, there is simultaneously a widespread sense of despair about reason's superior status and role. Instead of sovereignly guiding hu-

---

1. In the following, I refer to "reason" and "intellect" as fundamentally the same faculty. However, each stands for a particular aspect, insofar as reasoning is the discursive movement of the intellect. That is, "reason" carries the active connotation of the verbal form "to reason." The one implication of this internal differentiation that matters most in the following is that the faculty of the will has a larger effect on the discursive movement of reasoning than on the most basic act of apprehending intelligible truth. Similarly, I regard speculative and practical reasoning as particular aspects of the same faculty. As will become clear later, I follow in this Thomas Aquinas. Cf. esp. his *Summa theologiae* I, q. 79, aa. 8-11. (In the following chapters, all citations from the *Summa theologiae* [*ST*] in English are taken from the translation of the Fathers of the English Dominican Province, *St. Thomas Aquinas Summa Theologica* [New York: Benziger Brothers, 1948]. The Latin original offered in the footnotes is taken from Sancti Thomae de Aquino, *Summa Theologiae*, 3rd ed. [Turin: Edizioni San Paolo, 1999], which offers an improved version of the Leonine edition.)

man affairs to their clearly defined and well-considered ends, human reason seems to be little more than a coping mechanism or a regulative fiction driven and directed by instincts and desires it can hardly perceive, much less rule. The academic disciplines that traditionally draw upon reason's reflexive, integrative, and directive capacities — as exercised by humanity in the act of understanding and interpreting both world and self — have fallen into a state of internal disarray while finding themselves exiled into what by all accounts seems to be a state of permanent marginalization within the late modern university. Reason triumphing in the form of instrumental rationality has produced its own demise as famously analyzed in Max Horkheimer and Theodor Adorno's *Dialectic of Enlightenment*.[2]

This arguable state of affairs is obviously not just an ivory-tower phenomenon, remote from and largely irrelevant to human society at large. Rather, the simultaneous triumph of and despair about reason mirrors late modern society as such: We encounter breathtaking developments in artificial intelligence and biotechnology together with atmospheric epistemological skepticism and ontological nihilism. The very triumph of instrumental rationality seems to invite simultaneously the most radical questioning of reason itself: What drives reason relentlessly and breathlessly from success to success? Is it propelled by something situated "behind" its very gaze? If so, is reason's gaze directed in ways it can neither account for nor alter? Moreover, if reason were directed and driven in such a way, what actually would allow us to assume a sovereign — and, for that matter, first of all, coherent — self?

Precisely at the time when instrumental rationality came fully into its own, no one raised this suspicion more forcefully than Friedrich Nietzsche.[3] In many ways contemporary scientific reductionism is doing noth-

---

2. Max Horkheimer and Theodor W. Adorno, *Dialectic of Enlightenment: Philosophical Fragments*, ed. Gunzelin Schmid Noerr; trans. Edmund Jephcott (Stanford, CA: Stanford University Press, 2002).

3. Cf. Jürgen Habermas's way of situating Nietzsche's thought as the entrance into postmodernity in his *Philosophical Discourse of Modernity: Twelve Lectures*, trans. Frederick G. Lawrence (Cambridge, MA: MIT Press, 1987). Habermas's lecture on Nietzsche is especially instructive, because he rightly understands Nietzsche to be the catalyst both of *the critique of metaphysics* as developed by Heidegger and more recently by Derrida and of *skeptical science*, a science of suspicion based on the pervasiveness of the will to power in and behind all "knowing" as it was worked out in anthropological, psychological, and historical ways by Bataille, Lacan, and Foucault.

ing other than still catching up with Nietzsche's radical vision. Consider the following three samplings from Nietzsche's sprawling *oeuvre:*

> What then is truth? A movable host of metaphors, metonymies, and anthropomorphisms: in short, a sum of human relations which have been poetically and rhetorically intensified, transferred, and embellished, and which, after long usage, seem to a people to be fixed, canonical, and binding. Truths are illusions which we have forgotten are illusions; they are metaphors that have become worn out and have been drained of sensuous force, coins which have lost their embossing and are now considered as metal and no longer as coins.[4]

> There exists neither "spirit," nor reason, nor thinking, nor consciousness, nor soul, nor will, nor truth: all are fictions that are of no use. There is no question of "subject and object," but of a particular species of animal that can prosper only through a certain relative rightness; above all, regularity of its perceptions (so that it can accumulate experience). Knowledge works as a tool of power. Hence it is plain that it increases with every increase of power. The meaning of "knowledge": here, as in the case of "good" or "beautiful," the concept is to be regarded in a strict and narrow anthropocentric and biological sense. In order for a particular species to maintain itself and increase its power, its conception of reality must comprehend enough of the calculable and constant for it to base a scheme of behavior on it. The utility of preservation — not some abstract-theoretical need not to be deceived — stands as the motive behind the development of the organs of knowledge — they develop in such a way that their observations suffice for our preservation. In other words: the measure of the desire for knowledge depends upon the measure to which the will to power grows in a species: a species grasps a certain amount of reality in order to become master of it, in order to press it into service.[5]

> If the morality of "thou shalt not lie" is rejected, the "sense for truth" will have to legitimize itself before another tribunal: — as a means of the preservation of man, as *will to power.*

4. Friedrich Nietzsche, "On Truth and Lies in a Nonmoral Sense," in *Philosophy and Truth: Selections from Nietzsche's Notebooks of the Early 1870's,* trans. and ed. Daniel Breazeale (Atlantic Highlands, NJ: Humanities Press, 1979), p. 84.

5. Friedrich Nietzsche, *The Will to Power,* trans. Walter Kaufmann and R. J. Hollingdale (New York: Vintage Books, 1968), aphorism 480.

Likewise our love of the beautiful: it also is our shaping will. The two senses stand side-by-side; the sense for the real is the means of acquiring the power to shape things according to our wish. The joy in shaping and reshaping — a primeval joy! We can comprehend only a world that we ourselves have made.[6]

Nietzsche's aphorisms press the matter in a radicalness that goes well beyond the soft reductionism of contemporary science. Yet before we get locked into the question whether Nietzsche is right or wrong, it is of foremost importance to acknowledge the degree to which both the epistemological skepticism and the ontological nihilism implicit in his rigorous exercise of suspicion have become the unexamined conventional wisdom of the intellectual class that occupies the so-called humanities in countless college and university faculties.[7] Arguably, Nietzsche represents the end of a road that a relentless voluntarism, first theological and later philosophical, engendered.[8] One of the disturbing characteristics of this by now widely accepted voluntarism is the ease with which it is capable of accelerating the triumphs of instrumental reason while at the same time holding truth to be a by-product of this very process — a process that is meaningless in and of itself or, better put, simply self-referential, thereby tacitly affirming another tenet of Nietzsche's nihilism: the eternal return of things. Under the name of the god Dionysus, Nietzsche conceives being as a totality enfolded by the circularity of the eternal return. The very point of the eternal return is to negate the goal-oriented striving of the human, in short, to cancel out intentionality as well as teleology as the decisive parameters of human distinctiveness.

---

6. Nietzsche, *Will to Power*, aphorism 495.

7. The unexamined horizon is normatively Nietzschean in its fundamentally anti-metaphysical (that is, both anti-epistemological and anti-ontological) stance of celebrating "difference" for its own sake and of assuming "perspectivism" as an unquestioned first principle. Precisely because the intellect is driven and ruled by powers it can neither fully understand nor control, identity politics (being the uncritical acknowledgment of the ontological primacy of the will to power) has to replace discourse, reasoned argumentation, and the possibility of genuine insight. It does not much matter whether one favors Zizek's Lacanian reading of Schelling's *Ages of the World*, Vattimo's kenotic ontology, Rorty's neo-pragmatism, Foucault's archaeology of knowledge as a genealogy of power — for when hard-pressed, they all ultimately presuppose and rely upon an unexamined yet normatively assumed Nietzschean horizon.

8. Cf. Michael Allen Gillespie, *Nihilism before Nietzsche* (Chicago: University of Chicago Press, 1995) for a compelling account of the rise of modern nihilism from the seedbed of Ockham's voluntaristic theology.

Yet while the question whether Nietzsche is right or wrong can be postponed, it cannot be avoided. If it is indeed the case that reason is ultimately directed by something that can at best only partially become the object of its gaze but that nevertheless actually *makes* humans by their reason able to negotiate reality by ceaselessly creating coping mechanisms, does then human life not simply become identical with coping with reality, and, ultimately, coping as such? If reason indeed is nothing other than the extremely complex neural coping mechanism of a highly developed mammal, not only is reason then driven and directed by forces largely out of its control, but even more so, human reality becomes indistinguishable from the rest of the world, with the result that the intellectual procedure of scientifically penetrating reality must itself be understood as just a particularly effective moment of human coping. At the end of this road of scientifically objectifying human beings stands utter self-estrangement. As Robert Spaemann aptly put it, "The human being becomes an anthropomorphism to itself."[9] It seems quite obvious that, while the referents of such anthropomorphism can very well constitute the proper subject matter of scientific inquiry, a sheer anthropomorphism itself can hardly qualify as the proper subject and agent of such an inquiry. Yet because of scientism's determined avoidance of genuine philosophical reflection, this contradiction remains hidden to most, if not all, contemporary reductionist trends. However, as soon as reflection arises, it is hard to miss the fact that the very conditions of the possibility of science and scientific truth are of a metaphysical quality. That is, they are of immediate relevance to any scientific enterprise, yet at the same time, they antecede the particular set of subject matters of each individual science.

The assumption that there exists an investigation that is capable of exploring the principles of reality as they antecede and thus make possible the particular sciences is what has fallen into a deep crisis, a crisis intensely experienced since Nietzsche. To offer just one useful contemporary example, from the tradition of analytic philosophy, of what currently is in crisis: "We need to stand firm on the idea that the structure of elements that constitutes a thought, and the structure of elements that constitutes something that is the case, can be the very same thing."[10] The very fact that this

9. Robert Spaemann, "Ende der Modernität?" in *Philosophische Essays,* 2nd ed. (Stuttgart: Reclam, 1994), p. 240: "So wird der Mensch selbst sich zum Anthropomorphismus."
10. John McDowell, quoted in Fergus Kerr, *After Aquinas: Versions of Thomism* (Oxford: Blackwell, 2002), p. 29.

idea needs to be articulated, that it calls for a philosophical defense in light of its pervasive questioning, that ultimately it might need to be held as a conviction instead of simply constituting the unstated horizon of philosophical investigation precisely reflects what some lament as the "crisis of metaphysics" and most laud as the "end of metaphysics."[11]

Theology is deeply affected by the crisis of metaphysics, and this not only because theologians have drawn upon and transformed the tradition of metaphysics for at least fifteen hundred years.[12] Rather, the reason theology is affected by the crisis of metaphysics is of a genuinely *theological* nature. If the logos that elicits faith and legitimates theology is a contingent word spoken, a willful positing, such that it can in no way be related to the way things are and vice versa, and, more importantly, such that the way things are cannot be disclosed by this logos, such a "logos" only intensifies the specter of the will by placing one willful positing over against others, so that the last ground of reality is nothing but the agonism of warring wills and their contingent positings. Yet precisely because Christian theology is bound to the God whose Logos is from all eternity God, properly Christian theology will always have a metaphysical moment, in that it rightly expects

11. Readings of this "crisis" or "end" abound. For an accessible and representative reading, cf. Jürgen Habermas, *The Philosophical Discourse of Modernity* and his *Post-metaphysical Thinking: Philosophical Essays,* trans. William Mark Hohengarten (Cambridge, MA: MIT Press, 1992). Part of modern philosophy itself can be read as the crisis of metaphysics in the mode of its reflection, while other parts represent conscious efforts to overcome the crisis or to disprove the end of metaphysics. For the former, see Walter Schulz, *Philosophie in der veränderten Welt* (Pfullingen: Neske, 1972), and *Ich und Welt: Philosophie der Subjektivität* (Pfullingen: Neske, 1979). For the latter, see the remarkable intellectual heritage of Catholic philosophy in the nineteenth and twentieth centuries documented in *Christliche Philosophie im katholischen Denken des 19. und 20. Jahrhunderts,* ed. Emerich Coreth, S.J., Walter M. Neidl, and Georg Pfligersdorffer, 3 vols. (Graz: Styra, 1987-1990). Currently, one can observe a surprising return to metaphysical themes in analytic philosophy. See esp. John McDowell, *Mind and World* (Cambridge, MA: Harvard University Press, 1994) and Robert Brandom, *Making It Explicit: Reasoning, Representing, and Discursive Commitment* (Cambridge, MA: Harvard University Press, 1994). See also Philip Clayton, *The Problem of God in Modern Thought* (Grand Rapids: Eerdmans, 2000), pp. 3-49.

12. David Bentley Hart's essay, "The Offering of Names: Metaphysics, Nihilism, and Analogy," in *Reason and the Reasons of Faith* (henceforth *Reason*), ed. Paul J. Griffiths and Reinhard Hütter (New York: T&T Clark International, 2005), pp. 255-91, offers a penetrating theological meditation on the problems that arise when metaphysics emancipates itself from its theological roots. For a more extensive treatment, see his recent *Atheist Delusions: The Christian Revolution and Its Fashionable Enemies* (New Haven, CT: Yale University Press, 2009).

that the structure of the world and the structure of the human mind should indeed correspond because they were *made* to correspond.[13]

The crisis of metaphysics is by now well established in the form of moments of "postmetaphysical thought," characterized by the familiar agonistic strategies of "situating," "outbidding," "unmasking," and "overcoming." It is quite difficult for theology not to fall into this trap of contending discursive strategies and their agonistic positings. For, indeed, Nietzsche's challenge cuts to the very core of the human being; indeed, his is a quasi-theological challenge that he wants to be understood as such. Would it not be most natural to face this challenge with a counterchallenge, that is, to posit theology's own normative horizon with the same apodicticity with which Nietzsche is eager to presuppose quite a different horizon? Yet it is theology's normative horizon itself that disallows it to succumb to this agonistic temptation, precisely because of the very nature of the horizon. For the following three fundamental beliefs constitute the horizon of theology: First, the world is created, that is, it is in its nature completely different from, and in its existence completely dependent upon, God. Second, the human being is created in the image of God. Third, the human being is called to a communion of vision and love with the God who is love. An important entailment of these three beliefs is the further belief that in this communion human beings receive a fulfillment that assumes and infinitely surpasses its created capacity so that truth, freedom, and love are seen and experienced as one and the same reality. The epistemic key and ontological cornerstone to these three fundamental beliefs are the person and work of Jesus Christ. While the following remarks do not unfold an explicit Christology, they are possible only in light of the Chalcedonian convictions of Christian orthodoxy. To put it more strongly, it is precisely Chalcedonian Christology in conjunction with a doctrine of creation that must conceptually unfold *creatio ex nihilo* and that suggests, if not entails, what I will call a "metaphysics of creation."

Under postmetaphysical conditions, these three fundamental beliefs, constituting the horizon of theology, seem very much like a willful positing, yet they are not. Rather, they convey a truth that is first of all suffered, like all genuine truth, and therefore is in no way a product of theology and hence at its disposal.[14] Precisely in order to resist the temptation of agonis-

---

13. Cf. Josef Pieper, *Philosophia Negativa: Zwei Versuche über Thomas von Aquin* (Munich: Kösel, 1953), pp. 20ff.

14. Cf. my *Suffering Divine Things: Theology as Church Practice* (Grand Rapids: Eerd-

tics, theology has to be attentive to the metaphysical moment that simply is entailed in the belief that the world is created. Thus, while it can be argued on the basis of the truth of the Christian faith that epistemological skepticism and ontological nihilism are false, it is equally important to press the criterion of internal consistency by showing that they involve a significant moment of performative self-contradiction.[15] Again, the reason for the latter's importance is not to propagate a philosophy "pure" of theological commitments but rather to avoid the agonistics of willful positing by allowing theology to show on grounds other than its own substantive commitments that epistemological skepticism and ontological nihilism are untenable positions. This way of unfolding its metaphysical moment does not weaken Christian theology. Nor is this metaphysical moment to be confused with the modern apologetic strategy of defending the truth of the Christian faith on terms alien to its substance. On the contrary, its very metaphysical moment strengthens Christian theology simply by putting the fundamental belief to work that creation makes sense and communicates this sense to the intellect. It is thus especially in the middle of the crisis of metaphysics that theology cannot afford to embrace the postmetaphysical Zeitgeist.

Indeed, Christian theology cannot remain indifferent to the challenge posed by epistemological skepticism and ontological nihilism, for at least two reasons. First, the very practice of theology as faith seeking understanding depends on the assumption that rational inquiry is not simply a function of sub- and preconscious drives, be they directed to human

---

mans, 2000); and Bruce Marshall, "*Quod Scit Una Uetula*: Aquinas on the Nature of Theology," in *The Theology of Thomas Aquinas*, ed. Rik Van Nieuwenhove and Joseph P. Wawrykow (Notre Dame, IN: University of Notre Dame Press, 2005), pp. 1-35; 14, where he quotes Thomas: "The name of this sort of knowledge is 'wisdom, a kind of knowledge by taste' — a wisdom which comes not first from learning, but from 'suffering divine things' *(patiens divina)*" (quoting *ST* I, q. 43, a. 5, ad 2 and referring also to *ST* II-II, q. 45, a. 2; II-II, q. 97, a. 2, ad 2; and I, q. 1, a. 6, ad 3).

15. While it usually does not amount to a conclusive argument, such a demonstration can, next to relentlessly uncovering the performative self-contraction embedded in the positions criticized, address their unresolved problems and the paucity of the conceptual resources employed to answer those problems. For such ways of discursive demonstration, see Alasdair MacIntyre, *Three Rival Versions of Moral Inquiry* (Notre Dame, IN: University of Notre Dame Press, 1990), esp. ch. 9, "Tradition against Genealogy: Who Speaks to Whom?"; and Robert Spaemann, *Personen: Versuche über den Unterschied zwischen "etwas" und "jemand"* (Stuttgart: Klett-Cotta, 1996), as well as in many of his essays collected in his *Grenzen: Zur ethischen Dimension des Handelns* (Stuttgart: Klett-Cotta, 2001).

survival or to the expression of an allegedly omnipresent and omni-efficient will to power. And second, it is only Christian theology that has achieved a full conceptual recognition and analysis of the will by develop-ing profound accounts of the epistemological effects of sin.[16] In multiple ways, the postmetaphysical privileging of the will's rule over reason is to be best appreciated as simply parasitic on the Christian intellectual tradi-tion. Yet deprived of their crucial hamartiological, christological, and ul-timately soteriological contexts, these postmetaphysical accounts neces-sarily become distorted and wreak epistemological and ethical havoc. Ironically, because of their broad cultural diffusion, tacit Nietzschean as-sumptions have become the normal, if not normative, intellectual and ethical horizon for numerous Christians who are culturally literate but catechetically illiterate.

It is this confused and confusing mixture of cultural literacy and catechetical illiteracy that we find forcefully addressed in Pope John Paul II's encyclical, *Fides et Ratio* (1998). After critically assessing the vari-ous problems implied in contemporary philosophical eclecticism, scient-ism, and pragmatism, the encyclical touches upon the central feature of modern reductionism:

> The positions we have examined lead in turn to a more general con-ception which appears today as the common framework of many phi-losophies which have rejected the meaningfulness of being. I am re-ferring to the nihilist interpretation, which is at once the denial of all foundations and the negation of all objective truth. Quite apart from the fact that it conflicts with the demands and the content of the word of God, nihilism is a denial of the humanity and of the very identity of the human being. It should never be forgotten that the neglect of being inevitably leads to losing touch with objective truth and there-fore with the very ground of human dignity. This in turn makes it possible to erase from the countenance of man and woman the marks of their likeness to God, and thus to lead them little by little either to a destructive will to power or to a solitude without hope. Once the truth is denied by human beings, it is pure illusion to try to set them free. Truth and freedom either go hand in hand or together they per-ish in misery. (§90)

16. See most recently Merold Westphal, "Taking St. Paul Seriously: Sin as an Epistemological Category," in *Christian Philosophy*, ed. Thomas P. Flint (Notre Dame, IN: University of Notre Dame Press, 1990), pp. 201-26.

While a theology engulfed by the crisis of metaphysics may laud postmetaphysical thought as a welcome moment of relief, such celebrations are as shortsighted as they are short-lived. Rather, by attending to the question of how reason and will relate, contemporary theology acknowledges the crisis of metaphysics and with it the dominating specter of the will. Yet how might we go about this task under present circumstances? Alasdair MacIntyre once said to me in a personal conversation that if one does not know anymore how to go forward, it is helpful to trace one's steps backward in order to find another way forward. Heeding this recommendation, I will proceed in the following argument largely by moving backward.

First, I will offer a sketch of the grammar of Christian thought of how faith, reason, and will interrelate in multiple and complex ways. While primarily a delineation of the constraints upon properly Christian thought about *ratio* and *fides,* what is said in this section is in principle also open to being found illuminating and possibly convincing to non-Christians. (The latter is crucial if the agonism of willful positing is to be avoided.) In the course of this preliminary meditation, the fundamental reality of judgment comes into view so as to offer a path on which to retrace our steps concerning the question of reasoning's directedness.

Second, I will turn to Thomas Aquinas in order to explore his complex yet rewarding way of analyzing the relationship between intellect and will. I have chosen Thomas as my main interlocutor for more than one reason. First, I have been convinced by MacIntyre's argument in *Three Rival Versions of Moral Inquiry* that Thomas is the most promising point to which to retrace our steps from the swampy regions of late modern discourse we currently find ourselves in. Moreover, I have chosen Thomas for ecumenical reasons. He is the one theologian of the common tradition whose work still has to endure the most withering attacks by unwarranted Protestant prejudice: an Aristotelian distorting and obfuscating of the kerygma; a facile theology of glory oblivious to the centrality of Christ and his cross; an intellectualism that falls short of appreciating human depravity and especially the bondage of the will; and finally, a theology that harmfully privileges Pseudo-Dionysius and Aristotle over against the witness of Scripture. While recently both Catholic and Protestant scholarship have addressed and refuted most, if not all, of these false assumptions, the arguments fall on deaf ears for those eager to hold on to prejudices that help cement the walls between divided Christian communities. Hoping against hope, I have returned to Thomas in order to invite Protestants to take, next to St. Augustine, this arguably most important theologian of the common Western tradition with a renewed seriousness. Finally, I have chosen Thomas because I think he offers the most fruitful answer to the problem I have sketched above. If there is a way forward, it is a way with and from Thomas, a way that I will intimate toward the end of this chapter. My engagement of Thomas will simply follow the way the central activity of judgment — involving both the act of the intellect and that of the will — is affected by the great disturbance of and offense to all self-sufficient wisdom: the reality of sin and the centrality of Christ. It thus will take the following form: judgment of *esse* — judgment in crisis — redeemed judgment — the conflict of judgments.

An account of the judgment of *esse* will provide the necessary backdrop for exploring how Thomas relates intellect and will. An all-too-facile intellectualist reading of Thomas will be called into question by considering his treatment of the intellectual vice of curiosity, which paradigmatically displays the reality of judgment in crisis. Thomas's penetrating analysis of curiosity offers surprisingly fresh insight into why a "philosophy of genuinely metaphysical range" *(Fides et Ratio)* is a necessary component of his overall theological project and why it takes the form of a metaphysics of being. When transfigured by the normative horizon of the Christian faith, that is, by a redeemed judgment, the metaphysics of being is open to being elevated and assumed into the metaphysics of creation.[17] Finally, I will address with and from Thomas the ongoing conflict of judgments we will encounter as long as reason remains for many "a prisoner to itself."[18] It is a metaphysics of creation that in the very conflict of judgments prevents theology itself from becoming just a willful positing and from thus becoming trapped by that agonism that flourishes wherever the specter of the will looms large.

II. Reason, Faith, and the Centrality of Judgment

Fides and *ratio* are highly complex force fields that constantly overlap and presuppose each other, although not in strictly reciprocal ways. Faith rea-

---

17. See Martin Bieler, "The Theological Importance of a Philosophy of Being," in *Reason,* ed. Griffiths and Hütter, pp. 295-326, for a penetrating analysis of Thomas's metaphysics of *esse* and its theological relevance.

18. *Fides et Ratio,* no. 23, referring to Rom. 1:21-22. The full quote reads in the English translation: "The eyes of the mind were no longer able to see clearly: reason became more and more a prisoner to itself. The coming of Christ was the saving event which redeemed reason from its weakness, setting it free from the shackles in which it had imprisoned itself."

sons in order to explore the reasons of faith *(fidei ratio)*.[19] Yet reason in its own comprehensive reaching toward truth constantly anticipates — in a kind of faith, *rationis fides* — an antecedent coherence that is already presupposed in any process of inquiry.[20] As an inherently teleological activity, rational inquiry needs to anticipate the existence of the goal for which it aims (this goal being not a particular object but an insight in which the inquiry's investigative motion comes to rest).[21] The *rationis fides* differs substantively from the *fides* that ultimately is the gift of the Spirit and the beginning of participation in God's life. How is this so? Let us first consider *rationis fides,* which is constituted in a twofold manner.

First, *rationis fides* is constituted by *being ordered toward truth.* Let me formulate this claim in the form of a thesis: *Rationis fides* is the anticipation of the unity of the truth that is the *telos* of any ordered inquiry. This thesis is not uncontroversial. Some might concede that philosophy is in some sense an "ordered inquiry." Yet based on an argument like the following, they would deny that this makes it teleological: "Order" can be used to designate only formal relations among concepts, for example, in mathematics or predicate calculus. Yet here, I think, we need to distinguish between purely logical investigations based on analytic judgments that bracket any consideration of reality, on the one hand, and inquiries directed to aspects of what is, on the other. In the case of the former, truth is contained in the logic of the terms themselves; in the case of the latter, truth of being itself is the end that the inquiry anticipates in its investigative intention.

On a deeper level, we need to maintain that truth is the end of *ratio,* that toward which *ratio* is always directed and ordered and in which *ratio* finds its fulfillment. While this is unquestionably a reasonable assumption, it is difficult to demonstrate. It seems that there are at least two ways of ar-

19. See Karl Barth, *Anselm: Fides Quaerens Intellectum: Anselm's Proof of the Existence of God in the Context of His Theological Scheme,* trans. Ian W. Robertson (London: SCM Press, 1960).

20. See esp. Michael Polanyi, *Personal Knowledge: Towards a Post-Critical Philosophy* (Chicago: University of Chicago Press, 1962). One of the key problems of modernity is the erosion of the faith that grounds reason, that is, the *rationis fides* that reason has to have in the teleological coherence of both reality and its own "intelligere" of reality. This is a problem that is acutely reflected in Kant's "Critique of Teleological Judgment" (*Critique of Judgment,* §§61-91).

21. Since the insight gained will not be exhaustive but will raise new questions, there will never be a final rest to the intellect's motion of inquiry.

guing for this claim. The first is negative: We say that everyone who argues against this claim commits a performative contradiction (i.e., in the very act of reasoned argumentation, reason displays its directedness toward truth — otherwise, why argue in the first place?). The second is positive: We interpret the phenomenon of *ratio* as something whose reception we cannot antecede — in short, as a given. Givenness, in turn, must be understood either as emergence or as gift. The strategy of explaining reason as an emergent phenomenon has to face the problems inherent in reductionism; it needs to think about reason in ways that contradict the very act of thinking itself, an act that has ontological and teleological implications that defy any reductive strategies. Therefore, we need to understand *ratio* as a gift integrally given in the comprehensive giftedness of creation. As an integral element of the gifted matrix of creation, *ratio* can rightly be assumed to have an end *(telos)* that is capable of being fulfilled. Yet every end is the end of a potentiality. The recognition of truth is the end of *ratio*'s potentiality.

Thus Christian theologians should be committed to the view that *ratio* is teleologically ordered toward truth, with rational inquiry being reason's proper pursuit of its actuality and *rationis fides* being the confidence in *ratio*'s directedness toward truth.

Second, *rationis fides* is constituted by *being informed and directed by the will*. *Rationis fides* contains the tacit assumption of the *liberum arbitrium,* a will that is free in that it is reason's own capacity to choose not only the goal of inquiry but also all the means necessary to pursue it. In critical reflection we are free to relate to the way we do things. However, we are unable to relate freely to our critical relating — unless we are liberated by being drawn into a freedom that allows us to relate to our relating by being shaped, rectified, and transformed in ways we could not have even anticipated without this liberation. Thus the *rationis fides* rests on something that transcends its capacity of anticipation: the quality of its willing. Yet reason in being ordered toward truth does not seem to have the capacity to determine or transform the quality of that will that directs it.

At this point the fundamental problematic of our inquiry arises: As long as the will remains unthematized, *rationis fides* remains untroubled. But as soon as the will is thematized, the question of reason's directedness by the will (and consequently reason's liberation from the will's incurvature) emerges with full force.

After having considered *rationis fides,* we need now to turn to faith itself. In its strict theological sense, *fides* must be clearly differentiated from *rationis fides,* for *fides* is the *active reception* of an inexhaustible yet concrete personal truth, a reception in and through which the believer begins to participate in the divine freedom. By desiring communion with God as the highest good, the believer's will is rectified and thus is conformed to the *telos* of God's own will in Christ. Thus, faith is inseparably both reception and actualization of this truth, which is characterized by the following constitutive elements: (a) *existentially, fiducia* as the comprehensive existential relying on the gift and its giver in the gift; (b) *intellectually,* the intellect receiving a new formal object — revealed truth as its first truth; (c) *volitionally,* the will being directed to communion with God as its highest good; and (d) *intentionally,* the will being conformed to God's own will in Christ. Thus, both intellect and will become part of the actualization of the gift.

Fidei ratio signifies the conceptual as well as substantive exploration (*fides quaerens intellectum*) of this received truth as *ratio* is guided and informed by faith. This exploration occurs through reason's participation in the freedom that *is* the will's conformation to the *telos* of God's will. Yet at the same time, this exploration continuously draws upon concepts forged by a reason that enacts its faith in the prolepsis of the unity of truth (*rationis fides*). Because of the nature of *fides, fidei ratio* brings to the fore what remains hidden to the inquiring process of *ratio* as such, being essential to its gaze: the constitution of the human as a self (the human's *concrete existence* and his/her relationship to himself/herself)[22] and the central role of the will in it.

In order to conclude our preliminary considerations, we need to consider *judgment.* The "red thread" between faith and reason seems to be *iudicium,* "judgment." There can be no sustained process of rational inquiry without continuous judgments regarding the subject matter at hand and the arguments advanced so far. In the course of any rational inquiry, the *rationis fides* is enacted in and through the act of judging. Similarly, there can be no *fidei ratio* without continuous judgments regarding the subject matter at hand and the arguments advanced. The decisive question seems to be: Is "judgment" simply a matter of the intellect as such, or does it somehow involve the will's operation — not just concerning the obvious case of external action but concerning the less obvious case of what one might call reason's activity of judging? The "will" here addressed might

22. Søren Kierkegaard remains the most important analyst of this complex and ultimately unfathomable reality. See esp. his *Sickness unto Death,* ed. and trans. Howard V. Hong and Edna H. Hong (Princeton, NJ: Princeton University Press, 1980).

better be described as reasoning's directedness — that which constitutes the horizon of the gaze in which judgments are made. This gaze is not just conceptual but volitional. Not only does the intellect move the will in light of particular judgments, but the will also exacts a constant impact on the intellect by directing it in light of the good to which the will is drawn. "Rectitude of mind" indicates an intellect directed by the will that is drawn to the ultimate good. Yet rather than remaining an abstraction, the ultimate good, the triune God, through efficacious grace, heals and redirects the will so that a fundamentally renewed mind "may discern what is the will of God — what is good and acceptable and perfect" (Rom. 12:2). And for "discern" we could as well say "judge," since a renewal of discernment always issues in a renewal of judgment. Thus, discerning or judging what the will of God is presupposes the renewal of our mind. Yet this renewal of our mind, which we cannot "will" but can only receive, presupposes an antecedent misdirectedness of our will. By implication, therefore, our mind is directed in ways we de facto intend (and thus our judgments are always the uncompelled and, in this sense, "free" enactment of our reasoning) but are neither able to perceive nor free to change.[23] (Willfully changing our reason's directedness would have to assume a will^y that would redirect our will^x.)

We have reached the appropriate point for formulating the guiding thesis of this inquiry. If what has been posited above obtains, we can meaningfully raise the question of reasoning's directedness only from within a horizon in which the problem, at least in principle, is already overcome. *Only within the horizon of faith, reason now being informed by a renewed will that is beginning to be redirected toward communion with God as its highest good, can the will as such become a sufficient object of reason's inquiry and can* fidei ratio *therefore consider the will's incurvature and thus appreciate what was and is at stake in its own directedness to proper ends.*

Before we turn to Thomas, it is important to register three central assertions that are constitutive of *fidei ratio*. First, *credere* must always be conceived as the effect of grace in which we are liberated to participate freely and thus "decide" not *for* grace but *on the basis* of grace. Second, the cross stands for the ultimate and most radical establishment of wisdom

---

23. This relationship between willing and thinking (here *phronein*) can also be observed in Phil. 2:5 and 13. In Phil. 2:13 it is emphasized that God effects the willing and the doing, and it is precisely on this basis that the exhortation in Phil. 2:5 ("Let the same mind be in you that was in Christ Jesus") gains real momentum. The redirection of the mind implies a changing of the will that must be effected by God.

received in faith. And the reception of this wisdom entails the reception of a freedom in which the will is absorbed in its ultimate good, that is, conformed to God's will. *This is the genuine freedom in which reason can confidently develop again its genuine and original metaphysical range of inquiry.* Third, *iudicium* is central. If grace either perfects or re-creates human nature (and the one must be conceived of in ways as radical and fundamental as the other), we will need to assume that *iudicium*, "judgment" — standing at the very core of the human's interaction with everything else, including himself/herself — is most centrally affected by this perfection or re-creation.

We have finally reached the point of turning our attention to Thomas. What will an engagement of Thomas bequeath? It will open the possibility of a theological reading of the will that avoids the trap of an unrestrained voluntarism. At the same time, such an engagement will open up the space for a metaphysics of creation. More than just a particular philosophy, it is a necessary location for being able to think on the basis of creation and to expect conceptual and substantive guidance from creation — even and especially when judgment is in crisis.

III. Thomas Aquinas on the Directedness of Reasoning

Judgment of Esse

The concept of judgment is the central pillar of Thomas's metaphysics of creation. This concept secures the realism fundamental to the whole, that is, it preserves the inherent coherence and integrity of creation by starting with the central assumption of the intellect's essential fittingness and thus unfathomable connectedness to reality.[24] Because the world, being creation, must be conceived antecedently as thought *(gedacht)* — or, better, as thought out *(erdacht)* — by God, the intellect grasps the simple essence of things and thus arrives at true judgments about them.[25]

---

24. For a detailed historical account of Thomas's metaphysics, see John F. Wippel, *The Metaphysical Thought of Thomas Aquinas* (Washington, DC: The Catholic University of America Press, 2000); and for a more systematically constructive interpretation, W. Norris Clarke, S.J., *Explorations in Metaphysics: Being — God — Person* (Notre Dame, IN: University of Notre Dame Press, 1994), pp. 45-64, 102-22.

25. I am drawing here on the section "Wahrheit als Erdachtsein," in Josef Pieper, *Philosophia Negativa*, 20-23. See also my discussion in chapter 6, pp. 205-15.

Despite the strengths of this concept, one must wonder whether "judgment," conceived as fitting *in rebus naturalibus,* is nevertheless abstracting from a fundamental aspect of reality and thus remaining an abstract ideal in problematic ways. Why? This concept of judgment does not reflect on the concrete existence under the condition of sin of the one who judges, an existence that raises the pressing question of reasoning's directedness. While correct judgments about pencils, dogs, roses, rectangles, and black holes are not endangered and called into question in principle by this reservation, at least all judgments that appertain to the existence of the ones who judge — that is, persons — are fundamentally affected by it, or so it seems. And insofar as reflection upon the previously listed kinds of largely unproblematic judgments (whether implicitly or explicitly, but always inherently) involves the concrete *existence* of the one who reflects upon them, reasoning's directedness under the condition of sin unavoidably comes into play.

Is our excursion into Thomas's thought on this matter already over before it really begins? It simply depends on whether we attempt to read his metaphysical account of the judgment of *esse* in an implicitly modern sense, that is, as an epistemology that is isolated from the concrete existence of the person who thinks, wills, and judges, or whether we understand Thomas's account of judgment in the wider encompassing horizon of his theology. Crucially, Thomas's wider, theologically informed horizon addresses the interrelationship between intellect and will that underlies the act of judgment. Thomas addresses this interrelationship, first, by identifying intellect and will as distinct powers of the soul (*ST* I) and, second, by inquiring into their concrete enactment under the condition of sin (*ST* I-II and *ST* II-II). As will become sufficiently clear in the course of my argument, in order to be able to address both, Thomas's account presupposes the very horizon of a redeemed judgment in which theology's discursive knowledge is informed by *sacra doctrina* increasingly bearing the stamp of the *scientia Dei* itself (*ST* I, q. 1, a. 3. ad 2).

The Human Being — Made in God's Image

Before plunging into the deep waters of Thomas's account of the complex interaction between intellect and will, we need to acknowledge the warning that a noted Aquinas scholar recently expressed: "No one can do justice to Aquinas's theory of the will in a few pages. It is rich, complicated, and controversial, and a thorough treatment of it would require a book-length study."[26] Moreover, it is important to realize that in his *Summa theologiae*, Thomas places his inquiry into the nature of the human being squarely into an explicitly *theological* horizon. He does so by drawing upon Augustine's *imago*-doctrine, which he received by way of Peter Lombard's *Sentences*. Yet this dependence upon Augustine is not simply a matter of the history of ideas. It is, rather, a matter of substance. Thomas's anthropology represents nothing less than a philosophically argued yet theologically motivated and driven line of reasoning about the human being as created in the image of God. And if it indeed obtains that the human being is created in God's image, this quality must constitute the first formal principle of any subsequent claims about human nature. Thomas locates this first formal principle in the form of the human, that is, the soul. He does so by distinguishing between, on the one hand, the end, or terminus, of God's act of creation and, on the other, perfection of this image through grace and the light of glory, that is, the gratuitous gift of communion with the triune God.[27] In short, Thomas's anthropology is governed by a multilayered, complex structure: the human created in the image of God yet deeply wounded by the reality of sin and gratuitously directed toward restoration and perfection of the image, which reaches its completion only as human beings find themselves in personal communion with God, a communion gratuitously granted by the triune God through the Spirit in Christ and enacted as a communion of knowing and loving.[28]

26. Eleonore Stump, "Intellect, Will, and the Principle of Alternate Possibilities," in *Christian Theism and the Problems of Philosophy*, ed. Michael D. Beaty (Notre Dame, IN: University of Notre Dame Press, 1990), p. 266. I have profited greatly from Stump's concise account of Thomas's complex theory of the will, esp. as she unfolds it in her most recent magisterial account, *Aquinas* (London: Routledge, 2003).

27. Cf. D. Juvenal Merriell, *To the Image of the Trinity: A Study in the Development of Aquinas' Teaching* (Toronto: Pontifical Institute of Medieval Studies, 1990), pp. 153-235, esp. 168-69.

28. *ST* I, q. 93, esp. aa. 5 and 8; but see also *ST* I, q. 45, a. 7 and q. 43, a. 3. The subsequent 114 questions of the *Prima secundae* and 189 questions of the *Secunda secundae* need to be read as an interpretation of this dynamic *imago Dei* or, better, as an investigation of all those aspects through which the human being already is the image of God and still — gratuitously — is to be restored and perfected in that image. Cf. Otto Hermann Pesch, *Die Theologie der Rechtfertigung bei Martin Luther und Thomas von Aquin* (Mainz: Matthias-Grünewald, 1967), pp. 401ff.; and Yves Congar, O.P., "Le sens de l'économie' salutaire dans la 'théologie' de S. Thomas d'Aquin (Somme theologique)," in *Festgabe Joseph Lortz*, vol. 2, *Glaube und Geschichte*, ed. Erwin Iserloh and Peter Manns (Baden-Baden: Bruno Grimm, 1958), pp. 73-122, esp. 105.

Intellect and Will

In order accurately to appreciate Thomas's analysis of the intricate interrelationship between intellect and will, we need to understand the subtle development of his thought from an earlier "intellectualist" leaning, up to the completion of *ST* I, a later mature position that comes to the fore with the inception of *ST* I-II and especially in *De malo* 6.[29] We need to gain first a solid appreciation of the earlier, intellectualist emphasis[30] in order to appreciate the nature of the development of his later, nuanced position in which the will plays a more distinct role.

Thomas understands intellect and will as two distinct yet mutually interrelated powers of the soul, the intellect naturally and of necessity adhering to the first principles[31] and the will adhering to the universal good as its proper object (*ST* I, q. 82, a. 1). Thus, perceiving in abstraction from the concrete enactment of these two potencies, that is, simply according to their proper nature, Thomas regards the will as the striving that emerges from the intellect's power of cognition. The movement of the will is the inclination toward something. Yet being a property inherent in the intellect's potency, the will is an essentially intellectual capacity and therefore an inclination to a good that is recognized as such. Thus the will inheres in the intellect as that unique ground which moves it toward the good that the intellect has perceived as such.

---

29. Rather than a radical change of mind, I want to interpret this development as a change of emphasis and as a final clarification of the will as a power of the soul that while being informed by the intellect is fully independent from the intellect. My account of Thomas's mature position depends on Otto H. Pesch's detailed study "Philosophie und Theologie der Freiheit bei Thomas von Aquin in quaest. Disp. 6 De malo," *Münchener Theologische Zeitschrift* 13 (1962): 1-25. I find convincing Pesch's chronological arguments that suggest that *De malo* was written shortly after *ST* I-II, qq. 1-21 (i.e., between 1270 and 1272, during Thomas's second stay in Paris) and thus represents the latest state of Thomas's reflections on the relationship between intellect and will. On the particular historical cause for Thomas's change of emphasis, see Pesch, "Philosophie und Theologie der Freiheit," pp. 4-5.

30. For the sake of economy, I will draw exclusively upon *ST* I in order to establish Thomas's earlier account in its most accomplished and concise form.

31. That is, *prima intelligibilium principia.* These principles are the first concepts formed by the intellect when a human being comes into contact with the sensible. On the historical context of Thomas's discussion of sense and intellect, see the instructive account by Edward P. Mahoney, "Sense, Intellect, and Imagination in Albert, Thomas, and Siger," in *The Cambridge History of Later Medieval Philosophy,* ed. Norman Kretzmann, Anthony Kenny, Jan Pinborg, and Eleonore Stump (Cambridge: Cambridge University Press, 1982), pp. 602-22.

Despite the clear distinction between intellect and will insofar as they are considered in principle, there obtains an intricate interrelationship between the two, which Thomas discusses first under the question of "Whether the Will Is a Higher Power Than the Intellect?" (*ST* I, q. 82, a. 3). The upshot of Thomas's complex analysis in this article is that both powers include one another in accordance with their proper natures. For this reason the will itself can be the proper object of the intellect's inquiry.[32] Moreover, for the same reason, the will moves the intellect — but only in one particular way. On the one hand, Thomas draws upon the distinction between the intellect's inherent relationship to the first principles and the will's orientation toward the universal good, and on the other hand, upon their particular interrelationship in the interplay of all the powers of the soul. This distinction allows for the following relationship: "But if we consider the will as regards the common nature of its object, which is good, and the intellect as a thing and a special power, then the intellect itself, and its act, and its object, which is truth, each of which is some species of good, are contained under the common notion of good. And in this way, the will is higher than the intellect, and can move it" (*ST* I, q. 82, a. 4, ad 1). Thus, insofar as the intellect's act and its object — that is, truth — are subsumed under the common notion of good, both of them fall under the common nature of the will's object — that is, that toward which the will is unfailingly bent: the good. In other words, because the will moves all faculties of the soul to their proper end, the will moves the operation of the intellect[33]

---

32. *ST* I, q. 82, a. 4, ad 1: "If, however, we take the intellect as regards the common nature of its object and the will as a determinative power, then again the intellect is higher and nobler than the will, because under the notion of being and truth is contained both the will itself, and its act, and its object. Wherefore the intellect understands the will, and its act, and its object, just as it understands other species of things, as stone or wood, which are contained in the common notion of being and truth." If, supposedly, the will were superior or prior to the intellect, an investigation of the will would be a futile enterprise, since in this case the will would be both the agent and the object of the investigation, the result of which consequently would be only a play of forces contingent upon the will's particular whims. Interestingly, these "whims," by sleight of hand, assume a certain intellectual capacity of the will itself, yet a capacity clearly in service of desires that have no intellectual ground but rather form a preintellectual vortex of forces.

33. Following Aristotle's *De anima*, Thomas distinguishes between the capacity of abstraction, that is, the agent intellect *(intellectus agens)* that abstracts from sense experience of particular things to form (confused) ideas, and the capacity of understanding, that is, the possible intellect *(intellectus possibilis)* that receives those ideas and develops them via the process of discursive reasoning into concepts. Underlying the agent intellect and the possi-

to its proper end. And so Thomas concludes his reflection upon the interrelationship between intellect and will with the following summary: "From this we can easily understand why these powers include one another in their acts, because the intellect understands that the will wills and the will wills the intellect to understand. In the same way, good is contained in truth, inasmuch as it is an understood truth, and truth in good, inasmuch as it is a desired good" (*ST* I, q. 82, a. 4, ad 1).[34] In short, the will moves the intellect as an efficient cause, while the intellect moves the will as a final cause; that is, the will wills the intellect to understand, and therefore the will itself can be a proper object of the intellect's inquiry, while the intellect's understanding offers the will those goods toward which it inclines itself.[35]

As stated above, we can observe a subtle development from Thomas's teaching in *ST* I, which reflects and systematizes his earlier thought, to his later work in *ST* I-II and especially in *De malo* 6. Instead of moving the will, as a final cause, the intellect's operation is reduced to that of a formal cause, that is, to the role of presenting the object to the will and thereby offering a specification of the will's act.[36] In other words, the intellect as the will's formal cause does not suffice anymore to activate the will. Rather, lest the origin of the will's movement be thought to rest solely in the will itself — the will thus becoming its own prime mover, which would entail denying the will to be part and parcel of creation — God must be understood as the first mover of the will.[37] This development, however, does not

---

ble intellect is a more fundamental receptive act of the intellect that earlier Aristotelian commentators called *nous pathetikos*. Thomas gestures to this primal intellective act of undergoing or suffering reality in *ST* I, q. 79, a. 2 ("Et sic intelligere nostrum est pati") and in *De malo*, q. 3, a. 4 c., where he refers to the intellect as "cuius actus consistit in recipiendo ab exteriori: unde dicitur quod intelligere est pati quoddam." For detailed accounts of Thomas's complex way of relating active and possible intellect, see Robert E. Brennan, O.P., *Thomistic Psychology: A Philosophic Analysis of Man* (New York: Macmillan, 1941), esp. ch. 6; and most recently, Robert Pasnau, *Thomas Aquinas on Human Nature: A Philosophical Study of Summa theologiae 1a, 75-89* (Cambridge: Cambridge University Press, 2002), ch. 10.

34. "Ex his ergo apparet ratio quare hae potentiae suis actibus invicem se includunt: quia intellectus intelligit voluntatem velle, et voluntas vult intellectum intelligere. Et simili ratione bonum continetur sub vero, inquantum est quoddam verum intellectum; et verum continetur sub bono, inquantum est quoddam bonum desideratum" (ST I, q. 82, a. 4, ad 1).

35. The intellect also comprehends its own operation as intellect (*ST* I, q. 87, a. 3, ad 1).

36. *ST* I-II, q. 9, a. 1.

37. Cf. *ST* I-II, q. 10, a. 4 and *The* De Malo *of Thomas Aquinas,* ed. Brian Davies, trans. Richard Regan (Oxford: Oxford University Press, 2001), 463 (*De malo,* q. 6, ad 4). On the

at all affect the intellect's distinct and proper mode of operation. Rather, now the will's unique character and operation come into much sharper relief. Hence, while most emphatically not being its own first cause, the will is the proximate cause of its own motion: "The will when moved by God contributes something, since the will itself acts even though God moves it. And so the will's movement, although from an external source as the first source, is nevertheless not coerced."[38]

Judgment in Crisis

How are intellect and will now affected by sin? Thomas approaches this question with a fundamental Augustinian commitment, quoting in the *sed contra* of *ST* I-II, q. 74, a. 1 Augustine's statement that "it is by the will that we sin, and live righteously."[39] On the basis of his previous discussion of the nature of will and intellect as powers of the soul, Thomas identifies the will, being the principle of voluntary acts, as the principle of sins.[40] This fundamental insight gains crucial importance as Thomas turns to original sin and asks "Whether Original Sin Infects the Will before the Other Powers?" (*ST* I-II, q. 83, a. 3). In full consequence of his Augustinian position, he claims that original sin regards first of all the will. Recall Thomas's earlier claim that the will moves the intellect as its efficient cause and his later claim that the intellect does not move the will, that is, as its final cause, but rather operates merely as its formal cause, presenting the object to the will. Both claims now bear surprising fruit in the specification of original sin. Consider Thomas's remarks in *ST* I-II, q. 83, a. 3, ad 3: "The intellect precedes the will, in one way, by proposing its object to it. In another way, the will precedes the intellect, in the order of motion to act, which motion per-

once hotly debated question of the "praemotio physica," see the concise discussion in Gallus M. Manser, O.P., *Das Wesen des Thomismus*, 3rd enlarged ed. (Freiburg: Paulusverlag, 1949), pp. 603-25.

38. De Malo *of Thomas Aquinas*, 461 (*De malo*, q. 6 c.).

39. "Voluntas est qua peccatur, et recte vivitur" (*Retractationes* I.9; PL 32, 596).

40. "Et ideo sequitur quod peccatum sit in voluntate sicut in subiecto" (*ST* I-II, q. 74, a. 1). Already in *ST* I, q. 17, a. 1 ("Whether Falsity Exists in Things") Thomas establishes the will as the principle of sin: "In things that depend on God, falseness cannot be found, in so far as they are compared with the divine intellect; since whatever takes place in things proceeds from the ordinance of that intellect, unless perhaps in the case of voluntary agents only, who have it in their power to withdraw themselves from what is ordained; wherein consists the evil of sin. Thus sins themselves are called untruths and lies in the Scriptures."

tains to sin."[41] Here it is very important to remember Thomas's earlier distinction between external acts (falling under the category of *poiesis*, "making") and internal acts (falling under the category of *praxis*, "doing"), that is, desire and knowledge (*ST* I-II, q. 74, a. 1). The one internal act we are most interested in here is the act of the speculative intellect *(iudicium speculativum)*, or, in its Aristotelian rendition, *theoria*.[42] However, Thomas does not ask explicitly how *theoria* might be affected by the will's sinfully misdirecting the intellect. Rather, because of the particular thrust of *ST* I-II, where the intellective and volitional movement of humans is perfected by grace and led toward their gratuitous ultimate end, Thomas focuses on a particular class of internal moral acts, namely, those "acts which do not pass into external matter, but remain in the agent, e.g. to desire and to know: and such are all moral acts, whether virtuous or sinful" (*ST* I-II, q. 74, a. 1). Does this mean that *theoria*, the act of knowing that is directed to that which is solely and properly the intellect's object, can never be affected by the will and therefore by sin? In short, are we, according to Thomas, at least epistemologically free from the effects of original sin?

One of the strengths of Thomas's way of relating intellect and will is his ability to account for how the intellect's proper capacity has not been destroyed by human sin. The intellect is able to come to knowledge and judge properly (yet not inerrantly) in highly complex and nontrivial ways. Might therefore the question of reasoning's directedness, in its very own domain as *theoria*, be a moot one from Thomas's point of view? Would one therefore, in order to approach this question at all, have to descend the slippery slope of voluntarism? Is this the very problematic where the late Augustine and the late Thomas might part ways and companionship, the first allegedly calling forth Ockham and Luther, Pascal and Jansenius, the latter the rationalistic self-confidence of nineteenth-century neo-scholasticism?

When we turn to Thomas's discussion of the vice of curiosity (indeed, a very Augustinian theme),[43] we will realize that Thomas allows for

---

41. "[I]ntellectus quoddam modo praecedit voluntatem, inquantum proponit ei suum obiectum. Alio vero modo voluntas praecedit intellectum, secundum ordinem motionis ad actum: quae quidem motio pertinet ad peccatum."

42. On Aristotle's *bios theoretikos*, see Joseph Dunne, *Back to the Rough Ground: 'Phronesis' and 'Techne' in Modern Philosophy and in Aristotle* (Notre Dame, IN: University of Notre Dame Press, 1993), pp. 237-44.

43. For a profound, illuminating, and distinctly Augustinian treatment of this topic, see Paul J. Griffiths, *Intellectual Appetite: A Theological Grammar* (Washington, DC: The Catholic University of America Press, 2009).

theoria, while not being cognitively defective, to be nevertheless deeply affected by a will sinfully turned away from the ultimate good. Thomas's mature understanding of the specific and asymmetrical reciprocity of intellect and will upon each other allows for a nuanced account of reasoning's directedness without falling into the trap of voluntarist skepticism.

The Virtue of Studiousness and the Vice of Curiosity — A Paradigmatic Test Case

Thomas's treatment of the vice of curiosity is to be found in the *Secunda secundae* of his *Summa theologiae,* an extensive treatment of the virtues, the vices, and the gifts, beatitudes, and fruits of the Holy Spirit that he discussed in the *Prima secundae* in briefer and more formal ways. Curiosity and the respective virtue of studiousness pertain to the cardinal virtue of temperance, that is, the moral excellence that rightly restrains and channels the bodily and intellectual passions that sustain but also endanger human flourishing.[44] In slightly more technical language, Thomas would regard studiousness as "a subordinate virtue annexed to a principal virtue," that is, temperance, and "to be comprised under modesty" (*ST* II-II, q. 166, a. 2 c.), a virtue that in turn is "annexed to temperance as its principal" (*ST* II-II, q. 160, a. 1 c.).

It strikes me as important to register early on that seriously discussing studiousness as well as curiosity may look to many contemporary readers like indulging in a most irrelevant intellectual exercise. Yet nothing could be further from the truth than precisely this prejudice. Late modern societies that are fundamentally shaped by the overwhelming presence of electronic media and the obscene inundation of every aspect of human life by pictures and sounds have turned the vice of curiosity into a prescribed way of life. In a world in which curiosity rules, unmasking curiosity as a destructive and offensive vice therefore amounts to nothing less than a most radical critique of a culture of systemic superficiality and constant distraction.[45]

---

44. "[I]t belongs to temperance to moderate the movement of the appetite, lest it tend excessively to that which is desired naturally" (*ST* II-II, q. 166, a. 2 c.).

45. For fundamentally different thinkers converging in their critique of a culture that breeds curiosity and an ensuing superficiality, see Herbert Marcuse's decrying the "tyranny of tolerance" in his *One Dimensional Man: Studies in the Ideology of Advanced Industrial Society* (Boston: Beacon, 1966), and Josef Pieper offering a biting critique of a culture of multimedial distraction in the section "Disciplining the Eyes," in his *The Four Cardinal Virtues* (Notre Dame, IN: University of Notre Dame Press, 1966), pp. 198-202.

Studiousness   Because it provides the crucial backdrop for fully appreciating the deeply problematic nature of curiosity, I will attend first to Thomas's discussion of the virtue of studiousness. After establishing that the appropriate matter of studiousness is knowledge, Thomas turns to the question "Whether Studiousness Is a Part of Temperance?" (*ST* II-II, q. 166, a. 2). In a striking way, a quote from Augustine in the *sed contra* contrasts the three arguments that deny the question and, more importantly, anticipates Thomas's telling answer: "'We are forbidden to be curious: and this is a great gift that temperance bestows.'[46] Now curiosity is prevented by moderate studiousness. Therefore studiousness is a part of temperance." Precisely because the human being is not just a body but a body informed by an individual intellective soul,[47] the human naturally desires what is appropriate to his soul: *cognoscere aliquid,* to know something.[48] Unsurprisingly, "the moderation of this desire pertains to the virtue of studiousness." The real and exciting complexity of this seemingly straightforward position only emerges in Thomas's responses to the objections, two responses in which the problematic of reasoning's directedness is immediately and dramatically relevant.

One of the objections raises the problem that knowledge has no connection with the moral virtues of which temperance and therefore also modesty and studiousness are a part. This is because they root in the appetitive part of the soul, that is, in the will. Knowledge, consequently, seems to pertain only to the intellectual virtues (prudence and its subordinate virtues), which arise from the soul's cognitive part, that is, the intellect. In his response, by implicit reference to *ST* I-II, q. 9, a. 1, Thomas first restates the way in which the will directs the intellect: "The act of a cognitive power is commanded by the appetitive power, which moves all the powers." This fundamental insight into the way the will moves all the powers of the soul to their appropriate ends, as discussed above, allows Thomas to make a critical differentiation. It is the differentiation between the twofold good with respect to knowledge. There is, first, the one that is connected with the act of knowledge itself: "[T]his good pertains to the intellectual virtues, and

46. "Curiosi esse prohibemur: quod magnae temperantiae munus est" (*De Moribus Ecclesiae,* Cap. 21: PL 32, 1327).

47. That is, the substance of the human being is determined comprehensively by the intellect *(mens,* or *intellectus).* The *anima intellectiva* is the sole substantial form of the human being; it also governs all of the body's functions. Cf. *ST* I, q. 76, aa. 1-4.

48. It should come as no surprise when Thomas quotes in this very instance the familiar opening line from Aristotle's *Metaphysics:* Πάντες ἄνθρωποι τοῦ εἰδέναι ὀρέγονται φύσει (All human beings naturally desire knowledge).

consists in man having a true estimate about each thing." There is, second, the one that belongs to the act of the appetitive power, that is, the will. And this good "consists in man's appetite being directed aright in applying the cognitive power in this or that way to this or that thing" (*ST* II-II, q. 166, a. 2, ad 2). Being able to form the appetite aright in order that this power of the will might rightly apply the cognitive power is what makes studiousness a virtue in the first place. To turn Thomas's point around: Only because the will indeed does have a specific effect on the intellect does a particular moral virtue pertain to the cognitive power.

Let us turn to the other pertinent objection. Studiousness cannot be a subordinate virtue of temperance, because the former does not resemble the latter in the mode of its operation. While temperance is a kind of restraint that opposes the vice of excess, studiousness seems to be first of all the application of the mind to something that opposes the vice of neglect. Thomas again responds with a distinction, now between contrary inclinations. He prepares this distinction by drawing upon Aristotle's teaching that in order to be virtuous, one must avoid all that to which one is most naturally inclined. The virtue of studiousness has two seemingly contrary aspects because of the contrary inclination the human being displays regarding knowledge: "For on the part of the soul, he is inclined to desire knowledge of things; and so it behooves him to exercise a praiseworthy restraint on this desire, lest he seek knowledge immoderately: whereas on the part of the bodily nature, man is inclined to avoid the trouble of seeking knowledge" (*ST* II-II, q. 166, a. 2, ad 3). Consequently, as it pertains to the first inclination, studiousness constitutes a kind of restraint, but insofar as it pertains to the second inclination, "this virtue derives its praise from a certain keenness of interest in seeking knowledge of things; and from this it takes its name." Thus studiousness restrains, channels, directs, and applies the cognitive power in a concentrated, sustained, and keenly interested way to the arduous task of gaining knowledge that is appropriate as well as profound.

Curiosity   With the virtue of studiousness as necessary backdrop, we are now able finally to turn to the vice of curiosity. How does Thomas treat the vice of curiosity, and how might the intellect's speculative power, *theoria*, be affected by it? In *ST* II-II, q. 167, a. 1, Thomas goes right to the core of the matter by asking "Whether Curiosity Can Be About Intellective Knowledge?" First, he reports three objections, a not untypical assemblage of some of the ways strict intellectualists would want to defend the intellect's supremacy from any incursions from the side of the will. Yet again,

Thomas's choice of the *sed contra,* this time not from Augustine but from Jerome, is quite a foreboding of the kind of response that is about to come: "'Is it not evident that a man who day and night wrestles with the dialectic art, the student of natural science whose gaze pierces the heavens, walks in vanity of understanding and darkness of mind?' Now vanity of understanding and darkness of mind are sinful. Therefore curiosity about intellective sciences may be sinful."[49]

Fully consistent with what he has previously established, Thomas maintains that while knowledge as such is always good, the desire for and study in pursuit of knowledge of the truth may be right or wrong. First, acquiring a particular knowledge may be accidentally linked to evil. Second, the appetite and study that is directed at the knowledge of truth may itself be inordinate. This can be the case in four ways: First, in turning from one's primary obligation to a less useful occupation (as the pastor who, instead of persistently studying the Scriptures and continuing to develop the linguistic and conceptual tools necessary for this task, turns to other, more "interesting" intellectual pursuits such as computer programs or Web sites with ready-to-go sermons, liturgies, and other aids). Second, in seeking knowledge from persons by whom it is illicit to be taught (as the medical student who wants to study the human response to extreme cold with a Nazi physician who gained his knowledge by systematically freezing concentration camp inmates to death). Since I will dwell longer on the third way, I will immediately move to the fourth: in studying "to know the truth above the capacity of [one's] own intelligence, since by so doing men easily fall into error." As already pointed out above, for Thomas, reasoning is the discursive activity of the intellect, and because any extended and complex argument about the truth of something that transcends epistemic obviousness *(this is a chair; this is a pencil)* easily brings the uninstructed person to the limit of his/her own intellectual possibilities, error becomes increasingly likely, and instruction prior to the informed engagement of one's discursive powers in complex inquiries and their discursive disciplines increasingly necessary. Curiosity in these matters can only amount to dangerous dabbling, while studiousness implies the modesty to acknowledge the necessity of prior instruction.

Finally, we turn to the way most pertinent to our purposes in which

49. "Nonne vobis videtur in vanitate sensus et obscuritate mentis ingredi qui diebus ac noctibus in dialectica arte torquetur, qui physicus perscrutator oculos trans caelum levat?" (*In Ephes.,* Lib. II, super IV[17]; PL 26, 536).

the appetite to know can itself be inordinate: in desiring "to know the truth about creatures, without referring [one's] knowledge to its due end, namely, the knowledge of God."[50] Here we finally have Thomas identifying an inherently restricted — and in this precise sense, misdirected — act of the speculative intellect, or *theoria*. A knowledge of creatures that is not directed to its dutiful end, namely, the knowledge of God, is a distorted, sinful knowledge not because it is faulty in and of itself (that is, there need not be any cognitive defect in this knowledge). Rather, this knowledge becomes distorted, sinful knowledge by its lack of reference to and reverence for the One who grants being in the first place. Knowing "the truth about creatures" unquestionably refers to *theoria*, the speculative act of the intellect directed to everything that is not God or one of God's operations — in short, the full scope of the *ens inquantum ens*. It is Thomas's response in the *ad primum* that offers additional warrant for this assumption: "Hence there may be sin in the knowledge of certain truths, in so far as the desire of such knowledge is not directed in due manner to the knowledge of the sovereign truth, wherein supreme happiness consists."[51] What a sweeping anticipatory indictment of the whole range of modern immanentism this is, be it in philosophy, natural science, or the so-called humanities.

Thus, Thomas assumes also *theoria* to be affected by sin in that the intellect in its concrete operation is moved in a way that restricts or distracts it from its proper end, the knowledge of the ultimate truth and the supreme good, and in this sense misdirects it without necessarily causing a cognitive defect in what is known. Thomas's understanding of the specific, asymmetrical reciprocity between intellect and will undercuts the kind of voluntarist skepticism that eventually will arise from the assumption that the will rules unaccountably and irresistibly over the intellect.[52]

Knowing and Reasoning

It is here that Thomas's subtle distinction between intellect and reason — and hence between knowing and reasoning — to which I alluded ear-

---

50. "Tertio, quando homo appetit cognoscere veritatem circa creaturas non referendo ad debitum finem, scilicet ad cognitionem Dei."

51. "Et ideo potest esse vitium in cognitione aliquorum verorum, secundum quod talis appetitus non debito modo ordinatur ad cognitionem summae veritatis, in qua consistit summa felicitas."

52. For a lucid account of this distinctly modern development of thought, see Michael Allen Gillespie, *Nihilism before Nietzsche* (Chicago: University of Chicago Press, 1996).

lier does some surprisingly helpful work. It allows us to gain a clearer grasp of the way reasoning can be profoundly misdirected while the intellect's epistemic capacity per se remains unaffected.[53] The latter is actually the very presupposition necessary for reasoning to be misdirected in the first place: Even while being discursively misguided, the intellect always continues to perceive some truth, since this is precisely what allows it to remain in error and not in a state of undifferentiated delusion. Therefore, "the intellect cannot be false in its knowledge of simple essences; but is either true, or it understands nothing at all" (*ST* I, q. 17, a. 3 c.). Hence, it is not in the primal intellective act but in the discursive process of reasoning, of linking intellective judgments in one or another way into complex arguments and theories, that the will, and hence the agent, comes into play.[54]

It is useful to remember at this point Thomas's insight that similar to the intellect, the will is moved in two ways: first, so far as concerns the exercise of its act and, second, so far as concerns what seems to be — or indeed is — a particular good, that is, "the specification of the act, derived from the object" (*ST* I-II, q. 10, a. 2 c.).[55] While the will is not able to influence the intellect's basic operation, it is quite able to will that the intellect not continue thinking about something particular and to direct the intellect instead to consider something else. This accounts

53. Cf. *ST* I, q. 17, a. 3 c. ("Whether Falsity Is in the Intellect?"): "Now as the sense is directly informed by the likeness of its proper object, so is the intellect by the likeness of the essence of a thing. Hence the intellect is not deceived about the essence of a thing, as neither the sense about its proper object. But in affirming and denying, the intellect may be deceived, by attributing to the thing of which it understands the essence, something which is not consequent upon it, or is opposed to it. For the intellect is in the same position as regards *judging* of such things, as sense is as to judging of common, or accidental, sensible objects. *There is, however, this difference, as before mentioned regarding truth (Q. 16, A. 2), that falsity can exist in the intellect not only because the knowledge of the intellect is false, but because the intellect is conscious of that knowledge, as it is conscious of truth;* whereas in sense falsity does not exist as known, as stated above (A. 2)" (my emphasis).

54. Thomists therefore distinguish between the "order of specification," arising from the object of the (intellective) act, and the "order of exercise," arising from how the agent exists.

55. Eleonore Stump rightly points out that according to Thomas, "if the will is presented by the intellect with an object which can be considered good under some descriptions and not good under others, then the will is not necessarily moved by that object either. . . . It is open to the will not to will that object by willing that the intellect not think about it" (Stump, "Intellect, Will, and the Principle of Alternate Possibilities," p. 268; cf. *ST* I, q. 82, a. 2).

for the easy distractibility of reasoning in practical as well as theoretical matters.[56]

Instead of considering complex large-scale examples of misdirected reasoning from the history of science, such as "Aryan physics" (opposing Einstein's theory of relativity), or from dialectical-materialist sociology, economy, and history (acknowledged core disciplines of all the universities in the bygone Communist regimes), consider the simple case suggested by Eleonore Stump and applicable by family resemblance:

> Suppose that Anna has just won some money in a contest and that she plans to use the money to buy a frilly pink canopy bed for her daughter, something she has been coveting but unable to afford. As she sits reading a magazine, she comes across an advertisement urging readers to give money to support children in third-world countries and showing a picture of a ragged, emaciated child. Anna no sooner glances at the ad than she turns the page. Why does she do so? The answer to the question will, of course, involve the will's issuing commands which result in Anna's turning the page; *but underlying these commands is something like the will's directive to the intellect not to think about the ad and the needy children it describes.* The will makes this directive in virtue of a hasty calculation on the part of the intellect that looking at the

---

56. Thomas offers a complex discussion of this matter in *ST* I-II, q. 17 ("Of the Acts Commanded by the Will"), in which he applies and extends the highly complex feedback system between intellect and will. Command is an act of reason, yet the very fact that reason moves by commanding is due to the power of the will: "Consequently it follows that command is an act of reason, presupposing an act of the will, in virtue of which the reason, by its command, moves (the power) to the execution of the act" (*ST* I-II, q. 17, a. 1 c.). However, the aspect most pertinent to our concern is found in article 6 ("Whether the Act of Reason Is Commanded?"), where Thomas distinguishes between the exercise of the act (which is always commanded "as when one is told to be attentive, and to use one's reason") and the object of the exercise of reason. Here we encounter the crucial distinction between the uncommanded aspect and the aspect that is open to command: "One is the act whereby it apprehends the truth about something. This act is not in our power: because it happens in virtue of a natural or supernatural light. Consequently the act of reason is not in our power, and cannot be commanded. The other act of the reason is that whereby it assents to what it apprehends. If, therefore, that which the reason apprehends is such that it naturally assents thereto, e.g., the first principles, it is not in our power to assent or to dissent to the like. . . . But some things which are apprehended do not convince the intellect to such an extent as not to leave it free to assent or dissent, or at least suspend its assent or dissent, on account of some cause or other; and in such things assent or dissent is in our power, and is subject to our command" (*ST* I-II, q. 17, a. 6). Cf. also *De malo*, q. 3, a. 3 c.

ad is not good. . . . Informing or influencing this calculation will be Anna's coveting of the frilly pink canopy bed for her daughter, a passion in Aquinas's sense. Perhaps without the influence of that coveting Anna's calculation about the ad might have been different.[57]

Thomas's analysis of the vice of curiosity makes it plain why Stump's example, while pertaining to a matter of practical reasoning, can easily be applied to the act of speculative reasoning as well.[58]

Toward the Redemption of Judgment

Curiosity's Horizon of Discovery (Metaphysics of Creation) and Its Cure (Grace)

If it is the case that curiosity is the vice that affects *theoria* by restricting and distracting the intellect and by misdirecting the discursive process of reasoning, we need now to ask: What constitutes the horizon from which the vice of curiosity can be identified in the first place? And how can a redirected gaze of *theoria* be suggested at all? Thomas's third argument in *ST* II-II, q. 167, a. 1 c., and especially his response to the first objection, implies that this horizon is nothing less than a theologically motivated and informed metaphysics of creation. How so? Let us recall both passages. First, the pursuit of knowledge may be wrong "when a man desires to know the truth about creatures, without referring his knowledge to its due end, namely, the knowledge of God. Hence Augustine says that 'in studying creatures, we must not be moved by empty and perishable curiosity; but we should ever mount towards immortal and abiding things'" (*ST* II-II, q. 167, a. 1 c.). Second, since the sovereign good of humanity consists in the knowledge of the sovereign truth, Thomas avers, "there may be sin in the

---

57. Eleonore Stump, "Intellect, Will, and the Principle of Alternate Possibilities," p. 269 (my emphasis).

58. See Thomas's discussion of "Whether Falsity Is in the Intellect?" in *ST* I, q. 17, a. 3 and the concise summary he offers in *De malo*, q. 3, a. 3 c. of the ways the intellect and the will are moved and are not moved. Here again "regarding the intellect, things necessarily linked to naturally known first principles necessarily move the intellect. . . . But the intellect is not compelled to assent to conclusions if they be not necessarily linked to naturally known first principles, as is the case with contingent and probable things. Likewise, neither does the intellect necessarily assent to necessary things necessarily linked to first principles before it knows there is such a necessary connection" (De Malo *of Thomas Aquinas,* pp. 245, 247).

knowledge of certain truths, in so far as the desire of such knowledge is not directed in due manner to the knowledge of the sovereign truth, wherein supreme happiness consists" (*ST* II-II, q. 167, a. 1, ad 1).

What happens in both cases is that in order to specify curiosity as an intellectual vice, as sinfully misdirected reasoning, Thomas consistently presumes what Robert Sokolowski calls "the Christian distinction" between the Creator and everything *(ta panta)*.[59] However, it is precisely this distinction that constitutes the defining mark of the metaphysics of creation over against any other form of metaphysics.

To put it in the form of a thesis: A metaphysics of creation is the necessary horizon *(a)* to understand why curiosity is a vice and *(b)* to direct the intellect's gaze to its proper object, the ultimate truth. Yet what do I mean by a *theologically* motivated and informed metaphysics of creation? What differentiates it from other versions of metaphysics, especially an Aristotelian metaphysics, as the science of being as being *(ens inquantum est ens)?* To put it in terms that are possibly too condensed, while a metaphysics of being presupposes the ontological difference between being and beings, a metaphysics of creation admits its dependence "from above" by presuming a second, and ultimately more fundamental, difference. It is the difference between *esse commune/esse ipsum* — an absolute abundant *actus essendi* that is open to both participation (creation) and subsistence (God) and, while abstracting from both, is to be found in both — and *ipsum esse subsistens,* that is, God.[60] Hence, while remaining implicit in the metaphysics of *esse,* the dependence upon *sacra doctrina* and its normative distinction between the Creator and everything else becomes explicit in the metaphysics of creation.

Yet why does the metaphysics of creation antecedently depend upon the metaphysics of being? I cannot improve upon the answer given by Martin Bieler: Precisely because it is "the way of being." Thomas shows "that creation consists in the gift of being *(esse):* 'Creare autem est dare esse.' The 'way of being' is the 'dare esse' by which God in his care is present in all things."[61] Because it allows for the best conceptual expression of the *dare esse,* of the gift of creation, the metaphysics of being is open to being ele-

---

59. Robert Sokolowski, *The God of Faith and Reason: Foundations of Christian Theology* (Notre Dame, IN: University of Notre Dame Press, 1982), pp. 32-33.

60. For a short and accessible account, see Josef Stallmach, "Der actus essendi und die Frage nach dem Sinn von 'Sein,'" in *Actus omnium actuum: Festschrift für Heinrich Beck zum 60. Geburtstag,* ed. Erwin Schadel (Frankfurt: Lang, 1989), pp. 47-58.

61. Bieler, "Theological Importance," p. 311.

vated and assumed by the second difference into the metaphysics of creation.[62] And because the metaphysics of creation is an extension of *sacra doctrina* into the metaphysics of being, that is, an expression of *fides quaerens intellectum* that reads the world as God's creation, this move makes the metaphysics of creation vulnerable, dependent upon the conceptual and substantive veracity of the metaphysics of being that it assumes.

A theologically informed metaphysics of creation is constituted by the second, onto-theological, difference because the first, or ontological, difference is dramatically insufficient for understanding the world as *creatio ex nihilo* and, moreover, fundamentally incapable of establishing the horizon that enables us to appreciate the true nature of curiosity in the first place. Rather, only the onto-theological difference between *esse ipsum* and *ipsum esse subsistens,* in which *esse* itself is analogically conceived, fulfills the theological requirement to understand the world as creation.[63]

A metaphysics of creation (a) is able analogically to consider and interrelate all of reality, all of what is, thereby reflecting the intelligible unity in the difference of creation; (b) is inherently directed to and participationally dependent upon divine transcendence because of the centrality of the second difference; and (c) is therefore able intellectively to present to the will the ultimate object of desire, its due end. However, the intellect cannot reform or redirect the will so that the good of the second difference becomes the will's definitive end of desire. Thus, the metaphysics of creation begs the question of the will's primal mover and especially its renewal or healing through grace, so that, as the intellect is being informed by faith, the will may be informed by charity. In short, a genuine metaphysics of creation always begs Christology and can only achieve its purpose ultimately "after Christ."

Thomas's discussion of the relationship between intellect and will, assuming reasoning's directedness under the condition of sin, yields at least three crucial insights: First, the metaphysics of creation is a necessary implication of *fides quaerens intellectum,* lest creation remain a closed

---

62. For an extraordinary account of the openness of the metaphysics of *esse* to the metaphysics of creation, see Heinrich Beck, *Der Akt-Charakter des Seins* (Munich: Max Hueber, 1965).

63. Thomas draws in his metaphysics of creation upon both Aristotle and Plato, yet in the form of a superior synthesis that is made possible by the antecedent assumption of the intellect's due end as also desired by a rectified will, namely, the supreme truth and good. It is precisely the second difference that accounts for why the supreme truth and good do not need to become operative (as knowledge *simpliciter*) in the process of intellectual inquiry.

book to the *fidei ratio.* Second, the metaphysics of creation becomes a criterion for a critical Christian engagement of the philosophies of the day.[64] Third, Thomas' short remark amounts to a profound indictment of all forms of modern "unbiased" and supposedly strictly empirical research.[65] There is, though, one question that still needs to be addressed: If the metaphysics of creation here identified is understood to be informed by theology, how do the metaphysics of creation and theology relate to each other?

The Explicit Dependence of a Metaphysics of Creation on Theology

The metaphysics of creation explicitly depends on a theological a priori.[66] This is the case, first, because it is ordered by the second difference and, second, because its proper operation presupposes a rectified will that indeed desires what the intellect points to in posing the second difference. Thus, a volitionally sustained and, only therein, successful metaphysics of creation depends on an intervention of grace that is by definition beyond its intellective scope. It is this dependence on a reality it can gesture toward yet cannot account for in the horizon of its proper object of inquiry that makes the metaphysics of creation a disreputable discipline in the modern, post-Enlightenment academy. For the second difference introduces analogicity and, with it, a moment of corrective negativity that will prevent the construction of a conceptually closed "system" or of a dialectical machinery bent on the comprehensive conceptual penetration of reality.[67]

64. For some programmatic reflections in this direction, see Hans Urs von Balthasar, *Von den Aufgaben der katholischen Philosophie in der Zeit,* 2nd ed. (Freiburg: Einsiedeln, 1998).

65. Moreover, in light of Thomas's perspective, Heidegger's critique of modern metaphysics and science under the category "forgetfulness of being" needs to be understood as a weaker version of Thomas's own indictment. Heidegger's "forgetfulness of being" is ultimately fated, especially since Heidegger's "last god" remains playfully and painfully hidden in and under being's withdrawal and granting. Thus Heidegger's way of rendering the issue allows skeptical and nihilistic consequences impossible in Thomas's thought. For a penetrating critique of Heidegger, see Hart, "Offering of Names."

66. This dependence does not, however, entail that a metaphysics of being (supposing the will's rectification) is in itself unable to grasp the ontological difference between *esse commune* and *esse subsistens!*

67. Therefore, a metaphysics of creation in the spirit of Thomas would fall neither under the by now quite fashionable *Metaphysikkritik* developed in various forms by Heidegger and Derrida nor under the anti-Hegelian *Systemkritik* of Adorno and his students. On the fundamental difference between a metaphysics of the concept in which dialectic rules (Hegel)

While its arguments are in principle universally accessible (assuming the absence of error), a metaphysics of creation will be less than universally acceptable, not just because philosophy is an intrinsically controversial phenomenon,[68] but more importantly because it requires a seeing and willing, informed by a particular practice of judgment, that is shared only in historically contingent ways. In other words, a metaphysics of creation presupposes a tradition of discourse with a certain formation of thought and character as well as a will restored to its original destination, namely, desire for the ultimate good. Therefore, the *duplex ordo cognitionis,* the twofold order of knowledge, (as it is implied in a genuine metaphysics of creation) obtains — to use Thomas's own terms — *simpliciter;* yet under the condition of sin, it obtains only *secundum quid.* Differently put, precisely because the *duplex ordo cognitionis* is the result not of a primal intellective act but, to the contrary, of discursive reasoning, it is in need of magisterial affirmation (Vatican I).

The metaphysics of creation cannot afford to obscure its own dependence upon the appropriate directedness of reason, lest the proper activity of judgment be bent by the vice of curiosity. Moreover, it has to reflect upon the fundamental requirement of the formation of thought and character; a will restored to its original destination, necessary for a full judgment of *esse,* becomes vulnerable to the argument from history — a quite strong yet, in and of itself, inconclusive argument. It is a truism and borders on the banal that no tradition and/or school of philosophical inquiry has put forth a set of arguments that has resisted being thoroughly critiqued and eventually undermined by competing schools (yet not necessarily in conclusive ways).[69] And this vulnerability also is true of the metaphysics of creation. Yet by hamartiologically qualifying its concept of judgment by attending to reasoning's directedness in the concrete existence of the one who judges, the metaphysics of creation would be able to offer an account for the reason that it is just a school of thought. At the same time, however, this kind of theologically schooled metaphysics of

---

and a metaphysics grounded in the second difference and hence ruled by analogy, see Bernhard Lakebrink, "Analektik und Dialektik: Zur Methode des Thomistischen und Hegelschen Denkens," in *Perfectio Omnium Perfectionum: Studien zur Seinskonzeption bei Thomas von Aquin und Hegel,* ed. C. Günzler et al. (Vatican City: Libreria Editrice Vaticana, 1984), pp. 9-37.

68. Cf. Robert Spaemann, "Die kontroverse Natur der Philosophie," in *Philosophische Essays* (Stuttgart: Reclam, 1994), pp. 104-29.

69. Cf. Spaemann, "Die kontroverse Natur der Philosophie."

creation would have the tools necessary to understand itself as a tradition of discourse and inquiry not matched by any other philosophical school. This is the case precisely because of its dependence upon a rectification it cannot produce on its own but can only gesture toward in its concrete discursive activity. Hence, hamartiologically humble and historically reflective, the metaphysics of creation could interpret the veritable collection of dead — that is, "overcome" — theories that litter the battlefields of philosophical argument as philosophy caught in the incurvature of human existence under the condition of sin and thus fated to exist in the form of the eternal return of its conceptual possibilities. In other words, the metaphysics that draws upon its own history as a tradition of discourse in the horizon of the Christian faith can constructively face the challenge of the coming and going of philosophical schools and trends.[70] Yet at the same time, the metaphysics of creation operates *argumentatively*, like any other rational discourse, very well aware that, as Leibniz once put it, ultimately every argument is an argument *ad personam*, but aware as well that some arguments are coherently and comprehensively better than others.

The Implicit Dependence of Theology on a Metaphysics of Creation

Theology intends the reliability and veracity of its central concepts and their rootedness in the way things are. Only this reliability and veracity open the possibility of a genuine analogical discourse in theology, without which there is neither doctrine nor dogma. Scripture either suggests these concepts explicitly or begs them implicitly. Yet because of their rootedness in the way things are, it should be possible to unfold them, so to speak, on their own — that is, it should be possible for them to make sense on their own. Thus, the metaphysics of creation is ultimately normed by Scripture insofar as it is the latter's fundamental witness that constitutes the horizon

---

70. It might be conceivable to read the work of the later MacIntyre in this very way, especially his Gifford Lectures, *Three Rival Versions of Moral Inquiry*. I should hasten to emphasize that the disputability and vulnerability characteristic of a theologically — or, better, hamartiologically — reflective metaphysics of creation is by no means a necessarily unique advantage. Of course, genealogical accounts (Nietzschean, Foucaultian) of philosophy's nature and history might very well be able also to offer reasons for their own contingency and disputability. In other words, this advantage does not decisively separate a (Christian) metaphysics of creation from other meta-accounts of philosophy's nature — and this again is a good thing, precisely because of the very vulnerability and disputability of a metaphysics of creation.

that ultimately informs it. Yet insofar as the metaphysics of creation shapes the concepts with which theology operates, it also has a norming effect. But what is this norming effect all about?

Metaphysics of Creation — Metaphysics of Esse

As I averred at the beginning of this inquiry, Christian theology is bound to the God whose Logos is from all eternity God, and therefore Christian theology will always have a "metaphysical moment" in that it expects the structure of the world and the structure of the human mind to correspond because they were *made* to correspond; hence the metaphysics of creation. Yet Thomas teaches us to take this moment a step further by following the implication of "creation" to its very end. If the theocentric character of being obtains all the way down, if *ta panta* is creation all the way down, Christians should not be surprised to encounter fragments of a philosophical path or to be able to reconstruct such a path that allows this truth to be argued from the structure of being itself. Thomas's philosophy of being, drawing upon the fragments of this path encountered in Plato, Aristotle, and neo-Platonism, constitutes his own full reconstruction of the kind of metaphysics that must hypothetically be possible if indeed being is theocentric all the way down. In other words, theology must at least hypothetically be able to encounter its own metaphysical moment as external to itself — "external" because the economy of salvation relies upon the prior gift of creation, and "its own" because the gift of creation is in no way alien to the economy of salvation. It is this externality that has an appropriate norming effect on theology, since indeed all of being is governed by and ordered to God. Yet, ironically, this externality of a pure metaphysics of *esse* remains hypothetical unless it is concretely assumed into the metaphysics of creation. It is precisely here that — as governed by God's providence — the norming externality of creation is met by reasoning redirected to its ultimate good.

IV. Redeemed Judgment

We can raise the question of the directedness of reasoning meaningfully only in a horizon in which the problem is, at least in principle, already overcome. To put it in stark theological terms, only in the horizon of redemption can the fall be understood — that is, only retrospectively.[71] Similarly, Thomas's account of curiosity presupposes a horizon in light of which the problem under discussion is, at least inchoately, overcome. In other words, being able to inquire into the directedness of reasoning under the condition of sin presupposes a redirected reasoning and thus a redeemed capacity of judgment. Here Thomas assumes the epistemic and volitional reality of what Paul called the eschatological existence "in Christ," which begins inchoately in and through faith.

Let us first consider the end, the beatific vision. In contrast to human existence under the condition of sin, in the beatific vision God's goodness is clearly beheld "through the certitude of the Divine Vision." Beholding the divine essence, that is, the infinity of God's goodness, means to adhere to God of necessity: "[T]he will of the man who sees God in His essence of necessity adheres to God, just as now we desire of necessity to be happy" (*ST* I, q. 82, a. 2 c.). It is important to understand, however, that this necessity, far from destroying human freedom, constitutes the very fulfillment of freedom. For it is God's goodness that inexhaustibly fulfills the intellect's as well as the will's specific desires of truth and happiness.

Yet short of the beatific vision, where "the essence of God itself becomes the intelligible form of the intellect" (*ST* I, q. 12, a. 5 c.), we have to settle for faith. And it is fascinating to realize how, according to Thomas, faith needs to be understood as a fundamentally redirected reasoning, a dynamic in which the will commands the intellect to assent to God's revelation. Here is Thomas's succinct definition of faith, as found in *ST* II-II, q. 2, a. 9 c.: "Now the act of believing is an act of the intellect assenting to the Divine truth at the command of the will moved by the grace of God." The line of movement is from grace to will to intellect. Hence, it is grace that reorients the will to command the intellect to believe. In other words, the whole operation in which the human's will and intellect are active according to their proper created function nevertheless fully pertains to grace, that is, God's operation.[72] Bruce Marshall puts the whole matter in a beautifully clear way:

71. To put it in exegetical terms, only in light of Rom. 1:16-17 and 3:21ff. can the Apostle Paul thematize Rom. 1:18–3:20.

72. Thomas states this point in especially clear ways when it comes to justification: "God does not justify us without ourselves, because whilst we are being justified we consent to God's justification (*justitiae*) by a movement of our free-will. Nevertheless, this movement is not the cause of grace, but the effect; hence the whole operation pertains to grace" (*ST* I-II, q. 111, a. 2, ad 2).

The will, Aquinas argues, elicits the mind's assent to the teaching of scripture and creed. Even though the mind can "see" neither that the content of this teaching must be true, nor that its status compels assent, the will clings to the good which is held out in this teaching, and induces the intellect to hold it true. . . . Lit by grace, the heart (as we might now say) finds in the triune God of whom this teaching speaks its true desire, and so cleaves to this teaching not only as true, but as the first truth, "which is the goal of all our desires and actions."[73]

The reorientation of the will, caused by grace, is the source of redeemed judgment. It establishes now with faith's unique certainty (a) God's triune identity and Christ as the truth per se, and (b) the Creator/creature distinction, that is, the condition of the possibility of assuming the metaphysics of being into the metaphysics of creation. Redeemed judgment shows immediately forth in that fact that theology's genuine task, according to Thomas, is not to prove but to judge, to exercise and apply the judgment of faith in a sustained, comprehensive, and rigorous way. Marshall puts it thus: "The epistemic primacy of sacred doctrine is of a negative or limiting kind (i.e., *sacra doctrina* does not prove, but judges). No true statement can be inconsistent with the contents of Christian teaching."[74] Yet since one central entailment of *sacra doctrina* is the Creator/creature distinction, the second difference, theology applies its practice of redeemed judgment most consistently and comprehensively by assuming the metaphysics of being into a metaphysics of creation, that is, by realizing the Creator/creature distinction conceptually.[75] Redeemed judgment realizes being's beckoning.

The Gaze of Faith and the Wisdom of the Cross — With Thomas beyond Thomas

Faith has nothing less than an iconic effect. For the baptismal dynamic of faith (dying and rising) is not metaphorical but eschatological, and thus,

---

73. Bruce Marshall, *"Quod Scit Una Uetula,"* p. 13.

74. Bruce Marshall, *"Quod Scit Una Uetula,"* p. 16.

75. Martin Bieler puts it succinctly in his significant book *Freiheit als Gabe: Ein schöpfungstheologischer Entwurf* (Freiburg: Herder, 1991): "There is no Christian tradition without metaphysics lest it be ready to abandon the difference between Creator and creature and with it renounce itself. The question is not *whether* metaphysics but only *which* metaphysics is appropriate to the biblical tradition" (p. 78; my translation).

thanks to the will's restoration by grace, it provides a reconstituted gaze, the gaze of faith, as through a glass darkly. The human capacity to reason does not have to be destroyed and reinvented in this dying and rising. Rather, the will's orientation is now constantly informed in a substantive, albeit inchoate, way by its ultimate good, God. Yet this fundamental reorientation, this eschatological restoration of our gaze, is experienced under the condition of sin as an encounter with a Logos contra to our "logos" and its particular (mis)directedness, in other words, as an encounter with the Counter-Logos, the Wisdom of the Cross. What has to die and rise is not our reasoning capacity as such but rather the fundamental orientation of our reasoning under the condition of sin, the will that, instead of being fulfilled by participating in God's will and being thus genuinely freed, is locked *incurvatus in se* after having forfeited its ultimate good.[76]

Reasoning's directedness now participates through faith, inchoately, in the directedness of the Logos to the Father that *is* the Spirit, the triune identity that is the eternal law of triune love.[77] This participation in the Spirit, caused by the Spirit through faith, elicits a redeemed capacity of judgment that originates in a horizon constituted by *Gelassenheit* (the human will resigning to and thus participating in God's will) and by the complete release of any *Machtförmigkeit* of our epistemic gaze (the "let it be" that is the root of a metaphysics of creation in contrast to an onto-theology). Thus a complex cotemporality of all three realities of judgment — redeemed judgment, judgment of *esse*, and judgment in crisis — reflects the struggle over reason-

---

76. In an interesting essay, Jean Porter has shown that Thomas's account of the virtues is able to answer for the surprising possibility that infused cardinal virtues might cause significant tensions in the justified person. Infused cardinal virtues "can exist in the presence of contrary habits, that is, vices, which render their operation difficult and unpleasant (I-II, q. 65, a. 3, ad 2). . . . Indeed, the infused cardinal virtues can and do exist, at least potentially, in those who lack the use of reason altogether, as well as those who have some capacities for moral action but lack the maturity necessary to the full development of the acquired virtues." Porter, "The Subversion of Virtue: Acquired and Infused Virtues in the *Summa Theologiae*," in *Annual of the Society of Christian Ethics* (1992): 19-41; 32. For a more recent, very lucid treatment of this complex but utterly fascinating aspect of Thomas's doctrine of the infused moral virtues, see Michael F. Sherwin, O.P., "Infused Virtue and the Effects of Acquired Vice: A Test Case for the Thomistic Theory of Infused Cardinal Virtues," *The Thomist* 73, no. 1 (2009): 29-52.

77. See Bruce Marshall, *Trinity and Truth* (Cambridge: Cambridge University Press, 2000), on the epistemic role of the Spirit: "The action whereby the Spirit induces us to love God by sharing in the mutual love of the Father and the Son is epistemically decisive: from it ultimately stems our willingness to hold true the narratives which identify Jesus and the triune God, and to order the rest of our beliefs accordingly" (p. 209).

ing's directedness and thereby substantiates the conflictual relationship between theology and philosophy (with the exception of a metaphysics of creation). Philosophy, *ex sua natura*, is equally blind to the fall as to Christ and, as post-Christian, that is, modern, tends either to integrate and subsume from theology what it might regard as speculatively relevant (Hegel) or to fundamentally distance itself from the theological horizon, thus becoming crypto-theological by reclaiming and recasting central theological topoi (as with Kant, Nietzsche, and Heidegger).

V. The Metaphysics of Creation in the Conflict of Judgments

Yet even the metaphysics of creation will remain an exercise of thinking *in peregrinatione,* "on the way" — that is, an exercise in the middle of the conflict of judgments. Hence, while theology must use metaphysical argumentation in order to avoid the agonistics of one willful positing against another, so that reason(ing) may be sapientially assumed into the horizon of faith, such a theologically assumed philosophical reason(ing) will precisely *not* expect its arguments to be probative of the truth of the Christian faith (with the exception, of course, of the *praeambula fidei*). Rather, all that this sapiential mode of argumentation can do is, as Thomas put it, show how and why arguments against the Christian faith can be refuted (*ST* I, q. 1, a. 8). Hence, precisely under the specter of a seemingly sovereign postmetaphysical Zeitgeist — a repelling Janus-head of instrumental reason and ontological nihilism — Christian theology cannot afford to jettison the task of reading the world as governed by and ordered to God all the way down. It is the latter exercise that prevents Christian theology from becoming just one more willful positing, one more instantiation of the alleged will to power triumphing in an ultimate directing of reason. Yet in order to argue that there exists no such will to power but rather a humanity under the condition of sin, still governed by, and more importantly, called to communion with the triune God, Christian theology draws upon a metaphysics of creation in its rigorous reading of the world as governed by and ordered to God. Hence, because the conflict of judgments continues, this reading of the world as God's can ultimately be only a case of rigorous instruction, of sapiential catechesis at its highest level.

Epistemological skepticism and ontological nihilism on the one side and the triumphalism of instrumental reason on the other, while conceivably capable of being analyzed and criticized argumentatively, cannot be overcome by the force of argument alone. Thus, foundationalist strategies that breed the next round of skeptical rejoinders in their attempt to overcome the last round, as well as reductive strategies that commit performative contradictions in their very act of reduction, while predictably finding their disciples, will lead nowhere, because they obscure the concrete existence of the person who judges. Only if the very fact of existence comes into view, and, with it, the problem of existence as one essentially already overcome, can the crisis of reason as well as its instrumentalization be overcome. Yet this ultimately is a matter of conversion from the created things to the Creator, and of a corresponding catechesis. And the latter is nothing less than the initiation into a whole tradition of discourse and an exercise in the renewal of judgment. Therefore, only the conflict of judgments, including the conflict between a metaphysics of creation and other versions of philosophical discourse or style, points to a problem that otherwise would not even be perceptible. It is the offense of the wisdom of the cross, the offense of *Fides et Ratio*'s optimism about reason's full metaphysical range as it is informed by wisdom *(philosophari in Maria)*,[78] and the offense of a metaphysics of the second difference that lead into the conflict of judgments. This conflict is by no means to be avoided. On the contrary, it is a reflection of freedom, because only here in the difference between redeemed and unredeemed judgment — between reasoning directed to the creature alone, thereby precisely obscuring it as creature, and reasoning redirected to the Creator — shines forth the status of a world and existence over which the spiritual battle, the Spirit's battle, has not yet come to an end.

The drama of misdirected reasoning is not that it simply fails and knows nothing. On the contrary, misdirected reasoning is distressingly and shockingly successful in its reductive focus on the creature. Here a metaphysics of creation offers a discursive witness and argumentative pressure by creating a coherently argued difference in judgment and thus provoking the kind of intellectual conflict and crisis that is necessary in order fully to appreciate what in all its depth, *de facto* only grace followed by catechesis can give.

Yet the metaphysics of creation does more than that. In the form of

---

78. Cf. Ferdinand Ulrich, *Homo Abyssus: Das Wagnis der Seinsfrage,* with an introduction by Martin Bieler, 2nd ed. (Freiburg: Johannes Verlag Einsiedeln, 1998), pp. 275-76, and especially the way Martin Bieler unfolds this notion in the final section, *"Philosophari in Maria,"* of "Theological Importance," pp. 317-26.

an admittedly indirect sapiential *catechesis*, it would analogically unfold the very "grain of the universe" that reason properly directed is called audaciously to explore and to comtemplate. This ideal setting of a most rigorous and advanced catechesis in the horizon of redeemed judgment is the source of Thomas's inexhaustible trust in the intellect's capacity for truth, a trust deeply foreign to most late moderns, but one shared by and mirrored in the encyclical *Fides et Ratio*.

Dust Bound for Heaven —
Contemplating Human Nature and Destiny

A. Human Nature Wounded but Not Destroyed —
   The Passions, the Common Good, and the Natural
   Love of God under the Condition of Sin

CHAPTER 3

"Body Politics beyond Angelism and Animalism" — The Human Passions and Their Irreducible Spiritual Dimension

The formal cause of a thing is generally explained to be that which con-
stitutes it what it is; thus the soul may be said to be that which changes
the dust of the earth into an organized and living body.

John Henry Newman,
Lectures on the Doctrine of Justification

The lower part of the soul has some share of reason.

Summa theologiae I, q. 57, a. 4, ad 3

I. The Two Horns of the Modern Anthropological Dilemma: Angelism vs. Animalism

About thirty years ago, in her essay "From Passions to Emotions and Sentiments," the noted American philosopher Amélie Oksenberg Rorty astutely
observed:

> [In] [c]ontemporary philosophical and psychological debates about
> the emotions . . . [t]here is, as one might expect, combat on all sides,
> singularly unreflective polemics about whether the passions are
> evaluative judgments or physical states; about whether they can be vol-
> untarily controlled; about whether there are some culturally invariant
> basic passions; about whether altruism can be the consequence of

purely prudential considerations or whether it requires special development. . . . The problem is that our theories of the passions — and thus at least some of our experiences of what we call emotional states — are formed from the picturesque ruins of previous views. *We are a veritable walking archaeology of abandoned theories, even those that have claimed to vanquish one another.*[1]

Rorty's characterization of the modern failure to develop a stable and lasting theory of the emotions has a striking similarity to Alasdair MacIntyre's analysis, in his by now classic *After Virtue,* where he offers a profound analysis of the modern failure to sustain a satisfying theory of the virtues. What McIntyre has shown to be the case for the virtues is arguably also the case for the emotions.

Two reasons for such a connection between the modern failure to sustain a satisfying account of the virtues and the failure to sustain a satisfying account of the passions suggest themselves rather immediately. First, as already Aristotle and then especially Thomas Aquinas were fully aware of, there is a significant connection between the acts of the sense-appetite (and these acts, the "passions," have in modern discourse become the "emotions")[2] and the virtues. Thomas's treatment of both the passions and the virtues in the *Summa theologiae* demonstrates his exquisite sensitivity to the fact that losing appreciation of the acts of the sense appetite, the passions, as integral for human flourishing would be tantamount to the failure to understand the integral role the passions play in the development of the virtues. For Thomas, there simply cannot be a true formation of moral character without the passions being fully integrated into this formation.

Second, much of the contemporary philosophical debate about passions, emotions, or sentiments turns out to be irresolvable because this debate shares a set of tacit presuppositions that are the very cause for the debate's irresolvability. These presuppositions, I submit, are to be found in the early modern rejection of the Aristotelian-Thomist doctrine of hylemorphism and its concomitant faculty psychology, a rejection that makes it impossible to understand passions (1) as acts of the human soul (and more precisely, as acts of the soul's faculty of the sense appetite — in

---

1. Amélie Oksenberg Rorty, "From Passions to Emotions and Sentiments," *Philosophy* 57, no. 220 (1982): 159-72, p. 171f. (my emphasis).

2. For a detailed account, see Thomas Dixon, *From Passions to Emotions: The Creation of a Secular Psychological Category* (Cambridge: Cambridge University Press, 2003).

distinction from the acts of the intellectual appetite, that is, the will), and (2) as ordained — by way of their perfection through the moral virtues — to human flourishing and ultimately to human happiness in God. Hence, the contribution of the passions is indispensable for a full human flourishing so that a human life without the acts of the sense appetite would be always a severely diminished life.

Early modern theorists of the passions such as Descartes and Hobbes were still familiar with contemporaneous commentaries on Thomas's treatise on the passions in his *Summa theologiae*.[3] Thomas understands what the moderns tend to call "emotions" as acts of the sense-appetite that the human composite, the rational soul and the body together, "suffer" — hence "passions." Differently put: the passions do not act exclusively on the soul, but rather on the whole human composite. However, in the course of abandoning the hylemorphic constitution of the body-soul composite together with the comprehensive teleology of a transcendent perfection of the human life in favor of "regional" teleologies of immanent subjective well-being and flourishing, these thinkers undertook momentous changes in the construal of the passions. After the demise of the teleologically ordered integrity of human nature that the Aristotelian-Thomist hylemorphic doctrine afforded, we can discern in the subsequently emerging modern discourse on passions, emotions, and eventually sentiments two mutually exclusive and warring strands of reconceptualization, reflecting the fundamental options of a primarily idealist or a primarily materialist re-interpretation of the human being. Each strand has its distant antecedent in a once prominent Greek school of philosophy: Stoicism and Epicureanism.

The first, neo-Stoic strand leads from Descartes to Kant and is characterized by an understanding of the passions as bodily upheavals disruptive of the life of the intellect, a danger that can only be banned by way of the intellect's virtuous mastery and instrumentalization of the passions for the sake of the intellect's proper ends. In Descartes's words: "Even those who have the weakest souls could acquire absolute mastery over all their passions if we employed sufficient ingenuity in training and guiding

---

3. On the scholastic discussion of the passions contemporary to Descartes, see A. Levi, S.J., *French Moralists: The Theory of the Passions 1585-1649* (Oxford: Clarendon Press, 1964), pp. 1-39, and on the influences on Descartes's treatise on the passions in general, see R. Ariew, "Descartes and Scholasticism: The Intellectual Background to Descartes' Thought," in *The Cambridge Companion to Descartes*, ed. John Cottingham, pp. 58-90 (Cambridge: Cambridge University Press), pp. 58-90.

them."[4] In his theory of the passions, Descartes departs from the classical Christian theory (informed by Augustine and Aquinas) in two decisive ways: first, in accounting for the passions, he exchanges the traditional model of perception for a model of movement; second, he replaces the hylemorphic unity in differentiation of soul and body as one *res* with a co-ordinated substantial duality of the *res cogitans* (intellect) and the *res extensa* (body). Passions now are somewhat confused perceptions caused by the action of the body (that is, very fine parts of the blood or "animal spirits") on the soul.[5] Subtly but significantly, Descartes reassigns the relationship of activity and passivity such that passions now are conceived of as acts of the body that the soul "suffers." Only with him do the passions become strictly *passions de l'âme*. In his instructive study *From Passions to Emotions,* Thomas Dixon states: "This definition of 'passions of the soul' was to have significant theological and psychological consequences, most notably (not in Descartes himself, but ultimately) the disappearance of the will as the locus of human agency, and its gradual replacement by the passions and affections (and later 'emotions') themselves and, finally, by the body."[6]

The other, neo-Epicurean strand leads from Hobbes's mechanistic construal of the internal life as matter in motion and Hume's consistent identification of virtue with the movement of the passions themselves to the pervasive contemporary understanding of the emotions as biochemical states of the brain that, to a very large degree, account for human behavior. One quotation from Hume's programmatic *A Treatise of Human Nature* will suffice:

> ◁ Reason is, and ought only to be the slave of the passions, and can never pretend to any other office than to serve and obey them. . . . A passion

4. René Descartes, *The Passions of the Soul,* Part I, article 50, in *The Philosophical Writings of Descartes,* vol. 1, trans. John Cottingham, Robert Stoothoff, and Dugald Murdoch, pp. 325-404 (Cambridge: Cambridge University Press), p. 348. "[E]t que ceux même qui ont les plus faibles âmes pourraient acquérir un empire très absolu sur toutes leurs passions, si on employait assez d'industrie à les dresser et à les conduire" (René Descartes, *Les Passions de l'âme,* introduction by Michel Meyer and commentary by Benoît Timmermans [Paris: Librairie Générale Française, 1990], p. 75).

5. "This transformation of the scholastic view is characteristic of Descartes, replacing the model of the passions as fundamentally directional with one which makes them sudden and overwhelming physical responses to be resisted in various ways by the will" (Eileen C. Sweeney, "Restructuring Desire: Aquinas, Hobbes, and Descartes on the Passions," in *Meeting of the Minds,* ed. Stephen F. Brown, pp. 215-33 [Turnhout: Brepols, 1998], p. 223).

6. Dixon, *From Passions to Emotions,* p. 77.

is an original existence, or if you will, modification of existence, and contains not any representative quality, which renders it a copy of any other existence or modification. When I am angry, I am actually possest with the passion, and in that emotion have no more a reference to any other object. . . . 'Tis impossible, therefore, that this passion can be oppos'd by, or be contradictory to truth and reason; since this contradiction consists in the disagreement of ideas, consider'd as copies, with those objects, which they represent.[7]

In Hume's psychology the faculties of the soul have been replaced by multifarious passions, sentiment, desires, and emotions. "Will" is just one among the passions which seem to have been for Hume original realities, complete in themselves. Dixon rightly observes that we encounter in Hume's claim "an inversion of traditional Christian psychology in two ways. First, it deliberately inverted the hierarchical psychology in which 'reason' governed the passions and appetites. Secondly, the assertion that reason should be the slave of the passions depended on a Hobbesian view of the mind as a stream of passions and desires which were mini-agents in themselves."[8]

The stand-off between the two dominant strands of modern theorizing about the passions betrays a fundamental dilemma: Is the human principally a subsistent intellect that uses the body as a necessary, but external instrument for ends proper to the intellect, such that, ideally, the emotional life is to be controlled and ruled by the will similar to the body's movements? Or is the human being principally an animal that uses its advanced cognitive and ratiocinative capacities as internal instruments for proper animal ends to which the emotions prompt the intellect's operations?

In the following, I shall name the strand that opts for the first position "angelism," because despite its neo-Stoic thrust, the human being is conceptualized first and foremost as a subsisting intellect extrinsically coordinated with a body. I shall name the strand that opts for the second position "animalism," because of its consistent materialist monism and the consequent reduction of the intellectual operation to an emergent epiphenomenon of complex bio-chemical processes. I hold the modern conflict over the proper philosophical understanding of human emotions to be irresolvable, because each strand absolutizes a partial truth but is un-

7. Hume, *A Treatise of Human Nature*, 2nd ed., rev. by P. H. Nidditch (Oxford: Clarendon Press, 1981), p. 415.

8. Thomas Dixon, *From Passions to Emotions*, p. 106.

able to account for the other strand's central insight, the reason being that both strands reject the hylemorphic and teleological framework that would afford a comprehensive integration of the emotions in an overall account of human flourishing. The common rejection of the integrative scholastic framework by both strands and their respective emphasis on and transformation of different parts of this synthesis account for the characteristic modern vacillation between the opposing anthropological misconstruals of "angelism" and "animalism." Where contemporary philosophical thought is deeply influenced by the natural sciences, the latter strand finds strong support — with the regrettable, but rarely noticed side-effect that in light of such an understanding of the human being the scientific search for truth itself must turn into an anthropomorphism.[9] And this aporia of "animalism" — intrinsic to every interpretive strategy that reduces the intellect to an epiphenomenon of bio-chemical processes — is a sure indicator that the other modern strand, "angelism," has a strong point for itself, namely the very irreducibility of intellect to material processes. In short, the modern dilemma between "angelism" and "animalism" is genuine and, on the terms of each strand, irresolvable.

In such a situation where "we are a veritable walking archaeology of abandoned theories, even those that have claimed to vanquish one another" (Rorty), the best way forward seems to me to consist in going upstream and listening to the sources, which means in our particular case to consider afresh the subtle hylemorphic synthesis Thomas presents on the human being — in the very core of which stands the irreducible spiritual dimension of the sense-appetite and its acts, the passions.

II. The Integrity of Human Nature According to Thomas and the Centrality of the Passions

Thomas adopts, systematizes, and intensifies Aristotle's hylemorphic solution to the body-soul problem that preoccupied much of Plato's thought. The classical Aristotelian-Thomist definition is that the human rational soul is the substantial form of an ensouled body. The rational soul informs comprehensively the physical, vegetative, and sense aspects of the body such that the soul penetrates the body in uninterrupted continuity all the

9. Robert Spaemann, "Ende der Modernität?" in *Philosophische Essays*, 2nd ed. (Stuttgart: Reclam, 1994), p. 240.

way down to the pure receptivity of prime matter. This complete information of the body by the soul, however, does emphatically not mean that the
soul transforms the body into itself. While completely informed by the rational soul, the physical, vegetative, and animal aspects of the body retain a
reality of their own such that it would be a serious error to say that the soul
"is" the body. What is true is that body and soul form a composite unit of
two co-constitutive, though asymmetrical principles such that the human
soul is not fully intelligible (nor for that matter operative) without its body
and the human body is not the body (but a mere corpse) unless it is substantively informed by the rational soul.

Because of the fundamental difference between the two co-
constitutive principles of the human composite, it is crucial to distinguish
between the substantial unity of the human being, on the one hand, and
the differentiation of the order of faculties or powers (vegetative, sensitive,
intellectual) on the other hand. The powers are essentially different from
each other but have their common source in the one rational soul. In the
order of faculties or powers of the soul, the sense powers hold a special
place. For they are the very linchpin between the higher powers of the soul,
on the one hand, and the body, on the other hand. The rational soul of the
human being is of a kind[10] that requires sense powers for its proper operation and the sense powers in turn require the body as their instrument. By
way of the bodily performance *(executio)* that accompanies the actuation
of the sense-appetite in this or that passion, the body is fully implicated in
the spiritual nature and supernatural ordination of the human being. In
one of the best and most comprehensive studies of Thomas's doctrine of
the passions, Paul Gondreau states in a most felicitous way what is to be recovered from Thomas for the contemporary philosophical deliberation on
the human animal:

> One of the principal reasons Thomas adopts a favorable view toward
> human affectivity is because of his hylemorphism, whereby he sees the
> totality of the human person — body and soul combined — as inte-
> grally involved in the teleological pursuit of the true end of human life.

---

10. The reason for being this kind of rational soul is ultimately ontological. The principle of individuation of the "anima humana" is a kind of relation to the body: "Sic igitur
esse animae est a Deo sicut a principio activo, et est in corpore sicut in materia. Nec tamen
esse animae perit periente corpore, ita et individuatio animae, etsi aliquam relationem habet
ad corpus, non tamen perit corpore periente" (Thomas Aquinas, *Quaestiones de anima*, ed.
James H. Robb [Toronto: Pontifical Institute of Medieval Studies, 1968], q. 1, ad 2).

Aquinas refuses to isolate the sensible dimension of human life from the rational and spiritual one, with the treatise on the passions offering constant points of convergence between the two, such as between the passion of love and spiritual love, or between emotional pleasure and spiritual pleasure. As *human* acts, the passions *de facto* share in human freedom and morality. It bears insisting that in the perspective of Aquinas the passions are teleologically ordained to happiness in God by means of the virtues, the gifts of the Holy Spirit, and grace; the passions can in no sense be severed from the spiritual movements of the soul.[11]

Leading twentieth-century Dominican commentators and interpreters of Thomas have contributed significantly to bringing to the attention of a wider audience the absolutely central role the acts of the sense-appetite, the passions, play in Thomas's thought for a proper understanding of embodied human agency. In a seminal essay, "Reappropriating Aquinas's Account of the Passions," Servais Pinckaers, O.P., observes that the treatise on the passions constitutes the single largest treatise in the entire *Summa theologiae*, comprising twenty-seven questions of one hundred and thirty-two articles. And Jean-Pierre Torrell, O.P., in his important study on Thomas, *Spiritual Master,* states that, "in fact, this passage in his work has scarcely attracted the attention of moralists."[12] Since Torrell made this observation in 1996, the situation has changed considerably. In an important review essay from 2004, Luc-Thomas Somme, O.P., could

11. Paul Gondreau, *The Passions of Christ's Soul in the Theology of St. Thomas Aquinas* (Münster: Aschendorff, 2002), p. 109.

12. Jean-Pierre Torrell, O.P., *Saint Thomas Aquinas,* vol. 2, *Spiritual Master,* translated by Robert Royal (Washington, DC: The Catholic University of America Press, 2003), p. 259. He continues significantly: "Following an often-repeated parallel, just as our knowledge begins with sense perception, so too our first subjective reactions begin at the level of sensitive appetite (or affectivity), which is to say at the level of the *natural tendency* that inclines the living being *toward its good* (or what appears as such). This natural tendency is also found, to be sure, at the intellectual level, and is then called the will that *tends toward the good under its universal aspect of good.* . . . At the level of sensitive affectivity, on the contrary, reactions occur with respect to *particular goods or evils,* and it is precisely these reactions that Thomas calls 'passions,' because the subject suffers them more than he is their master. They are, then, in the realm of the involuntary. Which is to say, the word 'passion' does not have for Thomas the pejorative connotation that it has for us, who automatically think of it as suggesting debauchery and excess. *Passion simply designates the movement of sensibility.* It begins with the lightest impression and it occurs in every affective movement, sentiment, or emotion" (pp. 250f.; my emphasis).

even speak of a "resurrection of the passions," a claim confirmed by three important studies in the course of 2009 and 2010 in the English-speaking world alone.[13]

There are two principal reasons why in *ST* I-II, qq. 22-48, Thomas engages in an exceptionally extensive analysis of the acts of the sense appetite, the passions: (1) The journey of the human being to God is one of the *whole* human being, body and soul. Integral to this journey is the ordering of the passions by reason and the cardinal virtues of courage and temperance as well as their sanctification by way of the infused moral virtues (*ST* I-II; II-II). (2) A proper understanding of Christ's human nature requires an account of the passions of Christ's soul (*ST* III, q. 15). Absent such an account would in Thomas's estimation gravely endanger the full commitment of any orthodox Christology to the dogma of Chalcedon. In his placement of this investigation in the overall order of the *Summa* and in his execution of it, Thomas applies the principle "agere sequitur esse" (*ST* I-II, q. 55, a. 2, ad 1). A study of the ontology of human nature has to antecede an analysis of human psychology. Consequently, in *ST* I, qq. 84-89, after considering assimilative powers by which the soul takes in, Thomas discusses the ways the soul "goes out" to things: powers of will, sense-appetite, and locomotion. Yet an analysis of the very acts of the sense appetite, the passions, has to wait until the order of human agency itself is considered in *ST* I-II. In the practical order, the order of agency, the end is considered first. Hence *ST* I-II commences with the treatise on happiness (qq. 1-5) which is followed by the consideration of the ontology and the moral quality of human acts (qq. 6-21) by way of which happiness is to be achieved. With the subsequent extensive discussion of the acts of the sense-appetite, the passions (qq. 22-48), Thomas clearly indicates the centrality of the various movements of sensitive affectivity for the moral status of human acts. Because of the irreducible spiritual dimension of the human passions, human affectivity has an ineluctable moral quality.

---

13. Luc-Thomas Somme, O.P., "La résurrection des passions," *Revue thomiste* 104, no. 4 (2004): 657-66; Robert Miner, *Thomas Aquinas on the Passions: A Study of Summa Theologiae 1a2ae 22-48* (Cambridge: Cambridge University Press, 2009); Diana Fritz Cates, *Aquinas on the Emotions: A Religious-Ethical Inquiry* (Washington, DC: Georgetown University Press, 2009); and Nicholas E. Lombardo, O.P., *The Logic of Desire: Aquinas on Emotion* (Washington, DC: The Catholic University of America Press, 2010). See also the concise and informative article by Kevin White, "The Passions of the Soul (IaIIae, qq. 22-48)," in *The Ethics of Aquinas,* ed. Stephen J. Pope (Washington, DC: Georgetown University Press, 2002), pp. 103-15, from which I have profited greatly.

Thomas's Grammar of Appetitus and Passio

In all previous and future instances in this chapter where terms like "sense appetite," "natural appetite," or "intellectual appetite" have been or will be used, the notion "appetite" is nothing but a transliteration of the Latin *appetitus*. *Appetitus*, however, has important resonances absent from the English word "appetite" as it is currently in use. For it denotes first and foremost the universal tendency of anything to seek its completion.[14] *Appetitus* is the natural inclination of some form to a term that completes it. Hence, the notion carries with it connotations of tendency, inclination, attraction, and even desire.

Different from inanimate things whose natural appetite is deter-mined to their natural being solely by their form, living beings with the ca-pacity for knowledge are determined to their own actual being by their natural substantial form in such a way that they are naturally receptive of the species of other things: sense receives the species of all things sensible and the intellect receives the species of all things intelligible.[15] To put the matter into its Aristotelian nutshell: Apprehension *(aisthesis)* is what brings the sensible or intelligible species to the human being, while appe-tite *(orexis)*, on the contrary, moves the human being toward the thing — note, not just to its species, but the thing itself. Therefore, significantly, both in the natural as well as in the supernatural order, "the union caused by love is closer than that which is caused by knowledge."[16] Yet, at the same time sense appetite and intellectual appetite always follow apprehension, because the appetible only moves the appetite as it is apprehended.[17]

So much about *appetitus*, or "appetite" in general. Now, "*sense* appe-tite" is the sensual movement following from sense apprehension. Sense appetite regards all that pertains to naturally corruptible things, and this in two distinct respects: first in respect of acquiring what is suitable to and avoiding what is harmful for sustaining oneself; and secondly, in respect of resisting forces or overcoming obstacles that prevent acquiring what is suitable or that might harm or do damage. It is for this reason that Thomas distinguishes two species of the generic power of sense appetite: the

14. *ST* I, q. 80, a. 1: "[Q]uamlibet formam sequitur aliqua inclinatio."

15. *ST* I, q. 80, a. 1.

16. *ST* I-II, 28, a. 1, ad 3: "[C]ognitio perficitur per hoc quod cognitum unitur cogno-scenti secundum suam similitudinem. Sed amor facit quod ipsa res quae amatur, amanti aliquo modo uniatur. . . . Unde amor est magis unitivus quam cognitio."

17. *ST* I, q. 80, a. 2, ad 1.

concupiscible sense appetite and the irascible sense appetite. All acts of sense appetite fall under one or the other of these two species.

The treatise on the acts of the sense appetite follows a clear scheme. The passions are considered under the overall umbrella of the human act before habit and virtue because they are common to animals and human beings. In a first step, the passions are considered in general (qq. 22-25); in a second step (qq. 26-48), they are considered in particular as belonging either to the species of the concupiscible appetite or to the species of the irascible appetite. Thomas considers them in pairs of attraction to the good *(bonum)* or repulsion from the bad *(malum)*. Under the species of the concupiscible appetite Thomas considers *amor — odium; desiderium — fuga; gaudium — tristitia;* under the species of the irascible appetite he considers them in relationship first to the *bonum arduum (spes — desperatio)* and subsequently in relationship to the *malum arduum (timor — audacia)* and the *malum praesens arduum (ira)*.[18]

We finally need to clarify Thomas's use of the term *passio*, "passion." Different from (but related to) Thomas's other uses of *passio* in other respects, in the specific context of the sense appetite, *passio* denotes an act of the sense-appetite with a concomitant bodily change *(executio)*. As simple movement of sensuality subsequent to sense apprehension, a passion is "suffered" by the whole human composite (not just the soul), and in this respect passions are — at least incipiently — involuntary. Since the higher faculties integrate the lower, the universal apprehension of reason interprets the sense apprehension. This specific integration occurs through the "cogitative power" or "particular reason," which apprehends and compares *intentiones* or "values" that are as such not visible in objects of the outer senses. The mediation of the cogitative power is crucial, for by way of it universal premises can produce particular conclusions which in turn modify the passions.

As sense apprehension is integrated by way of the cogitative power into intellectual apprehension (the lower faculty into the higher, for, remember, proper integration after all always occurs top-down), so also is sense appetite integrated into intellectual appetite: human passion, the movement of human sensibility, does not instantaneously or inevitably result in a determinate bodily performance. On the contrary, human passion, rightly formed, awaits approval or disapproval by the higher appetitive power, the will:

18. Thomas discusses the eleven passions also in *In Sent.* III, dist. 26, q. 1, a. 3c.; *De veritate,* q. 26, a. 4c.; *In Ethic.* II, lect. 5.

85

> For wherever there is order among a number of motive powers, the second only moves by virtue of the first: wherefore the lower appetite is not sufficient to cause movement, unless the higher appetite consents. And this is what the Philosopher says (*De Anima* iii.11), that *the higher appetite moves the lower appetite, as the higher sphere moves the lower.* In this way, therefore, the irascible and the concupiscible are subject to reason.[19]

We encounter in this answer a crucial consequence of Thomas's teaching that the rational soul is the substantial form of the body, this consequence being the consistent integration of the sense apprehension and sense appetite into the higher intellectual cognitive and appetitive powers. This integration comes about by way of the elevation of the lower power into the operative order of the respective higher power. In the course of this elevation, the lower power is neither abolished nor transmuted. It is also not the case that the higher power somehow emerges from the lower as a complex epiphenomenon (an ontological impossibility), nor is it necessary for the higher power interminably to struggle with the lower in order to overpower it instead of being overpowered by it, or to instrumentalize it for its own specific ends. No: sense appetite remains distinct from intellectual appetite. At the same time, the sense appetite is ordered to the higher appetitive power such that by informing and guiding the sense appetite the higher appetitive power perfects the lower. Simultaneously, by way of the proper participation of the lower power in the operation of the higher, the goodness of an action is greatly enhanced.

This participation of the lower in the proper operation of the higher power and hence the former's proper perfection by the latter relies on a comprehensive ontology of the good: a natural tendency inclines every living being toward its good: on the level of sense appetite to a particular good or away from a particular evil and on the level of the intellectual appetite in respect to the universal aspect of good.

There are three features of Thomas's synthesis that in light of the modern dilemma deserve special profiling: first, the irreducible spiritual character of the sense appetite; second, the distinct political rule exercised

---

19. *ST* I, q. 81, a. 3: "In omnibus enim potentiis motivis ordinatis, secundum movens non movet nisi virtute primi moventis: unde appetitus inferior non sufficit movere, nisi appetitus superior consentiat. Et hoc est quod Philosophus dicit, in III *de Anima*, quod *appetitus superior movet appetitum inferiorem, sicut sphaera superior inferiorem.* — Hoc ergo modo irascibilis et concupiscibilis rationi subduntur."

by the intellectual appetite over the passions; and third and consequently, the ineluctable moral quality of the acts of the sense appetite.

(1) The Irreducible Spiritual Dimension of the Passions

The irreducible spiritual dimension of the passions becomes obvious when we grasp it as a ripe implication of the integrity of the human nature that has its root in the human rational soul being a spiritual substance in its own proper ontological integrity, and as such, qua spiritual substance the substantial form of the body. Anton C. Pegis, in an important, but largely forgotten essay, "St. Thomas and the Unity of Man," advances Thomas's crucial insight in ways most pertinent for a contemporary anthropological discussion shot through with reductionist presuppositions. Pegis recapitulates the core of Thomas's teaching on the integrity of the human nature when he states that

> St. Thomas knew and said that the soul is both an intellectual substance in its own right and also a form of matter. But St. Thomas did not stop with saying that the soul is a substance and a form. For if one and the same soul is, and this is its very nature, both substance and form, then the soul must be *a substance as a form.* And this is what St. Thomas says, and it is in this notion that we must seek the proportion between soul and body and the meaning of human nature.[20]

He concludes:

> The soul is, therefore, not a substance *and* a form, but a substance *as* a form, a substance whose spiritual nature is essentially suited to informing matter. And it is in the soul that the reason for this union is to be found; whatever the human body is, this it is for the sake of, and in view of, the human soul.[21]

This unique essential suitability of the human soul for informing matter, however, gives rise to an important question: "How does it happen that the soul, which is an immaterial and intellectual substance, has *lesser* than in-

---

20. Anton C. Pegis, "St. Thomas and the Unity of Man," in *Progress in Philosophy: Philosophical Studies in Honor of Rev. Doctor Charles A. Hart,* ed. James A. McWilliams, S.J., pp. 153-73 (Milwaukee, WI: Bruce Publishing Co., 1955), p. 168.
21. Pegis, "St. Thomas and the Unity of Man," p. 168.

tellectual powers?"[22] Pegis answers this question by following Thomas's lead. The intellect as the highest human power is the key to the integrity of human nature:

> The crux of the matter lies in seeing that, though man has powers in addition to the intellect, he is not *more* than intellectual. . . . [T]hough man is a composite being, we must not make him or his nature a compound being. If all the powers of man are rooted in the soul; if, furthermore, one and the same intellectual soul has within its nature both intellectual and sensible powers, this fact must mean, not that the soul has more powers than the intellect, but that the human intellect is not fully an intellect *without the sensible powers*. . . . [T]he *intellect and the senses taken together* constitute in their togetherness the adequate intellectual power of the human soul as an intellectual substance.[23]

In virtue of the lower powers of the human soul participating in an order determined by the highest power, the intellect, the human being is (1) an embodied intellect that due to its specific nature requires for its proper function (2) sense apprehension as well as sense appetite; these sense powers, in turn, require (3) the body as their instrument. In the case of the human being, the body exists for the sake of the rational soul, a spiritual substance uniquely ordained for embodiment and therefore functioning essentially as substantial form of its body. For this reason the passions most fundamentally are in potency to and indeed indispensable for a moral and spiritual formation that is integral to achieving the twofold human end. It is the full integration of the sense appetite into the operative order of the intellective power that constitutes the irreducible spiritual dimension of the human passions.

(2) Reason's "Political Rule" over the Passions[24]

If, however, it is the case — as Thomas as well as experience teaches — that the sense appetite has its own proper acts upon the higher powers of the soul and a concomitant bodily *executio*, how is it that reason does govern the acts of the sense appetite? The question is only the *how* of this gover-

22. Pegis, "St. Thomas and the Unity of Man," p. 168.
23. Pegis, "St. Thomas and the Unity of Man," p. 169.
24. Reason *(ratio)* denominates here and in the subsequent discussion the close interplay of intellect and will in the order of human agency.

nance, for the *that* is given in virtue of (1) the rational soul being the substantial form of the body and (2) the principle that the higher powers govern the lower powers. The *how* Thomas accounts for by conceiving the sense appetite as what we might call a semi-autonomous sub-system, integrating a lower level, and being itself integrated into a higher level system. This semi-autonomous sub-system has the power of bringing about effects in an even lower sub-system, a bodily *executio*, as well as on the higher level — where it is immediately received (though not necessarily checked) by reason.

In order to illustrate this partial self-possession of sense appetite and its simultaneous participation in the higher faculty of the rational soul, Thomas offers a psychologically subtle and astute analogy from the political realm. He inverts an analogy Aristotle uses in the *Politics* (Bekker 1254b5) between the rule of the human body and the rule of the body politic in order to give precision to the kind of governance reason exercises over the appetitive sense faculty.[25] Thomas distinguishes between a despotic and a political, kingly rule that under present political conditions might best be updated into the distinction between a dictatorship and a constitutional monarchy (or any other constitutional government of free citizens), the subject of the former being nothing but a slave, the subject of the latter being a citizen with constitutional rights and duties. In *ST* I-II,

25. "And he then shows that the ruling power in the parts of an animal is like external ruling power. For, regarding the human animal, we can consider two kinds of rules in relation [to] its parts, namely, the despotic kind by which masters rule over slaves, and the political kind by which the ruler of the political community rules over free persons. For we find among the parts of human beings that the soul rules over the body, and this is by a despotic rule in which the slave can in no way resist the master, since the slave as such belongs absolutely to the master, as he has said before [chap. 2, n. 11]. And we perceive that bodily members such as hands and feet immediately execute their functions at the soul's bidding and without any resistance. We also find that the intellect, or reason, rules over the will, although by a political and kingly rule, one over free persons, and so the latter can resist in particular things. And the will likewise sometimes does not follow reason. And the reason for this difference is that only the soul can move the body, and so the latter is completely subject to the former, but the senses as well as reason can move the will, and so the latter is not totally subject to reason.

"And in both regimes, it is clear that the subjection is by nature and expedient. For it is natural and expedient for the body that the soul rule over it, and likewise for the emotional part (i.e., the will subject to emotions) that the intellect, or reason, rule over it. And it would be harmful for both regimes if the part that should be ruled were to be equal or contrary to the part that should rule. For the body would be destroyed unless it were subject to the soul, and desire would be inordinate unless it were subject to reason" (Thomas Aquinas, *Commentary on Aristotle's Politics*, trans. Richard J. Regan [Indianapolis: Hackett, 2007], p. 29).

q. 17, a. 7, Thomas considers the question "whether the act of the sensitive appetite is commanded," and states:

> [I]t happens sometimes that the movement of the sensitive appetite is aroused suddenly in consequence of an apprehension of the imagination of sense. And then such a movement occurs without the command of reason: although reason could have prevented it, had it foreseen. Hence the Philosopher says (*Polit.* i.2) that the reason governs the irascible and the concupiscible not by a *despotic supremacy*, which is that of a master over his slave, but by a *politic and royal supremacy*, whereby the free are governed, who are not wholly subject to command.[26]

The concupiscible appetite and the irascible appetite might resist reason initially, because reason is not the only power to move the appetite. Rather, the appetite is moved also by sense apprehension and sense imagination. And being moved by either one or both of them, the appetite can and does in principle — and at least initially — resist the command of reason.

Now, this is human nature considered according to its *ontological structure*. In respect of the *historical existence of human nature* in the extant order of providence, Thomas distinguishes between the original state of innocence and the state of fallen human nature. In the original state of innocence "the inferior appetite was wholly subject to reason, so that in that state the passions of the soul existed only as consequent upon the judgment of reason."[27] Yet after the fall, "at times our passions forestall and hinder reason's judgment."[28] When first unforeseen and subsequently un-

---

26. *ST* I-II, q. 17, a. 7: "Contingit etiam quandoque quod motus appetitus sensitivi subito concitatur ad apprehensionem imaginationis vel sensus. Et tunc ille motus est praeter imperium rationis: quamvis potuisset impediri a ratione, si praevidisset. Unde Philosophus dicit, in I *Polit.*, quod ratio praeest irascibili et concupiscibili non *principatu despotico*, qui est domini ad servum; sed *principatu politico aut regali*, qui est ad liberos, qui non totaliter subduntur imperio." Already in *ST* I, q. 81, a. 3, ad 2, Thomas uses the same analogy and emphasizes that "the sensitive appetite is naturally moved, not only by the estimative power in other animals, and in man by the cogitative power which the universal reason guides, but also by the imagination and sense. Whence it is that we experience that the irascible and concupiscible powers do resist reason, inasmuch as we sense or imagine something pleasant, which reason forbids, or unpleasant, which reason commands." Thomas concludes significantly: "And so from the fact that the irascible and concupiscible resist reason in something, we must not conclude that they do not obey."

27. *ST* I, q. 95, a. 2: "In statu . . . innocentiae inferior appetitus erat rationi totaliter subiectus: unde non erant in eo passiones animae, nisi ex rationis iudicio consequentes."

28. *ST* I, q. 95, a. 2: "Aliter tamen quam in nobis. Nam in nobis appetitus sensualis, in

---

checked by reason, such an "antecedent passion" may gain a decisive influence over human beings such that they simply follow the impulse of the passion. Thomas is a subtle psychologist and clearly distinguishes this case (which is not infrequent for incontinent persons) from one we encounter even more often. Consider *ST* I-II, q. 10, a. 3:

> Now this influence of a passion on man occurs in two ways. First, so that his reason is wholly bound, so that he has not the use of reason: as happens in those who through a violent access of anger or concupiscence become furious or insane, just as they may from some other bodily disorder; since such like passions do not take place without some change in the body. . . . Sometimes, however, the reason is not entirely engrossed by the passion, so that the judgment of reason retains, to a certain extent, its freedom: and thus the movement of the will remains in a certain degree. Accordingly, in so far as the reason remains free, and not subject to the passion, the will's movement, which also remains, does not tend of necessity to that whereto the passion inclines it. Consequently, either there is no movement of the will in that man, and the passion alone holds its sway: or if there be a movement of the will, it does not necessarily follow the passion.[29]

In *ST* I-II, q. 77, a. 1, where Thomas considers the cause of sin on the part of the sense appetite, he asks whether and if so how the will can be moved by the sense appetite — never directly, but indirectly, and this in two ways. I give the full citation of Thomas's text, because it displays very clearly Thomas's very subtle and psychologically astute understanding of the complex interaction between the act of the sense-appetite, the judgment of reason, and the will's movement:

---

quo sunt passiones, non totaliter subest rationi: unde passiones quandoque sund in nobis praevenientes iudicium rationis, et impedientes."

29. *ST* I-II, q. 10, a. 3: "Huiusmodi autem immutatio hominis per passionem duobus modis contingit. Uno modo, sic quod totaliter ratio ligatur, ita quod homo usum rationis non habet: sicut contingit in his qui propter vehementem iram vel concupiscentiam furiosi vel amentes fiunt, sicut et propter aliquam aliam perturbationem corporalem; huiusmodi enim passiones non sine corporali transmutationem accidunt. . . . Aliquando autem ratio non totaliter absorbetur a passione, sed remanet quantum ad aliquid iudicium rationis liberum. Et secundum hoc remanet aliquid de motu voluntatis. Inquantum ergo ratio manet libera et passioni non subiecta, intantum voluntatis motus qui manet, non ex necessitate tendit ad hoc ad quod passio inclinat. Et sic aut motus voluntatis non est in homine, sed sola passio dominatur: aut, si motus voluntatis sit, non ex necessitate sequitur passionem."

First, by a kind of distraction: because, since all the soul's powers are rooted in the one essence of the soul, it follows of necessity that, when one power is intent in its act, another power becomes remiss, or is even altogether impeded, in its act, both because all energy is weakened through being divided, so that, on the contrary, through being centered on one thing, it is less able to being directed to several; and because, in the operations of the soul, a certain attention is requisite, and if this be closely fixed on one thing, less attention is given to another. In this way, by a kind of distraction, when the movement of the sensitive appetite is enforced in respect of any passion whatever, the proper movement of the rational appetite or will must, of necessity, become remiss or altogether impeded.

Secondly, this may happen on the part of the will's object, which is good apprehended by reason. Because the judgment and apprehension of reason is impeded on account of a vehement and inordinate apprehension of the imagination and judgment of the estimative power, as appears in those who are out of their mind. Now it is evident that the apprehension of the imagination and the judgment of the estimative power follow the passion of the sensitive appetite, even as the verdict of the taste follows the disposition of the tongue: for which reason we observe that those who are in some kind of passion, do not easily turn their imagination away from the object of their emotion, the result being that the judgment of the reason often follows the passion of the sensitive appetite, and consequently the will's movement follows it also, since it has a natural inclination always to follow the judgment of the reason.[30]

---

30. *ST* I-II, q. 77, a. 1: "Uno quidem modo, secundum quandam abstractionem. Cum enim omnes potentiae animae in una essentia animae radicentur, necesse est quod quando una potentia intenditur in suo actu, altera in suo actu remittatur, vel etiam totaliter impediatur. Tum quia omnis virtus ad plura dispersa fit minor: unde e contrario, quando intenditur circa unum, minus potest ad alia dispergi. Tum quia in operibus animae requiritur quaedam intentio, quae dum vehementer applicatur ad unum, non potest alteri vehementer attendere. Et secundum hunc modum, per quandam distractionem, quando motus appetitus sensitivi fortificatur secundum quamcumque passionem, necesse est quod remittatur, vel totaliter impediatur motus proprius appetitus rationalis, qui est voluntas.

Alio modo, ex parte obiecti voluntatis, quod est bonum ratione apprehensum. Impeditur enim iudicium et apprehensio rationis propter vehementem et inordinatam apprehensionem imaginationis, et iudicium virtutis aestimativae: ut patet in amentibus. Manifestum est autem quod passionem appetitus sensitivi sequitur imaginationis apprehensio, et iudicium aestimativae: sicut etiam dispositionem linguae sequitur iudicium

Each of the possibilities envisioned so clearly by Thomas points forward to two indispensable and connected components of the moral life Thomas considers subsequently to his treatment of the passions: habit (*ST* I-II, qq. 49-54) and virtue (*ST* I-II, qq. 55-67). For what checks antecedent violent passions best is nothing but the deep, acquired or infused habituation in especially two cardinal virtues: temperance in relationship to the concupiscible sense appetite;[31] and fortitude in relationship to the irascible sense appetite. *From incontinent to continent to virtuous: this is the moral journey that the rational animal has to undertake in order to become a true political ruler of the passions.* They have something of their own which contributes to the good of the whole human being, and therefore reason is to govern them differently from bodily limbs which are strictly instrumental. At the same time, the passions must be ruled, that is, properly informed and ordered by right reason to those goods that themselves are rightly ordered to the common good of the universe — God.

In the state of original righteousness, the proper internal ordering of all the powers in relation to each other and the highest in relation to God, there exists only "consequent passion," passion properly governed by reason and shaped by the virtues. After all, because the rational soul is the substantial form of the body, the whole human being is intellectual. Hence, while having something of its own and the body as its instrument, the sense appetite is eminently governable by reason. For sense appetite is, after all, the soul's own appetitive faculty, that is, a power intrinsic to the substantial form of the body. And despite the fact that reason is sometimes surprised and overwhelmed by the passions, because of the inherent governability of the sense powers by the higher power of the soul, there obtains an ineluctable moral quality of the acts of sense appetite.

---

gustus. Unde videmus quod homines in aliqua passione existentes, non facile imaginationem avertunt ab his circa quae afficiuntur. Unde per consequens iudicium rationis plerumque sequitur passionem appetitus sensitivi; et per consequens motus voluntatis, qui natus est sequi iudicium rationis."

31. Nota bene: temperance does not order the antecedent passion! Rather, temperance prevents antecedent passions from arising or renders them so docile that they never need to be fought against by the temperate person in order to maintain reason's control over the action. For an excellent interpretation of Thomas's account of the passions on this important point, see Gusiseppe Butera, "On Reason's Control of the Passions in Aquinas's Theory of Temperance," *Medieval Studies* 68 (2006): 133-60.

(3) The Passions and the Human Body

Before we turn to a closer consideration of the ineluctable moral quality of the passions, we must, however, briefly attend to the relationship between the human body and the sense appetite. In *ST* I-II, q. 17, a. 7, ad 2, with but a few very suggestive strokes Thomas adumbrates the particular relationship between the sense appetite and the lower subsystem with its own very limited, but nevertheless genuine semi-autonomy:

> The condition of the body stands in a twofold relation to the act of the sensitive appetite. First, as preceding it: thus a man may be disposed in one way or another, in respect of his body, to this or that passion. Secondly, as consequent to it: thus a man becomes heated through anger. Now the condition that precedes, is not subject to the command of reason: since it is due either to nature, or to some previous movement, which cannot cease at once. But the condition that is consequent, follows the command of reason: since it results from the local movement of the heart, which has various movements according to the various acts of the sensitive appetite.[32]

There is always a bodily condition that precedes the movements of sense-appetite. This condition can obtain, first, as antecedent bodily movements or changes. Some movements just come from the body itself, movements which cannot cease at once, and which sense-appetite, informed by sense-imagination, might increase through respective passions, or which are intercepted by a command of reason, a re-directing of the sense-imagination, or an activity that engages the sense-appetite and the body into a completely different direction. This condition can obtain, second, as a bodily predisposition to certain passions. The condition that is consequent to the act of the sense-appetite stands under the command of reason. Why? Because the acts of sense-appetite themselves are, as we have seen, eminently governable by reason. That means, if the will lets the passions run their course, this act of omission is itself voluntary and therefore, though defi-

32. *ST* I-II, q. 17, a. 7, ad 2: "[Q]ualitas corporalis dupliciter se habet ad actum appetitus sensitivi. Uno modo, ut praecedens: prout aliquis est aliqualiter dispositus secundum corpus, ad hanc vel illam passionem. Alio modo, ut consequens: sicut cum ex ira aliquis incalescit. Qualitas igitur praecedens non subiacet imperio rationis: quia vel est ex natura, vel ex aliqua praecedenti motione, quae non statim quiescere potest. Sed qualitas consequens sequitur imperium rationis: quia sequitur motum localem cordis, quod diversimode movetur secundum diversos actus sensitivi appetitus."

cient, still under the command of reason. Being an astute and careful observer of human reality, Thomas understands the instrumentality of the body not in a quasi-modern technical way, but proper to the constitution of the human body as enlivened by the soul such that certain vegetative and animal functions are exercised by the sub-system of the body, outside of the range of the rule of reason and will, and also somewhat independently from the sense appetite. Hence, at times, the body "surprises" the sense-appetite as well as reason and will. Nevertheless, being the lowest subsystem, the body stands under a threefold rule. First it stands under the sense-appetite's direct rule, a rule that pertains to the bodily effects of the passions *(executio)*. It stands, secondly, under the direct rule of reason and will, a rule that pertains to specifically intended bodily movements. It stands finally under the indirect governance of reason and will, a governance that results from their direct "political" governance of the acts of sense-appetite.[33] Hence, the condition of the body that is consequent to acts of the sense appetite acquires a distinct moral quality. Contrary to many modern thinkers, Thomas does not hold that the condition of the human body per se is always pre-moral or morally indifferent. Rather, only as antecedent condition is it pre-moral (but as we will see, even this antecedent condition is already charged with a potential moral quality, a tendency or weakness consequent upon human sin), and this antecedent condition is always only momentary or a condition that obtains until diagnosed (in the case of an illness). In all other cases, that is, especially in regard to long-term care and schooling of the body, the body's condition is consequent and hence has a moral quality to it.

(4) The Ineluctable Moral Quality of the Passions

Now we have reached the point to consider directly the ineluctable moral quality of the passions. In *ST* I-II, q. 24, Thomas considers this matter with typical care and nuance. First, he considers the question whether any moral quality at all pertains to the passions of the soul. In themselves, as movements of the sense appetite, they have no moral quality. However, considered as subject to the command of reason and will, they do indeed have a moral quality. Consider Thomas's argument:

---

33. For a brief, but lucid analysis of the way reason's political rule of the passions is conceived by Thomas, see Lombardo, *The Logic of Desire*, pp. 99-101.

Because the sensitive appetite is nearer than the outward members to the reason and will; and yet the movements and actions of the outward members are morally good or evil, inasmuch as they are voluntary. Much more, therefore, may the passions, in so far as they are voluntary, be called morally good or evil. And they are said to be voluntary, either from being commanded by the will, or from not being checked by the will.[34]

As soon as the will has something to act upon by way of command (even the slightest instant of an incipient motion of the sense appetite) the moral quality of the passion is established.

In a second step, Thomas addresses the question whether such moral quality of a passion might in principle be negative. Is a passion — being a non-rational motion — in and of itself evil? In his answer Thomas offers a nuanced discussion of the Stoic and the Peripatetic views of the passions. Needless to say that he decisively sides with the Peripatetic position. In his response to the third objection Thomas offers a pithy summary of why the spiritual dimension of the sense appetite accounts for the moral quality of the passions: "The passions of the soul, in so far as they are contrary to the order of reason, incline us to sin: but in so far as they are controlled by reason, they pertain to virtue."[35]

With this principle in place Thomas already determines the thrust of the answer for the third question: "Whether passion increases or decreases the goodness or malice of an act?" There can hardly be a greater praise of the passions and of their indispensable role in the moral life imaginable than the one found in Thomas's answer to this question:

[I]f we give the name of passions to all the movements of the sensitive appetite, then it belongs to the perfection of man's good that his passions be moderated by reason. For since man's good is founded on reason as its root, that good will be all the more perfect, according as it extends to more things pertaining to man. Wherefore no one questions

34. *ST* I-II, q. 24, a. 1: "Propinquior enim est appetitus sensitivus ipsi rationi et voluntati, quam membra exteriora; quorum tamen motus et actus sunt boni vel mali moraliter, secundum quod sunt voluntarii. Unde multo magis et ipsae passiones, secundum quod sunt voluntariae, possunt dici bonae vel malae moraliter. Dicuntur autem voluntariae vel ex eo quod a voluntate imperantur, vel ex eo quod a voluntate non prohibentur."

35. *ST* I-II, q. 24, a. 2, ad 3: "[P]assiones animarum, inquantum sunt praeter ordinem rationis, inclinant ad peccatum: inquantum autem sunt ordinatae a ratione, pertinent ad virtutem."

the fact that it belongs to the perfection of moral good, that the actions of the outward members be controlled by the law of reason. Hence, since the sensitive appetite can obey reason, as stated above . . . , it belongs to the perfection of moral or human good, that the passions themselves also should be controlled by reason. Accordingly, just as it is better that man should both will good and do it in his external act; so also does it belong to the perfection of moral good, that man should be moved unto good, not only in respect of his will, but also in respect of his sensitive appetite: according to Ps. 84:2[3]: *My heart and my flesh have rejoiced in the living God:* where by *heart* we are to understand the intellectual appetite, and by *flesh* the sensitive appetite.[36]

Reason governing the passions by aligning them by way of the moral virtues to the order of right reason is intrinsic to the perfection of the moral good. And therefore, passions that are principally to be cultivated are passions consequent upon the judgment of reason, while passions that are principally to be curbed — or transformed into consequent passions — are passions antecedent to the judgment of reason. "[S]ince [antecedent passions] obscure the judgment of reason, on which the goodness of the moral act depends, they diminish the goodness of the act; for it is more praiseworthy to do a work of charity from the judgment of reason than from the mere passion of pity."[37] Passions consequent to the judgment of reason can come about and increase the goodness of an action in two ways:

---

36. *ST* I-II, q. 24, a. 3: "[S]i passiones simpliciter nominemus omnes motus appetitus sensitivi, sic ad perfectionem humani boni pertinet quod etiam ipsae passiones sint moderatae per rationem. Cum enim bonum hominis consistat in ratione sicut in radice, tanto istud bonum erit perfectius, quanto ad plura quae homini conveniunt, derivari potest. Unde nullus dubitat quin ad perfectionem moralis boni pertineat quod actus exteriorum membrorum per rationis regulam dirigantur. Unde, cum appetitus sensitivus possit obedire rationi, ut supra dictum est, ad perfectionem moralis sive humani boni pertinet quod etiam ipsae passiones animae sint regulatae per rationem. Sicut igitur melius est quod homo et velit bonum, et faciat exteriori actu; ita etiam ad perfectionem boni moralis pertinet quod homo ad bonum moveatur non solum secundum voluntatem, sed etiam secundum appetitum sensitivum; secundum illud quod in *Psalmo* 83, [3] dicitur: *Cor meum et caro mea exultaverunt in Deum vivum,* ut *cor* accipiamus pro appetitu intellectivo, *carnem* autem pro appetitu sensitivo."

37. *ST* I-II, q. 24, a. 3, ad 1: "[C]um obnubilent iudicium rationis, ex quo dependet bonitas moralis actus, diminuunt actus bonitatem: laudabilius enim est quod ex iudicio rationis aliquis faciat opus caritatis, quam ex sola passione misericordiae."

First, by way of redundance: because, to wit, when the higher part of the soul is intensely moved to anything, the lower part also follows that movement; and thus the passion that results in consequence, in the sensitive appetite, is a sign of the intensity of the will, and so indicates greater moral goodness. — Secondly, by way of choice; when, to wit, a man, by the judgment of his reason, chooses to be affected by a passion in order to work more promptly with the co-operation of the sensitive appetite. And thus a passion of the soul increases the goodness of an action.[38]

In the positive line Thomas presses here a very important point: the passions, and via *executio,* the bodily effects, if governed by the judgment of reason, serve a similar function to the sound body of a violin: they greatly enhance the sound which the vibration of the strings produces.[39] The shining examples of such a life of perfected passions are, of course, the saints.[40]

(5) Implications

Because the sense appetite and its acts, the passions, are governed by reason, in virtue of this "political" governance the consequent passions participate in reason's own participation in the eternal law. In virtue of this "participated participation," the passions fall under the purview of the natural as well as the revealed law. Moreover, again because of the "participated participation," all antecedent passions are to be elevated to rightly informed consequent passions. Differently put, *the moral schooling of the*

38. *ST* I-II, q. 24, a. 3, ad 1: "Uno modo, per modum redundantiae: quia scilicet, cum superior pars animae intense movetur in aliquid, sequitur motum eius etiam pars inferior. Et sic passio existens consequenter in appetitu sensitivo, est signum intensionis voluntatis. Et sic indicat bonitatem moralem maiorem. — Alio modo, per modum electionis: quando scilicet homo ex iudicio rationis eligit affici aliqua passione, ut promptius operetur, cooperante appetitu sensitivo. Et sic passio animae addit ad bonitatem actionis." See also *ST* I-II, q. 59, a. 2, ad 3.

39. Growth in moral character does not entail repression of the acts of the sense appetite, but an ever improving alignment of them with reason's judgment. This alignment is brought about by the moral virtues which are inherently connected to the passions. (The exhaustive account of the virtues and the vices of *ST* II-II is unthinkable without the antecedent study of the passions in *ST* I-II, 22-48.)

40. Finally, in article 4 of question 24, Thomas considers whether there are inherently good and inherently evil passions, which he confirms in regard to consequent passions, that is, voluntary passions. He mentions compassion and shame as examples of intrinsically good passions, and envy as an example of intrinsically evil passions.

passions entails a moral schooling of the body. And this schooling is most natural and not at all a foreign imposition of some extrinsic rule upon the body, for after all, the human body being informed substantially by a rational soul acquires a distinct moral quality.

The appropriate moral appreciation of the spiritual dimension of the sense-appetite consists not in the mastery or subjugation of its acts, the passions, but rather in their proper formation according to reason's "political rule" over them. Hence, neither repression nor idolization of the passions is called for, but their proper formation in service of moral and spiritual perfection, that is, in service of achieving the twofold human end: "Perfection of moral virtue does not wholly take away the passions, but regulates them; for the temperate man desires as he ought to desire, and what he ought to desire, as stated in *Ethic.* iii. 11."[41]

III. Conclusion: Moving Beyond the Modern Anthropological Dilemma of Angelism versus Animalism by Retrieving Thomas's Integral Doctrine of Human Nature

Having gone up-stream and listened to the source, Thomas's doctrine of the passions, has yielded a distinct result — a forceful reminder that the human animal is an embodied intellect made for understanding the truth and loving the good. The acts of the sense appetite are to support and intensify the acts of reason such that the embodied intellect advances ever more efficaciously on the road toward the true and the good; the *homo viator* is ever to proceed in order to achieve his or her twofold final end. And because grace does not destroy but perfect nature, sanctifying grace (by way of the infused theological and moral virtues) reaches all the way down to heal and re-order the passions and allow them to contribute even more fully to the perfection of the moral act. Both angelism and animalism fail to appreciate this fact, animalism by taking the unformed, de facto passions as quasi-moral sentiments, angelism by regarding the passions as a detrimental intrusion of an alien dynamic into reason's moral existence, an intrusion that must be solved by way of a repressive subjugation of the passions. This characteristic modern dilemma between angelism and ani-

---

41. *ST* I, q. 95, a. 2, ad 3: "[P]erfecta virtus moralis non totaliter tollit passiones, sed ordinat eas: *temperati* enim *est concupiscere sicut oportet, et quae oportet,* ut dicitur in III *Ethic.*"

malism arises from the failure to appreciate the passions as acts of the human soul, that is, as acts of the soul's sense appetite, acts that are ordained to contribute to the comprehensive human flourishing, a flourishing that is neither pre- nor trans-moral, but the flourishing of the embodied soul and the ensouled body, a flourishing that is as embodied irreducibly spiritual and moral. That is, proper passions are consequent upon evaluative judgments of the cogitative power, but on the level of sensibility only, and even as such — *pace* Hume — they are not an original existence.

And here a second failure comes into play. Not only do angelism and animalism fail to appreciate the teleological structure and de facto ordination of the human being to a twofold final end. They also fail to appreciate the qualification of the passions by the concrete historical human nature in the extant order of providence. For antecedent passions always already are the result of the complex interplay of bodily dispositions, of the infirmity of fallen human nature, and the impact of healing and sanctifying grace. That is, their antecedence entails the consequence of a primordial condition: Consequent to the first sin, "all powers of the soul are left, as it were, destitute of their proper order, whereby they are naturally directed to virtue; which destitution is called a wounding of nature."[42] This wounding of nature pertains to the irascible as well as the concupiscible sense appetite: "[I]nsofar as the irascible is deprived of its order to the arduous, there is the wound of weakness; and insofar as the concupiscible is deprived of its order to the delectable, moderated by reason, there is the wound of concupiscence."[43] Consequently, the passions are distinct and immediate, but never "original" in the strict sense. Rather, they always already are antecedently charged with a potency for evil or good — in a privative sense due to the wound of nature consequent upon sin, and in a perfective sense due to the restoration and elevation of nature consequent upon healing and sanctifying grace.

In light of this integral doctrine of human nature — ensouled body and embodied soul — as teleologically ordered to a twofold final end, the warring modern accounts come into view as exactly what they are, fragments that fail to stand in for the whole. Hence they always are confronted

42. *ST* I-II, q. 85, a. 3: "Et ideo omnes vires animae remanent quodammodo destitutae proprio ordine, quo naturaliter ordinantur ad virtutem: et ipsa destitutio vulneratio naturae dicitur."

43. *ST* I-II, q. 85, a. 3: "[I]nquantum vero irascibilis destituitur suo ordine ad arduum, est vulnus infirmitatis; inquantum vero concupiscentia destituitur ordine ad delectabile moderatum ratione, est vulnus concupiscentiae."

with some puzzling remainder: be it the emotions as erratic and disruptive bodily upheavals of the life to which a pure, subsistent intellect is called, or be it the intellect and its own appetite, the will, as curious epiphenomena of the subconscious *Triebleben* of a highly advanced animal. Being a fragment, each of the two modern strands misses the human being and its specific dignity. Neither a bundle of instincts nor an encaged angel, but *animal rationale* — the singular meeting place of the spiritual and the material universe.

CHAPTER 4

"Democracy after Christendom" — Sovereign Secularism, Genuine Liberalism, and the Natural Love of God: What Thomas Can Teach Us about Modernity's Fraternal Twins

Introduction: Sovereign Secularism, Genuine Liberalism, and the Natural Love of God

Scholars of notable erudition and eminence have written — not infrequently at considerable length — on the secular age as well as on the origins of and the passage to modernity.[1] But only few of them have considered sovereign secularism and genuine liberalism as fraternal but not identical twins born of one and the same parent, modernity. By the end of this chapter, I hope, it will be clear why a theological analysis — and, indeed, a Thomist analysis — of the natural love of God above all and of the state of fallen human nature proves fruitful in order to fully uncover and elucidate the family relationship between sovereign secularism and genuine liberalism.

But before I go any further, I wish to offer a brief explanation of two concepts: "sovereign secularism" and "genuine liberalism." While these terms obviously spring from the discursive context of modern political theory, the distinction I shall draw in this chapter between "sovereign secularism" and "genuine liberalism" does not immediately arise from nor directly depend on any one specific theory of secularization or modernity. Rather, the distinction I shall be using throughout this chapter is

---

1. See representatively among others, Louis Dupré, *The Passage to Modernity* (New Haven: Yale University Press, 1993), Charles Taylor, *A Secular Age* (Cambridge, MA: The Belknap Press of Harvard University Press, 2007), Michael Allen Gillespie, *The Theological Origins of Modernity* (Chicago: The University of Chicago Press, 2008).

prompted by a *theological* analysis of problems much older and deeper than the relatively recent arrival of modernity.

Let me turn briefly to the first notion: *sovereign secularism.* I take sovereign secularism to be the programmatic ideological effort of understanding and affirming reality in intentional independence from any transcendent source in general and from revealed religion in particular. It is a program that, specifically, stands in intentional and often aggressive opposition to Christianity (in formerly Protestant countries) or to the Catholic Church (in formerly Catholic countries). Secularism regards religious practice and belief of any kind as at best irrelevant and at worst inimical to human flourishing. In short, secularism is constituted — not exclusively, though largely — by a negative freedom *from* religion and consequently, in its pure form, by a more or less tacit structural atheism, and not infrequently by a substantive and quite explicit atheism. I am calling this ideological program of comprehensive, immanentist self-sufficiency "sovereign secularism," not in order to distinguish it from some other putative species of "secularism." Rather, I wish to make explicit what secularism per se entails: an arrogation to itself of the divine attribute of sovereignty. As a primarily ideological, and in that pseudo-theological, program, sovereign secularism has appeared under the guise of monarchical, democratic, plutocratic, fascist, and socialist forms of political organization and will continue to appear under them. In short, the political self-expression of sovereign secularism is varied, or more precisely, legion.

Considered theologically, even in the most generous terms of a practice of "religio," sovereign secularism is gravely deficient. For, unlike liberalism, sovereign secularism discourages and, in many instances, represses as much as possible the publicly visible practice of "religio," the practice of due honor paid to God through interior acts of prayer, devotion, and adoration, and through exterior acts of public worship and visible commitments.[2] Because of its intentional, systemic omission and indeed inhibition of the public practice of "religio," sovereign secularism encourages and feeds the sins of irreligiosity and irreverence as well as the sin of unbelief. Worse, sovereign secularism structurally has to fill the intentional, intellectual, affective, and social space reserved for the practice of "religio" to God. Under the rule of sovereign secularism, in order to stabilize its *"novus ordo seclorum"* of comprehensive immanentism, the practice of "religio" is

2. The practice of "religio" in all of its components is nothing but the exercise of the virtue of justice in relationship to God. See *ST* II-II, qq. 81-100.

ever so subtly directed to some alternative immanent transcendence, the nation-state, the putative superiority of some race or class, the Enlightenment project, the greatest good for the greatest number, genetic optimalization, or planetary welfare. Consequently, sovereign secularism not only encourages and feeds irreligiosity, irreverence, and unbelief, but ultimately also idolatry, that is, treating a finite good as the putative ultimate good.

Under the parentage of modernity, sovereign secularism appears in close proximity to its non-identical twin: *liberalism.* However, unlike sovereign secularism, liberalism embraces some version of positive freedom *for* religion, a notion of human flourishing that is not only open to, but indeed includes the encouragement of the public practice of "religio." In the following, I will call liberalism that is enlightened about its limits and its dependency upon what transcends its very limits, *"genuine liberalism."* For, unlike sovereign secularism, and for that matter, also unlike *mere liberalism,* genuine liberalism is fully aware of the fact that a society can only be truly free, when it is just, and that there cannot be a just society in which the virtue of justice is not practiced comprehensively. But the virtue of justice can only be practiced comprehensively and thus properly when everyone receives his or her due, which pertains first and foremost to the Source of all being and good. Hence, the comprehensive and therefore proper practice of the virtue of justice must needs include the public practice of "religio"; and if there is a divinely revealed and instituted "religio," it must needs include its public practice.

Now, this is an Augustinian-Thomist way of putting the matter. To put the same insight in the terms of genuine liberalism, I should say that a truly just and therefore free society lives from moral sources that transcend its scope, sources that liberalism per se cannot provide and replenish on its own terms, but on which a truly free and just society at the same time vitally depends.[3] These sources are fundamentally connected with and ac-

---

3. This way of conceiving of "genuine liberalism" has its proximate origin in the thought of the German Catholic expert of constitutional law, Ernst-Wolfgang Böckenförde. He famously coined the dictum: "Der freiheitliche, säkularisierte Staat lebt von Voraussetzungen, die er selbst nicht garantieren kann." The longer, precise quotation reads the following way: "The liberal secular state lives on premises that it cannot itself guarantee. On the one hand, it can subsist only if the freedom it consents to its citizens is regulated from within, inside the moral substance of individuals and of a homogeneous society. On the other hand, it is not able to guarantee these forces of inner regulation by itself without renouncing its liberalism" (Ernst-Wolfgang Böckenförde, *Staat, Gesellschaft, Freiheit: Studien*

cessed by way of the practice of "religio." And this practice of "religio" will be ideally and preferably Christian, because it is nothing but the Christian understanding of the human being that is presupposed in the tenets and the program of genuine liberalism: the human being as created in the image of God and therefore endowed with an indelible dignity and an intrinsic orientation toward transcendence, an orientation expressed first and foremost in humanity's universal desire for knowledge and happiness.

Let me offer an example each of genuine liberalism and of sovereign secularism, as I have been experiencing both in the course of my own life. For about half a century, post-WWII West Germany embodied genuine liberalism in an almost prototypical way, unlike the newly emerging European Union and also increasingly unlike the reunified, post-1990 Germany, both of which are ruled by administrative elites with an increasingly tenacious commitment to sovereign secularism — admittedly, though, the EU more so than Germany. In its political constitution, by way of a substantively positive conception of the freedom of religion as freedom *for* religion, genuine liberalism encourages the public practice of worshipping the transcendent Source of all being and good from which it draws in order that human beings may flourish comprehensively and thus support the common good genuinely and to a maximum. Sovereign secularism, on the contrary, obstructs and suppresses the acknowledgement that any comprehensively flourishing society necessarily relies upon the transcendent Source of all being and good precisely because such an acknowledgement would question and eventually undo secularism's claim to sovereign self-sufficiency. It is for this very reason, I submit, that any substantive reference to Christianity had to be suppressed in the preamble to the new European Constitution.

Unlike genuine liberalism, sovereign secularism is an intentionally post-Christian ideology and state of existence. Driven by an immanentist humanism of metaphysical and moral self-sufficiency, sovereign secularism aims at a comprehensive public system of a negative freedom *from* religion, employing political, legal, and educational power to disenfranchise Christianity as a social, political, and educational force in particular, and

---

zur Staatstheorie und zum Verfassungsrecht [Frankfurt: Suhrkamp, 1976], p. 60). Obvious traces of his thought can not only be found in the thought of most Catholic and Protestant theologians in the Germany of the old federal republic, but also in the thought of Pope Benedict XVI about the constructive role of religion in late modern societies. See especially the Pope's most recent encyclical letter, *Caritas in veritate.*

all public and normative religious practice in general. It is important to realize that since the arrival of modern constitutional states, sovereign secularism cannot always be easily identified, because of its relative similarity to genuine liberalism and because of its constant attempt to present itself as a consistent liberalism, and hence as the true perfection of liberalism itself. Thus, in democratically organized political bodies sovereign secularism not infrequently appears in the role of the "undertaker" of genuine liberalism.

There are two readings of sovereign secularism at hand that are polar extremes to each other. There is first the pseudo-theological self-interpretation of sovereign secularism as the liberation of humanity from the fetters not only of revealed religion but of any form of practice of "religio" that might be due to God — all of this in the name of the recovery of the true "natural" state of humanity. But if indeed sovereign secularism genuinely recovered the "natural" state of humanity, should one not expect that whatever points to mere human nature, undefiled and undistorted by the unnatural impositions of revealed religion, should become transparent under the conditions of sovereign secularism: natural law should be pervasively understood and effective, natural rights should be respected, and human nature discernible without dispute. This, however, is empirically not the case.

The polar opposite to this pseudo-theological self-interpretation of sovereign secularism is a hyper-theological reading that takes sovereign secularism as the epitome of the complete post-lapsarian corruption of human nature to the point that under a pervasively ruling sovereign secularism it becomes absolutely pointless to use the terms "nature" or "natural" in reference to human beings, their desires, inclinations, actions and the way they direct themselves by way of reason. Appeals to "natural law" and "human nature" are epistemically ineffective and ontologically hollow because they refer to a state humanity has lost — the state of integral nature — and will remain meaningless until humanity has been comprehensively drawn — indeed catechized — by grace into the very restoration of its true, original nature. Sovereign secularism only brings crassly into daylight what has been the case for humanity since that fateful fall. Such an extreme reading of sovereign secularism proves no less convincing. For even under the conditions of sovereign secularism, human nature is still recognizable (as the act of a substance) and human reason, even if in gravely deficient ways and to a minimal degree, still directs human agency by way of the natural law.

It seems to me that neither the pseudo-theological self-interpretation of secularism nor the hyper-theological reading of secularism as the genuine exemplification of the total post-lapsarian corruption of human nature is tenable. While the first seems to amount to little more than a glorified self-deception about sovereign secularism's programmatic nature, the second seems to overshoot the goal by failing to identify the difference between sovereign secularism and its non-identical twin, genuine liberalism. And the latter, genuine liberalism, I take it, cannot be read in an accurate theological way, on the supposition of a completely corrupt human nature. Hence, in order to read sovereign secularism theologically in the right way and at the same time avoid the two possible and, indeed, not uncommon misreadings, two theological considerations strike me as indispensable: first, a consideration of the wounds of human nature consequent upon sin, and second, a consideration of the natural love of God above all. It seems to me that such a consideration, guided by Thomas Aquinas's analysis of the states of human nature — integral, corrupt, restored, and glorified — will help us understand better the difference and similarity between modernity's non-identical twins and help us understand why mere liberalism (that is, liberalism indifferent to and hence unsupported by the deliveries of the sources from which it lives) is prone eventually to mutate into sovereign secularism — unless liberalism remains vigilant (and thereby genuine) in nourishing its core tenets by encouraging the practice of "religio" as an integral part of its public life.

I understand the following as a modest Thomist contribution to elucidating the inherent tendency, the *pondus,* of genuine liberalism to decline into mere liberalism — the increasing indifference to the sources of transcendence vital for its own flourishing — and then sooner or later the fall from mere liberalism into sovereign secularism. Thomas offers a comprehensive account of the human condition, integrating two constitutive aspects: first a theological analysis of human existence and historicality in the extant order of providence and salvation; and second, a metaphysical analysis. It is the former, the theological analysis of human existence that allows us to gain some understanding of humanity in the state of corrupt nature, and it is the latter, the metaphysical analysis that helps us to gain an appreciation for the ontological identity underlying the various states of human nature: the state of integral nature, the state of corrupt nature, the state of restored nature, and finally the state of glorified nature. Thomas's consistent integration of an auxiliary metaphysical analysis of human nature in a dominant theological framework affords a nuanced analysis of the state of corrupt human nature in contrast with the state of integral human nature which in turn affords a theological appreciation of the difference between modernity's non-identical twins, sovereign secularism and genuine liberalism.

The true flourishing of any human society depends on the natural love of God above all. It is this love that orders a society to the common good and underwrites the structure of a genuine practice of "religio" as integral to that society's orderedness to the common good of all. Genuine liberalism has a lingering intuition that the natural love of God above all is necessary for it to flourish comprehensively, and that it cannot restore, let alone produce, on its own the natural love of God above all. What liberalism does not and cannot know on its own, and hence needs to be taught by the Church, is the fact that the natural love of God above all that orders a society to the common good is no longer efficaciously operative in the state of wounded human nature. It is a natural love to which human nature must needs be restored by healing grace. When liberalism embraces such a catechesis it becomes explicitly genuine, theologically enlightened liberalism. When it rejects this catechesis, it declines into mere liberalism. For mere liberalism characteristically assumes a pure human nature in which such a love of God above all is supposed to be efficaciously operative and, moreover, regards this natural love of God above all as the only relevant aspect of a functional transcendence that is ascertained independently of any discrete practice of "religio." Sooner or later mere liberalism will discover this to be a faulty supposition. Disillusioned about and even disgusted by its failed ideal, mere liberalism eventually rejects what it regards now as the false promise of a natural transcendence and embraces immanentism together with its bastard transcendence — and the fall into sovereign secularism has occurred.

Let me now suggest how Thomas's understanding of the natural love of God above all and the wounds of human nature consequent upon sin enable, nay, strongly suggest such a theological reading of modernity's non-identical twins.

I. The Natural Love of God above All: Human Nature Metaphysically Considered

Drawing upon Aristotle as well as Pseudo-Dionysius, Thomas, most extensively in his *Summa contra gentiles,* argues for an ontological constitution of nature in which each created object is directed not only to its own perfection, but even more so to the twofold good of the universe: the order among the parts and the ordering of the whole universe to God.[4] Thomas holds it to be an entailment of divine perfection that God in all eternity by an act of the divine will intends the end of a perfect universe as the true manifestation of the divine goodness. No single creature, however, is able perfectly to manifest the divine goodness. Therefore, God created an abundance of diverse beings with a plethora of different perfections. Thereby creation as a whole more perfectly manifests and participates in the divine goodness. Thomas rightly stresses, however, that creatures are more like God when they act and cause being *(ens)*. It is for this very reason, he argues, that God created all things in a state of potency to their particular type of action. When each creature performs its particular type of action, it contributes to the perfection of the universe, to the common good of all. And because God creates and guides creatures to their proper perfection in light of the same end (the perfection of the whole), each creature acts in accord with its particular mode of participation in *esse* which is its substantial form. Through these acts, which are its secondary perfections, a creature reaches its specific end. These secondary perfections are the way a creature participates in the eternal law, the *ratio* by way of which God governs the universe.[5]

Because God brings into being and guides creatures to their proper perfection in light of the same end (the perfection of the whole), every creature naturally desires the good of the whole more than its own good. According to Thomas, even the will has such an implicit desire for the good of the whole over a particular good. This implicit desire explains why it is natural for human beings to prefer the common good to their own good.

In order to understand Thomas's argument for the natural love of God above all, we need to grasp his teaching on the natural inclination and its relation to the intellectual appetite, the will. The commandment to love God above all belongs to the natural law because of the ontological partici-

4. See esp. *Summa contra gentiles* I, 29; III, 23-32. On this topic, now available in English, see the important essay by Charles De Koninck, "The Primacy of the Common Good against the Personalists," in *The Writings of Charles De Koninck*, vol. 2, ed. and trans. Ralph McInerny (Notre Dame, IN: University of Notre Dame Press, 2009), pp. 63-108.

5. For a lucid discussion of this complex topic, from which I learned a lot, see John Rziha, *Perfecting Human Actions: St. Thomas Aquinas on Human Participation in Eternal Law* (Washington, DC: The Catholic University of America Press, 2009).

pation of all created reality, including all rational beings, in God's eternal law, the *ratio* by way of which God governs the universe. Creatures endowed with intellect have a unique form of participation in this *ratio;* it is a natural cognitive participation called "natural law" (*ST* I-II, q. 91, a. 2). God's ratio, the eternal law, has imprinted upon all creatures ontologically natural inclinations to their natural ends, and among these inclinations is first and foremost the natural love of God above all. And precisely because the rational creature's participation of the divine *ratio* is the natural law, the commandment to love God above all must be a precept of the natural law.

Now, Thomas clearly and explicitly distinguishes between two loves — the natural love of God and charity — by referring to the different ways in which God is good. First, God is the good of the universe to which all creatures are naturally directed. The human being's elective love of God imitates this natural inclination. Second, God intends human beings to share a personal union of vision and charity with him, a life shared through a type of friendship, which is initiated by sanctifying grace and perfected by divinization. Such divinization does suppose a supernatural knowledge of God as well as God's gift of charity. Although Thomas uncontrovertibly thinks that human beings never existed in a state of pure nature, he nevertheless discusses what love would be like in such a hypothetical state of pure nature in order to show the extent of the natural powers of the human being. On account of the Fall, however, even these natural powers have been corrupted. Because grace does not destroy, but perfects nature, God's grace does not just add to human nature, but it first of all heals the defects of wounded nature. Hence, as Thomas Osborne puts it saliently:

> Fallen humanity's inability to love God more than self is in no way natural, since it contradicts the inclination of created human nature. For every single created being has an inclination to love God more than self.[6]

Now, what exactly is the situation in the state of corrupt nature? Has the natural inclination to love God above all been utterly destroyed? Is the state of corrupt nature identical with the Hobbesian state of natural man?

6. Thomas M. Osborne, Jr., *Love of Self and Love of God in Thirteenth-Century Ethics* (Notre Dame, IN: University of Notre Dame Press, 2005), p. 112. For a lucid analysis and presentation of the natural love of God above all in Thomas's thought, see esp. chapter 3.

Has the inclination of nature become a sheer equivocation of whatever drives a human being? To see how Thomas would treat these questions, we most usefully turn to his treatise on sin in *ST* I-II, and especially to q. 85, *de effectibus peccati,* on the effects of sin.

II. The Wounds of Human Nature Consequent upon Sin: A Theological Phenomenology of the State of Corrupt Human Nature

Allow me first to recall briefly Thomas's fundamentally Augustinian concept of *malum* and *peccatum.* Evil is a partial privation of good, and more specifically the absence of a specific good that is due. Sin is the absence of a due act, interior or exterior, in reference to God. Sin cannot undo the "primary perfection," the distinct subsistent terminus of the act of being, which is the substantial form of the rational creature. Sin does, however, have a profoundly negative impact on the "secondary perfections," the realization of the good of a rational creature by way of that creature's proper acts.

In *ST* I-II, q. 85, a. 1, Thomas asks whether and if so how precisely sin diminishes the good of human nature. In his answer, he distinguishes between three goods of human nature. The first good of human nature is its "primary perfection," that is, the very principles which constitute human nature and the properties that follow from them, such as the powers of the soul (the intellect, the will, and the sense appetites). The second good of human nature is the natural inclination to virtue.[7] Every form causes a corresponding inclination. Hence, the inclination that results from the rational soul, the substantial form of the body, is proper operation in accord with reason, which is virtue. The third good of human nature pertains to humanity's state of integral nature. In order to indicate the distinct difference of this third good from the other two, Thomas sends a subtle linguistic signal. The gift of original righteousness, conferred on the whole human nature in the person of the first human being *may be* called — "potest dici" — a good of nature. It is, arguably, a good of human nature for its properties to be rightly ordered, and hence for a rational creature to be rightly ordered internally (reason ruling the sense appetites), and in regard to the source of all being, reason being perfected by God and subject to God in all things. Because this good of human nature orders human beings rightly to what infinitely transcends the created nature as such and is a

---

7. See *ST* I-II, q. 60, a. 1; q. 63, a. 1.

good that is not proportionate to the powers of human nature, it is a good that is uniquely distinct from the first and the second good of nature, and therefore was later called "preternatural" in contradistinction from "supernatural," the principle of the divine life itself.

Thomas's characterization of the three goods of human nature reflects his consistent integration of a metaphysical analysis (the first and the second good of human nature, that is, the primary and the secondary perfections) within the dominant framework of the economy of salvation (the third good of human nature, the state of integral nature). The first and the second good pertain to human nature considered ontologically. The third good of human nature pertains to the proper internal ordering of the faculties of this created nature in its historical existence as personally related to an essentially transcendent reality. This concrete and gratuitously granted internal ordering of all faculties and their ordering in a concrete *relatio* to God brought about an accidental perfection of human nature that surpassed its mere ontological constitution. Thomas's careful way of indicating that this "integral nature" may be called, "potest dici," a good of nature, signals a subtle analogical shift in the meaning of "nature," a shift from "nature" identifying the essence or the quiddity of the species, that is, what belongs *de iure* to human nature, to "nature" signifying now the inclusion of a perfection that human nature de facto received when first created. The three goods of human nature together constitute the *state of integral nature*. Note well, the *state of original righteousness* — which in the extant order of providence is from the first instance of the creation of the human being identical with the state of integral nature — includes also the gratuitous gift of sanctifying grace, the principle of the divine life infused in the human soul.

From the consideration of human nature in its integrity, Thomas turns to the consideration of human nature as wounded by original as well as actual sin. The first mentioned good of human nature, the constitutive principles of human nature and their properties, are neither destroyed nor diminished by sin. The third good of human nature, human nature rightly ordered in a concrete "relatio" to God, was entirely destroyed by original sin. The second good of human nature, the natural inclination to virtue, however, is not destroyed but diminished by sin. How so? Here we need to recall the principle Thomas establishes in *ST* I-II, q. 50, a. 1: Human acts produce an inclination to like acts. From the fact that a thing becomes inclined to one of two contraries, its inclination to the other contrary is necessarily diminished. As sin is opposed to virtue, from the fact that a human being sins, there results a diminution of that good of nature, which is the inclination to virtue. But beware, it is still the good of nature that is diminished. "Diminishing" is after all an action that a patient suffers. How can sin that, as a privation, is like an accident in a subject (the good of nature), act on a subject? Thomas argues that an accident does not act effectively, but does act *formally* on the subject. The consequence of such a formal impact of the diminution of the inclination to the good is the *inordinateness of action*.[8]

But does such a continuous diminution of the good of human nature not eventually have to end in the total destruction of human good by sin? The first objection of *ST* I-II, q. 85, a. 2, where Thomas addresses this important question, is of considerable interest. For this objection anticipates a position that is only all too familiar since the Protestant Reformation with its singular insistence, at least among Lutherans and Calvinists, on the total corruption of human nature after the fall. It would seem, so this first objection goes, that the entire good of human nature can be destroyed by sin. Because human nature itself is finite, the good of human nature must also be finite. Now, as we all know, any finite thing is entirely taken away, if the subtraction be continuous. Since the good of nature can be continuously diminished by sin, it seems that in the end it can be entirely taken away. In his "sed contra," Thomas marshals Augustine as the decisive authority:

> *"Evil does not exist except in some good"* (*Enchiridion* xiv). But the evil of sin cannot be in the good of virtue or of grace, because they are contrary to the evil of sin. Hence, it must be in the good of nature, and consequently it does not destroy the good of nature entirely. (Translation modified)

Thomas's response builds upon Augustine's argument in three important steps. First, we already know from the previous question that it is the inclination to virtue that is diminished by sin. And this is perfectly fit-

8. *ST* I-II, q. 85, a. 1, ad 4: "An accident does not act effectively on its subject, but it acts on it formally, in the same sense as when we say that whiteness makes a thing white. In this way there is nothing to hinder sin from diminishing the good of nature; but only in so far as sin is itself a diminution of the good of nature, through being an inordinateness of action. But as regards the inordinateness of the agent, we must say that such like inordinateness is caused by the fact that in the acts of the soul, there is an active, and a passive element: thus the sensible object moves the sensitive appetite, and the sensitive appetite inclines the reason and will. . . . The result of this is the inordinateness, not as though an accident acted on its own subject, but in so far as the object acts on the power, and one power acts on another and puts it out of order."

ting, Thomas argues, because, after all, human beings are rational beings; and it is indeed due to the fact that they are rational beings that they perform acts in accord with reason which is synonymous with acting virtuously. Second, in consequence, sin can in no way remove entirely from humans their ontological constitution as rational beings. For in such a case they would no longer be capable of sin in the first place. Third, Thomas locates precisely where the diminution occurs. It occurs in regard to the inclination toward virtue. How so? The natural inclination toward virtue holds a middle position between its root which is human nature, and its term which is virtue. As we know, there can be no diminution by sin on the part of the root of the inclination. Rather, the diminution by sin occurs on the part of the term, "insofar as an obstacle is placed against its attaining the term." Such an obstacle is a specific sinful act that produces an inclination to like sinful acts. Such a secondary, acquired inclination to like sinful acts hinders the inclination brought forth by the root (human nature) to result in virtuous acts. And so, by anticipation, Thomas can respond to a central tenet of the Protestant Reformation: The entire good of human nature would be destroyed by sin if the diminution by sin were one of subtraction. But since the diminution of the good of nature by sin comes about by raising obstacles, that is, by producing contrary inclinations, "this neither diminishes nor destroys the root of the inclination."

Such a decisive rebuttal of anthropological pessimism might encourage in turn anthropological optimism to raise its head and to press the following question: If sin indeed neither diminishes nor destroys the root of the inclination, is it not then the case that we arrive at a fine distinction between a human nature, unblemished in its root, on the one hand, and on the other hand, a historically contingent and individually variant conglomeration of obstacles of acquired inclinations toward sin? If these obstacles were properly removed by a therapeutic counter-education of the will and a training in the acquired virtues (supported by the moral efficacy of the sacraments), should we not assume that eventually the unblemished root of human nature would elicit again its proper inclinations toward virtue? Would it then not be even possible to understand the supernatural virtues as just an intensified mode of the acquired virtues and the Church as primarily a religio-pedagogical institution, a training in the acquisition of the proper virtues? In short, should we not understand the Church first and foremost as a comprehensive ecclesial pedagogy aimed at systematically overcoming structures of and habituations in sin, aided by the moral efficacy of the sacraments? Such a line of thinking is not at all impossible, if one takes the state of corrupt human nature as an alleged state of pure nature absent of sanctifying grace, a pure nature faced with a contingent history of obstacles that prevent the inclination toward virtue from reaching its term, obstacles that in principle can be removed by way of a persistent moral pedagogy.

Thomas most decidedly does not follow such a path and does not facilitate such a line of thinking that would transpose the *metaphysical* analysis of the created structure of human nature into a *theological* analysis of human existence in the historicality of the economy of salvation. *Thomas understands the historicality of sin to go all the way down. Theologically considered, human nature after the fall is always already adversely affected in a twofold way, by original as well as by actual sin.*

This becomes eminently evident in *ST* I-II, q. 85, a. 3, where Thomas draws upon a text (unknown to us) from the Venerable Bede, presumably in order to remove any possible ambiguity about the state of fallen human nature and in order to discourage any undue anthropological optimism of whatever Pelagian shade. Human nature has received four wounds consequent upon sin, original as well as actual: the wounds of weakness, ignorance, malice, and concupiscence. Thomas discusses wounded nature in reference to integral nature which includes the third good of human nature in virtue of which reason had a perfect hold over the lower parts of the soul (the sense appetites), while reason was perfected by God and subject to God. Consequent upon original sin, all powers of the soul are left destitute of their *proper order,* whereby they are *naturally* directed to virtue. It is this *destitution of proper order* that Thomas has in mind when he discusses the four wounds of human nature consequent upon sin.

You will recall that Thomas holds there to be four essential powers or faculties of the soul that can be the subject of virtue. These four powers are reason, will, the irascible sense appetite, and the concupiscible sense appetite, and each of these powers has been wounded by sin. The wound of *ignorance* pertains to reason where prudence resides. Reason is deprived of the order to the true, especially in regard to moral matters. The wound of *malice* pertains to the will where justice resides. The will is deprived of its order to the good. The wound of *weakness* pertains to the irascible sense appetite where fortitude resides. The irascible sense appetite is deprived of its order to the arduous. The wound of *concupiscence* pertains to the concupiscible sense-appetite where temperance resides. The concupiscible sense appetite is deprived of its order to the delectable moderated by reason.

Note well, according to Thomas, these four wounds of human nature are the consequence of original as well as actual sin. First and foremost, "the four wounds are inflicted upon the whole of human nature as a result of the first parent's sin." That is, all human beings, with the exception of the Blessed Mother, even if they never committed a single mortal or *per impossibile* even never committed a single venial sin, still live under a condition in which the four essential powers of their souls that can be subject to virtue are left destitute of their proper order, whereby they are naturally directed to virtue (see *ST* I-II, q. 109, a. 8). The historical condition of fallen human nature is thus that the proper orderedness that seems to be characteristic of the natural directedness of all powers toward virtue is profoundly disturbed and that some divine *auxilium* seems to be required in order to account for the proper operation even of the acquired virtues (see *ST* I-II, q. 109, a. 6 and ad 2; q. 109, a. 7).

Through actual sin reason is made dull (first and foremost, in moral matters), and the will is hardened against the good. In consequence, good actions become increasingly difficult and concupiscence becomes increasingly impetuous.[9] Irrespective of the dire state of wounded human nature, however, the ontological structure of human nature and its natural inclination toward virtue remain incorrupt and hence in potency to healing grace. How does Thomas envisage this incorrupt and indeed incorruptible root whence the natural inclination to virtue, and for that matter, the natural love of God over self arises?

Thomas's treatise on grace is the place to turn for an answer: In *ST* I-II, q. 109, a. 2, Thomas considers whether a human being can wish or do any good without grace. He develops his answer by way of a twofold distinction, first, the distinction between integral and wounded nature and, secondly, between God as the first mover of every good act and wish and the human proximate cause (that is, the sufficient operative power proportionate to human nature) of human acts and wishes. He emphasizes first what is common to both states, namely that in each state the human being relies on God as the first mover to do *(facere)* or even to wish *(velle)* any good whatsoever. In the order of exercise as well as in the order of intention, in each state, God is the first mover of every good act and every good intention.

Now to the crucial difference between the two states of human na-

---

9. "Et maior difficultas bene agenda accrescit; et concupiscentia magis exardescit" (*ST* I-II, q. 85, a. 3).

ture: In the state of integral nature, "as regards the sufficiency of the operative power" *(quantum ad sufficientiam operativae virtutis)* human beings were able to do and wish the good proportionate to their nature, such as the good of acquired virtue — by their natural endowments *(per sua naturalia)*. This is not the case anymore in the state of corrupt nature. Allow me to cite Thomas at this point. For the terseness and gravity of his assessment of the state of wounded nature is worth meditating:

> [I]n the state of corrupt nature, [the human being] falls short of what he could do by his nature, so that he is unable to fulfill it by his own natural powers [*per sua naturalia*]. Yet because human nature is not altogether corrupted by sin, so as to be shorn of every natural good, even in the state of corrupted nature it can, by virtue of its natural endowments [*per sua naturalia*], work some particular good, as to build dwellings, plant vineyards, and the like; yet it cannot do all the good natural to it [*totum bonum sibi connaturale*], so as to fall short in nothing; just as the *sick man* [*homo infirmus*] can of himself make some movements, yet he cannot be perfectly moved with the movements of one in health, unless by the help of medicine he be cured. (*ST* I-II, q. 109, a. 2; my emphasis)

An all too fast and facile reading of Thomas's answer might suggest a striking agreement between the self-sufficiency that an immanentist sovereign secularism hopes to achieve and what Thomas thinks human nature in virtue of its natural endowment *(per sua naturalia)* is able to achieve in the state of corrupt human nature: *ars* or *techne* ordered to the needs and the flourishing of the human being as a highly advanced, social animal. Yet this is not quite so. In the state of corrupt nature, human beings cannot do all the good natural to them. The utopia of effortless sensual pleasure, arguably guiding the capitalist as well as the communist versions of sovereign secularism, is nothing but that, a utopia, a daydream entertained by Thomas's "sick man" (the *homo infirmus*) about living a life of health. What for sovereign secularism is the desired terminus to be achieved by means of increasing technological sophistication, is for the theologian, who considers wounded nature in light of integral nature, just an utterly reduced state of human flourishing, indeed a "sickness unto death" (Kierkegaard), as Thomas stresses in *ST* I-II, q. 85, a. 5.[10] So, anthropologi-

---

10. See also *ST* II-II, q. 10, a. 4, "Whether every act of an unbeliever is a sin": "[M]ortal sin takes away sanctifying grace, but does not wholly corrupt the good of nature. Since there-

cal optimism, the pure nature dream of a sovereign secularism is nothing but a strategy devised by the *homo infirmus* to avoid facing his sickness unto death.

But does such a strong rebuttal of anthropological optimism not entail the sheer impossibility of genuine liberalism? Do we, after all, have to acknowledge the de facto total corruption of human nature, at least regarding all secondary perfections? Does not the irreversible sickness unto death make the noble pagan nothing but a benign illusion at best and a dangerous one at worse? In short — to stay with Thomas's metaphor — how sick is the *homo infirmus*?

One way to get at this issue is to ask whether the *homo infirmus* is able to acquire any true virtue at all. Will there be only a semblance of virtue in the *homo infirmus*? To put it differently: Are all true virtues infused virtues?

In *ST* II-II, q. 23, a. 7, in the context of the treatment of the theological virtue of charity, Thomas considers at length the question whether any true virtue is possible without charity:

> Virtue is ordered to the good. . . . Now the good is chiefly an end, for things directed to the end are not said to be good except in relation to the end. Accordingly, just as the end is twofold, the last end, and the proximate end, so also, is good twofold, one, the ultimate and universal good, the other proximate and particular. The ultimate and principal good of man is the enjoyment of God, according to Ps. lxxiii. 28: *It is good for me to adhere to God,* and to this good man is ordered by charity. Man's secondary and, as it were, particular good may be twofold: one is truly good, because, considered in itself, it can be directed to the principal good, which is the last end; while the other is good apparently and not truly, because it leads us away from the final good.

---

fore, unbelief is a mortal sin, unbelievers are without grace indeed, yet some good of nature remains in them. Consequently it is evident that unbelievers cannot do those good works which proceed from grace, viz. meritorious works; yet they can, to a certain extent, do those good works for which the good of nature suffices. Hence it does not follow that they sin in everything they do; but whenever they do anything out of their unbelief, then they sin. For even as one who has the faith can commit an actual sin, venial or even mortal, which he does not refer to the end of faith, so too, an unbeliever can do a good deed in a matter which he does not refer to the end of his unbelief." As a self-consciously post-Christian phenomenon, sovereign secularism is systematic unbelief (a conscious rejection of belief) and as a ruling set of assumptions therefore a constant invitation to sin. Good things though can still be done under the rule of secularism "in matters which do not refer to the end of unbelief."

Accordingly, it is evident that simply true virtue is that which is directed to man's principal good; thus also the Philosopher says (*Phys.* vii, text 17) that *virtue is the disposition of a perfect thing to that which is best:* and in this way no true virtue is possible without charity.

If, however, we take virtue as being ordered to some particular end, then we may speak of virtue being where there is no charity, in so far as it is directed to some particular good. But if this particular good is not a true, but an apparent good, it is not a true virtue that is ordered to such a good, but a counterfeit virtue. . . . If, on the other hand, this particular good be a true good, for instance the welfare of the state, or the like, it will indeed be a true virtue, imperfect, however, unless it be referred to the final and perfect good. Accordingly, no strictly true virtue is possible without charity. (*ST* II-II, q. 23, a. 7)[11]

He first reminds his readers that a good is first and foremost an end. And because the human end is twofold *(duplex est finis, unus ultimus et alius proximus),* the last end and the proximate end, so also the human good is twofold, the ultimate and universal good, that is the enjoyment of God to which the human being is ordered by charity, and the proximate and particular good (to which the human being is ordered by prudence and the natural law). Thomas, interestingly and importantly, makes the following distinction regarding the proximate and particular good. The proximate good is truly good only if it can be directed to the universal good, the ultimate end. If, on the contrary, the proximate good leads away from the ultimate good, it is only apparently good. This distinction yields the following taxonomy of virtue: First, simply true virtue is directed to the principal good, which is the final end. In this respect, no true virtue is possible without it being informed by charity. Second, virtue as ordered to some proximate and particular good

11. See the corresponding earlier discussion in his treatise on virtues, *ST* I-II, q. 65, a. 2: "Whether Moral Virtues Can Be Without Charity?" "[I]t is possible by means of human works to acquire moral virtues, in so far as they produce good works that are directed to an end not surpassing the natural power of man: and when they are acquired thus, they can be without charity, even as they were in many of the Gentiles. But in so far as they produce good works in proportion to a supernatural last end, thus they have the character of virtue, truly and perfectly; and cannot be acquired by human acts, but are infused by God. Such like moral virtues cannot be without charity. . . . It is therefore clear from what has been said that only the infused virtues are perfect, and deserve to be called virtues simply: since they direct man well to the ultimate end. But the other virtues, those namely, that are acquired, are virtues in a restricted sense, but not simply: for they direct man well in respect of the last end in some particular genus of action, but not in respect of the last end simply."

needs to be distinguished the following way: If this particular good is only apparently good, then the virtue is counterfeit. If this particular good, however, is a true good, like, as Thomas suggests, the welfare of the state *(conservatio civitatis)*, the virtue being ordered to it is a true, albeit imperfect virtue — unless the particular good is ordered by charity to the principal good which would perfect the virtue under discussion.

Since sin cannot destroy particular goods and since in the state of corrupt nature human beings can still work particular goods, we encounter in the state of corrupt nature the mixture of apparent virtues ordered to some apparent good (the apparent virtue of thriftiness and miserliness ordered toward the accumulation of wealth) and of true, even if imperfect virtues ordered to a true good (the true, though imperfect virtue of studiousness ordered to the attainment of some particular truth) that can itself be ordered to the principal good, as every truth can be ordered to the First Truth.

Because of sovereign secularism's constitutively negative freedom *from* the public practice of religion, sovereign secularism is necessarily ordered to what is only apparently a universal, principal good, namely the utopia of a purely immanent and essentially sensualist notion of human flourishing. Therefore, sovereign secularism per se can encourage and produce nothing but apparent virtues. That is, if true, albeit imperfect, virtues do de facto occur under the regime of sovereign secularism, they do so despite of it, not because of it. Genuine liberalism, on the contrary, being at least somewhat theologically enlightened, is ordered to genuine goods of human flourishing, one of which is the welcome and encouraged public practice of "religio." In other words, the goods of human flourishing in genuine liberalism are not merely apparent, because they can, in principle, by way of the public practice of "religio" be ordered to the principal good and ultimate end. Hence, it is far from an unreasonable expectation that true, albeit imperfect virtues are encouraged and fostered under the rule of genuine liberalism. The United States of America, in the better parts of its history, has produced impressive numbers of persons shaped by these true, albeit imperfect, virtues. However, because genuine liberalism as a whole is not ordered to the universal good and ultimate end — that is, the enjoyment of God — the virtues genuine liberalism is able to encourage and to foster will remain essentially imperfect and profoundly vulnerable to the consequences of sin.[12]

12. Thomas reminds us (*ST* I-II, q. 65, a. 2) that the only truly perfect moral virtues are those that are infused together with the theological virtues, for unlike the acquired moral

But if genuine liberalism indeed encourages the public practice of "religio," and relies for its flourishing on those transcendent sources it cannot provide itself, should we then not assume that genuine liberalism, ideally conceived, is an indication that somehow a natural love of God above all remains operative even in the state of corrupt human nature?

III. The Natural Love of God above All in the State of Integral Human Nature and in the State of Corrupt Human Nature

Thomas addresses this question squarely in the third article of *ST* I-II, q. 109, the opening question of his treatise on grace.[13] In this article he

---

virtues, the infused moral virtues are always informed by charity, and therefore they are formally referred to the ultimate good, that is God: "Charity loves God above all things in a higher way than nature does. For nature loves God above all things inasmuch as He is the beginning and the end of natural good; whereas charity loves Him, as He is the object of beatitude, and inasmuch as man has a spiritual fellowship with God. Moreover, charity adds to natural love of God a certain quickness and joy, in the same way that every habit of virtue adds to the good act which is done merely by the natural reason of a man who has not the habit of virtue" (*ST* I-II, q. 109, a. 3, ad 1).

13. "[M]an in a state of perfect nature [human nature rightly ordered], could by his natural power, do the good natural to him without the addition of any gratuitous gift, though not without the help of God moving him. Now to love God above all things is natural to man and to every nature, not only rational but irrational, and even to inanimate nature according to the manner of love which can belong to each creature. And the reason of this is that it is natural to all to seek and love things according as they are naturally fit (to be sought and loved) since *all things act according as they are naturally fit* as stated in *Phys.* ii.8. Now it is manifest that the good of the part is for the good of the whole; hence everything, by its natural appetite and love, loves its own proper good on account of the common good of the whole universe, which is God. Hence Dionysius says (*Div. Nom.* iv) that *God leads everything to love of Himself.* Hence in the state of perfect nature man referred the love of himself and of all other things to the love of God as to its end; and thus he loved God more than himself and above all things. But in the state of corrupt nature man falls short of this in the appetite of his rational will, which, unless it is cured by God's grace, follows its private good, on account of the corruption of nature. And hence we must say that in the state of perfect nature man did not need the gift of grace added to his natural endowments, in order to love God above all things naturally, although he needed God's help to move him to it; but in the state of corrupt nature man needs, even for this, the help of grace to heal his nature" (*ST* I-II, q. 109, a. 3).

"When it is said that nature cannot rise above itself, we must not understand this as if it could not be drawn to any object above itself, for it is clear that our intellect by its natural knowledge can know things above itself, as is shown in our natural knowledge of God. But we are to understand that nature cannot rise to an act exceeding the proportion of its

considers explicitly whether by his own powers and without grace the human being can love God above all things. Quite predictably by now, Thomas first considers human nature in the state of integrity, *in sui integritate*. And as is clear from what we discussed previously, in this state, Thomas holds, human beings could do the good that is natural to them by their natural power *(poterat operari virtute suae naturae bonum quod est sibi connaturale)*. Thomas adduces the guiding metaphysical principle for his argument from Aristotle's *Physics* II, 8: *All things act according as they are naturally fit.* Hence it is natural for all to seek and love things as they are naturally fit to be sought and loved. But since the good of the part is manifestly for the good of the whole, everything loves its proper good by its natural love on account of the common good of the universe, which is God. And therefore to love God above all is natural to every nature, rational and irrational, according to the manner of love which can belong to each creature. In the case of human nature, this obtains for the state of integral nature. However, in the state of corrupt nature, the matter is quite different. Here the human being falls short of the appetite of the rational will with which he or she — in the state of integral nature — would love its own proper good on account of the common good of the whole universe. But on account of the woundedness of nature — remember the wound of nature consequent upon sin that pertains to the will: malice, the will's deprivation of its order to the good — the appetite of the rational will follows its private good, the *"bonum privatum."*

How the *homo infirmus*, under the conditions of modernity, relates to this private good turns out to be the *discrimen* between genuine liberalism and sovereign secularism. Is the private good always one that stands in need of being ordered toward the common good of the whole and thus toward the transcendent good of the universe — God? Or has the *bonum privatum* turned into the *bonum privativum*, the private good into the putative principal good itself, which is one version of sovereign secularism, the other being the destruction of the *bonum privatum* by a collectivist *bonum privativum*, the greatest good of the greatest number, for the sake of which the good of the few, the unborn, the elderly, the handicapped, and the incurably ill must be sacrificed? Thomas's terse observation about the dire state of corrupt human nature encourages a phenomenology of sovereign secularism and its travails *avant la lettre*: the errancy of reason in

---

strength. Now to love God above all things is not such an act; for it is natural to every creature, as was said above" (*ST* I-II, q. 109, a. 3, ad 2).

moral matters, the darkening of conscience regarding the fundamental questions of human life and dignity: abortion, euthanasia, economic and sexual exploitation of the poor, genocide etc.; a pervasive loss of magnanimity and humility (two essential virtues perfecting the irascible and the concupiscible sense appetites); the celebration of pride, vanity, greed, and egotism as broadly accepted characteristics of an acknowledged way of life; the will to power and lust reigning individually and collectively. But because neither original nor actual sin can destroy the root from which the inclination to virtue arises, the possibility — albeit the greatly unlikely possibility — of recovering genuine liberalism is never completely lost. In other words, while the possibility of recovery always obtains, the instrument of such a recovery has to be supplied from quite another domain. I will return to the question whence the instrumental help for such a recovery arrives, in the last section of this chapter.

In light of Thomas's analysis of what human beings in the state of corrupt nature are and are not capable of *per sua naturalia,* it becomes clear that liberalism would work quite well in the state of integral nature. In other words, liberalism is a political program perfectly fit for the human being — only, alas, quite less than perfectly fit for the state of corrupt human nature. Because liberalism accords properly only to integral human nature, the perennial fragility and inherent instability of mere liberalism should not come as a surprise at all to those who had Augustine as their theological teacher.[14]

Mere liberalism is nothing but the modern instantiation of the *homo infirmus* Thomas uses to describe the limited scope of particular goods humanity in the state of corrupt nature can achieve *per sua naturalia.* Unlike

14. It might be pertinent to recall in this very context what Thomas considers to be the capacity of persons by their own natural powers and without grace, in short, of persons in the ideal state of political liberalism, to fulfill the commandments of the law: "There are two ways of fulfilling the commandments of the Law. The first regards the substance of the works, as when a man does works of justice, fortitude, and of other virtues. And in this way man in the state of perfect nature could fulfill all the commandments of the Law; otherwise he would have been unable to sin in that state, since to sin is nothing else than to transgress the Divine commandments. But in the state of corrupted nature man cannot fulfill all the Divine commandments without healing grace. Secondly, the commandments of the law can be fulfilled, not merely as regards the substance of the act, but also as regards the mode of acting, i.e., their being done out of charity. And in this way, neither in the state of perfect nature, nor in the state of corrupt nature can man fulfill the commandments of the law without grace. . . . Beyond this, in both states they need the help of God's motion in order to fulfill the commandments, as stated above (AA 2, 3)" (*ST* I-II, q. 109, a. 4).

mere liberalism, genuine liberalism is somewhat, though not fully enlightened about humanity's state of sickness and hence willingly and sometimes even eagerly receives all the medication it can lay hands on in order to restore and expand the scope of the particular goods to be achieved in a genuinely liberal polity and society.

Thomas's balanced and integrated analysis of human nature helps us understand why genuine liberalism depends vitally on the transcendent source that enables a restoration of the natural love of God above all. By neglecting and eventually rejecting this source, genuine liberalism inevitably declines into mere liberalism and from there quickly into sovereign secularism, the prototypical, profoundly "unnatural" Hobbesian state of human society devoid of any tangible remnants of the natural love of God above all.[15]

Does this theological reading of liberalism and secularism in light of the natural love of God above all and the wounds of human nature consequent upon sin shed any light upon the Church's perennial and hence also contemporary vocation? Let me offer a few concluding observations — observations in which I distinguish between the Church's overarching ultimate vocation, to be *"Ursakrament,"* and her perennial proximate, political vocation. A distinction is not a dichotomy and hence what is distinguished here, forms in reality one inseparable unity.

IV. The Church's Perennial Proximate Political Vocation

The Church's perennial proximate "political vocation" has been and continues to be a restoration of humanity, a healing of the *homo infirmus,* a healing and strengthening of the natural love of God above all. The Church fulfills this task first and foremost as a teacher of conscience. Through public witness of the divine law and through public argumentation in light of and based on the natural law as well as the divine law, she instructs conscience and thereby begins to remove the dullness of practical reason consequent upon sin. Of at least equal if not greater importance, though, is her public sacramental and liturgical presence in unity with her

---

15. The de facto state of corrupt nature is the only "nature" secularism knows. This is why in concrete practical terms — quite different from the pronounced theories — fascists, communists, and secularist liberals fundamentally distrust human beings and hence never tire of devising political, social, and managerial strategies of control.

hidden spiritual presence of prayer, penance, and the cultivation of holy lives. For in the end it is only the unity of truth and charity that heals, guides, and edifies. There are remarkably diverse ways of embodying the Church's proper spiritual and her proximate political vocation — by lay persons like Thomas Moore, religious like Catherine of Siena, priests like Miguel Pro, bishops like Oscar Romero, and Popes like John Paul II.

Such was the Church's political vocation in her encounter with a pagan Roman empire, in her encounter with barbarian monarchies, and such is her encounter with modernity's fraternal twins, sovereign secularism and genuine liberalism.[16] Note well: this perennial proximate political vocation is subordinate, though integral to the Church's proper and principal vocation (which is nothing but being the instrumentality of the integration of humanity into the mystical body of Christ, that body that in unity with its head is to enjoy the life of the triune God in all eternity). But insofar as sanctifying grace also always heals, the Church's divinizing instrumentality has always a humanizing effect upon all political systems that are intrinsically open to such humanization (and, alas, not all political systems are), including modern constitutional democracy: the natural love of God above all is ready to be awakened by the Church's appeal by way of witness, catechesis, and publicly accessible argumentation to reason's proper participation in the eternal law. The good causes to which persons of good will dedicate themselves are an indication that despite the grave wounds of nature consequent upon sin, the source from which the natural inclination to virtue arises is still active, and with it, even in the state of corrupt human nature, a faint echo of the natural love of God above all.

It is in this precise sense that mere liberalism is in desperate need of the Church's principal as well as her proximate vocation, in need of a healing of that sickness that in its direst condition becomes the terminal, unnatural state of sovereign secularism. As the twentieth century has taught us by way of genocides, gulags, and concentration camps, and as the still young twenty-first century is already teaching us by way of aborturaries, euthanasia programs, genetic engineering, sex-tourism, and the transnational, corporate economic exploitation of the poor, sovereign secularism is anti-humanism pure, a lethal condition for human beings (especially the

---

16. For spelling out this proximate political vocation of the Catholic Church in the current US-American context, see the recent book, as accessible as astute, by the archbishop of Philadelphia, Charles J. Chaput, O.F.M. Cap., *Render unto Caesar: Serving the Nation by Living Our Catholic Beliefs in Political Life* (New York: Doubleday, 2008).

unborn, the handicapped, the elderly, and the poor) and hence profoundly unnatural.[17] Because it is so profoundly unnatural a condition, sovereign secularism also cannot sustain itself but must always eventually collapse, most often by quite literally consuming its own children.

In Europe and also in the United States, where the Church is presently faced with a quite sickly and waning mere liberalism and a newly budding and waxing sovereign secularism, it is appropriate, indeed urgent, to recall the following words from *Gaudium et Spes:*

> [T]he church is fully aware that its message is in harmony with the deepest desires of the human heart when it champions the dignity of the human calling and restores hope to those despairing of any higher destiny. Far from diminishing humankind, this message spreads light, life and liberty for its progress, and nothing less can satisfy the human heart. "It is for yourself that you have made us," Lord, "and our hearts are restless, until they repose in you."
>
> In fact, it is only in the mystery of the Word incarnate that light is shed on the mystery of humankind. For Adam, the first human being, was a representation of the future, namely, of Christ the lord. It is Christ, the last Adam, who fully discloses humankind to itself and unfolds its noble calling by revealing the mystery of the Father and of the Father's love. (GS 21 and 22)[18]

It is, after all and ultimately, only our participation in the body of Christ, our ever deeper union with Christ in charity and through the sacraments, that the wounds of human nature consequent upon sin are healed and our natural love of God above all is restored. Genuine liberalism nourishes itself from the crumbs that fall from the Lord's table. For the natural love of God above all has not been destroyed in the state of corrupt human nature, only starved into momentary inefficacy. Feed it with the Word of truth and the bread of life, and it will begin to stir again.

---

17. Of course, in the state of advanced moral and social corruption, the unnatural can indeed take on the appearance of the natural. For an astute analysis of this all too often neglected phenomenon, see J. Budziszewski, "The Natural, the Connatural, the Unnatural," in *The Line Through the Heart: Natural Law as Fact, Theory, and Sign of Contradiction* (Wilmington, DE: ISI Books, 2009), pp. 61-77.

18. For an incisive interpretation of *Gaudium et Spes* 22 that is fully consonant with the analysis advanced in this chapter, see Thomas Joseph White, O.P., "The 'Pure Nature' of Christology: Human Nature and *Gaudium et Spes* 22," *Nova et Vetera* (English) 8, no. 2 (2010): 283-322.

B. CREATED FOR HAPPINESS, BOUND FOR HEAVEN —
   NATURE AND THE SUPERNATURAL

"Palaeothomism?" — The Continuing Debate over the Natural Desire for the Vision of God

I. What Is the Human Being? — Two Overarching Types of Answers

One might propose that the fulcrum on which theology is balanced is an answer to the question, or some version of it, What is the human being?, or in more precise theological terms, What is the ultimate end of the human being, and in which way and to what degree is this end constitutive of human nature? The answers theologians offer to this question belong largely to one of two overarching types.

One type of answer begins with a statement, for some of almost canonical status, from Augustine's *Confessions:* "[I]nquietum est cor nostrum, donec requiescat in te."[1] Resting in God is the ultimate end of humanity and, short of reaching this end, human life will remain essentially unfulfilled and, in the end, pointless. For rational creatures such a resting in God can be nothing short of "seeing God face to face," that is, contemplating the infinite ocean of God's essence forever, which constitutes the rational creature's perfect felicity. Hence for some theologians human beings are creatures hardwired by God for communion with God such that theology has to stipulate a fundamental obligation for God to fulfill this destiny that human beings as creatures, by definition, cannot reach on their own. But such an exigency placed by creation on the Creator might very well go too far — and indeed, such a problematic version of Augus-

---

1. St. Augustine, *The Confessions,* introduction, translation, and notes by Maria Boulding, O.S.B. (Hyde Park, NY: New City Press, 1997), p. 39: "[O]ur heart is unquiet until it rests in you."

tinianism as contended by the sixteenth-century Louvain theologian Michael Bajus was condemned by the Church's magisterium.[2] If, however, the Augustinianism of Bajus went too far in stipulating a divine obligation, might it at least be the case that the ultimate end of human fulfillment in the beatific vision is anticipated in the form of an inmost desire for this end, a desire rooted in the unfathomable depths of human nature, deeper even than the most characteristic faculties of the human soul, intellect, and will? Might it be the case that this very desire is ontologically constitutive of the human being per se, that is, identical with the rational soul or spirit itself and thus the very source of the inner dynamic of intellect and will? Might this desire, without entailing any exigency for God to fulfill it, form the essential human élan for transcendence, the profundity of which can only be grasped in the inchoate moments of a completely gratuitous fulfillment, when the desired end begins to inform the human being from above as faith, hope, and love? Is the human being always made essentially for communion with God, such that the incarnate Son, the eternal God-Man, not only represents the prototype of the ultimate end of humanity, of genuine human fulfillment in the beatific vision, but also anticipates the destiny of indeed all creatures, the universal *apokatastasis?* Is human nature, due to its constitutive end being genuinely transcendent, already originally graced in a way such that the inchoate dynamic fulfillment of this end must be understood as an intensification — albeit an infinite intensification — of this original grace to its eventual fulfillment and vice versa, the original grace as nothing else than the very anticipation of the eventual fulfillment? In short, isn't it all a matter of fundamentally the same grace, just of gradations in intensity? Isn't human nature itself most fundamentally but a function of grace? This type of answer — that takes its patronage from Origen of Alexandria and Gregory of Nyssa, and finds its most brilliant Eastern Orthodox voice in the twentieth century in Sergei Bulgakov — is most prominently represented in the Western Catholic tradition in a highly nuanced form in the theology of Henri de Lubac, and has

---

2. One of the theses condemned in Pope Pius V's bull *Ex omnibus afflictionibus* (1567) claims: "Humanae naturae sublimatio et exaltatio in consortium divinae naturae debita fuit integritati primae condicionis, et proinde naturalis dicenda est, et non supernaturalis" (Heinrich Denzinger, *Enchiridion symbolorum definitionum et declarationum de rebus fidei et morum. Kompendium der Glaubensbekenntnisse und kirchlichen Lehrentscheidungen.* Lateinisch-Deutsch. Ed. Peter Hünermann, 40th ed. [Freiburg/Basle/Vienna: Herder, 2005]; this latest edition will subsequently be cited as DH followed by the section number. The 1975 edition, ed. Adolf Schönmetzer, will be cited as DS followed by the section number).

been recently radicalized by the Anglican theologian John Milbank in his Bulgakovian reading of de Lubac's theology.

Another type of answer, however, begins with Psalm 8: "What is man that thou art mindful of him and the son of man that thou dost care for him?" (Ps 8:4 RSV). The human being is a fragile creature with a limited lifespan, prone to all kinds of deficiencies of a physical, moral, and intellectual kind, surely a rational creature, but one whose intellect even in its highest flights of abstraction and speculation remains earthbound, limited by the exigencies of space, time, the deliverances of the senses, and the corruptibility of the body. Moreover, human beings are creatures whose nature is deeply wounded by original sin and whose concrete existence is burdened and diminished by a dense web of personal and systemic sin. According to this type of answer, Christ became incarnate first and foremost because of and in response to human sin, for the sake of salvation, and not primarily to perfect creation by inchoately ushering in its transcendent end.

And what about a natural desire for the vision of God? Like Abraham having not the slightest inkling about his eventual calling and surely no desire for it, but being unexpectedly and inexplicably called and following the call, like Israel being created out of the "nothingness" of Egyptian slavery and being called to something (Lev 19:2) for which it had no antecedent desire whatsoever of its own, so also "the many" (Mk 10:45)[3] from Israel and the nations are called to a supernatural destiny categorically transcending the range of human imagination and desire. This destiny grants its own supernatural desire with the call to it, and a fulfillment of the destiny in a glory of such utter transcendence that human nature can only be elevated by God to such a state. "'What no eye has seen, nor ear heard, nor the heart of man conceived, what God has prepared for those who love him,' God has revealed to us through the Spirit" (1 Cor 2:9-10a RSV). Because the human being, qua intellect and will, has been made capable for this end *(capax Dei)* by God such that human nature indeed is characterized by a genuine openness to and capacity for God. For this very reason, human nature is in no way transmuted into something else by being elevated to such a surpassing end. However, since this end so utterly transcends every aspect of created human nature, there can be no innate,

---

3. In the Eucharistic Prayers I-IV of the Novo Ordo Mass, the words of consecration over the cup read: "hic est enim cadix sanguinis mei . . . qui pro vobis et *pro multis* effundetur" (my emphasis).

unconditional natural desire in the human being for this specific end, the vision and hence the participation of God's very substance. Heavenly beatitude is as categorically different from earthly felicity as is God from creation. Hence the desire for the former cannot be innate in human nature (whereas desire for the latter indeed is) but must be in and of itself a gift from above. However, in order to perfect human nature instead of transmuting it, this gift from above must indeed be met by a corresponding conditional desire, hence a desire not *innate* to human nature itself, but *elicited*. That such elicitation can and indeed does most properly occur, is due to the very structure of human nature itself. This unique, conditional openness to the supernatural, the attainment of God, has at times been understood as a specific obediential potency, *specific* because of the very constitution of the human rational soul and its intellective and volitional faculties.

This type of answer finds its patronage in the late Augustine, was deepened and nuanced by Thomas Aquinas, was developed variously as well as controversially by the Thomist commentatorial tradition (partially in reaction to Bajanism as well as Jansenism), and has deeply informed Catholic theology until the middle of the twentieth century.

II. The Controversy over *la nouvelle théologie*

These variant types of answers to the question concerning the "nature and destiny of man" informed the most significant and intense theological battle among Catholic theologians in the middle of the twentieth century. The argument erupted between what was at the time a dominant neo-scholastic Thomism (predominantly the French Dominican Thomism of Marie-Michel Labourdette[4] and the "Thomism of the strict observance," represented at the Angelicum in Rome first and foremost by Reginald Garrigou-Lagrange[5]) and an emerging movement, dubbed very early on by Reginald Garrigou-Lagrange as *la nouvelle théologie*, which after a pe-

---

4. For a commemorative volume of his largely forgotten contribution, see *Un maître en théologie: Le Père Marie-Michel Labourdette*, O.P., *Revue thomiste* 92, no. 1 (1992).

5. For a very accessible introduction to the person and work, see Richard Peddicord, O.P., *The Sacred Monster of Thomism: An Introduction to the Life and Legacy of Reginald Garrigou-Lagrange*, O.P. (South Bend, IN: St. Augustine Press, 2005), and for a lucid overview of his sprawling oeuvre, see Aidan Nichols, O.P., *Reason with Piety: Garrigou-Lagrange in the Service of Catholic Thought* (Naples, FL: Sapientia Press, 2008).

riod of marginalization in the wake of the encyclical *Humani generis* (August 12, 1950) became the avant-garde and eventually with and after Vatican II the dominant theological movement.[6] Arguably, the very center of the debate, the eye of the storm, was formed by the collision of two variant overall theological visions, the one informed by Gregory of Nyssa's reception of Origen, and the other by Thomas Aquinas's reception of the late Augustine. However, many other complex issues informed the controversy and contributed to its acrimonious nature. A tightly interconnected set of questions were (and continue to be) involved, including:

1. the nature and method of theology and its proper discourse;
2. the role of metaphysics (Thomistic, Scotist, or Suarezian) in the constitution of theological arguments and
   a. the philosophical question of a natural teleology and its theological interpretation as well as
   b. the relationship between philosophical and theological knowledge;
3. the role and method of the interpretation of Scripture as informing theological discourse;
4. the role of the patristic Western and especially Eastern theological tradition for contemporary theology;
5. the interpretation of the genesis of "modernity," its subtle influence on Baroque scholasticism and hence also on neo-scholastic theology;
6. the place and role of the *nouvelle théologie* in general and Henri de Lubac's theology in particular before, during, and after Vatican II, as well as the specific issue whether Pope Pius XII's encyclical *Humani generis* indeed aimed at Henri de Lubac's early work; and, underlying all of the previous questions,
7. the correct method of interpreting and receiving the theological as well as philosophical thought of Thomas Aquinas.[7]

This struggle had its root and beginning in pre-WWII France and focused initially on two projects launched by the French Jesuits, the two series *Sources Chrétiennes* and *Théologie*. Both series, each in its own particu-

---

6. For a helpfully nuanced account of this historically as well as theologically complex controversy, see Aidan Nichols, O.P., "Thomism and the Nouvelle Théologie," *The Thomist* 64 (2000): 1-19.

7. There was indeed also a political context to this conflict accounting in part for its particularly acrimonious nature. See Nichols, "Thomism and the Nouvelle Théologie," pp. 8f.

lar way, were seen to question and challenge more or less directly the principles and methods of neo-scholastic theology. The book, however, around which the theological conflict became most intense, was Henri de Lubac's monograph *Surnaturel*,[8] which appeared in 1946 in the series *Théologie*.

The contended issues that came to a head with the publication of *Surnaturel* and the subsequent theological conflict are far from dead and gone. That they remain *quaestiones disputatae* is plainly documented by a number of noteworthy publications since 2001: *Surnaturel: Une controverse au coeur du thomisme au XXe siècle*, edited by Serge-Thomas Bonino;[9] Lawrence Feingold, *The Natural Desire to See God According to St. Thomas Aquinas and His Interpreters;*[10] Georges Cottier, O.P., *Le Désir de Dieu: Sur les Traces de Saint Thomas;*[11] John Milbank, *The Suspended Middle: Henri de Lubac and the Debate concerning the Supernatural;*[12] David Braine, "The Debate between Henri de Lubac and His Critics";[13] Steven A. Long, *Natura Pura: On the Recovery of Nature in the Doctrine of Grace;*[14] and Matthew B. Mulcahy, *Aquinas's Notion of Pure Nature and the Christian Integralism of Henri de Lubac and Radical Orthodoxy: Not Everything Is Grace.*[15]

While various essays from the conference volume *Surnaturel,* as well as Cottier's valuable book will play a central role in my re-lecture of Thomas in chapter 6 of this volume, I shall focus here in this chapter on Feingold's and Milbank's recent interventions in the debate over the natural desire for the vision of God. For it is by way of Feingold's and Milbank's glaringly variant normative frameworks in which they access Thomas Aquinas — for the one the Thomist commentatorial tradition, for the other a radicalized Lubacianism — that the underlying theological issues entailed in the question of the natural desire for the vision of God are coming into starkest relief.

8. Henri de Lubac, *Surnaturel: Études historiques. Nouvelle édition avec la traducion intégrale des citations latines et grecques* (Paris: Desclée de Brouwer, 1991). For a very instructive introduction to *Surnaturel* and the ensuing conflict, see Bernard Sesboüé, S.J., "Le Surnaturel chez Henri de Lubac," *Recherches de Science Religieuse* 80 (1992): 373-408.

9. A special publication of *Revue thomiste* (Toulouse: École de théologie, 2001).

10. 1st ed. (Rome: Apollinaire Studi, 2001); 2nd ed. (Naples, FL: Sapientia Press, 2010).

11. Paris: Éditions Parole et Silence, 2002.

12. Grand Rapids: Eerdmans, 2005.

13. *Nova et Vetera* (English) 6, no. 3 (2008): 543-89.

14. New York: Fordham University Press, 2010.

15. New York: Peter Lang, 2011.

III. Lawrence Feingold's Thomist Provocation of the Settled Lubacian Consensus vs. John Milbank's Radicalized Lubacianism

Others destroy the gratuity of the supernatural order, since God, they say, cannot create intellectual beings without ordering and calling them to the beatific vision.

Encyclical *Humani generis* (August 12, 1950), n. 26[16]

Lawrence Feingold's study *The Natural Desire to See God According to St. Thomas Aquinas and His Interpreters*[17] constitutes a contribution of rather far-reaching historical and doctrinal implications, sufficiently controversial to amount to a serious scholarly provocation. To put it in the briefest way: Feingold, in an opus more extensive in scope than *Surnaturel* itself, substantially challenges the charge of Henri de Lubac — now widely accepted — that much of the Thomistic commentatorial tradition, first and foremost Cajetan, introduced "renaissance distortions" into their interpretation of Thomas Aquinas and so rather profoundly obfuscated the authentic teaching of the *doctor communis,* especially regarding the relation between human nature and the vision of God. For de Lubac and his Jesuit confrères, as Aidan Nichols aptly put it, "the true 'nouvelle théologie' was the late Scholasticism defended *à l'outrance* by Garrigou and with much more nuance by Labourdette. *This* was the upstart theology alien not only to the Fathers but the Golden Age of the thirteenth century itself."[18]

Feingold's challenge of this widely received and settled notion is indeed not a minor provocation. In his recent opuscule, *The Suspended Middle: Henri de Lubac and the Debate concerning the Supernatural,* John Milbank characterizes Feingold's work as "arch-reactionary," "written to reinstate a Garrigou-Lagrange type position," and his exegetical method as "much like that of the proof-texting of a Protestant fundamentalist," hence representing the "die-hard," "palaeolithic" neo-Thomism. The readers of Milbank's treatise — most of whom in all likelihood are neither experts in the thought of Thomas Aquinas, Henri de Lubac, or Reginald Garrigou-

---

16. "Alii veram *'gratuitate' ordinis supernaturalis* corrumpunt, cum autument Deum entia intellectu praedita condere non posse, quin eadem ad beatificam visionem ordinet et vocet" (DH, 1094, #3891).

17. 2nd ed. (Naples, FL: Sapientia Press, 2010).

18. Nichols, "Thomism and the Nouvelle Théologie," pp. 17.

Lagrange in particular nor of Catholic theology in general — are thus invited to entertain the suspicion of some sinister right-wing ecclesiastical conspiracy.

What has elicited Milbank's ire? Three questions are indicative of a larger dispute: (1) whether de Lubac's critique of key Thomist commentators, especially Cajetan, obtains; (2) the correct interpretation of Thomas Aquinas's thought on the exceedingly complex subject of the *desiderium naturalis visionis Dei;* and (3) how theology itself is to be done and how it relates to philosophy. Milbank has a high stake in all three questions insofar as he is interested in presenting de Lubac as "along with Sergei Bulgakov, one of the two truly great theologians of the twentieth century"[19] (the former's *Surnaturel* is "arguably the key text of the twentieth century"),[20] and in drafting both for his own particular project — in marked contrast to Hans Urs von Balthasar[21] — into a vision that, like Sergei Bulgakov's,[22] is ultimately indebted to Origen of Alexandria, a vision "at once more strictly orthodox and more radically humanist." In short, de Lubac is assigned the role of forerunner to the self-proclaimed movement of Radical Orthodoxy and its continuation of "Origen's vision

19. John Milbank, *The Suspended Middle: Henri de Lubac and the Debate concerning the Supernatural* (Grand Rapids: Eerdmans, 2005), p. 104.

20. Milbank, *Suspended*, p. 3.

21. The student, close friend, and translator of de Lubac's works into German who, according to Milbank's intimations, never fully understood de Lubac's vision, and therefore — again for Milbank a regrettable theological deficiency — made more substantive concessions to the encyclical *Humani generis* than his mentor de Lubac was ever willing to do. According to Milbank, von Balthasar's capitulation to *Humani generis* can be clearly discerned "in the way von Balthasar's dogmatics seems to float free of ontological conceptualizations into a 'mythical' realm that is highly voluntarist and personalist, and in the end at times only tendentiously orthodox" (13). One not only wonders what the normative point of reference of Milbank's use of the term "orthodox" is ("Radical Orthodoxy"?), but also whether the deep and explicitly acknowledged indebtedness of Hans Urs von Balthasar to the metaphysics of being as advanced by the two twentieth-century Thomist philosophers Gustav Siewerth and Ferdinand Ulrich must have been a form of subtle self-deception, not to mention the form of self-deception exercised in his small, but weighty book on de Lubac. For a critique as concise as devastating of Milbank's reading of von Balthasar's theology, see the instructive review essay by Edward T. Oakes, S.J., "On Milbank's *The Suspended Middle,*" *Nova et Vetera* (English) 4 (2006): 667-96, esp. pp. 682ff.

22. Bulgakov's theological vision — thoroughly impressive in its systematic coherence, comprehensive scope, and speculative penetration — can possibly be best appreciated in his late work, *The Bride of the Lamb,* trans. Boris Jakim (Grand Rapids: Eerdmans, 2002).

of apocatastasis: the universal Christological salvation of spirits and through this, the eternal re-establishment of all things."[23]

It is precisely Milbank's consistently Bulgakovian reading of Henri de Lubac and his tendency to receive Thomas's thought in as neo-platonic or Dionysian way as possible that makes Feingold's book so irritating for him. While Milbank's project is neither guided nor framed by the norms and criteria of Catholic theology — and indeed it should not expected to be — his reaction is nevertheless indicative of how not a few contemporary Catholic theologians might react to Feingold's book as well. For Feingold indeed challenges numerous assumptions received and settled in the first three decades after Vatican II. The first is methodological: in the wake of neo-Marxist sociology, the linguistic turn in Anglo-Saxon philosophy, and the hermeneutical and poststructuralist developments in continental philosophy, theology for many a contemporary Catholic theologian can only be conceived as defensible and intelligible in a thoroughly historical-contextualist and constructivist mode. Every theological claim must needs be advanced, read, and assessed in light of the historical, communal, and political context in which it is produced and to which it is addressed. The only way to forward arguments is by situating and out-narrating opponents as well as offering rhetorical and aesthetic appeals leading to the volitional as well as conceptual conversion of the interlocutor. Propositional discourse as informed by metaphysical realism and discursive, conceptual argumentation is therefore at present widely dismissed as a suspiciously disembodied and philosophically outdated mode of speculative theology, oblivious to the historical, pragmatic, and practice-oriented nature of theology itself and thus vulnerable to being constantly co-opted by deeply entrenched as well as concealed discourses of power and interest. This wholesale rejection of what was seen as the ossified discourse of textbook neo-Scholasticism was accompanied — in the wake of Heidegger as well as Wittgenstein — by hailing the "end of metaphysics" in general and the Aristotelian Thomist metaphysics in particular. And since — on the basis of Leo XIII's encyclical *Aeterni patris* — Thomas Aquinas had again been instantiated as the loadstar of a renewed Catholic philosophy, according to an understanding that interpreted Vatican II as the license to break with that very tradition, he had to be put aside as outmoded too.

Yet in recent years, there has occurred a remarkable revival of interest

---

23. Milbank, *Suspended*, p. 108.

in Thomas Aquinas's thought. However, this revival, for the most part, is eager not to steer again a course of confrontation with the meanwhile well-established *nouvelle théologie*. Rather, this Thomist renewal — in the wake of Chenu and Torrell[24] — characteristically draws on the very best of the historical reconstruction of an authentic Thomas behind the interpretative discourse of the once greatly esteemed, but now equally widely despised Thomist commentatorial tradition, a Thomas whose theology is properly foregrounded and again linked to its original *Sitz im Leben* in the contemplative tradition of Dominican spirituality. At the same time, an increasing philosophical interest in Thomas has reemerged, but one much more attentive to the historical and social embeddedness of philosophical discourse (Alasdair MacIntyre), in dialogue with analytic philosophy of religion (Norman Kretzmann, Eleonore Stump et al.) as well as post-Wittgensteinian philosophy of language (Victor Preller, Cornelius Ernst, Herbert McCabe, Fergus Kerr, and David Burrell).

A large part of Feingold's provocation rests in the fact that he advances his enquiry and arguments as if none of the above had ever happened. There are no nods of even the slightest acknowledgement into the directions of any of these more recent forms of Thomism. Rather, he concentrates exclusively on Thomas Aquinas, Duns Scotus (as well as some Scotists), the Thomist commentators (including Suárez) up to Garrigou-Lagrange, and Henri de Lubac. The reason for what seems to be a narrow-minded obsession with the "Thomism of the strict observance," its interlocutors, and critics is that the scope of his enquiry corresponds with quite appropriate precision to the one in which de Lubac advances his critique of most of the Thomist commentatorial tradition on the question of nature and the supernatural.

Moreover and possibly more importantly, Feingold provokes by operating in a mode of discourse very unfamiliar to theological readers by now largely unaccustomed to the conceptual precision and rigor once cultivated by the "schoolmen." Differently put, Feingold's mode of discourse is highly mimetic of the virtually forgotten tradition of Thomist commentators. Hence his *modus operandi* can arguably be understood, precisely by way of his eventual engagement of de Lubac, to continue and thereby help

24. Still indispensable as a resource is Marie-Dominique Chenu, O.P., *Toward Understanding Saint Thomas* (Chicago: Regnery, 1964), while the first address for a comprehensive, up-to-date, and magisterial biography is Jean-Pierre Torrell, O.P., *Saint Thomas Aquinas: The Person and His Work* (Washington, DC: The Catholic University of America Press, 1996).

reinstate a particular tradition of discourse (MacIntyre), a move that can be described as "arch-reactionary" *or* as "prophetically proleptic" *or* even as "radically orthodox" depending on what one thinks to be at stake in the very recovery of such a discourse of scholastic enquiry and argumentation. Surely the macro-issue ultimately is whether to interpret what is properly Augustinian and properly Thomist by way of an Origenist and Bulgakovian vision (like Milbank) of the eternal God-man (entailing, by a Bulgakovian "necessity" of love — that is, of ultimately irresistable sophianization — the *apokatastasis ton panton*),[25] or whether to receive what is properly Augustinian and properly Thomist on the predestination of the saints as well as on gratuitous, efficient grace by way of the theology of the late Augustine as received by the Second Council of Orange (529),[26] as confirmed in the late theology of grace in Thomas Aquinas, and as re-confirmed by the Council of Trent.[27]

The more proximate, but also more implicit dispute between Feingold and de Lubac, however, is over *how* to access and interpret the interpretation of the Thomist commentators itself. What makes Feingold so provocative is that the *form* of his discourse — in stark contrast to de Lubac's way of reading the commentators — is shaped not by a historical hermeneutic but by reconstructing and thus entering their own way of conducting a speculative theological enquiry, a mimetic exercise reconstructing and thus continuing the commentators' discursive mimesis of Thomas. In his own very attempt of retrieving an even older form of theology, de Lubac, on the contrary, transposes the speculative theological discourse of the commentators into a historical-hermeneutical frame of enquiry (this transposition ironically forming nothing but a quite charac-

25. Bulgakov, in logical consequence, applies what he calls "the necessary principles of universal salvation" (p. 518) to Satan: "Satan's very being, his createdness by the omniscient God, is, so to speak, an ontological proof of the inevitability of his future salvation. Even Satan in his madness does not have the power to overcome the fact of his own being, its divine foundation, that is, the sophianicity of all creation, by virtue of which 'God will be all in all.' Satan cannot fail to be convinced by his own nature of the insanity of seeking freedom in self-willfulness rather than in knowledge of truth, which alone can give true freedom. 'Liar and the father of lies' who 'abode not in the truth' (John 8:44), he will end up by subordinating himself to the truth, and evil will thereby disappear completely from God's creation" (*The Bride of the Lamb*, p. 517).

26. See DH, pp. 370-400.

27. "Hoc concilium, utpote solummodo provinciale plurimis ignotum et mox per saecula oblivioni traditum, disputationibus demum Concilii Tridentini memoriae redditum est" (DS, p. 131). See chapter 7 for a more detailed discussion of this topic.

DUST BOUND FOR HEAVEN

teristic move of critical scholarship in a genuinely modern sense, and as such completely extrinsic and foreign to the *modus operandi* of the commentators). Hence what might look to a reader uninitiated into the discursive habits of the commentators like the equivalent of "Protestant fundamentalism" and its propositionalist proof-texting (a charge that the modern Protestant theologians in the Enlightenment tradition liked to place onto the threshold of the scholasticism of Lutheran and Reformed Orthodoxy) represents in Feingold's case the proper way of *entering* the commentatorial tradition with its propositional-discursive mode of operation and, moreover, turning this mode of operation consistently and cogently against de Lubac's interpretation of the commentators as well as his interpretation of Thomas. In other words, Feingold refuses to engage de Lubac in the discursive mode by way of which the latter chose to critique the commentators, that is, by way of a primarily historical exegesis of theological language, its development and use, and the related development and flux of theological ideas.[28] Rather, Feingold insists on engaging de Lubac's own account by way of the metaphysical realism (which makes his work a "Garrigou-Lagrange type position"[29]) and its rigorous discourse in which the Thomist commentators conducted their interpretation and enquiry.

This particular conflict opens up wide-ranging questions on the nature of the relationship between thought and language and more specifically on what the relationship between the broadly historical (of ideas, concepts, motives) and the strictly speculative and discursive should be in the interpretation of the oeuvre of Thomas Aquinas. Feingold provokes by returning to and, by implication, rehabilitating an older discursive tradition (albeit, and here the *nouvelle théologie* is unquestionably right, not *the* oldest way of doing theology) and submitting de Lubac's theology to the conceptual rigor of this tradition. In light of the fact that the recent encyclical *Fides et ratio* has pointed out that the historical-hermeneutical approach is not sufficient for the full task of Catholic theology, but that Catholic theology's commitment to the truth requires a genuine speculative

28. One of the most paradigmatic studies in which this approach comes clearest to the fore is de Lubac's *Corpus Mysticum: L'Eucharistie et L'Église au Moyen Age* (Paris: Aubier-Montaigne, 1949); English translation: *Corpus Mysticum: The Eucharist and the Church in the Middle Ages,* ed. Laurence Paul Hemming and Susan Frank Parsons, trans. Gemma Simmonds, C.J., with Richard Price and Christopher Stevens (Notre Dame, IN: University of Notre Dame Press, 2006).

29. Milbank, *Suspended,* p. 26, n. 10.

mode of operation,[30] Feingold's approach might not be exactly as untimely as it could seem at first hand to those deeply shaped by the intellectual conventions of the last forty years.

Moreover, it should be noted that, one might say, ironically, Feingold displays a historical consciousness sui generis, one present in Milbank (in significant contrast to de Lubac's *de facto* operation) only in form of its negation. Both de Lubac and Feingold, *in* their very dispute over the right interpretation of the Thomist tradition, are highly aware of the conceptual as well as speculative exigencies caused by Bajanism as well as Jansenism and their condemnation, in addition to other developments up to and including the encyclical *Humani generis.* In short, de Lubac and Feingold occupy the same ecclesial ground, with a shared, even if variously interpreted, set of doctrinal norms and magisterial decisions. Milbank's interpretation of de Lubac is, on the contrary, notably unencumbered by the normative doctrinal commitments that inform the horizon shared by de Lubac and Feingold, unencumbered to the degree that he interprets de Lubac's modification, in light of the concerns expressed in the encyclical *Humani generis,* of his early *Surnaturel* in the later two volumes *The Mystery of the Supernatural,*[31] and *Augustinianism and Modern Theology*[32] as a purely extrinsic form of deference to magisterial pressure.[33] Simultaneously, Milbank's dis-

30. "With regard to the *intellectus fidei,* a prime consideration must be that the divine Truth 'proposed to us in the Sacred Scriptures and rightly interpreted by the Church's teaching [Saint Thomas Aquinas, *Summa theologiae,* II-II, q. 5, a. 3, ad 2] enjoys an innate intelligibility, so logically consistent that it stands as an authentic body of knowledge. The *intellectus fidei* expounds this truth, not only in grasping the logical and conceptual structure of the propositions, in which the Church's teaching is framed, but also, indeed primarily, in bringing to light the salvific meaning of these propositions for the individual and for humanity. . . . For its part, *dogmatic theology* must be able to articulate the universal meaning of the mystery of the One and Triune God and of the economy of salvation, both as a narrative and, above all, in the form of argument" (*Fides et ratio,* §66). Cf. also *Fides et ratio,* §§95-98.

31. *The Mystery of the Supernatural,* trans. Rosemary Sheed (New York: Herder and Herder, 1965) (*Le mystère du surnaturel* [Paris: Aubier, 1967]).

32. *Augustinianism and Modern Theology,* trans. Lancelot Sheppard (New York: Herder and Herder, 1969) (*Augustinism et théologie moderne* [Paris: Aubier, 1965]).

33. Milbank, *Suspended,* pp. 35ff. Feingold and Milbank agree in the judgment that the encyclical indeed did, while Henri de Lubac and many de Lubac scholars think the encyclical, as a matter of fact, did not aim at his work. See on this question the instructive introduction by David L. Schindler to the 1998 edition of the English translation of Lubac's *Mystery of the Supernatural,* esp. pp. xxiff, as well as de Lubac himself in his *At the Service of the Church: Henri de Lubac Reflects on the Circumstances That Occasioned His Writings,* trans. Anne Elisabeth Englund (San Francisco: Ignatius 1993), pp. 60-79, 89-90.

missal of von Balthasar's theological project is largely fueled by the impression that, allegedly unlike de Lubac, the former took the encyclical *Humani generis* too seriously to heart by presumably submitting to some version of nature-grace-extrinsicism.[34] However, it might never have really occurred to Milbank that neither Henri de Lubac, nor Hans Urs von Balthasar, nor Lawrence Feingold, nor for that matter any of the Catholic theologians and philosophers adverted to in his small book, would want to take the stance that a happily unencumbered oppositionalism to the Church's magisterium and the normative dogmatic tradition is intrinsic to the role and vocation of the Catholic theologian.[35] The deeper issue, not only but especially for Catholic theology, which Milbank's situating of Henri de Lubac in his own project and his dismissal of Feingold's defense of the commentatorial tradition opens up is the following: Theologians who operate under the presupposition that the dogmatic tradition and the living magisterium substantively inform theology will take heed of the concerns expressed in the encyclical *Humani generis* about the enduring importance of maintaining a hypothetical state of pure nature. They will therefore assume that the magisterial rejection of Bajanism and Jansenism has lasting implications for the way the gratuity of the supernatural order is theologically conceived. If there is a legitimate and productive disagreement and critical engagement possible about the above questions, the mode of discourse in which such an engagement takes place might lean more to the historical-hermeneutical mode as advanced by the *nouvelle théologie* or more to the speculative-discursive mode as advanced by Dominican Thomism. In either mode, however, the critical theological engagement will be shaped by a fundamental fidelity to the Church's doctrinal tradition as well as the living ordinary magisterium.[36] It seems that Henri de Lubac and Hans Urs von Balthasar

34. See Edward T. Oakes's trenchant critique of this aspect of Milbank's construal in "On Milbank's *The Suspended Middle*."

35. In the case of Milbank's own criteriology, it remains unclear by what normative criteria Hans Urs von Balthasar should be understood as only marginally orthodox, Henri de Lubac fully, or even radically, orthodox, and Reginald Garrigou-Lagrange, by implication, heterodox — other than those subjectively entertained by the author.

36. For an important recent introduction to the irreplaceable, irreducible, and entirely salutary function of the magisterium for Catholic theology per se, see Avery Cardinal Dulles, S.J., *Magisterium: Teacher and Guardian of the Faith* (Naples, FL: Sapientia Press, 2007). That this function does not contradict, but indeed protects and promotes the genuine freedom of Catholic theology has been argued convincingly in Joseph Ratzinger's (Benedict XVI's) slim, but weighty volume, *The Nature and Mission of Theology: Essays to Orient Theology in Today's Debates* (San Francisco: Ignatius, 1995).

occupy a terrain of normative doctrinal and theological commitments shared with Reginald Garrigou-Lagrange and Lawrence Feingold that Milbank can only dismiss as the regrettable submission to the purely extrinsic pressures of dogma and magisterium, the truth-claims of which consequently make little if any difference in his reconstruction of Henri de Lubac's theological project.

IV. Thomas Aquinas — the "Other"

The question whether, and if so, to what degree Milbank's intensification of de Lubac's theology along Bulgakovian lines is legitimate cannot be pursued at this point. However, some remarks are in order pertaining to the reading of Thomas Aquinas he advances to foster such an intensification. Appealing to recent French philosophers of religion and philosophical theologians Courtine, Boulnois, Marion, Schutz, and Lacoste, Milbank stresses three motives, which in their combined force presumably give Thomas Aquinas himself a rather Bulgakovian appearance: "first, spirit as intrinsically linked to grace; second, the entire *cosmos* as drawn through humanity to beatitude; third, grace as gratuitous because a gift can be a gift without contrast to gift."[37] A bit further on, a fourth moment emerges, this time unequivocally negative: "the regime of pure nature."[38] While Milbank rightly emphasizes that, according to Thomas, "Adam was created from the outset with the reception of grace,"[39] the very rendition "regime of pure nature" signals a profound misunderstanding: for Thomas as much as for any other of the scholastic theologians there could never have been some "regime" that would not simply be identical with the execution of divine providence, that is, divine governance. Hence, either the state of pure nature is assumed (as it is not in Thomas) to belong — even as an instance — to the extant providential order as it coincides with the economy of salvation, or "pure nature" is assumed as hypothetically obtaining in another order of divine providence (as it is in Thomas). Because of frequent confusions regarding this latter topic, I will take it up first. Next, I shall turn to the question of the fundamental and indispensable difference between nature and grace, the ensuing double gratuity, and finally, by drawing upon

---

37. Milbank, *Suspended,* p. 88.
38. Milbank, *Suspended,* p. 89.
39. Milbank, *Suspended,* p. 89.

Thomas's teaching on predestination, address the Bulgakovian dynamic of the entire cosmos being irresistibly drawn through humanity to beatitude. Finally, I will briefly address the question whether the rational creature is "intrinsically linked to grace."

In the following consideration of Thomas's thought, I am going to adduce texts primarily of the later Thomas, that is, of his Roman period and of his second Parisian regency in order to make strange the Thomas proposed by Milbank's radical Lubacianism. For during his Roman period Thomas, for the first time, had direct access to the full text of such important treatises of the late Augustine as *De gratia et libero arbitrio*, *De correptione et gratia*, *De dono perseverantiae*, and *De praedestinatione sanctorum* and possibly came across echoes of the widely lost and forgotten canons of the Second Council of Orange — an encounter with a salutary impact on his late theology of grace which ever so subtly promotes the new, contingent, and supernatural gratuity of grace above and beyond the ontological thrust of the exitus-reditus-scheme.[40] These texts from Thomas serve as pointers to a significant strand of thought in his later theology on the specific gratuity of grace, texts that strongly suggest that the commentators first and foremost continue conceptually to unfold the implications of his theology of grace. Moreover, these texts paradigmatically represent central strands in Thomas's theology that strongly resist an adoption of the *doctor communis* into an overarching theological scheme shaped by the visions of Origen and Bulgakov.

1. The Hypothetical State of Pure Nature as Entailed in the Notion of Differing Orders of Divine Providence: De malo, q. 5, a. 1, ad 15

While Thomas never assumed an extant state of pure nature, he explicitly entertained as a legitimate thought the possibility of a state of pure nature in a different order of divine providence. Entertaining the thought of a hypothetical state of pure nature, however, presupposes the relative integrity of the principle of nature, both ontologically as well as epistemically. We

40. For detailed accounts of this rather complex matter see Henri Bouillard, *Conversion et Grace chez S. Thomas d'Aquin* (Paris: Aubier, 1944), pp. 97-102; Max Seckler, *Instinkt und Glaubenswille nach Thomas von Aquin* (Mainz: Matthias Grünewald, 1961), pp. 90-98; Joseph P. Wawrykow, *God's Grace and Human Action: "Merit" in the Theology of Thomas Aquinas* (Notre Dame, IN: University of Notre Dame Press, 1995), pp. 266-76. See also my discussion of this topic in chapter 7.

find these matters quite instructively addressed by Thomas in *De malo,* q. 5, a. 1, ad 15.

In *De malo* q. 5, a. 1,[41] Thomas treats the question "Is Privation of the Vision of God a Fitting Punishment for Original Sin?" and defends the position that indeed the privation of the vision of God is a fitting punishment for original sin. He does so by arguing that if two things belong to something's perfection — the first being capable of a great good but with significant external help, the second needing no or little help but being a small good — then the first is still far better than the second. Hence it is much better to attain a great good with much help than to attain a little good with little or no help at all. "Therefore, rational creatures surpass every other kind of creature in being capable of the highest good in beholding and enjoying God, although the sources from their own nature do not suffice to attain it, and they need the help of God's grace to attain it."[42]

Thomas emphasizes up front that to attain the perfect end of the beatific vision, every rational creature — be it angel or human — is in need of a particular divine help, sanctifying grace. However, due to the particular constitution of the human nature, it being an essentially composite nature of soul and body, an additional help is necessary, namely original justice:

> [I]f the body and the senses be left to their nature, as it were, they burden and hinder the intellect from being able freely to attain the highest reaches of contemplation. And this help was original justice, by which the mind of human beings would be so subject to God that their lower powers and their very bodies would be completely subject to them, nor would their reason impede them from being able to tend toward God. And as the body is for the sake of the soul, and the senses for the sake of the intellect, so this help, whereby the body is under the control of

41. As is often the case so also here, Thomas addresses in the first article of a particular question the most central issue and lays it out in such a way that it provides the basic structure of how the rest of the articles tackling other aspects of the question are ordered.

42. *De malo* q. 5, a. 1 c. (*The De Malo of Thomas Aquinas,* with facing-page translation by Richard Regan, ed. with introduction and notes by Brian Davies [Oxford: Oxford University Press, 2001], p. 409): "Creatura ergo rationalis in hoc preeminet omni creaturae, quod capax est summi boni per diuinam uisionem et fruitionem, licet ad hoc consequendum naturae propriae principia non sufficiant, set ad hoc indigeat auxilio diuinae gratiae" (p. 408). (In the following, this edition will be refered to as *De malo,* Davies edn.)

the soul, and sense powers under the control of the intellect, is almost a disposition for the help whereby the human mind is ordained to see and enjoy God.[43]

Original justice, being gratuitously given *to* what has been created and hence to be distinguished from human nature per se, is a quasi disposition for the help of sanctifying grace. Hence, sanctifying grace acts upon a human nature readily fit for such an operation, the one being neither intrinsic nor extrinsic to the other, but of a perfect and perfectly gratuitous fittingness *(convenientia)*. Original sin, however, destroys this quasi disposition, the help of original justice, as the result of which sanctifying grace — that is, "the help, whereby the human mind is ordained to see and enjoy God" — is withdrawn as the fitting punishment:

> And when persons by sinning cast away the means whereby they were disposed to obtain a good, they deserve that the good that they were disposed to obtain be taken away. And the very taking away of the good is a fitting punishment for the sin. And so the fitting punishment of original sin is the taking away of grace and thereby of the vision of God for which grace ordains human beings.[44]

Thomas clearly distinguishes in this question between (1) a *composite nature,* that is, a reality to be intellectually grasped according to its proper constituents, that is, as species, irrespective of the particular *state* (original justice), (2) the specific gratuitous help of *original justice,* being not integral to human nature, but rather constitutive of the particular *state* in which created humanity originally existed according to the given providential order, this original justice being the disposition for (3) the help of

---

43. *De malo,* Davies edn., p. 409. "[Q]uae quodammodo si suae naturae relinquantur, intellectum aggrauant et impediunt ne libere ad summum fastigium contemplationis peruenire possit. Hoc autem auxilium fuit originalis justitia, per quam mens hominis sic subderetur Deo ut ei subderentur totaliter inferiores uires et ipsum corpus, neque ratio impediretur quominus posset in Deum tendere. Et sicut corpus est propter animam et sensus propter intellectum, ita hoc auxilium quo continetur corpus sub anima et uires sensitiuae sub mente intellectuali, est quasi dispositio quaedam ad illud auxilium quo mens humana ordinatur ad uidendum Deum et ad fruendum ipso" (p. 408).

44. *De malo,* Davies edn., p. 409: "Cum autem aliquis peccando abicit a se id per quod disponebatur ad aliquod bonum acquirendum, meretur ut ei subtrahatur illud bonum ad quod optinendum disponebatur, et ipsa subtractio illius boni est conueniens poena eius. Et ideo conueniens poena peccati originalis est subtractio gratiae et per consequens uisionis diuinae, ad quam homo per gratiam ordinatur."

sanctifying grace, both helps being categorically different from the created nature and also different in kind from each other.

It is axiomatic for Thomas that only sanctifying grace ordains human beings effectively to the vision of God. Hence the natural desire for the vision of God per se is *not* an ordination to the vision in any strict sense — though, as will be seen in chapter 6 of this volume, Thomas can also employ the term "ordination" in a wider sense that denotes a genuine, dynamic openness to and capacity for, albeit per se ineffective, the vision of God. I will show there that according to Thomas the natural desire for the vision of God is entailed in the ontological structure of the created intellect or rational soul. In a nutshell: The natural desire for the vision of God constitutes the metaphysical condition for the gratuitous realization in the economy of salvation by sanctifying grace to ordain effectively the human being to the vision of God without having to transform human nature into something else. Rather, grace presupposes the natural desire for the vision of God and perfects it by elevating it into a supernatural desire for the beatific vision.

Let us consider now objection 15. This important objection denies that the privation of the vision of God is a fitting punishment for original sin, which goes like this: If human beings had been endowed with just natural powers *(homo naturalibus constitutus)* and had never sinned, they would have been indeed without the vision of God (which in any case can only be attained by grace). But since punishment is rightly owed for sin, the deprival of the vision of God cannot be called punishment for original sin. Thomas responds to this objection that humans endowed with only natural powers *(homo in solis naturalibus constitutus)* would indeed be without the divine vision if they were to die in such a supposed state (precluding hence any further divine agency before the separation of body and soul); however, this lack of the divine vision would in no way be punitive, since "the debt of not having it" would not apply to them: "For it is one thing, not to be bound to have, which does not have the nature of punishment but of defect only, and it is another thing to be bound not to have, which does have the nature of punishment."[45]

Thomas is unquestionably entertaining here the concept of a *hypothetical state of pure nature,* hypothetical because under the present order

---

45. This translation, which I prefer to the one offered by Richard Regan in the Davies edition, is to be found in St. Thomas Aquinas, *On Evil,* trans. John A. Oesterle and Jean T. Oesterle (Notre Dame, IN: University of Notre Dame Press, 1995), p. 214. "Aliud est enim non debere habere, quod non habet rationem poenae sed defectus tantum, et aliud debere non habere, quod habet rationem poenae" *(De malo,* q. 5, a. 1, ad 15, *De malo,* Davies edn., p. 412).

of providence such a state clearly never obtained.[46] The obtaining order of providence, on the contrary, coincides with the economy of salvation, according to which the human being, as created, was originally gifted with the help of original justice and elevated by sanctifying grace. To put it differently, according to Thomas — and as Milbank rightly emphasizes — humanity was originally created immediately in a state of grace. However, another order of providence seems for Thomas hypothetically entertainable in a perfectly legitimate way, and under such an order the non-attainability of the divine vision seems also to be perfectly thinkable. What seems, by entailment, also to be perfectly conceivable in his answer to the objection is the continuity of the self-same human nature under different orders of providence. Consequently, the state of graced nature presupposes an anterior created nature, the latter never de facto obtaining without the former, however being an ontological principle with its own integrity, the two being related to each other by way of a supreme fittingness, but without any intrinsic continuity between each other. For different orders of providence do not entail an ontological transmutation of the human being, nor is the rational soul — while *capax Dei* — becoming something else in a hypothetical order in which the human being is ordered to a lesser felicity than the vision of God. Hence, for Thomas, the creation of a rational soul, capable of and open to the vision of God, yet destined to a lesser felicity does not seem to be a contradiction in the very created nature itself, nor to constitute a punishment per se. However, in comparison to the de facto obtaining providential order, Thomas characterizes such a lesser felicity as a *defectus*. Arguably, *defectus* in this context must be understood rather neutrally as the absence of that which simply was never supposed to be there in the first place. Nevertheless, there seems a clear connotation ever so subtly suggested by Thomas that indicates that this *defectus* indeed

46. *De malo*, q. 5, a. 1, ad 1: "Human beings would have been created uselessly and in vain if they were to be unable to attain happiness, as would be the case with anything that cannot obtain its ultimate end. And so, lest human beings begotten with original sin be created uselessly and in vain, God from the beginning of the human race intended a remedy for them by which they would be freed from such frustration, namely, Jesus Christ, the very mediator between God and human beings. And the impediment of original sin could be removed through faith in him" (Davies edn., p. 409): "Ad primum ergo dicendum quod homo frustra et uane factus esset si beatitudinem consequi non posset, sicut quaelibet res quae non potest consequi ultimum finem. Vnde ne homo frustra et uane factus fieret cum peccato originali nascens, a principio humani generis proposuit Deus homini remedium per quod ab hac uanitate liberaretur, scilicet ipsum mediatorem Dei et hominum Ihesum Christum, per cuius fidem impedimentum peccati originalis subtrahi posset" (p. 408).

signifies a distinctly lesser felicity and that the rational soul is indeed capable of and open to a surpassing supernatural ultimate end. In chapter 6 I will reconstruct Thomas's metaphysical analysis of the ontological structure of the created intellect, an analysis that allows us to appreciate why such a *defectus* indicates both the simple absence of something never supposed to be there in the first place and at the same time the awareness that in such a hypothetically supposed order of divine providence a surpassing, utterly gratuitous ultimate end, to which the human being is essentially open, was never granted.

While Thomas does not employ the term *natura pura* but rather the more precise and restrictive notion *constitutus in solis naturalibus,* it is hard to deny the substance of the matter, namely that the possibility of reflecting about a *hypothetical state of pure nature* — instead of a retrospective projection of the Thomist commentators — is clearly intrinsic to Thomas's own discourse, where it admittedly, and indeed significantly, plays a rather marginal role. Such reflection, however, entails that God's creative activity in so far as it results in a subsistent reality, in distinct species, obtains ontologically and is hence epistemically accessible as well as intelligible in a multitude of created "natures," including the human nature, quite independently from superadded divine helps and gifts to that nature. This is the case even though in the de facto obtaining providential order these helps and gifts were indeed given, according to Thomas, from the first instance of human existence; one of which (original justice) was destroyed by the fall and the other (sanctifying grace) withdrawn in consequence of it. While human nature remains structurally constant under a variety of hypothetical divine providential orders, the superadded divine helps and gifts belong to the de facto economy of grace known solely by divine revelation.

Moreover, it is indeed important to emphasize that for Thomas human nature under the condition of sin in the present order of providence is emphatically not to be understood as the result of a fall into some state of "pure nature." Rather, original sin has affected human nature in such a way that in the present order of providence, after the loss of original justice, human nature is wounded. That is, because of the first sin, human nature is now continuously marked by the deficiency of a disordered disposition *(peccatum naturae),* which antecedes the free exercise of the will (*ST* I-II, qq. 82-83).[47] Hence, Thomas consistently differentiates between the

47. Thomas's treatment of sin in general and of original sin in particular deserves renewed serious attention. For two substantive treatments, covering the spectrum of Thomist

concrete historical condition of human nature *sub conditione peccati* which belongs to the extant order of providence as it coincides with the economy of salvation on the one hand, and on the other hand a *hypothetical state* of pure nature — in his own words in *De malo*, the possibility of *homo in solis naturalibus constitutus*. What is presupposed by such a nuanced and theologically indispensable differentiation is the relative integrity of the principle of nature, ontologically as well as epistemically. Put differently, the relative integrity of the principle (or the order) of nature is the necessary condition for the possibility of differentiating properly between the realities of creation, creation *sub conditione peccati,* and redemption. Failing to do so would inevitably lead to deficient theological positions, such as doctrines denying sin's impact on human nature, or doctrines defending the essential corruption (allegedly due to original sin) or the essential transmutation (presumably due to deification) of human nature. Hence, it is not accidental at all that Thomas defends the necessity of the sacraments as a healing remedy after sin based on this principle: "Man's nature is the same before and after sin, but the *state* of his nature is not the same. Because after sin, the soul, even in its higher part, needs to receive something from corporeal things in order that it may be perfected: whereas man had no need of this *in that state*."[48]

2. "Desiderium naturae" versus "desiderium gratiae": Thomas on 2 Corinthians 5:5-10

For Thomas, as for all Christian theology, everything that is, is God's gift *(creatio ex nihilo)*. However, there is — in the present order of providence

---

forms of reception of Thomas and engagement of more recent developments and problematics, see Marie-Michel Labourdette, O.P., *Le péché originel et les origines de l'homme* (Paris: Alsatia, 1953), esp. pp. 79-95 (more easily accessible for most readers will be three of his more recent essays on this topic: "Le péché originel," *Revue thomiste* 83, no. 3 [1983]: 357-93; "Le péché originel dans la Tradition vivante de l'Église," *Revue thomiste* 84, no. 3 [1984]: 357-98; "Aux origines du péché de l'homme d'après saint Thomas d'Aquin," *Revue thomiste* 85, no. 3 [1985]: 357-98); and Otto Hermann Pesch's extensive commentary in *Die Deutsche Thomas-Ausgabe: Summa Theologica. Deutsch-lateinische Ausgabe,* vol. 12, *Die Sünde* (Vienna: Styria, 2004).

48. *ST* III, q. 61, a. 2, ad 2 (my emphasis): "AD SECUNDUM dicendum quod eadem est natura hominis ante peccatum et post peccatum, non tamen est idem naturae *status*. Nam post peccatum anima, etiam quantum ad superiorem partem, indiget accipere aliquid a corporalibus rebus ad sui perfectionem: quod *in illo statu* homini necesse non erat."

as coinciding with the economy of salvation — a second gift: sanctifying grace that initiates friendship with God and, if not resisted, is perfected in the beatific vision, the union with God. Because God is the giver of both gifts and because the second (sanctifying grace) has to come by way of the first (being), there indeed cannot obtain an essential heterogeneity between them in respect of their origin. At the same time, however, what we might arguably call the *donum primum* and the *donum ultimum* do not simply represent two aspects of the self-same gift. Rather, there obtains a significant difference between both gifts: While God is the omnipotent *first* cause of both gifts, God, being the *sole* cause of the first gift, creation, grants the rational creature proper *secondary* causality in the comprehensive realization of the second gift, beatitude. While the first gift brings about free will by constituting it via God's exclusive creative agency, the second gift involves the proper actualization of free will in the realization of the gift (not, however, in a constitutive, but in an appropriately accompanying way).[49] Moreover, the second gift is to be differentiated from the first gift in that (1) the second gift necessarily presupposes the first gift (not in the chronological order, but in the logical as well as ontological orders) while the second gift is not necessarily entailed by the first; (2) the second gift brings the first gift, in the case of the human being, to a gratuitous, ultimate supernatural perfection and fulfillment; (3) the second gift discloses in the case of the rational creature — in perfecting the first gift — the ontological openness of creation for grace and hence the intrinsic orderedness of the first gift, created human nature, to such a supernatural perfection; and (4) the second gift is all of this without canceling out the relative integrity of the connatural, proportionate end that is entailed in the prior gift, created human nature.

A quite remarkable instance of how Thomas clearly distinguishes between the relative integrity of such a connatural end, and the respective desire directed to it, from an end that is infinitely disproportionate to human nature and hence requires the distinct supernatural desire that corresponds to such an end, can be found in one of Thomas's commentaries on the Pauline corpus of letters: 2 Corinthians 5:5-10.[50] In lectures I and II of his com-

---

49. I regard Bernard Lonergan's early study *Grace and Freedom: Operative Grace in the Thought of St. Thomas Aquinas,* ed. Frederick E. Crowe and Robert M. Doran in the *Collected Works of Bernard Lonergan,* vol. 1 (Toronto: University of Toronto Press, 2000) still to be the benchmark analysis of Thomas's profound treatment of this utterly complex topic.

50. 2 Cor 5:1-10: "(1) For we know that if the earthly tent we live in is destroyed, we have a building from God, a house not made with hands, eternal in the heavens. (2) Here in-

mentary on 2 Corinthians 5, Thomas distinguishes between a *desiderium naturae* and a *desiderium gratiae*[51] and displays the subtle dynamic between the two in this difficult passage of St. Paul's text. Thomas begins his second lecture (on verses 5-10) with the observation that in this section of his letter the apostle shows us that the author of the desire for the heavenly habitation is, in a very specific way, God, and that this desire is quite different from, indeed in contradiction to, the *desiderium naturae:*

> Here he discloses the author of the supernatural desire for a heavenly dwelling. For the cause of a natural desire that we be not despoiled is that the soul is naturally united to the body, and vice versa. But the desire to be clothed upon with a heavenly dwelling is not from nature but from God.[52]

Since the human being is a composite nature, the soul is naturally united with the body (being the sole substantial form) such that there is a natural desire to abhor the separation of the two, which is natural death. Hence, the *desiderium naturae* is an innate, necessary desire for the ongoing integrity of the human composite nature. It is a desire that reflects the very constitution of human nature per se in its relative integrity as an ontological principle with perfect epistemic intelligibility. However, the desire "to put on our heavenly dwelling" does not come from our nature, but from God in a distinct and quite specific way. Most interesting here is the contrasting use of *ex natura* and *ex Deo*. *Ex natura* is, of course, nothing else than the

---

deed we groan, and long to put on our heavenly dwelling, (3) so that by putting it on we may not be found naked. (4) For while we are still in this tent, we sigh with anxiety; not that we would be unclothed, but that we would be further clothed, so that what is mortal may be swallowed up by life. (5) He who has prepared us for this very thing is God, who has given us the Spirit as a guarantee. (6) So we are always of good courage; we know that while we are at home in the body we are away from the Lord, (7) for we walk by faith, not by sight. (8) We are of good courage, and we would rather be away from the body and at home with the Lord. (9) So whether we are at home or away, we make it our aim to please him. (10) For we must all appear before the judgment seat of Christ, so that each one may receive good or evil, according to what he has done in the body" (RSV).

51. In order to make the same distinction, he also uses the pair *naturalia desideria* versus *supernaturalia desideria*.

52. Trans. Fabian R. Larcher, O.P. ("Hic ostendit auctorem supernaturalis desiderii de habitatione caelesti. Causa enim naturalis desiderii quod nolumus expoliari est, quia sc. anima naturaliter unitur corpori, et e converso. Sed hoc, quod caelestem inhabitationem superindui cupiamus, non est ex natura, sed ex Deo" [*S. Thomae Aquinatis in omnes S. Pauli Apostoli epistolas commentaria*, vol. 1 (Turin: Marietti, 1929), p. 449]).

singular effect of God's creative agency *(creatio ex nihilo* as well as *creatio continuans).* In contrast, *ex Deo* must refer here to an act (1) categorically distinct from the former, (2) in no ways in any prospective intrinsic continuity with it, (3) but rather in a surprising, *newly gratuitous* relationship with and hence in clear distinction from the former:

> The reason for this is that upon every nature follows a desire suited to the end of that nature, as something heavy naturally tends downward and seeks to rest there. But if a thing's desire is above its nature, that thing is not moved to that end naturally, but by something else, which is above its nature. Now it is evident that to enjoy eternal glory and to see God by his essence, although it is appropriate to a rational creature, is above its nature. Therefore, the rational creature is not moved to desire this by nature, but by God himself, *who prepared us for this very thing.* How this is accomplished he adds, saying, *who has given us the Spirit as a guarantee [pledge].* In regard to this it should be noted that God produces natural desires and supernatural desires in us: the natural, when he gives us a natural spirit suited to human nature: *'God breathed into his nostrils the breath of life'* [Gen. 2:7]; but he gives the supernatural desires when he infuses in us the supernatural spirit, i.e., the Holy Spirit. Therefore he says, who has given us the Spirit as a guarantee, i.e., the Holy Spirit producing in us the certainty of this thing, with which we desire to be filled: *'You were sealed with the Holy Spirit, which is the guarantee of our inheritance'* [Eph. 1:13-14].[53]

This text speaks for itself. According to Thomas, God effects in us natural as well as supernatural desires: *Deus efficit in nobis naturalia desideria et*

---

53. Trans. Larcher. ("Cuius ratio est, quia quamlibet naturam consequitur appetitus conveniens fini suae naturae, sicut grave naturaliter tendit deorsum, et appetit ibi quiescere. Si autem sit appetitus alicujus rei supra naturam suam, illa res non movetur ad illum finem naturaliter, sed ab alio quod est supra naturam suam. Constat autem quod perfrui caelesti gloria, et videre Deum per essentiam, licet sit rationalis creaturae, est tamen supra naturam ipsius, non ergo movetur rationalis creatura ad hoc desiderandum a natura, sed ab ipso Deo, *qui in hoc ipsum efficit nos,* etc. Sed quomodo hoc efficit subdit, dicens: *Qui dedit pignus, etc.* Circa quod sciendum est, quod Deus efficit in nobis naturalia desideria et supernaturalia. Naturalia quidem quando dat nobis spiritum naturalem convenientem naturae humanae. *Inspiravit in faciem ejus, etc.* [Gen 1]. Supernaturalia vero dat quando infundit in nobis supernaturalem spiritum, sc. Spiritum Sanctum. Et ideo dicit: *Dedit nobis pignus spiritus,* id est, Spiritum Sanctum causantem in nobis certitudinem hujus rei qua desideramus impleri. *Signati estis Spiritu promissionis Sancto, etc.* [Ephes 1]" [*S. Thomae Aquinatis in omnes S. Pauli Apostoli epistolas commentaria,* vol. 1, p. 449].)

supernaturalia. The former are understood in this context strictly per se (as integral to a distinct species in its natural constitution), that is, *not* exclusively as desires as they might characterize the human being extant *sub conditione peccati* (although they even more intensely also do that), but as desires of a composite *nature* irrespective of the providential order in which it is found. Because of their natural spirit *(spiritus naturalis),* as it is fitting for human nature, human beings are endowed with *naturalia desideria.*

As I will show in the next chapter, "Thomist Ressourcement," in virtue of this *spiritus naturalis* being *intellectus,* that is, being able to apprehend intelligible truth, indeed to encompass the entire horizon of being, there is among the multiple *naturalia desideria* one that pertains to this ultimate horizon of being: the natural desire for the vision of God. What is difficult to grasp about this particular natural desire — which is categorically different from all the others — is that it reflects the ontological structure of the rational soul, which due to its ability to encompass the full horizon of being, is *capax Dei,* has the capacity for the vision of God. As I will argue, it is precisely this conditional desire, reflective of the ontological structure of *intellectus* per se, that is perfected by grace into the unconditional, supernatural desire for the beatific vision. For sure, God is the ultimate source for the natural desire for the vision of God, however, simply *ex natura* reflecting the ontological structure of the rational soul. The supernatural desires are, on the contrary, given by God, *ab ipso Deo* over and above all of the *naturalia desideria.* Categorically different from the former, the supernatural desires are the distinct effect of the Holy Spirit's mission, desires which indeed are the very pledge of the Spirit Himself.

Most decisive, however, is the explicit statement:

> But if a thing's desire is above its nature, that thing is not moved to that end naturally, but by something else, which is above its nature. Now it is evident that to enjoy eternal glory and to see God by his essence, although it is appropriate to a rational creature, is above its nature. Therefore, the rational creature is not moved to desire this by nature, but by God himself.[54]

---

54. Trans. Larcher ("Si autem sit appetitus alicujus rei supra naturam suam, illa res non movetur ad illum finem naturaliter, sed ab alio quod est supra naturam suam. Constat autem quod perfrui caelesti gloria, et videre Deum per essentiam, licet sit rationalis creaturae, est tamen supra naturam ipsius, non ergo movetur rationalis creatura ad hoc desiderandum a natura, sed ab ipso Deo" [*S. Thomae Aquinatis in omnes S. Pauli Apostoli epistolas commentaria,* vol. 1, p. 449]).

Thomas operates here very clearly with the distinction between an appetite or desire proportionate and connatural to human nature and being capable of directing human beings toward their connatural end, and a supernatural desire, given from above, directing human beings to their ultimate, supernatural end. Although the fruition of heavenly glory and the vision of God's essence is a permitted end *("licet"!)* for the rational creature, because it utterly transcends human nature the rational creature cannot be moved naturally to this end but must be moved to this end by God by way of a supernatural desire given by the Holy Spirit.

Hence it hardly amounts to a retrospective projection of a deplorable Baroque severance between nature and grace back into Thomas when the seventeenth-century French Dominican theologian and Thomist commentator Jean Baptiste Gonet claims that "[i]nnate appetite is from God as author of nature, and as the Creator of natural forms. However, the desire for the clear vision of God cannot be from the author of nature. Therefore, there cannot be an innate appetite for it."[55] In order to confirm Gonet's thesis, Feingold rightly draws upon Thomas's commentary on II Corinthians 5 and states: "According to this text, nature herself does not give an innate natural desire for an end that is above the nature of the creature. Such an ontological desire directly for a supernatural end must be infused directly by God, working above the natural order, through the gift of sanctifying grace. Surprisingly, de Lubac claims that the distinction between love of 'God as author of the natural order' and 'God as author of the supernatural order,' or between 'God as the object of natural beatitude' and 'God as the object of supernatural beatitude,' is not found in St. Thomas."[56] Feingold displays a significant number of texts by Thomas that prove the contrary.[57] He concludes:

> Thus it is clear that for St. Thomas, the natural love of God is not directed to God in His inner life, but to God as the source and end of

55. Feingold's translation from Jean Baptiste Gonet, O.P., *Clypeus theologiae thomisticae contra novos ejus impugnatores*, 6 vols. (Bordeaux 1659-69; Lyons 1681; Paris 1875), vol. I in I, q. 12, disp. 1, a. 5, §2, n. 86, p. 224, cited in Feingold, *Natural Desire*, p. 417, n. 75.

56. Feingold, *Natural Desire*, pp. 417-418.

57. Feingold, *Natural Desire*, pp. 418f., n. 78: *ST* I, q. 60, a. 5, ad 4; *ST* I, q. 62, a. 2, ad 1; *ST* I, q. 63, a. 1, ad 3; *ST* I-II, q. 62, a. 1, ad 3; *ST* I-II, q. 109, a. 3, ad 1; *ST* II-II, q. 26, a. 3; *Quodl.*, I, q. 4, a. 3 [8], ad 1; *De car.*, q. 1, a. 2, ad 16; *De spe*, q. 1, a. 1, ad 9; *In I Cor.*, c. 13, v. 13, lect. 4; *De malo*, q. 16, a. 4, ad 14 and 15; *De malo*, q. 5, a. 3, ad 4; *Comp. theol.*, I, q. 174, n. 2; *In II Sent.*, d. 3, q. 4, ad 1; *In II Sent.*, d. 33, q. 2, a. 2, ad 5; *In III Sent.*, d. 27, q. 2, a. 2, ad 4.

natural perfections, which love generates a "natural friendship" with God. The love or desire for God insofar as He can be seen face to face is spoken of by St. Thomas as charity, a love which is exclusively the product of grace. . . . It is clear, therefore, that for St. Thomas it would be very wrong to suppose that there is an *innate* natural desire or love for God insofar as He can be participated in only through grace. A love for God directed to union with Him in the beatific vision must itself be the product of a *supernatural* intervention of God, infusing the theological virtues and creating a supernatural friendship with Him.[58]

Feingold's correct emphasis on the sole efficient causality of God's supernatural intervention in eliciting the supernatural desire, however, does *not* per se invalidate the insistence upon a natural desire for the vision of God.[59] We find in this text two clearly distinguished operations of God — and corresponding gifts from God — one being the very constitution of human nature as a subsistent reality (with ends proportionate to this nature and its corresponding natural desires), the other being God's sovereign salvific operation in relationship to extant human beings, a second gift drawing the first beyond the confines of its original giftedness and thus not destroying but perfecting it in a way prospectively as inconceivable as unanticipatable, yet retrospectively to be understood as perfectly fitting the first gift as it has been ordered for and is intrinsically open to the reception of the second gift. The necessary precondition for the fitting reception of the second gift, however, must be a readiness in the first gift for the second, a potential in the first gift that allows for a transnatural expansion (elevation), an expansion infinitely disproportionate to human nature. However, because it is a genuine potential of the first gift, its infinitely disproportionate expansion does not transmute the particular constitution of the first gift, its specific nature, into another nature. That is, in the beatific vision, human beings remain human beings. (They are not, in an Eckhartian sense, "melted" into the divine essence itself.) Would such a specific natural potential of the first gift (the technical term in the Thomist tradition became "specific obediential potency"),[60] however, not require a

58. Feingold, *Natural Desire,* p. 420.

59. See chapters 4–10 for a detailed argumentation of this point.

60. See Steven A. Long's astute treatment and defense of this concept in his important essays "Obediential Potency, Human Knowledge, and the Natural Desire for the Vision of God," *International Philosophical Quarterly* 37, no. 1 (1997): 45-63 and "On the Loss, and Recovery, of Nature as Theonomic Principle: Reflections on the Nature/Grace Controversy,"

corresponding, proper natural desire? While such a desire would need to correspond in potency to the second gift (hence a desire for the vision of God), it could not be a desire innate to human nature itself (i.e. a *desiderium naturae*), because such a desire would necessarily reflect the connatural end of the composite human nature. Rather, this natural desire for the vision of God would need to be elicited by the same faculties by way of which the second gift is received: intellect and will. And precisely in the vicinity of this elicited desire, quasi preparing and undergirding it, we find the proper instantiation of that ontological élan so often emphasized by Milbank as the comprehensive dynamic of the creation's *reditus* to God. Such an élan indeed plays a fundamental and indispensable role in the thought of the *doctor communis*.

This élan, however, is treated by Thomas in a highly nuanced way. For it falls, first and foremost, under the category of "natural love" and, more precisely, comprises the equivalent of what Jacques Maritain, in his brilliant analysis of the four necessary loves (developed by Thomas in the treatise on the angels in his *Summa theologiae*), has identified as the first and the second love. The first is a love, by which

> every creature naturally loves the supreme Whole more than itself with a radical élan consubstantial with its essence. . . . It naturally exists in *every creature, with or without senses or reason,* and is not free. It is inamissible; a being cannot lose it except by losing its nature and ceasing to exist. It continues to exist in the sinner and in the demon.[61]

The second love is a version of the first, namely the love

> through which *every creature capable of knowledge* loves the supreme Whole more than itself, instinctively or by a spontaneous élan and not because it knows Him, due solely to the fact that it loves necessarily, and with an *elicited* love, whatever is its *good of nature.* . . . Here there is no knowledge of God properly speaking, no idea of God from which an elicited love for God might proceed.[62]

---

in *Natura Pura: On the Recovery of Nature in the Doctrine of Grace* (New York: Fordham University Press, 2010), pp. 10-51.

61. Jacques Maritain, *The Sin of the Angel: An Essay on a Re-Interpretation of Some Thomistic Positions,* trans. William L. Rossner, S.J. (Westminster, MD: Newman Press, 1959), p. 20.

62. Maritain, *Sin of the Angel,* pp. 20-22.

These first two loves, according to Thomas, cannot fail; they endure even in hell. Not so the next two. The third is the

> *elicited love-of-nature* which, before any option or election, arises at once in every intellectual creature as a spontaneous, immediate movement of the rational appetite at the instant and by the mere fact that the intellect knows the existence of the Principle of all good, the Self-subsisting Good which is the common good of all.[63]

While a movement necessary in itself, this love depends indirectly on the free will, "insofar as it can be prevented by free will, like any other indeliberate motion of the elicited appetite."[64] Finally,

> in every intelligent creature there exists a natural inclination . . . to love the supreme Whole more than himself with an elicited love of *free option*. The intelligent creature is inclined by his nature to this love which is essentially free in its very mode of emanation.[65]

Hence, de Lubac's famous dictum from *Surnaturel* that "the spirit is the desire for God"[66] is indeed correct — on the ontological level of natural love. As will become sufficiently clear later, for Thomas neither the innate ontological love pure and simple, nor the intra-elicited ontological love of God above all, translates into an *innate* natural desire for the vision of God. For, as Maritain rightly stresses, according to Thomas, the human being, as composite nature fundamentally different from the angel, receives all knowledge by way of the senses. Hence, since there is no *innate* knowledge of God,[67] the human being's *natural* desire for the vision of God, if it is an *intellective* desire (which, according to Thomas, it is), must be called forth via the senses by the first gift, creation, as it points, by way of its causal order, not ineluctably, but consistently, to its primal origin, the Giver of the gift. It must, hence, be an *elicited* desire, intending a transnatural and ultimately infinitely disproportionate end that, however, be-

63. Maritain, *Sin of the Angel*, p. 23.

64. Maritain, *Sin of the Angel*, p. 24.

65. Maritain, *Sin of the Angel*, p. 26.

66. Feingold, *Natural Desire*, p. 302 ("L'esprit est donc désir de Dieu," *Surnaturel*, p. 483).

67. The *intellectus agens*, pace Milbank, does not provide such a knowledge, even most implicitly. On *intellectus agens* in Thomas, see the excursus on *intellectus* in the subsequent chapter, pp. 208-15.

cause of the nature of the intellect, remains integral to the connatural human end as proportionate to human nature — short of the gift of sanctifying grace.[68]

3. Double Gratuity

Milbank, in his Bulgakovian radicalization of de Lubac and by entailment of Thomas argues that the two gifts, the second in a unique way perfecting the first, are to be seen in a continuum, a seamless dynamic of varying intensity, reflecting a fundamental ontological élan drawing the entire cosmos through humanity to beatitude. Can Thomas's theology be drafted for a project that assumes a single non-contrastive gratuity, seamlessly connecting creation and deification in a comprehensive unitary and universalistic vision? On the contrary, Thomas's theology of grace entails a clear double gratuity; moreover, his doctrine of predestination forestalls any attempt to claim his patronage for such a theological project.

In his profound and, in light of the widespread contemporary theological confusions about Christology, highly relevant treatise on the hypostatic union in the *Tertia pars* of the *Summa theologiae,* questions 1-15, Thomas dedicates the second *quaestio* to the problem of the precise mode of the union of the Incarnate Word with the human nature. Relevant for our particular problem is article 10 of question 2, where he asks whether the union of the incarnation took place by grace. In his response, Thomas

---

68. This elicited desire indeed needs to be satisfied supernaturally for an absolutely perfect human felicity to occur. The Thomist who, according to my lights, got the matter exactly right *ad mentem S. Thomae* is Jacques Maritain — and Feingold's long analysis is in substantive agreement with Maritain on this point: "Beatitude signifies perfect felicity, *ultima perfectio rationalis seu intellectualis creaturae* (the ultimate perfection of the rational or intellectual creature) [*ST* I, q. 62, a. 1]. And the very notion of perfect felicity might well be understood in various senses which are more or less strict, from the *eudaimonia* of the sage of antiquity, to the joy which surpasses all that the mind of man has ever conceived. As far as I am concerned, I do not much like the expression 'natural beatitude,' for I do not think that there is any *absolutely* perfect felicity as long as the natural (trans-natural) desire to see God (a desire which in the Angel must be still much more profound than in man) is not supernaturally satisfied. Nevertheless, I shall use the expression 'natural beatitude' . . . because quarrels over words are uninteresting, and because St. Thomas himself does not hesitate to use the word beatitude ['Quodammodo beatitudo . . . dicitur,' *ST* I, q. 62, a. 1] in order to designate the state of pure natural happiness . . . in which the Angel was created" (Maritain, *Sin of the Angel,* p. 97).

first offers a crisp summary of his definition of grace originally submitted in question 110, article 1 of the *Prima Secundae:* "[G]race is taken in two ways: — first as the will of God bestowing something; secondly, as the free gift of God."[69]

First, according to this definition, one might want to assume that Thomas regards creation itself as the first grace, since it surely is the first and foremost of all gifts.[70] However, quite interestingly, Thomas does not mention creation in this context at all. Rather, he immediately relates grace to human nature, a principle of relative but distinct ontological integrity and hence relative but distinct epistemic accessibility: "Now human nature stands in need of the gratuitous will of God in order to be lifted up [*elevetur*] to God, since this is above its natural capability."[71]

Second, a crucial term — if not *the* crucial term — in the above quote is the verb "to be lifted up," in the Latin passive *elevari* (active: *elevare;* noun: *elevatio*). Human nature — notice that Thomas does not say here, the "human person" — stands in a *passive* relationship to a *specific* agency of God, an agency fundamentally distinct from *creatio ex nihilo* and *creatio continuans,* in that it is an agency that presupposes human nature (notice, however, not a subsistent "*state* of pure nature") as a distinct species, sufficiently conceptually penetrable in its distinction from other natures in order to make relevant ontological claims about it and in relationship to which grace operates qua *elevatio,* because "*hoc sit supra facultatem naturae suae.*"

Third, Thomas distinguishes between two ways of *elevatio,* one *per operationem,* another *per esse personale.* The first, by operation, occurs "as the saints know and love God." The second, by personal being, occurs only in Christ, "in Whom human nature is assumed so as to be in the Person of the Son of God."[72] As Thomas reminds his readers in the *Tertia pars* of the

---

69. "Respondeo dicendum quod, sicut in Secunda Parte dictum est, gratia dupliciter dicitur: uno modo, ipsa voluntas Dei gratis aliquid dantis; alio modo, ipsum gratuitum donum Dei."

70. For a profound metaphysical meditation on creation as gift, see Kenneth L. Schmitz, *The Gift: Creation* (Milwaukee: Marquette University Press, 1982).

71. *ST* III, q. 2, a. 10, c.: "Indiget autem humana natura gratuita Dei voluntate ad hoc quod elevetur in Deum: cum hoc sit supra facultatem naturae suae."

72. *ST* III, q. 2, a. 10 c.: "Elevatur autem humana natura in Deum dupliciter. Uno modo, per operationem: qua scilicet sancti cognoscunt et amant Deum. Alio modo, per esse personale: qui quidem modus est singularis Christo, in quo humana natura assumpta est ad hoc quod sit personae Filii Dei."

Summa theologiae, question 4, article 1, ad 2, the elevation bringing about a union by operation is indeed possible because of "the likeness of image found in human nature." This likeness consists in human nature being *capax Dei,* namely, "by attaining to Him through its own operation of knowledge and love," which are the essential characteristics of the intellectual soul. And it is precisely this *capax Dei,* this inherent potentiality in human nature that grace reduces to act, to unitive knowledge and love, whereby human nature is elevated to God *per operationem.* Both ways of elevation presuppose the integrity of the prior gift, even *sub conditione peccati,* and by entailment the supplementary nature of the second gift. It is not explicitly denied by Thomas in this place that the second gift, quasi by infinite intensification of the first, extends efficaciously and hence infallibly to all rational creatures. However, it is by no means accidental that in *Summa theologiae* III, question 2, article 10 Thomas chose his "sed contra," preparing his response in light of the objections, from St. Augustine's late work *De praedestinatione sanctorum,* where Augustine argues that it is a mystery why faith is given to some and not to others and that the elect are not called because they believe, but that they may believe. The quote from the "sed contra" itself is taken from book 15 in which Augustine argues that the incarnation provides the supreme example of grace's specific gratuity, for Christ's human nature could have done nothing to deserve to be united to the Word.[73] What is clearly presupposed in this article, namely a distinct double gratuity, is constitutive of the whole architecture of Thomas's mature theology of grace.

The clear and categorical distinction between the first gift of creation and the grace of elevation is rooted deeply in Thomas's doctrine of God, and especially in his Trinitarian reflections. In his discussion of the missions of the Son and Spirit in the *Prima pars* of the *Summa theologiae,* question 43, article 3, he starts with the axiomatic distinction between two kinds of God's presence: first, "God is in all things by His essence, power, and presence, according to His one common mode, as the cause existing in the effects which participate in His goodness." There is, however, a second, special, and superior mode according to which God is present, a mode characterized by Thomas with the terms "above and beyond" *(super)* and "in a new way" *(novo modo):*

---

73. "Ea gratia fit ab initio fidei suae homo quicumque Christianus, qua gratia homo ille ab initio suo factus est Christus" (Cap. 10; PL 44, 982). Thomas continues: "Sed homo ille factus est Christus per unionem ad divinam naturam. Ergo unio illa fuit per gratiam."

Above and beyond this common mode, however, there is one special mode belonging to the rational nature wherein God is said to be present as the object known is in the knower, and the beloved in the lover. And since the rational creature by its operation of knowledge and love attains to God Himself, according to this special mode God is said not only to exist in the rational creature, but also to dwell therein as in His own temple. So no other effect can be put down as the reason why the divine person is in the rational creature *in a new mode,* except sanctifying grace.[74]

It is the latter claim, that the Holy Spirit dwells within the human being in the gift of sanctifying grace *(in ipso dono gratiae gratum facientis)* that perfectly justifies that, while human nature qua rational soul is surely capable of it, this "indwelling" of the Spirit by way of elevating human nature through sanctifying grace is infinitely beyond and categorically different from God's presence in the first mode, the presence of the Creator in the creation. If one turns to Thomas's discussion of the mission of the divine persons, it might indeed be perfectly defensible to call the very indwelling in the mind of the Trinity by sanctifying grace (*ST* I, q. 43, a. 5) a *donum ultimum* since by this very gift "the soul is made like to God *(animam per gratiam conformatur Dei) (ST* I, q. 43, a. 5, ad 2), resulting in an ultimate beatitude to be obtained "by the power of God alone, by a kind of participation of the Godhead, about which it is written (2 Pet. i.4) that by Christ we are made *partakers of the Divine nature*" (*ST* I-II, q. 62, a. 1). Different from this *donum ultimum,* the gift of union with God by the indwelling of the Trinity by sanctifying grace, is the very precondition for it, a first and fundamental gift, which we might want to call the *donum primum,* creation as the gift of a real relation to God that arises from a procession of creatures caused and upheld by the triune God's exemplar, efficient, formal, and final causality, a real relation that, therefore, subsists in its own relative, but proper integrity.

74. *ST* I, q. 43, a. 3 (my emphasis): "Est enim unus communis modus quo Deus est in omnibus rebus per essentiam, potentiam et praesentiam, sicut causa in effectibus participantibus bonitatem ipsius. Super istum modum autem communem, est *unus specialis,* qui convenit creaturae rationali, in qua Deus dicitur esse sicut cognitum in cognoscente et amatum in amante. Et quia, cognoscendo et amando, creatura rationalis sua operatione attingit ad ipsum Deum, *secundum istum specialem modum* Deus non solum dicitur esse in creatura rationali, sed etiam habitare in ea sicut in templo suo. Sic igitur nullus alius effectus potest esse ratio quod divina Persona sit *novo modo* in rationali creatura, nisi gratia gratum faciens" (*ST* I, q. 43, a. 3; my emphasis).

Let us now move further back in Thomas's doctrine of the Trinity in the *Prima pars* of the *Summa theologiae,* question 38, article 1, where Thomas asks whether "gift" is a personal name. For here again we encounter the sheer absence of a simple seamless continuity of infinite intensification between the two forms of divine presence as well as of some kind of intrinsic dynamic leading from the one to the other in a way already "inscribed in" or "anticipated by" the first. Rather, we encounter a twofold differentiation, the first by now being quite familiar: there obtains a crucial difference between the nature of the rational creature, on the one hand, and all other creatures, on the other hand. For only rational creatures can enjoy a divine person by being united to God. "Other creatures can be moved by a divine person, not, however, in such a way as to be able to enjoy the divine person, and to use the effect thereof." There is, however, a second crucial differentiation to be made regarding the *donum ultimum,* now pertaining specifically and exclusively to the rational creature. For "[t]he rational creature does *sometimes* [*quandoque*] attain thereto; as when it is made partaker of the divine Word and the Love proceeding, so as freely to know God truly and to love God rightly."[75] The rational creature qua rational is endowed with the, albeit purely passive, capability of being united to God by way of its own powers acting according to their proper secondary causality; this capability is reduced to act by the Holy Spirit Himself, who is given from above by way of sanctifying grace which simultaneously elevates human nature for the reception of such an infinitely disproportionate gift. However, unlike the gift of creation which is perfectly universal and by way of which God is present by essence, power, and presence, the enjoyment of the divine persons occurs *quandoque, sometimes.*

That the qualification *quandoque* is far from being a casual side remark finds its possibly clearest expression in Thomas's treatment of predestination in the *Prima pars* of the *Summa theologiae,* question 23, wherein he answers affirmatively the question whether human beings are predestined by God, resting his response to the objections on a "sed contra" in which he cites Romans 8:30: "And those whom he predestined he also called" (RSV). The opening sentence of his response is crucial: "*Deo conveniens est homines praedestinare.*" It is fitting for God to predestine human beings. The *convenientia* or fittingness refers to the end to which pre-

---

75. "Ad quod quandoque pertingit rationalis creatura, ut puta cum sic fit particeps divini Verbi et procedentis Amoris, ut possit libere Deum vere cognoscere et recte amare."

destination pertains. As Thomas argued in the preceding question 22, divine providence directs all things to their proper ends (*ST* I, q. 22, aa. 1-2). However, regarding the human being Thomas distinguishes between a twofold *(duplex)* end:

> one which exceeds all proportion and faculty of created nature; and this end is life eternal, that consists in seeing God which is above the nature of every creature. . . . The other end, however, is proportionate to created nature, to which end created being can attain according to the power of its nature. Now if a thing cannot attain to something by the power of its nature, it must be directed thereto by another; thus, an arrow is directed by the archer towards its mark. Hence, properly speaking, a rational creature, capable of eternal life, is led towards it, directed, as it were, by God.[76]

Here again we have the clear distinction between a final end proportionate to created nature (something that must be perceptible in its own right and makes sense ontologically as a subsistent reality in order to have ends clearly proportionate to it) and an ultimate end "which exceeds all proportion and faculty of created nature *(qui excedit proportionem naturae creatae et facultatem)*." Moreover, the use of the term *convenientia* signals that the relationship between the two ends cannot be captured by the all too simple alternatives "intrinsic" or "extrinsic." There is no continuity from the first end to the second, a continuity that might suggest some kind of innate and inchoate anticipation of the second in the first; nor is the first "closed up" to the second, such that it can only be "opened up" for the second gift by being miraculously transformed by the latter into something essentially foreign to its specific natural constitution. *Convenientia* rejects these alternatives by referring the matter to the mystery of God's goodness which is identical with God's justice as well as mercy, utterly unfathomable in the glorious simplicity of the divine perfection. The ineradicable difference, however, between the first gift and the grace of predesti-

---

76. *ST* I, q. 23, a. 1 c.: "Unus, qui excedit proportionem naturae creatae et facultatem: et hic finis est vita aeterna, quae in divina visione consistit, quae est supra naturam cuiuslibet creaturae, ut supra habitum est. Alius autem finis est naturae creatae proportionatus, quem scilicet res creata potest attingere secundum virtutem suae naturae. Ad illud autem ad quod non potest aliquid virtute suae naturae pervenire, oportet quod ab alio transmittatur; sicut sagitta a sagittante mittitur ad signum. Unde, proprie loquendo, rationalis creatura, quae est capax vitae aeternae, perducitur in ipsam quasi a Deo transmissa."

nation is marked by an echo of the oblique *quandoque* in two other instances. First, in question 23, article 2 (again with a *sed contra* from Augustine's *De praedestinatione sanctorum*) Thomas returns to Romans 8:30 in his response to the question whether predestination places anything in the predestined. Denying the question he emphasizes that

> providence is not anything in the things provided for; but is a type in the mind of the provider, as was proved above (22, 1). But the execution of providence which is called government, is in a passive way in the thing governed, and in an active way in the governor. Whence it is clear that predestination is a kind of type of the ordering of some persons [*aliquorum*] towards eternal salvation, existing in the divine mind. The execution, however, of this order is in a passive way in the predestined, but actively in God.[77]

Second, in question 23, article 7, where on this particular matter Thomas stands in clear agreement with the late St. Augustine: "The number of the predestined is certain . . . not only by reason of His knowledge, because, that is to say, He knows how many will be saved . . . ; but by reason of His deliberate choice and determination."[78] The reason for the *quandoque* as well as the *aliqui* is the mystery of God's principal preordination.[79] And it

---

77. "Providentia autem non est in rebus provisis; sed est quaedam ratio in intellectu provisoris, ut supra dictum est. Sed executio providentiae, quae gubernatio dicitur, passive quidem est in gubernatis; active autem in gubernante. Unde manifestum est quod praedestinatio est quaedam ratio ordinis aliquorum in salutem aeternam, in mente divinis existens" (*ST* I, q. 23, a. 2 c.).

78. That this account is far from some type of "blue print" statically and quasi-mechanistically imposed upon thing-like rational creatures, is implicitly addressed in q. 8, ad 3, where he makes the crucial metaphysical distinction between the first universal cause and secondary causes: "Secondary causes cannot escape the order of the first universal cause . . . , indeed, they execute that order. And therefore predestination can be furthered by creatures, but it cannot be impeded by them."

79. Thomas does not avoid the difficult question of reprobation either. It is important, however, to note that he implicitly follows the canons of the Second Council of Orange in rejecting any notion of an active divine reprobation. Rather, God permits some [*aliquos*] to fall away from the ultimate end (which entails the reality of sufficient grace); ("Unde, cum per divinam providentiam homines ordinentur in vitam aeternam, pertinet etiam ad divinam providentiam, quod permittat aliquos ab isto fine deficere. Et hoc dicitur reprobare" [*ST* I, q. 23, a. 3 c.]). However, as divine providence entails both the divine intellect (providence in the narrow sense) and the divine will (divine governance as the execution of providence), the divine permission not only entails the divine knowledge of such a falling away but includes the will to permit a person to fall into sin: "Sicut enim

is at this particular place where the irresolvable differentiation between God's loves becomes most pertinent. In his treatise on grace, *Summa theologiae* I-II, question 110, article 1, Thomas distinguishes between two aspects of God's love to the creature:

> For one is common [*dilectio generalis*], whereby He loves *all things that are* (Wis. xi. 25), and thereby gives things their natural being. But the second is a special love [*dilectio specialis*], whereby He draws the rational creature above the condition of its nature to a participation of the Divine good; and according to this love He is said to love anyone simply, since it is by this love that God simply wishes the eternal good, which is Himself, for the creature.[80]

Hence, Thomas explains, "grace" can signify something that is bestowed by God on the human being. Then he emphasizes again the logic of the *quandoque:* "Nevertheless the grace of God sometimes signifies God's eternal love, as we say the grace of predestination, inasmuch as God gratuitously and not from merits predestines or elects some."[81]

The very fact that Thomas describes the efficacious elevation of some to the beatific vision as the grace of predestination is a clear indication that in his theology there obtains an explicit and distinctive double gratuity such that the first gift, created human nature, originally gifted with the help of original justice and through sanctifying grace ordained for the vision of God, differs categorically from the ontological élan reflected in the first two loves, according to Maritain's analysis, as mentioned above. These two loves, however, indicate an antecedent fittingness of the first for the second gift, as becomes increasingly clear by reflecting upon the first gift, the rational creature qua particular nature in its proper integrity, in

---

praedestinatio includit voluntatem conferendi gratiam et gloriam, ita reprobatio includit voluntatem permittendi aliquem cadere in culpam, et inferendi damnationis poenam pro culpa" (*ST,* I q. 23, a. 3 c.).

80. *ST* I-II, q. 110, a. 1 c.: "Una quidem communis, secundum quam *diligit omnia quae sunt,* ut dicitur *Sap.* 11, [25]; secundum quam esse naturale rebus creatis largitur. Alia autem est dilectio specialis, secundum quam trahit creaturam rationalem supra conditionem naturae, ad participationem divini boni. Et secundum hanc dilectionem dicitur aliquem diligere simpliciter: quia secundum hanc dilectionem vult Deus simpliciter creaturae bonum aeternum, quod est ipse."

81. *ST* I-II, q. 110, a. 1 c.: "Quandoque tamen gratia Dei dicitur ipsa aeterna Dei dilectio: secundum quod dicitur etiam gratia praedestinationis, inquantum Deus gratuito, et non ex meritis, aliquos praedestinavit sive elegit."

light of the second gift, the elevation of human nature *per operationem* to personal communion with the triune God. Passages like the above suggest that Thomas was intent upon preserving the strict gratuity of the grace of predestination by operating with the logic of a double gratuity, first the gift that constitutes its own reception (creation), then the gift that infallibly, though entailing the proper secondary causality of free will, constitutes communion with God, the Giver of both gifts.

In the course of this brief excursion we encounter a Thomas who thoroughly resists Milbank's attempt of assimilating his theology into the latter's radicalized Bulgakovian Lubacianism for at least two reasons: first, while Thomas never assumed a state of pure nature in the present order of providence, he clearly assumes the principle of nature — and hence a hypothetical state of pure nature — with its own relative but proper integrity as an entailment of creation that ontologically obtains and is accessible to the intellect; second, Thomas's doctrine of the grace of predestination makes it impossible — despite the very prominent role of the ontological exitus-reditus-scheme in the overall architectonic of his thought — to press his theology into the service of an overarching Origenist-Bulgakovian vision of universal *apokatastasis.* The ontology of the exitus-reditus is a necessary precondition entailed in the first gift in order for grace "to come on the way of being,"[82] that is, to elevate human nature to a supernatural perfection without its transmutation into another species. The complexity of this position (ontological élan *as well as* grace of predestination) is precisely reflected in the way Thomas deals with the question of natural desire for the vision of God.

V. Is the Rational Creature "Intrinsically Linked to Grace"? Feingold's Thomist Engagement of Henri de Lubac's Position

Before we will turn to the question of the natural desire for the vision of God by way of a re-lecture of Thomas in the next chapter, one intermediary step will be necessary. For the principal obstacle for such a re-lecture is the presently widespread assumption, as dominant as it is unexamined, that on the question of the natural desire for the vision of God, Thomas Aquinas can meaningfully only be accessed by way of Henri de Lubac's re-

---

82. Ferdinand Ulrich, *Homo Abyssus: Das Wagnis der Seinsfrage,* ed. Martin Bieler and Florian Pitschl, 2nd ed. (Freiburg: Johannes Verlag, 1998), p. 333.

covery of a more authentic and original patristic vision, shared in significant parts by Thomas, but profoundly distorted by the Thomist commentatorial tradition. While the accuracy of the historical analysis did not go unchallenged at earlier points, such criticisms do not make much of a difference as long as de Lubac's own constructive position remains an unexamined given, in light of which all too often Thomas's position is read. It is one of the merits of Feingold's opus to submit de Lubac's philosophical premises and the inner coherence of his theological proposal on the natural desire for the vision of God to a penetrating analysis. His critical engagement opens an avenue to some of the central aporias and tensions hidden deep in the foundations of de Lubac's account and thereby makes possible a renewed appreciation for the approach taken by Thomas on this all too elusive but crucial question of the natural desire for the vision of God. Moreover, I regard this as the opportune place to give voice to Feingold himself. I choose this approach primarily because the subsequent extended citations may offer at least an initial appreciation of the utterly serious and substantive nature of Feingold's study and hence should form a direct antidote to Milbank's all too hasty disqualification of Feingold's interrogation of Henri de Lubac.

1. Feingold's Reconstruction of Henri de Lubac's Position on the desiderium naturale visionis Dei

a. De Lubac's fundamental concern: The intrinsic nature of a spiritual creature's finality:

De Lubac argues that the supernatural finality of a spiritual creature is intrinsic and cannot be changed without changing its nature. . . .

De Lubac's fundamental concern is to remove an "extrinsicist" view of man's relation to his supernatural end, a view which he thinks is inherently linked to the theory of the possibility of a state of pure nature, as put forward by Suárez, and to the way the natural desire to see God was interpreted by authors such as Cajetan, Báñez, Suárez, and those who followed them.

For de Lubac, the "essential finality" of man is the vision of God. This finality cannot be changed without changing his nature. Man as he is today has only one end that is in harmony with his nature as it now exists — the vision of God. This end, therefore, is "inscribed" or "imprinted" on man's nature as he concretely exists, prior to any gift of grace. (297)

b. De Lubac's central philosophical argument: The actual final end of a concrete nature:

This conception is based on a fundamental philosophical notion, central to de Lubac's position, according to which the actual final end of a thing is necessarily something which ontologically determines the nature of the thing. Since we know by faith that we have been destined to a supernatural end, it follows that even before we receive the gift of grace, our nature must be intrinsically determined by our destination to this supernatural end. One and the same "concrete nature" cannot have two distinct possible finalities, one natural and the other supernatural, which God could assign by an external decree, without changing the nature itself. Such a notion implies a "watered-down idea of what finality is." Rather, two different finalities determine two different natures (or two different "concrete natures" or "historic natures"). In other words, *the actual finality of a thing is always the "essential finality" of a thing, postulated by its very essence.*

Thus de Lubac opposes the idea that our supernatural end is something "super-added" by God above and distinct from a "natural end" to which our nature would be directed in virtue of its own intrinsic principles. . . . It is precisely this possibility of two distinct ends for human nature — natural and supernatural — that Lubac rejects as a notion that is philosophically and religiously unacceptable, contrary to the authentic notion of finality. (298f.; my emphasis)

c. The finality of the spiritual creature expressed in the natural desire to see God, understood as the innate inclination for the actual final end:

De Lubac's interpretation of the natural desire to see God is intimately connected with his understanding of finality in the spiritual creature. He understands natural desire as the innate inclination of a being for its actual final end, or as the "expression" of the finality of a thing. Therefore, he infers that man's elevation to a supernatural end necessarily determines a natural desire for that supernatural end. The natural desire to see God is thus nothing other than the necessary attraction of spiritual beings to the end imprinted on their nature by God. It is precisely the presence of our finality, inscribed within us, for the vision of God. . . . [See the important section from *The Mystery of the Supernatural,* pp. 70-72, cited at this point.]

De Lubac is affirming here a natural appetite for beatitude with regard to the *particular* object in which it actually consists (the vision of God), and not just for beatitude in *general.* Since the end for which God has ordained us is quite determinate in the mind of God — the beatific vision — de Lubac concludes that our natural desire must be equally determinate.

Since de Lubac identifies the actual end of the spiritual creature with the end *called for by its nature,* or "imprinted on its nature," he consequently understands the innate natural desire of the rational creature as the desire for its actual final end, which is supernatural, and not for a connatural final end proportionate to the creature, as understood by Suárez and the Thomistic tradition. (299ff.)

Therefore, de Lubac can assert both that a state of pure nature is impossible for human nature as we now possess it, and that God could perhaps create other rational creatures without ordering them to the vision of God, and without giving them a natural desire for the vision. Thus the possibility of a state of pure nature for *other* rational beings is left open, neither being asserted nor denied. However, the possibility of a state of pure nature is clearly denied with regard to men possessing the same "concrete" nature as ourselves. (307)

2. Feingold's Characterization of the Central Metaphysical Issue at Stake between Thomas Aquinas (and the Commentators) and Henri de Lubac

a. Thomas Aquinas: The metaphysical principle "form determines end" and the supernatural finality superadded by the principle of grace and the supernatural virtues:

For St. Thomas, everything is ordered to an end by reason of its form. In *ScG* III, ch. 150, he states that "each thing is ordered to the end that is fitting to it according to its form, for to different species there belong different ends." From this he concludes . . . that a new supernatural

form — *sanctifying grace* — must be "super-added" to human nature
so that it can be fittingly ordered to an end that is "above human nature." ["But the end to which man is directed by the help of divine
grace is above human nature. Therefore, some supernatural form and
perfection must be super-added to man whereby he may be ordered
suitably to the aforesaid end."][83]

This clearly implies that human nature in itself is not naturally or
essentially ordered — and *cannot be fittingly ordered without grace* —
to an end that is above human nature. (318)

*b. Henri de Lubac: The imprinting of a supernatural finality upon
human nature prior to the gift of grace:*

For de Lubac, on the contrary, the "imprinting of a supernatural finality" upon our nature is actually prior to the gift of grace, and is involved
in the very constitution of our nature, as it concretely exists in us from
conception. The first fundamental problem with this position is recon-
ciling the denial that our nature is *ordered* to the vision of God prior to
grace . . . with his repeated assertion that a supernatural finality has been
imprinted on our nature, prior to grace. Being intrinsically ordered to an
end and having a finality imprinted on one's nature seem to be equivalent notions. It appears therefore that de Lubac's position entails an unresolved tension or contradiction, and that he must logically choose between (1) his repeated affirmation that our nature itself is intrinsically
determined by having received a supernatural finality (also referred to as
an "essential finality"), prior to the reception of grace, and (2) his clear
avowal — following St. Thomas — that our nature itself is *not intrinsically ordered* to a supernatural end without sanctifying grace. (318f.)

De Lubac presupposes that the actual or de facto end must necessarily
be the natural end, inscribed in the nature.

However, we cannot conclude that because God has destined man
for an end that is above his nature, such an end must therefore be a finality "imprinted on the nature" itself, or an "intrinsic" or "ontological" end, or an "essential finality." All that we can conclude is that if

83. Translation from *Summa Contra Gentiles*. Book Three: *Providence*, Part II, trans.
Vernon J. Bourke (Notre Dame, IN: University of Notre Dame Press, 1975), p. 232. "Sed finis
in quem homo dirigitur per auxilium divinae gratiae, est supra naturam humanam. Ergo
oportet quod homini *superaddatur* aliqua supernaturalis forma et perfectio, per quam
convenienter *ordinetur* in finem praedictum."

God has eternally destined us to a supernatural end, it is fitting that He give a *new form,* "added on" to our nature, by which we are suitably ordered to that supernatural end. This new accidental form, which is sanctifying grace, must necessarily be *above our nature,* so as to make us proportionate to an end above our nature, connatural only to God.

If this new form which determines us to a supernatural end is above our nature (and given to us in Baptism), then this supernatural finality cannot be said to be "imprinted on our nature itself." Nor can the finality generated by this supernatural form be spoken of as an "essential finality." It is *ultimately contradictory to suppose that our nature or being itself — without the addition of a supernatural principle — could be intrinsically determined by a supernatural finality,* or have a supernatural finality inscribed upon it, or have an "essential finality" that is supernatural. If this were the case, our nature itself would be supernatural or divine, for every nature is defined by its end. *A nature with a divine end can only be the divine nature.* A creature can be intrinsically ordered to a supernatural end only by receiving — above nature — a supernatural principle of being, which is sanctifying grace. By giving us a participation in the divine nature, grace orders us to a participation in the end that is proper to the divine nature. An end that is actually imprinted on our nature itself (an "essential finality") can never truly be supernatural. Thus it should be said that for St. Thomas, our supernatural finality is "imprinted on our being first by sanctifying grace." (321-22)

c. The different meanings of "grace super-added"
in de Lubac and in Thomas:

For de Lubac, our nature is intrinsically finalized and inclined exclusively to our supernatural end in virtue of the imprinting of a supernatural finality on the soul in the moment of its creation. Nothing need be super-added to the concrete nature to give it this "determination" to a supernatural end and the corresponding natural desire. Super-added principles are necessary only with regard to the means to attain this end. In other words, for de Lubac, sanctifying grace should be conceived as "super-added" to our nature only insofar as it renders us properly disposed and capable of achieving the end which was already somehow inscribed in our nature prior to the gift of grace.

However, for St. Thomas, grace is not conceived as a necessary means to achieve an end to which our nature is already essentially ordered. On the contrary, grace is necessary first for us to have a *being and dignity* such that the vision of God is a fitting and proportionate end for us. Sanctifying grace inscribes a supernatural finality in our being by giving us a mysterious proportionality with the divine nature. On the basis of that foundation, hope and charity give our will an adequate inclination to that supernatural good, and the infused moral virtues are necessary so that we may work for that supernatural end. (323f.)

3. Feingold's Characterization of the Central Tension in Henri de Lubac's Account of the desiderium naturale: The Created Spirit

a. The innate appetite or natural inclination being necessarily directed to the actual final end:

The vision of God is certainly not "proportionate" to human nature without grace, as de Lubac also recognizes. [*The Mystery of the Supernatural,* pp. 111-112: "However profound, however lofty it may be, created spiritual nature is in no way 'proportionate' — except 'as the effect to the cause, or the potency to the act' — to what infinitely surpasses it."] However, he fails to draw the necessary conclusion from this. According to St. Thomas, the natural inclination of our will is directed to the end that is *proportionate* to our nature (loving contemplation of God through the mirror of creation), and not to the *actual* end to which God has destined us, which is supernatural. A supernatural end necessarily exceeds the proportionality of the nature which has been elevated to it, by definition. Therefore, it necessarily also exceeds the natural inclination or innate appetite of that nature, since natural inclination is based on proportionality and similarity. De Lubac's fundamental deviation from St. Thomas in this matter consists in supposing that natural inclination or innate appetite is necessarily directed to the *actual* final end to which God has destined a creature, and not rather to the end *proportionate* to the nature of the creature. (326)

b. The natural inclination or innate appetite generated by the natural form according to Thomas Aquinas:

Natural inclination or innate appetite must be based on the nature of the creature, since, being prior to knowledge, it can only be generated by the natural form that is possessed. Clearly there is nothing in the *natural form* of the creature, prior to the gift of grace, that could generate a natural inclination or innate appetite for the vision of God. A natural desire for the vision of God, prior to grace, can only be an elicited desire caused by some knowledge of God's effects, and thus it will be directed to knowledge of God's essence as first cause. The presence of sanctifying grace, on the other hand, generates a new "super-added" pre-cognitional inclination directly for the vision of God, as the object of our supernatural beatitude. This new inclination follows on grace as its innate impetus *(pondus gratiae)*.

In short, there is no basis for the thesis that the end to which God actually destines a creature — if that end is *supernatural* — necessarily generates a corresponding innate appetite or natural inclination for that end in the creature, prior to the reception of sanctifying grace. (327)

c. The unresolved tension in de Lubac's account: The natural desire to see God — purely natural, or also somewhat divine?

This creates an unresolved (and I would say unresolvable) tension in de Lubac's thought as to whether the natural desire to see God should be conceived as purely natural, or as also somehow divine. According to the logic of his system, there are strong reasons for both affirmations. It must be considered as natural, on the one hand, insofar as it is identified either with the nature itself, or with its foundation and depths. On the other hand, however, it must be considered to be somehow divine or supernatural (even though he firmly denies this consequence) for it to accomplish the role he assigns to it. The imprinting of a supernatural finality on our nature — the innate inclination to our supernatural end which de Lubac understands as God's "call" — can only be the result of the gift of a *supernatural* form added to our nature. (330f.)

If our nature can make no claim to the supernatural finality that has been imprinted on it, and does not in itself imply that finality, *then the imprinting of that finality cannot properly belong to the nature itself,* for otherwise my nature would "claim" it and "imply" it, as an essential constituent element. For example, our nature itself "claims" and "implies" the presence of reason, hands and feet, ordination to a fitting final end, and so forth. St. Thomas expresses this through the notion of *debitum naturae.* Therefore, this finality, if it is truly not claimed by the nature, must logically be something *super-added* to it.

This implies that what de Lubac refers to as our "concrete" or "historical" nature should really be conceived — in order to be coherent — as a composite formed by two elements: (1) our nature itself, as such ("abstract" or "pure"), and (2) a supernatural finality imprinted on that nature from the beginning which determines in us a natural desire to see God. This "imprint" would logically itself be a supernatural element, and thus this interpretation would coincide basically with the solution of Karl Rahner. (333)

4. The Resolution of the Tension in de Lubac's Account: Either Thomist or Bulgakovian/Milbankian

One ironic outcome of Feingold's critique and Milbank's modification of de Lubac's position is that Milbank's radicalized Bulgakovian Lubacianism constitutes precisely the other side of Feingold's Aristotelian Thomism. Both Feingold and Milbank agree that (a) the concern expressed in *Humani generis* was indeed aimed at de Lubac and (b) that the later de Lubac's way of responding to the encyclical's concern was not fully satisfying — for both because de Lubac never jettisoned the fundamental assumption about the constitution of the created spirit for a single supernatural end expressed in the *innate* natural desire for the vision of God.

a. The tension summarized:

[I]n order to coherently hold that our supernatural finality is truly "essential" in the proper sense of the word, de Lubac would logically have had to eliminate his novel distinction of abstract and concrete human nature altogether, and maintain that human nature as such is necessarily determined by a supernatural finality, which thus would be included in man's definition itself. According to this solution, an "uncalled" rational nature would not be human nature at all, but a completely different nature or species, having a different definition, with a different essential finality. This would mean discarding the possibility of an abstract human nature different from our actual human nature in not containing a supernatural finality imprinted on it.

Although this solution would be philosophically more coherent, and is supported by several passages of *The Mystery of the Supernatural* in which de Lubac implies that members of a hypothetical "uncalled" humanity would really have a different nature, such a solution poses insuperable theological problems, defining a created nature, as such, by a supernatural end. In any case, the mature de Lubac clearly chose not to take this step so as not to turn our supernatural end into a mere *sequela creationis,* and also so as not to be in conflict with the teaching of *Humani generis.* In fact, such a solution would render impossible de Lubac's threefold distinction, seen above, between (1) the creation of a spiritual nature, (2) the imprinting of a supernatural finality, and (3) the offer of grace, such that the first does not imply the second, and the second does not imply the third. (336f.)

b. The alternative resolutions:

In conclusion, de Lubac is in perfect harmony with St. Thomas and with the Catholic tradition in denying that our nature itself, as it actually exists, has the slightest supernatural element. However, this cannot be reconciled with his interpretation of the natural desire to see God as the expression of a supernatural finality imprinted on our nature in creation itself, prior to the reception of grace, determining us to an inevitably supernatural end. A choice must be made. Either the supernatural finality imprinted on our nature must be recognized to flow from a *supernatural element given with our constitution itself,* as Karl Rahner seems to affirm with his "supernatural existential," or one must reject altogether the thesis that a supernatural finality has been imprinted on our nature prior to grace, and maintain instead that an ordination to our supernatural end is impressed on our being *first by sanctifying grace.* Clearly the principles of St. Thomas and the Christian tradition demand the latter option. (339)

c. Feingold's rejection of "grace extrinsicism": the specific obediential potency of the rational creature, that is, the rational creature's natural openness to the supernatural:

The existence of an elicited natural desire to know the essence of God shows that a call by God to the beatific vision is tremendously fitting, since it is the only end in which we can find perfect beatitude and in which all natural desire can come to rest [my emphasis]. . . .

In addition, St. Thomas combats a certain type of "extrinsicism" by showing that our ordering to a supernatural end is realized through principles which are truly possessed by us in the form of supernatural *habits* (sanctifying grace and the theological virtues) which generate a new inclination, so that our supernatural end is attained in a "connatural" way. Although these principles ordering us to the vision of God remain extrinsic to our *nature* (for they are supernatural and thus "super-added" to the nature), they are not extrinsic to the *person* who possesses these supernatural habits, but inwardly transform and sanctify him.

The key difference between de Lubac and St. Thomas on this matter is that for the latter, this intrinsic ordering and inclination comes through "super-added" and directly supernatural principles, whereas for de Lubac, it comes through the nature itself, as it is historically realized in us, bearing an *innate and absolute* natural desire for its actual end. (340f.)

It is certainly true, as de Lubac emphasizes, that rational creatures constitute a special case with regard to their finality. St. Thomas notes that the great dignity of the rational creature lies in the fact that it can be raised to an end exceeding its natural faculties and proportionality; it alone is naturally *open* to the supernatural in virtue of the very nature of the faculties of intellect and will. Thus the rational creature can be elevated through the gift of grace to a new and higher end to which its nature itself is not intrinsically ordered, although it naturally desires that end.

This unique openness has been analyzed above as a *specific obediential potency* of the rational creature made in the image of God. (341f.)

d. The novelty or paradox of de Lubac's position:
The idea of an innate natural desire for the vision of God:

Just as it is a contradiction to say that the natural desire to see God is both absolute and imperfect, so too it is contradictory to assert with de Lubac that it is both absolute and inefficacious. (345)

Innate appetite, since it derives directly from the natural form possessed, is always directed to an object *proportionate* to the nature of the creature, to which it *gravitates,* as it were. . . . However, elicited natural desire, proper to the spiritual creature, is not limited in the same way! This is because elicited natural desire is based on knowledge. *Knowing our limitations, we can desire to transcend them. This desire for self-transcendence is only possible for the rational creature, and can only* manifest itself as an elicited desire based on knowledge of our limits. . . . This is precisely how St. Thomas shows the existence of a natural desire to see God in men and angels. . . . (401f.)

e. Avoiding the paradox; or, the philosophical and theological necessity of the possibility of a state of pure nature:

[T]he existence of an innate appetite for the vision of God logically implies the impossibility of [a state of pure nature]. However, the possibility of a state of pure nature is necessary for both philosophical and theological reasons, and has been taught by the Church's Magisterium. It is philosophically necessary for the coherence of the natural order, and theologically necessary to preserve the full gratuitousness of grace.

If there is only one final end (or only one beatitude) that is possible for man's nature as such — the vision of God — then that end, together with the means necessary to obtain it, will be due to human nature. In such a case, the vision of God, together with grace and the theological virtues, would no longer be gratuitous in the proper sense of the word. (424f.)

5. Thomas Transcending the Alternatives of the "Extrinsicism" and "Intrincisism" of Grace

Finally, it must be noted that Feingold captures with admirable nuance the intriguingly complex as well as precise position of Thomas and the Thomist tradition over against the rather crude alternatives of the alleged Thomist submission to a "grace-extrinsicism" on the one hand and the proposed panacea of the intrinsicism of a "grace-continuum of infinite intensification" on the other hand:

It should be noted that the assertion of the "possibility of a state of pure nature" — which should be understood as the possibility or non-absurdity for an intellectual nature to be created, and yet not to be called to a supernatural end — does *not* imply that it would be equally fitting for God to elevate an intellectual creature, as not to elevate him! On the contrary, St. Thomas shows that it is much more fitting to our nature and its natural aspirations, for God to elevate us to the supernatural end of the vision of God. This is shown by means of the natural desire to see God. *Perfect* beatitude, simply speaking, is possible only in the vision of God, for only this can bring to rest all natural desire.

Nevertheless, despite the fittingness of our elevation, it is very important to assert that it would not have been absurd or incoherent for human nature to have existed without being elevated to a supernatural end, in which case we could only have attained an imperfect beatitude. Such a thing would not have been impossible with regard to the order of God's providence or justice. However, the existence of a truly *innate* and unconditional natural appetite for the vision of God — as affirmed by Jansenius and his followers, together with the Augustinian theologians Noris, Bellelli, and Berti, and finally, in a somewhat different way, by de Lubac — would make it not merely less fitting for human nature to exist without being elevated to a supernatural end, but ultimately *absurd.*

Therefore, in order to coherently affirm the possibility of a state of pure nature, one must reject the existence of an innate appetite for the vision of God, as Suárez maintained in opposition to the earlier solution of Scotus, de Soto, Toledo, and St. Robert Bellarmine, all of whom maintained an innate appetite for the vision of God while also affirming the possibility of a state of pure nature. (425f.)

The subtle and nuanced argumentation of this last section gives the lie to Milbank's characterization that Feingold resurrects an "arch-reactionary," "die-hard," "palaeolithic" neo-Thomism intent on defending a "regime of pure nature." Moreover, Feingold himself advances at this very point the kind of aesthetic argument of ontological fittingness, based on *convenientia,* that Milbank hails as the latest achievement of what he characterizes as only a very recent Fribourg-Toulouse Thomism, presumably chastened by the *nouvelle théologie.* Hence it is not really surprising that Milbank fails to recognize that for Feingold, *convenientia* in this section has nothing whatsoever to do with the mere "epistemological likelihood," which according to Milbank is Reginald Garrigou-Lagrange's (and by implication Feingold's) understanding of *convenientia.*[84] Finally, in light of this particular passage, it becomes clear that the question of whether there exists in the human being an *innate* natural desire for the vision of God is a question debated in highly nuanced ways long before the days of Reginald

84. Milbank, *Suspended,* pp. 84f.

Garrigou-Lagrange, O.P., and Henri de Lubac, S.J., and hence in all likelihood a question that will continue to be debated long after them, though now in light of the concern expressed in *Humani generis*.[85]

Coda

In the course of this chapter it has become clear, first, that how the question of nature and grace is resolved has in at least some cases a subtle, but nevertheless immediate, impact on resolutions to the question of the nature and scope of salvation. In other words, if, as the early de Lubac states in *Surnaturel* and as Milbank likes to take him, spirit indeed *is* the desire for God, then Bulgakov's universal *apokatastasis* offers itself most irresistibly as the logical explication of a fundamental entailment of de Lubac's theological vision of a Christian humanist universalism.

It has become furthermore clear that it is ultimately unconvincing on the question of the natural desire for the vision of God to drive a consistent and comprehensive wedge, "all the way down," between the thought of Thomas Aquinas on the one hand and the tradition of the Thomist commentators on the other hand. The very fact that the greatest among the commentators were premier theologians and philosophers in their own right, that they interpreted Thomas in light of more recent philosophical challenges (Scotism, Nominalism, and eventually Cartesianism) as well as significant theological movements (Reformation and Jansenism), and that there obtain notable differences of style, emphasis, and interpretation between them, rather, must be understood as characteristic of what constitutes a living and authentic tradition of discourse in the precise sense Alasdair MacIntyre developed it in his classic *Three Rival Versions of Moral Enquiry*. How to assess individual instantiations of such a tradition as well as their specific faithfulness to the original vision in simultaneity with their successful treatment of a new and pressing philosophical or theological challenge is a matter of close and scrutinizing study. Feingold has challenged the present post-Lubacian consensus of regarding the Thomist commentators as a multi-layered burial-sheet over the corpse of

85. For a sobering reminder that the mid-twentieth century controversy over Henri de Lubac's *Surnaturel* is only a small segment of a much older, much longer, and much more complex debate over the precise philosophical and theological understanding of comprehensive human fulfillment *(beatitudo)*, see the bibliography in S. M. Ramírez, O.P., *De Hominis Beatitudine Tractatus Theologicus*, vol. 1 (Matriti: Aldecoa, 1942), pp. 103-154.

Thomas's thought by offering a strong account of the overarching inner coherence of the commentatorial tradition — well aware of differences and tensions — as well as its deep coherence with the most central tenets of Thomas's thought and thereby reminded us forcefully what the very point of a discursive tradition is.

Finally, it has become clear that the reading of Thomas's theology of grace as exclusively reconstructed in light of an Areopagite ontology of participation, in order to help warrant the vision of a Bulgakovian Lubacianism, simply is untenable. The humanism Thomas advances is integrally united with an Augustinian theological position on predestination and grace as stated in the Second Council of Orange and reconfirmed at the Council of Trent.

I should add, nevertheless, that while the universal *apokatastasis* was never adopted as a comprehensive dogmatic position by East or West,[86] universal human salvation remains a legitimate theological expression of the infused, supernatural virtues of hope and charity and hence a matter of fervent prayers of intercession, as consistently argued by Hans Urs von Balthasar.[87] Transposing universal salvation, however, from the scope of Christian hope and prayer to the core of Christian doctrine and theology would at the very least be a grave mistake of categories, if not the unwarranted anticipation of divine judgment in the form of theological speculation, even be it a Christological speculation as brilliant and gospel-centered as in the case of Karl Barth's doctrine of election.[88]

86. Indeed, it was explicitly rejected by the Fifth Ecumenical Council, that is, the Second Council of Constantinople (553), in a first, formally pre-conciliar, anathema, a statement issued by the assembly of bishops, in which they confirmed in an elaborated version the anti-Origenean canon promulgated by the Synod of Constantinople in 543. (For the anti-Origenean canon of 553 see *Acta Conciliorum Oecumenicorum* [Berlin, 1914ff], vol. IV/1, pp. 248ff.) The statement can be interpreted minimalistically as a rejection of the idea that one can know certainly that no one will be eternally damned; more straightforwardly and less minimalistically read, it seems simply to condemn any position that would want to deny the concrete possibility of eternal damnation for some, as argued already by Augustine in *De Civitate Dei* XXI, 17.

87. See for a discussion more accessible than the sprawling *Theo-Drama*, Hans Urs von Balthasar, *Dare We Hope "That All Men Be Saved"? with a Short Discussion on Hell* (San Francisco: Ignatius, 1988) and the insightful discussion of von Balthasar's nuanced position by Geoffrey Wainwright, "Eschatology," in *The Cambridge Companion to Hans Urs von Balthasar*, ed. Edward T. Oakes and David Moss (Cambridge: Cambridge University Press, 2004), pp. 113-27.

88. Karl Barth, *Church Dogmatics* II/2 (Edinburgh: T&T Clark, 1957), pp. 1-506. The remarkable sophistication of Barth's speculative Christological anticipation consists in the

Hence, to return to the beginning of these observations, the first type of answers to the question, What is the human being?, in all its profound humanist attraction suffers from the speculative excess of a premature systematic closure, precisely at the point where theology has to practice the *askesis* of leaving the end to God. Although, obviously, the second type of answers does not follow by necessity from the argument thus far advanced — an argument primarily pertaining to the correct interpretation of Thomas Aquinas — I shall nevertheless insist upon submitting that it is indeed in the second type of answers where we find such *askesis* most properly practiced. And in order to sustain the proper theological *askesis* this side of the eschaton, it strikes me to be indispensable as well as of eminent *convenientia* not only to acknowledge the proper difference that obtains *realiter* between nature and grace, in order to do justice to the specific gratuity of the grace of predestination, the *donum ultimum,* but moreover, and presently more importantly, to develop a coherent account of the relative and limited integrity of the principle of nature, which preserves the proper gratuity of the first gift, the *donum primum,* and hence does justice to the ineluctable double gratuity entailed in the economy of salvation. Where everything is grace all the way down in one and the same way, albeit of infinitely differing intensity, everything that has been brought into being, must have its end in God, by necessary ontological entailment. While undoubtedly a grandiose speculative vision, it, however, is neither the teaching of the Scriptures nor of the Church.

---

very fact that he stops short of stating explicitly what is clearly entailed by the logic of the argument itself for, as Barth himself acknowledges, there indeed is no explicit biblical warrant for universalism. To which degree Barth's restraint at this point remains a merely dialectical, rather than eschatological, reserve, however, depends on whether one reads the long concluding exegetical excursus on Judas Iscariot (pp. 458-506; esp. pp. 496f. and p. 506!) as a question mark or rather as an exclamation mark to his whole doctrine of election!

CHAPTER 6

"Thomist Ressourcement" — A Rereading of Thomas on the Natural Desire for the Vision of God

Thomas ist ein schwieriger Denker, der sich im Licht verbirgt und niemals seinen ganzen Gedanken auf einmal sagt.[1]

Josef Pieper

Josef Pieper's apt observation has special pertinence when one approaches the interpretive as well as the speculative challenge of comprehending Thomas Aquinas's thought on the natural desire for the vision of God. This teaching was contested among interpreters of Thomas long before Henri de Lubac contributed to the debate in 1946 with his influential and controversial study *Surnaturel.*[2]

William O'Connor, in an unjustly forgotten, instructive study from 1947, *The Eternal Quest: The Teaching of St. Thomas Aquinas on the Natural Desire for God,*[3] argued that since the days of the principal sixteenth-century commentators on Thomas's thought on the natural desire for the vision of God, one can usefully distinguish between a tradition of minimizing and a tradition of maximizing interpreters. These two tendencies of interpretation draw in differing ways upon two series of texts in the vast

---

1. "Thomas is a demanding thinker who so conceals himself in the light that he never reveals his complete thought at once without remainder."

2. Henri de Lubac, *Surnaturel: Études historiques,* ed. and intro. by Michel Sales, S.J. (Paris: Desclée de Brouwer, 1991). On the background of the controversy that erupted shortly after the publication of *Surnaturel,* see Aidan Nichols, O.P., "Thomism and the Nouvelle Théologie," *The Thomist* 64, no. 1 (2000): 1-19.

3. New York and London: Longman, Green, and Co., 1947.

corpus of the angelic doctor. In the first series of texts, Aquinas understands the desire to know the essence of the First Cause as a natural desire; in the second series he holds that the desire to know the divine essence is supernatural. Both series of texts run from the early through the later works and Thomas sees no need anywhere to reconcile them.[4]

O'Connor argues that the tradition of "minimizing" interpretations has its roots in the commentatorial work of the Italian Dominican theologian Thomas de Vio Cajetan (1469-1534) and of the Spanish Dominican theologian Dominicus Bañez (1528-1604), while the tradition of "maximizing" interpretations emerges from the commentaries of the Italian Dominican theologian Sylvester of Ferrara (1474-1528) and the Spanish Dominican theologian Dominicus Soto (1494-1560).[5] Cajetan and Bañez strongly privilege the first series of texts and prefer to interpret the natural desire in terms of an "obediential potency," a nonrepugnance or even a suitability in the created spiritual nature for the vision of God as he is in himself. Sylvester of Ferrara and Soto, on the other hand, read Thomas as teaching a genuine natural desire for the vision of God, although with the significant difference that Soto understands this desire primarily as a *pondus naturae,* a profound, innate natural impulse toward the vision of God as true human beatitude, while Sylvester of Ferrara takes the genuine desire to be not an innate, but an elicited desire that follows upon cognition.

All four interpreters of Thomas react to the profound impact Duns Scotus had on this debate with his strict Augustinian insistence that God in his divine substance is the natural end of the human being. All human volitions, Scotus argues, are ordained to the divine substance as to their ultimate end. Scotus's doctrine had such discursive weight that it inevitably impacted the subsequent interpretations of Thomas's thought, especially in the fifteenth and sixteenth centuries when Scotism had become a veritable philosophical and theological school in its own right.[6] Hence, not only did the maximizing and the minimizing interpretations draw differently on the two famous series of texts in the corpus of Thomas; they also were the result of Thomist commentators *post Scotum* having to consider and

4. O'Connor, *Eternal Quest,* pp. 7-23. For a complete listing of all the relevant passages in Thomas's writings, see Jorge Laporta, *La destinée de la nature humaine selon Thomas d'Aquin* (Paris: J. Vrin, 1965), pp. 147-61.

5. O'Connor, *Eternal Quest,* pp. 24-39, 55-72. For a concise introduction to these eminent interpreters of Thomas Aquinas, see Romanus Cessario, O.P., *A Short History of Thomism* (Washington, DC: The Catholic University of America Press, 2005).

6. O'Conner, *Eternal Quest,* pp. 40-54.

respond in their speculative interpretations of Thomas's doctrine to a subtle metaphysical and theological doctrine at variance with the *doctor angelicus.*[7]

It is possible to trace these interpretive traditions of Thomas's thought through the course of the subsequent centuries, with Cajetan's reading gaining predominance in the Dominican neo-Thomist revival of the late nineteenth and early twentieth centuries. With the appearance of de Lubac's *Surnaturel* and the expanded sequels *The Mystery of the Supernatural*[8] and *Augustinianism and Modern Theology,*[9] the tradition of a maximizing interpretation of Thomas along the lines of Soto found an unexpected but sustained renaissance. Put in a nutshell, de Lubac reads Thomas's teaching as establishing that human nature tends in itself necessarily toward God, that is, toward the supernatural end. In *Surnaturel* he states his thesis — and with it his reading of Thomas Aquinas on this matter — in provocative brevity: "'Natural desire for the supernatural': most theologians who reject this formula, reject together with it the very doctrine of St. Thomas Aquinas."[10] His position has become a widely accepted view, if not a majority consensus, among contemporary theologians in the English-speaking world as to how Thomas should best be understood on this difficult topic.[11]

When recently this consensus was challenged by Lawrence Feingold's substantive study *The Natural Desire to See God according to St. Thomas Aquinas and His Interpreters,*[12] the response was one of considerable irrita-

7. For a recent Scotist way of pointing out some of the significant differences, see Richard Cross, *Duns Scotus* (New York: Oxford University Press, 1999).

8. Henri de Lubac, S.J., *Le mystère du surnaturel* (Paris: F. Aubier, 1965); English edn., *The Mystery of the Supernatural,* trans. Rosemary Sheed (New York: Crossroad, 1998).

9. Henri de Lubac, S.J., *Augustinianisme et théologie moderne* (Paris: F. Aubier, 1965); English edn., *Augustinianism and Modern Theology,* trans. Lancelot Sheppard (New York: Crossroad, 2000).

10. "'Désir naturel du surnaturel': la plupart des théologiens qui repoussent cette formule, repoussent avec elle la doctrine même de saint Thomas d'Aquin" (De Lubac, *Surnaturel,* p. 431).

11. For one characteristic representative, see Fergus Kerr, O.P., *After Aquinas: Versions of Thomism* (Oxford: Blackwell, 2002), pp. 134-61, and *Twentieth Century Catholic Theologians: From Neo-Scholasticism to Nuptial Mysticism* (Oxford: Blackwell, 2007), pp. 67-86.

12. Rome: Apollinare Studi, 2001, 2nd ed. (Naples, FL: Sapientia Press, 2010). For a beginning conversation around this important work, see the Book Symposium with contributions by Harm Goris, Reinhard Hütter, Steven A. Long, and Guy Mansini in *Nova et Vetera* (English) 5, no. 1 (2007): 67-198; and David Braine, "The Debate between Henri de Lubac and His Critics," *Nova et Vetera* (English) 6, no. 3 (2008): 543-90.

tion. Such irritation in the English-speaking world is only explicable if one assumes that two earlier significant challenges or at least qualifications of this post-Lubacian consensus, advanced by French Dominicans and Thomist scholars, went largely unnoticed: first, the volume *Surnaturel: Une controverse au coeur du thomisme au XXe siècle;*[13] second, Georges Cottier, O.P., *Le désir de Dieu: Sur les traces de saint Thomas.*[14] In light of these recent substantive contributions to the discussion it is hard to deny that de Lubac's intervention, while arguably unsettling, in a possibly irreversible way, a once dominant minimizing interpretation of Thomas, turns out not to have been the last word on this matter. At the same time it is obvious that a renewed consideration of this intricate topic cannot simply go back behind de Lubac's intervention and give in to the temptation of pretending that *Surnaturel* and its sequels never had been written in the first place.

In this chapter I will attempt not to settle the matter, but to take a step "after Lubac" toward *a way of reading as one* the two sets of texts of Thomas on the natural desire for the vision of God. In order to be manageable, such a reading of Thomas has to be exemplary and paradigmatic and needs to be backed by an equally exemplary and paradigmatic engagement of de Lubac's central thesis. Therefore, this chapter falls into two parts. In the first part, I will focus on book 3 of the *Summa contra Gentiles*, since in any maximalizing interpretation of Thomas this book, and especially chapter 25, tends to play a pivotal role. Consequently, any rereading of Thomas on the natural desire for the vision of God "after Lubac" will have to attend to Thomas's exact use of the concept *desiderium naturale* in the context of his overall argument in book 3 of the *Summa contra Gentiles.*

In the second part, I will reconsider one of the most astute and nuanced early Thomist engagements of *Surnaturel*. While now largely forgotten, the constructive and critical analysis of *Surnaturel* by Marie-Joseph Le Guillou, O.P., encapsulates a promising Thomist reception of de Lubac's genuine concern as well as an apt critique of the excessive elements in de Lubac's reading of Thomas. In short, there is still much to learn from Le

---

13. Ed. Serge-Thomas Bonino, O.P., Actes du colloque organisé par l'Institute Saint-Thomas-d'Aquin les 26-27 mai 2000 à Toulouse (Toulouse: *Revue thomiste*, 2001); English edn. published as *Surnaturel: A Controversy at the Heart of Twentieth-Century Thomistic Thought*, trans. Robert Williams, trans. rev. by Matthew Levering (Naples, FL: Sapientia Press, 2009).

14. Paris: Éditions parole et silence, 2002.

Guillou's Thomist engagement of *Surnaturel,* an engagement as balanced as it is penetrating and astute.

I. *Summa contra Gentiles* III, c. 25 in Its Discursive Context: A Relecture

> *Since all creatures, even those devoid of understanding, are or-*
> *dered to God as to an ultimate end, all achieve this end to the ex-*
> *tent that they participate somewhat in His likeness. Intellectual*
> *creatures attain it in a more special way, that is, through their*
> *proper operation of understanding Him. Hence, this must be the*
> *end of the intellectual creature, namely, to understand God.*[15]

> *Besides, a thing has the greatest desire for its ultimate end. Now,*
> *the human intellect has a greater desire, and love, and pleasure,*
> *in knowing divine matters than it has in the perfect knowledge of*
> *the lowest things, even though it can grasp but little concerning*
> *divine things. So, the ultimate end of man is to understand God,*
> *in some fashion.*[16]

In the first part of this chapter, I will argue that Thomas's discourse in book 3 of the *Summa contra Gentiles,* as it pertains to our specific topic under discussion, is best understood as a metaphysical enquiry into the *onto-logical structure of created substance.* The emphasis of Thomas's enquiry falls upon created substances, hence substance not absolutely considered, but considered under the perspective of creation, that is, as the contingent effect in relationship to its first and final cause, the Creator. At the same

---

15. Thomas Aquinas, *ScG* III, c. 25, 1. All citations from the *Summa contra Gentiles* are taken from the following edition, which offers an improved version of the Leonine text: Thomas von Aquin, *Summa contra Gentiles,* 5 vols. (Darmstadt: Wissenschaftliche Buchgesellschaft, 1974 [2nd ed., 2001]): book 1, ed. and trans. Karl Albert and Paulus Engelhardt with cooperation by Leo Dümpelmann; book 2, ed. and trans. Karl Albert and Paulus Engelhardt; books 3/1 and 3/2, ed. and trans. Karl Allgaier; book 4, ed. and trans. Markus H. Wörner. The English citations are taken from Saint Thomas Aquinas, *Summa contra Gentiles* (Notre Dame, IN: University of Notre Dame Press, 1975): book 1, trans. Anton C. Pegis; book 2, trans. James F. Anderson; books 3/1 and 3/2, trans. Vernon J. Bourke; book 4, trans. Charles J. O'Neil. The English citations follow this edition in its practice of listing in sequence book, chapter, and chapter section, e.g., *ScG* I, c. 1, 1.

16. *ScG* III, c. 25, 7.

time, however, his analysis pertains primarily to the constitutive structure, that is, the respective nature of particular created substances — first and foremost among them the *substantia intellectualis*. Book 3 of the *Summa contra Gentiles,* hence, is to be understood as first and foremost an investigation into the principle of nature in its relative integrity and hence as properly accessible to metaphysical enquiry.[17] Consequently, while this primarily metaphysical enquiry is part and parcel of a wide-ranging consideration of divine providence, Thomas is not concerned here with the concrete givens of the one obtaining order of providence in which angels[18] and humans de facto exist. Any attempt to read particular statements or conclusions from Thomas's precisely delimited metaphysical argumentation here as *prima facie* theological claims about the obtaining order of providence as it coincides with the economy of salvation can only obfuscate the status of the conclusions reached. In short, as will be shown, the *desiderium naturale visionis Dei* as considered in book 3 of the *Summa contra Gentiles* belongs to the principle of nature in its relative integrity as it pertains to the metaphysical constitution of the *intellectus.*

By insisting upon the fundamentally metaphysical nature of the discourse undertaken here, I do not intend to resurrect the outdated thesis

17. See Lawrence Dewan, O.P., "Nature as a Topic for Metaphysical Inquiry," in *Form and Being: Studies in Thomistic Metaphysics* (Washington, DC: The Catholic University of America Press, 2006), pp. 205-28.

18. In the subsequent discussion the existence of angels is simply assumed. A philosophical defense of their existence obviously falls outside the range of this chapter. There seems to me to exist not the slightest need to "de-mythologize" the biblical witness to superior subsistent intelligences, even if for most contemporaries superior intelligences without bodies fall into the category of science-fiction movies or New-Age phantasies. Such pervasive contemporary inability to consider angels — and, alas, very widespread among Christians *pace* the recent New-Age rediscovery of "angels" as a quasi-personalistic transcendence at the expense of God — displays not only a disconcerting lack of theological imagination but metaphysical acumen as well. The present enquiry presupposes Thomas's argumentation in *ScG* II, cc. 46ff., and *ST* I, qq. 99ff., and, more importantly, the Church's unequivocal affirmation that the existence of angels pertains to the Christian faith. The theologically inclined reader might want to consult, next to the indispensable *Catechism of the Catholic Church* (nn. 327-30; 350), Lateran Council IV, c. 1, *De fide catholica* (*DS* 800); Vatican I, Dogmatic Constitution *Dei Filius,* c. 1 (DS 3002); and Pope Paul VI, *Sollemnis professio fidei,* 8 (*AAS* 60 [1968]: 436), known in English as "Credo of the People of God: Solemn Profession of Faith" (30 June 1968). The philosophically interested reader should consult Mortimer J. Adler, *The Angels and Us* (New York: Macmillan, 1982), as well as Benedict Ashley, O.P., "The Existence of Created Pure Spirits," in *The Ashley Reader: Redeeming Reason* (Naples, FL: Sapientia Press, 2006), pp. 47-59.

that the *Summa contra Gentiles* represents Thomas's "philosophical *summa.*" Far from it — though, as often, there may be a grain of truth in even such a misguided characterization. Indeed, as Jean-Pierre Torrell expresses the current consensus on the matter, "the *Summa contra Gentiles* is indeed a theological work" — and adopting a rendition fashionable in some contemporary academic circles, I might want to add, "all the way down."[19] However, it is obvious beyond dispute and hence in all likelihood significant for its particular purpose that the organization and mode of discourse of the *Summa contra Gentiles* is markedly different from that of the later *Summa theologiae.* In the *Summa contra Gentiles* we find a stronger separation than in the *Summa theologiae* between a primarily metaphysical enquiry (in books 1 through 3), an enquiry in which Thomas seems to engage head-on the Graeco-Islamic intellectual culture and especially Islamic Aristotelianism — hence an enquiry intelligible and pertinent equally to a broad range of Jewish, Muslim, and Christian theologians and philosophers of Thomas's day and age — and on the other hand, a properly Christian theological discourse, based on revelation (in book 4). However, a strict and clean separation between these two parts is not possible.[20] Elements of the one are clearly present in the other.

19. Jean-Pierre Torrell, O.P., *Saint Thomas Aquinas,* vol. 1, *The Person and His Work,* trans. Robert Royal (Washington, DC: The Catholic University of America Press, 1996), p. 114. Cf. the whole of chapter 6 (pp. 96-116), and the brief remarks in Jean-Pierre Torrell, O.P., *Aquinas's Summa: Background, Structure, and Reception,* trans. Benedict M. Guevin, O.S.B. (Washington, DC: The Catholic University of America Press, 2005), pp. 8f.

20. It is for this very reason that Michel Corbin, in his massive study *Le chemin de la théologie chez Thomas d'Aquin* (Paris: Beauchesnes, 1974) on the development of Thomas's theological thought, assigns the *Summa contra Gentiles* an "intermediary" location between the ingenious, but still youthful *Scriptum* on Lombard's *Sentences* and the mature and masterful *Summa theologiae.* Corbin comes to this assessment because he takes the conception of theology as the science of faith, as *sacra doctrina,* to be the perfect end point of an increasingly maturing spectrum, on which the *Summa contra Gentiles* also must find its place. Why does Corbin see the *Summa contra Gentiles* as falling short of the conceptual perfection of the *Summa theologiae?* Because he finds a tension between *Summa contra Gentiles* I-III, attending to truths of faith accessible to reason, and *Summa contra Gentiles* IV, attending to truths of faith unaccessible to reason, he discerns a less-than-perfect integration of the philosophical enquiry into the overarching theological task and hence regards it as a stage beneath the perfect mode of integration to be found in the *Summa theologiae.* While Corbin's thesis is complex and argued in great detail (pp. 491-692!), it seems to depend too much on the governing assumption that Aquinas was aiming at one single overarching goal, namely, that of fully integrating philosophical inquiry into an overall theological task of which the *Summa theologiae* represents the stage of perfection. Hence, I agree with Rudi te

The metaphysical enquiry in books 1 through 3 often takes a particular route due to matters that concern the truth of faith;[21] moreover, the theological discourse in book 4 consistently draws upon metaphysical argumentation in order to refute objections raised by unbelievers against revealed truth.

Thomas's foreword to book 4, therefore, merits a close reading. Here I can give only a brief adumbration of the aspects most pertinent to our discussion. First, Thomas opens the specific discourse of book 4 with a succinct summary of the topic that preoccupies us in these pages:

> The human intellect, to which it is connatural to derive its knowledge from sensible things, is not able through itself to reach the vision of the divine substance in itself, which is above all sensible things and, indeed, improportionately above all other things. Yet, because man's perfect good is that he somehow know God, lest such a noble creature might seem to be created to no purpose, as being unable to reach its own end, there is given to man a certain way through which he can rise to the knowledge of God: so that, since the perfections of things descend in a certain order from the highest summit of things — God — man may progress in the knowledge of God by beginning with lower things and gradually ascending. (*ScG* IV, c. 1, 1)[22]

Second, Thomas sketches two paths of metaphysical contemplation by way of which the human intellect may rise to the knowledge of God: one by a descent of perfections from God, the other by beginning with lower things and gradually ascending to the first cause. However, despite

---

Velde when he avers, "I see no reason why the *Contra Gentiles* should not be approached as a work in its own right, with an intention different from the *Summa theologiae* and an intelligible structure adapted to that intention" ("Natural Reason in the *Summa contra Gentiles*," in *Thomas Aquinas: Contemporary Philosophical Perspectives,* ed. Brian Davies [Oxford: Oxford University Press, 2002], pp. 117-40, at 119).

21. See, for example, *ScG* II, c. 46, 1.

22. *ScG* IV, c. 1: "Intellectus humanus, a rebus sensibilibus connaturaliter sibi scientiam capiens, ad intuendam divinam substantiam in seipsa, quae super omnia sensibilia, immo super omnia alia entia improportionabiliter elevatur, pertingere per seipsum non valet. Sed quia perfectum hominis bonum est ut quoquo modo Deum cognoscat, ne tam nobilis creatura omnino in vanum esse videretur, velut finem proprium attingere non valens, datur homini quaedam via per quam in Dei cognitionem ascendere possit: ut scilicet, quia omnes rerum perfectiones quodam ordine a summo rerum vertice Deo descendunt, ipse, ab inferioribus incipiens et gradatim ascendens, in Dei cognitionem proficiat."

the intellectual rigor required and the insights gained on these different, but ultimately complementary, paths of metaphysical enquiry, Thomas emphasizes that "because of the weakness of the intellect we are not able to know perfectly even the ways [of metaphysical enquiry] themselves" (*ScG* IV, c. 1, 3).[23] And if that were not enough of a blow against the confidence of the all-too-routinized metaphysician, Thomas adds only shortly afterwards, "and because that source [of these imperfectly known ways of enquiry] transcends the above-mentioned ways beyond proportion, even if we knew the ways themselves perfectly we would yet not have within our grasp a perfect knowledge of the source" (*ScG* IV, c. 1, 3).[24] In short, as Rudi te Velde rightly emphasizes, "[i]t is characteristic of the *Contra Gentiles* that natural reason, in its search for truth, is constantly reminded of its human point of departure."[25]

It no longer comes as a surprise that Thomas characterizes the knowledge of God to be reached by these ways of metaphysical enquiry as feeble *(debilis cognitio)*. We would gravely misunderstand Thomas, however, if we were to put aside this feeble knowledge of God gained in books 1 through 3 in a quasi-Barthian fashion as at best irrelevant, outdated rubble (or worse, dangerously misleading natural theology), and expect Thomas to announce a "new beginning" with book 4, a "post-metaphysical" theology solely based on revelation's grammar as unfolded in the biblical narrative. On the contrary, feeble knowledge is not ignorance, error, or delusion, but still knowledge. And indeed, for Thomas the feeble knowledge gained by way of the intellectual labors of the first three books is the indispensable precondition for a comprehensive actuation of the *intellectus fidei* as well as for an effective defense of faith's truth against its philosophical detractors.[26] For Thomas, the perfection

23. "Per has igitur vias intellectus noster in Dei cognitionem ascendere potest, sed, propter debilitatem intellectus nostri, nec ipsas vias perfecte cognoscere possumus."

24. "Quod quia sine proportione excedit vias praedictas, etiam si vias ipsas cognosceremus perfecte, nondum tamen perfecta principii cognitio nobis adesset."

25. Te Velde, "Natural Reason in the *Summa contra Gentiles*," p. 120.

26. Consider the last remark in *ScG* IV, c. 10, 15 regarding those who would argue by way of reason against the possibility of a divine generation: "[B]ecause truth is strong in itself and is overcome by no attack, it must be our intention to show that the truth of faith cannot be overcome by reason." ("[Q]uia veritas in seipsa fortis est et nulla impugnatione convellitur, oportet intendere ad ostendendum quod veritas fidei ratione superari non possit.") The emphasis lies here on "the truth that the Catholic faith *professes*," as te Velde rightly emphasizes ("Natural Reason in the *Summa contra Gentiles*," p. 121). He stresses at another point that "Aquinas proposes to show, to his fellow believers, that the Catholic claim

of wisdom entails both, in the proper distinction and in the right order: wisdom gained by way of human enquiry, an operation essential to an embodied intellect, and wisdom gained gratuitously by way of revelation, a wisdom infinitely surpassing all human knowledge. Only if we remember that the perfection of wisdom is the unifying source and goal of the *Summa contra Gentiles* are we able to appreciate the subtle synthesis between the predominantly metaphysical enquiry of books 1 through 3 and the primarily theological discourse of book 4. Te Velde captures Thomas's intention accurately when he states: "It is Aquinas's declared intention to assume the task of someone wise *(officium sapientis).* With this 'office,' Aquinas creates something new, an intellectual point of view that is formally different from theology as well as philosophy."[27]

Wisdom

Thomas pursues the *officium sapientis* by way of the overarching and integrating vision of an order of wisdom. Thomas Hibbs, in his important work *Dialectic and Narrative in Aquinas,* offers the following felicitous characterization of Thomas's project as he summarizes the achievement of the first book of the *Summa contra Gentiles:*

> Wisdom is a way of life, replete with joy, that satisfies all human longing, unites man to God in friendship, and warrants the name of blessed. The first book is itself an enactment of that life of wisdom, an enactment that culminates in a recognition of the pursuit of wisdom as a participation in the exemplary cause of the whole, a sharing in the life of that first and highest cause whose contemplation is the goal of philosophy. The previous arguments on behalf of God's desire to communicate his goodness to creatures provide grounds for an unex-

---

to truth can in fact be understood and self-consciously affirmed, against the numerous alternative claims, as a reasonable claim to truth" (p. 122). "It seems to me that Aquinas's immediate aim is not to prove the validity of the Catholic claim before others *(infideles)*. . . . On the contrary, the office is needed because of the threatening effect the various errors have on the Christian consciousness of truth. Natural reason, according to its historical reality in Greco-Islamic philosophy, calls the Christian perception of truth into question. In this sense, the *Contra Gentiles* seems to me comparable to Maimonides' *Guide of the Perplexed"* (p. 123).

27. Te Velde, "Natural Reason in the *Summa contra Gentiles,*" p. 121.

plained and audacious assertion of the prologue: the life of wisdom establishes friendship between us and God.[28]

Later, in book 3, Thomas will show how the wise person imitates God in the perfection of wisdom achieved by way of contemplating God's goodness. Hence, unsurprisingly, the whole of the *Summa contra Gentiles* is structured according to an order of wisdom: the first book treats the perfection of the divine nature, the second book the perfection of the divine power, and the third the perfect authority and dignity insofar as God is the end of all things and executes his government over all of them — in short, as perfect as God is in being and causing, so he is perfect in the ruling of all things, especially in the ruling of the intellectual creatures, angels and humans. Saint Thomas regards this threefold consideration as accessible to natural reason as it rises up in metaphysical contemplation toward God. However, while throughout the *Summa contra Gentiles* he insists on the validity of this contemplation by way of metaphysical inquiry as belonging to the proper domain of natural reason, he emphasizes with equal insistence the incomplete character of the knowledge thus gained, an imperfection deriving first of all structurally from the weakness of the human intellect, the lowest in the order of spirits. It is for this reason that he finally considers in book 4 a perfection surpassing all other perfections, the perfection of God's goodness. For God offers humanity a path by way of which human beings are elevated to a perfect knowledge of him, the unmediated vision of God that effectively unites human beings to him such

---

28. Thomas S. Hibbs, *Dialectic and Narrative in Aquinas: An Interpretation of the "Summa Contra Gentiles"* (Notre Dame, IN: University of Notre Dame Press, 1995), p. 62. Hibbs continues by stating: "Still, the dominant mode of discourse in the first book is *via negativa,* a mode that accentuates the gap between the human pursuit of wisdom and the divine possession of it (I, 102). As Thomas puts it, 'false and earthly felicity' is nothing but a 'certain shadow' *(quandam umbram)* of divine blessedness" (p. 62). Hibbs here seems to suggest that the human pursuit of wisdom does fall into the category of "false and earthly felicity." Such a claim — with too narrowly Augustinian a thrust, if I may say — seems to be dubious. For in *ScG* I, c. 102, Thomas lists as instantiations of such "false and earthly felicity" only pleasure, riches, power, honor, and fame. These are all forms of felicity refuted in *ScG* III, cc. 27-32. It is important to note that the philosopher's *admiratio,* the metaphysical contemplation of the first cause, which is the term of philosophical wisdom, is not contained in either of these lists. Hence, while clearly not identical with the participation in God's own beatitude and therefore a less than perfect felicity, this philosophical wisdom seems to amount to something considerably more than "false and earthly felicity," namely, the fragile realization of that kind of imperfect albeit genuine felicity that results from contemplating God, the first cause, by way of his created effects — *via causalitatis, via negativa, via eminentiae.*

that they become "partakers of the divine nature" (*divinae consortes naturae* [2 Pet 1:4]). And so we find in book 4 the treatment of the revealed mysteries that lie by definition outside the range of the kind of contemplation by way of metaphysical enquiry to which natural reason is able to rise, and that are solely the object of faith.[29]

Throughout the following reading of the *Summa contra Gentiles* it should be kept in mind that the whole argument Thomas advances in book 3 is (a) part of a consideration of divine providence — God's perfect dominion — (b) in the context of a structural-metaphysical analysis that (c) demonstrates that, and displays in which way precisely, God is the end and good of all things.

God's Being and Participated Being

The axiomatic beginning of such a metaphysical demonstration is, as always with Thomas, the consideration of God's being:

> That there is one First Being, possessing the full perfection of the whole of being, and that we call Him God, has been shown in the preceding Books. From the abundance of His perfection, He endows all existing things with being, so that He is fully established not only as the First Being but also as the original source of all existing things. Moreover, He has granted being to other things, not by a necessity of His nature but according to the choice of His will. (*ScG* III, c. 1, 1)[30]

Contrary to those who would want to claim that "creator" is an intrinsic characteristic of God — echoes of a Neoplatonic notion of emanationism (reverberating not incidentally in the Origenist tradition)[31] — because as es-

---

29. It is in book 4 that Thomas most explicitly inquires into the concrete path that carries with it the promise of leading to the partaking in divine wisdom, a fullness of possession never to be attained by the human pursuit of wisdom. However, even in book 4, for displaying the logical possibility of these mysteries and for their defense against objection and error, metaphysical contemplation and argumentation are still of paramount importance.

30. "Unum esse primum entium, totius esse perfectionem plenam possidens, quod Deum dicimus, in superioribus est ostensum, qui ex sui perfectionis abundantia omnibus existentibus esse largitur, ut non solum primum entium, sed et principium omnium esse comprobetur. Esse autem aliis tribuit non necessitate naturae, sed secundum suae arbitrium voluntatis."

31. See Sergius Bulgakov, *The Bride of the Lamb*, trans. Boris Jakim (Grand Rapids:

sentially self-diffusive *summum bonum* God ineluctably emanates an inexhaustible surplus of participated being, Thomas holds rightly that creation, that is, the totality of partipated being, is a surpassingly gratuitous act of the divine will.[32] God is not captive to some intrinsic aspect of his essence, the infinite act of being itself, but remains in his essence transcendently free, such that even if there were an eternal creation, it would still subsist as contingent relation to God, a relation originating from the divine will.

This relation constitutes the internal structure as well as the overarching purpose of creation:

> Now, each of the things produced through the will of an agent is directed to an end by the agent. For the proper object of the will is the good and the end. As a result, things which proceed from will must be directed to some end. Moreover, each thing achieves its ultimate end through its own action which must be directed to the end by Him Who gives things the principles through which they act. (*ScG* III, c. 1, 2)[33]

Eerdmans, 2002) for a subtle defense of such a notion: "God is both God in Himself and the Creator, with a completely equal necessity and freedom of His being. In other words, God cannot fail to be the Creator, just as the Creator cannot fail to be God. The plan of the world's creation is as co-eternal to God as is His own being in the Divine Sophia. In *this* sense (but only in this sense), God cannot do without the world, and the world is necessary for God's very being. And to this extent the world must be included in God's being in a certain sense. (But by no means does this inclusion signify the crude pantheistic identification of God and the world, according to which God is the world and the world is God)" (pp. 45f.). While the fundamental difference between Bulgakov's account and pantheism might readily be granted, attentive readers of his undoubtedly brilliant speculation, noting his characterization of the Scholastic differentiation between God *in se* and God as creator as "utterly alien to Scripture," will nevertheless be unable to dismiss the all-too-strong impression that they might be witnessing the wedding feast of Origenist intuition with Schellingian speculative daring — a phenomenon hardly more scriptural than is Scholastic conceptual precision.

32. Rudi te Velde, in his important study *Aquinas on God: The "Divine Science" of the Summa Theologiae* (Aldershot, U.K., and Burlington, VT: Ashgate, 2006) puts the matter succinctly: "Against the Neoplatonic doctrine of necessary emanation, Aquinas argues that the infinite essence of the first cause cannot express itself with natural necessity in any finite creature. Creation cannot be a matter of divine natural self-expression. God produces the universe of creatures according to the manner in which He wills them to exist, distinct from his own manner of existence" (p. 176).

33. "Eorum autem quae per voluntatem producuntur agentis, unumquodque ab agente in finem aliquem ordinatur: bonum enim et finis est obiectum proprium voluntatis, unde necesse est ut quae ex voluntate procedunt, ad finem aliquem ordinentur. Finem autem ultimum unaquaeque res per suam consequitur actionem, quam oportet in finem dirigi ab eo qui principia rebus dedit per quae agunt."

While the principle of an all-encompassing teleology must strike many a contemporary reader as utterly counterintuitive and outright strange, Thomas calmly enunciates it as one of the first metaphysical principles of creation as an order of participated being brought about as the result of the will of a transcendent, infinitely intelligent first cause. Everything that is (i.e., that has participated being) is directed to an end. As Georges Cottier puts it quite succinctly: "The universality of the final cause, without which any action were to remain inexplicable, is a principal given of reality."[34] Based on the universal teleology established in the first chapter of book 3, Thomas unfolds in the subsequent sixty-two chapters what is entailed in understanding God as the end of all things: if God has created everything because of his will, there must be an ultimate end to what God has willed; but the only possible ultimate end is God himself. The perfection of every participated being — being an effect of the First Cause — is achieved by reaching its ultimate end, which is nothing but its proper return to its source. In the second book of the *Summa contra Gentiles,* where Thomas considers creation, he lays the groundwork for this all-encompassing teleology:

> An effect is most perfect when it returns to its source; thus, the circle is the most perfect of all figures, and circular motions the most perfect of all motions, because in their case a return is made to the starting point. It is therefore necessary that creatures return to their principle in order that the universe of creatures may attain its ultimate perfection. Now, each and every creature returns to its source so far as it bears a likeness to its source, according to its being and its nature, wherein it enjoys a certain perfection. (*ScG* II, c. 46, 2)[35]

Primary and Secondary Perfection

As soon as Thomas has established the overarching teleology of participated being, he reintroduces a crucial distinction: the primary perfection

---

34. Georges Cottier, *Le désir de Dieu: Sur les traces de saint Thomas* (Paris: Éditions parole et silence, 2002), p. 190.

35. "Tunc enim effectus maxime perfectus est quando in suum redit principium: unde et circulus inter omnes figuras, et motus circularis inter omnes motus, est maxime perfectus, quia in eis ad principium reditur. Ad hoc igitur quod universum creaturarum ultimam perfectionem consequatur, oportet creaturas ad suum redire principium. Redeunt autem ad suum principium singulae et omnes creaturae inquantum sui principii similitudinem gerunt secundum suum esse et suam naturam, in quibus quandam perfectionem habent."

of every created being by virtue of its nature and the secondary perfection of every created being by virtue of its operation. While distinct, the perfections are inherently related to each other. Every being, in virtue of its nature, is intrinsically oriented toward its proper operations. Thomas puts the matter most succinctly in the discussion of divine providence: "Each thing appears to exist for the sake of its operation; indeed, operation is the ultimate perfection of a thing" (*ScG* III, c. 113, 1).[36] A longer and more important instantiation of this distinction is to be found in the second book of the *Summa contra Gentiles* — with immediate implications for the opening argument of book 3:

> A thing's second perfection . . . constitutes an addition to its first perfection. Now, just as the act of being and the nature of a thing are considered as belonging to its first perfection, so operation is referred to its second perfection. Hence, the complete perfection of the universe required the existence of some creatures which return to God not only as regards likeness of nature, but also by their action. And such a return to God cannot be made except by the act of the intellect and will, because God Himself has no other operation in His own regard than these. The greatest perfection of the universe therefore demanded the existence of some intellectual creatures. (*ScG* II, c. 46, 3)[37]

We can see this distinction at play in the following, easily overlooked section at the beginning of book 3, which is central to all that follows. Thomas emphasizes that as God is perfect in being and causing, so he is also in ruling. The result of this rule is, however, diverse:

> [T]he result of this rule is manifested differently in different beings, depending on the diversity of their natures. For some beings so exist as God's products that, possessing understanding, they bear His likeness and reflect His image. Consequently, they are not only ruled but are

---

36. "Omnis enim res propter suam operationem esse videtur: operatio enim est ultima perfectio rei."

37. "Perfectio secunda in rebus addit supra primam. Sicut autem esse et natura rei consideratur secundum primam perfectionem, ita operatio secundum perfectionem secundam. Oportuit igitur, ad consummatam universi perfectionem, esse aliquas creaturas quae in Deum redirent non solum secundum naturae similitudinem, sed etiam per operationem. Quae quidem non potest esse nisi per actum intellectus et voluntatis: quia nec ipse Deus aliter erga seipsum operationem habet. Oportuit igitur, ad perfectionem optimam universi, esse aliquas creaturas intellectuales."

also rulers of themselves, inasmuch as their own actions are directed to a fitting end. If these beings submit to the divine rule in their own ruling, then by virtue of the divine rule they are admitted to the achievement of their ultimate end; but, if they proceed otherwise in their own ruling, they are rejected. (*ScG* III, c. 1, 4)[38]

Thomas posits a direct relationship for beings possessing understanding (i.e., angels and humans) between submitting to the divine rule and achieving one's ultimate end. Concerning the manner of this rule, he states, "as regards those intellectual beings who are led by Him to their ultimate end, which is Himself [the Psalmist], uses this expression: 'For the Lord will not cast off His people'" (*ScG* III, c. 1, 8).[39]

Thomas establishes here three claims of paramount importance: (1) God is the infallible agent of that rule by virtue of which intellectual beings can achieve their ultimate end. (2) Whatever is constitutive of intellectual beings (i.e., inherent to their primary perfection, their nature) is not in and of itself efficacious in achieving their final end, for intellectual beings are, as the rest of created beings, fallible. It is their secondary perfection, operation, which itself is in need of divine help, that leads them to their ultimate end. (3) Intellectual beings can resist the divine rule and guidance and hence miss their ultimate end (as permitted by God).

Agency

In chapter 3, Thomas lays out the broad metaphysical contours of what is constitutive of an "agent" that "intends" and "acts." It is important to take note that throughout book 3 the notions of "agent," "intending," and "acting" do not denote at all the kind of "rational agent" and the kind of "intelligible actions"[40] that name the *terminus a quo* and the *terminus ad quem*

38. "Huius vero regiminis effectus in diversis apparet diversimode, secundum differentiam naturarum. Quaedam namque sic a Deo producta sunt ut, intellectum habentia, eius similitudinem gerant et imaginem repraesentent: unde et ipsa non solum sunt directa, sed et seipsa dirigentia secundum proprias actiones in debitum finem. Quae si in sua directione divino subdantur regimini, ad ultimum finem consequendum ex divino regimine admittuntur: repelluntur autem si secus in sua directione processerint."

39. "Et quidem quantum ad intellectualia, quae, eius regimen sequentia, ab ipso consequuntur ultimum finem, qui est ipse: et ideo dicit, *Quia non repellet Dominus plebem suam.*"

40. See Alasdair MacIntyre, "The Intelligibility of Action," in *Rationality, Relativism,*

of the will's exercise *(usus)* under the intellect's rule *(imperium)*. The latter is indeed the principal context in which we are used to encounter the notions of "agency," "intention,"[41] and "moral act."[42] However, in book 3 of the *Summa contra Gentiles* these notions have a broader, analogical application. They denote various aspects entailed in the fundamental principle of secondary perfection executed by every participated being, which is operation properly advancing its perfection toward the ultimate end. As W. Norris Clarke aptly put it, "Action is the primary bond of similarity between different kinds of being and thus is the ontological ground justifying the application of the same analogous term to them."[43] Everything that achieves its secondary perfection by way of its operation "intends" and "acts" in the broadest sense, be it inanimate as fire is, animate as trees or birds are, or intelligent as humans or angels are. Thomas thus argues that in acting every agent intends an end, and that the ultimate end is that beyond which the agent seeks nothing else.

> For every agent the principle of its action is either its nature or its intellect (*ScG* III, c. 2, 6). [T]he end is that in which the appetitive inclination of an agent or mover, and of the thing moved, finds its rest. Now, the essential meaning of the good is that it provides a terminus for appetite, since "the good is that which all desire." Therefore, every action and motion are for the sake of a good. (*ScG* III, c. 3, 3)[44]

Two things are especially noteworthy here. First, Thomas can use the term "agent" analogically because God is the first and foremost agent, who brings about creation. And since every effect has a certain similarity to its cause, creation indeed imitates its first cause in the most important respect: agency. Moreover, since God as perfect agent acts for an ultimate end, which necessarily can be nothing else but God, and since, from the

---

and Human Sciences, ed. J. Margolis, M. Krausz, and R. M. Burian (Dordrecht: Nijhoff, 1986), pp. 63-80.

41. On intention see the classic treatment by G. E. M. Anscombe, *Intention*, 2nd ed. (Ithaca, NY: Cornell University Press, 1963).

42. For a recent, astute introduction into this complex topic in Thomas Aquinas, see Steven A. Long, *The Teleological Grammar of the Moral Act* (Naples, FL: Sapientia Press, 2007).

43. W. Norris Clarke, S.J., *The One and the Many: A Contemporary Thomistic Metaphysics* (Notre Dame, IN: University of Notre Dame Press, 2001), p. 47.

44. "Finis est in quo quiescit appetitus agentis vel moventis, et eius quod movetur. Hoc autem est de ratione boni, ut terminet appetitum: nam 'bonum' est 'quod omnia appetunt' [*Eth.* I 1]. Omnis ergo actio et motus est propter bonum."

perspective of creation, God's efficient and final causality ultimately coincide, the final cause's "pull" constitutes the ultimate end which every creature's operation "intends" by way of its action. Finally, since God is perfectly and infinitely in act, *actus purus* (*ScG* I, c. 16, 5),[45] created substances, in virtue of their participated being, imitate the first cause by being "in act" as well. However, their being "in act" not only imitates the first cause's agency. Rather, because the first cause and the final cause are identical, the final causality of the *actus purus* is the reason why all participated beings desire *(appetunt)* as their proper good their own perfection and thereby the final cause as the ultimate good. As Cottier aptly puts it:

> Under the attraction of God, ultimate end and *summum bonum*, created being tends, in the measure according to which it is possible for it, toward a maximum of actualized being. This is indeed a dynamic vision. It arises from the doctrine of act, of which St. Thomas makes good all the implications, especially in light of the metaphysics of the final cause.[46]

In short, we find in Thomas's use of "agent" an analogical attribution *secundum prius et posterius,* based on a participation by imperfect similitude:[47] "[A] created thing tends toward the divine likeness through its operation" (*ScG* III, c. 21, 2).[48] Only the first transcendent cause of the uni-

---

45. "Primum igitur agens, quod Deus est, nullam habet potentiam admixtam, sed est actus purus."

46. Cottier, *Le désir de Dieu,* p. 192.

47. Bernard Montagnes, O.P., *The Doctrine of the Analogy of Being according to Thomas Aquinas,* trans. E. M. Macierowski, rev. Pol Vandervelde, ed. with revisions Andrew Tallon (Milwaukee: Marquette University Press, 2004), p. 39: "[P]articipation establishes a relation of formal causality between beings and God and that analogy conveys at the conceptual level the unity of order by reference to a primary instance that the analogates imitate and whose likeness they bear. A formulation of Thomas summarizes this doctrine: '*omne ens quantumcumque imperfectum a primo ente exemplariter deducitur*' [Sent. II, d. 3, q. 2, a. 3, ad 2]. There is a community of analogy between beings and God because creatures imitate God as best they can." However, Clarke rightly emphasizes in addition that beings themselves are not analogous. Rather, in the analogy of attribution (the relation of causal participation of many different analogates to a common source) "the analogous term (thought and word) gives linguistic expression to an objective *metaphysical structure of participation:* many real beings possessing in various limited ways a common attribute, received from a common source, which possesses the same attribute in unlimited fullness" (Clarke, *The One and the Many,* p. 56).

48. "Tendit enim in divinam similitudinem res creata per suam operationem."

verse is agent in the full and proper sense. Every participated being — being an effect of the first cause's agency — reaches its own proper perfection in someway imitating the first cause's agency; consequently, every participated being, properly, albeit analogically, is predicated as an "agent" that "intends" and "acts."[49]

Second, Thomas's metaphysical analysis pertains to the whole range of participated being, encompassing every created substance, from ants to angels and from humus to humans. The end is that in which the agent's *appetitus* comes to a rest. That end constitutes the good of the agent in light of which it "acts." And "good" is that — here Thomas simply regards Aristotle's famous definition as expressing the normative philosophical consensus — "which all things desire."[50] Hence "appetite" *(appetitus)* and "good" *(bonum)* must also be understood in the widest analogical sense. Consequently, on the level of metaphysical analysis and in this analogical sense of agency, any premature projection onto the text of the alternatives between an unelicited, innate, and unconditional desire and an elicited, conditional desire is clearly out of place at this point. While the metaphysical inquiry pertains to the primary perfection (nature) as well as to the secondary perfection (operation), it remains an inquiry into the ontological structure, the principle of nature in its relative integrity. For the analysis and demonstration pertain exclusively to the formal constitution of every created being seeking its perfection in its proper good, that good which terminates its appetite because the secondary perfection has been achieved. The sole criterion St. Thomas mentions is the creature's specific capacity *(quantum in se est)* to be moved to its proper perfection:

> [I]f anything lacks a proper perfection, it is moved toward it, in so far
> as lies within its capacity [*quantum in se est*], but if it possess it the

49. In *Aquinas on God,* te Velde offers a succinct characterization of the "analogical agent" in Thomas's thought: "[T]he analogical agent concerns a type of causality in which the effect falls short with respect to the perfection of its cause. In this case the effect receives merely a diminished and remote likeness of its cause — a likeness which cannot be reduced to a specific or even generic identity, but which is merely according to a certain analogy. . . . Analogy, as it is used here, is clearly of a Neoplatonic origin; it is intrinsically connected with the idea of a causal hierarchy, with the notion of participation, and with the 'descent' of the effect from the cause. Analogy is meant to designate the intelligible connection between cause and effect" (p. 110).

50. *ScG* III, c. 16: "[S]ic enim philosophi diffiniunt bonum, *quod omnia appetunt.*" Thomas cites here from Aristotle's *Nicomachean Ethics* 1.1.1094a 2.

thing rests in it. Therefore, the end of each thing is its perfection. (*ScG* III, c. 16, 3)[51]

As we shall see soon, the defining referent for the *quantum in se est,* that is, the specific capacity of angels as well as humans, is the *intellectus.*

God: The Final End of All Things

Let us return to the overarching teleology Thomas unfolds in the opening chapters of book 3. In chapters 17–25, Thomas elaborates more extensively how God is to be understood as the end of physical as well as intellectual beings. As I have already emphasized, his metaphysical-structural argument encompasses all creatures (separate substances [i.e., angels], humans, animals, inanimate things). All things are ordered in at least three respects to one ultimate end that is God: (1) by way of the substantial act of being, (2) by way of everything that pertains to a thing's perfection, and (3) by way of the thing's proper operation.

Having established in chapter 17 that God is the end of all things, in chapter 18 Thomas specifies how precisely this is the case. One could very well assume that God is the end of all things in the sense of an ideal, or in the sense of being something produced, or in the sense of something being added to God, or in the sense of something being obtained for God. It is not hard to recognize in these rejected positions an uncannily perceptive anticipation of the emasculated modern simulacra of teleology as one can encounter them in Kant, Hegel, and process philosophy. In chapter 13 of book 1 of the *Summa contra Gentiles* — a chapter worth meditating on at length — Thomas refutes the premodern precursors of these positions on the basis of the proofs of God's existence as well as God's categorical transcendence in relationship to participated being. It is, however, only in chapters 17 and 18 of book 3 that Thomas argues that God is simultaneously first agent and ultimate end. For our particular concern, the most relevant argument is the last one proffered in chapter 18:

> Moreover, the effect must tend toward the end in the same way that the agent works for the end. Now, God, Who is the first agent of all things,

51. "Unumquodque autem, si perfectione propria careat, in ipsam movetur, quantum in se est: si vero eam habeat, in ipsa quiescit. Finis igitur uniuscuiusque rei est eius perfectio."

does not act in such a way that something is attained by His action, but in such a way that something is enriched by His action. For He is not in potency to the possibility of obtaining something; rather, He is in perfect act simply, and as a result He is a source of enrichment. So, things are not ordered to God as to an end *for which* something may be obtained, but rather so that they may attain Himself from Himself, according to their measure [*sed ut ab ipso ipsummet suo modo consequantur*], since He is their end. (*ScG* III, c. 18, 5)[52]

Since God is in perfect act, nothing can enrich or improve or contribute to his perfection as final end. On the contrary, things are ordered solely to him as their final end so that everything may obtain God from God *suo modo*. This small but decisive qualifier *suo modo* is a crucial anticipation of the role that the *intellectus* plays in obtaining God from God. Yet what can the creature — as creature and without ceasing to be creature — obtain from God but the *divina bonitas,* God's own very goodness according to the measure of the creature's specific nature?

Being — Similar to God

In chapter 19 Thomas introduces the Platonic concept of "similitude." It is, Thomas argues, in virtue of created things *(res creatae)* attaining divine goodness that they are made like unto God. And because everything tends toward God in order to obtain God's goodness, it follows that the ultimate end of all things is to become like God. Again we turn to the argument most relevant for our particular concern. It builds upon the general principle *omne agens agit sibi simile* ("every agent produces its like"). In consequence of this universal metaphysical principle, all created things must be understood as images — in the broadest analogical sense of similitude — of the first agent. Their similitude obtains in virtue of their primary perfection — they exist as participated beings — and especially in virtue of their secondary perfection, by way of which they are ordered to God in or-

---

52. "Oportet quod eo modo effectus tendat in finem quo agens propter finem agit. Deus autem qui est primum agens omnium rerum, non sic agit quasi sua actione aliquid acquirat, sed quasi sua actione aliquid largiatur: quia non est in potentia ut aliquid acquirere possit, sed solum in actu perfecto, ex quo potest elargiri. Res igitur non ordinantur in Deum sicut in finem cui aliquid acquiratur, sed ut ab ipso ipsummet suo modo consequantur, cum ipsemet sit finis."

der to obtain divine goodness and hence attain to the divine likeness according to their measure. We must note at this point again that the concept of *similitudo* is an analogical concept, for similitude is realized according to diverse modalities, which Thomas considers eventually in chapter 22.

In chapters 20 and 21 Thomas analyzes in detail the likeness arising from the secondary perfection, operation:

> So, if each thing tends toward a likeness of divine goodness as its end, and if each thing becomes like the divine goodness in respect of all the things that belong to its proper goodness, then the goodness of the thing consists not only in its mere being, but in all the things needed for its perfection, as we have shown. It is obvious, then, that things are ordered to God as an end, not merely according to their substantial act of being, but also according to those items which are added as pertinent to perfection, and even according to the proper operation which also belongs to the thing's perfection. (*ScG* III, c. 20, 8)[53]

Each thing tends toward being and act which is the same as tending to its perfection and goodness. It is important to realize that with chapter 21 Thomas moves his consideration to the *order of operation*. However, also in this regard, he focuses his enquiry strictly upon the *ontological structure* of such operations as a particular nature actuates them.

> In fact, a created thing tends toward the divine likeness through its operation. Now, through its operation, one thing becomes the cause of another. Therefore, in this way, also, do things tend toward the divine likeness, in that they are the causes of other things. (*ScG* III, c. 21, 2)[54]

The order of proper secondary causality itself reflects God's first causality: things by way of their operation bring forth other things and in that tend to divine likeness.

---

53. "Si autem res quaelibet tendit in divinae bonitatis similitudinem sicut in finem; divinae autem bonitati assimilatur aliquid quantum ad omnia quae ad propriam pertinent bonitatem; bonitas autem rei non solum in esse suo consistit, sed in omnibus aliis quae ad suam perfectionem requiruntur, ut ostensum est: manifestum est quod res ordinantur in Deum sicut in finem non solum secundum esse substantiale, sed etiam secundum ea quae ei accidunt pertinentia ad perfectionem; et etiam secundum propriam operationem, quae etiam pertinet ad perfectionem rei."

54. "Tendit enim in divinam similitudinem res creata per suam operationem. Per suam autem operationem una res fit causa alterius. Ergo in hoc etiam res intendunt divinam similitudinem, ut sint aliis causae."

Intellect and Its Proper Appetite, the Will

In the midst of the seemingly seamless analogical range of predication of agency, Thomas finally in chapter 22 attends to the diverse mediations under which this similitude comes about by way of diverse modes of agency. Again, note that we are not leaving the realm of an enquiry into the general ontological structure of such modalities. In this chapter, Thomas finally introduces the far-reaching fundamental distinction between those agents whose secondary perfection comes about simply by way of their *natures* and those agents whose secondary perfection comes about by way of their *intellect.* It is in natural agents alone that the end is determined by the ontological *appetitus.* For agents endowed with *intellectus,* on the contrary, the end is determined by the *ratio boni,* the intellect's consideration of the good by way of which the good becomes the object of the will. This distinction is most clearly stated in the following passage:

> One kind of operation pertains to a thing as the mover of another, as in the actions of heating and sawing. Another is the operation of a thing that is moved by another, as in the case of being heated or being sawed. Still another operation is the perfection of an actually existing agent which does not tend to produce a change in another thing. And these last differ, first of all, from passion and motion, and secondly from action transitively productive of change in exterior matter. Examples of operations in this third sense are understanding, sensing, and willing. Hence, it is clear that the things which are moved, or passively worked on only, without actively moving or doing anything, tend to the divine likeness by being perfected within themselves; while the things that actively make and move, by virtue of their character, tend toward the divine likeness by being the causes of others. Finally, the things that move as a result of being moved tend toward the divine likeness in both ways. (*ScG* III, c. 22, 2)[55]

---

55. "Nam quaedam operatio est rei ut aliud moventis, sicut calefacere et secare. Quaedam vero est operatio rei ut ab alio motae, sicut calefieri et secari. Quaedam vero operatio est perfectio operantis actu existentis in aliud transmutandum non tendens: quorum primo differunt a passione et motu; secundo vero, ab actione transmutativa exterioris materiae. Huiusmodi autem operatio est sicut intelligere, sentire et velle. Unde manifestum est quod ea quae moventur vel operantur tantum, sine hoc quod moveant vel faciant, tendunt in divinam similitudinem quantum ad hoc quod sint in seipsis perfecta; quae vero faciunt et movent, inquantum huiusmodi, tendunt in divinam similitudinem in hoc quod

Here Thomas intimates the most decisive characteristic of human beings, their capability of intransitive operations, that is, operations that do not affect an external object: understanding, sensing, and willing. The first and the last kind of operation human beings share with angels, the second operation they share with animals, a fact that for Thomas as for the whole classical Christian tradition clearly indicated the precise place of humanity in the hierarchy of being: the highest in the order of beings composite of form and matter and the lowest in the order of spiritual beings. And again, it is according to the formal metaphysical analysis and not under the aspect of the particular instantiation of an operation that Thomas establishes tersely the relationship between intellect and will:

> [T]hings that know their end are always ordered to the good as an end, for the will, which is the *appetite for a foreknown end*, inclines toward something only if it has the rational character of a good, which is its object. (*ScG* III, c. 16, 4; emphasis added)[56]

It seems that for Thomas knowing one's end is a precondition for any thing to be ordered to the good as its end. But did we not learn earlier that things deprived of any knowledge also "act" in view of an end, also tend toward their perfection, toward divine likeness? The possibility to hold both claims together is the very point of the doctrine of divine providence, the consideration of God's perfection as governor and ruler of what he brought into being and continues to hold in being:

> [I]t is also evident that every working of nature is the work of an intelligent substance, because an effect is more fundamentally attributed to the prime mover, which aims at the end, than to the instruments which have been directed by it. And because of this we find that the workings of nature proceed toward their end in an orderly way, as do the actions of a wise man. (*ScG* III, c. 24, 5)[57]

---

sint aliorum causae; quae vero per hoc quod moventur movent, intendunt divinam similitudinem quantum ad utrumque."

56. "Sed ea quae cognoscunt finem, semper ordinantur in bonum sicut in finem: nam voluntas, quae est appetitus finis praecogniti, non tendit in aliquid nisi sub ratione boni, quod est eius obiectum."

57. "Unde etiam patet quod quodlibet opus naturae est opus substantiae intelligentis: nam effectus principalius attribuitur primo moventi dirigenti in finem, quam instrumentis ab eo directis. Et propter hoc operationes naturae inveniuntur ordinate procedere ad finem, sicut operationes sapientis."

The whole universe is the product of an infinite, subsistent *intellectus* in act, and hence ordered to him as *finis ultimus* and *summum bonum*.

> Hence, it becomes obvious that even things which lack knowledge can be made to work for an end, and to seek [*appetere*] the good by a natural appetite [*naturali appetitu*], and to seek the divine likeness and their own perfection. And there is no difference between saying one of these things or the other. For, by the fact that they tend to their own perfection they tend to the good, since a thing is good to the extent that it is perfect. Moreover, by virtue of tending to be good it tends to the divine likeness, for a thing is made like unto God in so far as it is good. (*ScG* III, c. 24, 6)[58]

It is of paramount importance that Thomas states (a) that there is *no* difference between saying that everything seeks the good by way of an *appetitus naturalis,* saying that everything seeks divine likeness, and saying that everything seeks its own perfection; and (b) that everything tends to the divine likeness by virtue of tending to be good. Tending to the divine likeness is the fundamental ontological condition of every created substance.

What then is the difference in tending to divine likeness between, on the one hand, things devoid of knowledge and, on the other hand, intellectual beings? Consider the following argument of St. Thomas:

> It is evident . . . that the more perfect something is in its power, and the higher it is in the scale of goodness, the more does it have an appetite for a broader common good [*tanto appetitum boni communiorem habet*], and the more does it seek and become involved in the doing of good for beings far removed from itself. Indeed, imperfect beings tend only to the good proper to the individual, while perfect beings tend to the good of their species. But more perfect beings tend to the good of the genus, while God, Who is most perfect in goodness, tends toward the good of being as a whole. (*ScG* III, c. 24, 8)[59]

58. "Planum igitur fit quod ea etiam quae cognitione carent, possunt operari propter finem; et appetere bonum naturali appetitu; et appetere divinam similitudinem; et propriam perfectionem. Non est autem differentia sive hoc sive illud dicatur. Nam per hoc quod tendunt in suam perfectionem, tendunt ad bonum: cum unumquodque in tantum bonum sit in quantum est perfectum. Secundum vero quod tendit ad hoc quod sit bonum, tendit in divinam similitudinem: Deo enim assimilatur aliquid inquantum bonum est."

59. "Ex quo patet quod quanto aliquid est perfectioris virtutis, et eminentius in gradu bonitatis, tanto appetitum boni communiorem habet, et magis in distantibus a se bonum

If the power in question is *intellectus,* it seems clear that the natural appetite for the *bonum commune* is categorically higher in angels and humans qua their ontological constitution than in any creature devoid of *intellectus.* Moreover, on the basis of what has been established so far, it seems equally clear that the good has become explicit — that is, known to the *intellectus* in order for it to become the *telos*/end of this agent's proper operation. Contrary to those beings whose perfection comes about simply by their nature and which hence are brought to perfection by entelechy, the intellectual substance needs to understand its proper good in light of the *bonum commune* for it to become its proper end or, differently put, the end of its proper perfection. The will — that is, *the appetite for a foreknown end* — can incline only toward that which is presented by the intellect as a good. Only what the intellect presents — and *a fortiori* is able to present — as a good, does the will incline to.[60] In short, I can only be drawn by my rational appetite, the will, to a good that I first of all understand as a worthwhile end. In order to desire with my rational appetite, that is, in the way proper for me as an intellectual substance, the ultimate end — the end in which my perfection rests — I must understand enough of this ultimate end for it to become the overarching good for my rational appetite. But we are rushing ahead. Before we finally turn to the crucial chapter 25 of book 3 in the *Summa contra Gentiles,* we need to gain a somewhat better sense what Thomas means by *intellectus.* For it is as axiomatic for him as for all theologians of the patristic and medieval period — as it should be for contemporary theologians — that angels and humans share something extraordinary with God that separates them categorically from the rest of creation — *intellectus.*

Intellectus

It might seem — and indeed be — preposterous, in a brief excursus — to attempt an incipient clarification of *intellectus* in Thomas's thought. Be-

---

quaerit et operatur. Nam imperfecta ad solum bonum proprii individui tendunt; perfecta vero ad bonum speciei; perfectiora vero ad bonum generis; Deus autem, qui est perfectissimus in bonitate, ad bonum totius entis."

60. Thomas understands intellect and will as two distinct yet mutually interrelated powers of the soul. The will, as efficient cause, moves the intellect, while the intellect, as final cause, moves the will: that is, the will wills the intellect to understand, while the intellect's understanding offers the will those goods toward which the will then inclines.

cause *intellectus* is utterly central to, if not constitutive of, his metaphysics, we need to limit ourselves to what is most crucial for our present consideration without, however, doing grave injustice to the utter profundity of the vision entailed.[61] Hence, this quite preliminary adumbration of *intellectus* in Thomas takes as its delimiting parameters two fundamental insights. On the one end stands Thomas's insight into the peculiar way the human *intellectus* operates. Because the differentiating characteristic of *intellectus* in the case of human beings is the condition of its essential embodiment, human beings have to advance in knowledge discursively by way of enquiry and discovery. On the other end stands Thomas's insight, rather difficult for us to grasp, that in a certain respect *intellectus* pertains to and encompasses everything that is. But we are rushing ahead. Let us turn to the first of the two parameters.

In order not to get stuck immediately in the deadend of merely lexical variations, we shall simply take note of the fact that when considering the human mind, Thomas is comfortable with the use of various terms to intend the same thing: *mens, ratio,* and *intellectus.* In the *sed contra* of question 79, article 8 of the *Prima Pars,* after quoting from Augustine's literal commentary on Genesis, he states tersely: "Reason, intellect, and mind are one power."[62] In the body of the article, however, he distinguishes between two fundamentally different aspects in the one power of the human mind, two aspects that do not simply reflect a lexical variation, but that indeed represent a substantive differentiation in the constitution of one single power: "[T]o understand is simply to apprehend intelligible truth: and to reason is to advance from one thing understood to another, so as to know an intelligible truth."[63] The difference between these two aspects of the one power is indeed crucial for a proper understanding of how, according to Thomas, human knowing comes about. The latter aspect is the one

---

61. For two remarkably profound attempts to probe the depths of Thomas's thought on "intellectus," see Gustav Siewerth, *Thomismus als Identitätssystem,* 2nd ed. (Frankfurt: Schulte-Bulmke, 1961), and Ferdinand Ulrich, *Homo Abyssus: Das Wagnis der Seinsfrage,* with an introduction by Martin Bieler, 2nd ed. (Freiburg: Johannes Verlag Einsiedeln, 1998).

62. "Ratio . . . et intellectus et mens sunt una potentia" (*ST* I, q. 79, a. 8 sed contra). The citation from Augustine's *De genesi ad litteram* is to be found in book 3, chapter 20: "Illud quo homo irrationabilibus animalibus antecellit, est ratio, vel mens, vel intelligentia, vel si quo alio vocabulo commodius appellatur" (PL 34, 292).

63. "Intelligere enim est simpliciter veritatem intelligibilem apprehendere. Ratiocinari autem est procedere de uno intellecto ad aliud, ad veritatem intelligibilem cognoscendam" (*ST* I, q. 79, a. 8).

that seems intrinsically obvious: Human reasoning is discursive, that is, it advances from one thing to another in order to arrive at the knowledge of intelligible truth. Human reasoning proceeds in the medium of time. The Latin verb *discurrere* denotes this mental movement — discourse as the mind's journey of enquiry and discovery. Thomas uses for it the technical term *ratiocinari*, reasoning. Why does the human intellect operate this way? Human beings qua their embodiment do not receive intelligible truth by way of a perfect, immediate intuition, but by way of what is proper to their essential embodiment, that is, by way of the senses. I must hasten to add, however — lest Thomas be mistakenly identified as a proto-Lockean epistemologist — that according to Thomas, in virtue of the rational soul being the substantial form of the human body, *intellectus* subsists in the human being antecedent to any sense-impressions. As form, *intellectus* activates the principal operation of understanding *(intellectus agens)*, informing the mind by abstracting the forms from the senses' deliverance and thus realizing (reducing from potency to act) specific knowledge *(intellectus possibilis)* that in turn forms the basis for the reasoning process.[64] The principal operation of understanding itself *(intellectus agens)*, however, subsists as a *habitus* of the human soul, as an inventive capacity intrinsic to its nature. It is, to be precise, the *habitus* of all first principles of knowledge, whether theoretical or practical principles, implicitly known in and of themselves, indemonstrable yet indispensable for any discursive knowledge. The source that keeps the *intellectus qua* form unceasingly in act is none but God: "Divina substantia est . . . totius intellectualis cognitionis principium" ("The divine substance is the . . . principle of all intellectual cognition" [*ScG* III, c. 54]). Human understanding is thus always gifted with the intuitive knowledge of first principles — certain things simply understood. From those principles the human being in the process of reasoning must discursively move forward by way of enquiry and discovery, and then in turn analyze these findings scientifically by way of a return to the first principles.

By contrast, angels, as subsistent intellects or separate substances, "who, according to their nature, possess perfect knowledge of intelligible

---

64. For a detailed account of Aristotelian-Thomist epistemology, see Jacques Maritain, *The Degrees of Knowledge*, translated from the fourth French edition under the supervision of Gerald B. Phelan (New York: Charles Scribner's Sons, 1959), pp. 110-35; and more recently the very useful and clear summary in Benedict M. Ashley, O.P., *The Way toward Wisdom: An Interdisciplinary and Intercultural Introduction to Metaphysics* (Notre Dame, IN: University of Notre Dame Press, 2006), pp. 101-14.

truth, have no need to advance from one thing to another; but apprehend the truth simply and without mental discussion."[65] Thomas puts the similarity and difference between angelic intuitive understanding and human discursive reasoning the following way: "Reasoning . . . is compared to understanding, as movement is to rest, or acquisition to possession; of which one belongs to the perfect, the other to the imperfect."[66]

Are we to conclude from this relationship between movement and rest, between the imperfect and the perfect, that since God is universally perfect (as Thomas argues in *ScG* I, c. 29), *intellectus* must first and foremost be identical with God, the subsistent act of being? That this indeed is the case, Thomas argues extensively in chapters 45 and 46 of the first part of the *Summa contra Gentiles,* and summarizes crisply in an important argument about "the supreme and perfect grade of life which is in the intellect, for the intellect reflects upon itself and the intellect can understand itself" (*ScG* IV, c. 11, 5).[67] So, if indeed the perfect grade of life rests in the *intellectus,* what would the ultimate perfection of life be? Here is Thomas's answer:

> The ultimate perfection of life belongs to God, in whom understanding is not other than being, as has been shown [*ScG* I, c. 45]; accordingly, the intention understood in God must be the divine essence itself. Now, I mean by the "intention understood" what the intellect conceives in itself of the thing understood. (*ScG* IV, c. 11, 5-6)[68]

Now we are at the point where we can appreciate that "light" has been the predominant metaphor for *intellectus.* God, pure act at perfect rest, is fully transparent to himself in the single perfect act of comprehension: "in God, because He understands Himself, the intellect, the thing understood, and

---

65. "Et ideo angeli, qui perfecte possident, secundum modum suae naturae, cognitionem intelligibilis veritatis, non habent necesse procedere de uno ad aliud; sed simpliciter et absque discursu veritatem rerum apprehendunt" (*ST* I, q. 79, a. 8).

66. "Patet ergo quod ratiocinari comparatur ad intelligere sicut moveri ad quiescere, vel acquirere ad habere: quorum unum est perfecti, aliud autem imperfecti" (*ST* I, q. 79, a. 8).

67. "Est igitur supremus et perfectus gradus vitae qui est secundum intellectum: nam intellectus in seipsum reflectitur, et seipsum intelligere potest."

68. "Ultima igitur perfectio vitae competit Deo, in quo non est aliud intelligere et aliud esse, ut supra ostensum est, et ita oportet quod intentio intellecta in Deo sit ipsa divina essentia. Dico autem 'intentionem intellectam' id quod intellectus in seipso concipit de re intellecta."

the intention understood are all identical" (*ScG* IV, c. 11, 7)[69] — light from light in light. As creatures, in proportion to our nature, we participate in this divine perfection. Hence, we are able by way of a faint analogical glimpse to surmise what the perfection of *intellectus* must be like, starting from the basic insight that *intellectus* is the power to apprehend intelligible truth. The perfection of *intellectus* must indeed be the identity of the act of understanding with the very act of being: "divinum intelligere est eius esse" ("God's understanding is his being").[70] And precisely this Thomas establishes in book 1, chapter 45 of the *Summa contra Gentiles.* We recall Thomas's argument "that the perfection of the universe required the existence of some intelligent creatures" (*ScG* II, c. 46).[71] For only these are able to return to God by way of their very action, an action that resembles God's own being in act which is understanding.

If such a relationship indeed obtains between the divine perfection of *intellectus* and some created participation in this perfection, the two, divine *intellectus* and created *intellectus,* cannot be absolutely foreign to each other:

> The divine substance is not beyond the capacity of the created intellect in such a way that it is altogether foreign to it, as sound is from the object of vision, or as immaterial substance is from sense power; in fact, the divine substance is the first intelligible object and the principle of all intellectual cognition. But it is beyond the capacity of the created intellect, in the sense that it exceeds its power. (*ScG* III, c. 54, 8)[72]

Here we have reached the point of closest proximity in Thomas's work to the deep Augustinian intuition that fuels Henri de Lubac's vision as well as

---

69. "Cum ergo in Deo sit idem esse et intelligere, intentio intellecta in ipso est ipse eius intellectus."

70. This axiom is the point of departure for Gustav Siewerth's profound speculative essay, *Der Thomismus als Identitätssystem,* a work written with Hegel and Heidegger as primary points of reference for a discussion of Thomas's work. While this might make a contemporary reception less likely, Siewerth's work has lost nothing of its relevance, this side of "analytic Thomism" and "ordinary language philosophy."

71. "Quod oportuit ad perfectionem universi aliquas creaturas intellectuales esse."

72. "Divina enim substantia non sic est extra facultatem creati intellectus quasi aliquid omnino extraneum ab ipso, sicut est sonus a visu, vel substantia immaterialis a sensu, nam divina substantia est primum intelligibile, et totius intellectualis cognitionis principium: sed est extra facultatem intellectus creati sicut excedens virtutem eius, sicut excellentia sensibilium sunt extra facultatem sensus."

his subtle polemic against most Thomism since the early sixteenth century. Let us give expression to this Augustinian intuition by way of a sentence from Augustine himself, from his treatise *De quantitate animae:* "Just as we must acknowledge that the human soul is not what God is, so is it to be set down that among all things that God has created nothing is nearer to God"; it is in fact equal to an angel.[73] If the human soul is to be understood as equal to an angel, would this entail that the human being, similar to an intellectual substance, is *essentially* spirit? Here it is imperative to realize that Thomas does not follow this admittedly attractive, albeit not unproblematic Augustinian inspiration. Rather, he develops his position by drawing upon and by deepening the *prima facie* obvious fact that human beings in respect to the essentially composite nature of their substance are not pure spirits. However, not being a pure spirit could still mean, as de Lubac arguably might press, that the intellectual soul is nevertheless what is *truly* human in the human being. Thomas would not agree with such a qualified insistence either, for even in this modified form such a claim simply disregards the indispensable significance of human embodiment for an accurate grasp of human nature, of which the rational soul undoubtedly is the substantial form. It is the latter fact, human embodiment as integral to the nature of the human soul, that leads Thomas to hold that the human being *essentially* is not only spirit. We find a striking argument for this position hidden away in the disputed questions *De potentia.* The objection is posed that the real human being is the soul:

> The end of man is a perfect assimilation to God. Now seeing that God has no body, the soul without the body is more like God than when

73. Saint Augustine, *De quantitate animae,* c. 34: "[I]ta praesumendum, nihil inter omnia quae creavit, Deo esse propinquius" (St. Augustine, *The Measure of the Soul,* trans. Francis E. Tourscher, O.S.A. [Philadelphia: The Peter Reilly Co.; London: Herder, 1933], p. 206). Regarding the similarity to the angel: "Si quid vero aliud est in rerum natura praeter ista quae sensibus nota sunt, et prorsus quae aliquod spatium loci obtinent, quibus omnibus praestantiorem animam humanam esse diximus: si quid ergo aliud est eorum quae Deus creavit, quiddam est deterius, quiddam par: deterius, ut anima pecoris; *par, ut angeli;* melius autem nihil" ("Whatever therefore is in the nature of things other than these realities that are known by the organs of sense, things which through and through occupy some dimension of space, than which we have said, the human soul is more excellent: — If there is any thing else, therefore, of things that God created, something is less excellent, something equal: less excellent, as the soul of the brute animal, *equal* [by reason of its spiritual substance] *as the angles* [sic]; but nothing more noble [in created nature]" [p. 208; emphasis added]).

united to the body. Therefore in the state of final beatitude the soul will be without the body. (*De Pot.*, q. 5, a. 10, obj. 5)[74]

Thomas responds:

The soul is more like God when united to the body than when separated from it, because its nature is then more perfect. For a thing is like God forasmuch as it is perfect, although God's perfection is not of the same kind as a creature's. (*De Pot.*, q. 5, a. 10, ad 5)[75]

Here, in this crucial claim — crucial for all that follows — we have Thomas's insistence most clearly expressed: intrinsic to the *nature* of the human soul is to be the substantial form of the body. That is, the human soul is essentially ordered to the body such that its nature is perfected in its act of embodiment, of informing the body and thus realizing the human being. Hence, while able to subsist in separation from the body, in such a state the nature of the human soul is severely diminished. Not only is this one of Thomas's strongest arguments for bodily resurrection, it is also one of the clearest reminders that the body is integral to the perfection of the nature of the human intellectual soul. Consequently, while the human *intellectus* is capable of self-knowledge, of grasping universals, and therefore ultimately *capax Dei,* human understanding, while antecedently enabled from within, arises concretely from without. "Without" is the body, the very way by which human beings are integrally part of the material world: "[T]he diversity of man's capacity to perform various acts of the soul arises from the diverse dispositions of the body."[76] By way of the body human beings "suffer" reality and are available to each other and to the world. Consequently, whatever is proportionate to the human intellect's nature in its proper perfection pertains to the intellectual soul as the substantial form of the body. To put it differently, the body does not diminish the perfection of the human soul's nature. It rather is its guarantor. For, as

74. "[F]inis hominis est perfecta assimilatio ad Deum. Sed Deo, qui incorporeus est, magis assimilatur anima corpore absoluta, quam corpori unita. Ergo in illo statu finalis beatitudinis, animae absque corporibus erunt."

75. "[A]nima corpori unita plus assimilatur Deo quam a corpore separata, quia perfectius habet suam naturam. Intantum enim unumquodque Deo simile est, in quantum perfectum est; licet non sit unius modi perfectio Dei et perfectio creaturae."

76. *De memoria,* lect. 1 (St. Thomas Aquinas, *Commentaries on Aristotle's "On Sense and What Is Sensed" and "On Memory and Recollection,"* trans. Kevin White and Edward M. Macierowski [Washington, DC: The Catholic University of America Press, 2005], p. 185).

Thomas puts it in his commentary on Aristotle's *On the Soul*, "The nobility of the soul corresponds to a good bodily constitution, because every form is proportioned to its matter" (II *De Anima*, lect. 19).[77] And here lies the profound difference in the constitution of human beings and angels: both are signified as *intellectualis creatura*, yet categorically different in the way the proper perfection of *intellectus* is realized in each.

Intelligere Deum — finis omnis intellectualis substantiae

Let us now turn to the crucial chapter 25, the heading of which is, "To understand God is the end of every intellectual substance" *(Quod intelligere Deum est finis omnis intellectualis substantiae).*

(1) It is of paramount importance to note the concept designating the particular kinds of agents under discussion here: *intellectualis substantia* or *intellectualis creatura*. The context is that of a primarily metaphysical enquiry into the very structure of divine providence: the ordering of every created substance, proper to its nature, to God as its ultimate end. The overarching category under consideration in book 3 is created substances, and in chapter 25 Thomas focuses on one particular and in some ways unique subset of created substances: the intellectual substances, angels and humans. Angels and humans, as just discussed, are unique in the universe in that they share something extraordinary with the Creator of the universe that separates them categorically from the rest of creation — *intellectus*. Hence, pertaining to the primary perfection, the perfection of nature, the metaphysical analysis of the last end does not differ for intellectual substances that subsist separately (i.e., as nonmaterial subsistent forms [angels]) and those that subsist as composites of form and matter (i.e., human beings). The conclusion to which Thomas's eight arguments in chapter 25 converge is that for every intellectual substance, be it angel or human, the ultimate end is to understand God. We will, however, see later that it matters greatly for Thomas that the gift of the intellect operates in fundamentally different ways for angels and for humans. And it is precisely this difference, in the order of secondary perfection (operation), we shall see, that matters for grasping the difference in the way the natural desire for the vision of God comes to play in angels and in humans.

---

77. "Ad bonam autem complexionem corporis sequitur nobilitas animae: quia omnis forma est proportionata suae materiae" (Marietti edn., #485).

Here is Thomas's opening thesis:

> Since all creatures, even those devoid of understanding, are ordered to God as to an ultimate end, all achieve this end to the extent that they participate somewhat in His likeness. Intellectual creatures attain it in a more special way, that is, through their proper operation of understanding Him. Hence, this must be the end of the intellectual creature, namely to understand God. (*ScG* III, c. 25, 1)[78]

In unfolding his argument, Thomas reminds his readers first of one fundamental axiom of divine providence informing the very structure of participated beings: "[E]ach thing intends, as its ultimate end, to be united with God as closely as is possible for it" (*ScG* III, c. 25, 2).[79] As said above, material participated beings, which were primarily under consideration until this chapter, attain God by way of realizing their own proper perfection — which represents a distant similitude of the *summum bonum*. Now, quite obviously, the ultimate end each thing intends is achieved to a greater degree if something attains to God's very essence in some manner. The latter is accomplished when one knows something of the divine substance. For "knowing" or "understanding" is to attain the object itself, because "understanding is becoming the other intentionally in its property as other."[80] By way of the concept — the object's form abstracted by the agent intellect — one comes to know the thing itself. Because of this very ontological structure of knowledge, it constitutes a more perfect form of union with God. For "understanding" does not proffer a distant and mediated similitude of the known to the knower. Rather, by way of knowledge, an immediate presence occurs of the known to the knower. Cottier, drawing on Sylvester of Ferrara's commentary on the *Summa contra Gentiles*, felicitously names the distinction Thomas makes here as that between a *via assimilationis* and an infinitely superior *via cognitionis*.[81] "Therefore, an intellectual substance tends to divine knowledge as an ultimate end" (*ScG*

---

78. "[C]um autem omnes creaturae, etiam intellectu carentes, ordinentur in Deum sicut in finem ultimum; ad hunc autem finem pertingunt omnia inquantum de similitudine eius aliquid participant: intellectuales creaturae aliquo specialiori modo ad ipsum pertingunt, scilicet per propriam operationem intelligendo ipsum. Unde oportet quod hoc sit finis intellectualis creaturae, scilicet intelligere Deum."

79. "Intendit igitur unumquodque sicut ultimo fini Deo coniungi quanto magis sibi possibile est."

80. Cottier, *Le désir de Dieu*, p. 198.

81. Cottier, *Le désir de Dieu*, p. 198.

III, c. 25, 2).[82] The intellectual substance attains its ultimate end by way of knowledge. Why so and how so, exactly?

(2) In order to demonstrate how precisely the intellectual substance attains its ultimate end, Thomas turns from a consideration of the order of being (*ScG* III, c. 25, 2) to a consideration of the order of operation (*ScG* III, c. 25, 3). As he had argued earlier, since the proper operation of every thing is its secondary perfection, proper operation is a genuine end for every created substance. And because the act of understanding *(intelligere)* is the proper operation of an intellectual substance, this act is its proper end. Since every operation is specified by its object, operations of *intelligere* are specified by their objects through which these operations are known, and the more perfect the object, the more perfect the operation. In other words, the perfection of the operation of *intelligere* depends completely on the perfection of the object understood. Consequently, to understand the most perfect intelligible object, God must be the most perfect thing in the genus of the operation of understanding; hence it is the ultimate end of that being whose proper operation is *intelligere.* Consequently — and utterly counterintuitive to the present pervasive preference for reductively materialist and quantitatively measurable forms of knowledge tending to ends of a more or less Epicurean kind — for Thomas, the most imperfect knowledge of God is infinitely more valuable than the most comprehensive knowledge of comparatively imperfect things, be they quarks, genes, and galaxies, or combustion engines, computer chips, and cosmetic surgery. In short, Thomas's evaluation reflects that mode of the human being as perfected by wisdom *(sapientia),* and hence characteristic of the *homo sapiens,* while the contemporary reductively materialist view is more reflective of what the ancients and, for that matter Thomas too, would have described as the way of thinking characteristic of the *homo insipiens.* For "dixit insipiens in corde suo non est Deus [Vulgate]" ("The fool says in his heart, 'There is no God'" [Ps 14:1 (RSV)]). And precisely because his metaphysical analysis remains properly restricted to the ontological structure, Thomas does not refer in this place to the absolutely most perfect understanding of God, the *scientia Dei et beatorum* of questions 1 and 12 of the *Prima Pars* of the *Summa theologiae* — which is essentially supernatural — but only to the structurally or formally most perfect understanding of God that is entailed in the formal characteristics of the *substantia intellectualis.*

---

82. "Substantia igitur intellectualis tendit in divinam cognitionem sicut in ultimum finem."

(3) Unsurprisingly, Thomas focuses next on the structure of cognition and understanding, the process of *admiratio* that culminates in first philosophy or *scientia divina*, the natural theology that constitutes the acme of metaphysical enquiry (*ScG* III, c. 25, 6-9 and the preparation for 11).[83] And understanding elicited by cognition is indeed the sole and proper way by which intellectual substances — angels as well as humans — tend to God. Thomas offers the following argument:

> [A] thing has the greatest desire for its ultimate end. Now, the human intellect has a greater desire, and love, and pleasure, in knowing divine matters than it has in the perfect knowledge of the lowest things, even though it can grasp but little concerning divine things. So, the ultimate end of man is to understand God, in some fashion [*quoquo modo*]. (*ScG* III, c. 25, 7)[84]

If read in isolation from its context, one could easily mistake this statement for an empirical observation from which Thomas draws an inference. The discursive context of this argument, however, makes it plain that this is not the case. The opening sentence lays down a comprehensive metaphysical principle pertaining to every created thing. The subsequent sentence continues a strictly metaphysical analysis of the ontological structure of the intellect, as derived from the earlier analysis. It does not describe the *de*

---

83. See Ralph McInerny, *Praeambula Fidei: Thomism and the God of the Philosophers* (Washington, DC: The Catholic University of America Press, 2006), for a compelling reconstruction of that metaphysical enquiry to which natural theology is the indispensable completion, and see Ashley, *The Way toward Wisdom,* for an outstanding, nuanced instantiation of such metaphysical enquiry of the *ens commune* — of which a consideration of the essence of the first cause is emphatically *not* an integral part (an essential difference between Thomist metaphysics on the one hand, and Scotist and Suarezian metaphysics on the other hand), but rather the goal of the metaphysical enquiry as such, a goal at best ever to be approximated. Thomas not only never questioned the validity of such a metaphysical enquiry, he rather assumed and practiced it in the context of his overall theological project. Eclipsing this element of his thought might make Thomas more palpable to the postmetaphysical presuppositions regnant among many contemporary theologians and philosophers, but will simply complicate and in the end prevent an accurate understanding of his complex integration of metaphysical enquiry into the superior wisdom of *sacra doctrina.*

84. "Unumquodque maxime desiderat suum finem ultimum. Intellectus autem humanus magis desiderat, et amat, et delectatur in cognitione divinorum, quamvis modicum quidem de illis percipere possit, quam in perfecta cognitione quam habet de rebus infimis. Est igitur ultimus finis hominis intelligere quoquo modo Deum."

facto operation of the human being *sub conditione peccati,* nor for that matter *in statu iustitiae originalis* or *in statu gratiae,* but the relative principle of human nature and the ontological structure of the most perfect operation proper to it as an intellectual nature.

In knowing only a little of divine matters the human intellect comes to a greater perfection — that is, it realizes its own proper end — than knowing a lot about the material world. Hence this kind of knowledge, however fragmentary, is desired more, due to the nature of the intellect itself. However, we must note the decisive qualification *quoquo modo* at the end of the above quotation, for the argument itself delivers nothing regarding the question of the mode of this operation. The conclusion at this point is that the final end of the human is the knowledge of God, attained in whatever mode, even the most imperfect. We need to return to the qualification *quoquo modo* when we consider again the natural desire in detail. We have here, however, a first inkling that this qualification refers to the way the structure of the intellect is actualized in the very order of knowledge, the end of which is the *scientia divina* of first philosophy (metaphysics).

Here is Thomas's argument in a nutshell. First comes the general principle: everything that is desirable for the sake of something else exists for something that is desirable in and of itself. Why so? Because, if the working of the appetite of nature *(appetitus naturae)* were to go on interminably, then the desire of nature *(desiderium naturae)* would be frustrated, for it is impossible to traverse infinity.

Now Thomas applies this principle to the order of knowledge. The practical sciences as well as the arts (including what we would call engineering and technology) are not directed toward knowledge, but toward operation, and hence they are means to an end, desired for the sake of something else. Only the speculative sciences are desirable in and of themselves, because their end is knowledge itself. Every human activity is ordered toward some other end with the exception of theoretical contemplation *(consideratio speculativa)*. As all practical sciences and arts are ordered toward the theoretical ones, so are all human activities ordered toward the theoretical contemplation of the intellect *(ad speculationem intellectus)*. And as all sciences and arts, ordered in such a way, have their end in that particular one which provides the ordering measure and rule for them *(praeceptiva et architectonica)*, all the theoretical sciences relate in a similar way to metaphysics *(philosophia prima)*, for the latter provides all the principles for the former. However,

[t]his first philosophy is wholly ordered to the knowing of God, as its ultimate end; that is why it is also called *divine science*. So, divine knowledge is the ultimate end of every act of human knowledge and every operation. (*ScG* III, c. 25, 9)[85]

Here, we receive a first commentary on the qualification *quoquo modo*. One way the knowledge of God is attained is by way of the operations of "first philosophy" which contemplates the first cause. The contemplation of the highest cause is the concrete terminus of the secondary perfection of the human intellect. This terminus is the condition for the possibility of a coherent architecture of the sciences and hence the order of human knowledge. Such a terminus and the structural possibility of attaining it is the condition for the desire of nature *(desiderium naturae)* to tend toward its fulfillment by way of the appetite of nature *(appetitus naturae)*, realized most eminently in the will, the rational appetite as it moves the intellect to its proper good and hence perfection in contemplating the most excellent object, the first cause.

However, as Thomas reminds us (*ScG* III, c. 25, 10), the absolutely superior mover is not the will, but rather the intellect, for the intellect moves the appetite by presenting it with its object. (It is only because embodied human thinking, also speculative contemplation, is discursive, and not intuitive, i.e., takes place by way of a discursive, temporal "procedere" that is vulnerable to exhaustion, distraction, and distortion, that the will is of importance in relationship to the intellect's proper operation.)

(4) There obtains a proper correspondence between the order of agents and movers and the order of ends, such that the end of the first agent and mover is the final end of all intermediate agents and movers. Thomas applies this general metaphysical principle to the human intellect:

[O]f all the parts of man, the intellect is found to be the superior mover, for the intellect moves the appetite, by presenting it with its object; then the intellectual appetite, that is the will, moves the sensory appetites, irascible and concupiscible, and that is why we do not obey concupiscence unless there be a command from the will; and finally, the sense appetite, with the advent of consent from the will, now moves the body. Therefore, the end of the intellect is the end of all human actions. 'But the end and good of the intellect are the true' [Aris-

85. "[I]psaque prima philosophia tota ordinatur ad Dei cognitionem sicut ad ultimum finem, unde et 'scientia divina' nominatur [*Met.* I 2]. Est ergo cognitio divina finis ultimus omnis humanae cognitionis et operationis."

totle, *Nicomachean Ethics,* VI, 2 (1139a 27)]; consequently, the first truth is the ultimate end. So, the ultimate end of the whole man, and of all his operations and desires, is to know the first truth, which is God. (*ScG* III, c. 25, 10)[86]

Cognoscere primum verum, to know the first truth, is the ultimate end of the human being and all his operations and desires *(omnium operationum et desideriorum eius).*[87] Again, it is noteworthy that Thomas makes reference only to all desires of the human being in their ontological structure, converging to one final end, the knowledge of the first truth. One of these desires, the *desiderium cognoscendi causam,* stands at the core of the next argument: "Besides, there is naturally present in all men the desire to know the causes of whatever things are observed" (*ScG* III, c. 25, 11).[88]

A natural reaction of *admiratio,* wonder, gives rise to increasingly disciplined and methodologically reflective philosophical enquiry. This quest is a movement that receives its élan from a natural desire elicited by the encounter with something[89] and that finds its rest or terminus in the contemplation of the cause of that thing — by way of which contemplation the thing itself is more perfectly understood. In principle, but only rarely in

86. "Inter omnes autem hominis partes, intellectus invenitur superior motor: nam intellectus movet appetitum, proponendo ei suum obiectum; appetitus autem intellectivus, qui est voluntas, movet appetitus sensitivos, qui sunt irascibiles et concupiscibiles, unde et concupiscentiae non obedimus nisi voluntatis imperium adsit; appetitus autem sensitivus, adveniente consensu voluntatis, movet iam corpus. Finis igitur intellectus est finis omnium actionum humanarum. Finis autem et bonum intellectus est verum [*Eth.* VI 2]: et per consequens ultimus finis primum verum. Est igitur ultimus finis totius hominis, et omnium operationum et desideriorum eius, cognoscere primum verum, quod est Deus."

87. The point needs to be pressed that *ScG* III, c. 25, 10 and 25, 11 must be seen in their specific order. *ScG* III, c. 25, 10 is the superior end, but can only be reached by way of 25, 11, because the human being is not an angel. At this point the specific constitution of the human soul as substantial form of the body as well as the way human knowledge comes about, needs to be taken fully into account. For such an account, see most recently Ashley, *The Way toward Wisdom,* pp. 101-14.

88. "Naturaliter inest omnibus hominibus desiderium cognoscendi causas eorum quae videntur."

89. Ashley puts the matter as succinctly as one can in two sentences: "We must begin our knowledge of all being with *ens mobile,* sensible being, as the only 'Being' that we can sense and thus know intellectually. But from that starting point, by observing the order of the sciences we can widen our understanding of beings, even until our notion of 'Being' analogically includes all created being, and through that, as the work of God, we get some idea of God as First Cause" (Ashley, *The Way toward Wisdom,* p. 63).

fact, this quest does not stop until the first cause is reached. The natural desire to know the causes arises from the very ontological structure of the intellect itself, for it is precisely knowing the causes that is the operation that perfects the intellect. Thomas extends this argument to the order of causes:

> [F]or each effect that he knows, man naturally desires to know the cause. Now, the human intellect knows universal being [*ens universale*]. So, he naturally desires to know its cause, which is God alone, as we proved in Book Two. Now, a person has not attained his ultimate end until natural desire comes to rest. Therefore, for human happiness which is the ultimate end it is not enough to have merely any kind of intelligible knowledge; there must be divine knowledge, as an ultimate end, to terminate the natural desire. So, the ultimate end of man is the knowledge of God. (*ScG* III, c. 25, 12)[90]

Thomas is not really arguing anything new here; rather, he is in a subtle way intensifying the previous arguments in an ascending line from the knowledge of the first truth to the knowledge of the first cause to the knowledge itself of God: *ipsa Dei cognitio*. Note however that *ipsa Dei cognitio*, the knowledge itself of God, is not to be confused with the knowledge of God himself, *cognitio Dei ipsius*, the latter being nothing but the beatific vision, the eternal participation of the blessed in the life of the Holy Trinity. The *ipsa Dei cognitio*, on the contrary, is the proper ultimate end of every created *intellectus*, the very knowledge of the essence of the first cause: "Omnis intellectus naturaliter desiderat divinae substantiae visionem" ("Every intellect naturally desires the vision of the divine substance" [*ScG* III, c. 57, 4]). However, for the created intellect a natural knowledge of the essence of the first cause independent from any created effects remains essentially unattainable. Hence the *felicitas* sought by way of metaphysical contemplation must necessarily remain incomplete. Nevertheless, it is the ontological structure of the created intellect in the first place that renders intelligible the ultimate significance of the Christian economy of salvation and its promise of perfect beatitude. Not only will

---

90. "Cuiuslibet effectus cogniti naturaliter homo scire causam desiderat. Intellectus autem humanus cognoscit ens universale. Desiderat igitur naturaliter cognoscere causam eius, quae solum Deus est, ut in Secundo probatum est. Non est autem aliquis assecutus finem ultimum quousque naturale desiderium quiescat. Non sufficit igitur ad felicitatem humanam, quae est ultimus finis, qualiscumque intelligibilis cognitio, nisi divina cognitio adsit, quae terminat naturale desiderium sicut ultimus finis. Est igitur ultimus finis hominis ipsa Dei cognitio."

the essence of God be known by the created intellect, but God will also make himself known to the intellect and thereby grant by way of friendship a created participation in his own triune life.

The natural desire to know the cause aims at *ipsa Dei cognitio* as its proper terminus. Again, we learn nothing here about the mode of this cognition. But then again, as in the earlier arguments the axiomatic assumption is that the *desiderium naturale* arises from the structure of the intellect itself in the encounter with the reality for which it is made. In other words, the *desiderium naturale* is not ontologically prior to the structure of the human intellect. Rather, it is its very entailment and arises simultaneously with the intellect's encounter with reality. An analysis of the precise modes of the intellect's operation in regard to the knowledge of God lies beyond the confines of chapter 25.

(5) Thomas, however, prepares the transition to this inquiry by introducing the notion of happiness or felicity:

> Now, the ultimate end of man, and of every intellectual substance, is called felicity or happiness, because this is what every intellectual substance desires as an ultimate end, and for its own sake alone. (*ScG* III, c. 25, 14)[91]

The chapter ends with the fascinating juxtaposition of the Evangelists Matthew and John on the one hand and Aristotle on the other:

> And so, it is said in Matthew (5:8): "Blessed are the clean of heart, for they shall see God"; and John (17:3): "This is eternal life, that they may know Thee, the only true God." (*ScG* III, c. 25, 15)[92]

> With this view, the judgment of Aristotle is also in agreement, in the last Book of his *Ethics,* where he says that the ultimate felicity of man is "speculative, in accord with the contemplation of the best object of speculation" [*Nicomachean Ethics,* X, 7 (1177a 18)]. (*ScG* III, c. 25, 16)[93]

---

91. "Ultimus autem finis hominis, et cuiuslibet intellectualis substantiae, *felicitas* sive *beatitudo* nominatur: hoc enim est quod omnis substantia intellectualis desiderat tanquam ultimum finem, et propter se tantum."

92. "Hinc est quod dicitur Matth. V: 'Beati mundo corde, quoniam ipsi Deum videbunt.' Et Ioan. XVII: 'Haec est vita aeterna, ut cognoscant te, Deum verum.'"

93. "Huic etiam sententiae Aristoteles, in ultimo *Ethicorum* [c. 7], concordat, ubi ultimam hominis felicitatem dicit esse speculativam, quantum ad speculationem optimi speculabilis."

While the proper term for the end which Matthew and John have in view is beatitude, Thomas neverthess uses *felicitas* in order to correlate Aristotle, at least in a preliminary way, to the two Evangelists. The reason Thomas prefers *felicitas* to *beatitudo* is arguably that he regards as a considerable part of his audience for the *Summa contra Gentiles* philosophers — that is, those who would agree with Aristotle, the Neoplatonic tradition and its Aristotelian commentaries, their reception in the Arabic tradition by Avicenna, Averroës, and others, and also with Maimonides, but would not accept the witness of the New Testament about the Son of God. Because of an explicitly assumed theological audience in the *Summa theologiae,* Thomas privileges there the term *beatitudo.*

There is, however, a deeper reason why Thomas correlates Aristotle's notion of the highest human felicity to the Christian notion of beatitude. He expresses this deeper reason at the beginning of the *Summa contra Gentiles,* where he states that "in so far as a man gives himself to the pursuit of wisdom, so far does he even now have some share in true beatitude" (*ScG* I, c. 2, 1),[94] and later more explicitly in the *Summa theologiae,* where he avers that "the consideration of speculative sciences is a certain participation of true and perfect happiness [*beatitudo*]."[95] Te Velde interprets Thomas's subtle reception of the Aristotelian *felicitas* succinctly:

> In Thomas' view the Aristotelian *felicitas* essentially retains an open and dynamic character as aiming at the perfect knowledge of the divine insofar as is possible through the speculative sciences. . . . The differentiation in happiness must . . . not be understood in the sense of their representing two wholly different kinds of happiness. They are related to each other in terms of imperfect and perfect; the happiness of philosophical contemplation shows a certain likeness with true happiness; seen from a Christian standpoint philosophical happiness points beyond itself to a more perfect happiness, to an adequate fulfilment of what the philosophical search for wisdom is aiming at.[96]

94. "[I]nquantum homo sapientiae studium dat, intantum verae beatitudinis iam aliquam partem habet."

95. *ST* I-II, q. 3, a. 6: "[C]onsideratio scientiarum speculativarum est quaedam participatio verae et perfectae beatitudinis."

96. Te Velde, *Aquinas on God,* p. 160.

Thomas's oblique correlation (in *ScG* III, c. 25, 14) of the acme of philosophical contemplation with the term of the Christian pilgrimage in the beatific vision is a telling reminder that in his metaphysical analysis of the ontological structure of the *intellectualis substantia* he is not interested in analyzing the concrete modes of elicitation, which differentiate the structurally one *desiderium naturale visionis Dei* de facto into two different desires — one elicited by way of creation's trace of the causes, leading philosophical *admiratio* to the contemplation of the first cause, with a *desiderium naturae* for happiness directed to the *bonum communi;* the other elicited by way of sanctifying grace with a *desiderium gratiae* for heavenly glory. As soon as he has to address explicitly the question of the ultimate human perfection, he does not shy away from using the proper theological term for this specific perfection *(beatitudo),* nor does he shy away from pointing to the necessity of the divine help *(auxilium)* of grace in order for human beings to attain this ultimate perfection, as plainly expressed in the title of chapter 147 of book 3 of the *Summa contra Gentiles:* "Quod homo indiget divino auxilio ad beatitudinem consequendam" ("That the human being needs divine help to attain beatitude"). Here in chapter 25 of the same book, by contrast, Thomas is principally concerned with the underlying ontological structure, the principle of nature in its own relative integrity. "Relative integrity" signifies here that human nature is not per se in act. Only particular human beings exist in the concrete order of providence in specific states; they do so, however, in virtue of one shared nature from which all acts characteristic of being human flow. Moreover, the principle of nature accounts for the gratuity of the concretely extant order of providence as it coincides with the economy of salvation. For the principle of nature allows one to affirm divine transcendent freedom: it is solely in virtue of divine *convenientia* and not due to any exigencies that might arise from human nature itself that the extant order of providence coincides with the economy of salvation. Furthermore, only by way of the relative integrity of the principle of nature is it possible to grasp the continuity of the identity of nature across various states of human nature in the economy of salvation.

II. The Desire for God: Sic et Non — Marie-Joseph Le Guillou's Response to Henri de Lubac's *Surnaturel*

> *S. Thomas est très maître de sa pensée et de son vocabulaire: il affirme le désir naturel de voir Dieu; il affirme aussi nettement —*

et selon nous, sans moindre contradiction — que l'esprit n'est pas effectivement proportionné à voir Dieu.[97]

Marie-Joseph Le Guillou (1920-90), a Dominican theologian from the Province of Paris, produced what is an unjustly forgotten, astute engagement of de Lubac's *Surnaturel*. Only Georges Cottier and Henry Donneaud have saved his remarkably nuanced and constructive Thomistic response to de Lubac's challenge from the fate of oblivion.[98] Le Guillou's engagement of *Surnaturel* rests on three principal points: (1) Unlike not a few other Thomist respondents, he readily recognizes a crucial insight that de Lubac rightly presses — the absolutely unique case of the created spirit, its fundamental ontological orientation toward God and hence its natural desire for the vision of God. (2) However, Le Guillou demonstrates convincingly that Thomas simultaneously maintains that the created spirit is not effectively proportioned for the vision of God and hence the positive supernatural character of the divine gift must be affirmed under all circumstances. These two truths neither contradict each other nor are they to be reconciled with each other by way of some notional or objective dialectic. Rather, according to Thomas, they are two complementary truths about the created spirit, the first being the result of a *metaphysical* enquiry into the ontological structure of the created spirit, the second the result of a *theological* enquiry into the concrete operations necessary for the beatific vision to occur, a discussion ultimately completed only in the *Summa theologiae* in the treatises on grace and the infused supernatural virtues of faith, hope, and love, as well as the gifts of the Holy Spirit. (3) Le Guillou rightly insists on the need to safeguard the proper integrity of the respective created natures. Consequently, he defends the position that the nonrealization of the transcendent end, the beatific vision, does not mutilate human nature, because the resources to reach this end simply do not belong to the nature itself.

97. Marie-Joseph Le Guillou, O.P., "Surnaturel," *Revue des sciences philosophiques et théologiques* 34 (1950): 226-43, at p. 234: "St. Thomas is very much master of his thought and of his terminology: he affirms the natural desire to see God; he also affirms straightforwardly — and in our mind without the slightest contradiction — that the [created] spirit is not *effectively* proportioned to see God."

98. See Cottier, *Le désir de Dieu*, pp. 228-32, and Henry Donneaud, O.P., "*Surnaturel* through the Fine-Tooth Comb of Traditional Thomism," in Bonino, ed., *Surnaturel*, pp. 41-57, at 51ff.

A Natural Desire for the Supernatural — Properly Speaking?

Le Guillou's remarkable essay might best be understood as a perspicacious engagement and refutation of the previously mentioned thesis forwarded by de Lubac in *Surnaturel:* "'Natural desire for the supernatural': most theologians who reject this formula, reject together with it the very doctrine of St. Thomas Aquinas."[99] Le Guillou argues that while Thomas indeed held the natural desire for the vision of God, this affirmation is fundamentally different from, albeit essentially related to, the desire for the supernatural, a desire elicited by the supernatural virtue of hope. The latter desire is fundamentally different because it is supernaturally elicited; however, it is essentially related to the natural desire, because it is that very natural desire (conditional by nature) that is presupposed as well as perfected by the supernaturally elicited desire. Thus Le Guillou will show that rejecting the formula "natural desire for the supernatural" in its precise sense does not entail a rejection of Thomas's teaching at all. On the contrary, on the basis of Thomas's teaching this formula must be rejected.

The Historical Context of Thomas's Argument: The Conviction That the Immediate Vision of God Is Impossible

Before anything else, Le Guillou puts great emphasis on the importance of recalling the historical context in which the problem of the natural desire for the vision of God arises for Thomas.[100] His insistence upon a natural desire for the vision of God constitutes his considered response to the strong contestation of the very possibility of any immediate vision of God by two quite different intellectual strands, both exercising a subtle influence on the thought of the day.

The first is a strand of Greek Christian apophaticism, mediated into the Western medieval debate by Scotus Eriugena, for whom the impossibility of the immediate vision of God does not constitute a problem, because for him the supposition suffices that an unfulfilled desire eternally links the beatified spirit to the invisible cause.[101] The second is a strand of

---

99. "'Désir naturel du surnaturel'" (De Lubac, *Surnaturel,* p. 431).

100. Le Guillou, "Surnaturel," p. 228.

101. Thomas handles this aspect of the question in a magisterial way in *ST* I, q. 12, where the *desiderium naturale* indeed figures prominently.

Neoplatonism inherited by Arabic philosophers who deny the very possibility of the immediate vision of God by the human being and instead propose that human felicity is attained by way of the contemplation of separate substances (angels) — that is, beings higher in the hierarchy of being than humans but lower than God. Only these separate substances would, according to this position, be capable of an immediate vision of the One.[102]

The philosophical contestation of the very possibility of an immediate vision of God constitutes the concrete discursive context of Thomas's argument for a *desiderium naturale*. The point of Thomas's whole line of argumentation is to establish, by way of arguments acceptable to the philosophical disputants, the suitability between the nature of the human spirit and its supernatural destiny. Le Guillou argues convincingly that the theologian Thomas, who knows by divine revelation that we are destined for a perfect beatitude, the immediate vision of God, intends to show by arguments of reason why such a perfect beatitude, though infinitely surpassing human nature, lies in direct line with its fulfillment. As we have seen above, the universal metaphysical principle from which Thomas develops such a philosophical argument in book 3 of the *Summa contra Gentiles* is the following: the ultimate perfection of each being consists in its unification with the principle or cause of its being.

Thomas, by applying this principle to the *creatura intellectualis,* develops the proper and immediate principles of the rational soul. He does so by embarking upon a metaphysical analysis of the structure proper to the *anima rationalis* in which he draws equally on the Augustinian *inquietum cor* and the Aristotelian and Arabic desire to know the essence of a thing *(quid est)*. Not only does this analysis allow him to lay bare the fundamental orientation of the created spirit toward the intellection of the divine essence;[103] more importantly, it allows him to demonstrate (in *ScG* III) the concrete possibility of the vision of God against its impossibility (Greek apophaticism) and against the failure of Arabic Neoplatonism to recognize its true meaning. And while Thomas does rely on the Augustinian tradition, which is so sensitive to an élan that "carries" the human being, so to speak, to the vision, Le Guillou rightly stresses that Thomas quite intentionally avoids the claim of that tradition that one may ascertain naturally and experientially such a call to the vision of God. Le Guillou help-

---

102. Thomas engages and refutes this position explicitly in *ScG* III, cc. 41-44.
103. Le Guillou, "Surnaturel," p. 229.

fully points out that, contrary to the sweeping Augustinian claim of a *natural desire for the supernatural,* Thomas remains more modest and restrained in his interest of proffering and defending solely a structural metaphysical analysis of a natural desire as it pertains to the respective principles of human and angelic nature in their proper relative integrity.

What Is a Desire?

In order to gain a deeper sense of the nature of *desiderium* according to Thomas, Le Guillou recalls Thomas's analysis of the passions:

> Properly speaking, desire may be not only in the lower, but also in the higher appetite. For it does not imply fellowship in craving, as concupiscence does; but simply movement towards the thing desired. (*ST* I-II, q. 30, a. 1, ad 2)[104]

Here we finally are offered a crisp definition of *desiderium:* "simplex motus in rem desideratam." Desire denotes the spontaneous reaction of the lower as well as the higher appetite to the apperception of a good, that is, the tendency toward a good that is inchoately understood and loved, yet not possessed. Unlike hope *(spes),* which regards something in the future that is "arduous and difficult to obtain," "desire . . . regards the future good absolutely."[105] For Thomas, desire is, so to speak, a distance covered by the rational appetite, the will, anterior to the intellect's consideration of the possibilities of its realization. The desire is an inchoate movement that be-

---

104. "[D]esiderium magis pertinere potest, proprie loquendo, non solum ad inferiorem appetitum, sed etiam ad superiorem. Non enim importat aliquam consociationem in cupiendo, sicut concupiscentia; sed simplicem motum in rem desideratam." See Le Guillou, "Surnaturel," p. 229, n. 4.

105. *ST* I-II, q. 40, a. 1: "Secundo, ut sit futurum: non enim spes est de praesenti iam habito. Et per hoc differt spes a gaudio, quod est de bono praesenti. — Tertio, requiritur quod sit aliquid arduum cum difficultate adipiscibile: non enim aliquis dicitur aliquid sperare minimum, quod statim est in sua potestate ut habeat. Et per hoc differt spes a desiderio vel cupiditate, quae est de bono futuro absolute" ("Secondly, that it is future; for hope does not regard that which is present and already possessed: in this respect, hope differs from joy which regards a present good. — Thirdly, that it must be something arduous and difficult to obtain, for we do not speak of any one hoping for trifles, which are in one's power to have at any time: in this respect, hope differs from desire or cupidity, which regards the future good absolutely").

comes one of a firm consistency only if there is for it the possibility of realization. Hence hope, which always presupposes desire, is an essential component of such a firmly consistent movement of the will, for hope considers the possibilities and difficulties of gaining the desired good.[106] To put it differently, while *desiderium* is a simple motion that belongs inherently to the nature of the created spirit and the principal operation of the rational appetite, *spes* belongs essentially to the embodied human existence in the extant order of providence as it coincides with the economy of salvation. For *spes* has to tackle the profound difficulties that arise from the loss of original righteousness. Consider Thomas's discussion of the twofold difficulty hope has to attend to:

> A thing is *difficult* which is beyond a power; and this happens in two ways. First of all, because it is beyond the natural capacity of the power. Thus, if it can be attained by some help, it is said to be *difficult;* but if it can in no way be attained, then it is *impossible;* thus it is impossible for a man to fly. In another way a thing may be beyond the power, not according to the natural order of such power, but owing to some intervening hindrance. . . . To be turned to his ultimate beatitude is difficult for man, both because it is beyond his nature, and because he has a hindrance from the corruption of the body and the infection of sin. (*ST* I, q. 62, a. 2, ad 2)[107]

Note that the *desiderium naturale* per se contributes effectively nothing besides providing the fundamental structural openness of the *intellectus* as well as the natural precondition of the simple motion to being turned to ultimate beatitude *(converti ad beatitudinem ultimam)*. The concrete possibility of realizing the ultimate end, the enjoyment of God, is de facto only opened by, and indeed occurs inchoately in, the gift of divine

---

106. *ST* I-II, q. 40, a. 1: "Quarto, quod illud arduum sit possibile adipisci: non enim aliquis sperat id quod omnino adipisci non potest. Et secundum hoc differt spes a desperatione" ("Fourthly, that this difficult thing is something possible to attain: for one does not hope for that which one cannot get at all: and, in this respect, hope differs from despair").

107. "*[D]ifficile* est quod transcendit potentiam. Sed hoc contingit esse dupliciter. Uno modo, quia transcendit potentiam secundum suum naturalem ordinem. Et tunc, si ad hoc possit pervenire aliquo auxilio, dicitur *difficile;* si autem nullo modo, dicitur *impossibile*, sicut impossibile est hominem volare. Alio modo transcendit aliquid potentiam, non secundum ordinem naturalem potentiae, sed propter aliquod impedimentum potentiae adiunctum. . . . Converti autem ad beatitudinem ultimam, homini quidem est difficile et quia est supra naturam, et quia habet impedimentum ex corruptione corporis et infectione peccati."

faith,[108] while the infection of sin is healed by the ensuing gift of sanctifying grace. Now, enlightened by faith, the intellect is able to present the ultimate end quite differently to the will as well as to consider quite concretely the means — the antecedent reality as well as the promise of the continuing aid by divine grace — of attaining the ultimate end. Thus the enlightenment of faith gives rise to hope, which in turn fortifies the will in striving toward attaining fully what the intellect already beholds in its assent of faith — the happiness of eternal life:

> [T]he hope of which we speak now, attains God by leaning on His help in order to obtain the hoped-for good. Now an effect must be proportionate to its cause. Wherefore the good which we ought to hope for from God properly and chiefly, is the infinite good, which is proportionate to the power of the divine helper, since it belongs to an infinite power to lead anyone to an infinite good. Such a good is eternal life, which consists in the enjoyment of God Himself. For we should hope from Him for nothing less than Himself, since His goodness, whereby He imparts good things to His creature, is no less than His Essence. Therefore the proper and principal object of hope is eternal happiness. (*ST* II-II, q. 17, a. 2)[109]

108. As Romanus Cessario, O.P., states in his astute theological treatment of Christian faith: "Faith as an act of judgment attains the uncreated Being of God — in scholastic shorthand, the *res;* thus, the oft-quoted adage of Thomas: '*Actus autem credentis non terminatur ad enuntiabile, sed ad rem*' ['the act of the believer does not reach its end in a statement, but in the thing']. . . . [*ST* II-II, q. 1, a. 2, ad 2.] The 'things' refers to all of the mysteries of the Christian religion, but, in an ultimate and foundational way, to God himself, as the object of theological faith" (*Christian Faith and the Theological Life* [Washington, DC: The Catholic University of America Press, 1996], p. 71). Hence, according to Thomas, the act of faith has its ultimate term in the divine life itself, such that faith begins the personal communion with God, the end of which St. Augustine adumbrates beautifully in *De civitate Dei* 22.30: "He shall be the end of our desires, who shall be seen without end, loved without cloy, praised without weariness. . . . There we shall rest and see, see and love, love and praise. This is what shall be in the end without end" (quoted in Cessario, *Chrisitan Faith and the Theological Life,* p. 54).

109. "[S]pes de qua loquimur attingit Deum innitens eius auxilio ad consequendum bonum speratum. Oportet autem effectum esse causae proportionatum. Et ideo bonum quod proprie et principaliter a Deo sperare debemus est bonum infinitum, quod proportionatur virtuti Dei adiuvantis: nam infinitae virtutis est proprium ad infinitum bonum perducere. Hoc autem bonum est vita aeterna, quae in fruitione ipsius Dei consistit: non enim minus aliquid ab eo sperandum est quam sit ipse, cum non sit minor eius bonitas, per quam bona creaturae communicat, quam eius essentia. Et ideo proprium et principale obiectum spei est beatitudo aeterna."

Note Thomas's employment in this article of the universal metaphysical principle "an effect must be proportionate to its cause." *An infinite good, the enjoyment of God, can only be brought about by a proportionate cause: God.* In an unexpected context, the question whether an angel needs grace in order to turn to God, Thomas offers a concise application of this principle:

> [T]he natural movement of the will is the principle of all things that we will. But the will's natural inclination is directed towards what is in keeping with its nature. Therefore, if there is anything which is above nature, the will cannot be inclined towards it, unless helped by some other supernatural principle. . . . Now it was shown above . . . when we were treating of God's knowledge, that to see God in His essence, wherein the ultimate beatitude of the rational creature consists, is beyond the nature of every created intellect. Consequently no rational creature can have the movement of the will directed towards such beatitude, except it be moved thereto by a supernatural agent. This is what we call the help of grace. (*ST* I, q. 62, a. 2)[110]

Hence the firm movement of the will toward the infinite good that is eternal happiness — in short, the habit of hope — can only be brought about by divine grace. Consequently, this hope is a supernatural, infused virtue. Such an elevation and perfection of natural hope indeed presupposes and draws upon the *desiderium,* the simple movement toward the desired thing. There is no movement of hope without the simple inchoate movement of *desiderium.* The former always presupposes the latter while the latter in and of itself is unable ever to reduce itself into a movement of firm consistency toward a specific end. The *desiderium,* however, has its own proper consistency, which arises from the very structure of the *intellectus* itself.

---

110. "Naturalis autem inclinatio voluntatis est ad id quod est conveniens secundum naturam. Et ideo, si aliquid est supra naturam, voluntas in id ferri non potest, nisi ab aliquo alio supernaturali principio adiuta. . . . Ostensum est autem supra, cum de Dei cognitione ageretur, quod videre Deum per essentiam, in quo ultima beatitudo rationalis creaturae consistit, est supra naturam cuiuslibet intellectus creati. Unde nulla creatura rationalis potest habere motum voluntatis ordinatum ad illam beatitudinem, nisi mota a supernaturali agente. Et hoc dicimus auxilium gratiae."

What Is the "Natural" Desire for the Vision of God?

In the case of the natural desire for the vision of God, the attribute "natural" denotes the consistency of the desire: a consistency arising from the nature of the *intellectus*.[111] It belongs to the very nature of the intellect consistently to give rise to the simple motion of the will to desire the human spirit's highest good. Hence it is precisely that consistently present, inchoate natural motion of the rational appetite which grace presupposes and perfects. The *desiderium* remains, however, an inchoate movement of the will, somewhat conditional, because it is less than a firmly realized movement of the rational appetite to a specific good. When we ask what it is that elicits this desire consistently as a *simplex motus*, Le Guillou points us to what the human intellect comes to know naturally: "Thomas calls it a natural desire, because it arises from the nature of the intellect as such, insofar as it is commended by natural knowledge."[112] Hence, Le Guillou emphasizes, the *desiderium naturale visionis Dei* is by no means a natural desire in the sense of a Scotist *pondus naturae,* a weight of nature pulling us inexorably toward the vision of God. Rather, it is a desire elicited by the very things the intellect comes to know, and hence a desire that is objectively directed at everything implied in our natural desire to know to the fullest degree by way of comprehending the causes of the things we come to know, an unlimited intellectual enquiry that continuously transcends known causes and eventually, at least in principle, leads to the first cause, the cause that cannot be transcended because it is the source and origin of all causes. Consequently, in the end this natural desire may develop into the full-fledged desire to come to know — to "see" by way of the *intellectus* — the essence of this first cause.[113]

Hence, it is crucial to realize in the debate over the *desiderium naturale visionis Dei* that Thomas's proof of the natural desire for the vision of God in book 3 of the *Summa contra Gentiles* is a proof properly at home in the desire to know essences and causes, which as such is the clear manifestation of the openness *(capacitas, aptitudo)* of the human *intellectus* for all being. Le Guillou reminds his readers at this apposite moment of the specific way in which Thomas understands the image of God to be in all human beings:

111. Le Guillou, "Surnaturel," p. 230, n. 4.

112. Le Guillou, "Surnaturel," p. 230.

113. Relevant here is the *admiratio* of the philosopher: *ST* I, q. 12, a. 1; I-II, q. 3, a. 8; *In Ioan.* I, lect. II; I *Metaphys.,* 1 (Marietti edn., pp. 1-4).

Since man is said to be to the image of God by reason of his intellectual nature, he is the most perfectly like God according to that in which he can best imitate God in his intellectual nature. Now the intellectual nature imitates God chiefly in this, that God understands and loves Himself. Wherefore we see that the image of God is in man . . . [f]irst, inasmuch as man possesses a natural aptitude for understanding and loving God; and this aptitude consists in the very nature of the mind, which is common to all men. (*ST* I, q. 93, a. 4)[114]

Note at this point that for Thomas the terms *capacitas* and *aptitudo* signify an exclusively receptive potency, contrary to *facultas*, which signifies an active potency.

What Is Special about the Natural Desire?

It is here where Le Guillou acknowledges the Thomist point of contact with de Lubac's Augustinian élan of nature for the supernatural. The natural desire appears in the consciousness as the difference between the proper object of the created spirit (which is the realm of all being) and its connatural object which is the consciousness of a nonaccordance between the nature of the *intellectus* and its very ground. Instead of committing the errors of ontologism or illuminationism, Le Guillou does nothing but offer a full acknowledgment of the gift of the active principle of the *intellectus*, the irreducible being-in-act of the intellect *(intellectus agens)* in every created spirit, an act which indeed begs the question of its source. However, while its very existence unavoidably raises the question of its source and giver, the *intellectus agens* by no means carries with and in itself an innate knowledge of God, in any remote form whatever.

114. "[C]um homo secundum intellectualem naturam ad imaginem Dei esse dicatur, secundum hoc est maxime ad imaginem Dei, secundum quod intellectualis natura Deum maxime imitari potest. Imitatur autem intellectualis natura maxime Deum quantum ad hoc, quod Deus seipsum intelligit et amat. Unde imago Dei . . . potest considerari in homine . . . [u]no quidem modo, secundum quod homo habet aptitudinem naturalem ad intelligendum et amandum Deum; et haec aptitudo consistit in ipsa natura mentis, quae est communis omnibus hominibus." Thomas distinguishes this image of creation from the image of re-creation, to be found in the just and consisting in the conformity of grace, and from the image of likeness, which is the likeness of glory to be found only in the blessed. See also *De Verit.*, q. 8, a. 1, ad 6; q. 14, a. 10, ad 4; *ScG* III, c. 54; III, c. 98; *ST* I, q. 12, a. 4, ad 3; *ST* I-II, q. 2, a. 3.

The human spirit aspires naturally to unite itself effectively to the one it divines negatively and ideally in its universality beneath the manifold species of its proper object (being) — God. This desire for union, however, is nothing but the desire to understand the truth, as Le Guillou's choice of citation from the *Summa contra Gentiles* shows:

> [U]ltimate felicity is to be sought in nothing other than an operation of the intellect, since no desire carries on to such sublime heights as the desire to understand the truth. Indeed, all our desires for pleasure, or other things of this sort that are craved by men, can be satisfied with other things, but the aforementioned desire does not rest until it reaches God, the highest point of reference for, and the maker of, things. (*ScG* III, c. 50, 9)[115]

It is indisputably the case that Thomas holds, in Le Guillou's words, "that in the very core of the human being there is an aspiration of a self-accomplishment in the order of the spirit, in a dimension somewhat divine."[116] Le Guillou is readily willing to grant this point to de Lubac and to affirm that a definition of the human being along the lines of Aristotle, as rational animal, does not exhaust at all the greatness of the human being. Acknowledging that much emphatically does not, however, entail agreeing with the Augustinian thesis that the human spirit's proper and only connatural object is God in and of himself. Rather, the being that is human is *qua intellectus* structurally oriented toward an enquiry into its spiritual identity up to its proper limits as a finite being, composite of rational soul and body.

The Natural Desire Denotes an Ordination to the Vision of God

After having reached the point of closest contact with de Lubac, Le Guillou rightly presses the point that Thomas's argument concerning the natural desire for the vision of God never passes beyond the idea of an ordination

---

115. "[I]n nullo alio quaerenda est ultima felicitas quam in operatione intellectus: cum nullum desiderium tam in sublime ferat sicut desiderium intelligendae veritatis. Omnia namque nostra desideria vel delectationis, vel cuiuscumque alterius quod ab homine desideratur, in aliis rebus quiescere possunt: desiderium autem praedictum non quiescit nisi ad summum rerum cardinem et factorem Deum pervenerit."

116. Le Guillou, "Surnaturel," p. 231.

in the sense of a real metaphysical possibility.[117] The argument amounts in each case always only to the defense of the possibility of the vision, as in the following:

> [I]t is impossible for natural desire to be unfulfilled, since 'nature does nothing in vain.' Now, natural desire would be in vain if it could never be fulfilled. Therefore, man's natural desire is capable of fulfillment [*implebile*]. (*ScG* III, c. 48, 11)[118]

It is only now, after a closer reading of the first twenty-five chapters of book 3 of the *Summa contra Gentiles* that this particular claim can be appreciated in its proper discursive context. The subsequent statement "So, it must be fulfilled after this life" ("Oportet igitur quod impleatur post hanc vitam") cannot be read as a kind of quasi-ontological necessity obeying a metaphysical exigency. Rather, it must be understood as an anticipation of what is intimated in book 3, chapters 51-63, and is fully developed only in book 4. In short, it is the *convenientia* of the economy of salvation itself that is in the one obtaining order of providence the concrete implementation of what on the basis of the principle of nature remains merely *implebile*. Consider again at this point what Thomas states in the opening chapter on divine providence about those creatures that "bear His likeness and reflect His image":

> [T]hey are not only ruled but are also rulers of themselves, inasmuch as their own actions are directed to a fitting end. If these beings submit to the divine rule in their own ruling, then by virtue of the divine rule they are admitted to the achievement of their ultimate end; but, if they proceed otherwise in their own ruling, they are rejected. (*ScG* III, c. 1, 4)

"To submit to the divine rule in their own ruling," however, was the primordial gift of original righteousness. Unlike the gift of nature itself, the primary perfection, the gift of an antecedent, habitually perfected secondary perfection can be refused and, alas, indeed was refused. After the initial refusal, any fulfillment of the natural desire rests upon a new, infinitely superior initiative of God (hence *felix culpa*), an initiative that infallibly,

---

117. Le Guillou, "Surnaturel," p. 231.

118. "Impossibile est naturale desiderium esse inane: 'natura enim nihil facit frustra' [Arist., *De caelo* II 11]. Esset autem inane desiderium naturae si nunquam posset impleri. Est igitur implebile desiderium naturale hominis."

though not irresistably, restores the original gift of habitually perfected operation in order, finally, to elevate the original gift to its infinitely surpassing perfection in the beatific vision.

The Natural Desire Is a Genuine Capacity — Reflecting the Fundamental Openness of the Human Being for God

Does Le Guillou then embrace the interpretation that such a desire, for Thomas, must simply and solely be a question of a passive natural potency or a simple obediential potency in the strict and limited sense? Interestingly, Le Guillou does not take this to be the consequence of Thomas's metaphysical analysis of the ontological structure of the created intellect. Rather, he astutely observes that wherever Thomas treats the natural desire for the vision of God *ex professo,* the *doctor communis* affirms that the natural desire reveals a capacity of the human spirit in regard to the vision of God.[119] Moreover, the fact that Thomas uses next to *capacitas* also the terms *ordinatio, habilitas, aptitudo,* and *inclinatio* indicates rather clearly that he intended to signal that the *desiderium naturale visionis Dei* is an altogether proper desire for the *creatura intellectualis* — created after all *ad imaginem Trinitatis.*[120]

"Capacity," according to Le Guillou, entails a purely passive ordination to the beatific vision, such that either the capacity is fulfilled by a determinate object or, if it is not, it simply remains unformed. The *desiderium naturale* "designates the real capacity which the created spirit has of opening itself to the vision of God, the possibility of a positive *convenientia,* which we can only await and to which the created spirit cannot adapt itself on its own."[121] However, by way of its natural desire, the ontological structure of the created spirit reveals its capability of a genuine reception: the vision of God can pour itself into the created spirit's activity without destroying or transmuting it, because it is — due to its ontological constitution as *intellectus* — *capax Dei.* Indeed, the beatific vision is the de facto return of the created spirit to its source. Le Guillou rightly draws attention to a crucial passage:

119. Le Guillou, "Surnaturel," p. 232.
120. Le Guillou, "Surnaturel," p. 232. He refers here to *ST* I, q. 93, a. 2 c. and ad 3; III, q. 9, a. 2; III, q. 4, a. 1.
121. Le Guillou, "Surnaturel," p. 232.

> The divine substance is not beyond the capacity of the created intellect
> in such a way that it is altogether foreign to it, as sound is from the ob-
> ject of vision, or as immaterial substance is from sense power; in fact,
> the divine substance is the first intelligible object and the principle of
> all intellectual cognition. But it is beyond the capacity of the created
> intellect, in the sense that it exceeds its power; just as sensible objects
> of extreme character are beyond the capacity of sense power. Hence
> the philosopher says that "our intellect is to the most evident things, as
> the eye of the owl is to the light of the sun" [Aristotle, *Metaphysics*
> 2.1.993b9]. So, a created intellect needs to be strenghened by a divine
> light in order that it may be able to see the divine essence. (*ScG* III,
> c. 54, 8)[122]

While the natural desire for the vision of God arises from the unique
structural kinship, by way of participation of the effect in the cause, between the divine substance and the created intellect, the fulfillment of this
desire lies utterly beyond the capacity of the created intellect. And since the
created intellect does not subsist per se but is realized in the existence of
separate substances (angels) as well as in the existence of human beings,
the natural desire, which in the structural analysis of the created intellect is
one, comes to operate only according to the specific nature of the extant
intelligent creatures. Hence, for angels, due to their specific nature as separate substances, this desire is an innate, unconditional desire. For human
beings, due to their specific nature as composites of soul and body, it is an
elicited and conditional desire.

Three Possible Objections from Thomas's Oeuvre

In order to advance our understanding of how precise, and how precisely
delineated, Thomas's notion of the natural desire for the vision of God is,

---

122. "Divinia enim substantia non sic est extra facultatem creati intellectus quasi aliquid omnino extraneum ab ipso, sicut est sonus a visu, vel substantia immaterialis a sensu, nam divina substantia est primum intelligibile, et totius intellectualis cognitionis principium: sed est extra facultatem intellectus creati sicut excedens virtutem eius, sicut excellentia sensibilium sunt extra facultatem sensus. Unde et Philosophus in II *Metaphys.* [2.1.993b10] dicit quod 'intellectus noster se habet ad rerum manifestissima sicut oculus noctuae ad lucem solis.' Indiget igitur confortari intellectus creatus aliquo divino lumine ad hoc quod divinam essentiam videre possit."

Le Guillou offers three paradigmatic instances from Thomas's work that seem to question, indeed, to negate the very possibility of such a natural desire for the vision of God.[123]

(a) "Natural desire can only exist for what can be obtained naturally." (III *Sent.*, d. 27, q. 2, a. 2, ad 4)[124]
(b) "Now in his nature man is proportioned to a certain end for which he has a natural appetite." (*De Verit.*, q. 27, a. 2)[125]
(c) "[T]his particular good (which he does not naturally desire) — for example, the vision of God." (*De Verit.*, q. 22, a. 7)[126]

Le Guillou correctly stresses that Thomas distinguishes three things from each other:

(1) the natural and necessary appetite for the beatitude *in communi,*
(2) the natural and elicited desire for the vision of the essence of God, and
(3) the effective choice of God as final end and hence the *desiderium gratiae* for the beatific vision.

The three texts that Le Guillou quotes as possible contradictory evidence from Thomas's *opus* address (1) and (3), but not (2). But what about passage (b)? Considering how the citation continues, should it not fall under

123. Le Guillou, "Surnaturel," p. 233.

124. "Desiderium autem naturale non potest esse nisi rei quae naturaliter haberi potest." The text continues beyond Le Guillou's quotation: "Wherefore the natural desire for the highest good is naturally in us to whatever extent the highest good can be participated in by us through a natural effect" ("Unde desiderium naturale summi boni inest nobis secundum naturam, inquantum summum bonum participabile est a nobis per effectus naturales").

125. The text continues: ". . . and for the obtaining of which he can work by his natural powers. That end is a contemplation of divine things [*aliqua contemplatio divina*] such as is possible to man according to the capabilities of his nature; and in this contemplation philosophers have placed man's ultimate happiness" (St. Thomas Aquinas, *Truth* [Chicago: H. Regnery Co., 1952-54], 3:315). ("Homo autem secundum naturam suam proportionatus est ad quemdam finem, cujus habet naturalem appetitum; et secundum naturales vires operari potest ad consecutionem illius finis, qui finis est aliqua contemplatio divinorum, qualis est homini possibilis secundum facultatem naturae, in qua philosophi ultimam hominis felicitatem posuerunt.")

126. St. Thomas Aquinas, *Truth*, 3:61. ("[H]oc speciale quod non naturaliter appetit, ut visionem Dei.")

(2)? Did Le Guillou misinterpret Thomas at this subtle point? At a first glance, passage (b), because of the way it appeals to the philosophers' metaphysical *admiratio,* seems to be pertinent to (2), despite the difference in terminology. However, if we take a closer look, the end to which the *appetitus naturalis* is directed in this passage is designated as *aliqua contemplatio divinorum,* which is not the intellectual vision of the divine essence, but rather what a natural theology as the very acme of metaphysical contemplation is indeed able to accomplish. Thomas is here interested only in that aspect of the philosophers' metaphysical *admiratio* that can be realized by human effort and ingenuity alone, resulting in a knowledge, albeit *debilis,* that is proportionate to the active potency, the faculty, of the human intellect, at its highest point of metaphysical contemplation. In the particular discussion, Thomas is after the distinct contrast between that end to which human nature is proportioned and for which, hence, it has a natural appetite, and

> an end for which man is prepared by God which surpasses the proportion of human nature, that is, eternal life, which consists in the vision of God by His essence. That vision is not proportionate to any creature whatsoever, being connatural only to God. (*De Verit.,* q. 27, a. 2)[127]

Now it becomes clear that this particular passage indeed falls under (1) as well as (3). Thomas distinguishes here between nature and grace, that is, between an end proportionate to human nature and a natural appetite directed toward such an end, on the one hand, and, on the other hand, an end infinitely surpassing human nature toward which the human being is directed by grace through the infused theological virtues of faith, hope, and charity. In book 3 of the *Summa contra Gentiles,* on the contrary, Thomas is not pursuing a contrastive analysis of nature and grace, but a metaphysical enquiry into the structure of the created intellect, as an effect that participates ontologically in its cause. And it is such an enquiry that yields the insight into the created intellect being *capax Dei* and into an ensuing natural desire for the vision of God that corresponds to the very ontological structure of the created intellect.

---

127. Aquinas, *Truth,* 3:315. ("Sed est aliquis finis ad quem homo a Deo praeparatur, naturae humanae proportionem excedens; scilicet vita aeterna, quae consistit in visione Dei per essentiam, quae excedit proportionem cujuslibet naturae creatae, soli Deo connaturalis existens.")

The Indispensable Elements Entailed in an Affirmation of the Natural Desire for the Vision of God

In conclusion, Le Guillou urges three fundamental and equally indispensable aspects of the consideration of the natural desire for the vision of God.

First, it is altogether necessary to affirm the significance of the natural desire for the vision of God:

> The very structure of the created spirit gives witness to a desired opening *in the prolongation of its proper perfection*, an opening toward a supernatural surpassing which would be the vision of God Himself, the divine essence. The realization of which, however, being absolutely out of the range of the created spirit, depends solely on God's good pleasure. Naturally powerless to realize the desire's fulfillment, the created spirit can only wait for the gratuitous gift, which can neither be accessed nor demanded.[128]

However, he also stresses that it is this very gift of the beatific vision that makes good the authentic symbiosis of the two orders, the natural and the supernatural. For the latter by no means simply redoubles the natural order in some heterogeneous and incomprehensible juxtaposition.

Second, it is altogether necessary to affirm the positive supernatural character of the divine gift. For only God is to himself his proper connatural object. Hence, the positive content of the word "supernatural" corresponds to that of an order of communion with God, accorded gratuitously. And God is absolutely free to communicate his divine life. The fact that God created a spirit capable of such communion in no way obligates him to grant the beatific vision.[129]

Third, it is altogether necessary to maintain the integrity of the respective created natures. "The created spirit is in its very structure raised above itself. It carries in its own structure the call to realize itself in a transcendent end."[130] Hence it aims always beyond its connatural end. However, the nonrealization of this transcendent end does not result in the loss of the created spirit's proper consistency, though it will not achieve perfect felicity. Indeed, the unsatisfied desire does not mutilate at all the nature of

---

128. Le Guillou, "Surnaturel," p. 240.
129. Le Guillou, "Surnaturel," p. 240.
130. Le Guillou, "Surnaturel," p. 240.

the spirit, simply because the resources necessary to fulfill it do not belong to the created spirit's nature itself. Rather, by way of its structure, the human spirit simply opens up to the divine gratuity, to the good pleasure of God.

In short, Le Guillou concludes, "the natural mystery of the created spirit consists in the fact that it structurally orients our attention to the mystery of God: the image of God points back to its model."[131] Furthermore, in the concretely obtaining order of providence, to be satisfied with humanity's connatural end amounts to a sin!

"Natura pura": The Integrity of the Relative Principle of Nature

After having secured these indispensable aspects of a correct consideration of the natural desire for the vision of God according to St. Thomas, Le Guillou once more returns to the relative integrity of the principle of nature. It is the very ontological structure of the created spirit that he understands to be referred to by the notion of "pure nature" *(natura pura):*

> It is for this very reason we deem it necessary to affirm the radical possibility of a "pure nature," which is not at all a nature closed in upon itself. For we see no other way to safeguard the affirmation of the new creation, which the first creation by itself does not require at all. Pure nature is not a nature which would be completely foreign to us. . . . It rather designates in our world the very structure proper to the created intellect. In our opinion, in a created world, in which the human being were not called to the beatific vision, the created spirit would still rise above itself.[132]

Insisting upon the contested concept of the *natura pura* (according to the above understanding) has a twofold value for Le Guillou: first, it puts into the right light the created structure of the spirit; second, it insists strongly on the absolute difference between the "created" and "uncreated" and hence allows to account for the gratuity of God's actual plan with the world. Here Le Guillou agrees explicitly with de Lubac that the theologian's task is to contemplate the gratuity of the actual plan of God and not some hypothetical plan. It is for this very reason that Le Guillou, on the

131. Le Guillou, "Surnaturel," p. 242.
132. Le Guillou, "Surnaturel," p. 242.

one hand, reclaims Jacques Maritain's rightly famous statement that, in fact, God would not have created human nature if he had not ordained it to the elevation by grace. On the other hand, he refuses for the reasons given to speak with de Lubac of a "natural desire for the supernatural."[133]

Conclusion

Sic

Le Guillou's response to Henri de Lubac's *Surnaturel* represents a highly nuanced position that in an exemplary way maintains the subtle synthesis of the *doctor communis* on this intricate topic. Le Guillou agrees with de Lubac on one point of surpassing importance: Human nature is *capax Dei*, is ontologically oriented towards the beatific vision. There is in the human being a positive fittingness, an opening inscribed into the very core of the nature of the human *intellectus*, created *ad imaginem Trinitatis.*

Et Non

However, the affirmation that the created intellect has only one concrete ultimate end is fully compatible with the distinction between two orders of finality. Indeed, positing one concrete ultimate end makes the distinction between such two orders of finality indispensable. For the genuinely surpassing gratuity of attaining the ultimate end can only be safeguarded if there obtains a finality that corresponds to the natural faculties of the created intellect. Without a proportionate proximate finality of human nature toward which humans are able to move on the basis of their nature, there would exist no active potency for sanctifying grace to presuppose and to perfect. In order for the human being — qua human — to be elevated to the ultimate end, and in this supernatural actuation neither to be transmuted into some other nature nor re-created *ex nihilo,* the gratuitous transcendence of the ultimate end requires the relative but proper integrity

---

133. Le Guillou, "Surnaturel," pp. 242f.: "[C]'est pourquoi nous reprendrions volontiers la formule de M. Maritain: '*de fait* il (Dieu) n'aurait pas créé la nature s'il ne l'avait pas ordonnée à la grâce.' Mais nous nous refusons à parler avec le P. de Lubac d'un désir naturel du surnaturel."

of a nature, including its proportionate finality, that is intrinsically open and waiting for such an elevation.

In a highly compressed passage in the *Compendium Theologiae*, Thomas holds both aspects together: on the one hand, qua structure of the *intellectus,* there obtains a *desiderium naturale* for evermore perfect knowledge up to and including the knowledge of the essence of the first cause; on the other hand, the *intellectus* is not effectively proportioned to see God and hence lacks the natural disposition for such knowledge. And since the intellect is by definition unable to present to the will the ultimate good, which is the essence of the first cause, the will does not actuate a fortified *desiderium,* a specific motion to this end as presented by the intellect. Hence the *desiderium naturale* has to remain a simple motion, conditional upon some future activation:

> [W]e cannot attain our ultimate end by the actuation of our intellect through the instrumentality of the agent intellect. For the function of the agent intellect consists in rendering *actually* intelligible the phantasms that of themselves are only *potentially* intelligible. . . . These phantasms are derived from the senses. Hence the efficacy of the agent intellect in reducing our intellect to act is restricted to intelligible objects of which we can gain knowledge by way of sense perception. Man's last end cannot consist in such cognition. The reason is that once the ultimate end has been reached, natural desire ceases. But no matter how much we may advance in this kind of understanding whereby we derive knowledge from the senses, there still remains a natural desire to know other objects. . . . Hence our natural desire for more perfect knowledge ever remains. But a natural desire cannot be in vain.
>
> Accordingly, we reach our last end when our intellect is actualized by some higher agent than an agent connatural to us, that is, by an agent capable of gratifying our natural, inborn craving for knowledge. So great is the desire for knowledge within us that, once we apprehend an effect, we wish to know its cause. Moreover, after we have gained some knowledge of the circumstances investing a thing, our desire is not satisfied until we penetrate to its essence. Therefore our natural desire for knowledge cannot come to rest within us until we know the first cause, and that not in any way, but in its very essence. This first cause is God. Consequently the ultimate end of an intellectual creature is the vision of God in His essence.[134]

134. St. Thomas Aquinas, *Compendium of Theology,* trans. Cyril Vollert, S.J. (St. Louis

Previous discussion has brought out the fact that no creature is associated with God in genus. Hence the essence of God cannot be known through any created species whatever, whether sensible or intelligible. Accordingly, if God is to be known as He is, in His essence, God Himself must become the form of the intellect knowing Him and must be joined to that intellect, not indeed so as to constitute a single nature with it but in the way an intelligible species is joined to the intelligence. For God, who is His own being, is also His own truth, and truth is the form of the intellect. . . . Our intellect is not equipped by its nature with the ultimate disposition looking to that form which is truth; otherwise it would be in possession of truth from the beginning. Consequently, when it does finally attain to truth, it must be elevated by some disposition newly conferred on it. And this we call the light of glory, whereby our intellect is perfected by God, who alone by His very nature has this form properly as His own. In somewhat the same way the disposition which heat has for the form of fire can come from fire alone. This is the light that is spoken of in Psalm 36:9: "In Thy light we shall see light."[135]

and London: Herder, 1952), pp. 109-11 (c. 104). (*Compendium theologiae,* c. 104, in S. Thomae Aquinatis Doctoris Angelici, *Opuscula theologica,* vol. 1: *De re dogmatica et morali* [Rome: Marietti, 1954], pp. 51f.: "208. Est autem impossibile nos ultimum finem consequi per hoc quod intellectus noster sic reducatur in actum: nam virtus intellectus agentis est ut phantasmata, quae sunt intelligibilia in potentia, faciat intelligibilia in actu, ut ex superioribus patet [cap. 83]. Phantasmata autem sunt accepta per sensum. Per intellectum igitur agentem intellectus noster in actum reducitur respectu horum intelligibilium tantum in quorum notitiam per sensibilia possumus devenire. Impossibile est autem in tali cognitione ultimum hominis finem consistere. Nam ultimo fine adepto, desiderium naturale quiescit. Quantumcumque autem aliquis proficiat intelligendo secundum praedictum modum cognitionis quo a sensu scientiam percipimus, adhuc remanet naturale desiderium ad alia cognoscenda. . . . Unde semper remanet naturale desiderium respectu perfectioris cognitionis. Impossibile est autem naturale desiderium esse vanum. 209. Consequimur igitur ultimum finem in hoc quod intellectus noster fiat in actu, aliquo sublimiori agente quam sit agens nobis connaturale, quod quiescere faciat desiderium quod nobis inest naturaliter ad sciendum. Tale est autem in nobis sciendi desiderium, ut cognoscentes effectum, desideremus cognoscere causam, et in quacumque re cognitis quibuscumque eius circumstantiis, non quiescit nostrum desiderium, quousque eius essentiam cognoscamus. Non igitur naturale desiderium sciendi potest quietari in nobis, quousque primam causam cognoscamus, non quocumque modo, sed per eius essentiam. Prima autem causa Deus est, ut ex superioribus patet [cap. 3; 68ff.]. Est igitur finis ultimus intellectualis creaturae, Deum per essentiam videre.")

135. Aquinas, *Compendium of Theology,* pp. 111-12 (c. 105). (*Compendium theologiae,* c. 105 [Marietti edn., pp. 52f.]: "211. Manifestum est autem ex superioribus [cap. 12, 13] quod

For Thomas, there cannot exist an innate, unconditional natural desire for the supernatural — the supernatural in the strict sense of the word being nothing less than the specific overarching good of God according to his proper quiddity, the Trinity of Father, Son, and Holy Spirit, as presented by revelation and inchoately embraced in the infused virtue of divine faith.[136] Henri de Lubac, with the thesis of a "natural desire for the supernatural," overshot the goal. What has to occur — and indeed what does occur in the economy of salvation via divine *convenientia* — is a perfecting of the natural, conditional desire by sanctifying grace into the unconditional desire of the infused virtue of hope to see "the God whom I know (by faith) *secundum suam propriam quidditatem* (and as the Trinity), the God whom I know as able to give Himself to me *according as He is the object of the divine knowledge itself.*"[137]

---

nullum creatum communicat cum Deo in genere. Per quamcumque igitur speciem creatam non solum sensibilem, sed intelligibilem, Deus cognosci per essentiam non potest. Ad hoc igitur quod ipse Deus per essentiam cognoscatur, oportet quod ipse Deus fiat forma intellectus ipsum cognoscentis, et coniungatur ei non ad unam naturam constituendam, sed sicut species intelligibilis intelligenti. Ipse enim sicut est suum esse, ita est sua veritas, quae est forma intellectus. 212. . . . Intellectus autem noster non est ex ipsa sua natura in ultima dispositione existens respectu formae illius quae est veritas, quia sic a principio ipsam assequeretur. Oportet igitur quod cum eam consequitur, aliqua dispositione de novo addita elevetur, quam dicimus gloriae lumen: quo quidem intellectus noster a Deo perficitur, qui solus secundum suam naturam hanc propriam formam habet, sicut nec dispositio caloris ad formam ignis potest esse nisi ab igne: et de hoc lumine in Psal. xxxv, 10 dicitur: *In lumine tuo videbimus lumen.*")

136. On theological faith, see Cessario, *Christian Faith and the Theological Life.*

137. Maritain, *Degrees of Knowledge,* p. 284, n. 1.

c. BOUND TO BE FREE, SUFFERING DIVINE THINGS —
GRACE AND THE THEOLOGICAL VIRTUES

"Thomas the Augustinian" — Recovering a Surpassing Synthesis of Grace and Free Will

Introduction

For many contemporary theologians, those who dare to treat the topic of grace and free will with a measure of conviction, however minimal, resemble fools rushing in where angels fear to tread. And I am indeed painfully aware that I might at least indulge in the vice of presumption with what I attempt to cover in this chapter. But I would submit that nothing less than the ensuing *tour d'horizon* will suffice to get to the core of the topic, as well as its contemporary relevance.[1] I will begin with the usual three apposite remarks of introduction, the last of which will be the thesis I wish to submit.

First, in the following when I speak of "grace and free will," I refer specifically to the question of how God and human interrelate in the first and fundamental act of salvation, the *initium fidei* — the beginning of faith, also referred to as the act of conversion.[2] Conversion, most fundamentally, is the turning from sin to God, a turning that is nothing else than God gratuitously as well as efficaciously turning us to himself as our ulti-

---

1. In the following, I am writing as neither a doctrinal nor a church historian. Rather, I am writing as a theologian. Hence, my brief remarks about Augustine and Thomas, as well as those about Erasmus of Rotterdam and Martin Luther, will all be painted with far too broad a brush. But this is the privilege of the theologian. Moreover, I am not interested in being original by offering some new insight. Rather, I am interested in remembering and holding on to a most profound insight put forth by Augustine and, more explicitly, Thomas, in the hope that this insight might again become fruitful in the present theological conversation.

2. To be more precise, *initium fidei* refers not to acts prior and extrinsic to faith but strictly to faith itself, albeit faith still lacking its full realization, as informed by charity.

mate, supernatural end to be consummated only in the beatific vision. The question of how divine grace and human free will interrelate in the act of conversion — of how God is able to move the human's will infallibly yet freely — is not simply a complex problem, eventually to be resolved; it is an unfathomable *mystery*, to be discerned ever more deeply. Mystery, understood aright, will always invite new theological efforts at interpretation.[3] Thus when I argue in the concluding section that Thomas has offered the most satisfying Augustinian interpretation to date of this mystery, I emphatically do not claim that his interpretation has thereby resolved once and for all a conceptual problem. Rather, I propose that in all his precision and profundity, Thomas has deepened our understanding of — and thereby preserved the very character of — the mystery itself.

Second, with the interrelationship of grace and free will, we step into the very heart of Augustinianism and its debates, debates that gave rise to ecclesiastical and political developments that culminated in the cataclysmic religious and political upheavals of sixteenth- and seventeenth-century Europe. Hence, the relationship between divine grace and human free will is a question of the greatest ecumenical importance. The mystery of grace and free will is most acutely present in the act of conversion. Here Western Christianity is irreversibly shaped by Augustine and Augustinianism — and rightly so. "Freedom," however, is a notoriously multivalent notion. Therefore, it will be imperative to keep in mind the fundamental distinction between what I will call in the following "natural," or "created," freedom on the one hand and "acquired" freedom on the other.[4] Natural, or created, freedom is the *liberum arbitrium,* the "free will," to choose between alternatives and to decide for or against a course of action. Acquired freedom, on the contrary, is the freedom to live as one ought. It is the freedom for which Christ has set us free (Gal. 5:1), or, as Thomas would put it

---

3. I am drawing here upon a most helpful distinction employed by Gabriel Marcel, Jacques Maritain, and Thomas G. Weinandy: "Maritain states that where there is mystery 'the intellect has to penetrate more and more deeply the *same* object.' The mystery, by the necessity of its subject matter, remains. . . . Many theologians today, having embraced the Enlightenment presupposition and the scientific method that it fostered, approach theological issues as if they were scientific problems to be solved rather than mysteries to be discerned and clarified. However, the true goal of theological inquiry is not the resolution of theological *problems*, but the discernment of what the *mystery* of faith is." Thomas G. Weinandy, O.F.M. Cap., *Does God Suffer?* (Notre Dame, IN: University of Notre Dame Press, 2000), pp. 31-32 (original emphasis).

4. See, comprehensively, Mortimer Adler, *The Idea of Freedom: A Dialectical Examination of the Conceptions of Freedom,* 2 vols. (New York: Doubleday, 1958-61).

by drawing upon the Gospel of John, the freedom to live as God's friends by sharing inchoately through charity the very life of the triune God.[5]

Finally, let me submit, in the form of a thesis, the rough contours of my modest proposal, which eventually requires a more nuanced elaboration than I can offer in this chapter. Augustine developed a profound account of the mystery of grace and free will. However, his account, with its ontology of participation remaining largely implicit, proved to be notoriously open to a variety of conflicting interpretations. The best example of such conflict, ostensibly based solely on the meaning of Scripture[6] — but with a philosophical background profoundly incompatible with Augustinian and Thomist forms of thought — is seen in the famous (or infamous) early-sixteenth-century debate on free versus enslaved will *(liberum arbitrium* versus *servum arbitrium)* between Desiderius Erasmus of Rotterdam and Martin Luther. In light of this epochal debate,[7] I would submit

---

5. On this topic, see Michael Sherwin, O.P., "Christ the Teacher in St. Thomas's *Commentary on the Gospel of John,"* in *Reading John with St. Thomas Aquinas: Theological Exegesis and Speculative Theology,* ed. Michael Dauphinais and Matthew Levering (Washington, DC: The Catholic University of America Press, 2005), pp. 173-93; esp. 190-91.

6. Erasmus: "De sensu scripturae pugna est" [Our battle is about the meaning of Scripture]. Erasmus von Rotterdam, *Ausgewählte Werke,* vol. 4 (Darmstadt: Wissenschaftliche Buchgesellschaft, 1969), p. 26.

7. I call the exchange between Erasmus and Luther epochal because, for a significant segment of Protestant as well as Roman Catholic theologians, it is still regarded as paradigmatic, to the effect that not a few Protestant theologians continue to hold Catholicism under suspicion of (Semi-)Pelagianism, while not a few Catholic theologians continue to charge Luther with theological determinism and even Manichaeism. It took several generations of intense ecumenical effort up to and including the recent Lutheran World Federation and Catholic Church's *Joint Declaration on the Doctrine of Justification* (1999) to begin officially to bury the mutual misconceptions on this crucial point. Now, I should add, there is an important way to construe Luther's theology differently, that is, by quite intentionally not making *De servo arbitrio* the sole hinge on which the rest of Luther's theology hangs. The new Finnish school of Luther research (see Carl E. Braaten and Robert W. Jenson, eds., *Union with Christ: The New Finnish Interpretation of Luther* [Grand Rapids: Eerdmans Publishing Company, 1998]; and esp. Tuomo Mannermaa, *Christ Present in Faith: Luther's View of Justification* [Minneapolis: Augsburg Fortress, 2005]) as well as the interpretations of Luther by George Lindbeck and his student David Yeago would be its most recent preeminent representatives. These reconstructions to a large degree bracket *De servo arbitrio* (as an unfortunate product of Luther's getting sidetracked by Erasmus's deficient attack) and focus on Luther's christocentric work, his commentaries on Romans and Galatians, his sermons on the Gospel of John, and his two catechisms. While this is a complex question of interpreting Luther's work as a whole, I tend to agree with Luther's self-interpretation, according to which he regarded *De servo arbitrio* as his most important theological work.

that (1) Thomas's account remains the most satisfying Augustinian way of interpreting and deepening Augustine's own account — an approach, for complex historical and intellectual reasons, that was either not available or not desirable to Erasmus and Luther. Moreover, (2) Thomas's particular way of antecedently avoiding erroneous Augustinianisms shows us that an anti-speculative (and hence anti-Scholastic) debate, purportedly solely on the grounds of Scripture, allows unarticulated philosophical presuppositions to rule. Furthermore, (3) I should like to propose that by way of the pivotal Thomist axiom that grace presupposes as well as perfects nature — as substantiated by Thomas's metaphysics of being, which climaxes in the surpassing beauty of divine transcendent causality — we can successfully avert the reductive alternatives of Erasmus's theologically as well as Luther's philosophically erroneous Augustinianism.

Hence, I will turn first to the epochal debate between Erasmus and Luther on free will; next, to the complex position of Augustine; and finally, to the profound account of Thomas.

I. Erasmus and Luther: Two Reductive Augustinianisms post Ockham

Martin Luther was brought up philosophically and theologically in the *via moderna,* that is, the school of William of Ockham, also called nominalism. As Étienne Gilson in his magisterial *Philosophy in the Middle Ages* argues:[8]

> [T]he essential characteristic of Occam's [*sic*] thought, and of nominalism in general, [is] a radical empiricism, reducing all being to what is perceived, which empties out, with the idea of substance, all possibility of real relations between beings, as well as the stable subsistence of any of them, and ends by denying to the real any intelligibility, conceiving God himself only as a Protean figure impossible to apprehend.[9]

Louis Bouyer astutely observes that in this kind of conceptual system, "a grace which produces a real change in us, while remaining purely the grace of God, becomes inconceivable. If some change is effected in us, then it

---

8. *La philosophie au moyen âge* (Paris, 1944), pp. 638-55. I cite Gilson because I think that his characterization of nominalism in its basic contours still obtains, pace recent attempts at philosophical as well as theological rehabilitation of nominalism in general and Ockham in particular.

9. I am quoting here Louis Bouyer's apt summary of Gilson's account in Bouyer, *The Spirit and Forms of Protestantism* (Westminster, MD: Newman, 1956), p. 153.

comes from us, and to suppose it could come also and primarily from God amounts to confusing God with the creature."[10] Thus, the first move of turning to God has to come either from God or from the human. And if, as the nominalist theologians were inclined to think, the human is to merit grace prior to any reception of grace, the human under the condition of sin must have the power to turn to God freely.[11] Consequently, the human's natural, or created, freedom must be understood as just this power, a power essentially unaffected by original sin. This, in a nutshell, is the position of the dominant theological school in Germany in the fifteenth and early sixteenth centuries[12] — a position with which also many humanists, not least Erasmus, sympathized.[13] Martin Luther received his philosophical and theological training in this school. However, under the influence of his intense study of the Apostle Paul and of the late Augustine,[14] he began to reject, branch and root, his school's *theological* account of grace and free will, rightly understanding its position to be incompatible with the teaching of St. Paul. But never rejecting the *philosophical* tenets of nominalism,[15] Luther's corrective move veered to the opposite extreme: God is not

10. Bouyer, *Spirit and Forms of Protestantism,* p. 153.

11. The nominalist theologians held that one has to merit the first grace *de congruo;* after this initial merit on the basis of *facere quod in se est,* God on the basis of his own liberality infuses first grace, thereby making condign merit possible. The strictness comes in that the initial move must lie completely with the human *(sub conditione peccati);* it can be a quite imperfect move, but it has to be the first move on the way to condign merit. See, in detail, Leif Grane, *Contra Gabrielem: Luthers Auseinandersetzung mit Gabriel Biel in der Disputatio Contra Scholasticam Theologiam* (Copenhagen: Gyldendal, 1962), pp. 214-22.

12. The leading German theologian of late medieval nominalism was Gabriel Biel. Still indispensable for a study of Biel's theology is Heiko A. Oberman, *The Harvest of Medieval Theology: Gabriel Biel and Late Medieval Nominalism* (Grand Rapid: Baker, 2000). Most decisive for our present concerns is that, according to Biel, "[t]he impact of original sin and its consequences leaves the freedom of the will intact" (p. 131).

13. For Erasmus's relationship to Scholasticism in general and nominalism in particular, see Christian Dolfen, *Die Stellung des Erasmus von Rotterdam zur scholastischen Methode* (Osnabrück: Meinders & Elstermann, 1936); and John B. Payne, *Erasmus: His Theology of the Sacraments* (Richmond: John Knox, 1970), esp. pp. 228-29, where Payne points out how Erasmus draws support for his position from Gerson, Durandus, and Biel.

14. Shortly before Luther delivered his *Lectures on the Epistle to the Romans* (1515-16), he had discovered Augustine's anti-Pelagian writings in volume eight of the Amorbach edition of Augustine's works from 1506.

15. On the complex discussion of this matter in Luther research, see Grane, *Contra Gabrielem,* pp. 9-42; and more recently, Graham White, *Luther as Nominalist: A Study of the Logical Methods Used in Martin Luther's Disputations in the Light of Their Medieval Background* (Helsinki: Luther-Agricola-Society, 1994).

merely the first but the sole agent of the act of conversion, with the human in a state of utter passivity. For, according to Luther, the human free will is not simply held captive by sin, as Augustine would maintain (*liberum arbitrium captivatum*). Rather, after the fall, "free will" — understood as the power to turn to God — becomes an "empty word." According to Luther, we continue to use this "empty word" only because the human being once had it, before the fall, and through grace can have it again.[16]

In the heat of polemic, in his response to the bull *Exsurge Domine*,[17] Luther pushed this position one step further by claiming that free will — that is, now any form of natural or created, freedom — is simply a fiction, because all things happen by absolute necessity.[18] Lest we do grave injustice to Luther, however, it is important to remember the context in and against which he formulated these extreme claims, as Harry McSorley rightly emphasizes:

> Luther's concern here was surely not to propagate a doctrine of absolute necessitarianism. His unquestionable concern was to refute and to

16. See Martin Luther, *Contra malignum Iohannis Eccii iudicium super aliquot articulis quibusdam ei suppositis Martini Lutheri defensio*, in idem, *D. Martin Luthers Werke: Kritische Gesamtausgabe*, ed. J. F. K. Knaake et al., vol. 2 (Weimar: Böhlau, 1883ff), p. 647, lines 10-13 (henceforth WA). As we will see later, even already in the Second Council of Orange (529) we can find the admittedly singular description of the *liberum arbitrium* after the fall as *amissum*, "lost." And in his *De servo arbitrio*, Luther avers: "Lost liberty, according to my grammar, is no liberty at all, and to give the name of liberty to something that has no liberty, is to employ an empty phrase." *Luther and Erasmus: Free Will and Salvation*, ed. E. Gordon Rupp and Philip S. Watson (Philadelphia: Westminster, 1969), p. 181; cf. Luther, *Kritische Gesamtausgabe*, vol. 18, p. 670).

17. *Bulla "Exsurge Domine,"* June 15, 1520, in Heinrich Denzinger and Adolf Schönmetzer, *Enchiridion Symbolorum: Definitionum et Declarationum de Rebus Fidei et Morum*, 36th ed. (Freiburg: Herder, 1976), nos. 1451-92. Canon 36: "Liberum arbitrium post peccatum est res de solo titulo; et dum facit, quod in se est, peccat mortaliter." Denzinger and Schönmetzer, *Enchiridion Symbolorum*, no. 1486.

18. *Assertio omnium articulorum M. Lutheri per bullam Leonis X novissimam damnatorum* (December 1520), Luther, *Kritische Gesamtausgabe*, vol. 7, p. 146, lines 3-12: "Unde et hunc articulum necesse est revocare. Male enim dixi, quod liberum arbitrium ante gratiam sit res de solo titulo, sed simpliciter debui dicere 'liberum arbitrium est figmentum in rebus seu titulus sine re'. Quia nulli est in manu sua quippiam cogitare mali aut boni, sed omnia (ut Viglephi articulus Constantiae damnatus recte docet) de necessitate absoluta eveniunt. Quod et Poeta voluit, quando dixit 'certa stant omnia lege,' Et Christus Matth. x 'Folium arboris non cadit in terram sine voluntate patris vestri qui in celis est et capilli capitis vestri omnes numerati sunt.' Et Esa. xli. eis insultat dicens 'Bene quoque aut male si potestis facite.'"

destroy the exaggerated Neo-Semi-pelagian view of free will that found its expression in the Ockham-Biel interpretation of the Scholastic axiom: *facienti quod in se est,* etc. From the beginning to the end of the *Assertio,* Luther attacks the Bielian doctrine "that free will is able to prepare itself to enter into grace."[19]

But with the extreme formulation of the *Assertio* — echoing and indeed at that point supporting a position held by Wyclif and condemned at the Council of Constance[20] — Luther made himself vulnerable to the charge of theological determinism. And it is precisely this determinism, or necessitarianism, that Erasmus intended to attack in his 1524 treatise *On the Freedom of the Will (De libero arbitrio)* — emulating in title as well as intention an early treatise of Augustine.[21] While rhetorically elegant, Erasmus's treatise lacked the precise conceptual organization of the Scho-

19. Harry J. McSorley, C.S.P., *Luther: Right or Wrong? An Ecumenical-Theological Study of Luther's Major Work, The Bondage of the Will* (New York: Newman; Minneapolis: Augsburg, 1969), p. 262. Oberman characterizes this central tenet of Biel's teaching thus: "Biel's explanation of the possibility of this *facere quod in se est* makes it clear that, though the *facere quod in se est* means different things for different people, everyone is by nature in a position to discharge this first duty. For God, however, the *facere quod in se est* means only one thing: He is obliged, because he has placed the obligation on himself, to infuse his grace in everyone who has done his very best" (idem, *Harvest of Medieval Theology,* p. 32). Because Biel appealed to the authority of Thomas in order to substantiate his own semi-Pelagian theology of grace, Luther came to think that not only the *doctores moderni* but also the *doctores antiqui* were Pelagians. For a highly instructive study of this matter, see John L. Farthing, *Thomas Aquinas and Gabriel Biel: Interpretations of St. Thomas Aquinas in German Nominalism on the Eve of the Reformation* (Durham/London: Duke University Press, 1988).

20. Sessio VIII on February 22, 1418; among the errors of Wyclif listed is canon 27: "Omnia de necessitate absoluta eveniunt." Denzinger and Schönmetzer, *Enchiridion Symbolorum,* no. 1177.

21. See Rupp and Watson, *Luther and Erasmus,* pp. 41, 43, and esp. 63-64, where he refers explicitly to Luther's *Assertio:* "What is the point of praising obedience if in doing good or evil works we are the kind of instrument for God that an ax is to a carpenter? But such a tool are we all if Wyclif is right. All things before and after grace, good equally with ill, yes even things indifferent, are done by sheer necessity. Which opinion Luther approves." Cf. Erasmus, *Ausgewählte Werke,* p. 88. We will see later that Thomas could use the example of the carpenter and the ax, however, with a dramatically different result, since he was able to conceive of divine causality as truly transcendent causality, a causality that includes the genuine contingency of the human *liberum arbitrium!* On Erasmus's life and thought, see the informative as well as sympathetic accounts by Cornelius Augustijn, "Erasmus, Desiderius (1466/69-1536)," *Theologische Realenzyklopädie,* 10:1-18; and Louis Dupré, *Passage to Modernity: An Essay in the Hermeneutics of Nature and Culture* (New Haven, CT: Yale University Press, 1993), pp. 194ff.

lastic discourse that his humanist tastes loathed. Even more fateful was the definition he offered of "free will," or "natural freedom": "By free choice . . . we mean a power of the human will by which a man can apply himself to the things which lead to eternal salvation, or turn away from them."[22] In light of the theological issue at stake and of Augustine's own mature position, this definition was shockingly deficient, for it seemed simply to underwrite the nominalist Semi-Pelagianism Luther so vigorously opposed. We might not go completely wrong in assuming that Luther stopped reading Erasmus's treatise at this very point, seeing his worst fears come true. It did not matter that later in the treatise Erasmus allowed grace to make an appearance in aiding the human will, and offered a tentative nod in the direction of the late Augustine and the Thomists as positions possible to hold.[23]

In his 1525 response, *On the Bondage of the Will (De servo arbitrio)*, Luther painted a picture of Erasmus as a humanist skeptic[24] who disingenuously offered a "probable" opinion about what for Luther was most central to the Christian faith and — worse — submitted a blatantly Semi-Pelagian definition of the free will, and this based on the alleged evidence of Scripture. Luther reacted most forcefully, and his theological intentions

22. Rupp and Watson, *Luther and Erasmus*, p. 47. "Porro liberum arbitrium hoc loco sentimus vim humanae voluntatis, qua se possit homo applicare ad ea, quae perducunt ad aeternam salutem, aut ab iisdem avertere." Erasmus, *Ausgewählte Werke*, p. 36. Cf. Luther's analysis of this definition, Rupp and Watson, *Luther and Erasmus*, pp. 169ff.; Luther, *Kritische Gesamtausgabe*, vol. 8, pp. 662ff.

23. Rupp and Watson, *Luther and Erasmus*, pp. 51ff.; cf. Erasmus, *Ausgewählte Werke*, pp. 50ff. Erasmus's eventual rejoinder to Luther's *De servo arbitrio*, a two-volume work with the title *Hyperaspistes* (liber I, 1526; liber II, 1527) in which he greatly clarified and nuanced his position — albeit without ever fully grasping Augustine's insistence on the primacy of God's agency in the act of faith — was largely ignored.

24. Erasmus had his critics also on the Catholic side. (For the long history of portrayals of Erasmus, see Augustijn, "Erasmus, Desiderius," pp. 12ff.) For a rather devastating account of him, see the *spiritus rector* of modern Catholic Reformation history, Joseph Lortz, *The Reformation in Germany*, vol. 1, trans. Ronald Walls (New York: Herder, 1939, 1968), pp. 144-56. "That is Erasmus' basic attitude — his vagueness. In theology, however, vagueness means to be a-dogmatic or un-dogmatic. In theology, Erasmus was a born relativist" (p. 150). More recent research on Erasmus, however, has brought the picture of the comprehensive skeptic into serious question. At least in light of his late work against Luther, *Hyperaspistes* I and II, it seems indisputable that Erasmus preferred a reticence of theological assertion in questions where the Church had not promulgated a binding teaching and opposed the declaration of premature definitions *(definire)*, but he allowed the making of theological assertions *(asserere)*. Cf. Erasmus, *Hyperaspistes I*, in *Ausgewählte Werke*, pp. 248 54.

were undoubtedly Augustinian:[25] "Rapt" *(rapi)* into communion by God, the human receives genuine freedom.[26] But in an effort to set the record straight once and for all, Luther went too far: God is not merely the first and final agent of human salvation but its sole agent, with the human remaining purely passive *(mere passive).*

We can observe this radical passivity in relationship to God in a central — albeit rhetorically overcharged — passage from Luther's text, which has given rise to the (false) charge of Manichean tendencies in Luther's thought:

> In short, if we are under the god of this world, away from the work and Spirit of the true God, we are held captive to his will, as Paul says to Timothy (2 Tim. 2:26), so that we cannot will anything but what he wills. . . . And this we do readily and willingly, according to the nature of the will, which would not be a will if it were compelled; for compulsion is rather (so to say) "unwill" [*noluntas*]. But if a Stronger One comes who overcomes him and takes us as His spoil, then through his Spirit we are again slaves and captives — though this is royal freedom — so that we readily will and do what he wills. Thus the human will is placed between the two like a beast of burden. If God rides it, it wills and goes where God wills. . . . If Satan rides it, it wills and goes where Satan wills; nor can it choose to run to either of the two riders or to seek him out, but the riders themselves contend for the possession and control of it.[27]

One might want to question the Satanology implied in this passage and also ask how any sensible account of personal responsibility for sin can be maintained under these proposed conditions.[28] However, much more cen-

---

25. See Rupp and Watson, *Luther and Erasmus,* p. 174; Luther, *Kritische Gesamtausgabe,* vol. 8, p. 665. Here Luther drew upon the second book of Augustine's late *Contra Iulianum,* where Augustine used, for the only time, the notion "servum arbitrium": "Utinam Dei dono, et non libero, vel potius servo proprie voluntatis arbitrio" (*Contra Iulianum* 2.8.23; PL 44:689). For the important differences between Augustine and Luther regarding the meaning of this concept, see Harry McSorley's pertinent excursus "The Meaning of 'Servum Arbitrium' in Augustine," in his *Luther: Right or Wrong?* pp. 90-93.

26. For the best recent interpretation of this undervalued but crucial aspect of Luther's *De servo arbitrio,* see Robert W. Jenson, "An Ontology of Freedom in the *De servo arbitrio* of Luther," *Modern Theology* 10 (1994): 247-52; and idem, *Systematic Theology,* vol. 2, *The Works of God* (New York: Oxford University Press, 1999), pp. 105-8.

27. Rupp and Watson, *Luther and Erasmus,* 140; Luther, *Kritische Gesamtausgabe,* vol. 8, p. 635.

28. Cf. the nuanced and detailed discussion of the question, "Does the devil cause sin?" in Aquinas, *De malo,* q. 3, a. 3, in which Thomas rightly concludes that "the will's move-

257

tral to our present concern is the fact that the ontological link between natural, or created, freedom and the acquired Christian freedom in the act of conversion is severed. Luther's legitimate Augustinian concern of rebutting even the subtlest form of (Semi-)Pelagianism is hampered by the burden of what looks all too similar to the formulation in the *Assertio* and hence all too much like theological determinism.[29]

The Erasmus-Luther exchange shows in a paradigmatic way that the twin problems of Semi-Pelagianism and theological determinism arise whenever theologians fail to uphold or straightforwardly deny the notion that divine providence operates infallibly by way of both necessity and contingency. The classical Thomist form of maintaining this notion was to insist on the real distinction between *necessitas consequentis* and *necessitas consequentiae*. In his *De servo arbitrio*, Luther explicitly dismissed this distinction as a sophistic wordplay; and this I regard as the most consequential *philosophical* error in Luther's treatise.

The classical illustration for this distinction is that of Socrates sitting or standing. When Socrates sits he sits, necessarily, as long as he is sitting (this by *necessitas consequentiae*, or *suppositionis*), the reason being that it is impossible for him to sit and not sit at the same time. However, Socrates sits contingently, or freely (that is, not by *necessitas consequentis*), because it is always possible for him to stand. On the other hand, consider a puppet sitting on a chair. Unlike Socrates, the puppet must remain sitting on the

---

ment directly comes from the will and God, who causes the will, who alone acts within the will and can incline the will to whatever he should will. But God cannot cause sin, as I have shown before. Therefore, we conclude that only the will directly causes human sin. Therefore, it is clear that the devil does not, properly speaking, directly cause sin but causes sin only as a persuader." Aquinas, *De malo*, in *The* De Malo *of Thomas Aquinas*, ed. Brian Davies, trans. Richard Regan (Oxford: Oxford University Press, 2001), p. 247. All subsequent quotations of *De malo* will be taken from this edition.

29. I agree with McSorley's judgment that "Luther's necessitarian argument *can* be interpreted in the sense of Thomas Aquinas, namely, that all things happen necessarily *(ex suppositione)* in view of God's immutable will, but not by an absolute necessity which would exclude free or contingent actions. We hold, further, that Luther's argument *must* be so interpreted if we are to avoid accusing Luther of that type of glaring contradiction which one rarely finds in thinkers of Luther's stature" (*Luther: Right or Wrong?* p. 329, original emphasis). The most important reason McSorley advances to support this judgment is that Luther indeed "explicitly and repeatedly affirms that man has *liberum arbitrium* 'in the realm of things below him' or 'in respect of what is below him' or 'in his own kingdom' where man 'is led by his own will and not by the precepts of another' and where God 'has granted him a free use of things at his own will'" (p. 327).

chair until it is removed by another force *(necessitas consequentis)*. Hence the crucial difference between the two types of necessity: Contingency is excluded only by absolute necessity, not by conditional necessity.

Thomas offered a version of this example in *De malo* and concluded: "And so as we most certainly see that Socrates is sitting when he is sitting, although it be not absolutely necessary on that account that he be sitting, so also the contingency of things is not taken away because God sees everything in itself that happens." Most instructively, Thomas's next point anticipates the thrust of the third and final part of this chapter:

> And regarding God's will, we should note that God's will universally causes being and every consequence of being, and so both necessity and contingency. And his will is above the ordination of the necessary and the contingent, as it is above the whole of created existing. And so we distinguish the necessity and contingency in things in relation to created causes, which the divine will has ordained in relation to their effects, namely, that there be immutable causes of necessary effects and mutable causes of contingent effects, not by the relationship of things to God's will, which is their universal cause.[30]

I will argue later that it is precisely Thomas's metaphysics of being that allows for the real distinction between *necessitas consequentis* and *necessitas consequentiae*.

Because Luther rejected this crucial distinction as a "playing with words," he could not regard genuine contingency as the result of God's will.[31] Rather, he saw it as

> fundamentally necessary and salutary for a Christian, to know that God foreknows nothing contingently, but that he foresees and purposes and does all things by his immutable, eternal, and infallible will. . . . From this it follows irrefutably that everything we do, everything that happens, even if it seems to us to happen mutably and contingently, happens in fact nonetheless necessarily and immutably, if you have regard to the will of God.[32]

---

30. *De malo*, q. 16, a. 7, ad 15; Davies, *The* De Malo *of Thomas Aquinas*, p. 911.

31. Rupp and Watson, *Luther and Erasmus*, 120; Luther, *Kritische Gesamtausgabe*, vol. 8, p. 617: "Quid autem istis ludibriis verborum efficiunt?"

32. Rupp and Watson, *Luther and Erasmus*, 118-19; Luther, *Kritische Gesamtausgabe*, vol. 8, p. 615.

Clearly, Luther had to exclude genuine contingency from consideration, because in his conceptual framework genuine contingency turns into a potential competitor with God's creative power. Only by embracing the distinction between *necessitas consequentis* and *necessitas consequentiae* and hence the kind of metaphysics of being that was put aside by nominalism would he have been able to conceive of God's creative power as genuinely transcendent, as a power that can operate through necessity as well as contingency and thus can very well effect even the free choices of humans. In his eagerness to undercut the semi-Pelagian error once and for all, by likening the human to a beast of burden with either God or Satan as its rider, Luther seems to have accepted the price that in the act of conversion the human being has to be less than a human person, less than the creature to whom God has granted the gift of created freedom. McSorley rightly states that "a personal, free decision of faith is explicitly excluded by Luther's over-extended concept of *servum arbitrium*."[33]

Both Erasmus and Luther seem to have operated under the de facto influence of a new and increasingly dominant notion of human freedom promoted by intellectual forces as substantively different and internally diverse as nominalism and humanism.[34] At the root of this new notion lay a libertarian account of spontaneity based on a concept of contingency operative on the same ontological plane as divine causality and hence in a competitive relationship with it. Erasmus seems to have entertained this

---

33. McSorley, *Luther: Right or Wrong?* p. 332. At the same time, McSorley discerns in the normative doctrinal teachings of Lutheranism, most expressly in the *Solid Declaration* of the *Formula of Concord*, a subtle yet significant modification of Luther's position in *De servo arbitrio*: "The clear implication of Article II, 18 is that the free will, illuminated and ruled by the Holy Spirit ("spiritu Dei illuminatum et rectum") *can* cooperate in man's conversion, justice and salvation and *can* 'believe and give assent when the Holy Spirit offers the grace of God.' Such a doctrine is in full harmony with the teaching of the Council of Trent that man's free will, *activated by God,* cooperates by assenting to God in order to obtain the grace of justification. The Lutheran confessional statements thus overcome one of the chief objections against DSA [*De servo arbitrio*], namely, that it leaves no place for man's free decision in faith. The doctrine of man's 'unfreedom' which is contained in the Lutheran confessional writings, especially in the *Formula of Concord,* corresponds closely to the biblical-Catholic doctrine that the free will of man is totally incapable of doing anything that is truly good *coram Deo* or of freeing itself from its sinful situation. It must *be* freed by the grace of Christ. Then it becomes, in a formula reminiscent of Augustine, a liberated will *(arbitrium liberatum).* The Holy Spirit *begins* the work of conversion in us; we are able to cooperate with him because of the new powers and the gifts he gives us." McSorley, *Luther: Right or Wrong?* pp. 361-62 (original emphasis).

34. See Louis Dupré, *Passage to Modernity,* pp. 120-44.

notion of freedom in the human's relationship to God, while Luther — in a vigorous (hyper-) Augustinian reaction — regarded it strictly as a divine attribute. The question of grace and freedom in the act of conversion thus became a strict "either-or." Either the human turns to God freely, that is, by way of an act of spontaneous, self-determining freedom, and God subsequently comes to the human's aid; *or* God irresistibly turns the human in an act in which the human remains completely passive. Bouyer aptly captures the emerging picture:

> For both Erasmus and Luther, to say that God and man act together in justification must mean that their joint action is analogous to that of two men drawing the same load. Consequently, the more one does, the less the other; whence, for Luther, realising anew that grace does everything in salvation, it follows of necessity that man does nothing. But Erasmus desired to uphold the other aspect of tradition; that salvation is truly ours implies that we are ourselves active.[35]

Should one wonder what the impact of Ockham's razor — entities are not to be multiplied beyond necessity — might have been in the centuries in which the *via moderna* unfolded?[36] A rigorous nominalist conception of *liberum arbitrium* just does not fit well with the notion of divine operative grace. If both agents are to act, the first cause of any form of co-operation must lie with one or the other. Luther took the one side and, in good Augustinian but equally good nominalist fashion, deleted the unnecessary factor, the "empty word," *liberum arbitrium.* Erasmus took the other side and, in good humanist but equally good nominalist fashion, defined

35. Bouyer, *The Spirit and Forms of Protestantism,* pp. 156-57.

36. Rega Wood insists that Ockham refrained from using the principle of parsimony, that is, the razor, in the economy of salvation. See Rega Wood, "Ockham's Repudiation of Pelagianism," in *The Cambridge Companion to Ockham,* ed. Paul Vincent Spade (Cambridge: Cambridge University Press, 1999), pp. 350-74, 358. Even so, that would not have prevented his students in the *via moderna* from applying the rule. Indeed, they might eventually have asked whether one would not want to be a bit more consistent across the board, especially if there are no overarching metaphysical reasons not also to economize the economy of salvation. An indication that this in fact was precisely the case in dismissing the distinction between *necessitas consequentis* and *necessitas consequentiae* can be found in the instructive study by Martin Seils, *Der Gedanke vom Zusammenwirken Gottes und des Menschen in Luthers Theologie* (Gütersloh: Gütersloher Verlagshaus Gerd Mohn, 1962), p. 98, where Seils points to Johannes Altenstaig's nominalist *Lexicon theologicum* (Leiden, 1580). Oberman, in the nominalist glossary at the end of his *Harvest of Medieval Theology,* refers to an earlier version, Altenstaig's *Vocabularius theologie* (Hagenau, 1517).

liberum arbitrium competitively, as the first cause of its proper agency, God then joining as an auxiliary cause strengthening and eventually securing the human effort. Hence, what became unavailable to both Erasmus and Luther was the radical, non-competitive transcendent causality of God as upheld explicitly by Thomas and implicitly in the late works of Augustine — a causality that allowed genuine contingency to fall utterly under the infallible divine providence and hence illuminate the real distinction between the *necessitas consequentis* and the *necessitas consequentiae,* or *suppositionis.*

When we characterize Erasmus's and Luther's positions as two reductive Augustinianisms *post-Ockham,* it would be false to assume that their respective accounts simply mirrored each other. The Erasmus of the *De libero arbitrio,* while capturing the early Augustine and displaying remarkable familiarity with Origen's account of human freedom, missed the central tenets of the late Augustine and remained disturbingly hospitable to the kind of Semi-Pelagianism that found a home among Ockhamist theologians as well as leading humanists. In other words, Erasmus's Augustinianism was erroneous primarily in matters theological. Conversely, Luther's account, while remaining fundamentally in accord with the central theological tenet of the late Augustine (and the Thomas of the second Parisian period) regarding the *initium fidei,* was erroneous primarily in matters *philosophical.*[37]

The epochal Erasmus-Luther exchange offers exemplary evidence of the fact that it is deeply problematic to discern the mystery of grace and free will ostensibly on the grounds of Scripture alone while leaving the implied philosophical conceptualities unaddressed. As we will see, both Erasmus and Luther could claim with some legitimacy to be Augustinians of sorts, Erasmus drawing exclusively upon the early Augustine up to and including *De libero arbitrio* and Luther relying completely on the Augustine of the late Pelagian controversies. But how was it possible for both to see themselves as apologists of Augustine, especially on the matter of grace and free will?

37. *Nota bene:* Luther's nominalist inability to conceive of a non-competitive account of divine and human causality/agency in the *ordo salutis* was arguably the cause of the serious theological deficiencies in other areas, especially in his inability to conceive "created grace" as a "second nature" and hence to grasp the divine-human cooperation, non-competitive and asymmetrical, in the order of grace as constitutively informed by the supernaturally infused virtues of faith, hope, and charity.

II. Augustine's Complex Position[38]

It is notoriously difficult to get a full grasp of the vast corpus produced by the preeminent "Doctor of Grace" during his long life. In his prolificacy he might be rivaled only by Thomas and Martin Luther. Throughout his life, Augustine maintained most of what he argued for in his relatively early work *On Free Will (De libero arbitrio)*.[39] However, on one single — albeit theologically decisive — point, he corrected his position. In a nutshell: The early Augustine, prior to his elevation to the episcopate in 395, taught the same error he later refuted most vigorously, namely, the Semi-Pelagian error, which attributed the beginning of salvation *(initium fidei)* to the human's free will. This claim is precisely what Thomas, by the time he was composing *Summa theologiae* I-II, identified as the error of the early Augustine,[40] what Erasmus submitted as his definition of "free will" in his *De libero arbitrio*, and what Luther most intensely attacked in his *De servo arbitrio*.

Augustine's mature position emerged in a complex process. Around the year 418, his doctrine of the divine operation of conversion, that is, of the *interior* operative grace, seems to have been in place. It was only around 426, when he began to compose his treatise *On Grace and Free Will* that he defended a second operative grace completing the first — the grace of perseverance.[41] For our purpose, three aspects of his mature position, handily available in *On Grace and Free Will,* are most pertinent. First, he continued to hold that God has revealed to us through his Holy Scriptures that there exists free will, *liberum arbitrium,* in the human being.[42] After settling the abundant scriptural evidence for this truth, he emphasized, second, that for an action of the free will to be genuinely good, the grace of

---

38. For a concise introduction to the complex controversy in which Augustine was involved toward the end of his life, see Marianne Djuth, "Initium fidei," in *Augustine through the Ages: An Encyclopedia,* ed. Allan D. Fitzgerald, O.S.A. (Grand Rapids: Eerdmans Publishing Company, 1999), pp. 447-51, and for a detailed historical reconstruction of Augustine's teaching on operative grace, see J. Patout Burns, *The Development of Augustine's Doctrine of Operative Grace* (Paris: Études Augustiniennes, 1980).

39. Augustine began to compose this work in 388, one year after his baptism, and completed it in 395.

40. *ST* I-II, q. 114, a. 5, ad 1. Cf. Augustine, *Retractationes* 1.23.

41. For a more detailed description, see the nuanced account in Burns, *Development of Augustine's Doctrine of Operative Grace,* pp. 141-82.

42. *De gratia et libero arbitrio,* 2.2: "Revelavit autem nobis per Scripturas suas sanctas, esse in homine liberum voluntatis arbitrium" (PL 44:880).

God must precede and accompany it.[43] Third, and most important, he argued that only after humans have received God's grace do they begin to have good merits.[44] It might be safe to say that Augustine's theology of grace reaches its very peak in the axiom that these merits are themselves God's gifts. And here we find the core of a theology of merit, sadly absent in the German pre-Reformation and early Reformation period: "If therefore your good merits are gifts of God, then God does not crown your merits insofar as they are your merits, but insofar as they are his gifts."[45] At the very core of this teaching of merit stands Augustine's crucial distinction between two moments, or types, of grace: first, operative grace *(gratia operans)*, through which God gives the good will itself to perform good acts; and second, cooperative grace *(gratia cooperans)*, through which God cooperates with the human free will in the actual performance of the good act. Hence, Augustine would maintain that God operates the good will in human beings without their assent, but when human beings will and do what is good, God cooperates with them. Put negatively, without God's operative and cooperative grace, neither faith, hope, and love nor good works are possible.[46]

Lest Augustine's teaching on the beginning of faith be dismissed as the bygone position of an all too dominant theological figure, and as just that — the teaching of one theologian in the Church's long tradition — consider the fact that Augustine's teaching on the *initium fidei* became the Church's teaching, at the Second Council of Orange.

An Augustinian Excursus: The Second Council of Orange

In 529, after a lengthy period of complex disputes between Augustinians and Semi-Pelagians in the Gallic Church, the Second Council of Orange, argu-

---

43. *De gratia et libero arbitrio*, 4.6.

44. *De gratia et libero arbitrio*, 6.13.

45. *De gratia et libero arbitrio*, 6.15: "Si ergo Dei dona sunt bona merita tua, non Deus coronat merita tua tanquam merita tua, sed tanquam dona sua" (PL 44:891). In a somewhat abbreviated form, the *Catechism of the Catholic Church,* in the section on merit, quotes from a sermon of Augustine: "Grace has gone before us; now we are given what is due. . . . Our merits are God's gifts" (Ante gratia donabatur, modo debitum redditur. . . . Dona Ipsius sunt merita tua). *Catechismus Catholicae Ecclesiae,* no. 2009.

46. Augustine draws upon Phil 2:13 and Rom 8:28 in order to support his notions of *gratia operans* and *cooperans,* respectively.

ably one of the most important provincial Church councils in the history of the Latin Church, declared Augustine's teaching on the *initium fidei* to be *de fide* — indispensable to the Christian faith. To cite, in only the briefest form, the teachings from Orange II most relevant for our concerns:[47]

> CANON III: "That the grace of God is not given at man's call, but itself makes man call for it."[48]

> CANON IV: "That God, to cleanse us from sin, does not wait for, but prepares our will."[49]

> CANON V: "That the beginning of faith is not of ourselves, but of the grace of God."[50]

> CANON VI: "That without the grace of God mercy is not bestowed upon us when we believe and seek for it; rather, it is grace itself which causes us to believe and seek for it."[51]

> CANON VII: "That by the powers of nature without grace we are not able to think or choose any good thing pertaining to our salvation."[52]

> CANON IX: "Of the help of God, by which we do good works — It is of God's gift when we think rightly, and keep our steps from falsehood and unrighteousness; for as often as we do good, God works in us and with us that we may work."[53]

---

47. The full text of the Latin original and an English translation can be found in F. H. Woods, *Canons of the Second Council of Orange, A.D. 529: Text, with an Introduction, Translation, and Notes* (Oxford: James Thornton, 1882). Except where noted otherwise, all quotations of the council text are taken from this edition.

48. "Quod gratia Dei non ad invocationem detur, sed ipsa faciat ut invocetur." Cf. Denzinger and Schönmetzer, *Enchiridion Symbolorum,* no. 373.

49. "Quod Deus, ut a peccato purgemur, voluntatem nostram non expectet, sed praeparet." Cf. *Enchiridion Symbolorum,* no. 374.

50. "Quod initium fidei non ex nobis, sed ex gratia Dei sit." Cf. *Enchiridion Symbolorum,* no. 375.

51. "Quod sine gratia Dei credentibus et petentibus misericordia non conferatur, cum gratia ipsa faciat ut credamus et petamus." Cf. *Enchiridion Symbolorum,* no. 376.

52. "Quod viribus naturae bonum aliquid quod ad salutem pertineat, cogitare aut eligere sine gratia non possimus." Cf. *Enchiridion Symbolorum,* no. 377.

53. "De adjutorio Dei, per quod bona operamur. Divini est muneris, cum et recte cogitamus, et pedes nostros a falsitate et injustitia continemus; quoties enim bona agimus, Deus in nobis atque nobiscum ut operemur operatur." Cf. *Enchiridion Symbolorum,* no. 379.

CANON XXII: "Of the things which properly belong to men — No man has anything of his own but falsehood and sin."[54] Which sounds like a quotation from Martin Luther, who would say: "Free will prior to grace is capable only of sinning."[55]

The Second Council of Orange maintains time and again that *liberum arbitrium* exists; it was not annihilated by original sin. At the same time, "through the sin of the first man, free choice was so biassed and weakened that no one can afterwards either love God as he ought, or believe in God, or work for God's sake what is good, unless the grace of Divine mercy prevents [e.g., goes before or precedes: R. H.] him."[56] These canons and definitions surely lack the conceptual sophistication and rhetorical brilliance of Augustine's own theology; nonetheless, they constitute the normative inscription of fundamental tenets of Augustinian theology into the tradition of the Latin Church.[57]

The fate of the Second Council of Orange, however, was a curious one. As Henri Bouillard has convincingly argued, until about the eighth century its decrees were held in high esteem. Yet, from the tenth to the middle of the sixteenth century, theologians seem to have been utterly unaware of the fact that there had been a Second Council of Orange and that

---

54. "De his quae hominum propria sunt. Nemo habet de suo nisi mendacium et peccatum." Cf. *Enchiridion Symbolorum*, no. 392.

55. Luther, *Contra malignum I. eccii iudicium*, idem, *Kritische Gesamtausgabe*, vol. 2, p. 647, lines 3ff.: "Eccius Lipsiae concessit, liberum arbitrium ante gratiam non valere nisi ad peccandum: ergo non valet ad bonum sed tantum ad malum. Ubi ergo libertas eius?"

56. Woods, *Canons of the Second Council of Orange*, p. 45. "Quod per peccatum primi hominis inclinatum et attenuatum fuerit liberum arbitrium, ut nullus postea aut diligere Deum sicut oportuit, aut credere in Deum, aut operari propter Deum quod bonum est possit, nisi eum gratia misericordiae divinae praevenerit" (p. 44). Canon 1 refers to the soul injured ("laesa") by the sin of the first human. Canon 8 refers to the *liberum arbitrium* as weakened ("infirmatum") and injured ("laesum") by it. In canon 13 we find an even stronger formulation. Not only is the choice of the will weakened in the first human ("in primo homine infirmatum"); it is also described as "lost" ("amissum"). Might this one word offer the key for an ecumenically constructive understanding of what Martin Luther was pursuing by way of rhetorical overkill in his *De servo arbitrio* in order to unmask and confront a pervasive Semi-Pelagianism in a theological landscape dominated by nominalism and humanism?

57. One important tenet of the late Augustine's theology, his teaching of double predestination, embraced by Luther and Calvin, was expressly rejected by the Council: "Aliquos vero ad malum divina potestate praedestinatos esse, non solum non credimus, sed etiam si sunt qui tantum malum credere velint, cum omni detestatione illis anathema dicimus." Woods, *Canons of the Second Council of Orange*, p. 46.

it had produced these normative teachings, to the effect that Augustine's late struggle against what was much later dubbed "Semi-Pelagianism" was lost on virtually all medieval theologians.[58] Only at the Council of Trent were these decrees rediscovered and reaffirmed.[59] Following Bouillard, Max Seckler and Joseph Wawrykow are inclined to think that Thomas probably did not have access during his Roman period to the acts of the Second Council of Orange, but quite likely did have access to the full text of such important treatises of the late Augustine as *De gratia et libero arbitrio, De correptione et gratia, De dono perseverantiae,* and *De praedestinatione sanctorum* — texts that were otherwise either unavailable to most medieval theologians or, at best, selectively available in the form of various collections of Augustinian *dicta.*[60] Hence, we should assume that Thomas, in his later life and antecedent to his second Parisian period, became a rare exception to the virtually collective medieval amnesia about Augustine's late theology of grace.[61]

In a day and age when not a few post–Vatican II theologians are eager to dilute or even jettison the Church's teaching on original sin, as well as prevenient grace, for the sake of an easier — but thereby misunderstood — evangelization, it is crucial to remember and reappropriate the canons of this council. Orange II's unwavering insistence on prevenient grace, as well as the arrant impotence of the *liberum arbitrium* in matters of salvation, constitutes a small but critical bridge across the Reformation divide. To put the matter differently, had the canons of the Second Council of Orange been alive and well in late medieval theology, Luther would not have been in need of "rediscovering" Augustine against the nominal-

---

58. Henri Bouillard, *Conversion et grâce chez S. Thomas d'Aquin* (Paris: Aubier, 1944), pp. 97-102. Notable exceptions are the Lombard, Gregor of Rimini, and students of Thomas such as John Capreolus and Henry of Gorkum. For an instructive study on this matter, see Denis R. Janz, *Luther and Late Medieval Thomism: A Study in Theological Anthropology* (Waterloo: Wilfrid Laurier University Press, 1983), esp. pp. 43-91.

59. Denzinger and Schönmetzer's *Enchiridion symbolorum,* 36th ed., puts it the following way: "Hoc concilium, utpote solummodo provinciale plurimis ignotum et mox per saecula oblivioni traditum, disputationibus demum Concilii Tridentini memoriae redditum est" (p. 131).

60. Consider the fact that Luther "discovered" the late Augustine only shortly before 1517 in the relatively recent (1506) Amorbach edition of Augustine's works.

61. See Max Seckler, *Instinkt und Glaubenswille nach Thomas von Aquin* (Mainz: Matthias-Grünewald, 1961), pp. 90-98; Joseph P. Wawrykow, *God's Grace and Human Action: "Merit" in the Theology of Thomas Aquinas* (Notre Dame, IN: University of Notre Dame Press, 1995), pp. 266-76.

ist theologians of the *via moderna* by rigorously appropriating, albeit in a new key, central tenets of the former's late theology. But alas, only at the Council of Trent were the canons of Orange II fully reclaimed and reinstated, and this by way of a thorough retrieval of the theology of the *doctor communis.*

III. Divine Transcendent Causality: Thomas's Surpassing Augustinian Synthesis

I shall conclude my *tour d'horizon* by turning finally and explicitly to the *doctor communis* himself. I should like to propose that by way of the pivotal Thomist axiom that grace presupposes as well as perfects nature[62] — as substantiated by Thomas's metaphysics of being, which climaxes in the surpassing beauty of divine transcendent causality — can we successfully avert the reductive alternatives of Erasmus's theologically as well as Luther's philosophically erroneous Augustinianism.

Undoubtedly, Thomas's salient axiom serves first and foremost to illuminate the supernatural end of humanity, the beatific vision, and the way God moves us to this end. Nevertheless, the same axiom also serves as a premier aid in understanding that the root of the mystery of divine and human operation in the act of conversion lies in the very nature of

---

62. *ST* I, q. 1, a. 8, ad 2: "Cum enim gratia non tollat naturam, sed perficiat, oportet quod naturalis ratio subserviat fidei; sicut et naturalis inclinatio voluntatis obsequitur caritati." ST I, q. 2, a. 2, ad 1: "Sic enim fides praesupponit cognitionem naturalem, sicut gratia naturam, et ut perfectio perfectibile."

For an instructive account of the emergence of the axiom "gratia supponit naturam" in the Patristic theologians to its full development in Bonaventure and Thomas, see J. B. Beumer, S.J., "Gratia supponit naturam: Zur Geschichte eines theologischen Prinzips," *Gregorianum* 20 (1939): 381-406. I would emphasize that in the subsequent discussion of Thomas I shall consider exclusively his mature views on the *initium fidei* from his second period of teaching at Paris (1268-72). On his biography, see exhaustively Jean-Pierre Torrell, O.P., *St. Thomas Aquinas,* vol. 1, *The Person and His Work,* trans. Robert Royal (Washington, DC: The Catholic University of America Press, 1996), esp. pp. 197-223; on the development of Thomas's thought on the *initium fidei,* see the definitive account by Bernard Lonergan, S.J., *The Collected Works of Bernard Lonergan, S.J.,* vol. 1, *Grace and Freedom: Operative Grace in the Thought of St. Thomas Aquinas,* ed. Frederick E. Crowe and Robert M. Doran (Toronto: University of Toronto Press, 2000), pp. 21-43, 98-104; and on the related topic of merit, see Wawrykow, *God's Grace and Human Action.* In the following, I am especially indebted to Lonergan's penetrating analysis of operative grace in Thomas's theology.

created freedom itself. For human free will, in its very natural structure, is a created reality all the way down. Hence, not only does it fall without remainder under the purview of divine providence,[63] but even more important, natural freedom as created reality is constituted and sustained by God's first gratuitous act *ad extra*, namely, his act of creation, which is to give being *(dare esse)*.[64] It is precisely in this regard that Thomas is most faithful to Augustine's mature intentions by developing a metaphysics of being that accounts for the ontological difference, that is, the principal difference between Creator and creature and, simultaneously, for utter creaturely contingency upon the Creator.[65] In the *dare esse*, the first and fundamental act of divine gratuity, God is the sole agent, such that *ipsum esse* is God's first effect.[66] This effect, however, does not subsist by itself but only in the plenitude of beings.[67] The latter we might conveniently abbreviate with the notion "nature."[68] Hence, in and through the act of being, God is always already closer to the creature than the creature to itself.[69]

Since quite obviously for Thomas, free will must be part and parcel

63. On this topic, see Stephen A. Long, "Divine Providence and John 15:5," in *Reading John with St. Thomas Aquinas,* ed. Dauphinais and Levering, pp. 140-52.

64. *1 Sent.,* 37.1.1c.: "Creare est dare esse." In elucidating divine transcendental causality primarily by way of Thomas's metaphysics of being, the subsequent modest and rather preliminary sketch does by no means claim to offer a sufficiently elaborated analysis of the human act in the *initium fidei.* Rather, a full account of the act of conversion would need to attend in much greater details than the scope of this chapter allows to Thomas's metaphysical psychology, which is as precise as it is compelling in its analytic rigor.

65. For a comprehensive and detailed recent historical reconstruction of Thomas's metaphysics of being, see John F. Wippel, *The Metaphysical Thought of Thomas Aquinas: From Finite Being to Uncreated Being* (Washington, DC: The Catholic University of America Press, 2000), and for attempts at reconstructing the metaphysics of being strictly *ad mentem Thomam,* see the numerous instructive and penetrating articles by Lawrence Dewan, O.P.

66. *Quaestiones disputatae de anima,* 6, ad 2: "Ipsum esse est actus ultimus qui participabilis est ab omnibus; ipsum autem nihil participat."

67. *Sententia libri Metaphysicae,* 12.1 (Marietti 2419): "Ens dicitur quasi esse habens, hoc autem solum est substantia, quae subsistit"; cf. *ST* I, q. 45, a. 4.

68. Thomas uses the notion of "nature" in numerous analogous ways. I refer here to his use of "nature" in the general sense of the whole order of creation ("Ipse est conditor et ordinator naturae." *De potentia* q. 1, a. 3, ad 1) and subsequently also to his use of "nature" as the essence of a thing, that is, that by virtue of which it is what it is, under the aspect of its characteristic action. See *De ente et essentia* 1, 45.

69. *ST* I, q. 8, a. 1 c.: "Esse autem est illud quod est magis intimum cuilibet, et quod profundius omnibus inest, cum sit formale respectu omnium quae in re sunt."

of creation all the way down, the substantiation of his theology of creation by his metaphysics of being obtains also, for our purposes most relevantly, for the reality of natural freedom. Consider his reasoning:

> The movement of the will is from within, as also is the movement of nature. Now although it is possible for something to move a natural thing, without being the cause of the thing moved, yet that alone, which is in some way the cause of a thing's nature, can cause a natural movement in that thing. . . . Accordingly man endowed with a will is sometimes moved by something that is not his cause; but that his voluntary movement be from an exterior principle that is not the cause of his will, is impossible.
>
> Now the cause of the will can be none other than God. And this is evident for two reasons. First, because the will is a power of the rational soul, which is caused by God alone, by creation, as was stated in the first part (q. 90, a. 2). Secondly, it is evident from the fact that the will is ordained to the universal good. Wherefore nothing else can be the cause of the will, except God Himself, Who is the universal good: while every other good is good by participation, and is some particular good, and a particular cause does not give a universal inclination. (*ST* I-II, q. 9, a. 6 c.)

Bernard Lonergan offers a succinct interpretation of Thomas's argument: "Because God creates the soul, he alone can operate within the will; again, because the will tends to the *bonum universale,* this tendency cannot be the effect of any particular cause but only of the universal cause, God."[70]

God causes the will — which is just one particular faculty of the soul, together with the soul itself — to be according to its own particular nature, that is, to tend to the *bonum universale,* whereby "inclinations of the will remain indeterminately disposed to many things"[71] depending on what the intellect proposes to the will as a good to tend to. Hence, the will in its particular nature is a function of God's *dare esse:*

> [W]hat first moves the intellect and the will is something superior to them, namely, God. And since he moves every kind of thing according to the nature of the moveable thing . . . he also moves the will according to its condition, as indeterminately disposed to many things, not in

70. Lonergan, *Grace and Freedom,* p. 103.
71. Aquinas, *De malo,* q. 6 c.; Davies, *The* De Malo *of Thomas Aquinas,* p. 457.

a necessary way. Therefore, if we should consider the movement of the will regarding the performance of an act, the will is evidently not moved in a necessary way.[72]

So also the external acts that result from deliberation *(consilium)* and choice *(electio)* — from the interplay between intellect and will[73] — that is, acts of genuine contingency, do not fall outside the divine giving of being and hence remain fully under the purview of divine providence: "And so it is not contrary to freedom that God cause acts of free choice."[74]

What we have considered thus far pertains to nature, the effect of the *dare esse,* God's first and fundamental gratuity *ad extra.* The *initium fidei* does not, however, belong to this effect; rather, it is the distinctive effect of grace. Grace in the precise sense must be understood as a *second,* unfathomable, surpassing gratuity (always already presupposing the gratuity of the *dare esse*) and, in that, fundamentally different from nature by (1) being contingent in relationship to nature, and (2) efficaciously turning human beings from sin to God, directing, and moving them to their supernatural end. Lest the fundamentally and exclusively Christological and pneumatological character of grace be lost, let me stress that for Thomas "the mystery of Christ's Incarnation and Passion is the way by which men obtain beatitude" (*ST* II-II, q. 2, a. 7 c.); specifically, "men become receivers of this grace through God's Son made man, Whose humanity grace filled first, and thence flowed forth to us" through the action of the Holy Spirit (*ST* I-II, q. 108, a. 1 c.). Consequently, grace is most intrinsically and hence constitutively the created effect of God in the human being of the Son's and the Spirit's saving mission (*ST* I, q. 43, a. 3).

Grace works by the logic of *convenientia* — a very Augustinian category — that is, by the logic of an unfathomable fittingness, calling forth praise and delight. But because nature is the "way of being," grace always comes "on the way of being."[75] For everything is included in the act of be-

72. Davies, *The* De Malo *of Thomas Aquinas,* p. 459.

73. For a more detailed account of the intellect's and the will's interaction, see chapter 2, pp. 47-59; and most recently, Michael S. Sherwin, O.P., *By Knowledge & By Love: Charity and Knowledge in the Moral Theology of St. Thomas Aquinas* (Washington, DC: The Catholic University of America Press, 2005), pp. 18-62.

74. Aquinas, *De malo,* q. 3, a. 2, ad 4; Davies, *The* De Malo *of Thomas Aquinas,* p. 239. "Et sic <non> repugnat libertati quod Deus est causa actus liberi arbitrii" (p. 238).

75. Ferdinand Ulrich, *Homo Abyssus: Das Wagnis der Seinsfrage,* 2nd ed., ed. Martin Bieler and Florian Pitschl (Freiburg: Johannes Verlag, 1998), p. 333.

ing.[76] Yet what does this mean for grace? Is grace to be understood as an intensification of being *(esse)*, on the same scale as nature, just infinitely more? No. For if it were so, the act of being would not be perfect in and of itself but would require grace for its perfection. Is grace then extrinsic to the act of being, a second act, foreign to and superimposed upon the first? Grace cannot be that either, since everything is contained in the act of being, the *actus ultimus*. Rather, the instantaneous unfolding of the *actus essendi* into the order and hierarchy of beings entails that everything is generally ordered to God, who is the universal good. This ordering comes about by way of the ordering of each being to its own proper final ends. As we will see, grace is the created effect of the gratuitous divine act — always coming on the way of being — that directs human beings to their supernatural end, that is, to God as their overarching specific end. But we are getting ahead of ourselves.

Remember at present that we are concerned exclusively with the initial conversion of the human being *sub conditione peccati* to God, an act that does not involve an infusion of habitual grace but solely the initial and fundamental operation of God converting the soul to himself — in short, operative grace. Hence, it should not surprise that the *initium fidei* is not the total conversion Thomas envisages but rather the very *beginning* of a comprehensive conversion in which the human — on the basis of habitual grace — increasingly takes part:

> Every movement of the will towards God can be termed a conversion to God. And so there is a threefold turning to God. The first is by the perfect love of God; this belongs to the creature enjoying the possession of God; and for such conversion, consummate grace is required. The next turning to God is that which merits beatitude; and for this there is required habitual grace, which is the principle of merit. The third conversion is that whereby a man disposes himself so that he may have grace; for this no habitual grace is required; but the operation of God, Who draws the soul towards Himself, according to Lamentations 5:21: "Convert us, O Lord, to Thee, and we shall be converted." *(ST* I, q. 62, a. 2, ad 3)

The conversion identified by Thomas in the third place is indeed the first and fundamental one, and the only one considered here.

Operative grace denotes the special act of God by which the human

---

76. *De potentia,* 1.1 c.: "[E]sse significat aliquid completum et simplex sed non subsistens."

being is efficaciously ordered to God as his or her supernatural end, that is, his or her overarching particular ultimate end. Put differently, operative grace is nothing other than the divine *initium* of the second gratuity by which God brings about the returning to God of the *actus essendi,* as it comes to subsist as human being, a returning that comes about by way of a gratuitous elevation of the human faculties of intellect and will. In order to understand the operation of grace correctly, we need to consider five distinctive, albeit closely interrelated, aspects of operative grace.

1. The Orientation of the Will

First, we need to call attention to the fact that in operative grace God acts on the will and not on the intellect. As Lonergan rightly avers: "The first act does not presuppose any object apprehended by the intellect; God acts directly on the radical orientation of the will."[77] Because the will is the efficient cause of all human acts and because it moves all the other powers of the soul to their acts, the will is the first principle of sin (*ST* I-II, q. 74, a. 1). And consequently, of all the powers of the soul, the will has been most fundamentally infected by original sin (*ST* I-II, q. 83, a. 3; *De malo,* q. 4, a. 2, c.). For this reason, it is the will that first and foremost needs to be restored. However, operative grace does not merely restore the will but orients the will such that God becomes the overarching specific ultimate end to which the will tends. It is on the basis of this gratuitous reorientation that the will commands the intellect to the act of faith.[78]

2. The Special Motion of Operative Grace

Next we need to emphasize that Thomas distinguishes the special motion of operative grace very clearly from the will's universal motion to the *bonum universale:*

77. Lonergan, *Grace and Freedom,* 128. Lonergan's insight does not contradict the fact that every free act of the will is informed by the intellect (*ST* I-II, q. 77, a. 2). Concrete sin is in the act of the *liberum arbitrium* and hence is the product of the will as well as the intellect: "Dicendum quod peccatum essentialiter consistit in actu liberi arbitrii, quod est *facultas voluntatis et rationis."* *ST* I-II, a. 77, a. 6 (emphasis added).

78. *ST* II-II, q. 2, a. 9 c.: "Now the act of believing is an act of the intellect assenting to the Divine truth at the command of the will moved by the grace of God"; *ST* II-II, q. 6, a. 1 c.: "Faith, as regards the assent which is the chief act of faith, is from God moving man inwardly by grace." For a detailed and nuanced account, see Sherwin, *By Knowledge & By Love,* pp. 119-46.

God moves man's will, as the Universal Mover, to the universal object of the will, which is good. And without this universal motion, man cannot will anything. But man determines himself by his reason to will this or that, which is true or apparent good. Nevertheless, sometimes God moves some specially [*specialiter*] to the willing of something determinate, which is good; as in the case of those whom He moves by grace. (*ST* I-II, q. 9, a. 6, ad 3)

Lonergan rightly points out that while this grace may be a habitual grace, "it may also be an actual grace that is a change of will."[79] In order to substantiate this claim, Lonergan refers to *De malo,* where Thomas states: "And an external cause alters free choice, as when God by grace changes the will of a human being from evil to good, as Proverbs 21:1 says: 'The heart of the king is in God's hands, and God will turn it whithersoever he willed.'"[80] This changing of the will from evil to good comes always on the way of being and consequently does not violate or contradict the will's proper operation. For "the will advanced to its first movement in virtue of the instigation [*instinctus*] of some exterior mover [*exterior movens*]" (*ST* I-II, q. 9, a. 4 c.), who is God himself (*ST* I-II, q. 9, a. 6 c.). Thanks to the divine *instinctus*,[81] the appetitive inclination of the will tends to God himself as the overarching specific good and ultimate end.

3. God's External, Transcendent Causality Operating Internally

Thomas uses the notion of an external cause to refer to God's alteration of free choice. "External" is here distinguished from "internal," where the latter is the proximate cause in the order of secondary causality. God as external cause is in no way extrinsic to the creature's nature or existence but external only to the creature's proximate causality. It is precisely the metaphysics of being that prevents this "externality" from being understood in the modern sense of a "first cause," issued by a "highest" or "perfect" being — that is, infinitely superior to all other causes and beings but still on an ontic continuum and hence in a competitive relationship with

79. Lonergan, *Grace and Freedom,* p. 104.

80. *De malo,* q. 16, a. 5 c.; Davies, *The* De Malo *of Thomas Aquinas,* p. 877.

81. At this point I can only stress the pivotal role the term "instinctus" plays in the development of Thomas's thoroughly anti-Semi-Pelagian theology of grace. For a full account, see Seckler, *Instinkt und Glaubenswille;* and more recently and accessibly, Sherwin, *By Knowledge & By Love,* pp. 139-44.

them because it does not transcend the ontological level of secondary causality. For Thomas, the external causality of grace remains transcendent causality all the way down and hence is not competitive with the internal proximate causality of the will — whose first universal mover is also God.

Lonergan, in his interpretation of Thomas's theology of operative grace, overcomes this nocuous modernist misunderstanding thanks to the "theorem of divine transcendence," which he sees at work in Thomas: "The Thomist higher synthesis was to place God above and beyond the created orders of necessity and contingence: because God is universal cause, his providence must be certain; but because he is a transcendent cause, there can be no incompatibility between terrestrial contingence and the causal certitude of providence."[82]

It would be a mistake, however, to create a competitive relationship between what Lonergan describes as a theorem and Thomas's metaphysics of being.[83] Rather, the theorem is consequent upon the cosmic emanation scheme operative in Thomas's metaphysics so that the former presupposes the latter: "For an instrument is a lower cause moved by a higher so as to produce an effect within the category proportionate to the higher; but in the cosmic hierarchy all causes are moved except the highest, and every effect is at least in the category of being; therefore, all causes except the highest are instruments."[84] David Burrell brings Lonergan's insistence upon God's transcendent causality (that is, transcending necessity as well as contingency) succinctly to the point when he states:

> So what freely comes forth from God in its very being can be brought to act freely by that same One who keeps it in existence. The how escapes

82. Lonergan, *Grace and Freedom,* pp. 81-82.

83. Lonergan characterizes a theorem as "something known by understanding the data already apprehended and not something known by adding a new datum to the apprehension, something like the principle of work and not something like another lever, something like the discovery of gravitation and not something like the discovery of America" (idem, *Grace and Freedom,* p. 147). David Burrell rightly points out that "we must speak here of *theorems* and of their *corollaries,* . . . because we cannot determine anything in the creature which indicates that it is an instrument. . . . That is, we know that the hammer did not build the house, yet that the carpenters who did are themselves instruments as well — that we cannot see. Yet we must assert it, although we can only assert it as a theorem." David B. Burrell, C.S.C., "Jacques Maritain and Bernard Lonergan on Divine and Human Freedom," in *The Future of Thomism,* ed. Deal W. Hudson and Dennis W. Moran (Notre Dame, IN: University of Notre Dame Press, 1992), p. 165 (original emphasis).

84. Lonergan, *Grace and Freedom,* p. 83.

us in both cases, of course, but using the language of 'theorems' links us expressly to the originating activity, and so reminds us that just as the how of creation escapes us (it is not a motion), so does the manner in which God causes agents to cause by "applying causes to effects."[85]

To summarize: Under the category of God as transcendent cause, operative grace is identical with the very act of the will willing God as supernatural ultimate end. Again quoting Lonergan: "God as external principle moves the will to the end, and in special cases He moves it by grace to a special end. Conspicuous among the latter is conversion, which is expressed entirely in terms of willing the end."[86]

4. Divine Instrumentality: The External Cause Moving Interiorly

When Thomas responds to the question whether human beings can prepare themselves for grace without the external aid of grace, he emphasizes that the gift of habitual grace is the precondition for right operation and enjoyment of God. In other words, the very medium for right operation and enjoyment of God is the acquired Christian freedom. But what is the first cause of this acquired freedom? Remember that it is precisely in this context that Thomas introduces the concept of the divine *instinctus*. Is the first cause of this freedom internal, intrinsic to its own proper causality — leading to an infinite regress of causes? Or is it external — violating the very nature of free choice itself? We must conclude that the first cause moves internally, interior to the will itself, but as external cause — the divine *instinctus*. Clearly, it is only a genuinely transcendent mode of causality that can fulfill these conditions. Hence, the divine *instinctus* cannot be simply the first in a chain of secondary causality. Rather, the whole sequence of secondary causality must relate instrumentally to the transcendent first cause.

Let us attend to Thomas's response at length:

> Now in order that man prepare himself to receive this gift, it is not necessary to presuppose any further habitual gift in the soul, otherwise we should go on to infinity. But we must presuppose a gratuitous gift of God, Who moves the soul inwardly or inspires the good wish. For in

85. Burrell, "Jacques Maritain and Bernard Lonergan on Divine and Human Freedom," p. 166.
86. Lonergan, *Grace and Freedom*, p. 125.

these two ways do we need the Divine assistance, as stated above (aa. 2, 3). Now that we need the help of God to move us, is manifest. For since every agent acts for an end, every cause must direct its effect to its end, and hence since the order of ends is according to the order of agents or movers, man must be directed to the last end by the motion of the first mover, and to the proximate end by the motion of any of the subordinate movers. . . . And thus since God is the first Mover simply, it is by His motion that everything seeks Him under the common notion of good, whereby everything seeks to be likened to God in its own way. Hence Dionysius says (*De Divinis Nominibus,* IV) that "God turns all to Himself." But He directs righteous men to Himself as to a special end [*ad specialem finem*], which they seek, and to which they wish to cling, according to Psalm 73:28, "it is good for Me to adhere to my God." And that they are *turned* to God can only spring from God's having *turned* them. Now to prepare oneself for grace is, as it were, to be turned to God; just as, whoever has his eyes turned away from the light of the sun, prepares himself to receive the sun's light, by turning his eyes towards the sun. Hence it is clear that man cannot prepare himself to receive the light of grace except by the gratuitous help of God moving him inwardly.[87]

Note the crucial sentence: "Now to prepare oneself for grace is, as it were, to be turned to God" *(Hoc autem est praeparare se ad gratiam, quasi ad Deum converti).* To prepare oneself for the gift of habitual grace, for acquired freedom, *is* to be turned to God. Such is the grammatical instantiation of understanding God as transcendent cause to move interiorly as a genuinely external cause.[88] In other words, one's own act of prep-

---

87. *ST* I-II, q. 109, a. 6 c. (original emphasis): "Sic igitur, cum Deus sit primum movens simpliciter, ex eius motione est quod omnia in ipsum convertantur secundum communem intentionem boni, per quam unumquodque intendit assimilari Deo secundum suum modum. Unde et Dionysius, in libro *de Divinis Nominibus* [c. 4 §10], dicit quod Deus 'convertit omnia ad seipsum.' Sed homines iustos convertit ad seipsum sicut ad specialem finem, quem intendunt, et cui cupiunt adhaerere sicut bono proprio; secundum illud *Psalmi* 72 [28]: 'Mihi adhaerere Deo bonum est.' Et ideo quod homo convertatur ad Deum, hoc non potest esse nisi Deo ipsum convertente. Hoc autem est praeparare se ad gratiam, quasi ad Deum converti: sicut ille qui habet oculum aversum a lumine solis, per hoc se praeparat ad recipiendum lumen solis, quod oculos suos convertit versus solem. Unde patet quod homo non potest se praeparare ad lumen gratiae suscipiendum, nisi per auxilium gratuitum Dei interius moventis."

88. Accordingly, the divine *instinctus,* introduced above, must be understood, not as a first cause in the chain of secondary causality, but as that transcendent cause to which the whole chain of secondary causality relates instrumentally.

aration is caused by God without that act losing its integrity as the will's proper operation, being drawn toward its end — but now being the special end of adhering to God. If this indeed obtains, there is no ontological difference between operative and cooperative grace; rather, they are to be understood as two moments of God's actual grace simply differentiated according to their different effects.[89]

5. *Operative and Cooperative Grace:* voluntas mota et non movens *and* voluntas mota et movens

Let us now attend more specifically to the particular distinction between operative and cooperative grace. In order to appreciate this distinction, we need to grasp that it presupposes a pivotal distinction in the voluntary action itself:

> Now, in a voluntary action, there is a twofold action, namely, the interior action of the will, and the external action: and each of these actions has its object. The end is properly the object of the interior act of the will: while the object of the external action is that on which the action is brought to bear. (*ST* I-II, q. 18, a. 6 c.)

While the interior action is concerned solely with the end itself, the external action pertains to the means that lead to the end, means that can entail proper proximate ends of their own, which are respectively objects of interior acts of the will.

This distinction is put to work as Thomas considers how God converts the soul to himself by giving himself to the will as a special good to be desired:

> Now there is a double act in us. First, there is the interior act of the will, and with regard to this act the will is a thing moved, and God is the mover [*istum actum, voluntas se habet ut mota, Deus autem ut movens*]; and especially when the will, which hitherto willed evil, begins to will good. And hence, inasmuch as God moves the human mind to this act, we speak of operating grace. (*ST* I-II, q. 111, a. 2 c.)

89. *ST* I-II, q. 111, a. 2, ad 4: "Operating and cooperating grace are the same grace; but are distinguished by their different effects."

Hence, the operative grace of conversion is the very act of the will willing God as the overarching special good to be desired, that is, as willing God as the supernatural end.[90] By giving himself as special end, God moves the will interiorly, since the will, being "wired" to desire good, is by internal premotion now oriented to God as ultimate end. Lonergan explains:

> The *voluntas mota et non movens* is the reception of divine action in the creature antecedent to any operation on the creature's part. So far from being a free act, it lies entirely outside the creature's power. But though not a free act in itself, it is the first principle of free acts, even internal free acts such as faith, fear, hope, sorrow, and repentance.[91]

Accordingly, the internal act of faith, arising from the new principle, is a free act, an act of *liberum arbitrium:* "Now the act of believing is an act of the intellect assenting to the divine truth at the command of the will moved by the grace of God, so that it is subject to the free-will [*liberum arbitrium*] in relation to God; and consequently the act of faith can be meritorious" (*ST* II-II, q. 2, a. 9, c.).

How does Thomas account for the second aspect of the "twofold action," the exterior acts by which the human person chooses (on the basis of the will's consent with the intellect's *consilium*) the means to attain the end?

> [S]ince [the exterior act] is commanded by the will, . . . the operation of this act is attributed to the will. And because God assists us in this act, both by strengthening our will interiorly so as to attain to the act, and by granting outwardly the capability of operating, it is with respect to this that we speak of cooperating grace. (*ST* I-II, q. 111, a. 2 c.)

Consequently, as Thomas emphasizes: "God does not justify us without ourselves, because whilst we are being justified we consent to God's justification *(justitiae)* by a movement of our free-will. Nevertheless this movement is not the cause of grace, but the effect; hence the whole operation

---

90. Though not irresistibly: "God does not cause grace not to be supplied to someone; rather, those not supplied with grace offer an obstacle to grace insofar as they turn themselves away from the light that does not turn itself away, as Dionysius says" (*De malo*, q. 3, a. 1, ad 8; Davies, *The* De Malo *of Thomas Aquinas*, p. 233). However, if God so wishes, God can move the will infallibly by inclining the person to good unto the end. Hence, "perseverance of the wayfarer does not fall under merit, since it depends solely on the Divine motion, which is the principle of all merit. Now God freely bestows the good of perseverance, on whomsoever He bestows it." *ST* I-II, q. 114, a. 9 c.

91. Lonergan, *Grace and Freedom*, p. 424.

pertains to grace."[92] The difference between *voluntas mota et non movens* and *voluntas mota et movens* is the difference between willing the end and willing the means leading to this end. Because this principle is constitutive of and therefore interior to the will's nature — albeit simultaneously as the relation of *dare esse* transcending it and thus constituting an external cause — its operation can also properly be described as the will's own preparation. Now, *voluntas mota et movens* simply renders the actualization of acquired freedom in the efficacious choice of means, as the will's proximate causality is now directed to its special end, God himself.[93]

What remained ontologically implicit in Augustine's controversial concerns becomes explicit by way of Thomas's metaphysics of being. Lonergan stresses rightly that

> in both cases the same theory of instrumentality and of freedom is in evidence: the will has its strip of autonomy, yet beyond this there is the ground from which free acts spring; and that ground God holds and moves as a fencer moves his whole rapier by grasping only the hilt. When the will is *mota et non movens, solus autem Deus movens, dicitur gratia operans*. On the other hand, when the will is *et mota et movens, dicitur gratia cooperans*. . . . In actual grace, divine operation effects the will of the end to become cooperation when this will of the end leads to an efficacious choice of means.[94]

Because it comes on the way of being *(esse)*, operative grace, by way of the divine *instinctus*, is closer to the human will than the will to itself.

92. *ST* I-II, q. 111, a. 2, ad 2: "Deus non sine nobis nos iustificat, quia per motum liberi arbitrii, dum iustificamur, Dei iustitiae consentimus. Ille tamen motus non est causa gratiae, sed effectus. Unde tota operatio pertinet ad gratiam." This act of consent, in which the will is moved and moves by itself, St. Thomas calls "cooperative grace," with God's act being logically as well as ontologically — yet not temporally — prior to the human act.

93. In his commentary on St. Paul's Epistle to the Romans — another of his late works — Thomas applies this actualization of the acquired freedom to the reality of the spiritual person, that is, the person who is moved by the higher prompting [*superiori instinctu*] of the Holy Spirit: "Homo spiritualis non quasi ex motu propriae voluntatis principaliter, sed ex instinctu Spiritus Sancti inclinatur ad aliquid agendum. . . . Non tamen per hoc excluditur quin viri spirituales, per voluntatem et liberum arbitrium operentur, quia ipsum motum voluntatis et liberi arbitrii Spiritus Sanctus in eis causat, secundum illud Phil. II: *Deus est qui operatur in nobis velle et perficere*" (*In ep. ad Romanos* c. VIII, l. III, in *S. Thomae Aquinitatis Doctoris Angelici in omnes S. Pauli Apostoli epistolas commentaria*, vol. 1, 7th ed. [Turin: Marietti, 1929], p. 111).

94. Lonergan, *Grace and Freedom*, p. 147.

Consequently, operative grace neither competes nor conflicts with the exercise of created freedom, or *electio humana,* as Thomas calls it. Rather, divine instrumentality and created freedom are the two sides of one and the same reality.

Now we have reached the apposite point to revisit the topic of necessity and contingency that drove the debate between Erasmus and Luther. Recall that Erasmus understood Wyclif's and Luther's "necessitarianism" to imply that humans are only instruments in God's hand, with their *liberum arbitrium* reduced to nothing and therefore their very humanity reduced to a subhuman form of existence. In an important sense, Luther agreed with Erasmus's judgment, except that he regarded such a humiliation as the most appropriate medicine to destroy the worst pathogen of original sin, *superbia,* pride. Neither Erasmus nor Luther was able conceptually to conceive divine transcendent causality in the way Thomas did. Thus the possibility of understanding instrumentality in a way that would encompass necessity as well as contingency was lost on them. And while Erasmus even referred to the Scholastic distinction between *necessitas consequentis* and *necessitas consequentiae* in order to score a point against Luther's position, he did not have the slightest clue how to put this crucial distinction to work conceptually. Had he not despised the discipline of Scholastic argumentation and been thoroughly uninformed with regard to Thomas's metaphysics of being, he might have been able to respond differently to Luther's alleged necessitarianism. Luther, as we have noted, rejected the distinction itself on clearly nominalist grounds and therefore faced the problem of a potential account of contingency that would be inherently competitive with the infallibility of the divine will and thus had to be rejected as well.

We have seen that an account of divine causality that transcends as well as encompasses both necessity and contingency depends on a metaphysics of being concordant with the notion that "God's will universally causes being and every consequence of being, and so both necessity and contingency."[95] Moreover, created freedom, the capacity to choose between alternatives and decide for or against a course of action, remains always intact, even *sub conditione peccati,* because the free will pertains solely to the interior act of deliberation in regard to the end(s), along with the *electio* of the external means to move toward the end(s). Regarding the end to which it is drawn, it is "wired" to the *bonum universale.* And under the

---

95. *De malo,* q. 16, a. 7, ad 15; Davies, *The De Malo of Thomas Aquinas,* p. 911.

condition of sin this can take the form of whatever seems to be a good, even to a person fully habituated into malice.[96] Only when the will's inclination is reoriented by God's particular operation of grace, the divine *instinctus,* to the special overarching end, indeed, the supernatural end per se — God himself — does the quality of the human's *electio* fundamentally change. Nonetheless, because God as transcendent, external cause, by way of operative grace, moves internally, the ensuing change is the person's own preparation.

So, my modest proposal is simply this: By way of his metaphysics of being, as it accounts for divine transcendent causality all the way down, Thomas offers a salutary way of preserving Augustine's fundamental insight that grace and free will do not need to come into a conflictual competition in the mystery of the *initium fidei.* On matters of grace and free will in the *initium fidei,* Thomas is a profoundly Augustinian theologian. This is obvious. What is less obvious and in need of recovery is the fact that even his metaphysics of being, rightly understood, ultimately serves none but proper Augustinian ends and that by way of his metaphysics of being Thomas is capable of achieving a surpassing Augustinian synthesis of unparalleled depth and beauty. The ongoing evangelical and hence ecumenical significance of this synthesis is that it offers a potent prophylactic against the pathogens of (semi-)Pelagian as well as (quasi-)necessitarian accounts of the *initium fidei,* numerously afloat in contemporary theology.[97]

---

96. *De malo,* q. 3, a. 12 c.: "And a habit sometimes inclines the will, when customary behavior has, as it were, turned the inclination to such a good into a habit or natural disposition for the transient good, and then the will of itself is inclined to the good by its own motion apart from any emotion. And this is to sin by choice, that is, deliberately, or purposely or even maliciously." Davies, *The De Malo of Thomas Aquinas,* p. 301.

97. Unfortunately, the important and original work by Dom M. John Farrelly, O.S.B., *Predestination, Grace, and Free Will* (Westminster, MD: Newman Press, 1964), came to my attention only after the completion of this chapter. In this noteworthy book — in good Benedictine fashion deeply immersed in the study of Scripture and the patristic tradition — Farrelly, not unlike Lonergan in the end, but by way of other means — argues for the surpassing superiority of Thomas's position in comparison to those advanced by the contestants in the (in)famous "De auxiliis" controversy. Anyone wishing to return to the speculative intricacies of this greatly instructive controversy cannot afford to bypass Farrelly's book, for the latter demonstrates convincingly that speculative theology can only afford to ignore at its own peril the rich wisdom accrued by positive theology's surpassing attention to Scripture and the patristic tradition. Contrary to some later scholastics, Thomas never committed this mistake, nor for that matter the opposite one we had the occasion to witness in Luther and Erasmus. This is one of the reasons why Thomas's work remains the single most important source for a proper theological ressourcement in the Latin tradition of the Church.

CHAPTER 8

"In Hope He Believed Against Hope" —
The Unity of Faith and Hope in Paul, Thomas,
and Benedict XVI

Etiam si occiderit me in ipso sperabo.

Job 13:15

Shaking the very foundations of the global economy, the financial implosions of 2008 and 2009 have been of an almost apocalyptic nature. Not the least of their many sobering effects is that we have acquired a renewed and deepened awareness of the fragility of all things human in general and more specifically, of all things modern. Such newly acquired keenness of view on the fragility of human matters lends urgency to looking afresh at the very core of the Christian faith. For it is here that the fragility of human matters, due to human nature as well as sin, is addressed most profoundly — and surpassingly saved. Even the most cursory *re-lecture* of Pope Benedict XVI's encyclical letter *Spe Salvi* amply demonstrates the importance of a contemporary ressourcement in the very core of the Christian faith in order to face in true Christian hope what amounts to just one more upheaval in the long crisis of modernity. Just consider the opening lines:

> *"SPE SALVI facti sumus"* — in hope we were saved, says Saint Paul to the Romans, and likewise to us (*Rom* 8:24). According to the Christian faith, "redemption" — salvation — is not simply a given. Redemption is offered to us in the sense that we have been given hope, trustworthy hope, by virtue of which we can face our present: the present, even if it is arduous, can be lived and accepted if it leads towards a goal, if we

can be sure of this goal, and if this goal is great enough to justify the effort of the journey. (§1)

To which goal does the present actually lead and how can we be sure of this goal? The recent global economic crisis has put into question the familiar hopes that have arisen from an all too attractive and seemingly secure goal — the endless growth of profit margins. These hopes, though, did not arise just yesterday on Wall Street or in any of the financial markets around the world. Rather, the roots of these hopes reach way down into what constitutes the self-understanding of the modern world, indeed, of modernity itself.[1] Pope Benedict addresses the matter straightforwardly:

> Again, we find ourselves facing the question: what may we hope? A self-critique of modernity is needed in dialogue with Christianity and its concept of hope. In this dialogue Christians too, in the context of their knowledge and experience, must learn anew in what their hope truly consists, what they have to offer to the world and what they cannot offer. Flowing into this self-critique of the modern age there also has to be a self-critique of modern Christianity, which must constantly renew its self-understanding setting out from its roots. (§22)

By beginning to ask again, what is the nature of Christian hope — in distinction from and contrast to all other human hopes — Christians have to turn to their own roots, and of these roots, the teaching of the apostle Paul is unquestionably one of the most essential and sustaining. Additionally, such a turning to the roots, such a ressourcement, will contribute, first, to a dialogue between Christianity and a modernity that in light of an impending economic and subsequent social collapse might be increasingly open to submit its most cherished convictions to a sustained critique. Second, such a dialogue would also contribute to a parallel proper self-critique of modern Christianity, that is, a Christianity that has increasingly defined itself by way of the project of modernity and its characteristic hopes, in short, has come to see itself almost exclusively as the religious aspect of modernity and consequently has become oblivious and even resentful of the faith that comes from the apostles.

---

1. For a recent astute reconsideration of Thomas's economic teachings as a critical contrast to the unexamined economic axioms entailed in the project of modernity, see Christopher A. Franks, *He Became Poor: The Poverty of Christ and Aquinas's Economic Teachings* (Grand Rapids: Eerdmans, 2009).

What would be the focus of such a self-critique of modernity and of modern Christianity in its midst? In *Spe Salvi,* Pope Benedict identifies two convictions most central to the self-understanding of modernity in its radical self-differentiation from all other epochs of history: first, *progress* guided by human reason, primarily understood as technological and managerial progress; and second, *freedom* as autonomous and rational self-determination. Due to modernity's ever increasing technological dominion over nature and a simultaneously ever-increasing autonomous self-realization, Pope Benedict sees as centrally related to the ideas of progress and freedom the respective faith and hope of modernity in an irreversible historical progress toward an ever better and brighter future.[2] But what does progress *really* mean? What is *true* progress? Presupposing hypothetically the modern understanding of rational progress and freedom, Pope Benedict advances a subtle argument. Roughly adumbrated, it goes like this: If progress is to be true progress, human reason cannot be merely technological reason. Rather, human reason must be deeply informed by moral reasoning, a reasoning that truly guides human freedom. And such a morally informed and guided reason must necessarily be open to the differentiation between good and evil, which is, the Pope emphasizes, identical with reason's openness to the saving forces of faith. He states:

> Only thus does reason become truly human. It becomes human only if it is capable of directing the will along the right path, and it is capable of this only if it looks beyond itself. Otherwise, man's situation, in view of the imbalance between his material capacity and the lack of judgment in his heart, becomes a threat for him and for creation. Thus where freedom is concerned, we must remember that human freedom always requires a convergence of various freedoms. Yet this convergence cannot succeed unless it is determined by a common intrinsic criterion of measurement, which is the foundation and goal of our freedom. Let us put it very simply: man needs God, otherwise he remains without hope. (§23)

2. In one brief phrase Pope Benedict indicates what such a Christian dialogue with the self-critique of modernity might look like: "We have all witnessed the way in which progress, in the wrong hands, can become and has indeed become a terrifying progress in evil. If technical progress is not matched by corresponding progress in man's ethical formation, in man's inner growth (cf. *Eph* 3:16; *2 Cor* 4:16), then it is not progress at all, but a threat for man and for the world" (§22).

In short, hope is only true hope if it is grounded in the truth. And it is here that Pope Benedict turns to the apostle Paul: "Paul reminds the Ephesians that before their encounter with Christ, they were 'without hope and without God in the world' (*Eph* 2:12)" (§2). What makes this apostolic statement radical is the explicit link between God and hope, that is, the claim that the only hope deserving the name is directed to attaining God, and such hope arises from the encounter with Christ. For only through Christ does eternal life with God become possible. And this surpassing good indeed gives rise to a hope — Christian hope — that infinitely transcends all ordinary human hopes. Because, however, Christ can only be received by way of faith, the relationship between faith and hope is paramount in order to understand the nature of true hope. But are not faith and hope actually almost the same, Pope Benedict asks; "'Hope', in fact, is a key word in Biblical faith — so much so that in several passages the words 'faith' and 'hope' seem interchangeable" (§2). Nevertheless: no. Faith and hope seem to be almost interchangeable because they are so intimately connected with each other. But while this is the case, they are still by no means simply interchangeable. For, as Pope Benedict emphasizes, "to come to know God — the true God — means to receive hope" (§3). To come to know God, the true God, in his personal identity comes about by no other way than by faith. It is by faith in the one true God that hope, the great hope, arises. For in faith we come to know the God of love whose face is Christ — a truth most eloquently expounded in Pope Benedict's first encyclical *Deus Caritas Est.* Hence, the structure of this chapter will emulate the theological grammar exemplified in *Spe Salvi,* first, by considering two constitutive aspects of faith; second, by analyzing the nature and structure of hope; and third, by attending to a saint of the modern period, Josephine Bakhita, in whose life Pope Benedict sees his hopeful pedagogy on hope realized: "In hope she believed against hope." In the first two sections, on faith and hope, I shall advance a Thomist *re-lecture* of *Spe Salvi,* not in order to force the encyclical letter into a Procrustean bed. On the contrary, I wish to demonstrate, first, that *Spe Salvi* does its own ressourcement in the thought of Thomas Aquinas and, second, that reading the encyclical letter in light of Thomas's theology of grace and of the theological virtues allows for a more comprehensive reception of the encyclical's teaching on faith and hope.

I. Faith — Substance of Things Hoped For

There is no other access to Christian hope than by way of faith.[3] Hence, in order to be able to elucidate the nature and scope of Christian hope, Pope Benedict has first to attend to the nature of faith. But has faith not become one of the most elusive and contested theological concepts, claimed and transmuted by the project of modernity itself? Where to turn in order to get a sure footing on this most central topic of Christian theology?

For an initial answer Pope Benedict does not turn immediately to the epistles of the apostle Paul but rather to an epistle that tradition for a long time — *pace* Origen — attributed to Paul, but that modern scholarly consensus now believes had another author: the Letter to the Hebrews.[4] Pope Benedict approaches the teaching of the apostle Paul by way of a prior consideration of a central passage in the Letter to the Hebrews. I will argue that Pope Benedict's consideration of faith and hope according to Hebrews 11:1 is meant first and foremost to protect the ongoing reception of Paul's apostolic teaching from the subjectivist distortions and existentialist reductions of not a few modern Protestant, as well as Catholic, scholars who too uncritically embraced the project of modernity.

Faith as Habitus: The Objective Internal Principle or Substance of the Things Hoped For (Heb 11:1)

Consider how Pope Benedict interprets the letter's famous definition of faith-based hope in Hebrews 11:1. Because of the overall importance of this passage, I have to indulge the reader's patience with a longer citation from the encyclical:

> In the eleventh chapter of the *Letter to the Hebrews* (v. 1) we find a kind of definition of faith which closely links this virtue with hope. Ever since the Reformation there has been a dispute among exegetes over the central word of this phrase, but today a way towards a com-

---

3. Thomas argues this point quite explicitly. In order to hope, that is, to aspire to an arduous good in the future, a good difficult but possible to attain, one must first know that good and the way to attain it (*Summa theologiae* II-II, q. 17, a. 7).

4. For a helpful recent discussion of the authorship of Hebrews, see Anthony C. Thiselton, "Hebrews," in *Eerdmans Commentary on the Bible*, ed. James D. G. Dunn and John W. Rogerson (Grand Rapids: Eerdmans, 2003), p. 1451.

mon interpretation seems to be opening up once more. For the time being I shall leave this central word untranslated. The sentence therefore reads as follows: "Faith is the *hypostasis* of things hoped for; the proof of things not seen." For the Fathers and for the theologians of the Middle Ages, it was clear that the Greek word *hypostasis* was to be rendered in Latin with the term *substantia*. The Latin translation of the text produced at the time of the early Church therefore reads: *Est autem fides sperandarum substantia rerum, argumentum non apparentium* — faith is the "substance" of things hoped for; the proof of things not seen. (§7)

At this point, significantly, Pope Benedict turns to no other theological authority but that of the *doctor communis,* in order to elucidate the nature of faith:

> Saint Thomas Aquinas, using the terminology of the philosophical tradition to which he belonged, explains it as follows: faith is a *habitus,* that is, a stable disposition of the spirit, through which eternal life takes root in us and reason is led to consent to what it does not see. The concept of "substance" is therefore modified in the sense that through faith, in a tentative way, or as we might say "in embryo" — and thus according to the "substance" — there are already present in us the things that are hoped for: a whole, true life. And precisely because the thing itself is already present, this presence of what is to come also creates certainty: this "thing" which must come is not yet visible in the external world (it does not "appear"), but because of the fact that, as an initial and dynamic reality, we carry it within us, a certain perception of it has even now come into existence. (§7)

I regard the following sentence to be the very center of this crucial passage on faith: "'In embryo' — and thus according to the 'substance' — there are already present in us the things that are hoped for: a whole, true life." Being a stable disposition of the spirit, faith is the beginning of eternal life in the believer. Significantly, at this important juncture of the encyclical, Pope Benedict draws heavily on Thomas's teaching in order to interpret the kind of definition of faith found in Hebrews 11:1.[5] I shall limit myself here to

---

5. Thomas argues, in a way too complex to reproduce here in full, that Hebrews 11:1 proposes indeed a fitting *(conveniens)* definition of faith. For his full line of argumentation, see *ST* II-II, q. 4, a. 1 and *Ad Hebraeos,* c. xi, pp. 405-8 (Marietti).

highlighting what I regard to be three central elements of Thomas's exposition of faith as echoed in *Spe Salvi*.

1. As a *habitus* (infused by habitual grace at justification), faith establishes in the believer a firm and continuous disposition to acts of faith. Through these acts of faith *(credere)* eternal life is begun in the believer "in embryo," that is, according to its "substance," and the intellect assents to what is non-apparent.[6]

2. What the intellect assents to, that is, embraces as true, is indeed the "substance" of eternal life. Pope Benedict indicates that Thomas in the context of interpreting Hebrews 11:1 understands "substance" in a modified sense, precisely along the lines that allow a notion of an objective embryonic presence of that which is hoped for in the believer by way of the supernatural, infused habit of faith. Thomas understands "substance" here analogically along the lines of something that is still to become or develop, but is already present in its principle. Thomas's analogical use of substance in *ST* II-II, q. 4, a. 1, ad 1 seems to be the source of Pope Benedict's expression "in embryo," a contemporary metaphorical way of adopting Thomas's technically more precise but also less accessible analogical use of substance: "in embryo" — and thus according to the 'substance' — there is already present in us the things that are hoped for" (§7).[7]

3. In his *Commentary on the Epistle to the Hebrews* — which antedates *Summa theologiae* II-II by several years — we encounter verbatim the definition of faith found in *ST* II-II, q. 4, a. 1: "Faith is the habit of the mind by which eternal life is begun in us, making the intellect to assent to things which are not apparent."[8] Among various interpretations on *argumentum/elenchos* put forward in the tradition of interpreting Hebrews 11:1, Thomas leans toward understanding *argumentum* as "an arguing of the mind"

---

6. *ST* II-II, q. 4, a. 1: "[F]ides est habitus mentis, qua inchoatur vita aeterna in nobis, faciens intellectum assentire non apparentibus."

7. *ST* II-II, q. 4, a. 1, ad 1: "*Substance,* here, does not stand for the supreme genus condivided with the other genera, but for that likeness to substance which is found in each genus, inasmuch as the first thing in a genus contains the others virtually and is said to be the substance thereof." "[S]ubstantia non sumitur hic secundum quod est genus generalissimum contra alia genera divisum: sed secundum quod in quolibet genere invenitur quaedam similitudo substantiae, prout scilicet primum in quolibet genere, continens in se alia virtute, dicitur esse substantia illorum."

8. Thomas Aquinas, *Commentary on the Epistle to the Hebrews*, c. 11, lect. 1, trans. Chrysostom Baer, O.Praem. (South Bend, IN: St. Augustine's Press, 2006), p. 231; *Ad Hebraeos*, c. xi, l. 1, p. 408 (Marietti): "[F]ides est habitus mentis qua inchoatur vita aeterna in nobis, faciens intellectum assentire non apparentibus."

(arguens mentem), such that the effect is taken for the cause, "since from the certitude of the thing it happens that the mind is forced to assent."[9] Pope Benedict affirms this long-standing interpretation: the substance or principle of a new reality within us makes the intellect assent to it. He contrasts this objective sense of *argumentum* with an understanding that would take it as a disposition of the subject, as a conviction held by the believer. Thomas makes brief mention that this alternative reading has some followers, but says no more on the matter.[10] Less than three hundred years after Thomas's death, a version of this other reading shall instantiate a powerful alternative tradition of interpreting the *argumentum* in Hebrews 11:1, a reading that in subsequent centuries, though arguably unintentionally, opened the floodgates for an eventual radical subjectivization of the faith. Significantly, Pope Benedict categorizes Martin Luther's position on this important matter in clear contradistinction to Thomas's position:

> To Luther, who was not particularly fond of the *Letter to the Hebrews,* the concept of "substance," in the context of his view of faith, meant nothing. For this reason he understood the term *hypostasis/substance* not in the objective sense (of a reality present within us), but in the subjective sense, as an expression of an interior attitude, and so, naturally, he also had to understand the term *argumentum* as a disposition of the subject. In the twentieth century this interpretation became prevalent — at least in Germany — in Catholic exegesis too, so that the ecumenical translation into German of the New Testament, ap-

9. *Commentary on the Epistle to the Hebrews,* p. 230; *Ad Hebraeos,* c. xi, l. 1, p. 408 (Marietti): "Vel si sequamur etymologiam nominis qua dicitur argumentum, quasi arguens mentem, tunc accipit effectum pro causa, quia ex certitudine rei provenit, quod mens cogatur ad assentiendum."

10. *ST* II-II, q. 4, a. 1 and *Commentary on the Epistle to the Hebrews,* p. 231: "For where we have *argument,* another reading has *conviction,* since by the divine authority the intellect is convinced to assent to those things which it does not see." *Ad Hebraeos,* c. xi, l. 1, p. 408 (Marietti): "Ubi enim nos argumentum habemus, habet alia littera *convictio,* quia per auctoritatem divinam convincitur intellectus ad assentiendum his quae non videt" (my emphasis). In private correspondence Jörgen Vijgen has pointed out to me the noteworthy fact that Thomas seems to use the term "convictio" only four times in his whole corpus of writings, and three of these four times in order to indicate that others have proposed "convictio" where he prefers "argumentum." Next to the two instances familiar to us — *ST* II-II, q. 4, a. 1 and *Ad Heb.,* c. 11, l. 1 — there is also *De veritate,* q. 14, a. 2. The fourth place is *II. Ad Thessalonicenses,* c. 3, l. 2, where "convictio" is yoked with "manifestatio." In short, it seems to be rather obvious that Thomas has no use whatsover for "convictio" in a true understanding of the nature of faith.

proved by the Bishops, reads as follows: *Glaube aber ist: Feststehen in dem, was man erhofft, Überzeugtsein von dem, was man nicht sieht* (faith is: standing firm in what one hopes, being convinced of what one does not see). This in itself is not incorrect, but it is not the meaning of the text, because the Greek term used *(elenchos)* does not have the subjective sense of "conviction" but the objective sense of "proof." Rightly, therefore, recent Protestant exegesis has arrived at a different interpretation. (§7)

And now follows what Pope Benedict would regard as the proper consensus between modern biblical scholarship and the traditional Catholic interpretation of Hebrews 11:1:

Faith is not merely a personal reaching out towards things to come that are still totally absent: *[faith] gives us something. It gives us even now something of the reality we are waiting for, and this present reality constitutes for us a "proof" of the things that are still unseen.* Faith draws the future into the present, so that it is no longer simply a "not yet." The fact that this future exists changes the present; the present is touched by the future reality, and thus the things of the future spill over into those of the present and those of the present into those of the future. (§7; my emphasis)[11]

11. Martin Luther dismisses the interpretation of *"argumentum/elenchos"* as "proof" — that is, as interior proof — in consequence of his prior, deeper, and theologically more detrimental rejection of faith as a supernatural, infused habit of sanctifying grace. Without presupposing such an infused habit, however, Luther must necessarily take the "proof" to be a merely external phenomenon of homiletical proclamation and theological discourse. On such an assumption, Luther, of course, has a hard time understanding how Adam or Abel could have ever been believers. And so it does not come as a surprise that Luther "could not be pleased" with the interpretation of *"argumentum/elenchos"* as "proof." What is, however, surprising is the ease with which Luther affords the omission of considering to any degree the arguments of the rejected tradition of interpretation, let alone of representing it correctly: "Here, however, they want 'argument' to be the 'proof,' the 'demonstration,' and, in general, what in dialectics is called the argument, so that there is some sure knowledge that certain things, that is, 'things invisible,' exist, namely, because this is how the patriarchs and other saints believed. This view does not please me, not only because from this opinion it would follow that Adam and Abel did not have faith — for, since they were the first believers, their faith was not certain for the reason that others had believed this way, but especially because it seems to be self-contradictory. For this way faith would be nothing else than one person's credulity of another person; and thus the apostle would be speaking not of the faith of all but only about a persuasion, and the proof would be passive, not active." *Luther's Works*, vol. 29, *Lectures on Titus, Philemon, and Hebrews*, ed. Jaroslav Pelikan

Arising from the principles of new life itself, the light of faith communicates this inchoate reality to the intellect to such a degree that the human will, presented with the surpassing good of this new life, commands the intellect to assent to this donation of the light of faith as a surpassing truth that renders certain things that are not apparent. Hence faith constitutes a stable disposition of the person — supernaturally given, not naturally acquired. This is the objective *internal* principle of faith. Human beings, however, are not angels. That is, human beings are essentially embodied and thus subject to the conditions of the material universe (space and time) and the respective intellectual configurations of such conditions: language, culture (family and society), and history. Integral to such a configuration is that truth can only be received, that is, understood, as well as communicated by way of propositions — irrespective of their narrative or discursive instantiation. Hence, in the case of human beings, the inner light of faith cannot deliver the truth without a corresponding external catechesis — the one as objective as the other — a linguistically configured and propositionally structured "form of teaching" by way of which the things hoped for are received as well as passed on. This indispensable external catechetical side of the faith is not simply a speculative theological stipulation based on the composite nature of the human being. It is, on the contrary, central to the apostle Paul's understanding of faith, although modern exegesis has largely neglected, or at least gravely underrated, it — arguably a result of the consistent subjectivization of faith in liberal Protestantism, the seedbed of modern Pauline exegesis.

---

and Walter A. Hansen (St. Louis: Concordia, 1968), p. 229; cf. *D. Martin Luthers Werke,* 120 vols. (Weimar: Böhlau und Nachfolger, 1883-2009) (henceforth *WA*), pp. 57-53, 226-27. Drawing exclusively on the homilies of Chrysostom on Hebrews and appealing to one reference in Lombard's *Sentences,* Luther regards faith as an internal, natural, though surely "given" operation of the believing subject, a "clinging to the Word of God" (*Luther's Works,* vol. 29, p. 230) ("adhaesio verbi Dei," from which follows the "possessio verbi Dei id est aeternorum bonorum" [*WA*, pp. 57-53, 228]). The attempt to regard faith as a human operation given by God, but without God's antecedent gift of internal illumination and the correlative infused habit of faith, leads to notorious ambiguities, insuperable difficulties, and hence interminable disagreements about the nature of faith in Protestant theology. For while faith is circumscribed by way of many illustrative and well-known metaphors, the nature of faith itself remains notoriously elusive. For a penetrating analysis of this problem at the very heart of the Protestant theology of justification by faith alone, see John Henry Newman's *Lectures on the Doctrine of Justification* from 1838, 3rd ed. (New York: Scribner, Welford, and Armstrong, 1874).

Faith as Assent: The Corresponding Objective External *"Form of Teaching"* (typos didaches) *(Rom 6:17)*

In a nutshell, the "form of teaching" *(typos didaches)* is Paul's answer to the question of how we receive and pass on what in the Letter to the Hebrews is called the substance of things hoped for. In the Letter to the Romans the new life of grace holds an exceedingly prominent place, for it constitutes the proximate terminus of the Christian existence: a life under a new obedience that begins in and with baptism. Becoming truly free is identical to being committed to the true Lord of the universe. This is what Paul has to say about the life of those who have been "buried . . . with [Christ] by baptism into death, so that as Christ was raised from the dead by the glory of the Father, we too might walk in newness of life" (Rom 6:4, RSV):

> What then? Are we to sin because we are not under law but under grace? By no means! Do you not know that if you yield yourselves to any one as obedient slaves, you are slaves of the one whom you obey, either of sin, which leads to death, or of obedience, which leads to righteousness? But thanks be to God, that you who were once slaves of sin have become obedient from the heart to the *standard of teaching* to which you were committed, and, having been set free from sin, have become slaves of righteousness." (Rom 6:15-19; my emphasis)

What is this "standard" or "form of teaching" (in Greek *typos didaches*, and in the Vulgate *forma doctrinae*) to which the Roman Christians "were committed," or, in some way more clearly, to which they "were given over"?

In order to offer at least the sketch of an answer to this complex question, I shall array three voices of the Catholic tradition of Biblical interpretation that give witness to a remarkable consonance of understanding. The most recent one is that of Heinrich Schlier, an eminent German New Testament scholar, who in the period right after World War II was one of Germany's most famous Lutheran converts to the Roman Catholic Church. In his commentary on the Letter to the Romans, he interprets *typos didaches* the following way:

> *Typos* is "form" or "shape," *typos didaches* is the form of teaching in the sense of a doctrine present in a specific form, resonating perhaps with the fact that a *typos* represents a pattern or model. Concretely, one might imagine the *didache* in the form of a baptismal symbol or even

as a catechetical formulation of doctrine in transmitted traditions. (cf. 1 Cor 11:23; 15:1ff)[12]

Schlier's interpretation resonates in remarkable ways with the reading put forth 1600 years earlier by the Cappadocian bishop and theologian Basil the Great. In his treatise *On the Holy Spirit* from the year A.D. 375, Basil takes both the baptismal event and the baptismal doctrine to be related with regard to the *typos didaches:*

> What makes us Christians? Faith, one says. How are we saved? Obviously through being born again in the grace of baptism. For how else? After we have seen that this, our salvation, is effected through the Father and the Son and the Holy Spirit, will we betray what we have received as the "form of teaching" (Rom 6:17)? . . . Those who do not perpetually adhere to the confession we made at our initiation, when we came over from idols to the living God (cf. 1 Thess 1:9), and do not cling to it their entire lives as to a secure shelter — they will exclude themselves from God's promises (cf. Eph 2:12) by setting themselves in opposition to that which they personally signed when they made the confession of faith.[13]

Let us finally turn to Thomas's *Commentary on Romans,* which date most likely from the last years of his life, 1272-73, years he spent in Naples. He understands "the form of teaching to which you were committed" as being "given over" by God to the *doctrina catholicae fidei,* the teaching of the Catholic faith. Thomas connects this "form of teaching" (in Latin *forma doctrinae*) with 2 Timothy 1:13: "Follow the pattern [the *forma*] of the sound words which you have heard from me."[14] To this *forma doctrinae* the catechumens were given over and to this they committed themselves com-

---

12. Heinrich Schlier, *Herders theologischer Kommentar zum Neuen Testament,* vol. 6, *Der Römerbrief,* 2nd ed. (Freiburg/Basel/Vienna: Herder, 1979), p. 209 (my translation).

13. Basil the Great of Caesarea, *Fontes Christiani,* vol. 12, *De Spiritu Sancto/Über den Heiligen Geist,* trans. and intro. by Hermann Josef Sieben, S.J. (Freiburg/Basel/Vienna: Herder, 1993), pp. 147-49; for the standard English edition, see *St. Basil the Great: On the Holy Spirit,* trans. David Anderson (Crestwood, NY: St. Vladimir's Seminary Press, 1980), pp. 46f.

14. "*[I]n eam formam doctrinae,* idest in doctrinam catholicae fidei (*Formam habens sanorum verborum quae a me audisti* [2 Tim 1:13]), *in quam traditi estis,* id est, cui vos totaliter subdidistis (*Semetipsos dederunt primum Deo, deinde nobis per voluntatem Dei* [2 Cor 8])." Aquinas, *In ep. ad Romanos,* c. VI, l. III, in *S. Thomae Aquinatis in omnes S. Pauli Apostoli epistolas commentaria,* vol. 1 (Turin: Marietti, 1929), p. 89.

pletely. In Thomas's interpretation, the interior baptismal equivalent to the exterior event of being given over or committed to the *forma doctrinae,* the *doctrina catholicae fidei,* is what Basil describes as the *paradosis,* the handing over of Father, Son, and Holy Spirit to the baptized person such that the Holy Trinity indwells the person who in baptism has received sanctifying grace.[15]

It is not accidental that we concluded this all too brief exegetical excursus on Paul's "form of teaching" with Thomas. For according to Thomas, faith as the supernatural, infused *inchoatio* of eternal life, and fidelity to the Church's teaching are nothing but two sides of the same coin. One of the most instructive commentaries on the inherent correlation between these two aspects of faith, *inchoatio vitae aeternae* as well as fidelity, can be found in Thomas's discussion of the object of faith in *ST* II-II, q. 1. Here, in the course of a single question, Thomas moves from considering in the first article the contemplation of the First Truth, God, to considering in the tenth article "Whether it belongs to the Sovereign Pontiff to draw up a symbol of faith?" We do not go wrong in assuming that Thomas suggests a profound interrelationship between the first and the tenth article. Christians are given over to the First Truth by way of the *forma doctrinae,* the standard of teaching, and the infused *inchoatio* of eternal life, faith, takes its concrete form as an act of fidelity, a deep commitment *(obsequium religiosum)* to the Church's teaching, to the *doctrina catholicae fidei.* Consider the opening section of the response from *ST* II-II, q. 1, a. 9:

> As the Apostle says (Heb. xi.6), *he that cometh to God, must believe that He is.* Now a man cannot believe, unless the truth be proposed to him that he may believe it. Hence the need for the truth of faith to be collected together, so that it might the more easily be proposed to all, lest anyone might stray from the truth through ignorance of the faith.[16]

---

15. *ST* I, q. 43, a. 3 and esp. a. 5: "The whole Trinity dwells in the mind by sanctifying grace, according to Job xiv.23: *We will come to him, and will make Our abode with him."* And *ST* III, q. 69, a. 4: "As Augustine says in the book on Infant Baptism (*De Pecc. Merit. et Remiss.* i), *the effect of Baptism is that the baptized are incorporated in Christ as His members.* Now the fullness of grace and virtues flows from Christ the Head to all His members, according to John i.16: *Of His fulness we all have received.* Hence it is clear that man receives grace and virtues in Baptism."

16. *ST* II-II, q. 1, a. 9: "[S]icut Apostolus dicit, *ad Heb.* 11, [6], *accedentem ad Deum oportet credere.* Credere autem non potest aliquis nisi ei veritas quam credat proponatur. Et ideo necessarium fuit veritatem fidei in unum colligi, ut facilius posset omnibus proponi, ne aliquis per ignorantiam a fidei veritate deficeret."

Hence, faith is *not* what it came to be in the wake of liberal Protestantism and a Catholic modernism eager to adopt such a notion, that is, faith as an existential, pre-conceptual act of trust, primordially and ineffably enacted in the depths of the religious subject and only subsequently expressed and confessed in community and in categories and expressions relative to the age, culture, and society in which they are made.[17] It is most likely in order to undercut from the outset this prevalent misunderstanding of faith in Paul that Pope Benedict turns to the Letter to the Hebrews before he turns to the apostle Paul. And by attending to an all too often neglected but crucial concept in Romans 6:17, we can better appreciate the profound consonance between faith as a supernatural, infused *habitus,* that is, as the objective *internal* principle or substance of the things hoped for, and the corresponding faith as assent to the *external* "form of teaching" in Paul.[18] To administer Thomist

---

17. George Lindbeck's widely accepted descriptor "experiential-expressivist" encapsulates still the most apt characterization of an understanding of faith that liberal Protestantism and Catholic modernism share. See George A. Lindbeck, *The Nature of Doctrine: Religion and Theology in a Postliberal Age,* 25th Anniversary Edition with a New Introduction by Bruce D. Marshall and a New Afterword by the Author (Louisville: Westminster/John Knox, 2009), pp. 17f. To be perfectly clear, the understanding of faith and religion largely shared by liberal Protestantism and Catholic modernism is not the understanding of faith held and defended by Luther and the subsequent generations of "Protestant orthodoxy." However, because of the notoriously elusive nature of faith that plagued Lutheran theology from early on (not to mention Luther's strong embrace of "convictio" as the key to understanding faith), matters changed drastically with the modern turn to the subject in matters of religion, a turn that arguably was facilitated by Luther's erroneous elevation — in matters of central truths of the Christian faith — of private judgment to prophetic judgment. Just consider the following telling remark of Luther's in his 1535 *Lectures on Galatians:* "[I]t is the gift of prophecy and our own effort, together with inward and outward trials, that opens to us the meaning of Paul and of all the Scriptures" (*Luther's Works,* vol. 26, *Lectures on Galatians 1535: Chapters 1–4,* ed. Jaroslav Pelikan and Walter A. Hansen [St. Louis: Concordia, 1963], p. 418). ("Ideo donum prophetiae et studium nostrum una cum tentationibus internis et externis aperiunt nobis sensum Pauli et omnium scripturarum" [WA 40/I, 634].) Based on what he regarded as an extraordinary, gratuitously granted fundamental insight or discovery, Luther claimed this gift of prophetic judgment exclusively for himself (and consequently also the entailed quasi-magisterial authority of advancing the true meaning of "Paul and all Scriptures"); however, the consequence of passing private judgment off as prophetic judgment was that every reader and hence interpreter of the Scriptures could with equally good reason claim for him- or herself what Luther should never have claimed for himself in the first place.

18. We must understand such a "symphonic" canonical reading of two distinct New Testament witnesses as the proper theological way of grasping the inner coherence of the apostolic *paradosis* across the New Testament, even and especially if instantiated in differing

conceptuality, the instrumental cause by way of which the intellect assents to what is to become a firm disposition of the human spirit, is nothing other than the "form of teaching" to which the faithful are given over, the apostolic *paradosis* as received in the Church's symbols.[19] Hence the substance of things hoped for is only to be had, is only accessible, in and through the Church's living faith,[20] which passes on publicly — for all to hear and to have — the "form of teaching," the *typos didaches,* to which one needs to be given over in baptism in order to receive in turn this new substance inwardly, the principle of the new life (the *inchoatio vitae aeternae*) that gives rise to the light of faith, an inner illumination which is the source of that certitude to which the intellect has to assent.[21]

---

and even heterogeneous worlds of thought. On this important topic of theological exegesis and hermeneutics of Scripture, I took guidance from Joseph Ratzinger/Benedict XVI, *Jesus von Nazareth* (Freiburg: Herder, 2007), pp. 15-20, as well as Joseph Cardinal Ratzinger, "Biblical Interpretation in Crisis," in *God's Word: Scripture — Tradition — Office* (San Francisco: Ignatius Press, 2008), pp. 91-126.

19. *ST* II-II, q. 1, a. 7: "The articles of faith stand in the same relation to the doctrine of faith as self-evident principles to a teaching based on natural reason." "[I]ta se habent in doctrina fidei articuli fidei sicut principia per se nota in doctrina quae per rationem naturalem habetur."

20. *ST* II-II, q. 1, a. 9, ad 3: "The confession of faith is drawn up in a symbol, in the person, as it were, of the whole Church, which is united together by faith. Now the faith of the Church is living faith; since such is the faith to be found in all those who are of the Church not only outwardly but also by merit. Hence the confession of faith is expressed in a symbol, in a manner that is in keeping with living faith, so that even if some of the faithful lack living faith, they should endeavor to acquire it." "[C]onfessio fidei traditur in symbolo quasi ex persona totius Ecclesiae, quae per fidem unitur. Fides autem Ecclesiae est fides formata: talis enim fides invenitur in omnibus illis qui sunt numero et merito de Ecclesia. Et ideo confessio fidei in symbolo traditur secundum quod convenit fidei formatae: ut etiam si qui fideles fidem formatam non habent, ad hanc formam pertingere studeant."

21. The present discussion of faith should not obscure the fact that — because faith is a participation in the divine Truth — the proper object of faith is God. This is what makes faith "theological faith" in the precise sense of the term: "The virtue of faith is an infused *habitus* that enables the human person to attain the transcendent God who is the First Truth." Romanus Cessario, O.P., *Christian Faith and the Theological Life* (Washington, DC: The Catholic University of America Press, 1996), pp. 57-58. Thomas puts the matter very curtly in his *Commentary on Romans:* "Credere autem, Deum demonstrat fidei materiam, secundum quod est virtus theologica, habens Deum pro objecto." *In ep. ad Rom.,* c. IV, l. 1, p. 58 (Marietti). On this complex topic, see the classical essay by Marie-Michel Labourdette, O.P., "La vie théologale selon saint Thomas: L'object de la foi," *Revue thomiste* 58 (1958): 597-622.

II. Hope

Its Foundation and Fulfillment in Christ

Having considered the objective internal, as well as the objective external, aspect of faith, we need to turn to one other aspect that marks the objective sense of the substance of things hoped for. For nowhere else but in baptism, as the apostle Paul explicitly stresses in Romans 6, does our future in Christ break into our lives, and "according to the 'substance' — there are already present in us the things that are hoped for: the whole true life" (*Spe Salvi,* §7). As already observed above, *Spe Salvi* clearly echoes Thomas, who holds that through faith, being a theological virtue and as such an infused, supernatural *habitus mentis,* eternal life has begun in us.[22] This *inchoatio* of the eternal life, however, has a distinct christoform configuration:

> We were buried therefore with [Christ] by baptism into death, so that as Christ was raised from the dead by the glory of the Father, we too might walk in newness of life. . . . So you also must consider yourselves dead to sin and alive to God in Christ Jesus. (Rom 6:4, 11)

And this whole true life present in the Christian is nothing but the life of Christ himself, or as Paul puts it in Colossians 1:27, "Christ in you, the hope of glory." *Christ himself, in us, is the real, objective foundation of hope.* And again the trajectory of Paul's fundamental insight leads us back to the Letter to the Hebrews where we hear a faint, but distinct echo: "We have this as a sure and steadfast anchor of the soul, a hope that enters into the inner shrine behind the curtain, where Jesus has gone as a forerunner on our behalf" (Heb 6:19-20a). Thomas offers the following commentary: "In Him Who is now veiled from our eyes he wants the anchor of our hope to be fixed."[23] The anchor of our hope can be fixed in Christ precisely because, in Pope Benedict's words, faith "gives us even now something of the reality we are waiting for, and this present reality constitutes for us a 'proof' of the things that are still unseen" (§7). Hope is stretched out between the fulfillment still veiled, on the one side, and on the other side, the very substance of the things hoped for, already infused in us as a new real-

---

22. *ST* II-II, q. 4, a. 1.

23. Thomas Aquinas, *Commentary on the Epistle to the Hebrews* c. 6, lect. 4, p. 139. "In illo ergo vult quod figatur anchora spei nostrae, qui est modo velatus ab oculis nostris" (Marietti, p. 359).

ity in an embryonic state, the *inchoatio vitae aeternae.* Hence the supernatural, infused habit of faith precedes and gives rise to supernatural hope, as Thomas argues in *ST* II-II, q. 17, a. 7:

> Absolutely speaking, faith precedes hope. For the object of hope is a future good, arduous but possible to obtain. In order, therefore, that we may hope, it is necessary for the object of hope to be proposed to us as possible. Now the object of hope is, in one way, eternal happiness, and, in another way, the Divine assistance . . . and both of these are proposed to us by faith, whereby we come to know that we are able to obtain eternal life, and that for this purpose the Divine assistance is ready for us, according to Hebrews xi. 6: *He that cometh to God, must believe that He is, and is a rewarder to them that seek Him.* Therefore it is evident that faith precedes hope.[24]

Its Nature and Structure

Having considered the foundation and fulfillment of hope in Christ, we need to turn to the unique inner structure of this hope. In order to begin such a consideration we shall again take our basic orientation from Paul, this time from his presentation of the prototype of faith-based hope in Romans 4:

> In hope he believed against hope, that he should become the father of many nations; as he had been told "so shall your descendants be." He did not weaken in faith when he considered his own body, which was as good as dead because he was about a hundred years old, or when he considered the barrenness of Sarah's womb. No distrust made him waver concerning the promise of God, but he grew strong in his faith as he gave glory to God, fully convinced that God was able to do what he had promised. (Rom 4:18-21)

24. *ST* II-II, q. 17, a. 7: "[F]ides absolute praecedit spem. Obiectum enim spei est bonum futurum arduum possibile haberi. Ad hoc ergo quod aliquis speret, requiritur quod obiectum spei proponatur ei ut possibile. Sed obiectum spei est uno modo beatitudo aeterna, et alio modo divinum auxilium. . . . Et utrumque eorum proponitur nobis per fidem, per quam nobis innotescit quod ad vitam aeternam possumus pervenire, et quod ad hoc paratum est nobis divinum auxilium: secundum illud *Heb.* 11, [6]: *Accedentem ad Deum oportet credere quia est, et quia inquirentibus se remunerator est.* Unde manifestum est quod fides praecedit spem."

We immediately perceive the profound inner connection between faith and hope in this passage. God's promise to Abraham constitutes the new substance of the things hoped for, an embryonic reality in him which is his faith. It is for this reason that "in hope he believed against hope." Paul is not waxing paradoxically at this point. For the two occurrences of the word "hope" in this sentence (παρ᾽ ἐλπίδα ἐπ᾽ ἐλπίδι) have two different meanings and the difference between these meanings discloses the very nature and structure of Christian hope in contrast to what we might want to call "ordinary hope."[25] For the hope, against which Abraham believed in hope, is the kind of ordinary hope we can find in all human beings to a smaller or larger degree.[26]

In order to differentiate between Christian hope and ordinary human hope, as well as to correlate the two kinds of hope, Pope Benedict draws upon conceptual resources developed most thoroughly by Thomas. For Thomas distinguishes clearly between (1) the passion of hope, (2) those virtues that are correlative to the passion of hope — humility and magnanimity, and (3) the supernatural, infused virtue of hope, that is, Christian hope proper.[27]

25. Thomas Aquinas, in his *Commentary on Romans,* is quite explicit about the contrast between Christian hope and ordinary hope: "[S]pes importat certam expectationem boni futuri, quae quidem certitudo est quandoque ex causa humana sive naturali, secundum illud I. Cor. ix: *Debet in spe, qui arat, arare:* quandoque vero certitudo expectantis est ex causa divina, secundum illud Ps. xxx: *In te, Domine, speravi, etc.* Hoc ergo bonum quod Abraham fieret pater multarum gentium, certitudinem habebat ex parte Dei promittentis; sed contrarium apparebat ex causa naturali sive humana. Ideo dicit: Qui contra spem causae naturalis vel humanae, credidit in spem, scilicet divinae promissionis." *In ep. ad Rom.,* c. iv, 1.3, pp. 64f. (Marietti).

26. Chrysostom, in his commentary *In epistulam ad Romanos* shares this interpretation: "Πῶς παρ᾽ ἐλπίδα ἐπ᾽ ἐλπίδι ἐπίστευσε; Παρ᾽ ἐλπίδα τὴν ἀνθρωπίνην, ἐπ᾽ ἐλπίδι τῇ τοῦ Θεοῦ." (I am indebted to Nathan Eubank for bringing to my attention this important passage in Chrysostom's commentary.)

27. On the complex topic of hope in Thomas's philosophical and theological thought, see Josef Pieper, *Über die Hoffnung* (Leipzig: Hegner, 1938); English edition: *On Hope,* trans. Mary Frances McCarthy (San Francisco: Ignatius, 1986); Servais Pinckaers, O.P., "La nature vertueuse de l'espérance," *Revue thomiste* 58 (1958): 405-42, 623-44; Marie-Michel Labourdette, O.P., *Cours de théologie morale,* vol. 9: *L'espérance (Thomas d'Aquin: Somme théologique* II-II, qq. 17-22) (Toulouse, 1959-1960); Ch.-A. Bernard, S.J., *Théologie de l'espérance selon saint Thomas d'Aquin* (Paris: J. Vrin, 1961); Albert Fries, C.Ss.R., "Hoffnung und Heilsgewißheit bei Thomas von Aquin," *Studia Moralia VII: Contributiones ad problema spei* (Rome: Desclée & Socii, 1969), pp. 131-236; Eberhard Schockenhoff, *Bonum hominis: Die anthropologischen und theologischen Grundlagen des Tugendbegriffs bei Thomas von Aquin*

1. The Passion of Hope

Passions are instinctive drives, or in Thomas's terminology, "acts of the sensitive appetite" that originate in the body and pertain to the soul "per accidens," that is, insofar as the soul is united with the body. The passion of hope is most essential for human life, for

> hope is a movement of the appetitive power ensuing from the apprehension of a future good, difficult but possible to obtain; namely, a stretching forth of the appetite to such a good.[28]

The strength of the movement of this appetitive power is proportionate to our present capacities, as well as to the nature of the good we aim to attain. Such hope is common and indeed indispensible to the human condition. Hope moves us constantly toward all kinds of arduous goods not yet attained. In light of the realization by the human mind that a desirable good, difficult to obtain, is in principle in reach and with persistence and effort of will can be attained, hope moves us toward this good. Hence by way of the anticipation of the good and the subsequent determination of the will toward it, as well as the appetitive movement toward it, our mind already participates in the good to be attained, whence arise confidence and a certain pleasure.[29] Remember, this is the kind of ordinary hope *against* which

---

(Mainz: Grünewald, 1987), pp. 286-351, 418-75; Bernard Schumacher, *A Philosophy of Hope: Josef Pieper and the Contemporary Debate on Hope,* trans. D. C. Schindler (New York: Fordham University Press, 2003).

28. *ST* I-II, q. 40, a. 2: "[S]pes est motus appetitivae virtutis consequens apprehensionem boni futuri ardui possibilis adipisci, scilicet extensio appetitus in huiusmodi obiectum."

29. Pertaining to the confidence to which such hope gives rise, see *ST* I-II, q. 40, a. 2, ad 2: "When a man desires a thing and reckons that he can get it, he believes that he will get it; and from this belief which proceeds in the cognitive power, the ensuing movement in the appetite is called confidence." "[I]llud quod homo desiderat, et aestimat se posse adipisci, credit se adepturum: et ex tali fide in cognitiva praecedente, motus sequens in appetitu fiducia nominatur." Pertaining to the pleasure such hope gives, see *ST* I-II, q. 32, a. 3: "[Q]uia maior est coniunctio secundum rem quam secundum similitudinem, quae est coniunctio cognitionis; itemque maior est coniunctio rei in actu quam in potentia: ideo maxima est delectatio quae fit per sensum, qui requirit praesentiam rei sensibilis. Secundum autem gradum tenet delectatio spei, in qua non solum est delectabilis coniunctio secundum apprehensionem, set etiam secundum facultatem vel potestatem adipiscendi bonum quod delectat. Tertium autem gradum tenet delectatio memoriae, quae habet solam coniunctionem apprehensionis." In contradistinction to the passion of hope, which gives rise to pleasure, the theological virtue of hope gives rise to joy — "rejoicing in hope" (Rom 12:12).

Abraham believed in hope. For such an ordinary hope arises solely from our specific capacities, skills, faculties, as well as experiences, and is consequently also limited by them.[30]

2. The Virtues Correlative to the Passion of Hope: Humility and Magnanimity

Remember, the object of the passion of hope is "a future good, difficult but possible to obtain," and the passion of hope "a movement of the appetitive power," "a stretching forth of the appetite to such a good."[31] Thomas characterizes this appetite as "irascible" (in contradistinction to a "concupiscible appetite"), because the former is directed to all kinds of goods that are hard to obtain and the obtaining of which might involve the overcoming of difficult obstacles. For the irascible appetite to be rightly governed by reason, namely, to be aiming at attaining the just mean, it must be informed by two specific moral virtues. Humility (rooted in the cardinal virtue of temperance) moderates the passion of hope and thus assists it in acting in conformity with the dictates of reason. Magnanimity (rooted in the cardinal virtue of courage) strengthens the passion of hope and directs attention to the subject of the moral act by aiming at the accomplishment of great deeds, as well as at the requisite honors that accompany the attainment of greatness.[32] Because of the central and sustaining role that magnanimity plays in governing the passion of hope, some interpreters of Thomas have understood, with good reason, the natural virtue of magnanimity as the natural virtue of hope.[33] If indeed the passion of hope is intrinsic to human nature, there must be a proximate virtue that perfects human agency insofar as it is informed by the passion of hope. It is therefore precisely in regard to magnanimity as the quasi-natural virtue of hope that Thomas characterizes the distinctive feature of the theological virtue of hope. A theological virtue has God for its object[34] and theological hope

---

30. *ST* I-II, q. 40, a. 5.

31. *ST* I-II, q. 40, a. 2.

32. *ST* II-II, q. 129, a. 1.

33. See R.-A. Gauthier, O.P., *Magnanimité: L'idéal de la grandeur dans la philosophie païenne et dans la théologie chrétienne* (Paris: J. Vrin, 1951), esp. pp. 295-371. The text of Thomas most centrally in support of understanding magnanimity as the natural virtue of hope is *In Sent.* III, d. 26, q. 2, a. 2, ad 4: "Sed tamen magnanimitas non est idem quod spes virtus; quia est circa arduum quod consistit in rebus humanis, non circa arduum quod est deus; *unde non est virtus theologica, sed moralis, participans aliquid a spe*" (my emphasis).

34. *ST* I-II, q. 62, a. 1.

therefore tends toward an arduous good "in reference to God as the last end, or as the first efficient cause."[35] About the natural virtue of magnanimity, in contrast, Thomas states:

> Magnanimity tends to something arduous in the hope of obtaining something that is within one's power, wherefore its proper object is the doing of great things. On the other hand, hope, as a theological virtue, regards something arduous, to be obtained by another's help.[36]

3. The Supernatural, Infused Virtue of Hope

A good that completely transcends human faculties and experiences can never become the object of the appetitive power of hope. For such a good must first be communicated by the First Truth Himself, as the apostle Paul emphasizes in 1 Corinthians 2:9-10: "What no eye has seen, nor ear heard, nor the heart of man conceived, what God has prepared for those who love him, God has revealed to us through the Spirit." The great hope against hope now, in which Abraham believed, is essentially a hope that arises from believing in the God who, as Paul so emphatically proclaims, "gives life to the dead and calls into existence the things that do not exist" (Rom 4:17). Christian hope is nothing other than the most perfect instantiation of this Abrahamic hope. This hope is a virtue and not simply a passion, for "the virtue of a thing is that which makes its subject good, and its work good likewise."[37] Every human act that attains its due rule, reason, or, surpassingly, God, is good. But the act of hope that is now considered does precisely this, it attains God:

35. *ST* II-II, q. 17, a. 5, ad 1: "in ordine ad Deum sicut ad ultimum finem et sicut ad primam causam efficientem."

36. *ST* II-II, q. 17, a. 5, ad 4: "[M]agnanimitas tendit in arduum sperans aliquid quod est suae potestatis. Unde proprie respicit operationem aliquorum magnorum. Sed spes, secundum quod est virtus theologica, respicit arduum alterius auxilio assequendum." See also *ST* II-II, q. 1, a. 3, ad 1: "Nevertheless neither can anything false come under hope, for a man hopes to obtain eternal life, not by his own power (since this would be an act of presumption), but with the help of grace; and if he perseveres therein he will obtain eternal life surely and infallibly." "Et tamen neque etiam spei subest falsum. Non enim aliquis sperat se habiturum vitam aeternam secundum propriam potestatem (hoc enim esset praesumptionis), sed secundum auxilium gratiae: in qua si perseveraverit, omnino infallibiliter vitam aeternam consequetur."

37. *ST* II-II, q. 17, a. 1: "Virtus uniuscuiusque rei est quae bonum facit habentem et opus eius bonum reddit." (Thomas cites the definition of a virtue offered by Aristotle in the *Nicomachean Ethics*, 1106a15.)

> [I]nsofar as we hope for anything as being possible to us by means of the Divine assistance, our hope attains God Himself, on Whose help it leans. It is therefore evident that hope is a virtue, since it causes a human act to be good and to attain its due rule.[38]

This virtue is a supernatural, infused virtue, because the *habitus* of this virtue flows from grace alone.[39] For not only is the attaining of the arduous good to which Christian hope is directed completely dependent upon God's initiating, accompanying, and completing causality (or agency). Rather, the arduous good is nothing short of eternal beatitude,[40] that is, the eternal union with God's own life of triune love, or as Pope Benedict puts it, "the supreme moment of satisfaction, in which totality embraces us and we embrace totality. . . . It would be like plunging into the ocean of infinite love, a moment in which time . . . no longer exists" (§12). Such an exceedingly extravagant and wild hope infinitely transcends the kinds of ordinary hopes we usually entertain on a daily basis:

> Eternal happiness does not enter into the heart of man perfectly, i.e., so that it be possible for a wayfarer to know its nature and quality; yet, under the general notion of the perfect good, it is possible for it to be apprehended by a man, and it is in this way that the movement of hope towards it arises. Hence the Apostle says pointedly (Heb. vi.19) that hope *enters in, even within the veil,* because that which we hope for is as yet veiled, so to speak.[41]

---

38. *ST* II-II, q. 17, a. 1: "Inquantum . . . speramus aliquid ut possibile nobis per divinum auxilium, spes nostra attingit ad ipsum Deum, cuius auxilio innititur. Et ideo patet quod spes est virtus: cum faciat actum hominis bonum et debitam regulam attingentem."

39. *ST* II-II, q. 17, a. 1, ad 2: "Ipse autem habitus spei, per quam aliquis expectat beatitudinem, non causatur ex meritis, sed pure ex gratia."

40. *ST* II-II, q. 17, a. 2: "[T]he hope of which we speak now, attains God by leaning on His help in order to obtain the hoped for good. . . . Such a good is eternal life, which consists in the enjoyment of God Himself. For we should hope from Him nothing less than Himself, since His goodness, whereby He imparts good things to His creatures, is no less than His Essence. Therefore the proper and principal object of hope is eternal happiness." "[S]pes de qua loquimur attingit Deum innitens eius auxilio ad consequendum bonum speratum. . . . Hoc autem bonum est vita aeterna, quae in fruitione ipsius Dei consistit: non enim minus aliquid ab eo sperandum est quam sit ipse, cum non sit minor eius bonitas, per quam bona creaturae communicat, quam eius essentia. Et ideo proprium et principale obiectum spei est beatitudo aeterna."

41. *ST* II-II, q. 17, a. 2, ad 1: "[B]eatitudo aeterna perfecte quidem in cor hominis non ascendit, ut scilicet cognosci possit ab homine viatore quae et qualis sit: sed secundum

Hence such a hope could not be entertained without it profoundly impacting all other ordinary hopes. And it must have such an effect, for without this hope our ordinary hopes would simply constitute the horizon of our hoping and thus squelch the great hope and consequently — and detrimentally — have Christian prayer be fueled by our ordinary hopes. But, as Thomas rightly insists against the dominant *Zeitgeist* to which not a few Catholics in the Western world have succumbed, it is solely the great hope that is to govern Christian prayer:

> We ought not to pray God for any other goods, except in reference to eternal happiness. Hence hope regards eternal happiness chiefly, and other things, for which we pray God, it regards secondarily and as referred to eternal happiness.[42]

Like Abraham, Christians, in entertaining the great hope, believe — at least initially — against these ordinary hopes. For the arduous goods to which the passion of hope is directed tend to be sensible goods. The arduous good to which the theological virtue of hope tends is, on the contrary, an essentially superintelligible good.[43] And much is at stake here, indeed. For not only is the great hope always a pure gift from above, but when this hope is genuinely embraced, it takes root in the Christian by becoming a firm disposition. And it is from this moment on that the relationship between the great hope and our small, ordinary hopes is able to change. For by becoming a firm disposition, the great hope is able eventually to perfect all our small, ordinary hopes:

> [W]e need the greater and lesser hopes that keep us going day by day. But these are not enough without the great hope, which must surpass

---

communem rationem, scilicet boni perfecti, cadere potest in apprehensione hominis. Et hoc modo motus spei in ipsam consurgit. Unde et signanter Apostolus dicit quod spes incedit *usque ad interiora velaminis:* quia id quod speramus est nobis adhuc velatum."

42. *ST* II-II, q. 17, a. 2, ad 2: "[Q]aecumque alia bona non debemus a Deo petere nisi in ordine ad beatitudinem aeternam. Unde et spes principaliter quidem respicit beatitudinem aeternam; alia vero quae petuntur a Deo respicit secundario, in ordine ad beatitudinem aeternam." It is not at all accidental that in the second, incomplete part, *De spe,* of Thomas's *Compendium theologiae,* prayer — and first and foremost the Lord's Prayer — figures prominently in relationship to the theological virtue of hope. Consider the heading of chapter 3: "Quod conveniens fuit ad consummationem spei, ut nobis forma orandi traderetur a Christo."

43. *ST* II-II, q. 18, a. 1, ad 1: "[I]rascibilis obiectum est arduum sensibile. Obiectum autem virtutis spei est arduum intelligibile; vel potius supra intellectum existens."

everything else. This great hope can only be God, who encompasses the whole of reality and who can bestow upon us what we, by ourselves, cannot attain. The fact that it comes to us as a gift is actually part of hope. God is the foundation of hope: not any god, but the God who has a human face and who has loved us to the end, each one of us and humanity in its entirety. (*Spe Salvi*, §31)

The way Pope Benedict relates the ordinary human hopes to the great, transcendent hope echoes Thomas's famous axiom "gratia non tollit sed perficit naturam."[44] The great hope, having become a firm disposition in the believer, will eventually conform these ordinary hopes to itself, will make them moments of anticipation, always transparent to the great hope.[45] Again Paul gives us a profound description of such a conformation of hope to the great hope:

44. *ST* I, q. 1, a. 8, ad 2: "Cum enim gratia non tollat naturam, sed perficiat, oportet quod naturalis ratio subserviat fidei; sicut et naturalis inclinatio voluntatis obsequitur caritati." *ST* I, q. 2, a. 2, ad 1: "[S]ic enim fides praesupponit cognitionem naturalem, sicut gratia naturam, et ut perfectio perfectibile." Already in 1963, in a contribution to a Festschrift for his mentor Gottlieb Söhngen, did Pope Benedict XVI treat this topic — from an explicitly Bonaventurian angle, but open to and in sympathy with the tenets of what he then called a non-reductive Thomism, that is, a Thomism still in contact with its Augustinian roots. See Josef Ratzinger, "Gratia praesupponit naturam," in *Dogma und Verkündigung* (Munich/Freiburg: Wewel, 1973), pp. 161-81.

45. In this regard, Thomas's all too brief, but very suggestive, remarks on the certainty of hope strike me as relevant for further consideration (*ST* II-II, q. 18, a. 4). Thomas would want to say that such conformation of our ordinary hopes to the great hope comes about first and foremost by way of the *infused* moral virtue of magnanimity. (On the infused moral virtues in distinction from the naturally acquired moral virtues, see Romanus Cessario, O.P., *The Moral Virtues and Theological Ethics* [Notre Dame, IN: University of Notre Dame Press, 1991], pp. 102-25.) Thomas distinguishes between two kinds of moral virtue, one kind being naturally acquired through our own efforts, the other being supernaturally acquired by way of infusion. Faith, hope, and love are the most central of these infused virtues, because they direct the human being completely to God by way of sanctifying grace, which is a participation in the divine life itself. While absolutely necessary for any human act pertaining to salvation, the infused theological virtues do not suffice. For, as Michael S. Sherwin, O.P., rightly stresses, "just as in our natural life the principles orienting us toward our natural end depend on the acquired cardinal virtues with regard to the means to that end, so too in the life of grace. Although the theological virtues orient us toward God as our ultimate end, we require other infused virtues — the infused cardinal virtues — in order to act rightly with regard to the means to that end. The analogy, therefore, is as follows: natural principles are to the acquired cardinal virtues as the theological virtues are to the infused cardinal virtues." Sherwin, "Infused Virtue and the Effects of Acquired Vice: A Test Case for the Thomistic Theory of Infused Cardinal Virtues," *The Thomist* 73 (2009): 29-52; 39. The in-

Through [Jesus Christ] we have obtained access to this grace in which we stand, and we rejoice in our hope of sharing in the glory of God. More than that, we rejoice in our sufferings, knowing that suffering produces endurance, and endurance produces character, and character produces hope, and hope docs not disappoint us, because God's love has been poured into our hearts through the Holy Spirit which has been given to us. (Rom 5:2-5)[46]

The link between the great hope and the ordinary hopes conformed to it is suffering, suffering for the sake of this great hope. And the hope that is born from suffering and produced by character does not disappoint us because it has its roots in the great hope of sharing in the glory of God. The "first installment" or "guarantee" *(arrabon/pignus)* of this hope is nothing other than the Holy Spirit, who is the love of God, dwelling in the hearts of the faithful (2 Cor 1:22).[47] Hence, suffering in love for Christ's sake, that is,

---

fused cardinal virtues (and by analogy those other moral virtues rooted in them, as, for example, magnanimity) pertain to those actions necessary for salvation. Hence it is the task of the infused moral virtue of magnanimity to conform the ordinary hopes to the great hope, that is, not to sustain these hopes against the great hope, but rather to enhance them toward and in perspective of the great hope.

46. For an illuminating commentary on this passage arising from the contemporary renaissance of Christian virtue ethics, see Stanley Hauerwas, "On Developing Hopeful Virtues," in *Christians Among the Virtues: Theological Conversations with Ancient and Modern Ethics,* by Stanley Hauerwas and Charles Pinches (Notre Dame, IN: University of Notre Dame Press, 1997), pp. 113-28.

47. Regarding this *arrabon/pignus,* Thomas invites us to consider two things, the substance itself, the Holy Spirit, indeed, the triune God who is eternal life, on the one hand, and on the other hand, the very mode in which we have it as *pignus* only such that it causes hope but remains in this life an imperfect way of having: "In pignore duo sunt consideranda, sc. quod faciat spem habendae rei, et quod valeat tantum, quantum valet res, vel plus, et haec duo sunt in Spiritu Sancto, quia si consideremus substantiam Spiritus Sancti, sic valet tantum Spiritus Sanctus quantum vita acterna, quae est ipse Deus, quia sc. valet quantum omnes tres personae. Si vero consideretur modus habendi, sic facit spem, et non possessionem vitae aeternae, quia nondum perfecte habemus ipsum in vita ista. Et ideo non perfecte beati sumus, nisi quando perfecte habebimus in patria." *II Ad Corinthios,* c. I, l. 5, p. 425 (Marietti). Might one understand the created gift — sanctifying grace — of this *arrabon/pignus,* the indwelling of the Holy Spirit, as the interior objective reality of the proof, the *argumentum,* of things not seen? One could pursue this question by drawing upon Thomas's reflections on the *nova lex* in *ST* I-II, q. 106, a. 1: "Id autem quod est potissimum in lege novi testamenti, et in quo tota virtus eius consistit, est gratia Spiritus Sancti, quae datur per fidem Christi. Et ideo principaliter lex nova est ipsa gratia Spiritus Sancti, quae datur Christi fidelibus."

also for the sake of truth and justice, is the great conformer of all our everyday hopes to the one great hope. Pope Benedict puts it most succinctly:

> Certainly, in our many different sufferings and trials we always need the lesser and the greater hopes too — a kind visit, the healing of internal and external wounds, a favorable resolution of a crisis, and so on. In our lesser trials these kinds of hope may even be sufficient. But in truly great trials, where I must make a definitive decision to place the truth before my own welfare, career and possessions, I need the certitude of that true, great hope of which we have spoken here. . . . Let us say once again: the capacity to suffer for the sake of the truth is the measure of humanity. Yet this capacity to suffer depends on the type and extent of the hope that we bear within us and build upon. The saints were able to make the great journey of human existence in the way that Christ had done before them, because they were brimming with great hope. (§39)

Turning to the witness of a saint's life might therefore be the only apt way to offer a concrete narrative capstone to any theological discussion on faith and hope. As a matter of fact, Pope Benedict offers exactly such a narrative account, albeit not as a concluding capstone, but rather as the kind of cornerstone that is part of the very foundation on which the theological reflection comes to stand.[48]

III. In Hope She Believed against Hope: Pope Benedict's Hopeful Pedagogy on Hope

For a powerful modern, almost contemporary example of the liberating and transformative effect of Christian hope, Pope Benedict narrates the life story of the Sudanese former slave girl Josephine Bakhita, beatified by Pope John Paul II on May 17, 1992 and canonized by him on October 1, 2000. After many years of suffering humiliation and abuse at the hands of

---

48. This move is indeed profoundly Bonaventurian in that holiness is the very foundation on which the edifice of any true theological reflection is to be erected. For a nuanced and enlightening discussion of this topic in Bonaventure, see Gregory LaNave, *Through Holiness to Wisdom: The Nature of Theology according to St. Bonaventure* (Rome: Istituto storico dei Cappuccini, 2005), and in a more Thomistic key, see his "Why Holiness Is Necessary for Theology: Some Thomistic Distinctions," *The Thomist* 74, no. 3 (2010): 437-59.

Sudanese slave masters and by a felicitous break in the seemingly endless cycle of being sold and bought and sold again, Josephine Bakhita ended up in Italy. There she encountered for the first time the good news of the living God, the God of Jesus Christ, and this good news was fundamentally life-changing for her. The encounter with the living God liberated her inwardly in a way that enabled her to take the bold step and refuse to return to Sudan. Instead she became a witness of Christ and eventually took the vows of a religious. Pope Benedict reads Josephine Bakhita's story as a salient reminder of what it means to encounter for the first time the love of the living God:

> She was known and loved and she was awaited. What is more, this master had himself accepted the destiny of being flogged and now he was waiting for her "at the Father's right hand." Now she had "hope" — no longer simply the modest hope of finding masters who would be less cruel, but the great hope: "I am definitively loved and whatever happens to me — I am awaited by this Love. And so my life is good." Through the knowledge of this hope she was "redeemed," no longer a slave, but a free child of God. She understood what Paul meant when he reminded the Ephesians that previously they were without hope and without God in the world — without hope *because* without God. Hence, when she was about to be taken back to Sudan, Bakhita refused; she did not wish to be separated again from her *"Paron."* On 9 January 1890, she was baptized and confirmed and received her first Holy Communion from the hands of the Patriarch of Venice. On 8 December 1896, in Verona, she took her vows in the Congregation of the Canossian Sisters and from that time onwards, besides her work in the sacristy and in the porter's lodge at the convent, she made several journeys round Italy in order to promote the missions: the liberation that she had received through her encounter with the God of Jesus Christ, she felt she had to extend, it had to be handed on to others, to the greatest possible number of people. The hope born in her which had "redeemed" her she could not keep to herself; this hope had to reach many, to reach everybody. (§3)

From this example of the radical transformation of the life of a modern slave girl from the modest everyday hopes of life getting incrementally less bad and abusive in this or that regard to the great hope of living for eternity in union with the God who is love, Pope Benedict takes the readers of *Spe Salvi* back to Paul's Letter to Philemon, the apostolic admonition of a first-century Christian slave owner. It is in this epistle where we encounter for the first time the fundamental Christological revolution between a Christian master and a Christian slave:

> Those who, as far as their civil status is concerned, stand in relation to one another as masters and slaves, inasmuch as they are members of the one Church, have become brothers and sisters — this is how Christians addressed one another. By virtue of their Baptism they had been re-born, they had been given to drink of the same Spirit and they received the Body of the Lord together, alongside one another. Even if external structures remained unaltered, this changed society from within. (§4)

But there was not only a new great hope for those belonging to the lower social strata of the Roman Empire; there was also new hope for the educated classes, those disillusioned by a petrified pagan religious ritualism and by the recondite rationalism of the philosophical schools. "The Divine was seen in various ways in cosmic forces, but a God to whom one could pray did not exist" (§5). The Gospel of Christ opened up a completely new and utterly hopeful perspective on the universe:

> It is not the elemental spirits of the universe, the laws of matter, which ultimately govern the world and mankind, but a personal God governs the stars, that is, the universe; it is not the laws of matter and of evolution that have the final say, but reason, will, love — a Person. And if we know this Person and he knows us, then truly the inexorable power of material elements no longer has the last word; we are not slaves of the universe and of its laws, we are free. (§5)

It is good — indeed indispensable — for Christians, in these latter days of a modernity imploding under the weight of hopeless skepticism and materialism, to be reminded again and again of the profoundly transformative and utterly liberating hope that fueled Christians from the days of the first martyrs and confessors right up to a Josephine Bakhita on the threshold of the twentieth century.

IV. God, Faith, Hope — an Offer to a Modernity in Crisis

When Christians return to their roots, they rediscover that the Gospel that elicits the great hope is first and foremost performative, because Christian hope, the supernatural virtue of hope, ineluctably transforms life. Thus transformed, human life becomes transparent to the fundamental *conditio humana,* the *status viatoris* of all humanity, that is, humanity existentially, as well as historically, being "on the way" to a destination of surpassing truth, goodness, and beauty — the *status comprehensoris,* the gratuitous, irreversible, that is, eternal participation in God's own life of love. The theological virtues of faith and hope (together with the infused moral virtues) are meant to sustain human existence *in statu viatoris* and on the pilgrimage unite us already in a certain way with the goal of the journey. Only the theological virtue of charity unites us as *viatores* already *simpliciter* with the goal with exactly the same charity in which the blessed are united with God as *comprehensores.*[49]

Pope Benedict strongly affirms that the apostle Paul — echoed by the Letter to the Hebrews — remains our prime apostolic teacher for how to become a living dialogue partner to an increasingly hopeless modernity, a late and tired modernity that hovers on the edge of cynicism and despair. In the stark words of *Spe Salvi:* "Man needs God, otherwise he remains without hope" (§23). More than ever Christians are called to enter the school of the apostle Paul and witness anew that "hope does not disappoint us, because God's love has been poured out into our hearts through the Holy Spirit which has been given to us" (Rom 5:5). In the salient words of *Spe Salvi:* "'In embryo' — and thus according to the 'substance' — there is already present in us the things that are hoped for: a whole true life" (§7). That this hope is not to be misunderstood as a romantic flirtation with a mode of religious enthusiasm Paul also adamantly maintains. The hope that does not disappoint has its exterior objective correspondence in the "form of teaching" to which we are given over at baptism. And the profound insight that the warrant for the truth of this faith is neither subjective sincerity or piety, nor a successful philosophical argument, but the authority of the apostolic Church, is well and alive in the first generation after the apostle Paul. Either Paul (according to the tradition) or one of his own very close disciples (according to modern critical consensus) characterized in 1 Timothy 3:15 the household of God as "the church of the living God, the pillar and bulwark of the truth."[50] Is it not a great consolation for

49. Cf. Josef Pieper, *Über die Hoffnung,* pp. 11-23: "Bemerkungen über den Begriff des status viatoris."

50. In his *lectura* on 1 Timothy, Thomas leaves no doubt about the importance of this utterly fundamental claim about the *veritas ecclesiae:* "Naturale est enim homini ut desideret

all Christians that — in deep consonance with the *doctor communis* — the present successor of St. Peter, whose office it is to take care that the Church infallibly continues her mission as the "pillar and bulwark of the truth," encourages all Christians to become in ever more fervent ways disciples of the apostle Paul, witnesses to the great hope that is in us — and in this way to become a gift of hope to a modernity without hope? For this great hope surpasses whatever hopes modernity can muster, and because this great hope cannot be shaken or destroyed by the crisis of modernity, it remains a genuine gift to modernity. For whatever are the true and legitimate hopes of modernity will not be destroyed, but saved, elevated, and thus perfected by Christian hope.

---

cognitionem veritatis, cum sit perfectio intellectus. Unde Augustinus dicit, quod beatitudo est finis hominis, quae nihil aliud est quam gaudium de veritate. Hoc innotuit philosophis per creaturas. Sed in hoc vacillabant, quia non habebant certitudinem veritatis, tum quia erant corrupti erroribus, tum quia vix invenitur apud eos, quod in veritate concordent. Sed in ecclesia est firma cognitio et veritas." *I. Ad Timotheum*, c. iv, l. 3, p. 204 (Marietti).

CHAPTER 9

"A Forgotten Truth?" — Theological Faith, Source and Guarantee of Theology's Inner Unity

Es ist mit der Wissenschaft über Gott die Gefahr verbunden, daß sie unser tiefstes Innere Gott entfremde, anstatt es Ihm zu nähern.[1]

Ceslaus Maria Schneider

Nihil est pauperius et miserius mente quae caret Deo et de Deo philosophatur et disputat.[2]

John Climacus

The considerations of this chapter arise from an indisputable, albeit regrettable fact: the pervasive fragmentation of contemporary Catholic theology and the consequent urgent need of renewal. Such renewal will have to come about by way of recovering theology's inner unity. And the latter requires nothing less than allowing theology's soul — supernatural, divine faith — to inform again the whole body of theology. The authority of America's foremost Catholic theologian, the late Avery Cardinal Dulles, S.J., shall suffice as a warrant for the way I characterize the present state of Catholic theology. In his important essay, "Wisdom as the Source of Unity for Theology," published shortly before his death, he observes:

1. "The science of God is accompanied by the danger that its pursuit estranges our innermost self from God instead of bringing it closer to Him."
2. "There is nothing more miserable and desolate than a mind bereft of God that speaks of and philosophizes about God."

Over the past fifty years we have all heard the repeated complaint, amounting sometimes to a lamentation, that theology has lost its unity. Like Humpty Dumpty it has suffered a great fall, and all the pope's theologians have not succeeded in putting it together again. Theology is splintered into subdisciplines that insist on their own autonomy without regard for one another. Biblical studies go in one direction, historical scholarship goes in another, ethics in a third, and spirituality in a fourth.

In addition to this fragmentation of disciplines, there is a growing breach between past and present. The classic statements of the faith are studied historically, in relation to the circumstances in which they arose. If their contemporary relevance is not denied, they are reinterpreted for today in ways that preserve little if anything of their original content. The Magisterium, which has traditionally been the guardian of theological orthodoxy, is simply ignored by some theologians and bitterly criticized by others. Dogmatic theology, which seeks to ground itself in official Catholic teaching, is shunned as being servile and unprogressive. . . . Each theologian is expected to be creative and is encouraged to say something novel and surprising. A theologian who reaffirms the tradition and fails to challenge the received doctrine is considered timid and retrograde.[3]

Cardinal Dulles's analysis is true in every respect. Furthermore, his constructive proposal is as salient as it is salutary in retrieving Thomas's three kinds of wisdom as the source of unity for theology: philosophical wisdom, theological wisdom, and infused wisdom. While *philosophical wisdom* arises from the natural capacity of the human intellect to investigate the structures of reality, *infused wisdom,* the immediate gift of the Holy Spirit, enables the believer to form right judgments by means of a divinely given connaturality. *Theological wisdom,* finally, considers all reality in light of revelation and is thus constitutive of theology as *sacra doctrina.*[4]

3. Avery Cardinal Dulles, S.J., "Wisdom as the Source of Unity for Theology," in *Wisdom and Holiness, Science and Scholarship: Essays in Honor of Matthew L. Lamb,* ed. Michael Dauphinais and Matthew Levering (Naples, FL: Sapientia Press, 2007), pp. 59-71; 59f.

4. Thomas never discusses the three kinds of wisdom together in one single place of his vast oeuvre. For a discussion of philosophical wisdom, see *In Metaph.,* I, lect. 1 and 2; for a discussion of theological wisdom, see *Summa theologiae* I, q. 1, a. 6; and for a discussion of infused wisdom, see *Summa theologiae* II-II, q. 45. In the twentieth century, French Thomists took Thomas's teaching on the three kinds of wisdom to offer the best possible access to the intricate interplay of sacred theology and metaphysics in Thomas's thought. See Réginald

In the following, I wish to build upon Dulles's proposal by expanding it in one important regard: the crucial connection between theological wisdom and the infused, supernatural virtue of faith. Such an attempt is not as far-fetched as it might at first seem. Recent magisterial teaching — Pope Benedict XVI's encyclical *Spe salvi* — encourages a genuine recovery of the supernatural character of the faith. By drawing out the implications of such a recovery for Catholic theology as a unified sapiential theology, the internal unity of which arises from its essential correlation to supernatural faith, I intend to receive this magisterial teaching as an impulse for a genuinely Thomist contribution to the renewal of contemporary Catholic theology.

It is worthwhile to quote again the pertinent passage from *Spe salvi* that I discussed at length in the previous chapter:

> In the eleventh chapter of the *Letter to the Hebrews* (v. 1) we find a kind of definition of faith which closely links this virtue with hope. . . . "Faith is the *hypostasis* of things hoped for; the proof of things not seen." For the Fathers and for the theologians of the Middle Ages, it was clear that the Greek word *hypostasis* was to be rendered in Latin with the term *substantia*. The Latin translation of the text produced at the time of the early Church therefore reads: *Est autem fides sperandarum substantia rerum, argumentum non apparentium* — faith is the "substance" of things hoped for; the proof of things not seen. Saint Thomas Aquinas, using the terminology of the philosophical tradition to which he belonged, explains it as follows: faith is a *habitus,* that is, a stable disposition of the spirit, through which eternal life takes root in us and reason is led to consent to what it does not see. . . . [T]hrough faith, in a tentative way, or as we might say "in embryo" — and thus according to the "substance" — there are already present in us the things that are hoped for: the whole, true life. And precisely because the thing itself is already present, this presence of what is to come also creates certainty: this "thing" which must come is not yet visible in the external world (it does not "appear"), but because of the fact that, as an initial and dynamic reality, we carry it within us, a certain perception of it has even now come into existence. . . . Faith is not merely a personal reaching out towards things to come that are still totally absent: it gives us something. It gives us even now something of

Garrigou-Lagrange, O.P., *Le sens du mystère et le clair-obscur intellectual: Nature et surnaturel* (Paris: Desclée de Brouwer, 1934), and Marie-Dominique Philippe, *Les trois sagesses: Entretiens avec Frédéric Lenoir* (Paris: Fayard, 1994).

the reality we are waiting for, and this present reality constitutes for us a "proof" of the things that are still unseen. Faith draws the future into the present, so that it is no longer simply a "not yet." (§7)[5]

In this crucial passage, the source for the renewal of contemporary Catholic theology is as plainly stated as is the name of the *doctor communis* who in his theology offers the very resources for such a renewal. To put the encyclical's teaching on faith into Thomas's somewhat more technical language: Faith is an infused *habitus,* that is, a stable supernatural disposition of the human spirit, indeed, the effect of the "new being" of sanctifying grace in believers, through which eternal life takes root in us such that reason is led to assent to what it does not see, and in consequence of which the human person is enabled to attain the transcendent God who is the First Truth.[6] It is this attaining of the transcendent God who is the First Truth that makes supernatural faith "theological" in the proper sense of the word. For in virtue of the infused *habitus* of faith, "'in embryo' — and thus according to the 'substance' — there are already present in us the things that are hoped for: the whole, true life" (*Spe salvi* §7). This is what the Thomist tradition used to call the "theological life," "la vie théologale."[7]

When Catholic theology becomes again intrinsically ordered to and informed by the supernatural dynamic and content of theological faith, it will recover its unity as *sacra doctrina* and thereby will undergo a salutary renewal. In this regard, I would like to submit, Thomism — which constantly teaches the essential correlation between theological faith and the sapiential character of theology, between the simple understanding of faith and the discursive and contemplative operation of theological wisdom — is in an advantageous position to make a salient contribution to such a contemporary renewal of Catholic theology.[8]

5. This and all further quotations from *Spe salvi* are taken from the Vatican website: http://www.vatican.va/holy_father/benedict_xvi/encyclicals/documents/hf_ben-xvi_enc_20071130_spe-salvi_en.html; accessed May 12, 2010.

6. *ST* II-II, q. 4, a. 1.

7. See M.-M. Labourdette, O.P., "La vie théologale selon saint Thomas," *Revue thomiste* 58 (1958): 597-622.

8. Instantiations of such Thomistic contributions to a renewal of Catholic theology indeed already exist. Arguably, one of them is Jean-Hervé Nicolas, O.P., *Synthèse dogmatique: De la Trinité à la Trinité* (Fribourg: Éditions Universitaires; Paris: Éditions Beauchesne, 1985), with a preface by the then Cardinal Joseph Ratzinger. Romanus Cessario, O.P., aptly characterizes Nicolas's *magnum opus* as taking the proper course between the reductive

In order to avoid the danger of vague and largely unsupported gener-
alizations about contemporary Catholic theology, however, I shall build
upon and advance Dulles's proposal by way of examining two paradigmatic sketches of the nature and task of Catholic theology. I shall first consider a programmatic post–Vatican II revision of the nature of Catholic
dogmatic theology. The author is the already then noted German Catholic
dogmatic theologian Walter Kasper, now cardinal and former president of
the Pontifical Council for Promoting Christian Unity. Kasper's treatise
originated in a lecture he presented at the first postconciliar Conference of
German Dogmatic Theologians, which met in Munich, January 2-5, 1967.
The German original was published the same year under the title "Die
Methoden der Dogmatik — Einheit und Vielheit" ("The Methods of Dogmatic Theology — Unity and Plurality").[9] In 1969 an English translation
appeared, although its title omitted what is most indicative of Kasper's
program: "Unity and Plurality."[10] This elimination was unfortunate, because Kasper is quite explicitly concerned with recovering the inner unity
of dogmatic theology and thereby contributing to the integration of all
branches of Catholic theology.[11]

---

alternatives of theological rationalism and theological positivism: "Theology, after all, according to the Thomist viewpoint, develops out of faith's seeking to deepen its understanding of revealed truth. Rationalism reduces theology to a purely human enterprise. Practitioners of this kind of theology perceive themselves either as peers of secular professors in
academic circles or the religious counterparts of other learned professions, like social work
or psychology. Whatever are the merits of the science of religious studies, theology in service
to the Church requires more than academic credentials to communicate a revealed doctrine.
Theological positivism, on the other hand, which relies on authoritarian pronouncements
to support Church doctrine, closes off the theological project by replacing demonstration
with the weakest form of argument, authority. Its practitioners find satisfaction with repeti-
tion of what the Church teaches, but recoil from the hard work of making that teaching intelligible to contemporary hearers. Father Nicolas offers the theologian a model to avoid
these unfortunate and disserviceable alternatives" ("Theology at Fribourg," *The Thomist* 51,
no. 2 [1987]: 325-66; 339-40).

9. Walter Kasper, *Die Methoden der Dogmatik — Einheit und Vielheit* (Munich: Kösel,
1967).

10. Walter Kasper, *The Methods of Dogmatic Theology,* trans. John Drury (Glen Rock,
NJ: Paulist Press, 1969).

11. "There is a growing splintering of methods within one and the same discipline
and by one and the same theologian. At one point the dogmatic theologian may utilize
exegetical, historical and philosophical arguments; at another point he may adopt a pastoral,
an anthropological, or a sociological approach. But if dogmatic theology is to avoid
dilettantism, if it is to remain a scientific discipline, then it must look for the one dogmatic

In the foreword to his treatise, Kasper emphasizes that this work claims to be nothing more than "a preliminary probe."[12] Yet precisely because of its experimental and preliminary character, Kasper's opuscule represents an instructive and indeed paradigmatic example of what, in the years immediately following the Second Vatican Council, was widely regarded as an overdue fresh theological venture.[13]

In a second step, I shall turn to an equally brief, programmatic treatise, "The Work of Theology,"[14] of the Spanish Dominican Francisco P. Muñiz, who taught at the Angelicum in Rome. Translated by the American Dominican John Reid, Muñiz's humbly titled "Work" was published in English in 1953, during those theologically and ecclesiastically complicated years leading up to the Second Vatican Council. Thus fifteen years before Kasper's treatise appeared in English and about ten years before the council, Muñiz's preoccupation with the unity of theology, with theology as a proper whole *(totum)*, and his creative use of Thomas's metaphysics of the the *totum potestativum*, was made available to an English-speaking theological readership.

One could hardly imagine two treatises on the renewal of Catholic

---

method" (Kasper, *Methods of Dogmatic Theology,* pp. 1f.). Kasper's express goal of his treatise is "to arrive at a single, unified epistemological process that is proper to theology" (p. 21).

12. Kasper, *Methods of Dogmatic Theology,* p. vii.

13. I do not know how more than forty years later Cardinal Kasper would assess this brief work. (For a complete bibliography of Walter Cardinal Kasper's impressive *opus,* see the Festschrift in honor of his seventy-fifth birthday, introduced with a personal salutation by Pope Benedict XVI, *Gott denken und bezeugen,* ed. Georg Augustin and Klaus Krämer [Freiburg: Herder, 2008].) While there are tangible influences of Kasper's important earlier scholarly work upon this treatise, in the following I will be unable to do full justice to the complex ways in which Kasper's opuscule depends on and departs from his doctoral dissertation on the concept of tradition in the nineteenth-century Roman school and his Tübingen *Habilitationsschrift* on the philosophy and theology of history in the later period of Schelling's thought: Walter Kasper, *Die Lehre von der Tradition in der Römischen Schule (Giovanni Perrone, Carlo Passaglia, Clemens Schrader),* Die Überlieferung in der neueren Theologie 5 (Freiburg: Herder, 1962); and *Das Absolute in der Geschichte. Philosophie und Theologie der Geschichte in der Spätphilosophie Schellings* (Mainz: Grünewald, 1965). See also his important early essay, "Grundlinien einer Theologie der Geschichte," *Theologische Quartalschrift* 144 (1964): 129-69.

14. Francisco P. Muñiz, O.P., *The Work of Theology,* trans. John P. Reid, O.P. (Washington, DC: The Thomist Press, 1953). For a brief account of the life and work of Muñiz, see the entry by Cepada Palomo, O.P., in vol. 3 of *Diccionario de Historia Eclesiástica de España,* ed. Quintín Aldea Vaquero et al. (Madrid: Instituto Enrique Flórez, Consejo Superior de Investigaciones Científicas, 1972-1975), p. 1970.

theology more different in rhetorical posture, intellectual orientation, and theological patrimony. Each bears the traces characteristic of the particular intellectual moment in which it was conceived in the history of Catholic theology. Muñiz's treatise embodies in an unencumbered way the conceptual rigor of Scholastic discourse, to which we have largely grown unaccustomed in the last fifty years. Kasper's treatise embraces in an equally unencumbered way the later Heidegger's consistent historicizing of being and Gadamer's version of a tradition-dependent universal hermeneutics, two philosophical interventions of undoubted importance that, however, forty years later — and especially outside of the confines of the German intellectual context — convey an indisputable datedness. Moreover, the all too conventional post–Vatican II hermeneutics of discontinuity, which is as superficial as it is erroneous, would most likely dismiss Muñiz's approach as a typical instantiation of a static, unhistorical metaphysical and theological framework and embrace Kasper's program as a properly dynamic and historically sensitive stance. Among other things, I hope to show that such a contrastive reading of pre– and post–Vatican II accounts of the nature of theology misses the real issues at stake, robs itself of a most salutary theological patrimony, and does justice neither to Kasper nor to Muñiz.

In what follows, I examine what Kasper and Muñiz have to say about (a) the nature and task of theology; (b) the nature of faith; (c) the relationship between faith and theology; (d) the impact of their variant understandings of the nature of faith on their respective accounts of theology; and finally (e) whether and, if so, how each programmatic proposal can be received in light of *Spe salvi*'s teaching on supernatural, divine faith.

I. Theology as a Historical-Hermeneutical Process

Walter Kasper's *Methods of Dogmatic Theology* is divided into five sections: (I) "The Present Crisis," (II) "The Historical Background," (III) "Theology's Starting Point," (IV) "History and Theology," and (V) "The Goal of Methodology." In the first section, "The Present Crisis," Kasper characterizes the intellectual situation of the 1960s as a "crisis of faith" in which "the fundamental principles of faith itself and the possibility of saying anything about God" (1)[15] have been called into question. He understands Vatican II

---

15. Parenthetical Arabic page numbers in this section refer to pages in *Methods of Dogmatic Theology.*

as addressing this critical situation with a call for "a new theology, a dogmatic methodology that was more biblically and pastorally oriented" (2). This new theology is to be fueled by "the new spirit which pervades [the Second Vatican Council's] statements and declarations. Dogmatic theology as a whole is presented as being more dynamic, more catholic, more oriented to this world and the future; moreover, in many respects, it is portrayed as something possessing less certainty than heretofore" (3).

According to Kasper, there is an urgent need for such a new theology, for he sees a real crisis threatening the foundations of theology, a crisis caused primarily by rapidly accelerating new developments: "Justifiable criticism of the a-worldliness of theology in the past now threatens to drive us to the other extreme, to give rise to a secular theology which has no real tradition" (3). In order to check the move to this extreme, Kasper explicitly recalls the traditional, sapiential understanding of theology:

> Theology belongs to a realm which tradition sums up under the word *sapientia* (wisdom). Through it we savor *(sapere)*, we come to know, "the glory of God shining on the face of Christ Jesus" (2 Cor 4,6). This is the type of experience which is proper to theology, and the modern-day emphasis on truth requires that this experience be given a new, more intensive form of methodological self-verification. For even though theology cannot simply appropriate one or other of the secular methods, it is not a purely whimsical process either. Theology, too, must be rigorous and serious. It, too, must draw reasonable conclusions. It, too, must use exactness in posing and answering questions. Theology, too, has its methods. (5)

Hence, in contrast to the newly emerging "secular theology," Kasper very much regards theology as a methodical inquiry into the truth, an inquiry in which tradition is an essential ingredient. To put it into MacIntyrean terms, for Kasper theology is irreversibly tradition-constituted: "Only tradition, dominated as it is by the quest for truth, can put us on the road where the search for truth is made" (6f.). The concept of ecclesial-doctrinal tradition that Kasper introduces and consistently applies throughout his treatise is deeply shaped by his interpretation of the doctrine of tradition held by the nineteenth-century Roman school.[16] More importantly, however, Kasper

---

16. We might not go completely wrong in finding echoes of Kasper's interpretation of Passaglia's and Schrader's interpretation of tradition in his own programmatic and eschatologically determined vision: "Die Tradition 'ist' nicht, sie geschieht, sie ereignet sich. Die

normatively contextualizes and thus interprets his understanding of ecclesial-doctrinal tradition further by way of a more comprehensive and indeed foundational philosophical-hermeneutical understanding of tradition that is explicitly indebted to Heidegger's late philosophy:

> Tradition discloses the truth and touches off the quest for it, but at the same time it also hides the truth. The answers of tradition can never fully handle the questions to which tradition gives rise; indeed, they often obstruct these questions and maintain a stranglehold on them. Historical reflection on the questions of the past leads inevitably to further exploration of the new and more radical possibilities of comprehending truth. Tradition sets us on the road to seek truth and, in so doing, it opens up new pathways for future theology. (7f.)[17]

Tradition ist der Akt, der von Christus im Heiligen Geist getragen ist, der durch den Dienst der Kirche geschieht, in dem und durch den allein das einmal gesprochene Wort aktuell wird, Da-sein besitzt für uns und aufsteht für unseren Glauben" ("Tradition 'is' not, it occurs, it takes place. Tradition is the act which is sustained by Christ in the Holy Spirit; which takes place through the Church's ministry; and in and by which alone the Word, after it has been spoken, becomes real, has existence for us, and supports our faith") (Kasper, *Die Lehre von der Tradition in der Römischen Schule,* 331). In short, objective tradition exists in the Church always only in the traditioning act as it occurs again and again — carried out by Christ and the Holy Spirit by way of the Church's ministry. The most recent and comprehensively normative event of this kind was for Kasper the Second Vatican Council. All previous tradition has existence only insofar as it is integral to this Spirit-suffused traditioning event.

17. Kasper explicitly acknowledges the profound influence of Heidegger's late philosophy in several places in his treatise. At the time of its composition, Heidegger's late philosophy held German intellectuals under a spell that retrospectively is as instructive as it is disconcerting. Few Catholic philosophers, among them most notably Robert Spaemann and Ferdinand Ulrich, resisted this bewitchment from the outset. It was only with the ascendency of the Frankfurt School (Adorno, Horkheimer, Habermas) that a spell-breaking, though no less problematic, intellectual alternative developed in the post-WWII intellectual discourse in Germany. While the generation of Catholic theologians to which Kasper (as well as Karl Cardinal Lehmann) belong shows a tangible indebtedness to Heidegger's thought (the Catholic philosophical reception of Heidegger is associated with the names of Bernhard Welte, Max Müller, Karl Rahner, S.J., and Johannes B. Lotz, S.J.), the subsequent generation of Catholic theologians in Germany (Kasper refers to this development in his treatise as "secular theology") fell to an even greater degree under the spell of the Frankfurt School and adopted as the philosophical point of reference for Catholic theology a Marx-inspired critical theory instead of a Heidegger-inspired history of being. In short, what happened was the (in)famous transition out of the frying pan into the fire. The abandonment of the *philosophia perennis* upon which Catholic theology had drawn prior

This passage demonstrates as well as any other the fundamental, ontological historicity Kasper assumes to obtain in regard to the human act of understanding in general.[18]

Thus it is that a philosophical hermeneutics inspired by Heidegger and Gadamer, in conjunction with what the German biblical exegesis of the 1950s and 1960s regarded as the newly recovered biblical notion of truth, provides the warrant for holding truth to be a fundamentally historical phenomenon and ultimately an eschatological promise:

> Truth and fidelity are closely tied together. A thing is true if it actually turns out to be what it purports to be. A thing is true if it has permanence and stability, if it stands the test of time. Thus the biblical notion of truth is characterized by its temporal orientation. It is concerned with things that have happened or will happen, not with things that are what they are by nature. In the biblical view, truth is an historical phenomenon and, ultimately, an eschatological promise. (53)

This authentic biblical notion of truth, purportedly retrieved just recently by the efforts of historical-critical exegesis, gives rise to a profound questioning of the received central concepts of theology:

---

to Vatican II had as a consequence the ever more rapid replacement of one philosophical point of reference or framework with another. So the journey went from Heidegger and Gadamer to Adorno, Horkheimer, and Habermas, and from there in more recent years to Foucault, Derrida, Deleuze, and Irigaray. Pope John Paul II's encyclical *Fides et ratio* has encouraged a more sober and penetrating reflection pertaining to the question of what kind of philosophy indeed meets best the exigencies of inquiring in essentially nonreductive ways into the truth of the human being and the world as a whole and thus best serves Catholic theology.

18. "The notion of historicity posited here involves more than the purely subjective historicity of man himself; it embraces reality as a whole and being as such. Thus it includes society, institutions, and the world" (*Methods of Dogmatic Theology*, p. 7, n. 6); "[N]ature and being only become real within the all-embracing cloak of history" (p. 55). This comprehensive philosophical claim aptly puts into a nutshell Heidegger's late philosophy, his ontological historicism which can be usefully encountered in his *Der Satz vom Grund* (Pfullingen: Neske, 1957) and *Nietzsche*, vol. II (Pfullingen: Neske, 1961). For an instructive introduction to the later Heidegger's thinking, see Julian Young, *Heidegger's Later Philosophy* (Cambridge: Cambridge University Press, 2002). In order to offer some background and backing to the notion of the history of being that he endorses, Kasper refers to the standard Heideggerian introduction to Heidegger's thought by Otto Pöggeler, *Der Denkweg Martin Heideggers* (Pfullingen: Neske, 1963) and to works of two eminent representatives of what has been called the "Catholic Heidegger-school": Max Müller and Bernhard Welte.

In these revolutionary days we simply must probe all our theological
concepts in depth, asking how relevant and how meaningful they are
for our concrete practice of the faith. Even the central concepts of theology — grace, salvation, sin, God — have become empty words to a
large extent. They do not say anything to men, and they have no foundation in the realm of experience. They often seem to represent a set of
values which cannot be discovered experientially in the Christian's life
of faith in history. (52)[19]

It is important to note that Kasper in no way intends to endorse relativism or skepticism. He rather argues exclusively in favor of substituting
what he calls a "static framework" with a historical framework of metaphysical structures.[20] He has no interest in theology being dissolved into a
"historical soup" (56), which he regards as the inevitable result of any radical attempt to historicize existence to such a degree that all perduring
metaphysical norms would prove illusory. Rather, he very much wants to
understand the "end of metaphysics" along the lines of the later Schelling
and the later Heidegger: "The end of metaphysics can only mean that we
are salvaging the intrinsic historicity of metaphysical thought from the
false trap of a *philosophia perennis* and a *theologia perennis*" (57).

A genuinely historical outlook, Kasper emphasizes, cannot, after all,
afford to jettison metaphysical categories *in toto*. And while theology is
embedded in the same comprehensive historicity of being and thinking as
fully as philosophy, "theology cannot dispense with universally valid metaphysical categories any more than philosophy can" (58). If one wonders
how according to Kasper's comprehensive historical-hermeneutical program, theology comes by such universally valid metaphysical categories,
one might have recourse to the universality of the eschatological promise
as the normative transhistorical point of reference for a theology that is
"historical through and through" (58). In order for theology not to fall into
the trap of fideism ("a particular truth is propounded apodictically as a
universally valid truth" [58]), the universality of this promise must be preserved in the concrete engagement of theology with all other ways and
kinds of thinking: "If theology is not to retire into freely chosen isolation,

19. In which remedy does Kasper put his hope? "If all our theological statements are
viewed as historical explications and interpretations of Christ's salvific promise, then men
will be able to comprehend and assimilate the truths of faith once again" (54).
20. "Theology views everything within the framework of a universal, eschatological
promise. Thus, from the start, it is historical through and through" (58).

then it must be able to show that its statements concretize, outstrip and fulfill the elements of anticipation and longing that stand out in the basic structures of every history" (58f.).

It is far from clear how such an illustration should show that the metaphysical categories entailed in theology are indeed true[21] and how such an illustration would protect theology from ending up in the very "historical soup" Kasper is rightly concerned about. It is, however, patent what the overarching goal of such a philosophical theology of history is: "to show that Christ is truly the *concretum universale . . .* the unique and irreducible concretization of history's universal essence" (59, 61).[22] This *concretum universale* constitutes the irreducible normative aspect of dogmatic theology that keeps it from becoming an exclusively historical enterprise. Consequently, "[t]he historical and speculative methods of dogmatic theology are two aspects of a single historical-hermeneutical

21. To be fair to Kasper's comprehensive historical-hermeneutical framework, this would not be a valid concern for him, for he regards the relationship itself of theology to philosophy as a historical process. Hence, "however much theology may need metaphysical categories, it cannot tie itself to a specific metaphysics if it is to remain its true self" (60). It is clear that according to Kasper, metaphysics is itself nothing but concrete historical thought. And therefore, "the use of hellenic notions was a necessary hermeneutic process at that point in history" (60). Because of the genuinely historical character of metaphysics, Kasper's program seems to entail that the central truths promulgated in the Trinitarian and Christological dogmas (and configured comprehensively in "hellenic notions") can only be retrieved in a hermeneutical process that is essentially extrinsic to these hellenistically conceived dogmas themselves. For the hellenic notions do not seem to be reflective of human "ratio" per se, and in principle and per se intelligible to human beings at all times and in all places, but are rather reflective of a particular historical instantiation of human "ratio" in specific time-bound philosophical tenets.

22. The inspiration behind this claim is quite obviously Schelling's late philosophy of history. In Kasper's reading, Schelling's late philosophy of history acquires a distinctly Christological character: "Die Dialektik wird so in der Spätphilosophie Schellings zur Dialogik, und dieser geschichtliche Dialog bleibt offen, weist auf eine Zukunft hin, die nur in hoffendem Glauben vorweggenommen werden kann; nicht das Wissen des Wissens ist das Letzte für den Menschen, sondern *docta ignorantia* im Akt eines sich in die Zukunft hinausstreckenden Glaubens. Vermittelt und getragen wird die Geschichte von Christus, in dem alles Bestand hat und auf den alles hin erschaffen ist (Kol 1,16f)" ("Thus in Schelling's late philosophy, dialectics turns into dialogics, and this historical dialogue remains open and points to a future that can be anticipated only by a faith that hopes; the ultimate goal of the human being is not self-reflective knowledge, but rather the *docta ignorantia* of a faith that stretches itself out towards the future. History is mediated and sustained by Christ, in whom all things hold together and with respect to whom all things were created") (*Das Absolute in der Geschichte,* 22).

process" (63). If we ask which of the two aspects governs the other, Kasper does not hesitate to draw a not altogether unproblematic, albeit perfectly consistent conclusion from his programmatic approach: there indeed is a speculative aspect of dogmatic theology, but "[s]peculative thought must be viewed as concrete, historical thought" (63). The reason for this is that "dogma can only be regarded as a relative, historical reality of purely functional significance" (25). The two poles or terms in relation to which dogma is relative are, on the one hand, "the pristine Word of God" and, on the other hand, "the questioning process of a given era" (25). Kasper stresses that: "Dogma itself, and the speculative reflection of dogmatic theology, must be viewed in terms of these two overriding considerations which go beyond them" (25). Consequently, dogmatic theology is a hermeneutical activity that stands between the poles of "the Word of revelation in Scripture and the present-day realities of Christian proclamation" (25).[23] Hence, "[t]he aim of speculative theology is to comprehend faith's universal claim in a concrete intellectual situation" (62). With explicit reference to Johann Sebastian Drey, Kasper conceives dogmatic theology as the "transmission of the faith to an ever enduring present" (64).[24]

---

23. By advancing this understanding of dogmatic theology, Kasper seems to approximate, if not to adopt, Karl Barth's understanding of the place and role of dogmatic theology, most exhaustively developed in his prolegomena to the monumental *Church Dogmatics*, in the opening sections of vol. I/1 and the concluding sections of vol. I/2. See Karl Barth, *Kirchliche Dogmatik*, vol. I/1, 10th ed. (Zurich: TVZ, 1981), §§1-2 and vol. I/2, 7th ed. (Zurich: TVZ, 1983), §§22-24. With respect to the precise role and understanding of dogma itself Kasper differs slightly, but importantly, from Barth's understanding. While Barth understands dogma in an exclusively eschatological sense (*Kirchliche Dogmatik* I/1, p. 284), Kasper stresses that dogma "shares the eschatological-definitive character of Christian revelation, and its historical cast. Dogma exemplifies the trait of 'already here' and 'yet to come' which characterizes the whole existence of the Church in this world" (p. 25, n. 6).

24. Johann Sebastian Drey (1777-1853) was an influential Catholic theologian who held a professorship of dogmatic theology and the history of dogma on the Catholic faculty of the University of Tübingen from 1817 to 1846. Drey was one of the most important representatives of a Catholic Enlightenment in conversation with Lessing, Schelling, and Schleiermacher. He is regarded as the founder of modern Catholic apologetics and fundamental theology, and as the intellectual initiator of the Catholic "Tübingen School." For an introduction to Drey's thought, see Max Seckler's informative essay, "Ein Tübinger Entwurf: Johann Sebastian Drey und die Theologie," in *Im Spannungsfeld von Wissenschaft und Kirche. Theologie als schöpferische Auslegung der Wirklichkeit* (Freiburg: Herder, 1980), pp. 178-98. Kasper understands his own program very much as a continuation of this tradition, which represents to him the best of Catholic theology of its day: "In the first half of the nineteenth century, theologians in Tübingen, Münster, Munich and Vienna strove to develop a

The point has arrived where it is apposite to ask how Kasper conceives of "faith." Analogous to theology, faith for Kasper has a historical as well as a normative aspect. The normative aspect of faith, the ultimate Christological and eschatological mystery of God, pertains to faith's existential *certitudo super omnia*. The historical aspect of the faith pertains to the concrete, historically configured articles of faith by way of which faith's universal claim takes concrete historical shape.[25] It is faith's normative aspect, its unshakable existential certitude in relationship to the *concretum universale,* Jesus Christ, that sets the theologian free to engage in an unrestrained questioning process of *fides quaerens intellectum* "beyond its ready-made concepts to the underlying reality" (64).[26] Therefore, "[s]trong in the faith and supported by the Church, the theologian is free to ask whatever he will. . . . [H]e can savor the delight of questioning everything" (64f.). "The wonder of faith is that its *certitudo super omnia* permits and even calls for such a questioning process" (64). In Kasper's own words, as already cited above, "[e]ven the central concepts of theology — grace, salvation, sin, God — have become empty words to a large extent" (52). Such provocative formulations make it difficult not to wonder whether such an unrestrained interrogative process should not indeed include a radical questioning of the very *concept* itself of the "articles of faith." But on these very articles seems to depend — according to Kasper — faith's universal claim in a concrete intellectual situation. One wonders: Might not such a radical comprehensive questioning of all central

---

theology that was both ecclesial (in the best sense of the word) and imbued with a sound theological liberalism. It was a theology produced by original minds who were at ease in the intellectual currents of their time. Men like Möhler and Döllinger championed the cause of the Church, but they were open-minded men who were recognized and respected by other contemporary scholars" (p. 19).

25. Kasper offers an instructive clarification of the nature of the articles of faith by interpreting some central assertions of the Vatican I Dogmatic Constitution "Dei Filius" "in an historical perspective" (p. 63): "1. The articles of faith prove to be the universal, concrete embodiment and fulfillment of history's questions. They are comprehended *'ex eorum quae naturaliter cognoscit analogia.'* 2. The articles of faith prove to be capable of protecting man's freedom and of answering his questions about the meaning of human life; they are comprehended *'e nexu cum fine hominis ultimo.'* 3. Faith becomes intrinsically comprehensible through a *reductio in mysterium.* All its individual statements are resolved, christologically and eschatologically, into the unique mystery of God. Faith is comprehended *'e mysteriorum nexu inter se'* (DS 3016)" (p. 63).

26. The only possible candidates for the "ready-made concepts" that stand in the way of the underlying reality that come to mind are the allegedly now outdated metaphysical concepts by way of which the articles of faith themselves are configured.

concepts for which faith's certitude seems to liberate the dogmatic theologian undo the last traces of any propositional content of the faith itself (which depends upon revealed principles and their correlative concepts that essentially transcend history: God, salvation, grace, and sin) and thereby lay bare the very nature of the concept of faith on which Kasper's account seems to rely?

The only notion of faith that seems to be essentially invulnerable to such a radical questioning process is faith as an existential relation (in the form of a conviction) to a singular trans-historical datum in history — the kerygma of Jesus Christ. Because of the strong substantive resonances between Kasper's concept of faith and a peculiar Lutheran, existential-hermeneutical understanding of faith dominant in the Germany of the 1950s and 1960s (Fuchs, Bultmann, Ebeling — all of whom Kasper refers to at various places in his treatise), it might not only be permissible but indeed salient at this point to recall the continuation of the crucial passage from *Spe salvi* cited above:

> To Luther, who was not particularly fond of the *Letter to the Hebrews,* the concept of "substance," in the context of his view of faith, meant nothing. For this reason he understood the term *hypostasis/substance* not in the objective sense (of a reality present within us), but in the subjective sense, as an expression of an interior attitude, and so, naturally, he also had to understand the term *argumentum* as a disposition of the subject. In the twentieth century this interpretation became prevalent — at least in Germany — in Catholic exegesis too, so that the ecumenical translation into German of the New Testament, approved by the Bishops, reads as follows: *Glaube aber ist: Feststehen in dem, was man erhofft, Überzeugtsein von dem, was man nicht sieht* (faith is: standing firm in what one hopes, being convinced of what one does not see). This in itself is not incorrect, but it is not the meaning of the text, because the Greek term used *(elenchos)* does not have the subjective sense of "conviction" but the objective sense of "proof." (§7)

One might wonder to what degree the notion of faith Kasper advances in his programmatic sketch on the nature and task of dogmatic theology is adversely affected by conceiving faith primarily as the subjective conviction of an essentially future truth that broke into history in the death and resurrection of Christ. Due to his pervasive emphasis on the "not yet" (while acknowledging marginally [i.e., in a footnote] an "already now"), it seems Kasper's predominantly existential-eschatological understanding of faith lacks the specific supernatural character that according to *Spe salvi* is essential to the faith:

> Faith is not merely a personal reaching out towards things to come that are still totally absent: it gives us something. It gives us even now something of the reality we are waiting for, and this present reality constitutes for us a "proof" of the things that are still unseen. Faith draws the future into the present, so that it is no longer simply a "not yet." The fact that this future exists changes the present; the present is touched by the future reality, and thus the things of the future spill over into those of the present and those of the present into those of the future. (§7)

While Kasper clearly does not want to jettison completely this "already" of the faith, he seems to be unable to account for it fully inside his pervasive historical-eschatological framework, which is governed by "the one eschatological mystery of God which unfolds in history" (54).[27] Faith is for Kasper first and foremost the conviction of the kerygma's truth as an eschatological promise; in such a notion of faith there obtains necessarily a foregrounding if not privileging of the "not yet." A faith thus conceived seeking understanding must unceasingly give rise to historically contingent and contextually situated explications and interpretations of the kerygma. The radical questioning in turn of earlier explications and interpretations by the selfsame faith seeking understanding seems to come at no real cost because faith's existential certitude remains unaffected by any of these time-contingent and context-dependent construals of meaning. All that the questioning undertaken by this faith seeking understanding can deconstruct and in turn construct anew are historically contingent interpretations of revelation — but never the normative, eschatological core of faith itself. Hence, for Kasper there is no necessary intrinsic transhistorical correlation between the faith and its object on the one side and, on the other side, the propositions of the articles of the faith as conveyed in the creeds and in dogma. Faith is the *convictio* of a kerygma that seems to transcend any propositionality because it rests solely in a person and his story, the *concretum universale*, Jesus Christ. The *prima veritas* is God's fu-

---

27. This understanding of faith seems to correspond rather well to what Kasper calls "our newly won realization that the Church is an eschatological entity, a reality in the making, a promise as yet unfulfilled, an instrument of service, not an end in itself" (p. 24).

ture eschatological mystery, to which the kerygma points; and tradition is the historically concrete application of the kerygma. Therefore, dogma is always relative to its particular time. All propositions are functions of the promise of a future that is not yet at hand, hence historically conditioned by this future and therefore to be interpreted in light of it. Because there is no perennial supernatural given of the faith, there can be no contemplation of the faith that rises above the flux of history toward God. Consequently, theology cannot per se acquire a sapiential character that views all historical change in light of God's transcendent, eternal wisdom. The gift of truth has been promised, but not yet given.

It is hard, if not impossible, to see how a theological program of this kind could account for and accommodate the following statement from *Spe salvi:*

> "[I]n embryo" — and thus according to the "substance" — there are already present in us the things that are hoped for: the whole, true life. And precisely because the thing itself is already present, this presence of what is to come also creates certainty: this "thing" which must come is not yet visible in the external world (it does not "appear"), but because of the fact that, as an initial and dynamic reality, we carry it within us, a certain perception of it has even now come into existence. (§7)

Because for Kasper faith is not a supernaturally given, objective disposition of the intellect (and hence essentially incapable of a contemplation that would transcend the vagaries of historical reception, interpretation, reinterpretation, and renewed radical questioning of received construals), the theological enterprise cannot be correlated to the deliveries of the faith that essentially transcend the vagaries of historically conditioned understanding. Hence, the single historical-hermeneutical process becomes inevitably a comprehensive teleological process and theology consequently a comprehensive historical-hermeneutical enterprise in service of the common heritage of human thought. Precisely by losing itself in this process, Kasper claims, theology will truly find itself — by showing "how its faith overcomes the world."[28]

---

28. "Theology can preserve its identity only if it has the courage to immerse itself in the alien realm of philosophy — not to commit suicide there or to degenerate into a philosophy of religion, but to truly find itself. In losing itself, theology will be able to show how its faith overcomes the world (1 Jn 5,4). In other words, theology cannot be reflected in the common heritage of human thought unless it moves this heritage beyond itself as well" (p. 60).

The unifying impact of dogmatic theology on the other theological disciplines rests on its historical-hermeneutical function (within the eschatological horizon of univeral history) of bringing the normativity of the kerygma to bear on the present. It is the correlation between the kerygmatic center of "a positive, historical revelation"[29] and the contemporary existential questions of life's meaning that keeps this historical-hermeneutical dynamic alive. The gift of truth has its root in the kerygma and its fulfillment in the eschatological mystery of God.[30] However, "in-between" kerygma and eschaton, the hermeutically gleaned and doctrinally affirmed truth of the kerygma is always relative to the particular historical situation of its reception.

Kasper's way of correlating history and truth in the wake of the later Schelling and the later Heidegger constitutes a *novum* in the history of theology. This fact can easily be illustrated by contrasting Kasper with the theologian who first brought the development of doctrine into explicit conceptual form: John Henry Newman. Kasper counts Newman among those theologians who "were viewed with suspicion and censured to a greater or lesser degree" in the aftermath of the "tragic controversy over Modernism" (20). However, contrary to the well-known tenets of theological Modernism, the catholic Newman clearly states in *The Idea of a University:*

> Induction is the instrument of Physics, and deduction only is the instrument of Theology. There the simple question is, What is revealed? all doctrinal knowledge flows from one fountain head. If we are able to enlarge our view and multiply our propositions, it must be merely by the comparison and adjustment of the original truths; if we would solve new questions, it must be by consulting old answers. The notion of doctrinal knowledge absolutely novel, and of simple addition from without, is intolerable to Catholic ears, and never was entertained by any one who was even approaching to an understanding of our creed. Revelation is all in all in doctrine; the Apostles its sole depository, the inferential method its sole instrument, and ecclesiastical authority its

---

29. "Theology is grounded on a positive, historical revelation which is accessible to us only through the historical testimony of the apostolic and (in a different way) the post-apostolic Church. Thus the historical argument from authority is constitutive for theology" (p. 33).

30. "Kerygma, which theology serves, is essentially recollection and eschatological, prognostic promise also" (p. 43).

sole sanction. The Divine Voice has spoken once for all, and the only question is about its meaning. . . . Christian Truth is purely of revelation; that revelation we can but explain, we cannot increase, except relatively to our own apprehensions.[31]

Kasper would have to reject Newman's understanding of Catholic theology as an all too typical expression of an outdated, because metaphysically erroneous, *theologia perennis.* However, if faith is indeed an infused disposition by way of which "we carry . . . within us [the whole, true life], . . . a certain perception of [which] has even now come into existence" (*Spe salvi* §7), then the light of faith corresponds to the gift of revelation in such a way that by way of the contemplation of the given of revelation the light of faith does indeed lead deeper and deeper into what revelation has given to faith.[32] What would a conception of theology that — instead of being united by the synthetic, hermeneutical-speculative exertions of dogmatic theology and practiced in correlation to an existential-eschatological faith — was theological wisdom that in each of its parts (biblical, historical, dogmatic, liturgical, spiritual) was informed by the theological faith, the "whole true life in us," the supernatural life of grace in the faithful, look like?

II. Theology as a Potential Whole

One specific instantiation of an answer to the above question is *The Work of Theology*,[33] by Francisco P. Muñiz, O.P. This opuscule, as dense as it is carefully organized and argued, must be understood as one of the smaller fruits of a genuine revival of Thomist theology around the middle of the last century. As such it belongs to the labor of at least two generations of Thomists who were sifting out, after Leo XIII's 1879 encyclical *Aeterni Patris,* the ker-

---

31. John Henry Cardinal Newman, *The Idea of a University* (The New Edition of the Works of John Henry Newman), ed. Charles Frederick Harrold (New York: Longmans, Green and Co., 1947), 197f.

32. The "given of revelation" is a central, but unfortunately somewhat forgotten concept of the Dominican Thomist tradition (building directly upon Thomas's discussion of the virtue of faith in *ST* II-II, q. 1, aa. 4 and 6): certain principles have been given in the supernaturally infused faith as definitive starting points and sign posts for *sacra doctrina.* See Ambroise Gardeil, O.P., *Le donné révélé et la théologie,* 2nd ed. (Paris: Editions du Cerf, 1932).

33. Parenthetical page numbers in this section refer to this work.

nel of Thomist theology and philosophy from the husks of a philosophically quite varied neo-Scholasticism. It is important to remember that this
neo-Scholasticism was dominated by Jesuit institutions and publications
that were not directly inspired by Thomas, to say the least. Instead, Thomas
was filtered through the philosophical and theological frameworks of
Suárez, Vásquez, Molina, and others, who interpreted his thought in a
philosophically heterogeneous milieu. Muñiz's treatise is an intentional recovery of Thomas's own understanding of the nature and task of theology.
However, the treatise is not organized along the *via inventionis,* culminating
in a primarily historical reconstruction of Thomas's genuine account.
Rather, Muñiz follows the *via doctrinae* from principles to conclusions. His
treatise falls into two main sections of unequal length.

In the first, rather brief section, "Theology as a Kind of Potential
Whole," Muñiz puts to a new constructive use Thomas's metaphysical distinction between three types of whole *(totum):* universal whole *(totum
universale),* integral whole *(totum integrale),* and potential whole *(totum
potestativum).*[34] Muñiz considers these types of wholes in order to identify
the type that allows a genuine retrieval of Thomas's proper understanding
of the unity of sacred theology in all of its parts:

> We call a universal whole one which enters into each and every one of
> its parts with its complete nature and with all its power; so, for exam-
> ple, animal is a universal whole in relation to horse and to man, be-
> cause the entire essence of animality as well as all of its force or perfec-
> tion are found both in horse and in man. Horse and man are said to be
> and in fact are subjective parts of animal.
>
> The integral whole is found to occupy the opposite extreme, since it
> enters into each and every one of its parts, neither in its nature nor in
> its power, but rather results from all the parts taken together. This is
> evident in a house or in the human organism, the essence and power

---

34. On the role of the distinction between *totum universale, totum integrale,* and
totum potestativum in Thomas's metaphysics, see Ludger Oeing-Hanhoff, *Ens et unum
convertuntur: Stellung und Gehalt des Grundsatzes in der Philosophie des hl. Thomas von
Aquin,* Beiträge zur Geschichte der Philosophie und Theologie des Mittelalters 37/3
(Münster: Aschendorff, 1953), pp. 156-78. For an astute application of Muñiz's treatise in the
context of ecumenism, see Richard Schenk, O.P., "Eine Ökumene des Einspruchs.
Systematische Überlegungen zum heutigen ökumenischen Prozeß aus einer römisch-
katholischer Sicht," in *Die Reunionsgespräche im Niedersachsen des 17. Jahrhunderts: Royas y
Spinola–Molan–Leibniz* (Studien zur Kirchengeschichte Niedersachsens, 37), ed. Hans Otte
and Richard Schenk (Göttingen: Vandenhoeck & Ruprecht, 1999), pp. 225-50, 237, 246.

of which are merely in actual contact with all of the parts, and not in any way one or several parts taken by themselves. . . .

Between these two types stands the *totum potestativum* or potential whole, which enters into its individual parts with its complete nature — wherein it agrees with the universal whole — but not with its total power — wherein it resembles the integral whole. (1f.)

Thomas's favorite example for the potential whole is the human soul which has three functions: vegetative, sensitive, and intellective. Consider Muñiz's succinct explanation:

It is the same human soul and the whole human soul which vegetates, which senses, and which enjoys intellectual knowledge. Thus the whole human soul is active in each of its functions. But its complete power is not active in each function, for in the function of vegetating, the sense and intellective powers play no part; and in the function of sensing the vegetative and intellective powers remain inactive, and so on. . . . It is clear from this illustration that a potential whole, from part of the essence, bears a strong and necessary similarity to the universal whole, but on the part of power, it approaches the terms of the integral whole. Therefore, it is properly designated by St. Thomas as a mean between the other two. (2f.)

As the human soul "includes within its powers a multiplicity and variety of operations" (3), so does sacred theology in virtue of its various potential parts. There is a further crucial characteristic, though, of the *totum potestativum:* potential parts participate more or less in the power of the whole. Consequently there must obtain among these potential parts an *order of super- and subordination* that reflects the degree to which the potential parts participate in the power of the whole. To put it differently, every potential whole entails a specific hierarchical order of its potential parts. Where this order of super- and subordination among the parts does not obtain, we are not dealing with a potential whole, but either another type of whole (universal or integral) or simply an agglomeration of heterogeneous elements.

If sacred theology were a *totum universale,* the whole would enter each and every one of its parts — that is, each of the subdisciplines — with theology's complete nature and power. The consequence would be a compartmentalization of sacred theology into independent subdisciplines that are all fully and sufficiently theological on their own.

If, on the contrary, theology were a *totum integrale,* the whole would result from all the parts, that is, from all subdisciplines of sacred theology taken together. Consequently, all subdisciplines would essentially remain pretheological academic disciplines until they are brought together in a grand theological synthesis. The practitioners of these subdisciplines would not have to hold themselves accountable theologically, but would defer such accountability to the eventual grand theological synthesis for which they provide strictly pretheological building blocks. The consequence would be a compartmentalization of theology into subdisciplines that remain essentially pretheological academic disciplines.

Hence, only as a *totum potestativum* can sacred theology avoid these two undesirable and indeed detrimental alternatives, both extant in contemporary Catholic theology. In the case of the *totum potestativum* the whole enters each and every part, each subdiscipline, but not with its total power. Consequently, while all subdisciplines are genuinely theological, they are not independently theological as would be the case if theology were a *totum universale.* Rather, the parts of the *totum potestativum* are essentially ordered and correlated parts. All subdisciplines have the whole potentially in them to different degrees and so contribute to the realization of the whole in different ways:

> [T]he potential parts of Theology are the various activities, functions, or offices which it exercises with regard to its object. In each of these parts the complete nature of Theology must be preserved, not, however, all of its force *(tota ejus virtus).* The whole essence of Theology must be retained, since it is entirely one and the same habit which elicits each and every one of the several activities, but not the complete power of Theology, because this complete power is not actuated in each activity. (7)

Sacred theology being a *totum potestativum* entails an order of super- and subordination between its various subdisciplines and consequently a mutual, but asymmetrical theological accountability among them.

In the second, larger section of the work, "The Potential Parts of Theology," Muñiz sketches first the nature of theology according to modern authors, then, the nature of theology according to Thomas, and, finally, the potential parts of theology according to Thomas. This *modus procedendi* serves the purpose of distinguishing Thomas's superior account from what Muñiz regards as the overly restrictive understanding of theology developed by "modern theologians" — theologians who comprise a range of representatives from Baroque to neo-Scholasticism. What distinguishes them collectively from Thomas and the Dominican Thomist commentatorial tradition is that they regard theology exclusively as a science that deduces conclusions. According to Muñiz, these modern theologians correlate faith and theology by way of the following analogy: faith is to theology as understanding is to science. Faith is a simple assent that embraces truths explicitly revealed, while theology is a discourse that focuses exclusively on truths implicitly and virtually revealed *(revelabilia)*.[35] Contrary to these modern Scholastic theologians, Muñiz argues — rightly, I think — that according to Thomas the relationship between faith and theology is to be conceived by way of the relationship between understanding and wisdom (instead of understanding and science): as understanding is to wisdom, so faith is to theology.[36] In consequence, theology's total and adequate object is *every* explicitly as well as implicitly revealed truth. Theology's scientific deductive component, the concern with truths implicitly and virtually revealed *(revelabilia),* has its proper and rightful place *within* a larger revelatory and sapiential whole.

The introduction of the concept of wisdom *(sapientia)* is crucial in Muñiz's recovery of Thomas and in many ways anticipates Dulles's constructive proposal adumbrated above:[37]

> Wisdom . . . has two distinct functions: first, that of explaining and defending principles; and secondly, that of inferring conclusions. In the exercise of the first function, wisdom attains the object which is proper to understanding, namely, principles or truths which are per se and immediately evident. In the exercise of its other function, wisdom attains the object which is proper to science, namely, truths that are known mediately or by demonstration. Therefore, the object of wisdom is broader *(amplius)* than the objects both of understanding and of science taken separately. It is broader than the object of understand-

35. It is worth observing at this point that both Kasper and Muñiz critically distance themselves from this increasingly narrow rationalistic performance of Scholastic theology in the modern period: Kasper in order to reconceptualize the constitutive framework of theology; Muñiz in order to find in Thomas a wider and more nuanced understanding of theology that would allow to correct and improve the tradition of sacred theology from within.

36. On this matter there is a deep agreement between Muñiz and Kasper, for the latter observes: "Faith is never simply an affirmation of belief. As a human act, it is something understood and accepted; it is incipient theology" (*Methods of Dogmatic Theology,* p. 12).

37. Dulles, "Wisdom as the Source of Unity for Theology," pp. 61-68.

ing because it extends to conclusions, which the habit of first principles does not touch; it is equally wider than the object of science, because it embraces principles, which science does not attain. (19)[38]

Therefore, according to Thomas, "Theology is at once an explication, a defense, and an unfolding of faith itself, objectively considered" (21). Explication and unfolding of the faith, objectively considered, are the two discursive operations of theology that identify its essential correlation to the
supernatural faith. Faith and theology differ only in that faith as understanding is concerned with what has been immediately and explicitly revealed, while theology as discursive operation of the mind is concerned
with truths that have been revealed immediately and formally as well as
those that have been revealed mediately and virtually.[39]

Yet how is theology as discursive wisdom guided, or, technically put,
what is the light *sub quo* of theology? Muñiz puts it succinctly: "The light
sub quo of Theology in its total extension is the natural light of reason, exercised under the light of divine revelation, or under the positive direction of
faith; it is 'reason guided by faith'" (23).[40] And so Muñiz arrives at the following definition of theology: "Discursive wisdom, exercised under the
light of divine revelation, on every truth revealed by God either immedi-

38. "Understanding grasps principles by simple assent, without any discourse; wisdom, however, is concerned with the same principles, but in a discursive and argumentative
mode" (p. 20).

"Now, then, if Theology be conceived as wisdom in relation to faith, by this very fact
it must be admitted that the theological habit should not only draw conclusions from the
truths of faith, but also should explain and defend these very truths" (p. 20).

"From this it follows that the *total* or *adequate* material object of Theology is not
truth which is only *virtually* revealed, *but every revealed truth whatsoever,* whether formally
and explicitly or mediately and virtually revealed. In a word, it embraces both principles and
conclusions. Therefore, the object of Theology is *broader* in scope than is the object of faith"
(p. 20).

39. "The true distinction between faith and Theology lies in this, that faith is concerned only with what has been immediately and explicitly revealed, and Theology is concerned with truths which have been revealed both immediately and formally as well as
mediately and virtually" (p. 20).

40. "Sacred Theology is a habit which stands mid-way between faith and natural
Theology, which is a part of philosophy. Therefore, it will have a light which is a mean between the light of faith and that of natural Theology. Now the light of faith is the supernatural light of divine revelation; while the light of natural Theology is that of pure reason.
Therefore, the intermediate light is one which partakes both of revelation and of reason: it is
the natural light of reason exercised under the light of divine revelation" (p. 22).

ately and formally or mediately and virtually" (28). First, theology is called wisdom because it both concerns itself with principles and deduces conclusions. It is a form of contemplation that learns to see all things in light of the first principles. Second, theology is discursive wisdom, because it thereby distinguishes itself from faith on the one side and the infused gift of wisdom on the other. Third, theology is exercised under the light of divine revelation which essentially distinguishes it from purely human wisdom, which is metaphysics in its highest mode, that is, natural theology.[41]

Muñiz draws directly on Thomas's teaching when he states the three things that are believed in every act of theological faith:

(1) an objective or ontological supernatural truth, a certain Divine mystery; (2) this truth has been revealed by God, for we assent to it in virtue of this divine revelation; (3) the fact or existence of Divine Revelation manifesting the aforesaid truth. (32)

What then is the precise nature of the correlation of sapiential theology to supernatural faith? Muñiz specifies: The truths believed by the habit of supernatural faith are the very principles of theology:

Therefore, Sacred Theology — in its sapiential function — should undertake to explain and defend those three things, which are believed as principles in every act of faith: (1) the fact of divine revelation, (2) the connection between God's revelation and the truth which is believed to have been revealed, and (3) the revealed truth itself. (32)

Hence, by way of its principles, theology participates in a certain way in supernatural faith itself, and therefore faith is the indispensable and supernatural foundation of theology as *sacra doctrina*.[42] Conceived in this way, sapiential theology is essentially one single whole, but it has what Muñiz calls potential parts: apologetics, positive theology (biblical, symbolic, patristic), and Scholastic speculation.

---

41. For a recent compelling argument for the auxiliary indispensability of philosophical wisdom for the theological task, see Thomas Joseph White, O.P., *Wisdom in the Face of Modernity: A Study in Thomistic Natural Theology* (Naples, FL: Sapientia Press, 2009).

42. Profoundly faithful to Thomas's understanding of *sacra doctrina*, Muñiz in fact adopts the explicit defense by John of St. Thomas against Vásquez of the position that theological faith is indeed the indispensable supernatural foundation of sacred theology. See John of St. Thomas, *Cursus Theologicus*, I, disp. 2, ed. the monks of Solesmes (Paris, Tournai; Rome: Desclée, 1931), vol. 1, pp. 350ff.

The difference between the subdisciplines of contemporary theology almost fifty years after Vatican II (and also after the integrative hermeneutical function of dogmatic theology has arguably disappeared into thin air) and Muñiz's Thomistically conceived sapiential theology is the difference between on the one hand a *totum integrale,* that is, a practically oriented gathering of various extrinsically related and essentially pre-theological subdisciplines, none of which are ordered to and informed by the supernatural faith in an actual, let alone intrinsic way, and on the other hand a *totum potestativum,* a single discursive wisdom, the potential parts of which are integrally ordered in relation to each other and the whole of which is intrinsically ordered to and informed by supernatural faith. The crucial difference between a largely disintegrated and compartmentalized contemporary Catholic theology and a Thomistically conceived sapiential theology is the difference between a *totum integrale* that remains formally unaffected by supernatural faith and a *totum potestativum* that is intrinsically informed by supernatural faith.

There is another important difference between Kasper's and Muñiz's proposals. By enclosing all theological disciplines under the historical-hermeneutical category of interpretive science, Kasper de facto isolates theology to a surprising degree. As an essentially historical-hermeneutical science, theology is by definition prevented from any substantive interaction with the natural sciences, let alone with philosophy. Kasper does not perceive this to be a problem, since according to the ontologically conceived historicism he advances, all sciences (including philosophy and the natural sciences) are essentially historical sciences. There would indeed not be much of a problem with this part of the proposal if the natural sciences and philosophy had indeed adopted such an understanding of themselves, which, however, seems hardly to be the case.[43]

Following Thomas, Muñiz, in contrast to Kasper, insists on three different functions of sacred theology in respect to all other sciences: First, theology judges all human sciences, both as regards their principles and as regards their conclusions. Second, theology orders or directs all the philosophical sciences. Third, theology uses all of them. To contemporary ears

43. The only discipline in which Kasper's historical-hermeneutical paradigm seems to have taken a hold for good is Catholic dogmatic theology — which by now, though, has quite obviously lost to a surprisingly large degree its integrative hermeneutical, let alone normative function, and — as Dulles has so aptly described — operates as just one increasingly specialized subdiscipline parallel to all the other compartmentalized subdisciplines of theology.

such a notion of theology sounds most likely presumptuous, as well as utopian. However, if properly correlated to supernatural faith and thus understood first and foremost as surpassing wisdom, the three functions of theology sound neither presumptuous nor utopian, but simply appropriate: *Wisdom* judges all human sciences, both as regards their principles and as regards their conclusions. *Wisdom* orders or directs all the philosophical sciences. *Wisdom* uses all of them. Since, in the Thomist understanding, theology is most truly wisdom[44] — clearly more so than metaphysics — the three functions mentioned above must indeed all be attributed to sapiential theology. Hence it is only on the basis of the gift of divine faith and theology's most thorough and consistent illumination by this supernatural gift that one can conceive it at all possible that sacred theology might indeed fulfill the task that, according to Muñiz, Thomas envisions for it:

> Sacred Theology considers God as He is the first existing Truth *(prima veritas in essendo)*, the cause and norm of all created truth. Hence it belongs to Theology to judge all created truth. "Whatever is found in other sciences contrary to a truth of this science must be condemned as entirely false." (37)[45]

It is obvious that Muñiz's understanding of sacred theology *ad mentem sancti Thomae* cannot simply be adopted as if nothing had happened theologically in the last sixty years, a time during which much of Catholic theology has placed itself on one of two horns of the dilemma between conceiving of its unity as that of a *totum universale* and conceiving it as that of a *totum integrale*. However, it is arguably apposite to the present state of a pervasive fragmentation, compartmentalization, and over-historicization of Catholic theology to remember that Muñiz's genuinely Thomist pro-

---

44. *ST* I, q. 1, a. 6 c.: "This doctrine is wisdom above all human wisdom; not merely in any one order, but absolutely. For since it is the part of a wise man to arrange and to judge, and since lesser matters should be judged in the light of some higher principle, he is said to be wise in any one order who considers the highest principle in that order. . . . Therefore he who considers absolutely the highest cause of the whole universe, namely God, is most of all called wise. Hence wisdom is said to be the knowledge of divine things, as Augustine says *(De Trin.* XII.14). But sacred doctrine essentially treats of God viewed as the highest cause — not only so far as he can be known through creatures just as philosophers knew Him . . . but also so far as He is known to Himself alone and revealed to others. Hence sacred doctrine is especially called wisdom."

45. The internal quotation is from *ST* I, q. 1, a. 6, ad 2.

posal offers a compellingly coherent account of the integral unity of sacred theology that is not only fully compatible with the understanding of theological faith taught explicitly in *Spe salvi* but indeed allows for a comprehensive theological reception of this teaching in the service of renewing Catholic theology by recovering its unity as *sacra doctrina* — to be precise, its unity as a *totum potestativum*.

III. Theological Faith, Source and Guarantee of Theology's Inner Unity

These reflections on the essential correlation of sacred theology to supernatural faith build upon and advance Avery Cardinal Dulles's retrieval of the sapiential dimension of Catholic theology in order to overcome its pervasive fragmentation. The first crucial point of reference that invites, indeed urges, this further step to be taken is Pope Benedict XVI's teaching on supernatural faith in *Spe salvi:*

> Faith is a *habitus,* that is, a stable disposition of the spirit, through which eternal life takes root in us and reason is led to consent to what it does not see. . . . [T]hrough faith, in a tentative way, or as we might say "in embryo" — and thus according to the "substance" — there are already present in us the things that are hoped for: the whole, true life. (§7)

The second crucial point of reference for this further step to be taken has been a well-known teaching of Thomas Aquinas that has been essential for Dominican spirituality and central to the Thomist doctrine of supernatural faith and of *sacra doctrina*. In his discussion of the missions of the Divine Persons in *Summa theologiae* I Thomas famously states:

> There is one special mode belonging to the rational creature wherein God is said to be present as the object known is in the knower, and the beloved in the lover. And since the rational creature by its operation of knowledge and love attains to God Himself, according to this special mode God is said not only to exist in the rational creature, but also to dwell therein as in His own temple. (*ST* I, q. 43, a. 3)[46]

46. *ST* I, q. 43, a. 3c: "Super istum modum autem communem, est unus specialis, qui convenit creaturae rationali, in qua Deus dicitur esse sicut cognitum in cognoscente et

Because of the simultaneously supernatural infusion of the theological virtues of faith, hope, and charity the Christian is able to achieve an initial, intentional union with the Triune God, which indeed is a "pati divina," a "suffering of divine things."[47] For God as First Truth constitutes both the medium (the mediating formal object or formal object *quo*) and the dis-

---

amatum in amante. Et quia, cognoscendo et amando, creatura rationalis sua operatione attingit ad ipsum Deum, secundum istum specialem modum Deus non solum dicitur esse in creatura rationali, sed etiam habitare in ea sicut in templo suo."

47. I am here primarily concerned with the *fact* of the divine indwelling. Pertaining to the question of *how* precisely Thomas understood the nature and mode of this divine indwelling similarly to as well as differently from his scholastic predecessors, see the instructive study by Francis L. B. Cunningham, O.P., *The Indwelling of the Trinity: A Historico-Doctrinal Study of the Theory of St. Thomas Aquinas* (Dubuque, IA: Priory Press, 1955), and pertaining to the defense and development of Thomas's doctrine in the Thomist commentatorial tradition, see Ambrose Gardeil, O.P., *La structure de l'âme et l'expérience mystique,* vol. 2 (Paris: Libraire Victor Lecoffre, 1927), pp. 6-60; and Reginald Garrigou-Lagrange, O.P., *The Love of God and the Cross of Jesus,* vol. 1, trans. Sr. Jean Marie (St. Louis: Herder, 1947; reprinted 1957), pp. 136-73, and *The Three Ages of the Interior Life,* vol. 1, trans. Sr. M. Timothea Doyle, O.P. (St. Louis: Herder, 1947), pp. 101-5. The particular way I put the matter in the text follows John of St. Thomas's interpretation in I, q. 43, disp. 17, a. 3 of *Cursus Theologicus,* vol. 4, ed. the monks of Solesmen (Paris, Tournai; Rome: Desclée, 1953), pp. 364-76, esp. 370ff. Noteworthy is John of St. Thomas's beautiful interpretation of Thomas's reference to the Dionysian rendition of *"patiens divina"* (*De Divinis nom.,* ch. 2) in *ST* II-II, q. 45, a. 2: "Pati autem divina, et experimentalem cognitionem de Deo habere, non solum pertinet ad statum gloriae, ubi intuitive Deus videtur, sed etiam ad statum viae: ubi adhuc Hierotheus erat, et ubi Deus, etsi obscure et per fidem cognitus, tamen quasi experimentali quodam tactu cognoscitur, etsi non visu. Sicut animam nostram non videmus, et tamen experimentiâ animationis sentimus quasi objectum praesens, quia et informat nos realiter, et informationis indicia nobis praesentat: sic Deus suam intimam presentiam, quam habet ut agens et principium totius esse per immensitatem, nobis specialiter per gratiam demonstrat tamquam objectum intime et experimentaliter cognoscibile, hic occulte et per indicia, in patria per visionem, sed tamen jam nobis specialiter et realiter praesens, et quasi stans post parietem" (p. 370). ("However, to suffer divine things and to have experiential knowledge of God, does not only pertain to the state of glory, where God is seen intuitively, but also to the state of pilgrimage; where Hierotheus was, there also was God, even if perceived obscurely and by faith, nevertheless, so to speak, known experientially by a kind of touch, although not by sight. Just as we do not perceive our soul, we, nevertheless, through the very experience of being animated by it, sense it like an object at hand, for the soul really forms us and presents to us the signs of us being thus formed. Likewise, in a special way by grace, God shows us his innermost presence [which he himself possesses as the agent and principle of all *esse* in his immensity] like an object that can be intimately and experientially known, on earth obscurely and by way of signs, in the fatherland by way of vision; but even now God is present to us in a particular way, just as if standing behind a partition wall.")

tinct subject (the terminative formal object or formal object *quod*) of theological faith.[48] Simultaneously, faith as human understanding, by way of acts of judgment, operates with the indispensable help of the instrument of propositions (secondary material objects), that is, a divinely received *doctrina* the ultimate source and center of which is Christ.[49] Through the instrumentality of the propositions *(enuntiabile)*, faith truly attains God as First Truth. Wisdom, now, is nothing but the analogical extension of faith's own understanding by way of a discursive reasoning that arises from and returns back to contemplation.

There are at least three distinct salient strengths of sapiential theology as retrieved by Muñiz *ad mentem Sancti Thomae.*

First, because the beginning and end of sapiential theology are essentially transhistorical (because essentially correlated to the intentional union of the believer with God), this theology can afford to accommodate all the genuine concerns of Kasper's proposal without having to adopt its comprehensive historical-hermeneutical approach and its correlative constrained concept of faith. Kasper introduces the kerygma as the normative point of reference and the eschaton as the normative frame of reference in order to check the inherently historicizing and thus relativizing tendency of a comprehensively historical-hermeneutical approach. However, these twin transhistorical points of reference, kerygma and eschaton, remain too weak to fulfill the assigned function of a normative integration because neither one of them informs faith "already now" in a substantively transhistorical way. Faith is not conceived of as essentially supernatural and infused, with the consequence that faith does not directly and objectively attend to the First Truth by way of the revealed transhistorical principles — the beginning of the divine life in us — which would inform faith substantively and to which all of theology is essen-

---

48. For an astute discussion of this important distinction between the formal object *quod* and the formal object *quo* of theological faith (a distinction introduced by the Dominican Thomist commentatorial tradition based on *ST* II-II, q. 1, a. 6, ad 2), see M.-M. Labourdette, O.P., "La vie théologale selon saint Thomas," *Revue thomiste* 58 (1958): 597-622, esp. pp. 607-13.

49. Cessario offers the important reminder that for Thomas, "[o]f course, Christ himself stands at the center of this entire process. For it is Christ who teaches both angels and men, and who alone fully communicates divine Truth to the world. The articles of faith serve as instruments of this universal outpouring of doctrine from God, which culminates in the offer of truth and friendship that Jesus extends as a free gift" (Romanus Cessario, O.P., *Christian Faith and the Theological Life* [Washington, DC: The Catholic University of America Press, 1996], p. 69).

tially correlated in what amounts to be a categorically transhistorical relation.[50]

Second, by understanding the unity of theology as that of a *totum potestativum,* Muñiz is able (1) to conceive each branch of theology as a distinct actualization of the *totum* of *sacra doctrina;* (2) to regard each particular discursive actualization in essential correlation to theological faith; (3) to suppose a distinct order of super- and subordination and hence of theological interdependence and accountability between the branches of theology; and (4) to anchor the essentially transhistorical character of *sacra doctrina* in the principles of theological faith itself. The genuinely historical character of biblical exegesis and historical theology is far from being suffocated or suppressed by being informed by the transhistorical principles of theological faith. Sapiential theology or *sacra doctrina* conceived of as *totum potestativum* allows the various parts of sacred theology to do their genuine work and contribute to the whole. Each part, in virtue of being part of the whole, is essentially correlated to supernatural faith and therefore essentially contemplative, that is, sapiential. Each part, however, will be sapiential in a different way that is ordered in relation to the other parts and thereby will realize the whole to a different degree. Unlike Kasper, Muñiz does not need to rely on dogmatic or systematic theology to integrate into a theological synthesis the various pretheological parts of theology that have long ceased to understand themselves as informed by supernatural faith and hence as sapiential.[51]

Instantiations of sacred theology that remain essentially correlated to supernatural faith are not completely absent from the Catholic theology

---

50. Kasper is aware of and writes about the "analysis fidei" in his earlier work (*Die Lehre von der Tradition in der Römischen Schule,* pp. 64, 398), but in this treatise, the reference point for faith is not the "already now" ("'[I]n embryo' — and thus according to the 'substance' — there are already present in us the things that are hoped for: the whole, true life" [*Spe salvi* §7]), but rather the future "yet to come." The essentially eschatological orientation of the faith allows it to be correlated to the historicizing of being as reflected in different but analogous ways in the later Schelling and the later Heidegger.

51. Dulles offers an apt characterization of the burden contemporary Catholic systematic theology is not able bear, the burden of attempting a theological integration and synthesis that cannot be achieved as long as the parts are essentially pretheological and therefore heterogeneous: "In many Catholic faculties dogmatic theology has been replaced by the traditionally Protestant discipline of 'systematic theology' — a discipline that seeks to synthesize the results of religious experience and positive historical research in the light of some freely chosen philosophical system, be it idealist, existentialist, phenomenologist, pragmatist, or whatever" (Dulles, "Wisdom as the Source of Unity for Theology," p. 60).

of the last fifty years, nor are they necessarily instantiations of Thomistic theology. Dominican theologians, however, are prime candidates for examples of this theology, be it in biblical theology (Adrian Schenker, Ceslaus Spicq, and Pierre Benoit), historical theology (Jean-Pierre Torrell, Guy Bedouelle), dogmatic theology (Jean-Hervé Nicolas, Gilles Emery, Benoît-Dominique de la Soujeole, Charles Morerod, and Serge-Thomas Bonino), or moral theology (Servais Pinckaers). What makes these Dominican (and in most cases Thomist) instantiations unique is that the correlation of sacred theology to the supernatural faith is always noticeable, if not explicitly reflected. If we were to allow simply an implicit correlation, a much wider field of instantiations would open up. But in such cases the correlation is connatural and not carried and passed on by an explicit reflective theological awareness as is the case in the various Dominican Thomist schools. Where such an explicit reflective theological awareness is missing the correlation remains at best fragile because it depends solely on a particular theologian's de facto correlation.[52]

Third, wherever in contemporary Catholic theology faith is not regarded as a supernatural, infused habit, the loss of access to the theological substance of patristic biblical exegesis, as well as to a proper theological interpretation of the *sacra pagina* itself, becomes a tangibly disconcerting reality. For the analogy of faith, which is a requisite for such a proper theological interpretation of the Sacred Scriptures, presupposes the light of faith, which is the supernatural quality of the disposition of faith. Muñiz's retrieval of Thomas's concept of *sacra doctrina* stands in remarkable proximity to the explicit teaching of the Second Vatican Council's Dogmatic Constitution on Divine Revelation *(Dei Verbum)* about the essential correlation between the light of faith, the study of the sacred page, and the inner unity of sacred theology:

> Sacred theology rests on the written word of God, together with sacred tradition, as its primary and perpetual foundation. By scrutinizing *in*

52. What has not been addressed in this chapter at all, but what is an indispensable component of a revival of the unity of Catholic theology by way of a recovery of its character as *sacra doctrina* is, first, the question of an overall coherent curriculum that would reflect the unity of sacred theology as a *totum potestativum;* second, the role a coherent philosophical formation would play in such a curriculum; and third, the institutional setting in which such a curriculum could be realized. (Regarding the latter — the institutions by way of which such curricula are carried out and sustained — see my discussion in chapter 11.) One place that not only has great potential in addressing all three components successfully but also has indeed a mandate to do so is the Dominican *studium.*

the light of faith all truth stored up in the mystery of Christ, theology is most powerfully strengthened and constantly rejuvenated by that word. For the Sacred Scriptures contain the word of God and since they are inspired really are the word of God; and so the study of the sacred page is, as it were, the soul of sacred theology. (*DV* 24; my emphasis)[53]

The sacred page can only be received and hence read as such — as sacred page — in the light of faith; that is, by way of the theological faith. Consequently, in the study of the sacred page the essential correlation of sacred theology to the theological faith becomes most obvious — and is most fundamentally at stake. No supernatural faith, no *lumen fidei;* no *lumen fidei,* no analogy of faith; no analogy of faith, no theological study of the sacred page; no theological study of the sacred page, no *sacra doctrina.*[54] In short, the sapiential character of theology, which is essentially correlated to supernatural faith, guarantees the permanent rootedness of all parts of theology in the written word of God and in sacred tradition.

Finally, if anything, it is sapiential theology that liberates the theologian for a genuine engagement of all kinds of intellectual disciplines of enquiry — historical, hermeneutical, or empirical. Wisdom, after all, uses all

53. The translation is taken from the Vatican website: http://www.vatican.va/archive/hist_councils/ii_vatican_council/documents/vat-ii_const_19651118_dei-verbum_en.html, accessed May 12, 2010. ("Sacra theologia in verbo Dei scripto, una cum sacra traditione, tamquam in perenni fundamento innititur, in eoque ipsa firmissime roboratur semperque iuvenescit, omnem veritatem in mysterio Christi conditam sub lumine fidei perscrutando. Sacrae autem scripturae verbum Dei continent et, quia inspiratae, vere verbum Dei sunt; ideoque sacrae paginae studium sit veluti anima sacrae theologiae." *Decrees of the Ecumenical Councils,* vol. II, *Trent–Vatican II,* ed. Norman P. Tanner, S.J. [London: Sheed & Ward Ltd.; Washington, DC: Georgetown University Press, 1990], p. 980.) Above I have called supernatural, infused faith theology's soul. In the quoted passage from *Dei Verbum,* however, the study of the sacred page is suggested to be — *veluti* — the very soul of theology. Do these two designations contradict each other? I do not think so. They rather imply each other. The word of God that is contained in the Sacred Scriptures can only be rightly received and understood in the light of faith, the *lumen fidei.* If we hold the rational soul (and what else could be the proper analogue for thinking about theology's soul?) to be a composite of *esse* and essence, would it go too far to understand the composition of theology's soul in such a way that the light of faith designates its *esse* and the study of the sacred page its essence?

54. It is for this very reason that articles 9 ("Whether Holy Scripture should use metaphors?") and 10 ("Whether in Holy Scripture a word may have several senses?") are absolutely indispensable components of the first question of the *Summa theologiae,* where Thomas discusses the nature and extent of *sacra doctrina.* Take away articles 9 and 10 and *sacra doctrina* has received a mortal blow.

human sciences. Sapiential theology thus reconceived would look remarkably different from the present accommodation of Catholic theology to the liberal nineteenth-century model of the modern Berlin-type research university, with its Procrustean bed cutting the body of theology into four heterogeneous parts (exegetical, historical, normative [systematics and ethics], and practical). But since this Procrustean bed has turned out to be the tomb of theology, a Thomistic effort at renewing the unity of sacred theology by retrieving its essential correlation to the supernatural faith would be nothing less than a proper Thomistic participation in the raising of the Lazarus of theology to the integral unity of a new and authentic sapiential life.

D. SEEKING TRUTH — WISDOM AND CONTEMPLATION

CHAPTER 10

"The Wisdom of Analogy Defended" —
From Effect to Cause, from Creation to God

Non enim possumus nominare Deum nisi ex creaturis.

Summa theologiae I, q. 13, a. 5

I. Introduction: Two Protestant Objections to Analogical Predication of God in Thomas: Anthropomorphism (Pannenberg) and Apophaticism (Jüngel)

It is not altogether insignificant for the shape of the theological dispute over the *analogia entis* in the twentieth century that the arguably two most eminent German Protestant theologians of their period, Wolfhart Pannenberg and Eberhard Jüngel, in their early formative years as theologians both deeply immersed themselves into the doctrine of analogy. Maybe their early immersion into this (for Protestant theologians) rather unlikely topic is not accidental, since after all, in Basel, Switzerland, each sat at the feet of the last century's greatest master of Protestant theology. And ever since, each — although one more than the other — remained a close reader of that master's *opus magnum*, the *Church Dogmatics*. And so it happened that Wolfhart Pannenberg as well as Eberhard Jüngel wrote their respective *Habilitationsschriften* on the topic of analogy, Pannenberg's bearing the title *Analogy and Revelation*[1]

1. Wolfhart Pannenberg, "Analogie und Offenbarung" (Habilitationsschrift Heidelberg, 1955), published in an altered and expanded version more than fifty years later, *Analogie und Offenbarung: Eine kritische Untersuchung zur Geschichte des Analogiebegriffes in*

349

and Jüngel's bearing the title *On the Origin of Analogy in Parmenides and Heraclitus*.[2]

And interestingly, neither Pannenberg nor Jüngel ever left the topic behind. Rather, each one in his respective *opus magnum* — Jüngel in his *God as the Mystery of the World*[3] and Pannenberg in his *Systematic Theology*[4] — develops his theology in marked contrast to what he holds to be profoundly problematic in the concept of analogy as it is used to predicate truths about God and, beyond that, to organize all theological knowledge itself.

There is something rather striking about the early Pannenberg's and Jüngel's respective accounts of the dangers of a theological use of analogy in what they identify as Thomas Aquinas's account of analogical predication. It is not that they differ somewhat in their respective post-Barthian assessments (which might be expected), but that their accounts of the use of analogy in Thomas and of the putatively detrimental theological problems arising from it are indeed diametrically opposed to each other. In a nutshell: The early Pannenberg of the unpublished *Habilitationsschrift* regards analogical predication in Thomas as a subtly camouflaged version of univocal predication. Analogy allegedly always presumes a "common logos" between creature and Creator. Hence, for Pannenberg the very concept of analogy itself entails "the structure of 'spiritual assault'" upon the mystery of God.[5] If consistently employed in theology, analogical predica-

---

der Lehre von der Gotteserkenntnis (Göttingen: Vandenhoeck & Ruprecht, 2007). On the original debate on the *analogia entis*, the analogy of being, between Erich Przywara and Karl Barth, see the instructive essays in *The Analogy of Being: Invention of the Antichrist or the Wisdom of God*, ed. Thomas Joseph White, O.P. (Grand Rapids: Eerdmans, 2011) and esp. White's introduction, "The *Analogia Entis* Controversy and Its Contemporary Significance," pp. 1-31.

2. Eberhard Jüngel, *Zum Ursprung der Analogie bei Parmenides und Heraklit* (Berlin: de Gruyter, 1964).

3. Eberhard Jüngel, *Gott als Geheimnis der Welt: Zur Begründung der Theologie des Gekreuzigten im Streit zwischen Theismus und Atheismus* (Tübingen: Mohr Siebeck, 1977; 5th ed., 1986); English trans., *God as the Mystery of the World: On the Foundation of the Theology of the Crucified One in the Dispute between Theism and Atheism*, trans. Darrell L. Guder (Grand Rapids: Eerdmans, 1983).

4. Wolfhart Pannenberg, *Systematische Theologie*, vol. 1 (Göttingen: Vandenhoeck & Ruprecht, 1988), esp. pp. 372-73; English trans., *Systematic Theology*, trans. Geoffrey W. Bromiley (Grand Rapids: Eerdmans, 1991), pp. 342ff.

5. Elizabeth A. Johnson, "The Right Way to Speak about God? Pannenberg on Analogy," *Theological Studies* 43 (1982): 673-92; 685. Johnson offers a lucid interpretation of Pannenberg's unpublished *Habilitationsschrift*. It is very instructive to see how deeply the

tion of God along Thomas's lines must unavoidably end in anthropomorphism — the mystery of God ineluctably drawn into the conceptual closure of the human mind and thus compromised in and eventually emptied of its infinite transcendence.

Jüngel, in contrast, regards Thomas as fatally implicated in the apophatic entailments of the analogy of attribution. Similar to Kant's account of analogical predication of God at a later stage, he sees already Thomas's account haunted by one central aporia culminating in the question "whether God is speakable only as the one who actually is unspeakable, and can be made known actually only as the one who is actually unknown."[6] Jüngel regards this aporia to be central to the analogy of attribution as — in his judgment — similarly employed by Thomas and Kant: "The analogy of attribution defines so precisely the unknownness of God that it vastly increases that unknownness into God's total inaccessibility."[7] He concludes that analogy employed in divine predication by Thomas as well as Kant "functions to keep God out of the world . . . and [thereby] to protect God from anthropomorphic talk — [from] dogmatic anthropomorphism."[8] For Jüngel, analogical predication in theology is a barely concealed version of equivocation — an instrument to prevent precisely what Pannenberg alleges it to lead into — anthropomorphism! If consistently employed in theology along Thomas's lines, Jüngel claims, analogical predication ineluctably leads to a profound agnosticism irrevocably muting the God of the Gospel.

A curious picture, to say the least, emerges: Thomas is charged by the one with exactly what, according to the other, Thomas is bent on avoiding at all costs. Of course, one reading might be right and the other wrong. But even if true — which it is not — such an answer would be less than satisfying. For Pannenberg's and Jüngel's assessments of Thomas on analogical

---

early Pannenberg in his reading of Thomas on analogy was influenced by Barth's profound concern over the *analogia entis* allegedly enabling theology to take a conceptual hold of God, to submit God to our grasp ("Zugriff") by way of the concept ("Begriff").

6. Eberhard Jüngel, *God as the Mystery of the World*, p. 277.

7. Eberhard Jüngel, *God as the Mystery of the World*, p. 278.

8. Philip A. Rolnick, *Analogical Possibilities: How Words Refer to God* (Atlanta: Scholar's Press, 1993), p. 208. I regard Rolnick's book as the most instructive analysis and discussion available of analogy in David Burrell, W. Norris Clarke, and Eberhard Jüngel. I am gratefully indebted to his nuanced interpretation and acute critique of Jüngel's (mis-)reading of Thomas — a critique that still holds and that in light of more recent research on the analogy of being in Thomas has become only more pertinent.

predication of God are not just variants but contradictories. And this circumstance points to a deeper problem and hence invites the simple question, How come?

In the following I will advance an answer to this question from the position under critique by arguing that the best position from which properly to understand the reason for the contradictory assessment of Thomas is indeed Thomas's own mature doctrine of the analogy of being and of analogical predication of God. I should like to propose that the very fact that Pannenberg and Jüngel misread Thomas in the precisely contrary way they do is profoundly indicative of the twin theological problems Thomas's doctrine of analogy is meant to address and avoid. Pannenberg and Jüngel, held captive by what both regard as the irreversible normative entailments of post-Cartesian philosophy, operate in their respective theologies from within the uniquely modern conceptualist metaphysical framework of what quite perceptively and famously has been diagnosed as the modern "forgetfulness of being." It strikes me as not an altogether unfair question to ask whether Pannenberg's and Jüngel's consistently modern rejection of the analogy of being might haunt their own respective theologies in problematic ways. In the following I will limit myself to the prolegomena of such an inquiry, that is, to reconsidering Thomas's mature doctrine of analogy. This account will unfold according to the usual three steps of exposition. First, I will offer a re-lecture of Thomas's mature doctrine of analogy; second, I will argue that Thomas's doctrine of analogy does not suffer from the flaws Pannenberg and Jüngel charge it to suffer from; and third, I will intimate the contours of a Thomist response to what amounts to the shared deficiencies in Pannenberg's as well as Jüngel's readings of Thomas's mature position on analogical predication of God.

My analysis will follow a line of recovery of Thomas's thought that (after certain recent detours around and flat denials of the central role of metaphysics in Thomas's synthesis) is returning to understanding his metaphysical insights as an integral part of his overall theological project. The following apt remark by Rudi te Velde captures well what I am going to argue: "Analogy, as applied to divine names, is firmly rooted in the metaphysical conception of being as the intelligible aspect under which the world of creatures is positively related to its divine origin."[9]

9. Rudi te Velde, *Aquinas on God: The "Divine Science" of the* Summa theologiae (Aldershot: Ashgate, 2006), p. 97. I am indebted to te Velde's excellent synthetic account of the metaphysics of participation and of transcendental analogy in Thomas.

II. Analogy in Thomas

Lest we cannot see the forest because of the trees, I shall first announce in broad sweeps the central themes that make up the core of this chapter. There is, first, the theme of the *predicamental use of analogy;* here a "formal content" of existence is attributed horizontally across the various predicamental modes of being so as to attribute being as something intrinsic to all that exists across the diversity of genera, or categories. The predicamental use of analogy makes possible eventually an attribution of being to God in a sense that relates in some way analogically to what creatures are intrinsically. For this reason predicamental analogy avoids a "merely extrinsic" equivocation, pace Jüngel.

The second theme is the transcendental predication of being, from creatures to God, based upon causality and participation. Transcendental predication allows one to attribute perfections in creatures to God as "divine names." Because *transcendental analogy* is based on the creative causality of the transcendent first cause, it avoids any form of mere univocal assimilation of God to creatures, a "conceptual essentialism" of the kind the early Pannenberg greatly worried about in his first works on analogy.[10]

Those who have traveled this road know that the topic of analogy in Thomas is as notoriously complex as it is subtle. Thomas never wrote a treatise on analogy. But from his very first work on, he thought about analogy, and over time his thought did indeed develop in notable ways. I am not interested, however, in offering a genealogy of the overall development of the doctrine of analogy in Thomas's thought. For this I would like to direct the reader to the exhaustive scholarly accounts advanced by Hampus Lyttkens, George P. Klubertanz, Cornelio Fabro, Bernard Montagnes, Rolf Schönberger, Rudi te Velde, John F. Wippel, and Gregory P. Rocca.[11]

10. See esp. his lengthy review essay "Zur Bedeutung des Analogiegedankens bei Karl Barth: Eine Auseinandersetzung mit Urs von Balthasar," *Theologische Literaturzeitung* 78 (1953): 17-24, as well as his essay "Analogy and Doxology," *Basic Questions in Theology,* vol. 1, trans. George H. Kehm (Philadelphia: Fortress Press, 1970), pp. 212-38, originally published in *Dogma und Denkstrukturen: Festschrift für Edmund Schlink,* ed. Wilfried Joest and Wolfhart Pannenberg (Göttingen: Vandenhoeck & Ruprecht, 1963), pp. 96-115.

11. Hampus Lyttkens, *The Analogy between God and the World: An Investigation of Its Background and Interpretation of Its Use by Thomas of Aquino,* trans. Axel Poignant (Uppsala: Almqvist and Wiksells, 1952); George Klubertanz, *St. Thomas Aquinas on Analogy: A Textual Analysis and Systematic Synthesis* (Chicago: Loyola University Press, 1960); Cornelio Fabro, *Participation et causalité selon S. Thomas d'Aquin* (Paris: Béatrice-Nauwelaerts; Louvain: Publications Universitaires, 1961); Bernard Montagnes, O.P., *The Doctrine of the Analogy of Being*

Rather, I would like to content myself with offering the contours of what can reasonably be defended as Thomas's mature doctrine of analogy as it came to bear most significantly on his way of predicating divine names.

Thomas's mature doctrine of analogy arises from a distinct synthesis of two strands of metaphysical thought, a synthesis arguably prepared by the Neoplatonic commentators of the Aristotelian corpus. The one strand — that of the unity of order by reference to a primary instance — is of Aristotelian provenance and belongs primarily, albeit (as we shall see) not exclusively, to the order of predication. The other strand — that of participation — is of Neoplatonic origin and belongs exclusively to the order of being.[12] The first element of this synthesis — the unity of order by reference to a primary instance — permanently underlies all the later developments and is to be found in the early opuscula *De principiis naturae* and *De ente et essentia* (both probably written between 1252 and 1256), as well as in his late commentary on Aristotle's *Metaphysics* (1270-71). The second element of this synthesis, participation, which enriches and completes the Aristotelian strand, but also integrates it into a higher metaphysical synthesis, is already fully at work in the *Summa contra Gentiles* (1259-65), as well as the *Summa theologiae* (1265-73), but can as well be observed in the *De potentia* (1265-66) and in full maturity late in the *De substantiis separatis* (1271).

Any attempt to understand the analogy of being in Thomas has to come to terms with the simple fact that the topic of analogy is present from the very first moment of Thomas's written work. At the danger of overstating the matter, there is simply no instance in Thomas's work where analogy is not tacitly presupposed or being treated without being named or simply being silently at work in the exercise of *sacra doctrina* itself.

---

according to Thomas Aquinas, trans. E. M. Macierowski, reviewed and corrected by P. Vandervelde, with revisions by A. Tallon (Milwaukee, WI: Marquette University Press, 2004; French original, *La doctrine de l'analogie de l'être d'après Saint Thomas d'Aquin* [Louvain: Publications Universitaires; Paris: Béatrice-Nauwelaerts, 1963]); Rolf Schönberger, *Die Transformation des klassischen Seinsverständnisses: Studien zur Vorgeschichte des neuzeitlichen Seinsbegriffs im Mittelalter* (Berlin: de Gruyter, 1986); Rudi te Velde, *Participation and Substantiality in Thomas Aquinas* (Leiden: Brill, 1995); John Wippel, *The Metaphysical Thought of Thomas Aquinas: From Finite Being to Uncreated Being* (Washington, DC: The Catholic University of America Press, 2000); Gregory P. Rocca, *Speaking the Incomprehensible God: Thomas Aquinas on the Interplay of Positive and Negative Theology* (Washington, DC: The Catholic University of America Press, 2004).

12. Montagnes, *Doctrine of the Analogy of Being,* p. 23. As will become clear in the following, on the relationship between the Aristotelian predicamental analogy and the transcendental analogy by way of participation I am substantively indebted to Montagnes' analysis.

Moreover, lest we immediately project definite preunderstandings of analogy onto Thomas — be they the mathematical analogy of the Pythagorean school or analogy as the structural principle of the cosmos in Plato's *Timaeus* — let us first note that Thomas's doctrine is part and parcel of a quite original interpretation of Aristotle advanced by the Christian schoolmen of the first half of the thirteenth century. Alexander of Hales, Albert the Great, and Bonaventure contribute to this emerging doctrine of analogy. In this Christian philosophical reception of Aristotle, analogy is first of all a distinct way of predication — in contrast with univocal predication — to be employed in transgeneric predication. The basis of such analogical predication is the unity of many meanings of one common word by reference to a primary instance. Thomas was fully part of this emerging Christian tradition of metaphysical inquiry and hence had no interest whatsoever in coming up with a new "theory" of analogy in the modern sense of philosophical patricide. Instead of aiming at intellectual replacement, Thomas aimed at a superior synthesis of what he regarded as the strongest strands of the received philosophical tradition, the Aristotelian account of the unity of order by reference to a primary instance, and the Neoplatonic account of ontological participation. I will first address the Aristotelian strand, then turn to the Neoplatonic one and the mutual integration of both, and finally to the predication of divine names.

The fundamental axiom, ontological and epistemological in one, operative behind this analysis, shared by the whole classical metaphysical tradition, is of an almost shocking naïveté for modern critical and skeptical sensibilities: the structure of the conceptual syntax that arises from the analysis of the way we predicate reality is isomorphic to this very reality. Hence the very predication of being discloses and renders intelligible the structures of being itself. This axiom is understood to be operative not unlike a first principle of the intellect. Consequently, it cannot be proven. Rather, it asserts itself in all modes of inquiry including allegedly a priori inquiries into the conceptual structures of reason or the manifold complexities of language itself. The very cornerstone of metaphysical realism, this axiom, however, can be reasonably accounted for and successfully defended against the criticisms raised against metaphysical realism from the perspectives of transcendental idealism, phenomenology, or poststructuralism. Such accounts and defenses have indeed been offered throughout the twentieth century.[13] The quite contingent but

---

13. Just to name one, by now classical, account: Jacques Maritain, *Distinguish to Unite or The Degrees of Knowledge*, trans. Gerald B. Phelan (New York: Charles Scribner's Sons, 1959).

not altogether insignificant fact that only few contemporary philosophers find such defenses convincing should not tempt us into assuming that therefore the axiom does not obtain. While I cannot get involved in any defense of metaphysical realism at this point, I should note that in the following I not only take this realist principle to be central to Thomas's metaphysical inquiry but also indeed to obtain per se. Hence the following presentation of Thomas on analogy, while primarily reconstructive, indeed holds the principle of Thomist realism to obtain and to enable a genuine inquiry into the structures of being.

Predicamental Analogy: The Likeness of Species and Genus

For Aristotle, being (ὄν) is predicated in irreducibly multiple ways. For being is primordially diverse. To put it in the terms of Aristotle's teacher, being does not have a single, pure, idea-like form and therefore cannot be determined by way of a definition. And consequently, neither can the unity of being be achieved by abstracting it like a genus from the multiplicity of beings — "being" (ὄν/*ens*) as something like the smallest common denominator of all beings. Rather, the very plurality of beings must be integrated into a differentiated unity of being by way of an analogy of proportion. Aristotle regarded this procedure as the only viable alternative to the procedure of definition — and the latter is obviously not possible. For in a definition, the specific difference is added *extrinsically* to the identity of the genus while the multiplicity of being is *intrinsic* to the unity of being. Consequently, for Aristotle, the multiplicity of being presents itself irreducibly by way of the ten categories, or genera, of being (substance, quantity, quality, relation, place, time, position, action, passion/reception, possession/condition). Furthermore, the multiplicity of being presents itself as fundamentally differentiated between substance and accidents and in the modes of actuality and potentiality.[14]

Following Aristotle, Thomas understands the categories, or predicamentals, as the different ways of predicating. And because in each way of predicating ineluctably "being" is predicated, the various modes of being, the *modi essendi,* are always already included in these ways of predication. Hence, logically considered, the categories or predicamentals are the most comprehensive genera by way of which we conceptually understand all of

---

14. See Aristotle, *Metaphysics,* book VII (Z), for an extensive treatment.

contingent reality. Ontologically considered, the categories, or predicamentals, are the most universal modes of being and as such subsist independently of human conceptual formation. It is for this reason that Thomas never pursues a logical deduction of the categories (as Kant did famously, if erroneously, in his *Critique of Pure Reason*). Rather, according to Thomas, the deduction of the categories must follow the analysis of reality. For insofar as in each way of predicating a mode of being is entailed, the categories, or predicamentals, are grounded in the nature of being itself.[15]

We can find an immediate echo of these considerations in Thomas's early *De ente et essentia:*

> [T]he term 'a being' [*ens per se*] in itself has two meanings. Taken one
> way it is divided by the ten categories; taken in the other way it signi-
> fies the truth of propositions. The difference between the two is that in
> the second sense anything can be called a being if an affirmative prop-
> osition can be formed about it, even though it is nothing positive in re-
> ality. In this way privations and negations are called beings, for we say
> that affirmation *is* opposed to negation, and that blindness *is* in the
> eye. But in the first way nothing can be called being unless it is some-
> thing positive in reality. In the first sense, then, blindness and the like
> are not beings.[16]

What matters for our consideration here, is the first sense only, by way of which something positive in reality is predicated by way of the ten categories or genera. For it is in the very context of this sense of "being" that Thomas conceives "analogy" in a largely unproblematic way as a property of common names and concepts — in short, as *predicamental analogy.* And it is for this reason that the division of predicates into three groups

15. For a more detailed discussion of how the diverse modes of being are proportional to the ways of predicating, see Thomas's commentary on Aristotle's *Physics,* lecture 5, no. 322.

16. Thomas Aquinas, *On being and essence,* trans. Armand Maurer (Toronto: PIMS, 1968), pp. 29-30; Thomas Aquinas, *De ente et essentia,* in *Opuscula philosophica* (Rome: Marietti, 1954), c. 1, p. 5: "[E]ns per se dicitur *dupliciter: uno modo,* quod dividitur per decem genera; *alio modo,* quod significat propositionum veritatem. Horum autem differentia est, quia secundo modo potest dici ens omne illud de quo affirmativa propositio formari potest, etiamsi illud in re ponat; per quem modum privationes et negationes entia dicuntur: dicimus enim quod affirmatio est opposita negationi, et quod caecitas est in oculo. Sed primo modo non potest dici ens, nisi quod aliquid in re ponit. Unde primo modo caecitas et huiusmodi non sunt entia."

occurs — into univocal, equivocal, and analogous predicates. *Univocation:* a term is predicated of several subjects with exactly the same *ratio,* or meaning. *Equivocation:* there is no commonality of the *ratio* or meaning between the subjects predicated, only the same word is used accidentally. *Analogical* predication comes to stand in the middle between univocation and equivocation. It occurs when the analogous term comprises in its meaning some similarity-in-difference across the *predicamental range* (substance and accidents) or across the *transcendental range* (different levels/perfections of being).[17] Thomas never debates this division between univocal, equivocal, and analogical predication, but always presupposes and uses it.[18]

De principiis naturae

In his very first work, *De principiis naturae,*[19] Thomas offers a brief but penetrating inquiry into the metaphysical principles that constitute reality

17. Thomas puts the matter succinctly in a late explanation of his mature doctrine of analogy in *ST* I, q. 13, a. 10 c.: "Univocal terms mean absolutely the same thing, but equivocal terms are absolutely different; whereas in analogical terms a word taken in one signification must be placed in the definition of the same word taken in other senses; as, for instance, *being* which is applied to *substance* is placed in the definition of being as applied to *accident;* and *healthy* applied to animal is placed in the definition of healthy as applied to urine and medicine. For urine is the sign of health in the animal, and medicine is the cause of health." For a very clear rendition of this matter, one to which I am here indebted, see W. Norris Clarke, S.J., "Analogy and the Meaningfulness of Language about God," in *Explorations in Metaphysics: Being — God — Person* (Notre Dame: University of Notre Dame Press, 1994), pp. 123-49.

18. As Montagnes has argued in *Doctrine of the Analogy of Being,* p. 24, this division was not introduced by Aristotle himself but by Arab Aristotelianism — to be precise, by Averroës. The other elements of predicamental analogy Thomas draws from Aristotle's *Metaphysics.* They pertain to the unity and diversity of the principles constituting reality, to the enumeration of the types of unity, and especially to the ordered diversity of the meaning of being. The doctrine of the unity and diversity of intrinsic principles appears in *Meta.* 12.4 and 5, 1070a31-1071b1; the enumeration of different types of unity appears in 5.6.1016b31-1017a2 and 5.9.1018a13, and the Aristotelian theory of the unity of the object of metaphysics (being is said in many ways but ways that are unified by reference to a fundamental meaning, which is that of substance) appears in 4.2.1003a33-b15; 7.4.1030a34-b3; 11.3.1060b31-1061a10.

19. Thomas Aquinas, *De principiis naturae,* in *Opuscula philosophica,* pp. 121-28; Thomas d'Aquin, *Les Principes de la réalité naturelle,* introd., trans., and notes by Jean Madiran (Paris: Nouvelles Éditions Latines, 1963); Thomas von Aquin, *De principiis naturae*

as we perceive it by way of the senses. The last chapter of the opusculum, the one most pertinent to our topic, is devoted to the analogy of principles and causes. Thomas's metaphysical resolution toward the constitutive principles of sensibly perceptible reality leads him to form and matter.[20] Thomas then asks, What kind of unity obtains between the diverse things composed of form and matter we encounter?[21] In order to grasp the kind of unity we find between such diverse things as stones, trees, and human beings Thomas appeals to the axiom of *proportional unity,* the unity of a standard-Aristotelian four-part proportion: The type of community and diversity of principles is identical to the type of community and diversity of the beings of which they are the principles. Thomas's late commentary on Aristotle's *Metaphysics* offers a helpful illustration for this axiom of pre-dicamental analogy by way of proportion. Here he is defending the attri-bution of act and potency, not only to the accidents of a reality (its opera-tions and powers), but also to substances. The ascription of act and potency is proportional and analogical, ascribed not only to accidents but also to substances:

> Then [Aristotle] shows that the term actuality is used in different senses; and he gives two different senses in which it is used. First, actual-ity means action, or operation. And with a view to introducing the dif-ferent senses of actuality he says, first, that we do not say that all things are actual in the same way but in different ones; and this difference can be considered according to different proportions. For a proportion can be taken as meaning that, just as one thing is in another, so a third is in a fourth; for example, just as sight is in the eye, so hearing is in the ear. And the relation of substance (i.e., of form) to matter is taken accord-ing to this kind of proportion; for form is said to be in matter.[22]

— *Die Prinzipien der Wirklichkeit,* intro., trans., and commentary by Richard Heinzmann (Stuttgart: Kohlhammer, 1999). Heinzmann's commentary is as profound as it is lucid. I happily acknowledge my indebtedness to Heinzmann's insights.

20. *De principiis naturae,* chaps. 1-5.

21. *De principiis naturae,* chap 6.

22. Thomas Aquinas, *Commentary on Aristotle's Metaphysics,* trans. John P. Rowan, preface by Ralph McInerny (Notre Dame, IN: Dumb Ox Books, 1995), 9.5.1828, p. 605; S. Thomae Aquinatis, *In Duodecim Libros Metaphysicorum Aristotelis Expositio* (Rome: Marietti, 1950), p. 437. Thomas continues in §1829: "There is another meaning of proportion inasmuch as we say that, just as this is related to that, so another thing is related to some-thing else; for example, just as the power of sight is related to the act of seeing, so too the power of hearing is related to the act of hearing."

There is a fundamental continuity between the early *De principiis naturae* and the late commentary on this crucial matter: *The principles of being for each of the categories identified by Aristotle are different, but they are also proportionally similar.*[23] Substances and their accidents are said to "be in act" in different ways. The very fact, however, that Aristotle already understands the principles of being to be *causal* principles allows Thomas to inquire more deeply into the precise nature of analogical unity. Following Aristotle, *he grounds the unity of proportion in the unity of order.*[24] For it is substance that gives causal order and unity to all the accidents of a specific being. Hence the principles of being do not only relate proportionately to each other but also by way of the causality of the primary instance — substance.[25]

At this very point Thomas introduces Aristotle's famous example of health:

> While 'healthy' can be predicated of an animate body as well as of its urine and its food, it does not mean in all three cases exactly the same. For 'healthy' is predicated of the urine as a sign of health, of the animate body as its subject, and of its food as its cause. However, all these three meanings relate to one single end, that is, to health.[26]

It is of principal importance to grasp the profound metaphysical insight conveyed by this unassumingly simple example — and even more so by the deceptively simplistic explanation that Thomas adds. As Montagnes rightly stresses, Thomas takes this reference to a primary instance of health as "a relation of ontological causality tying the analogates to the primary instance." For Thomas, most fundamentally, "analogical unity rests upon the causality that the primary instance exercises toward the analogates."[27] Notice however that

---

23. Montagnes, *Doctrine of the Analogy of Being*, p. 25.

24. Montagnes, *Doctrine of the Analogy of Being*, p. 25.

25. By extrapolating from the substance-accident-relation of causal unity, Thomas arrives at the insight that the analogical way of predication "applies to different beings each of which has its own nature and a distinct definition, but which have in common the fact that they are all in a relation to the one among them to which the common meaning primarily belongs" (*Doctrine of the Analogy of Being*, p. 26).

26. "Sicut sanum dicitur de corpore animalis et de urina et potione, sed non ex toto idem significat in omnibus tribus. Dicitur enim de urina ut de signo sanitatis, de corpore ut de subiecto, de potione ut de causa; sed tamen omnes istae rationes attribuuntur uni fini, scilicet sanitati" (*De principiis naturae*, no. 366, p. 127).

27. Montagnes, *Doctrine of the Analogy of Being*, p. 26.

the causality of the primary instance is not uniform. Sometimes it plays the role of final cause: in this way the different meanings of the term "healthy" designate realities that are ordered to the health of a living being as their end; sometimes it is the efficient cause: in this way the meanings of the term "medical" are taken by derivation from the medical practitioner who is the agent; sometimes it is the receptive cause: this is the case with being, which is said primarily of substance, then secondarily of quantity, quality, and the other accidents by reference to the substance which is their subject, their material cause. This is why being is not a genus, because it is attributed unequally *(per prius et posterius)* to the various categories.[28]

We will discuss at a later point an important aspect that remains implicit in *De principiis naturae.* It is the precise way in which the analogy of being resembles the analogy of health and how it differs from it. Since health can properly belong only to a living thing and hence neither to urine nor to medicine, the analogy of health remains an *extrinsic* analogy. In the case of the analogy of being, however, there obtains a formal participation between the analogates; hence the analogy is *intrinsic.* While this important difference is developed only in later works, it is indeed the case that already in his very first work, "Thomas connects proportional unity to unity of order and defines analogical unity by reference to a primary instance."[29]

Notice that Thomas designates to these two kinds of unity, proportional unity and unity of order, the same name: *analogical unity.* There obtains, however, a subordination of the proportional unity to the unity of order, since, as Thomas argues, proportional unity depends upon the unity of order.[30] In short, *on the level of substance and accidents, the analogy of order by reference to a primary instance is ontologically primary. The analogy*

---

28. Montagnes, *Doctrine of the Analogy of Being,* p. 26.

29. Montagnes, *Doctrine of the Analogy of Being,* p. 26.

30. "[A]nalogical unity is first and foremost the unity that is established by the ontological relations of final, efficient and material causality with respect to a primary instance, whence proportional likenesses result among the analogates" (Montagnes, *Doctrine of the Analogy of Being,* p. 27). "So, for Thomas, the name 'analogy' passes from proportion to relation: analogy is the theory laid out by Aristotle in Book IV of the *Metaphysics* to explain the diversity and unity of the meanings of being and secondarily mathematical proportion, i.e., the likeness of two or more relations. Each time that Thomas refers to the example of health and of the being of accidents and substance, he alludes implicitly but indisputably to Aristotle's *Metaphysics* and he understands analogy as unity of order by reference to a primary instance" (pp. 27-28).

of proportion must be understood in light of the primordial, causal analogy of order or attribution.

De ente et essentia

While in *De ente et essentia*, the second of Thomas's early metaphysical works, the term *analogia* does not occur a single time, this opusculum amounts nevertheless to an extensive inquiry into analogy, namely regarding the attributions of being in a unity of order by reference to a primary instance *(per prius et posterius)*. There are at least two aspects in *De ente et essentia* that pertain centrally to our topic: First, in continuity with *De principiis naturae* Thomas also argues in *De ente et essentia* that "the predicamental analogy of being is that which binds accidents to substance."[31] Substance is to be understood as principal being, being *in se,* and accident as relative being, ordered toward the substance. For its being the accident depends entirely upon substance; simultaneously, accident is the proper perfection of substance. Second, Thomas deepens his understanding of substance as principal being:

> In the order of being, there is a gradation by relation to a maximum which is cause: the perfection of being, realized without restriction in the substance, is participated derivatively by the accidents. The unity of order that relates accidental being to substantial being is no longer confined to an external relation of inherence; it is deeper: it is based upon a common nature, the *ratio entis,* unequally participated among the substance and the accidents.[32]

The key word in the last sentence is "participated": the *ratio entis* is unequally participated among the substance and the accidents. Already in *De ente et essentia* Thomas realizes that predicamental analogy must be conceived in terms of ontological participation. In the words of Bernard

---

31. Montagnes, *Doctrine of the Analogy of Being,* p. 29.

32. Montagnes, *Doctrine of the Analogy of Being,* p. 29. Thomas puts the matter the following way in *De ente et essentia,* c. 6: "Sed, quia illud quod dicitur maxime et verissime in quolibet genere, est causa eorum quae sunt post in illo genere . . . , ut in II *Metaphysicae* dicitur, ideo substantia, quae est principium in genere entis, verissime et maxime essentiam habens, oportet quod sit causa accidentium quae secundario et quasi secundum quid rationem entis participant" (Marietti, §36, p. 17).

Montagnes, "If substance is the primordial being, it is no longer merely a subject of accidents, but a maximum degree of a perfection that the accidents possess by participation of a lesser degree. At the level of the categories, the unity of order rests on a relation of participation."[33]

Let us step back for a moment and ask ourselves what the "analogy of being" signifies in Thomas's early philosophical work. Insofar as we can inquire into the causal principles of being, the unity and difference of being is reflected in the analogy of order that itself rests on the relation of participation. We are able to grasp the unity in difference because we understand the causal order that obtains between substance and accidents. Thomas always regards Aristotle's solution of predicamental analogy on the horizontal level as definitively established. From his early works on right up to his very last ones, he alludes to it in passing, clarifies it, but otherwise simply presupposes it.[34] However, what Thomas came increasingly to understand is that the relation of participation on which the analogy of order rests calls for further metaphysical resolution.

Now, let us prepare the transition from the predicamental to the transcendental order. Remember that in the predicamental order the predicates fall under a determinate category, or genus, with the exception of the most common predicate, being *(ens),* which is analogously shared or participated by all things of whatever category. Hence the *predicamental analogy* is transgeneric, or transcategorical, insofar as it applies analogically to the substance and to all the accidents, across the various genera, or categories. Following his teacher Albert the Great, Thomas calls names which are common to all things in this transgeneric sense "transcendentals," *transcendentia* (next to "being," also "true," "good," and "one").[35] The transcendentals are *modes of being,* because they transcend everything that is, by being common to and contained in everything that is.[36] The turn to the transcendental order occurs in the realization that the same diversity

---

33. Montagnes, *Doctrine of the Analogy of Being,* p. 29.

34. In the most extensive treatments of this matter in his commentary on the *Metaphysics,* Thomas presents the predicamental analogy of being as a unity of order by relation to this primary form of being, which is substance: 1.14.223-24; 4.1.534-43 (commentary on 4.2); 7.1.1246-59 and 7.4.1334-38 (commentary on 7.1); and 11.3 (commentary on 11.3).

35. On the derivation of the transcendentals, see Wippel, *The Metaphysical Thought of Thomas Aquinas,* pp. 192-94.

36. See Thomas Aquinas, *De veritate,* q. 1, a. 1. For the overall topic of transcendentals in Thomas, see the outstanding and, what strikes me as definitive, study by Jan Aertsen, *Medieval Philosophy and the Transcendentals: The Case of Thomas Aquinas* (Leiden: Brill, 1996).

of the transcendentals does not only obtain in relation to the diversity of created being but also obtains in their relation to the transcendent being of God as their ultimate cause.

At this point we have reached the threshold of the *transition from the predicamental to the transcendental order*. It is here, in light of the transcendentals, that for Christian thinkers in the medieval context the old metaphysical problem of the one and the many takes on a new urgency. For by now creation *ex nihilo* is known definitively by virtue of divine revelation, and is also coherently defensible on the philosophical level. And consequently, the central metaphysical challenge is not anymore the reduction to unity of multiple meanings of being by way of substance but the reduction of diverse beings to unity in relation to God. Bernard Montagnes puts the matter succinctly and in such a way that we immediately realize its striking relevance for contemporary theology:

> How to conceive the relation of beings to Being? If they are homogeneous with it, the monism that results leads necessarily to pantheism. And if they are heterogeneous to it, the mind comes up against a pluralism such that makes God unknowable. A God too close or too far, pantheism or agnosticism: how can we find a passage between these two dangers?[37]

This is what is at stake in the question — Is being univocal or equivocal? — when understood to refer to transcendental analogy.

Is Analogy a Purely Logical Tool — or Does It Pertain to Reality as Well?

At this point — *the very transition from predicamental to transcendental analogy* — we have to pause briefly for a fundamental sort of clarification pertaining to predicamental as well as to transcendental analogy. Our reading of *De principiis naturae*, as well as *De ente et essentia*, suggests that Thomas transitions in both works from logic to metaphysics, from the consideration of things according to the being which they have in the mind to a consideration of things according to their being in reality. And it is in the latter context, the metaphysical consideration, where Thomas

---

37. Montagnes, *Doctrine of the Analogy of Being,* p. 13.

develops the analogy of hierarchical participation of being. Some Thomists, however, deny such a transition from logic to metaphysics, from predicamental analogy that is concerned with logical *intentiones* to the analogy of being that is concerned with causal relations in reality. It is first and foremost Ralph McInerny who has extensively argued that the analogy of names belongs to logic alone, that it pertains exclusively to the mode of being things have in human intellection.[38] While it would exceed the scope of this chapter to enter into an extensive textual and speculative debate with McInerny, I shall rely in the following upon the extensive textual and speculative critique of his position advanced by Lawrence Dewan.[39] I find the latter persuasive as a reading of Thomas's texts, as well as a speculative position *secundum mentem S. Thomae* and in accord with major voices of the Thomist commentatorial tradition (John Capreolus and Sylvester of Ferrara). I shall briefly highlight three points as most salient for our concerns. They pertain to the fundamental relationship between metaphysics, or first philosophy, on the one hand, and logic, on the other hand. They make explicit the primordial nature of metaphysical inquiry of being as an inquiry that gives rise to notions that pertain properly to being and as defined by the metaphysician become the principles with which logic operates.

I also should stress that I do not regard these three points per se as advancing a probative argument against McInerny's position, though I think Dewan's developed position indeed does. All I regard these three points to do is, in light of McInerny's fundamental objection, to offer sufficient warrant to continue to maintain that there is terminologically as well as substantively speaking an analogy of being in Thomas.

First, according to Thomas as well as Aristotle, logic as a science depends on metaphysics and not vice versa. Following Aristotle, Thomas regards metaphysics as the science that considers the principles common to

---

38. Most recently Ralph McInerny, *Aquinas and Analogy* (Washington, DC: The Catholic University of America Press, 1996). But see also Charles De Koninck, "Metaphysics and the Interpretation of Words," *Laval théologique et philosophique* 17 (1961): 22-34, and Hyacinthe-Marie Robillard, *De l'analogie et du concept d'être* (Montréal: Les presses de l'Université de Montréal, 1963).

39. Lawrence Dewan, O.P., "St. Thomas and Analogy: The Logician and the Metaphysician," in *Form and Being: Studies in Thomistic Metaphysics* (Washington, DC: The Catholic University of America Press, 2006), pp. 81-95, and "Does Being Have a Nature? (Or: Metaphysics as a Science of the Real)," in *Approaches to Metaphysics,* ed. William Sweet (Dordrecht/Boston/London: Kluwer Academic Publishers, 2004), pp. 23-59.

all the other sciences.[40] Indeed, in some particular cases it is the metaphysician who gives the principles of some sciences to these sciences, which is the case with logic. For, as Dewan emphasizes, the definition of the genus, the species, and the analogue falls under the responsibility of the metaphysician: "To investigate genus and species is proper to the metaphysician, since they pertain properly to being as being."[41]

Second, from logic's dependence upon metaphysics follows that "more is included in the metaphysician's notions of univocity and analogy than the logician's notions of these *intentiones*."[42] This is a point as complex as it is crucial. Dewan draws upon Thomas's *Scriptum super libros Sententiarum* I d. 19, q. 5, a. 2, ad 1 in order to substantiate it. Next to two classifications of analogy we are familiar with (according to notion only and not according to being; according to notion and according to being), Thomas introduces a third one:

> Or else, [something is said according to analogy] according to being and not according to notion [*secundum esse et not secundum intentionem*]; and this occurs when many things are taken as equal [*parificantur*] in the notion [*in intentione*] of something common, but that common item does not have being of one intelligible character [*esse unius rationis*] in all: for example, all bodies are taken as equal in the notion of corporeity [*in intentione corporeitatis*]; hence, the logician [*logicus*], who considers only notions [*intentiones tantum*], says that this name "body" is predicated of all bodies univocally; however, the being of this nature [*esse hujus naturae*] is not of the same intelligible character [*ejusdem rationis*] in corruptible and incorruptible bodies; hence for the metaphysician and the physicist, who consider things according to their be-

---

40. "[T]hat science is pre-eminently intellectual which deals with the most universal principles. These principles are being and those things which naturally accompany being, such as *unity* and *plurality, potency* and *act*. Now such principles should not remain entirely undetermined, since without them a complete knowledge of the principles which are proper to any genus or species cannot be had. Nor again should they be dealt with in any one particular science; for, since a knowledge of each class of beings stands in need of these principles, they would with equal reason be investigated in every particular science. It follows, then, that such principles are treated by one common science, which, since it is intellectual in the highest degree, is the mistress of the others" (Thomas Aquinas, *Commentary on Aristotle's Metaphysics,* trans. and with an introduction by John P. Rowan [Notre Dame, IN: Dumb Ox Books, 1995], pp. xxix-xxx).

41. Dewan, "St. Thomas and Analogy," p. 84.

42. Dewan, "St. Thomas and Analogy," p. 88.

ing, neither this name "body," nor any other [name] is said univocally of corruptibles and incorruptibles, as is clear from *Metaph.* 10, text 5, from [both] the Philosopher and the Commentator.[43]

This classification is indeed crucial because here the difference between the metaphysician's consideration and that of the logician is starkest. There is one important instance, according to Thomas, where what is univocity for the logician is emphatically not univocity but analogy for the metaphysician. Hence, "there is a type of term which a logician sees as univocal and a metaphysician sees as analogical,"[44] and it is this latter instance that establishes the fact that more is included in the metaphysician's notions of analogy and univocity. In the case of corruptible and incorruptible bodies, Dewan rightly stresses, "it is not enough, according to the metaphysician, to have one *intentio* for *univocity.* One must have the same kind of matter."[45]

Third, because the metaphysician considers the constitutive causal principles of being and, by doing so, also investigates genus, species, and the analogue, Thomas properly uses the logical notions as "stand-ins" for metaphysical conceptions. As Thomas states in his commentary on Aristotle's *Metaphysics,* the metaphysician "considers the prior and the posterior, genus and species, whole and part, and other things of this sort, because these also are accidents of that which is inasmuch as it is that which is [*accidentia entis inquantum est ens*]."[46] As Thomas says elsewhere in his commentary, for the metaphysician's consideration "being *in* a subject" and "being *about* a subject"[47] do not differ. For genus and difference have

43. Dewan's translation, "St. Thomas and Analogy," p. 88. He points to *Summa contra Gentiles* I. c. 32 and *De potentia* q. 7, a. 7, ad 6 for examples of this sort of analogy and Thomas's explicit denial of its univocity.

44. Dewan, "St. Thomas and Analogy," p. 89.

45. Dewan, "St. Thomas and Analogy," p. 93. Dewan illustrates his point with *ST* I, q. 66, a. 2, ad 2, where Thomas argues that the word "genus" needs to be properly qualified according to its consideration by a logician compared to its consideration by a physicist, i.e. natural philosopher: "If genus is taken in a physical sense, corruptible and incorruptible things are not in the same genus, on account of their different modes of potentiality, as is said in *Metaph.* x, text 26. Logically considered, however, there is but one genus of all bodies, since they are all included in the one notion of corporeity."

46. Thomas Aquinas, *Commentary on Aristotle's Metaphysics,* 4.4.587, concerning Aristotle's *Metaphysics* 1005a13-18. Dewan's translation, "St. Thomas and Analogy," p. 84, n. 14.

47. Thomas Aquinas, *Commentary on Aristotle's Metaphysics,* 7.13.1576, concerning Aristotle's *Metaphysics* 1038b15-16.

a foundation in things, as it became clear in the connection of genus to matter in Thomas's treatment of "body" as an analogical name, metaphysically considered, when used in common for corruptible and incorruptible bodies.[48]

In conclusion, our transition from predicamental to transcendental analogy and from the logic of predication to the metaphysics of ontological participation merely reflects the *ordo doctrinae,* the pedagogical order from what is easier to what is more difficult. The order of being itself as it gives rise to the order of knowledge and of predication, in its distinction from the *ordo doctrinae,* is reflected in the hierarchical relationship between metaphysics as first philosophy and the science of logic, in that "it is the metaphysician who defines analogy, and does so in terms of *the foundations in reality* for the modes of discourse."[49] The analogy of being is the condition for the possibility of predicamental analogy and hence "the interest of the metaphysician in the *real* foundation for naming."[50] We understand *De principiis naturae* and *De ente et essentia* rightly only if we read them as exercises of a metaphysical inquiry into reality per se that provide the logician with the notions constitutive of his or her science but that simultaneously use these notions as "stand-ins" for metaphysical conceptions. It is for this very reason that in *Summa theologiae* I, q. 4, a. 3, when treating the metaphysical question of the likeness of some creature to God, Thomas identifies the similarity of the effect to the cause, the similarity of the creature to the Creator, as "according to a sort of analogy [*secundum aliqualem analogiam*]."[51] The question under consideration does not pertain exclusively to the analogy of names in the order of predication but indeed pertains first and foremost to the real relation of all beings, insofar as they are beings, to the first cause, the universal principle of being in its entirety. And it is the latter to which we shall now turn.

---

48. Dewan is here in fundamental agreement with Montagnes. Cf. the latter's instructive n. 100 on p. 60, where, in reference to the passage of Thomas's Sentences commentary under discussion, he states: "The logical equality of the generic notion conceals a real hierarchy of species; whence the logician is more aware of the notional unity, whereas the metaphysician is more attentive to the real diversity."

49. Dewan, "St. Thomas and Analogy," p. 94.

50. Dewan, "St. Thomas and Analogy," p. 95.

51. Also, as Dewan adds as additional text, Thomas characterizes the *natura entitatis* (i.e., the act of being) as one *secundum analogiam* in all creatures (*In II Sent.,* d. 1, q. 1, a. 1).

The Analogy of Participation:
The Likeness between Cause and Effect

It has been well established in recent scholarship on Thomas that, up to and including *De veritate,* Thomas is intensely searching for the proper way to conceive of transcendental analogy and the ensuing analogical predication of God.[52] Eventually he integrates all major elements of the earlier solutions into a mature synthesis, fully articulated first in *Summa contra Gentiles* I, 34, a synthesis that presents "a general theory of the analogy of being which applies to transcendental unity as well as predicamental unity."[53] It is of paramount importance not to get sidetracked by the temporary solution entertained in the prior *De veritate,* where indeed for a brief period Thomas does consider the analogy of proportionality as the ultimate, overarching framework for transcendental analogy. In light of the late Scotus's critique of the analogy of attribution *ad alterum,* first Thomas Sutton and later Cajetan and the ensuing Cajetanian tradition of conceiving analogy, anchor themselves in the particular proposal of *De veritate.* Recent scholarship, however, has established that Thomas drops this proposal never to return to it again, except in those instances of transcendental analogy in which the analogy of proportionality is guided and controlled by the primordial analogy of causal participation.[54]

It has been incontrovertibly demonstrated by L.-B. Geiger, Cornelio Fabro, W. Norris Clarke, John F. Wippel, Rudi te Velde, and others that the notion of ontological participation maintained by Neoplatonic philosophers — especially Proclus — and tacitly assumed by Aristotle's Neoplatonic commentators, became a central element in the development of Thomas's mature position on the analogy of being.[55]

---

52. For the following, see Cornelio Fabro, "The Intensive Hermeneutics of Thomistic Philosophy: The Notion of Participation," trans. B. M. Bonansea, *Review of Metaphysics* 27 (1974): 449-491 (486ff.).

53. Montagnes, *Doctrine of the Analogy of Being,* p. 14.

54. See the important recent work of Joshua Hochschild on this complex and controversial issue: *The Semantics of Analogy: Rereading Cajetan's* De Nominum Analogia (Notre Dame, IN: University of Notre Dame Press, 2010).

55. L.-B. Geiger, O.P., *La participation dans la philosophie de S. Thomas d'Aquin* (Paris: J. Vrin, 1942); Cornelio Fabro, *Participation et causalité selon S. Thomas d'Aquin* (Paris: Béatrice-Nauwelaerts, 1961); W. Norris Clarke, S.J., "The Limitation of Act by Potency in St. Thomas: Aristotelianism or Neoplatonism?" and "The Meaning of Participation in St. Thomas," in *Explorations in Metaphysics,* pp. 65-101; John F. Wippel, "Thomas Aquinas and

Thomas's decisive move was to deepen the analysis of *De ente et essentia* by way of the metaphysical method of resolution, that is, by tracing all things to the one first principle by which they are coordinated.[56] In the course of this inquiry toward increasing resolution — bearing fruit especially in *De potentia* — Thomas eventually realizes the following: *While God indeed is the source of all that exists with a formal or essential determination, God in his uniquely transcendent act of being as the efficient cause of their being is utterly distinct from the world of determinate created forms.* Such metaphysical resolution leads Thomas eventually to the first substantial act, which is *esse*. And more importantly even, the final consequence of such metaphysical resolution is to reduce the act of being by participation,

---

Participation," in *Studies in Medieval Philosophy,* ed. John F. Wippel (Washington, DC: The Catholic University of America Press, 1987), pp. 117-58; te Velde, *Participation and Substantiality in Thomas Aquinas;* see also Fabro, "Intensive Hermeneutics," pp. 468-69. Notice, however, that deepening his inquiry into ontological participation by way of the neo-Platonic tradition did not mean for Thomas to replace the Aristotelianism of his youth with an allegedly more mature neo-Platonic view that eventually "Platonized" Thomas's whole metaphysical approach. On the contrary, the profoundly Aristotelian *De ente et essentia* already entailed the potential for the unique metaphysical synthesis Thomas achieves late in his work, especially in *De substantiis separatis.* In that work, see c. 3, "De convenientia positionum Aristotelis et Platonis." According to Fabro, the importance of this text for Thomas's synthesis cannot be overrated: "The Thomistic synthesis is absolutely original: it accepts the metaphysical nucleus of Platonic transcendence (notion of creation, composition of *esse* and essence, doctrine of analogy) and welds it with the act of Aristotelian immanence (the unity of the substantial form, the intellective soul as substantial form of the body, the doctrine of abstraction). The originality of the dialectic of *esse* was fully developed by Aquinas especially in his later works because of a more direct knowledge of some Neoplatonic writings, such as those of Proclus and Porphyry. In *De substantiis separatis* (1272-73) he solves the classic Neoplatonic problem of the accord between Plato and Aristotle through his 'new' notion of participation. This he does in Chapter 3, *De convenientia positionum Aristotelis et Platonis,* where he shows the agreement of the two philosophers on such important doctrines as the real composition of essence and *esse* in creatures, the absolute immortality of spiritual substances, and the notion of divine Providence, while in chapter 4, *De differentia dictarum positionum Aristotelis et Platonis,* he shows that their differences concern only very secondary points" ("Intensive Hermeneutics," pp. 468-69).

56. Thomas Aquinas, *On the Power of God (Quaestiones Disputatae de Potentia Dei),* literally trans. by the English Dominican Fathers (Westminster: Newman Press, 1932), book I, q. 3, a. 6. In the body of the article he offers a highly condensed account of the discursive progress of metaphysical inquiry before Aristotle, at the end of which he states: "Consequently, all these various things must be traced to one first principle whereby they are coordinated: and for this reason the Philosopher concludes (*Meta.* 12.10) that there is one ruler over all" (p. 118).

the *actus essendi,* to the first principle, the *esse per essentiam,* that which is the act of being by way of its very essence.[57]

Here we can see immediately why participation and transcendental analogy converge: To participate is to have partially what another is without restriction.[58] Since being is participated by degrees beginning with that which is being by essence, there obtain simultaneously an essential diversity of participants and a unity of reference to the primary instance from which they obtain the common perfection.

Let us be very clear about one point here. For Thomas, being a creature means, not to be identical with one's *esse,* but to have *esse.* This *esse* is participated in by all creatures and hence is called *esse commune.* It is of central importance, not to get the relationship wrong between the *esse commune* and God, *the esse ipsum subsistens.* Are the two identical, or is God even contained in the *esse commune?* In his commentary on Denys's *Divine Names,* Thomas explicitly rejects such an identification.[59] Rather, the *esse commune* is the first of created realities. As such, the *esse commune* is an effect of God's creative agency and hence has no part whatsoever in God's essence but participates in some of the perfections of the *ipsum esse subsistens.* Consequently, God and the *esse commune* are as fundamentally distinct from each other as cause and effect are. Moreover, the *esse commune* does not subsist on its own; rather it is to be understood as a formal principle inherent in all beings.[60]

57. "[T]he notion of *actus essendi* appears beginning with the *Contra Gentiles,* where we meet the decisive affirmation: *esse actus est*" (Montagnes, *Doctrine of the Analogy of Being,* p. 43). Hence, for Thomas participation by way of the *actus essendi,* the act of all acts, "concerns the transcendental analogy of being, or, more precisely, the communication of being according to degrees, from the divine being, in which being subsists without restriction right down to partial realizations in the different substances" (p. 34).

58. "Ens . . . de quolibet autem creatura praedicatur per participationem: nulla autem creatura est suum esse, sed *est habens esse*" (Quodl. II, q. 2, a. 1).

59. Thomas Aquinas, *In librum beati Dionysii de divinis nominibus expositio* (Rome: Marietti, 1950), 5.2.660: "Deinde, cum dicit [279]: *Et ipsum* . . . ostendit quomodo esse se habeat ad Deum; et dicit quod *ipsum esse* commune *est ex* primo Ente, quod est Deus, et ex hoc sequitur quod esse commune aliter se habeat ad Deum quam alia existentia, quantum ad tria: primo quidem, quantum ad hoc quod alia existentia dependent ab esse communi, non autem Deus, sed magis esse commune dependet a Deo; et hoc est quod dicit quod ipsum *esse* commune *est ipsius Dei,* tamquam ab Ipso dependens, *et non ipse* Deus *est esse,* idest ipsius esse communis, tamquam ab ipso dependens."

60. See the illuminating discussion of this difficult metaphysical point by Martin Bieler, "The Theological Importance of a Philosophy of Being," in *Reason and the Reasons of Faith,* ed. Paul J. Griffiths and Reinhard Hütter (New York: T & T Clark International, 2005), pp. 295-326, esp. 314-15.

It is crucial to understand that in participation by way of the *actus essendi*, the act of being, there is no factor extrinsic to the *esse commune* itself that limits and pluralizes being. Rather, this limiting and pluralizing principle — in short, essence — must come by way of the *actus essendi* as the latter's proper perfection of differentiated subsistence. Remember what differentiates one thing from another. It is its essential determinations, that which makes it intelligibly different from something else.

But how exactly is this composite of the *actus essendi* and essence unified? It is in order to address this important metaphysical question that Thomas, in a rather bold speculative step of further metaphysical resolution, applies the Aristotelian principles of act and potency to the Neoplatonic dynamic of participation. We find this crucial move in *Summa contra Gentiles* I, c. 18: "Several things cannot become absolutely one unless among them something is act and something potency."[61] Hence, this metaphysical resolution leads Thomas to the axiom of first composition: *"the subject that participates is related to the participated perfection as potency to act."*[62]

It is indeed the case that, in this Aristotelian re-conception of the Neoplatonic concept of participation, the primacy of act and the priority of efficient causality condition each other. In other words, in the process of Thomas's metaphysical study of the composition of *esse* and essence in created things, participation remains governed by act and potency. *Participation signifies the communication of act to a subject in potency.*

Understanding participation rightly depends on not misunderstanding *esse* as a quasi essence. Rather, *ens* is essence in act. It is the "in act" that *esse* signifies. Let us unpack this fundamental point in three respects:

First, *esse* is always in act; hence a being *(id quod est)* can participate it, because a being is in potency to *esse*. God, who is *esse* without any potency admixed whatsoever, has nothing by participation but is what he is by virtue of his own essence: "As act free from potentiality, God grounds all participation and causes all beings."[63]

---

61. Thomas Aquinas, *Summa contra Gentiles. Book One: God,* trans. Anton C. Pegis (Notre Dame, IN: University of Notre Dame Press, 1975), p. 103 (SCG 1.18: "Non enim plura possunt simpliciter unum fieri nisi aliquid sit ibi actus, et aliud potentia"). For this point I am indebted to George Lindbeck's illuminating discussion in his essay "Participation and Existence in the Interpretation of St. Thomas Aquinas," *Franciscan Studies* 17 (1957): 1-22, 107-25.

62. Montagnes, *Doctrine of the Analogy of Being,* p. 40. "The participated perfection is the act of the subject in potency which receives it, and it is limited to the measure of this subject."

63. Montagnes, *Doctrine of the Analogy of Being,* p. 41. "*Esse,* which is infinite when it

Second, *esse* as act is not to be conceived as some primordial, undifferentiated *esse* that would only subsequently "actuate different essences as it were from the outside."[64] Rather, *esse* and essence are equally primordial and hence each must be understood in light of the other. Essence itself comes on the way of *esse* (Ferdinand Ulrich), the *esse commune*, for nothing falls outside the act of being; hence neither does essence as the perfection of differentiated potency to subsistence. Now to invert the perspective, essence is the measure and degree in which *esse* is participated.[65] Consequently, the *perfectio essendi*, the act of being — terminating in a concrete being *(hoc ens)* — includes indissolubly *esse*, essence, and the subject.

Third, it is utterly crucial to understand that there is no "common logos" of an ever so subtly hidden univocity at play in Thomas's understanding of ontological participation. For beings, by way of the measuring perfection of essence, are *intrinsically* diversified. Hence, in analogical predication of existence there is no univocity of the nature of essence whatsoever involved. Nevertheless, there still obtains an analogical unity, since all intrinsically diversified beings receive their specific limited perfection from the primary instance in which the respective perfection subsists without limitation.[66] This is to say that all things resemble the primary cause of existence and, insofar as they participate in existence, resemble one another. In light of the correlation between act and form, *esse* and essence, Thomas conceives transcendental analogy as a causal, as well as formal, ontological dependence of every being *(id quod est)* with respect to the *ipse esse subsistens*, God. Being *(ens)* is never univocal because it is always participated. And because there obtain two dimensions of participation, predicamental and transcendental participation, there are two corre-

---

is not received within a potency, can be participated according to the indefinitely varied measures that the different essences are; beings are to the extent that they participate *esse*, and they are more or less perfect according as they participate more or less the perfection of being that pertains to God by essence. Their measure of being establishes their degree of likeness to the one who is *ipsum esse*. Thus, every subject that receives *esse* without being identical to it possesses being by participation. This is why the essence of such a substance is to the *esse* that it participates as receptive potency to the act received" (p. 41).

64. Montagnes, *Doctrine of the Analogy of Being*, p. 41.

65. "The being that subsists in God without restriction communicates itself in virtue of the divine causality in a more or less limited way according to the measure of each being, and it is intrinsically and formally participated on each occasion" (Montagnes, *Doctrine of the Analogy of Being*, p. 41).

66. Montagnes, *Doctrine of the Analogy of Being*, p. 41.

sponding forms of the analogy of being, one between substance and accident, and the other between God and creature.

In his later works, that is, from the *Summa contra Gentiles* on, Thomas conceives of both dimensions of participation as an integral unity. In the order of knowledge one ascends from predicamental to transcendental analogy. In the order of being, predicamental participation depends on the ontologically prior transcendental participation.[67]

Now, remember Aristotle's analogy of health as employed by Thomas in *De principiis naturae*. Notice in what respect the analogy of being resembles the analogy of health and how it differs from it. Quite obviously, the analogy of health is an *extrinsic* analogy; there is no intrinsic formal participation involved, since health can only belong to a living thing. There would indeed be serious if not fatal consequences for transcendental analogy, if all being only were to belong to the primary instance. For in this case it would be necessary to affirm that God is the only being, the only perfect thing, and that everything else has being and perfection only by extrinsic denomination. To emphasize divine transcendence in this way would deprive the universe of all reality. However, on this matter Thomas is as clear as can be desired. For he stresses that the analogy of health obtains "according to the intellectual conception only, but not according to being."[68] The analogy of being, on the other hand, obtains "according to the intellectual conception as well as according to being,"[69] because it involves an intrinsic formal as well as causal participation. For this second kind of analogy by reference to a primary instance is constituted by causal dependence upon the first being and by an intrinsic possession of the perfection of being, albeit formally specified according to a hierarchy of essences.[70]

---

67. Montagnes puts the matter well: "In order to elaborate a coherent and unified theory of the analogy of being, Thomas strove to apply the predicamental analogy discovered by Aristotle to the relation of beings to God, i.e., to transcendental analogy. By doing this the unified diversity that one encounters at the horizontal level of the categories and that one finds on the vertical plane of substances pertain to one and the same principle of explanation: analogy by reference to a primary instance" (*Doctrine of the Analogy of Being*, pp. 43-44).

68. "Secundum intentionem tantum et non secundum esse" (*In I Sent.*, d. 19, q. 5, a. 2, ad 1).

69. "Secundum intentionem et secundum esse" (*In I Sent.*, d. 19, q. 5, a. 2, ad 1).

70. Montagnes, *Doctrine of the Analogy of Being*, pp. 44-45. In his instructive n. 100 on p. 60, Montagnes directs the reader to *De ver.*, q. 21, a. 4, ad 2, where Thomas distinguishes clearly between extrinsic and intrinsic analogy: "A thing is denominated with reference to something else in two ways. (1) This occurs when the very reference itself is the meaning of

There is, however, one further step of differentiation necessary in the precise specification of the intrinsic analogy by reference to a primary instance. In an important discussion in *De potentia* Thomas identifies two ways to conceive such an analogy.[71] One is the analogy of two to a third *(duorum ad tertium)*. An example would be to call the accidents of quality and quantity as being in relationship to the substance. And it is this analogy of two to a third that Thomas decidedly rejects for use in the analogical naming of God. For according to this kind of analogy, the transcendental "being" *(ens)* would embrace God as well as beings and would be superior to them, since "being" *(ens)* would relate to God and creatures as substance would to quantity and quality.

What Thomas embraces in his later works is the second way of conceiving such an analogy, the analogy of *unius ad alterum,* which is established exclusively between a secondary analogate and the primary instance. The example for this kind of analogy is that between substance per se and accident per se. For substance exists of itself *(substantia est quod per se est)* and accident is in something else *(accidentis esse est inesse)*. In this kind of predication one of the two precedes the other. Montagnes puts the matter succinctly:

> What it means is that on the categorical level accident and substance do not receive the attribution of being by reference to a form common

---

the denomination. Thus urine is called healthy with respect to the health of an animal. For the meaning of healthy as predicated of urine is 'serving as a sign of the health of an animal.' In such cases what is thus relatively denominated does not get its name from a form inherent in it but from something extrinsic to which it is referred. (2) A thing is denominated by reference to something else when the reference is not the meaning of the denomination but its cause. . . . It is in this way that the creature is called good with reference to God" (*Truth,* vol. 3, trans. Robert W. Schmidt, S.J. [Indianapolis: Hackett, 1994], pp. 20-21).

71. Thomas Aquinas, *On the Power of God,* book 3, p. 43: "We must accordingly take a different view and hold that nothing is predicated univocally of God and the creature: but that those things which are attributed to them in common are predicated not equivocally but analogically. Now this kind of predication is twofold. The first is when one thing is predicated of two with respect to a third: thus being is predicated of quantity and quality with respect to substance. The other is when a thing is predicated of two by reason of a relationship between these two: thus being is predicated of substance and quantity. In the first kind of predication the two things must be preceded by something to which each of them bears some relation: thus substance has a respect to quantity and quality: whereas in the second kind of predication this is not necessary, but one of the two must precede the other. Wherefore since nothing precedes God, but he precedes the creature, the second kind of analogical predication is applicable to him but not the first" (*De potentia,* q. 7, a. 7, c).

to each term, namely being; there is nothing prior to substance, and being is either substance in the first place *(per prius)* or else accident subsequently *(per posterius)*. . . . In the same way, on the transcendental level, being does not encompass both beings and God, since being is not prior to God. It is God who grounds the analogy of being, since beings receive by participation what He is by essence; there is no primary instance of being other than He.[72]

Lest we misunderstand the analogy of being, however, as a ladder that, having made possible the necessary ascent, can now safely be discarded, let me reemphasize the following by way of a summary of what the analogy of being amounts to in Thomas's thought. It is fair to say that, ultimately, in light of the final metaphysical *resolutio,* for Thomas the unity of being rests on the unity of the first cause of being. For only when one has arrived at the real unity of being, has the multiplicity of beings been reduced to one. Hence, there obtains a strict correspondence between the structure of analogy and the structure of participation, with analogy as the way of predicating the unity of being and participation as the real unity of being. In short, as a way of predication the analogy of being reflects the dynamic unity of causal order that obtains between beings and their first and universal principle.[73] Hence, for Thomas analogy is anything but a merely linguistic tool or logical operation in relation to divine predication. Rather, the analogy of being is the necessary predicamental entailment of an epistemological, as well as metaphysical, realism that finds its proximate metaphysical resolution in the *actus essendi* and its final resolution in the first and ultimate principle, *ipsum esse subsistens.*

The Analogical Predication of God: Transgeneric Likeness between Cause and Effect Based on the Analogy Unius ad Alterum

When we turn now to the analogical predication of God, we need to keep in mind that according to Thomas's mature doctrine, such analogical predication occurs exclusively on the basis of this latter analogy of *unius ad alterum.* For being the first and universal principle of everything, God is "extra omne genus." Hence, in the analogy of divine predication, the whole

72. Montagnes, *Doctrine of the Analogy of Being,* p. 71.
73. Montagnes, *Doctrine of the Analogy of Being,* p. 91.

of all categorically distinct things as such is transcended. As Rudi te Velde rightly observes:

> Seen in this light, it becomes clear why God cannot be addressed as some *particular* reality, the highest and first in the order of essences. God is not a being among others who is merely higher and more perfect than everything we know of. God cannot be approached in the line of "more of the same" — that is, the same as the perfections we encounter in the world of creatures, such as life, intelligence, goodness, and so on — but then enlarged to its maximum and purified from its imperfections.[74]

Rather than pursuing such a perfect-being ontology, as it won the day in later Leibnizian and Wolffian metaphysics, Thomas conceives of created reality as *esse commune* in its differentiated unity and hence as a whole that *as such* is related to God as the first and universal principle of the *actus essendi*. Hence, there obtains a specific metaphysical order between the first principle or cause and its effect. Since this order is transgeneric, it escapes, on the one hand, the univocal identity of the genus. On the other hand, the likeness that it entails, is "secundum analogiam tantum" (*ST* I, q. 4, a. 3, ad 3), only according to a certain analogy — that is, of course, the analogy "unius ad alterum."

At this point we need to come back to the first transcendental, "being" *(ens)*. Remember that for Thomas it was by way of considering the first transcendental as such, *ens inquantum ens,* that the final metaphysical resolution became possible, the resolution to the first and single universal principle of all being — God.

The entailment of this last resolution is that the relationship between God and the *esse commune* is a causal one. *Esse* designates the universal perfection, the perfection of all perfections that pertain to the essences of things. In the process of the metaphysical *resolutio* the many perfections of creatures are reduced to their one origin, the first causal principle. The very path of this *resolutio* consists in leaving behind, in bracketing, what pertains to the order of essence and its categorical differentiations.[75]

Now we have arrived at the key notion of analogical predication for Thomas — the names for divine perfections. These are names capable of signifying the very perfection of *esse* as the act of all acts and the perfection

74. Te Velde, *Aquinas on God*, p. 117.
75. See te Velde, *Aquinas on God*, p. 116.

of all perfections. Hence they are not restricted to the categorically specified way in which we come to know these perfections. Because of their
transcategorical nature the perfections they signify are not intrinsically finite, and therefore the names for divine perfections can properly be attributed to God.

Hence, Thomas emphasizes in *Summa theologiae* I, q. 13, a. 6 that

> these names are applied to God not as the cause only, but also essen-
> tially. For the words, *God is good,* or *wise,* signify not only that He is the
> cause of wisdom or goodness, but that these exist in Him in a more ex-
> cellent way. Hence as regards what the name signifies, these names are
> applied primarily to God rather than to creatures, because these
> perfections flow from God to creatures; but as regards the imposition
> of the names, they are primarily applied by us to creatures, which we
> know first.[76]

Thomas draws here a clear distinction between the order of being and the
order of knowledge in order to secure the absolute transcendence of God.
In the order of being or participation perfection belongs most eminently
to God and is only participated by the creature. Hence attributing perfection to God is not simply a virtual attribution. However, the perfection can
be named only from the proximate context in which it is accessible to us as
creatures. Rudi te Velde rightly stresses that all these multiple perfections
are perfections of being, "which means that 'being' expresses their common unity in which they reflect their common origin in God. Perfection
terms such as 'life,' 'wisdom,' 'good' signify more 'intense' aspects of the
likeness creatures are said to have of God insofar as they are *beings*."[77]

Because of the simultaneity of the order of participation and the order of predication, the likeness of being has to find expression in a twofold
analogous way. Regarding its *first* aspect, Thomas says: "Whatever is said of
God and creatures, is said according to the relation of a creature to God as
its principle and cause, wherein all perfections of things preexist excel-

76. *ST* I, q. 13, a. 6 c.: "[H]uiusmodi nomina non solum dicuntur de Deo causaliter,
sed etiam essentialiter. Cum enim dicitur *Deus est bonus* vel *sapiens,* non solum significatur
quod ipse sit causa sapientiae vel bonitatis, sed quod haec in eo eminentius praeexistunt.
Unde, secundum hoc, dicendum est quod, quantum ad rem significatam per nomen, per
prius dicuntur de Deo quam de creaturis: quia a Deo huiusmodi perfectiones in creaturas
manant. Sed quantum ad impositionem nominis, per prius a nobis imponuntur creaturis,
quas prius cognoscimus."

77. Te Velde, *Aquinas on God,* p. 116.

lently."[78] Here we have the analogy of *unius ad alterum*. But remember now that all perfections are perfections of being, and because being is inherently and primordially predicated in an analogous way,[79] Thomas emphasizes that "a term [i.e. a perfection of being] which is thus used in a multiple sense signifies various proportions to some one thing; thus *healthy* applied to urine signifies the sign of animal health, and applied to medicine signifies the cause of that same health."[80] Because the perfections of being participate variously but similarly in their common first cause, they signify various but similar proportions to their common first cause. Hence there is a proportional likeness between God and creatures entailed in the analogy *unius ad alterum*. This kind of analogy by reference to a primary instance is constituted by *causal* dependence upon the first being and by an intrinsic possession of the perfection of being, albeit formally specified according to a hierarchy of essences. Consequently, the analogy of attribution *unius ad alterum* by way of the *esse commune* always entails an analogy of proportion by way of reference to a primary instance. And this is the *second* aspect of the twofold way of the analogical predication of God. Because of the intrinsic possession of the perfection of being by way of participation, the proportion is *intrinsic* — quite unlike the analogy of health, where the proportion remains *extrinsic*. In short, the multiplicity of perfections (like life, goodness, being, etc.) all refer to God as "toward one" *(ad unum)* as proportional effects of God's being. The *proportio*, or relation, does not, however, depend on a "common logos," some shared identity, but only on a common first principle in the order of being. All that exists and all created ontological perfections refer to their one ultimate source, who as subsistent *esse* is perfect in an unsurpassable and ineffable way.

It is the order of being that requires the analogy of attribution *unius ad alterum* to be the logically primary one, and it is by way of this analogy that agnosticism as well as anthropomorphism are avoided. The logically

78. *ST* I, q. 13, a. 5 c.: "[Q]uidquid dicitur de Deo et creaturis, dicitur secundum quod est aliquis ordo creaturae ad Deum, ut ad principium et causam, in qua praeexistunt excellenter omnes rerum perfectiones."

79. *ST* I, q. 13, a. 5, ad 1: "[A]ll univocal predications are reduced to one first non-univocal analogical predication, which is being." ("[I]n praedicationibus omnia univoca reducuntur ad unum primum, non univocum, sed analogicum, quod est ens.")

80. *ST* I, q. 13, a. 5 c.: "[N]omen quod sic multipliciter dicitur, significat diversas proportiones ad aliquid unum; sicut *sanum*, de urina dictum, significat signum sanitatis animalis, de medicina vero dictum, significat causam eiusdem sanitatis."

subsequent analogy of intrinsic proportion secures that the perfections predicated of God are ascribed in a more than virtual sense such that a total apophaticism is also avoided.[81] God possesses the perfections we attribute to him in a preeminent way, from which creatures derive all that they are and all the perfections that pertain to them. Analogical names for divine perfection can be understood to refer to God not only eminently but indeed really and properly.[82] They truly signify God in himself as the *res significata* (the thing signified). But because God's essence indeed remains a mystery, the *modus significandi* of the perfection name (signifying *how* the perfection exists in God) denotes something that remains hidden in the abyss of the *ipsum esse subsistens* — which is *not* the definition of God's essence but merely a circumscription of the first principle in its pure, subsisting actuality.[83] While we know that God truly is preeminently existent, good, wise, and so on, we do not know what this existence, goodness, and wisdom are in themselves. God in his perfection remains an unfathomable mystery.

III. Conclusion: A Response *secundum mentem S. Thomae* to the Two Protestant Objections to Analogical Predication of God in Thomas

We have reached the appropriate point in light of this *re-lecture* of Thomas to reconsider the criticisms that Wolfhart Pannenberg and Eberhard Jüngel advanced against Thomas's theological use of analogy.

The late Pannenberg in the significantly revised and recently published version of his 1955 *Habilitationsschrift* offers a much more nuanced and perceptive reading of Thomas's doctrine of the analogy of being than

---

81. E. L. Mascall, in his unjustly forgotten *Existence and Analogy: A Sequel to "He Who Is"* (London: Longmans and Green, 1949), rightly stressed this important point: "[I]n order to make the doctrine of analogy really satisfactory, we must see the analogical relation between God and the world as combining in a tightly interlocked union both analogy of attribution and analogy of proportionality. Without analogy of proportionality it is very doubtful whether the attributes which we predicate of God can be ascribed to him in more than a merely virtual sense; without analogy of attribution it hardly seems possible to avoid agnosticism. Which of the two forms of analogy is prior to the other has been, and still is, a hotly debated question among scholastic philosophers. Sylvester of Ferrara, in his great commentary on the *Summa contra Gentiles,* asserted the primacy of attribution and alleged that in this he was expressing the true thought of St. Thomas" (pp. 113-14).

82. *ST* I, q. 13, a. 2 c.

83. *ST* I, q. 13, a. 3 c.

he did in his early work. Focusing in his critique of Thomas on the Neo-platonic causal scheme, he connects with it an axiom he sees entailed in Neoplatonic speculation, namely, that in us human beings capable of such rational speculation there must exist some identical core with the ultimate One. For without some point of identity of all things with the One, so Pannenberg maintains, an "Erfassung," that is, a proper speculative conceptual comprehension, of the One is impossible.[84]

In a nutshell, this is how Pannenberg's Hegelian argument goes: Any form of similarity presupposes a partial identity either of being or by way of a univocal conceptual comprehension. Since Thomas denies both, his analogical predication, says Pannenberg, is without any true conceptual traction and hence cannot deliver any genuine knowledge of God. In order to avoid this problem of a camouflaged equivocation, Pannenberg asserts that analogy has to be developed on the basis of a univocal concept of being (as Duns Scotus did). In this case, however, analogical predication of God becomes theologically problematic because of the serious danger of anthropomorphism entailed in this form of analogical predication. The one condition under which this double-pronged critique — either a univocal conceptual core or the meaninglessness of equivocation — gains true force is from the angle of a tacitly assumed, normative conceptualism: The question of analogous versus univocal predication is a question *exclusively* to be determined in relationship to the concept. Differently put, the concept by way of which essence is comprehended *(begriffen)* becomes the *sole* normative metaphysical frame of reference — very much along the lines of Hegel's fatal identification of logic and ontology. However, Thomas's doctrine of analogy does not operate at all within this conceptualist metaphysical frame of reference for an analysis of analogical language. Rather, this frame of reference is decisively transcended in Thomas by the realization of the real distinction between *esse* and essence and the priority of order that obtains between the *actus essendi* and the essence. In the framework of these fundamental metaphysical principles, it becomes perfectly intelligible and defensible to understand analogy as a way of predicating in which an analogous term comprises in its meaning some similarity-in-difference across the transcendental range of perfections of being. As we have seen, for Thomas the analogical naming of God from creatures is a transgeneric predication, not from one genus to another, but transcending all genera. The analogical naming occurs by way of the in-

---

84. See Pannenberg, *Analogie und Offenbarung,* 122.

trinsic attribution of a perfection name, where the similarity-in-difference expressed by the perfection comprises an intrinsic causal relation of participating in the *actus essendi*. In short, Thomas's analogy of being reaches to principles that decisively transcend the metaphysical conceptualism with its strong Hegelian undertones at work in Pannenberg's understanding of analogy.

Eberhard Jüngel, in his respective critique, reduces Thomas's doctrine of analogy essentially to Kant's way of defending the possibility of an analogical predication of God.[85] What is quite obvious in Kant, he sees also at play in Thomas, namely, that the analogy of attribution is of a purely *extrinsic* kind, functioning according to the logic of the analogy of proportionality: "God has a given perfection to God's being as the creature has the same perfection to that creature's being."[86] This reading and critique could perhaps function against Cajetan's doctrine of analogy, but misses Thomas's. Not unlike Pannenberg, Jüngel places Thomas into a tacitly assumed, overarching conceptualist framework — with the only difference that Pannenberg by putting Scotist pressure on Thomas forces on him the conceptualist alternative between either an analogous concept with a univocal core of identity or meaningless equivocation, while Jüngel, by mistaking Thomas for Cajetan — read in turn through Kant — reduces Thomas's way of analogical predication to conceptual proportionality.[87] Analogy is interpreted here merely as a mentally immanent system of comparison.

However, as we have seen, in Thomas the perfection names for God

85. Jüngel, *Gott als Geheimnis der Welt*, pp. 358-63; *God as the Mystery of the World*, pp. 263-66.

86. Rolnick, *Analogical Possibilities*, p. 206; see Jüngel, *God as the Mystery of the World*, p. 276. While a theoretical proof of God's existence is impossible according to Kant, he admits the possibility to think God coherently as a construct of pure reason by way of analogy. If such an analogy, however, is based upon concepts that (instead of receiving the intelligible by way of the sense data) impose intelligibility upon the sense data and hence when applied to that which lies outside the sensible world are entirely separate from it and receive no input of intelligibility from outside, the analogy of proportion based on these concepts of experience must necessarily be an analogy of *extrinsic* proportionality. The result of such an analogical procedure can indeed be nothing but a "mere thought-entity" (cf. *Critique of Pure Reason*, B 593-95).

87. The rejection of the real distinction between *esse* and essence and the denial of an analogous concept of being are at the core of this essentialist conceptualism: "Being is obviously not a real predicate, i.e., a concept of something that could add to the concept of a thing. It is merely the positing [*Position*] of a thing or of certain determinations in themselves. In the logical use it is merely the copula of a judgment" (*Critique of Pure Reason* B 626).

have a basis in the intrinsic being of creatures, and their likeness to God through causal participation. This viewpoint (because of the intrinsicism due to causality) avoids the danger of an absolute apophaticism. For the analogy of intrinsic attribution reflects the dynamic of causal participation, and it is this causal connection that grounds the analogical naming of God from creatures.[88] Contrary to Jüngel's interpretation, Thomas and Kant differ fundamentally in their respective doctrines of analogy. For, different from Kant, Thomas regards metaphysical causality as reflected by the predicamentals to be indispensable for the analogy of intrinsic attribution. However, in his *Critique of Pure Reason,*[89] Kant famously *construes* — and, I would say, consequently *misunderstands* — the categories as categories of the understanding (quantity, quality, relation, and modality) as *constitutive* of experience. For Kant, the categories (including causality) are valid when applied to the phenomenal order, but not valid when applied beyond it to the noumenal order. Hence, for Kant the categories, by definition, cannot reflect causal principles in the order of being, and consequently the only form of analogy left for a predication of God is one of a purely formal, conceptual proportionality that indeed must — and here Jüngel is exactly right — end up in the apophaticism of an utterly mute God *supra nos.* A second reason is that "causality" for Kant is inapplicable to the trans-sensible realm, and therefore it is not only the case that predicamental analogy is inapplicable to the things themselves. In addition, causal and transcendental analogies from creatures to God are inapplicable, since we can never refer from sensible existents to the transcendent "cause" of existence.

Jüngel misses or chooses to ignore this fundamental difference between Kant on the one side and Thomas on the other side when he argues that, in regard to analogical predication of truths about God, Kant, like Thomas, seems to relate the analogy of proportion to the analogy of attribution or relation. He refers to a footnote in Kant's *Critique of Judgment* (B 448) where Kant considers the identity of the relationship between causes and effects.[90] While the categories of the understanding (including causal-

---

88. "God is the exceeding *principle* of all things contained under different genera. This causal connection grounds the analogous naming of God from creatures" (te Velde, *Aquinas on God,* p. 112).

89. Immanuel Kant, *Kritik der reinen Vernunft* (Hamburg: Meiner, 1956), B 102-9; Immanuel Kant, *Critique of Pure Reason,* trans. Paul Guyer and Allen W. Wood (Cambridge: Cambridge University Press, 1997), pp. 210-14 (B 102-9).

90. Jüngel, *Gott als Geheimnis der Welt,* 363; *God as the Mystery of the World,* 266.

ity) can be applied validly only to the phenomenal order, they become invalid when applied to the noumenal order. Hence, because causes and effects cannot be extended beyond the sensible world, any supposed extension beyond it has to draw upon the pure (i.e., empty) conceptuality of reason. Correspondingly, any intrinsic proportion between finite effect and infinite first cause becomes impossible per se. Again, all we have here in Kant's discussion is the analogy of *extrinsic* proportionality that is explicitly excluded by Thomas in reference to God. (Moreover, the whole discussion in which this footnote occurs is part and parcel of Kant's consideration of the kinds of argument necessary for a valid *moral proof* of God's existence.) All of this is perfectly consistent within the specific conceptualism of Kant's critical transcendentalism. However, the whole approach rests on the unwarranted empiricist assumption that no intellectual nature can be abstracted from what the senses convey in combination with the rather unreasonable Cartesian mandate for clear and distinct ideas, as well as quasi-mathematical certitude in the deliveries of metaphysics. This unhappy union of two metaphysical reductions — empiricism and essentialist conceptualism — not only gave birth to the inherently patricidal monster of "modern philosophy" but remains under the fundamental critique of the uninterrupted tradition of Thomist metaphysics.[91]

And so the very difference between Thomas's and Kant's ways of analogical predication of God offers quite a bit of evidence to what Bernard Montagnes observes: "Each doctrine of analogy is a manifestation of a certain conception of being, of causality, of participation, of the unity of beings in being."[92] Fundamentally different from Kant, for Thomas analogical predication reflects the causal structure of being in the existent world and not merely a mentally immanent system of comparison.

Looked at from the Thomist perspective, Pannenberg's and Jüngel's

---

91. For a recent example of presupposing in a metaphysically unreflective way, that is, in a philosophically dogmatic way, the validity of the Kantian critique of the ascription of causality to "supersensible" reality, see Archie J. Spencer, "Causality and the *analogia entis*: Karl Barth's Rejection of the Analogy of Being Reconsidered," *Nova et Vetera* (English) 6, no. 2 (2008): 329-76. However, the very presupposition of the validity of this Kantian critique has been refuted consistently within the modern Thomist tradition, most recently by Thomas Joseph White, O.P., *Wisdom in the Face of Modernity: A Study in Modern Thomistic Natural Theology* (Naples, FL: Sapientia Press, 2009). For a substantive interrogation of Spencer's charges, see the astute response by Thomas Joseph White, "How Barth Got Aquinas Wrong: A Reply to Archie J. Spencer on Causality and Christocentrism," in *Nova et Vetera* (English) 7, no. 1 (2009): 241-70.

92. Montagnes, *Doctrine of the Analogy of Being*, p. 10.

critical readings of Thomas on analogy are held captive by the implicit Kantian and Hegelian presupposition that an essentialist notion of concept holds the place of honor in philosophy, a notion they tacitly assume antecedently also to be operative in Thomas's way of analogical predication of God. For Thomas, however, there is no concept of this kind operative in the analogical predication of God. Rather, the analogous term and concept comprises in its meaning some similarity-in-difference across the transcendental range of perfections of being. Hence, the analogy of being is primordially entailed in the concrete ways we ineluctably predicate being differently but always in the differentiated unity of substance and accident, of cause and effect. W. Norris Clarke puts the matter that is at stake at this point between univocity and analogy in the predication of God thus:

> The Scotus-Ockham analysis is geared primarily to the demands of deductive reasoning and the logical functioning of concepts. It also takes the word and concept as the fundamental unit of meaning, which remains intact in its own self-contained meaning no matter how it is moved around as a counter in combination with other concepts, including its use in a judgment, which is interpreted simply as a composition of two concepts, subject and predicate, without change in either. The Thomistic analysis is geared much more to the actual lived usage of the concept in a judgment, interpreted as an intentional act of referring its synthesis of subject-predicate to the real order, as it is in reality. Hence it tends to look right through the abstract meaning of the concept to what it signifies, or intends to signify *(intendit significare)*, in the concrete, and so adjusts the content of the concept to what it knows about its realization in the concrete.[93]

According to Thomas, it is precisely by this way of understanding the analogy of being that rationalism and apophatic agnosticism are excluded in the analogous predication of God by way of perfection names. It is by way of the analogy of being that neither the mere metaphor nor the essentialist concept is granted predominance in the predication of God. This is the limited but indispensable role Thomas assigns in *sacra doctrina* to the natural knowledge of God derived analogically from creatures by way of the transcendentals and the derived perfection names. But because *sacra doctrina* is a subaltern *scientia* and as such essentially informed by

93. W. Norris Clarke, "Analogy and the Meaningfulness of Language about God," in *Explorations in Metaphysics,* pp. 126-27.

the principles of the superior *scientia Dei et beatorum,* there is by definition no way that the analogy of being could ever determine or govern what infinitely surpasses it in dignity as well as depth. It is because of the infinitely surpassing superintelligibility of the *scientia Dei et beatorum* and the simultaneous limitation of our understanding, that the analogy of being remains a subaltern albeit integral *auxilium* in the science of theology. Short of the beatific vision, it is the case even in the state of grace, that for a proper theological intelligibility of the revealed truths, the modest *auxilium* of the analogy of being proves indispensable. "For," as Thomas puts it very dryly in the famous question 13 of the Prima Pars of his *Summa theologiae,* "we can name God only from creatures."[94]

For Thomas, the analogy of being reflects in our very way of predicating our ineradicable creatureliness and hence the primordial relationship between creature and God as one of *causal participation.* And thus the analogy of being is indeed the always already operative metaphysical condition for the surpassingly gratuitous salvific relation of God *quoad nos* to become analogically intelligible while remaining essentially *mysterium.*

---

94. *ST* I, q. 13, a. 5: "Non enim possumus nominare Deum nisi ex creaturis."

CHAPTER 11

"Seeking Truth on Dry Soil and under Thornbushes" — God, the University, and the Missing Link: Wisdom

> *Without the Creator the creature would disappear. . . . But when God is forgotten the creature itself grows unintelligible.*
>
> Pope Paul VI, Gaudium et Spes, §36

Pope Benedict XVI, in his famous lecture at the University of Regensburg on 12 September, 2006, "Faith, Reason, and the University: Memories and Reflections," makes this programmatic statement about reason and the modern university:

> The scientific ethos, moreover, is . . . the will to be obedient to the truth, and, as such, it embodies an attitude which belongs to the essential decisions of the Christian spirit. The intention here is not one of retrenchment or negative criticism, but of broadening our concept of reason and its application. While we rejoice in the new possibilities open to humanity, we also see the dangers arising from these possibilities and we must ask ourselves how we can overcome them. We will succeed in doing so only if reason and faith come together in a new way, if we overcome the self-imposed limitation of reason to the empirically falsifiable, and if we once more disclose its vast horizons. In this sense theology rightly belongs in the university and within the wide-ranging dialogue of sciences, not merely as a historical discipline and one of the human sciences, but precisely as theology, as inquiry into the rationality of faith.[1]

1. Available on the Vatican web site (http://www.vatican.va/holy_father/benedict_xvi/

387

Quite obviously, and not unlike his predecessor Pope John Paul II,[2] Pope Benedict has a keen interest in the modern university. In an equally important speech composed for the university "La Sapienza" — once the Pope's own university in Rome, today a secular Roman university — a speech that was, however, never to be delivered, because the invitation to the Holy Father was withdrawn in the last moment, the Pope points even more explicitly to a danger facing reason and consequently also the university in the Western world:

> The danger for the western world — to speak only of this — is that today, precisely because of the greatness of his knowledge and power, man will fail to face up to the question of the truth. This would mean at the same time that reason would ultimately bow to the pressure of interests and the attraction of utility, constrained to recognize this as the ultimate criterion. To put it from the point of view of the structure of the university: there is a danger that philosophy, no longer considering itself capable of its true task, will degenerate into positivism; and that theology, with its message addressed to reason, will be limited to the private sphere of a more or less numerous group. Yet if reason, out of concern for its alleged purity, becomes deaf to the great message that comes to it from Christian faith and wisdom, then it withers like a tree whose roots can no longer reach the waters that give it life. It loses the courage for truth and thus becomes not greater but smaller.[3]

In his Regensburg lecture, Pope Benedict makes a case for theology belonging to the very heart of what a university is about; in his lecture for "La Sapenzia" he makes a similar case for philosophy. Only if theology and

---

speeches/2006/september/documents/hf_ben-xvi_spe_20060912_university-regensburg_en .html).

2. See James V. Schall, S.J., ed., *The Whole Truth about Man: John Paul II to University Faculties and Students* (Boston: Daughters of St. Paul, 1981).

3. Available on the Vatican web site: (http://www.vatican.va/holy_father/benedict _xvi/speeches/2008/january/documents/hf_ben-xvi_spe_20080117_la-sapienza_en.html). It is not just the Popes who come to rather drastic judgments of this kind. The president of Viadrina European University in Frankfurt (Oder), Prof. Dr. Gesine Schwan, a political scientist and highly respected public figure of German cultural and political life (she has been twice candidate for the office of president of the German Federal Republic) anticipated many of Pope Benedict XVI's concerns and formulated even more stringent criticisms of late modern science. See her essay, "Das zerstörte Tabu. Ohne ein religiöses Fundament und ohne die Sehnsucht nach Wahrheit verrät die Wissenschaft ihre eigenen Ideale und verkommt zum Erfüllungsgehilfen der Wirtschaft," *Süddeutsche Zeitung,* 4 January 2003.

philosophy occupy an indispensable central role in the structure of the university will the university as an institution maintain the courage for truth, realize reason's inherent orientation toward transcendence, and thus be able to resist "the pressures of interest and the attraction of utility," in short, the familiar instrumentalization of the modern university for tangible ends in the material order. The modern research university prepares for its own disintegration by embracing a reductive notion of truth, by degrading philosophy from its original status as integrative meta-science (viz., metaphysics) to the status of one academic discipline among many — and more marginal than most — and by, at best, preserving theology in the semi-exiled reservation of a professional school of Christian ministry, a divinity school, or, at worst, simply banning it from its walls.

Pope Benedict XVI's assessment of the modern research university is echoed by one of the most highly respected and widely read philosophers presently teaching in the United States:

> To whom . . . in such a university falls the task of integrating the various disciplines, of considering the bearing of each on the others, and of asking how each contributes to the overall understanding of the nature and order of things? The answer is "No one," but even this answer is misleading. For there is no sense in the contemporary American university that there is such a task, that something that matters is being left undone. And so the very notion of the nature and order of things, of a single universe, different aspects of which are objects of enquiry for the various disciplines, but in such a way that each aspect needs to be related to every other, this notion no longer informs the enterprise of the contemporary American university. It has become an irrelevant concept. It makes little difference in this respect whether a university is professedly secular or professedly Catholic.[4]

This statement is taken from the first of two books to be discussed in this chapter, Alasdair MacIntyre's *God, Philosophy, Universities.* MacIntyre is one of two Catholic philosophers who have recently undertaken a most central but also most unfashionable task, namely, to rethink the unity of all academic disciplines by way of the integrative role of philosophy. MacIntyre pursues this task by unfolding a selective narrative account of the complex history of Catholic philosophy in relationship to the emergence

---

4. Alasdair MacIntyre, *God, Philosophy, Universities: A Selective History of the Catholic Philosophical Tradition* (Lanham, MD: Rowman & Littlefield, 2009), p. 16.

of the university. Benedict Ashley, O.P., in *The Way toward Wisdom: An Interdisciplinary and Intercultural Introduction to Metaphysics*,[5] pursues this task in dialogue with the sciences, especially the natural sciences, by way of an Aristotelian Thomist reconstruction of metaphysics as meta-science.

MacIntyre and Ashley share the concern for the integrative role of philosophy in the university: the first argues for it by way of a narrative account, the latter by displaying concretely how this integrative role of philosophy as meta-science actually works. Moreover, MacIntyre and Ashley share a fundamental normative presupposition, namely that the enterprise of the university should be essentially informed by "the very notion of the nature and order of things, of a single universe, different aspects of which are objects of enquiry for the various disciplines, but in such a way that each aspect needs to be related to every other."[6] The pursuit of such a substantive interdisciplinarity, such a "connected view or grasp of things," as John Henry Newman puts it in *The Idea of a University*,[7] is nothing but the pursuit of wisdom, and such a pursuit entails an ever widening horizon of reason, indeed, the inherent openness of reason to transcendence. It is by way of *teaching* such a "connected view or grasp of things" — or "*teaching* universal knowledge"[8] — that the whole of reality in its essential interconnectedness is attended to. For it is first and foremost the coherence of the curriculum of a particular science and the interrelationship between the university curricula that reflects best the "nature and order of things." This is the reason why for MacIntyre, as well as for Ashley, the extension of knowledge by way of teaching (as integral to education in a comprehensive sense) is the first and foremost task of the university. By attending primarily to this task, the university realizes and maintains best the unity and coherence between all academic disciplines.

The advancement of knowledge by way of research is, on the contrary, not absolutely essential to the normative understanding of the university defended by MacIntyre and Ashley. Highly advanced research can just as well be undertaken by globally networked academies, think tanks,

---

5. Benedict M. Ashley, O.P., *The Way toward Wisdom: An Interdisciplinary and Intercultural Introduction to Metaphysics* (Notre Dame, IN: University of Notre Dame Press, 2006).

6. MacIntyre, *God, Philosophy, Universities*, p. 16; cf. Ashley, *Way toward Wisdom*, p. 20.

7. John Henry Cardinal Newman, *The Idea of a University (The New Edition of the Works of John Henry Newman)*, ed. Charles Frederick Harrold (New York: Longmans, Green and Co., 1947), p. xxxiv.

8. Newman, *Idea of a University*, p. xxvii.

and laboratories sponsored by corporations and governments. Such research institutes and laboratories are not essentially directed toward the extension of knowledge by way of teaching and hence are also not in any need whatsoever of students. Consequently, a university that focuses primarily on research and only secondarily upon teaching — in short, the modern research university — will eventually become a victim of the systemic forces unleashed by making research, and hence knowledge production, its dominant purpose and end.[9] Both MacIntyre and Ashley hold that an increasing transmutation of universities into such conglomerates of advanced and ever-more-specialized knowledge production will necessarily increase those centrifugal, purely research-oriented forces that will lead to the all-too-familiar fragmentation of the university as a whole and of the field-specific curricula in particular. Consequently, for both authors the very nature and vitality of the university depend on the role philosophy as a meta-science plays in ensuring a "connected view or grasp of things." For a university cannot be "a place of teaching universal knowledge"[10] and hence of pursuing wisdom if it lacks interdisciplinary integrity and fails to reflect reason's openness to transcendence.

---

9. In the following I understand modern research universities to be institutions geared primarily to producing knowledge by way of highly specialized research (primarily in the natural and medical sciences) that is meant to serve interests that almost exclusively arise from the practical and technical demands of the modern world. Newman rightly anticipated what eventually would become the modern research university by way of Francis Bacon's method: "I cannot deny he has abundantly achieved what he proposed. His is simply a Method whereby bodily discomforts and temporal wants are to be most effectually removed from the greatest number; and already, before it has shown any signs of exhaustion, the gifts of nature, in their most artificial shapes and luxurious profusion and diversity, from all quarters of the earth, are, it is undeniable, by its means brought even to our doors, and we rejoice in them" (*Idea of a University*, p. 106). Immanuel Kant's intensely ironic and passive aggressive opuscule, *Der Streit der Fakultäten*, anticipates the present de facto hierarchy of university sciences in *late* modernity — a secular modernity that has now lost its optimistic élan and instead has become tired and cynical. In the agonistic world of irresistibly corruptible, interminably quarrelling, and tirelessly consuming bodies, hence a world in which the greatest dangers are disease, litigation, and the inability to consume, the hierarchy of university sciences stands in service of the avoidance of these evils: at the top is the medical school supported by all the auxiliary bio-sciences, followed by the law school and the business school supported by their respective auxiliary sciences — first and foremost computer science and mathematics, but also any useful remnants of the liberal arts. However, since it has been discovered that religious practices might contribute to health and longevity, the gods are making a comeback — of sorts!

10. Newman, *Idea of a University*, p. xxvii.

There is, however, a subtle difference between MacIntyre and Ashley in that the latter, possibly because of his extensive dialogue with the natural sciences, is more open than MacIntyre seems to be in regarding the university *also* as a legitimate place for the advancement of knowledge by way of research. While profoundly dedicated to a program of education in a Thomistic sense,[11] Ashley appears to allow space in the university also for a modern extension of Aristotle's comprehensive program of research. Possibly because of the central role Newman's understanding of the university plays for him, MacIntyre has a deeper and more exclusive commitment to the university as a place of the extension of knowledge by way of *teaching*. I will revisit this not-altogether-unimportant difference later, but at this point I shall turn to the ways MacIntyre and Ashley make their respective cases.

I. God, Philosophy, Universities

God, Philosophy, Universities grew out of an undergraduate course of the same title that MacIntyre taught for many years at the University of Notre Dame.[12] The book is remarkable in at least three respects. First, it is — as far as I can see — the only book in which MacIntyre, by way of explicit philosophical discourse, attends to God. Second, it is the one book in which MacIntyre offers his, so far, most ambitious and comprehensive philosophical narrative about philosophy. Stretching across a spectrum of one-and-a-half millennia on 180 compact and elegantly written pages, from Augustine to the late Pope John Paul II's encyclical *Fides et ratio,* the narrative pursues an intricate pattern made of three distinct but tightly interwoven strands: the philosophical contemplation of God, the tradition of Catholic philosophy, and the development of universities. Third, among MacIntyre's rich corpus, and especially in comparison with *After Virtue* and *Three Rival Versions of Moral Enquiry,* this book is his most disquieting, if not despairing, *pace* the invocation of hope in the book's very last line. The book's profoundly disquieting character does not pertain to the theistic discourse about God (though some theologians might wish for an

11. See Benedict M. Ashley, O.P., *The Arts of Learning and Communication: A Handbook of the Liberal Arts* (Chicago: Priory Press, 1957); Benedict M. Ashley, O.P. and Pierre Conway, O.P., *The Liberal Arts in St. Thomas Aquinas* (Washington, DC: The Thomist Press, 1959).

12. Parenthetical page numbers in this section refer to this book.

explicit Trinitarian identification of and discourse about God). Nor does it pertain to the tradition of Catholic philosophy per se (though MacIntyre prescribes to its contemporary practitioners a disquietingly ambitious and comprehensive agenda). Rather, *God, Philosophy, Universities* is most disquieting in its evident disdain for the present modern research university. More than twenty-five years ago, in one of those rare but important conversations that go to the very core of things, a German university professor of theology, who eventually became my *Doktorvater,* made the following remark to me: "It is only the students who still believe in the university as a corporate reality with an overarching, coherent telos. The professors have long ago ceased to do so." As a motivated student with not untypically high ideals, I was markedly disturbed by what struck me then as a rather alarming statement. Twelve years into teaching at a leading, Berlin-type, American research university, I now know only all too well what my *Doktorvater* then observed about his and my Berlin-type, German research university. In MacIntyre's words the observation sounds thus:

> Research universities in the early twenty-first century are wonderfully successful business corporations subsidized by tax exemptions and exhibiting all the acquisitive ambitions of such corporations.
>
> What disappears from view in such universities, and what significantly differentiates them from many of their predecessors, is twofold: first, any large sense of and concern for enquiry into the relationships between the disciplines and, second, any conception of the disciplines as each contributing to a single shared enterprise, one whose principal aim is neither to benefit the economy nor to advance the careers of its students, but rather to achieve for teachers and students alike a certain kind of shared understanding. Universities have become, perhaps irremediably, fragmented and partitioned institutions, better renamed "multiversities," as Clark Kerr suggested almost fifty years ago. (174)

Is MacIntyre chasing the memories of a long bygone past or is he musing over the contours of a utopia that never existed and never will exist? Should he, having himself been a professor at numerous distinguished modern research universities, better acknowledge the unavoidable or, even better, praise and defend the achievements of these "multiversities"? While it might arguably be inadvisable for persons sitting in a glass house to throw stones, it is very advisable, if not mandatory, for professors teaching in these kinds of institutions to raise overarching normative questions (of precisely the kind MacIntyre does) in order to critique the modern university. For who should raise such questions with greater legitimacy (and even a necessity internal to his or her very academic discipline) than a philosopher — or for that matter, a theologian?[13] The question of the relationship between all disciplines, and of the overall shared end of the university, must be raised inside the university if there is to be even the smallest indication of a genuine life of the intellect and hence of the capacity for a critical self-examination and self-reflexivity left in such an institution.

Such questions, moreover, are asked best in a proper scientific way, and this means in the context of a meta-science that deals with the nature, the mutual relationships, and the overall ordering of all academic disciplines, and hence with the nature and scope of the university as such. Were such a meta-science to occupy a central role in a university it could indeed achieve the kind of intrinsic coherence that not even the most advanced and sophisticated extrinsic managerial strategies and administrative tactics could ever hope to achieve.[14] What is so disquieting about MacIntyre's book is that even a cursory consideration of its narrative by any member of an average contemporary "multiversity" makes it plain how utterly removed these fundamental concerns are from the day-to-day business of such institutions, and hence in turn how utterly removed these activities are from what pertains to the essence of a university properly conceived. Might the application of the term "university" to such institutions have become just a craftily camouflaged case of equivocation?

A summary of the book's narrative is both easy and difficult to compose. MacIntyre has written this book with an educated Catholic lay audience in mind: persons of largely Catholic convictions, broadly educated in a variety of current matters, but not particularly informed by the Catholic philosophical tradition and hence unequipped to situate and assess in a constructive and meaningful way. By way of a broadly accessible, and hence necessarily selective narrative, MacIntyre intends to offer a map that will allow educated Catholics to negotiate a better path through the complexities and ambiguities of late modern thought and life by evaluating the

13. For two recent instructive theological engagements of these matters, see Gavin D'Costa, *Theology in the Public Square: Church, Academy, and Nation* (Malden, MA: Blackwell, 2005); and Stanley Hauerwas, *The State of the University: Academic Knowledges and the Knowledge of God* (Malden, MA, and Oxford: Blackwell, 2007).

14. Might the ludicrously inflated role of sports as a rallying, unifying, and motivating factor on American college and university campuses be directly proportional to the loss of the proper formal coherence of the modern research university?

underlying philosophical theses and claims and effectively distinguishing between the truth of some philosophical theses and the falsity of others. As in his earlier works, MacIntyre is interested in reclaiming the central role of philosophy for a wider, nonspecialized public. He thus conceives philosophy as the systematic development of questions that plain persons might raise, especially but not exclusively in light of their broadly theistic or concretely Catholic beliefs. The narrative MacIntyre unfolds, with an exemplary erudition, is indeed largely accessible to a nonspecialized readership. The prose is attractive and transparent; the narrative flows with an admirable ease and coherence, yet with subtle nuance.

According to MacIntyre, broadly theistic and specifically Catholic beliefs have historically given rise to three pre-eminent philosophical questions: first, the question of the compatibility between the existence of God and the scope of evil — natural, social, and moral — in a universe of finite beings; second, the question of the compatibility between divine transcendent causality and genuine secondary causality (i.e., between divine omnipotence and human freedom); and third, the question of true knowledge of and hence meaningful discourse about God. Catholic philosophy has had to consider these issues again and again. And because the engagement of these profound and difficult questions has occurred in socially, culturally, and institutionally embodied forms, the university has to be part of the narrative of Catholic philosophy.

Not altogether unpredictably, the narrative commences with Augustine. The eminent imperial rhetor and later even more eminent bishop of Hippo turns out to be also the first Catholic philosopher — offering consistent, frequent, and extensive philosophical argumentation in defense of the Catholic faith. The lucid treatment of Augustine's ontology forms part of a Patristic prologue that includes Boethius and the Pseudo-Dionysius and that tail ends in Anselm of Canterbury, who is presented as the first fully refined Catholic philosopher in the Augustinian tradition — a monastic thinker, however, in an eleventh-century Christian French kingdom devoid of any university. Before the university, or at least, the *studium generale* enters the stage for Catholic philosophy, another prologue has to be told: the pivotal role for Catholic philosophy of Muslim philosophy, especially the first encounter of Catholic philosophers with most of the *Corpus Aristotelicum* by way of its Muslim commentators. The encounter between the Augustinian tradition (having adopted and successfully adapted large neo-platonic strands of thought with select Aristotelian moments by way of Boethius) and a massive *Corpus Aristotelicum* (interpreted by highly sophisticated Muslim philosophers) created the critical mass that gave rise to the genesis of a Catholic philosophical tradition in the proper sense.

MacIntyre himself regards the convergence of three dynamic events as the birth hour of Catholic philosophy in its full sense: a large set of intellectually challenging new texts, a pool of profound thinkers, and the emergence of new institutions of higher learning — a *studium generale,* at Paris, Oxford, Bologna, and Naples. The hero of this part of MacIntyre's narrative is Thomas Aquinas (his most crucial forerunner, Albert the Great, and his role in founding the Dominican *studium* at Cologne — the seed of its later university — is regrettably absent). For it is with Thomas that a separate, proper philosophical discourse is assumed, not parallel with and indifferent to the Catholic convictions, but as a mode of inquiry informing these convictions while being informed by them. The marked decline MacIntyre observes in the decades after Thomas's death must not be understood, he stresses, as a willful departure by these thinkers from the position of the *doctor communis,* but rather as a proliferation of philosophical difficulties and rival philosophical conceptualities that could no longer be successfully resolved in one coherent and comprehensive philosophical discourse. The result of this failure was the formation of particular schools and traditions of Catholic philosophical enquiry (Thomism, Scotism, Ockhamism, Augustinianism), schools that allegedly marked themselves off from each other by way of increasingly arcane and protracted lines of argumentation.

With the rise of and in light of the challenges of Renaissance humanism, modern natural science, and early modern skepticism, the Catholic philosophical tradition underwent a series of transformations. The discovery and political subjugation of the Americas presented profound intellectual challenges to key representatives of the Catholic philosophical tradition in the Spain of the sixteenth century. However, this tradition was not able to achieve a coherent and compelling position on these novel and conceptually challenging, as well as politically pressing matters. Rather, the formation of particular schools of thought with complex speculative positions continued (Suarezianism forming a new school). The fact that these highly developed positions were in what seemed to the sharpest minds of the time an irresolvable and hence interminable conceptual conflict with each other gave rise to a Catholic version of skepticism. Descartes, Pascal, and Arnauld reacted to this in varying complex ways. Thus, having reached the threshold of modernity, the narrative continues to unfold according to the following basic pattern — after an ever increasing Baroque scholastic self-isolation,

Catholic philosophy eventually distinguishes itself by its complete absence. "Where philosophy flourished, Catholic faith was absent. Where the Catholic faith was sustained, philosophy failed to flourish" (133).

When does Catholic philosophy proper reemerge in the modern context? Parallel to the emergence of Catholic philosophy in the patristic era with Augustine and its medieval flourishing with Thomas, MacIntyre identifies a forerunner and a subsequent hero in the modern era: the forerunner is Antonio Rosmini-Serbati and the hero is John Henry Newman. Rosmini-Serbati, having intellectually confronted Kant and German idealism, was the first seriously to attempt to address modern philosophical problems as a Catholic thinker; and only Newman, having intellectually confronted British empiricism, was able to define the tasks confronting Catholic philosophy in modernity. However, Rosmini's engagement was not altogether successful, and even Newman did not fully identify, let alone muster, the resources necessary to address these daunting tasks. Only with Pope Leo XIII's coordinated effort — encapsulated in his famous 1879 encyclical letter *Aeterni Patris* and in the launching of the Leonine edition of the works of Thomas Aquinas — does the situation change. In one crucial regard, namely, the way Christian faith actually enables true rational enquiry, MacIntyre makes the link between Newman and *Aeterni Patris* explicit:

> Part of the gift of Christian faith is to enable us to identify accurately where the line between faith and reason is to be drawn, something that cannot be done from the standpoint of reason, but only from that of faith. Reason therefore needs Christian faith, if it is to do its own work well. Reason without Christian faith is always reason informed by some other faith, characteristically an unacknowledged faith, one that renders its adherents liable to error. (152f.)

Next to new ventures in personalism (Marcel et al.) and phenomenology (Hildebrand, Scheler, Stein, Marion), and quite a bit later in post-Wittgensteinian analytic philosophy (Anscombe, Geach, Dummett), MacIntyre identifies inside the ecclesiastically encouraged and endorsed neo-Scholastic form of Catholic philosophy various strands of neo-Thomism. The strand with the most lasting success and impact is the one that led to an increasingly sophisticated recovery of the full breadth and depths of Thomas's thought in its own medieval context. MacIntyre also discusses Transcendental Thomism and Aristotelian Thomism briefly. He keeps at a distance, subtly but firmly, all strands of Thomism that understand themselves as instantiations of a shared *philosophia perennis*. This is not because he would disagree with such an effort in principle, but rather because he seems to regard the performance of modern Thomist metaphysics as not quite true to the highest standards of the Catholic philosophical enterprise, standards presumably set by Augustine and Aquinas. In other words, he seems to be most rigorous in his expectations where the performance comes close to, but still falls somewhat short of, these highest standards.

Where is the journey of Catholic philosophy going? MacIntyre turns to the twentieth-century Catholic philosopher who became pope in 1978. He understands Pope John Paul II, in his 1998 encyclical letter *Fides et ratio*, as doing nothing short of reconceiving the Catholic philosophical tradition according to the highest possible standards: "It is within the Catholic philosophical enterprise, when it is true to its own highest standards, that philosophy is carried on as it needs to be carried on" (165). MacIntyre reads *Fides et ratio* as a most urgent invitation to Catholic philosophers to refocus on the deepest human concerns and what it is to be human, and thereby to carry on philosophy as it needs to be carried on. Such an account of what it is to be a human being will explain why human beings are capable of relevant self-knowledge. In other words, the integrative function of philosophy in the Catholic tradition will best be recovered by way of a comprehensively anthropological focus. For

> such an account will have to integrate what we can learn about the nature and constitution of human beings from physicists, chemists, and biologists, historians, economists, and sociologists, with the kind of understanding of human beings that only theology can afford. (177)

According to MacIntyre such an account would presuppose the theology of Augustine and would otherwise be largely Thomist (in questions of truth and of God as the first and final cause of all reality), but would draw upon seminal non-Catholic thinkers as Kierkegaard, Husserl, and Wittgenstein, while making the best of insights of key Catholic thinkers as different as Anselm, Scotus, Suárez, Pascal, Stein, and Anscombe. MacIntyre's adumbration of such an account culminates in the following programmatic remarks:

> If such an account were to accomplish its philosophical purposes, it would have to confront and overcome more than one kind of difficulty. It would have to enable Catholic philosophers to engage with the

contentions of the whole range of contemporary major philosophical positions incompatible with and antagonistic to the Catholic faith, including the whole range of versions of naturalism, reductive and nonreductive, the Heideggerian and post-Heideggerian romantic rejections of the ontology presupposed by the Catholic faith, pragmatist reconceptions and postmodern rejections of truth, and that so often taken for granted thin desiccated Neokantianism that is so fashionable in contemporary philosophy. (178)

I think he is exactly right. Needless to say, this program would be greatly helped by a contemporary recovery of the Thomist philosophical tradition according to Thomas's own highest standards (as, arguably, adumbrated in *Three Rival Versions of Moral Enquiry*), a program that would require the sustained cooperation of numerous Catholic thinkers in various fields of enquiry across a prolonged period of time. Moreover, such a program would require a well-functioning Catholic university roughly along the lines Newman conceived of in his book *The Idea of a University,* a university in which philosophy occupies a central, integrative position, essentially open toward theology (natural theology as well as *sacra doctrina*) on the one hand and, on the other hand, equally open to the human and natural sciences. The reality of contemporary Catholic universities, let alone secular universities, in America (and Europe, I venture to claim) is, however, strikingly hostile to such possibilities. For

> what in fact we find is that the most prestigious Catholic universities often mimic the structures and goals of the most prestigious secular universities and do so with little sense of something having gone seriously amiss. To the extent that this is so, the institutional prospects for the future history of the Catholic philosophical tradition are not encouraging, quite apart from the daunting character of its intellectual needs and ambitions. (179)[15]

15. In his important article, "The End of Education: The Fragmentation of the American University," MacIntyre speaks his mind with less constraint: "What should be the distinctive calling of the American Catholic university or college here and now? It should be to challenge its secular counterparts by recovering both for them and for itself a less fragmented conception of what an education beyond high school should be, by identifying what has gone badly wrong with even the best of secular universities. From a Catholic point of view the contemporary secular university is not at fault because it is not Catholic. It is at fault insofar as it is not a university. Yet the major Catholic universities seem unlikely to accept this calling, if only because their administrative leaders are for the most part hell-bent

Again the question of the university emerges forcefully. But before I return to this topic, I shall address, first, the overall narrative; second, strands one and two, God and Catholic philosophy, combined. Finally, I shall return to the third strand, the university.

MacIntyre's Narrative

In the preface to his book, MacIntyre anticipates that the selection under-lying his narrative will be a likely point of contention with many a reader of the book. And indeed, admirers of late medieval philosophy in general and of the thought of Scotus and Ockham in particular will be quick to observe that MacIntyre's narrative depends too much on Gilson's classic, but by now broadly challenged, account of the rise, progress, and decline of medieval Catholic philosophy from Augustine to the Renaissance. Ad-mirers of Catholic thought in the early modern period, especially the

---

on imitating their prestigious secular counterparts, which already imitate one another. So we find Notre Dame glancing nervously at Duke, only to catch Duke in the act of glancing nervously at Princeton. What is it that makes this attitude so corrupting? What has gone wrong with the secular university?" (*Commonweal*, October 20, 2006, p. 10). I think MacIn-tyre is exactly right. However, some might want to ask themselves why he only cared to men-tion, among Catholic universities, the University of Notre Dame. Are the others completely beyond repair? Or is so much at stake with the University of Notre Dame, because being the flagship of all Catholic universities in America, it matters greatly for the outcome of the bat-tle whether she goes under or survives the internal and external attacks of what Ashley has identified as the ideology of "Secular Humanism." One also might wonder to what degree MacIntyre's scathing analysis of the present situation of the American Catholic university represents an indirect assessment of the undesirable but foreseeable consequences of the 1967 "Land O' Lakes Statement" by which Catholic college leaders declared independence from the Catholic Church. More than forty years after this statement was issued it might be the time to take stock. A stimulant for such a re-assessment can be found in "Discourse IX: Duties of the Church toward Knowledge" of Newman's *The Idea of a University:* "If the Catholic Faith is true, a University cannot exist externally to the Catholic pale, for it cannot teach Universal Knowledge if it does not teach Catholic theology. This is certain; but still, though it had ever so many theological Chairs, that would not suffice to make it a Catholic University; for theology would be included in its teaching only as a branch of knowledge, only as one out of many constituent portions, however important a one, of what I have called Philosophy. Hence a direct and active jurisdiction of the Church over it and in it is necessary lest it should become the rival of the Church with the community at large in those theological matters which to the Church are exclusively committed, — acting as the repre-sentative of the intellect, as the Church is the representative of the religious principle" (p. 190).

Thomist tradition, might be quick to observe that the narrative in its modern period depends too much on an ever so subtle self-congratulatory attitude underlying virtually all of modern philosophy interpreting itself as a decisive break with previous traditions of philosophizing, arriving at insights to which Catholic philosophy has little or nothing to say in response. Such admirers of Catholic thought in the modern period would most likely want to question the following strong claim: "Where philosophy flourished, Catholic faith was absent. Where Catholic faith was sustained, philosophy failed to flourish" (133). They would also most likely regret that MacIntyre did not explicitly consider the possibility that if indeed his judgment were true it might simply be because modern post-Cartesian philosophers such as Hume, Rousseau, Diderot, and Robespierre regarded themselves as quasi-theologians intent on displacing theology first and foremost as *sacra doctrina* and eventually also as natural theology, integral to metaphysics (see 134). Wherever Catholic faith and its theological and philosophical reflection was sustained, there indeed was no need for, nor interest in, a philosophical discourse indifferent or inimical to the truth of revelation, let alone intent on setting up (a)theistic agendas, in the advancement of philosophical claims that were per se untenable in the considered judgment of the best of Catholic philosophers.

Moreover, some might want to point to not a few noteworthy instantiations of a Catholic engagement with and reception of Enlightenment philosophy, as soon as Catholic intellectual life had somewhat recovered from its persecution and repression in the French Revolution and its Central European aftermath. One thinks of the Dillinger circle, the Landshuter circle, and the Tübingen School. There are later names of intellectual significance and influence as well, such as, in Germany, Franz von Baader, Friedrich Schlegel, Joseph Görres, Anton Günther, Carl Werner, Hermann Schell, and Franz Brentano, or, on the French side, Louis de Bonald, Joseph de Maistre, François-René de Chateaubriand, and Félicité-Robert de Lamennais, et al.

Finally, since the French Revolution has already been mentioned, some might wonder why MacIntyre did not pay more attention to the oppressive and destructive effects of the French Revolution on the state of Catholic philosophy and the subsequent secularization and state confiscation of Church property, the suppression of monasteries and Catholic institutions of education, and the fundamental reconfiguration of what once were Catholic universities. In short, they might wonder whether Catholic philosophy was absent from a range of new intellectual developments, possibly not because it had nothing to say in response to them, but rather because the institutional basis for its flourishing had been willfully destroyed by state violence. If one consults the first of the three eight-hundred-page volumes of *Christliche Philosophie im katholischen Denken des 19. und 20. Jahrhunderts,*[16] a much more nuanced picture emerges, a picture that indicates quite an intense and substantive engagement of modern secular thought antedating Antonio Rosmini-Serbati's and John Henry Newman's respective engagements — not to mention Pope Leo XIII's *Aeterni Patris* — by a generation, if not more.

Others might wonder about the significance of MacIntyre's complete silence about the impact of the reception of Vatican II on the curriculum of Catholic philosophy, as well as, and even more importantly, on the curriculum of Catholic theology in most Catholic universities and seminaries. In light of MacIntyre's narrative it is hard if not simply impossible to regard the impact of this reception as anything other than an overzealous and underreflected, wholesale dismissal of increasingly sophisticated preconciliar efforts to recover Catholic philosophy, with a devastating result on Catholic philosophical formation in colleges and universities and a consequent weakening of the conceptual backbone and intellectual strength of Catholic theology.

Still others might wonder what ever happened to that fourth strand without which the narrative of Catholic philosophy in its relevant social and institutional embeddedness cannot possibly be told — the Church as visible institution and especially the relationship between episcopal authority and universities in Catholic countries. They might wonder whether indeed the relationship between Catholic philosophy, the Catholic universities, and the Catholic Church from the emergence of the universities in the Middle Ages to the French Revolution and even afterwards is purely extrinsic and contingent, so that the Church's magisterial role might indeed be negligible for such a narrative.

God and Catholic Philosophy

I shall turn now to the first and the second elements of MacIntyre's narrative: God and Catholic philosophy. The most important, albeit elusive

---

16. *Christliche Philosophie im katholischen Denken des 19. und 20. Jahrhunderts,* ed. Emerich Coreth, S.J., Walter M. Neidl, and Georg Pfligersdorfer (Graz: Styra, 1987-1990).

strand of MacIntyre's narrative is clearly his restrained but persistent philosophical reflection upon God. From his brief and brilliant opening adumbration of a theistic grammar of God to his concluding insistence that human beings can only comprehend themselves in even an approximately adequate way if they understand themselves as fundamentally directed towards God (an ever-so-careful allusion to the long and hotly debated *desiderium naturale visionis Dei*), his focus is evident. However, in MacIntyre's discourse, God-talk remains very distinctly and precisely that of philosophers — theistic philosophers, that is, of the Jewish, Christian, and Muslim variety — and never crosses over into the explicitly Christian discourse governed by the Trinitarian grammar of Scripture and tradition. MacIntyre states explicitly that Catholic philosophers qua Catholic are committed to the revealed truths of the Catholic faith. That is, the God of theistic philosophical enquiry is none other than the One who has revealed himself as the essentially and eternally triune God of love, Father, Son, and Holy Spirit. The revealed truths of the Catholic faith, however, are not the subject matter of Catholic philosophy properly conceived, but are rather the subject matter of *sacra doctrina,* the science of revealed truth.

MacIntyre's precision at this point is greatly to be welcomed. It identifies him not only as an astute student of Thomas but indeed as a Thomist. Any imprecision about and subsequent confusion between *doctrina fidei Christianae (Summa contra Gentiles)* or *sacra doctrina (Summa theologiae)* as the science of divinely revealed truth, on the one hand, and *philosophia humana (Summa contra Gentiles),* on the other, will be detrimental for both disciplines. MacIntyre seems to have a clearer sense than many contemporary theologians about the utter importance of this distinction, an importance not so much for the sake of philosophy, which as metaphysical enquiry has its proper completion in a natural theology, an enquiry into the first cause, but rather for the sake of *sacra doctrina.* The distinction is not simply between two kinds of enquiry, but between two *orders* of discourse. *Sacra doctrina* considers everything in light of an essentially supernatural principle, that is, divine revelation. The theistic discourse that MacIntyre affords is not at all the discourse of *sacra doctrina* proper, but rather a contemporary application of an important distinction Thomas introduces in the *Summa contra Gentiles* (*ScG* II, cc. 3-4). What he observes there about Thomas's distinction between theology (*doctrina fidei Christianae*) and philosophy (*philosophia humana*) holds true for the way he himself maintains the distinction between these two orders of discourse:

Philosophy begins from finite things as they are and from what belongs to them by nature. It leads us from them through an enquiry
into their proper causes to knowledge of God. Theology by contrast
begins from God and considers finite beings only in their relationship
to God. So, although there are matters of which theology treats and
philosophy does not and vice versa, they also have a common subject
matter. (74-75)[17]

It is this common subject matter, God, as first cause of all finite things, that
opens the space for a theistic discourse proper to the philosophical order.

One reason Thomas and Newman occupy such an eminent role in
MacIntyre's account — not unlike the two foci of an ellipse — is that both
serve as strategic signposts for how MacIntyre wants to understand the
proper distinction, as well as the relationship, between nature and grace,
reason and faith, and consequently between (Catholic) philosophy and
theology *(sacra doctrina)*. Most importantly, and most offensively for postmodern instincts, neither Thomas nor Newman evacuates nature and reason, and hence philosophy has an essentially unproblematic access to reality. Thomas puts it in characteristically brief terms: "The philosopher
considers such things as belong to them by nature" (*ScG* II, c. 4).[18] The nature of a thing is that by which its essential operation is characterized. All

---

17. What MacIntyre describes here in a possibly too epigrammatic manner must be
spelled out along the lines provided by Thomas in *ScG* II, c. 3. Ralph McInerny offers a more
detailed and precise rendition of Thomas's distinction, a distinction that applies to MacIntyre's, as well as to Ashley's, *modus operandi* of a theistic discourse proper to the philosophical
order: "1. The theologian treats God for himself and all other things with reference to God;
the philosopher treats nature and man for themselves and of God only as their cause. Call this
a matter of the object, the material object of the two. 2. The theologian treats the properties of
things that refer them to God, the philosopher treats the properties of things in themselves
and as they are. Call this a difference of formal object, but of the formal object *quod;* still the
formal object *quo,* the *ratio sub qua,* the matter of principles, is also involved. Thus if the
theologian and the philosopher should study the same things, they do so in the light of different principles; the philosopher, through their proper causes, the theologian with recourse to
the first cause. 3. In terms of method, the philosopher first studies nature and man, and then
through knowledge of them comes to knowledge of the first cause. But theology begins with
God, who is both its first object and its light, and then goes on to creatures that emanate from
God and are related to him" (*Praeambula Fidei: Thomism and the God of the Philosophers*
[Washington, DC: The Catholic University of America Press, 2006], p. 103).

18. "Philosophus . . . considerat illa quae eis secundum naturam propriam conve-
nient" (*Summa contra Gentiles.* Book 2: *Creation,* trans. James F. Anderson [Notre Dame, IN:
University of Notre Dame Press, 1975], p. 3).

those characteristics together as they are accessible to human natural powers form "nature" in a comprehensive sense, the sense to which Newman appeals in one important passage in *The Idea of a University:*

> By nature is meant, I suppose, that vast system of things, taken as a whole, of which we are cognizant by means of our natural powers. By the supernatural world is meant that still more marvellous and awful universe, of which the Creator Himself is the fulness [sic], and which becomes known to us, not through our natural faculties, but by superadded and direct communication from Him. These two great circles of knowledge . . . intersect; first, as far as supernatural knowledge includes truths and facts of the natural world, and secondly, as far as truths and facts of the natural world are on the other hand data for inferences about the supernatural. Still, allowing this interference to the full, it will be found, on the whole, that the two worlds and the two kinds of knowledge respectively are separated off from each other; and that, therefore, as being separate, they cannot on the whole contradict each other.[19]

MacIntyre's tangible reticence to trespass onto a discourse of an essentially supernatural order displays an awareness lost to many post–Vatican II Catholic theologians in Catholic colleges and universities in America, and to Catholic university faculties in Europe for whom theology — emancipated from magisterial tutelage — has ceased to be understood as *sacra doctrina.* Theology has for the most part turned into a form of practical "training" for a specific profession. The individual disciplines entailed in this "training" constitute "fields of enquiry" of essentially the same order as all the other academic pursuits of the modern research university. Catholic theology in this naturalized state has become as unspectacular as irrelevant, indeed largely superfluous. The setting is one in which philologists, linguists, historians, archaeologists, psychologists, and philosophers can do equally superb if not better research on the same "material" of which this kind of naturalized theology treats. This comes with the predictable consequence that typically theologians in the modern research university want to be nothing but excellent philologists, linguists, historians, archaeologists, and philosophers. In such a desolate situation, MacIntyre's discursive performance is a remarkable witness to a proper awareness of these categorically different orders of discourse.

19. Newman, *Idea of a University,* p. 310 (from the lecture "Christianity and Physical Science: A Lecture in the School of Medicine").

Meta-science and the Nature and Task of the University

What connects the narrative's first with its second strand (viz., the tradition of Catholic philosophy) and eventually with its third strand (viz., the nature and task of a university), is Thomas's fundamental operative assumption — following Aristotle — that there is a philosophical enquiry that integrates and orders all other scientific enquiries: metaphysics in the broad sense of the term or, in Benedict Ashley's apt terminology, "meta-science," the acme of which meta-science is nothing but an enquiry into the first cause of all being. MacIntyre seems to be in agreement with Thomas on this fundamental operative assumption, and it is significant that John Henry Newman in *The Idea of a University* entertains a similar operative assumption — only that he does not do it along Thomist lines and that he calls it more broadly "philosophy."[20]

Thomas and Newman constitute the normative points of reference around which MacIntyre's narrative is ordered. Both assume the inner coherence of each science and the overall coherence between all sciences. This intra- and inter-disciplinary coherence is for them constitutive of what makes a university a university. To remove this double coherence is to lose the university. Hence the disintegration of the curriculum and the internal disintegration of the academic fields go hand in hand.

The normative thrust of the argument underlying MacIntyre's narrative entails an ambitious agenda for Catholic philosophy. Arguably, Benedict Ashley's *The Way toward Wisdom* can be received most fruitfully as an equally ambitious implementation of MacIntyre's agenda *avant la lettre*.

II. *The Way toward Wisdom*

I can think of at least three good reasons why Ashley's *The Way toward Wisdom: An Interdisciplinary and Intercultural Introduction to Metaphysics*,[21]

---

20. "And further, the comprehension of the bearings of one science on another, and the use of each to each, and the location and limitation and adjustment and due appreciation of them all, one with another, this belongs, I conceive, to a sort of science distinct from all of them, and in some sense a science of sciences, which is my own conception of what is meant by Philosophy, in the true sense of the word, and of a philosophical habit of mind, and which in these Discourses I shall call by that name" (Newman, *Idea of a University*, p. 46).

21. Parenthetical page numbers in this section refer to this book.

though published three years previously, offers itself as a fit sequel to MacIntyre's *God, Philosophy, Universities.*

First, the school of modern Thomism that conversed most intensely with the modern natural sciences, that attended most extensively to Thomas's commentaries on Aristotle's works, and that reflected more than any other strand of modern Thomism on the proper ordering of all the sciences for a genuine liberal arts education, finds no mention in MacIntyre's brief sketch of the various strands of neo-Thomism developing after Leo XIII's encyclical *Aeterni Patris.* Next to the Canadian Charles De Koninck,[22] the American Ralph McInerny,[23] and the Dutch Leo Elders,[24] who all stand in a certain proximity to this strand, it is the River Forest School of Aristotelian Thomism (William H. Kane, O.P., James A. Weisheipl, O.P., William Wallace, O.P., Benedict Ashley, O.P., et al.) that has now found its late fruit in Ashley's *magnum opus.*

Second, *The Way toward Wisdom* throws more penetrating and consistent light onto the question of what MacIntyre might mean by "nature" in his selective history of the Catholic philosophical tradition. For the overlapping common ground between the understandings of "nature" in Thomas and Newman is none other than Aristotle. And Ashley offers a most instructive argument for the ongoing relevance of Aristotle's natural philosophy with more comprehensive and far-reaching implications than even MacIntyre entertains in *Dependent Rational Animals.*

Third, *The Way toward Wisdom* offers a most comprehensive and accurate account of how the sciences are to be ordered according to Thomas. And this ordering is far from a purely antiquarian interest for specialists in medieval thought or only relevant for a small band of disciples of Thomas. Rather, Ashley makes a compelling, 530-page case of showing in detail how Thomas's ordering of the sciences is the result of a remarkably successful meta-science in operation.

No one serious about meta-science and a vision that integrates the natural sciences and the humanities into a universe of knowledge ordered toward wisdom (universal knowledge in Newman's terms) can afford to

---

22. See most recently the first two volumes of a projected three-volume edition, *The Writings of Charles De Koninck,* trans. and ed. Ralph McInerny (Notre Dame, IN: University of Notre Dame Press, 2008-2009).

23. See most recently his *Praeambula fidei.*

24. From among his many works, see most recently his essay "St. Thomas Aquinas on Education and Instruction" (*Nova et Vetera* [English], 7, no. 1 [2009]: 107-24), which offers instructive resonances with Ashley's *The Way toward Wisdom.*

ignore Ashley's remarkable achievement. Following Thomas, Ashley displays an encyclopedic knowledge of the natural sciences as well as the humanities — not in the extrinsic alphabetical ordering of an encyclopedia, but ordered, engaged, and evaluated by a way of a meta-scientific enquiry.

In his *Commonweal* article (cited above), MacIntyre points out a pervasive problem haunting most nonspecialized but interdisciplinary conversations inside the modern research university and even more so beyond its borders in the wider public:

> Ours is a culture in which there is the sharpest of contrasts between the rigor and integrity with which issues of detail are discussed within each specialized discipline and the self-indulgent shoddiness of so much of public debate on large and general issues of great import. . . . One reason for this contrast is the absence of a large educated public, a public with shared standards of argument and inquiry and some shared conception of the central questions that we need to address.[25]

Ashley's work does nothing less than to outline the program of a liberal arts education that would help to eliminate this problem from its very roots up. That such a suggestion sounds all too utopian in light of the present state of colleges and universities only displays the lack of vision that plagues the imagination, the lack of understanding of the depth of the crisis of university education that plagues the intellect, and the lack of courage that plagues the will. Ashley, who wrote his *magnum opus* as an octogenarian, displays more intellectual vision, understanding, breadth, and courage than many a younger and, by contemporary academic standards, successful and recognized university scholar.[26]

Ashley intends this book "for the general reader as a sustained critical argument to show why metaphysics is still a valid intellectual endeavor, and what kind of metaphysics can justifiably claim to be true and useful today" (xix). Like MacIntyre, he is also profoundly concerned with "the fragmentation of knowledge that prevails in our modern colleges and universities" (xx) and hence intends this extensive introduction into meta-

---

25. MacIntyre, "End of Education," p. 14.

26. One fascinating aspect of Ashley's book I cannot pursue here is its rather obvious indebtedness to the kind of undergraduate education he received at the University of Chicago in the 1930s when there occurred a university-wide, meta-scientific debate about the hierarchy and coherence of all academic disciplines, a debate shaped by Richard P. McKeon's Aristotle Renaissance and Mortimer J. Adler's Great Ideas project.

"Seeking Truth on Dry Soil and under Thornbushes"

physics as meta-science primarily for the undergraduate student reader who is in need of a uniform fund of information. What Newman in *The Idea of a University* called "genuine philosophical knowledge" as the end of a true university education, Ashley names "wisdom," and the path to reaching this end he names "interdisciplinarity."

> [H]ow is a modern university, or any of our "think tanks," to engage in or promote multicultural dialogue unless it has reflected on the foundations of its own unity as an institution? To do this it must achieve genuine interdisciplinarity. (20)

In order to pursue the goal of genuine interdisciplinarity, the meta-science he unfolds must be essentially dialogical, not in order to achieve conversion or refutation, but in order to achieve *reconciliation*. The mode of this dialogic approach is analytic, "since it aims to formulate basic assumptions held by the dialogue partners so that what is true in both positions may be recognized" (19). It is the aim to achieve a genuine interdisciplinarity that drives Ashley's book and also accounts for the extraordinary scope of its discussion, from the religions and the wisdom of ancient cultures to modern astrophysics, from Aristotelian logic to contemporary mathematics. This book is the fruit of a life-long intellectual effort to achieve a comprehensive understanding of reality, and thus represents a precious gift to the university — a gift, however, I am not sure the contemporary university is capable of receiving:

> The very term "uni-versity" means many-looking-toward-one, and is related to the term "universe," the whole of reality. Thus, the name no longer seems appropriate to such a fragmented modern institution whose unity is provided only by a financial administration and perhaps a sports team. The fragmented academy is, of course the result of the energetic exploration of all kinds of knowledge, but how can it meet the fundamental yearning for wisdom on which each culture is based? (20)

In part 1, "Metaphysics: Nonsense or Wisdom?" (93-169), Ashley offers an astute and informative survey of the varieties of metaphysics in Western culture. Most helpful are his lucid characterizations of the varieties of twentieth-century Thomism. The subsequent discussion of part 1 represents a rigorous unfolding of the Aristotelian Thomism of the River Forest School's philosophy of nature. By way of Aristotle's *Posterior Ana-*

409

lytics and *Physics* (following Thomas's interpretation of both works), Ashley argues forcefully that (1) natural science is epistemologically first; (2) that the basics of Aristotle's *Physics* are still in harmony with modern science; and (3) that natural science establishes the ground for first philosophy or metaphysics — not the ground for its possibility, but indeed the ground for its necessity (and here his running disagreement with such Thomists as Clarke, Dewan, Knasas, Wippel, et al. becomes manifest).

In part 2, "The Properties of all Reality" (173-381), Ashley unfolds a comprehensive consideration of all branches of knowledge ordered and guided by the properties of all being, the transcendentals one, true, good (*unum, verum, bonum*) correlated to efficient, formal, and final causality. This approach allows for a concise, and always solid, consideration of the constitutive aspects of all central academic disciplines, from natural science and mathematics to the practical sciences and history. I know of no other contemporary philosopher who, between the covers of one book, so concisely discusses the unity of physical bodies, atoms, and particles, as well as the unity of contingent spiritual substances (that is, the unity of the embodied human spirit and the unity of the pure spirit, the angel). This part of the book strikes me as a paradigmatic instantiation of Pope Benedict XVI's mandate from his Regensburg Lecture (cited above) to broaden our concept of reason and its application and thereby disclose reason's vast horizons.

In part 3, "The First Cause or Absolute Principle of Reality" (385-430), Ashley's *The Way toward Wisdom* ascends finally to an enquiry into the First Cause, a discussion that can be read as an extended treatment of what MacIntyre condenses in the opening four pages of his book and presupposes for the rest of his discussion. MacIntyre follows the *ordo doctrinae* proper to unfolding a philosophical narrative and Ashley adopts the *ordo inventionis* proper to an immediate metaphysical enquiry. It is important to realize that Ashley follows Thomas in holding that the First Cause is not included in the proper subject of metaphysics, which is *ens commune*. Rather, the First Cause is but the goal of metaphysics, a goal that this science can never claim to comprehend. Unsurprisingly, Ashley emphasizes the crucial difference between this understanding of metaphysics (arguably the proper *Aristotelian* understanding as adopted by Thomas) and the one advanced by Scotus, adopted by Suárez, popularized by Wolff, rejected by Kant, and rightly submitted to the charge of "onto-theology" by Martin Heidegger, a charge echoed by Jean-Luc Marion and held as conventional wisdom by those announcing the post-metaphysical epoch in philosophy and theology. Ashley simply invites a closer and better philosophical rereading of Aristotle. At stake in this part is nothing less than the truth of monotheistic belief:

> In trying to achieve some understanding of the nature of the First Cause, the first question must be whether the world of human experience is really distinct from a First Cause who has freely created it out of nothing, or whether this world of experience is really identified with its First Cause. (385)

Ashley offers an astute discussion and withering critique of materialistic or nature monism, the panentheism of Whitehead, and the spiritual monisms of Neoplatonism and Idealism.

The subsequent chapter, "The One Creating First Cause" (403-430), would make an excellent study for those theologians, especially Protestant, who all too quickly might want to dismiss the deity of Aristotle's *Metaphysics* 12 (Lambda) as final causality elevated to the supreme level of "world *nous*" in charge of moving the outermost sphere of an eternal universe and otherwise simply contemplating itself — hence intrinsically unfit for any form of adoption by Christian theology. Ashley makes a convincing case to the contrary by arguing that, in principle, final causality can only be understood in light of efficient causality. Hence:

> [i]t is utterly contrary to Aristotle's whole thought to suppose that there could be a final cause that does not require a proportionate efficient cause. Final causality . . . is the predetermination of an efficient cause and could not exist without such a proportionate efficient cause. Since the total series of moved movers cannot move itself, how could the First Cause be the final cause of the motion of all things unless, by implication at least, it was the first *efficient cause* of their motion? (404)

Consequently, the discussion of the final cause in *Metaphysics* 12 (Lambda) must be read in light of the antecedent proof of the existence of the Unmoved Mover in *Physics* 7 and 8. The final cause of the universe is first and foremost the efficient first cause of the world. And as Thomas maintains, the efficient causality of the first cause pertains not only to the causality of motion, but to the very causality of substance itself.[27]

27. "Hence there are causes of beings as beings, which are investigated in first philosophy. . . . And from this it is quite evident that the opinion of those who claimed that Aris-

The subsequent enquiry into the perfection of the First Cause follows closely the first book of Thomas's *Summa contra Gentiles* and questions 3-25 of book I of the *Summa theologiae,* arguing "why and how the First Cause is one and why and how the First Cause is personal" (409). It is in this section that Ashley offers a compelling contemporary Thomistic answer to the three preeminent philosophical questions which, as MacIntyre claims, arose historically from broadly theistic and specifically Catholic beliefs: first, the question of the compatibility between the existence of God and the scope of evil — natural, social, and moral — in a universe of finite beings; second, the question of the compatibility between divine transcendent causality and genuine secondary causality (i.e., between divine omnipotence and human freedom); and third, the question of true knowledge of and hence meaningful discourse about God.

In part 4, "Wisdom, Human and Divine" (433-51), Ashley returns to the book's fundamental concern that strongly echoes Newman's *The Idea of the University* and his concern about liberal education. However, there are two differences to be noted between Newman and Ashley's Aristotelian Thomism, differences that remain unresolved in the way Thomas and Newman form the two foci of MacIntyre's narrative. First, following Thomas, Ashley affirms that the study of nature is basic to all disciplines;[28] second, also following Thomas, he affirms the fundamental connectedness of the intellectual and the moral virtues, and especially the preeminent role of prudence in uniting the virtues (228, 355) such that a proper liberal arts education along Thomistic lines should lead to an integral excellence of mind and character. Newman, on the contrary, stresses a principled dis-

---

totle thought that God is not the cause of the substance of the heavens, but only of their motion, is false" ("Unde sunt causae entium secundum quod sunt entia, quae inquiruntur in prima philosophia. . . . Ex hoc autem apparet manifeste falsitas opinionis illorum, qui posuerunt Aristotelem sensisse, quod Deus non sit causa substantiae caeli, sed solum motus eius" (Aquinas, *In Met.* 6.1, §1164 [Rome: Marietti, 1950] regarding Aristotle, *Metaphysics* 6, 1026a 11-18; translation in Aquinas, *Commentary on Aristotle's Metaphysics,* trans. and introduced by John P. Rowan [Notre Dame, IN: Dumb Ox Books, 1995], p. 402).

28. "[T]he basis of a liberal higher education for *all* students must be the natural sciences. Only then will the present need of all of us to live in a modern, scientifically oriented culture be adequately met. The division between the 'Two Cultures' of the sciences and the humanities can be overcome only by rooting the humanities in the objective truth of the 'hard' sciences" (p. 439). In order to appreciate this recommendation fully one needs to remember that Ashley maintains the inherent unity of natural philosophy (as paradigmatically executed in Aristotle's *Physics*) and natural science, and their full integration in a liberal arts curriculum that is ultimately directed toward the search of wisdom.

connection between the intellectual and the moral virtues. For Newman, the existence of "gentlemen" who are intellectually brilliant and socially refined, but who are also scoundrels, is something that in principle even the best liberal arts education cannot avoid.[29] Ashley would most likely agree that even the best liberal arts education along Thomistic lines can never *completely* exclude the possibility of such an undesirable outcome. However, with respect to such cases of gentlemanly scoundrels as Newman has in mind, Ashley would maintain that we must diagnose not only an obvious failure of moral formation but also some consequent deficiency in the comprehensive formation of the intellectual virtues. In short, the disagreement comes down to the question of whether a genuine liberal arts education is supposed to form the intellectual virtue of prudence and whether this virtue is integral to the overall pursuit of wisdom.[30]

29. "Knowledge is one thing, virtue is another; good sense is not conscience, refinement is not humility, nor is largeness and justness of view faith. Philosophy, however enlightened, however profound, gives no command over the passions, no influential motives, no vivifying principles. Liberal Education makes not the Christian, not the Catholic, but the gentleman. . . . Quarry the granite rock with razors, or moor the vessel with a thread of silk; then may you hope with such keen and delicate instruments as human knowledge and human reason to contend against those giants, the passion and the pride of man. . . . Liberal Education, viewed in itself, is simply the cultivation of the intellect, as such, and its object is nothing more or less than intellectual excellence" (Newman, *Idea of a University,* pp. 106f.).

30. The subtle but important difference that seems to me to obtain between Newman's position and that of the Thomist tradition deserves a more extensive and nuanced discussion than I am able to afford in the scope of this chapter. I shall mention for a starter, however, that in Thomas's doctrine of the cardinal virtues prudence holds a principal position insofar as this intellectual virtue constitutes the unifying link between the moral and the intellectual virtues. And while the other intellectual virtues indeed can be without moral virtue, prudence cannot (*ST* I, q. 58, a. 5). Hence, Thomas can account for the brilliant scoundrel. Prudence does not belong to those intellectual virtues that perfect the speculative intellect for the consideration of truth — and it is on the formation of those that, according to Newman, a university education exclusively concentrates. However, the pursuit of wisdom, which is the proper end of a liberal arts education along Thomistic lines, entails the refinement of habits of thought, as well as of action, for both pertain to the end of the human being. And since prudence is an intellectual virtue, its formation and refinement fall under the competency of a liberal arts education along Thomistic lines. Furthermore, since prudence is the intellectual virtue that perfects reason pertaining to things to be done (*ST* I, q. 57, a. 5), the formation of prudence is integral to a university education that is directed to the pursuit of wisdom as its ultimate end. For it is the case that for this pursuit to reach its end, many actions as means to advance best toward this end will need to be decided upon — and the habituation into such actions presupposes the virtue of prudence. For an instructive

Ashley demonstrates persuasively how the pursuit of wisdom along the lines of a recovery and expansion of the Aristotelian-Thomist trajectory of a meta-science is a nontrivial contribution to the proper flourishing of theology *(sacra doctrina)*. Much of contemporary "post-metaphysical" theology, especially in the dialogue between theology and science, naively adopts the deliveries of the sciences, adapting its own construals to them without fully employing the critical mediation afforded by meta-scientific reflection. It frequently follows that philosophically erroneous entailments of naturalism, materialism, and of programmatically atheistic versions of evolution theory tend to find their way into theology and contribute to deficient understandings of God, what it is to be human, and the world as creation "all the way down." Here theologians can receive fruitful lessons from Ashley's nondefensive, meta-scientific reflection on all branches of knowledge, which gives priority to the natural sciences and at the same time remains a nonreductive exercise of a consistent expansion of the horizons of reason. (This performance would have driven the Kant of the *Critique of Pure Reason* insane, but then again, Ashley makes a persuasive case that Aristotle was right and Kant was wrong — in matters of epistemology, as well as in matters pertaining to the validity of the proof from motion that a first immaterial efficient cause exits.) In short, *The Way toward Wisdom* represents a paradigmatic exemplification of Pope Benedict XVI's call of his Regensburg Lecture to overcome the self-imposed limitation of reason to the empirically falsifiable, and to once more disclose reason's vast horizons.

A book of such vast scope and ambition makes itself vulnerable, of course, to all kinds of shortcomings, weaknesses, and failures of nuance in multiple respects — though, from my own limited perspective, I encountered only a few. Because Ashley approaches the unity and order of all sciences by way of natural philosophy and natural science, the practical sciences, as well as history, in short, the "humanities," did not receive quite as extensive and nuanced a consideration as they deserve. Some Thomist metaphysicians (Clarke, Dewan, Knasas, Wippel, et al.) will want to challenge Ashley on the philosophical necessity of accessing the subject matter of metaphysics by way of natural philosophy and natural science. Additionally, students of Maritain will wonder whether, in light of the very nature of modern physics, the integral unity of natural philosophy and natu-

---

introduction into this topic, see Pierre H. Conway, O.P., *Principles of Education: A Thomistic Approach* (Washington, DC: The Thomist Press, 1960). Though much harder to find than Newman's *The Idea of a University*, it deserves no less serious a reconsideration.

ral science that Ashley defends can still be maintained or whether some greater distinction between natural philosophy and modern physics is necessary — with the entailed acknowledgement that a direct passing from modern physics to meta-science is impossible. While such objections and reservations represent some of the in-house debates among Thomists, other philosophers will raise quite predictably more fundamental objections and disagreements, many of which are anticipated and quite forcefully addressed in Ashley's work.

There is, however, a much simpler and at the same time much deeper problem as a result of which Ashley's accomplishment will go largely unnoticed. It is the problem to which MacIntyre points both at the beginning and end of *God, Philosophy, Universities.* For the single most serious, if not insuperable obstacle to any substantive reception of Ashley's book outside a narrow circle of Aristotelian and Thomist philosophers rests on the fact that most, if not all, contemporary university teachers and scholars have never been introduced to and habituated into any sustained intellectual practice of meta-scientific reflection, let alone the search for wisdom, and consequently do not comprehend that their particular fields of enquiry can only flourish as part of a larger search for wisdom. In short, the predicament of secular universities simply reflects the necessary outcome of abandoning any commitment to reason as a comprehensive operation in search of a shared, integral understanding. But for this to be the predicament also of Catholic universities amounts for MacIntyre to grave error in the intellectual order and to grave fault in the moral order. As mentioned already above, in contrast to MacIntyre, Ashley puts the challenge in slightly more positive terms and directs it especially to theologians and philosophers — not in Catholic universities in particular, but in Christian universities in general:

> Christian universities represent a great international culture that is inevitably a major player in any multicultural dialogue at the sapiential level. Christian culture has played a leading role in the historical development of the university, yet because its theologians and philosophers in the post-Galilean epoch withdrew from active dialogue with developing natural science, it remains isolated. Christians must now accept the laborious and even painful tasks of rethinking the foundations of natural science and of achieving a Metascience grounded in such a revised natural science. It will then be effective in a mediating, ecumenical role between Secular Humanism (which threatens to reduce all cul-

tures to its own ideological perspectives) and the cultures of the world that recognize spiritual reality.

In this task, a Christian university must not only promote dialogue with its monotheist partners — the Jews and the Muslims — but it must also learn to dialogue with the naturalist and spiritualist monism of most other cultures. (443)

As it turns out, the agenda Ashley prescribes for philosophers and theologians in contemporary Christian universities is no less ambitious than the one MacIntyre prescribes to contemporary Catholic philosophers. However, Ashley's approach and agenda seem more capable to accommodate the modern, Berlin-type research university with its ideal of an integral unity between research and teaching. Ashley's agenda, while admittedly not very likely to be adopted by any present research university, Christian or Catholic, let alone secular, still betrays more hope in the potential redeemability of such universities than MacIntyre's narrative does. For Ashley can acknowledge the modern research university as the great-grandchild of Aristotle's comprehensive program of research, from whence Ashley also sees arising the very potential for its internal reform. For in the case of the Aristotelian research program (and its modern adaptation by the River Forest School of Aristotelian Thomism), the advancement of knowledge by way of research always remains integral to a comprehensive program of education for which the teaching of universal knowledge holds primacy. MacIntyre, more deeply committed to Newman's exclusive vision of the university as "a place of *teaching* universal knowledge," will keep high the critical bar on the hopes Ashley entertains for Christian universities. For not only would theology and philosophy have to reoccupy a long lost central position (and in consequence reinvent themselves) in these Christian universities, but these Christian universities, in order to be in a position of adopting Ashley's agenda, would have to become again *primarily* places of *teaching* universal knowledge on the basis of curricula that would facilitate, indeed mandate, the interface between theology and philosophy with the natural sciences. These schools would only secondarily be places in which research agendas are also maintained for the sake of the expansion of knowledge.

But the fundamental question remains: From where would come the faculty who themselves had received the kind of integrated interdisciplinary education that would enable them to appreciate, adopt, and pursue Ashley's agenda? To questions of this kind, MacIntyre, has a rather blunt response:

We do possess the intellectual resources to bring about the kind of change I propose. What we lack, in Catholic and in secular universities, is the will to change, and that absence of will is a symptom of a quite unwarranted complacency concerning our present state and our present direction.[31]

Should we entertain any reasonable hope for Christian universities in general and Catholic universities in particular? I should say that any undergraduate curriculum that approximates the normative vision of the university shared by John Henry Newman, Alasdair MacIntyre, and Benedict Ashley — and for that matter, by the late Pope John Paul II and by Pope Benedict XVI, two former university professors — should be applauded. For resigning oneself to increasing curricula fragmentation, to acceleration of centrifugal forces of knowledge production — with its accompanying tendency to instrumentalize and commodify — and to dismissing philosophers like MacIntyre and Ashley as incurable romantics will only cement an already emerging reality: that the label "university" held by these late modern institutions is an illegitimate claim at best and quite simply an equivocation at worst.

MacInyre's and Ashley's books have indeed the touch of untimeliness to them. They are written for generations of university professors and students still to come, generations ready to receive the profundity of MacIntyre's and Ashley's insights and proposals as the gifts they are. For these future generations will eventually become disillusioned with the present celebration of knowledge production without end and will thirst again for a "connected view or grasp of things," in short, for wisdom, let alone, for God.

When this is going to happen, though, will depend largely on when it is that the first part of the conditional clause of Pope Benedict XVI's speech for "La Sapienza" ceases to obtain:

If our culture seeks only to build itself on the basis of the circle of its own argumentation, on what convinces it at the time, and if — anxious to preserve its secularism — it detaches itself from its life-giving roots, then it will not become more reasonable or purer, but will fall apart and disintegrate.[32]

31. Alasdair MacIntyre, "End of Education," p. 14.
32. While the Pope applies this conditional to the European culture, it arguably also obtains — *mutatis mutandis* — for the United States and Canada. In his meeting with the

DUST BOUND FOR HEAVEN

Are there presently any signs of hope, any instantiations of an institutional awareness of and concern for Pope Benedict XVI's sobering analysis and grave warning? That there are at least some liberal arts institutions that seem both aware of the Pope's somber analysis and capable of acknowledging MacIntyre's and Ashley's proposals can perhaps be gathered from the remarks of the late Dr. Thomas E. Dillon (1946-2009), president of Thomas Aquinas College:

> Our fundamental endeavor at Thomas Aquinas College is a modest one: to help you make a good beginning on the ascent to wisdom. . . . These four years at the College are a precious opportunity to develop your minds and refine your habits of thought and action. You will be reading and discussing the greatest works ever written; works that have defined eras and shaped civilizations. In a community of friends, and under the guidance of tutors who care deeply about your good, you will seek to make reasoned judgments about the nature of reality. You will be aided in your inquiries by the rich intellectual tradition of the Church as you study Her wisest teachers — wise especially because of their own docility to Christ and His Church. Liberal education concerns not what is servile and transient, but what is intrinsically worthwhile and permanent. By coming to Thomas Aquinas College, by devoting yourselves to four years of a liberal arts education, you are standing with Socrates and opting not for the life of convenience and trivial pleasure, but rather for the life rooted in the love of wisdom and ordered to virtue. Such a life is not easy, for it demands discipline and self-denial, but it is a life of genuine freedom and happiness.[33]

French intellectual, cultural, and political élite on 12 September 2008 at the Collège des Bernardins in Paris, Pope Benedict XVI stressed that what he has to say about the foundations of European culture does indeed pertain today to the basis of *any* genuine culture: "*Quaerere Deum* — to seek God and to let oneself be found by him, that is today no less necessary than in former times. A purely positivistic culture which tried to drive the question concerning God into the subjective realm, as being unscientific, would be the capitulation of reason, the renunciation of its highest possibilities, and hence a disaster for humanity, with very grave consequences. What gave Europe's culture its foundation — the search for God and the readiness to listen to him — remains today the basis of any genuine culture" (available on the Vatican web site: http://www.vatican.va/holy_father/benedict_xvi/speeches/ 2008/september/documents/hf_ben-xvi_spe_20080912_parigi-cultura_en.html).

33. "Commencement Day Remarks," *Communio* 35, no. 4 (2008): 672f. In the 2010 edition of the popular Princeton Review College guidebook, *The Best 371 Colleges* (New York: Random House, 2009), Thomas Aquinas College received a rating of 99 (out of 100) for its academics and is included in the "Top 50" colleges in the country.

An institution of higher education shaped in its core curriculum by such a vision provides the proximate context for an intelligent and fruitful reception of Ashley's *The Way toward Wisdom* and offers some warrant for the hope MacIntyre expresses at the very end of *God, Philosophy, Universities*. It is to liberal arts institutions shaped by a vision like the one expressed by Dr. Dillon that the modern research university will eventually have to turn in order to find the medicine that will cure it from the ruinous disease that has befallen it.[34] Neither an ivy-covered neo-gothic architecture, nor a top placement in international university rankings, nor the desperate acceleration of research production, nor the foundation of another research institute of bio-engineering will prevent the fatal consequences of the disease unless the medicine be taken from marginal and often belittled and ridiculed Christian, and especially Catholic, liberal arts institutions such as Thomas Aquinas College. Considering such medicine to be vital is the first step for resuscitating the heart of the modern university and restoring the pursuit of wisdom.

34. In order to find the proper cure it might often suffice for modern research universities simply to reform themselves along the lines of their founding charters. Here is Duke University's: "The aims of Duke University are to assert a faith in the eternal union of knowledge and religion set forth in the teachings and character of Jesus Christ, the Son of God, to advance learning in all lines of truth, to defend scholarship against all false notions and ideals, to develop a Christian love of freedom and truth, to promote a sincere spirit of tolerance, to discourage all partisan and sectarian strife, and to render the largest permanent service to the individual, the state, the nation, and the church. Unto these ends shall the affairs of this university always be administered."

Postlude — Mystery and Metaphysics

CHAPTER 12

"This Is My Body" — Eucharistic Adoration
and Metaphysical Contemplation

No one eats that flesh without first adoring it. . . . Not only do we not
commit a sin by adoring it, but we do sin by not adoring it.

St. Augustine[1]

Of all devotions, that of adoring Jesus in the Blessed Sacrament is the
greatest after the sacraments, the one dearest to God and the one most
helpful to us.

St. Alphonsus Liguori[2]

Introduction

The Roman Catholic Church in the United States and elsewhere has in recent years experienced nothing less than quite a remarkable resurgence of

---

1. Cited by Pope Pius XII, Encyclical Letter *Mediator Dei* (1947), §130: "[N]emo autem illam carnem manducat, nisi prius adorauerit . . . , et non solum non peccemus adorando, sed peccemus non adorando" (CCL 39, 1385, lines 23-26). This passage from Augustine's *Enarrationes in Psalmos* 98:9, as famous as it is difficult, has been invoked at least twice by Pope Benedict XVI in the context of encouraging the practice of Eucharistic Adoration. First in his address to the Roman Curia on December 22, 2005 (AAS 98 [2006], 44-45) and then again in his post-synodal apostolic exhortation *Sacramentum Caritatis* (2007), §66.

2. *Visite al SS. Sacramento e a Maria Sanctissima*, Introduction: *Opere Ascetiche*, Avellino 2000, 295, as cited in Pope John Paul II's 2003 encyclical letter *Ecclesia de Eucharistia*, §25.

devotion to the Real Presence of Christ in the Blessed Sacrament outside of the celebration of the Mass. In this postlude, I will, first, attend to the liturgical practice of Eucharistic adoration; second, adumbrate the intentionality inscribed in the liturgical practice itself; and third, undertake a re-reading of the Thomist doctrine of Eucharistic transubstantiation. I intend to submit the latter as one profound proposal of a philosophical hermeneutics in the service of theology, a proposal that offers a comprehensive interpretation of the mystery of Christ's lasting real, substantial and hence personal presence in the reserved Blessed Sacrament. Two introductory caveats are called for.

First, there is a fundamental assumption I will *not* argue for in this chapter, but simply will presuppose: in the Catholic Church it is an ancient,[3] venerable, and universally held principle that the Church's living tradition of prayer serves as an authentic guide for her faith[4] as authentically interpreted by the Church's magisterium.[5] Hence, I take the adoration of the Blessed Sacrament to be an *authentic* liturgical practice of the Catholic Church and, furthermore, since it has been embraced, affirmed, regulated, and encouraged by the Church's magisterium, it is not only *licit,* but indeed surpassingly *commendable.* The following consideration is therefore neither apologetic — that is, interested in defending this particular instantiation of the Catholic faith and practice against possible Protestant criticism and likely secular detraction; nor is the following consideration ecumenical in nature — that is, intended to contribute to a possible future consensus on the matter of Eucharistic adoration. Rather, my intention here is strictly *hermeneutical,* roughly along the lines of *fides quaerens intellectum.* Like any other Christian liturgical practice, Eucharistic adoration can and indeed should become the topic of faith seeking understanding. Every person encountering or involved in this liturgical practice might

---

3. The famous formula "ut legem credendi lex statuat supplicandi" — later abbreviated into "lex orandi, lex credendi" — is first to be found in the anti-Pelagian "Indiculus" (chapter) that was probably put together by Prosper of Aquitania in Rome some time between 435 and 442. See Denzinger-Hünermann §246 (Heinrich Denzinger, *Enchiridion symbolorum definitionum et declarationum de rebus fidei et morum,* 40th ed., ed. Peter Hünermann [Freiburg: Herder, 2005], 118).

4. See Vatican II, The Constitution on the Sacred Liturgy, *Sacrosanctum Concilium,* §10 and §33, in *Decrees of the Ecumenical Councils: Volume II (Trent–Vatican II),* ed. Norman P. Tanner, S.J. (London: Sheed & Ward; Washington, DC: Georgetown University Press, 1990), pp. 823 and 827.

5. See Pope Pius XII, *Mediator Dei* (1947), *AAS* 39 (1947), pp. 540-41.

want to ask, what is going on and how does one make explicit its most central implication, Christ's abiding substantial and hence personal presence in the reserved Blessed Sacrament?

Now, the second caveat. Because Christ's abiding and lasting presence in the Eucharistic elements has been affirmed by the Catholic Church's magisterium often and in manifold ways, and at the same time has been regarded as integral to the mystery of faith, any theological interpretation of this mystery that draws upon philosophical categories or even upon a comprehensive metaphysics, that is, a comprehensive philosophical interpretation of all that exists, nevertheless remains nothing but a way of making explicit what remains antecedently and inexhaustibly the mystery of faith.[6] An interpretation of this mystery is, hence, fundamentally different from "making sense" of it along the lines of resolving a philosophical puzzle — an attempt that a genuine mystery of faith will always and consistently frustrate. Consequently, even the most profound instantiation of making philosophically explicit what the act of faith assents to about the mystery of faith ever makes exhaustive or even indisputable sense of the mystery so that the act of faith might become a redundant add-on. The intentionality of the liturgical practice, as well as the act of faith entailed in it, *essentially* transcends the scope of making philosophically explicit this mystery of faith.[7]

In this postlude on "mystery and metaphysics," I wish to reconsider one particular tradition of philosophical interpretation that makes explicit Christ's lasting substantial and hence personal presence in the reserved Blessed Sacrament — the Thomistic account. While the majority of contemporary philosophers might disqualify the metaphysical approach taken by the Thomist tradition as simply not being "à jour," hermeneutically reconsidered, this philosophical interpretation makes explicit the liturgical practice's most central implication and at the same time remains invulnerable to the single most frequently raised charge against the liturgical prac-

---

6. Cf. the explicit emphasis on the mystery of faith in the opening pages of Pope Benedict XVI's post-synodal apostolic exhortation *Sacramentum Caritatis*, §6: "'*The mystery of faith!*' With these words, spoken immediately after the words of consecration, the priest proclaims the mystery being celebrated and expresses his wonder before the substantial change of bread and wine into the body and blood of the Lord Jesus, a reality which surpasses all human understanding. The Eucharist is a 'mystery of faith' par excellence: 'the sum and summary of our faith' [*Catechism of the Catholic Church*, §1327]."

7. For the understanding of "mystery" that I presuppose in the following discussion, see chapter 7, n. 3.

tice itself — namely, that it reflects and promotes a misplaced focus on some kind of "thing-like" presence of Christ and consequently perpetuates a reductive reification, and hence a disconcerting distortion of Christ's personal Eucharistic presence.

I shall proceed by offering first a brief word on the history of the slow emergence of the practice of Eucharistic adoration in the life of the Catholic Church; second, a rough adumbration of the practice itself together with its intentionality; third, a reconsideration of some central tenets of Thomas's metaphysical way of making explicit the substantial presence of Christ presupposed by and entailed in Eucharistic adoration; and fourth, by way of a methodological postscript an initial consideration of the proper relationship between theology, philosophy, and liturgy.

The Emerging Liturgical Practice of Eucharistic Adoration[8]

While the real presence of Christ in the Eucharistic species has arguably been recognized since apostolic times, and while we find early witnesses to the practice of the reservation of the Blessed Sacrament with the desert fathers and with St. Basil, the adoration of the Blessed Sacrament may have begun only in the sixth century in the Cathedral of Lugo, Spain. Certainly, from the eleventh century on, we can observe an increasing prevalence in devotion to the Blessed Sacrament reserved in the tabernacle, and we know that by the twelfth century, St. Thomas Becket is known to have prayed for King Henry II before the "majesty of the Body of Christ." The feast of Corpus Christi, instituted by Pope Urban IV in 1264, gathered much of the emerging Eucharistic piety into one feast that gave it focus and expression, and in the fourteenth century, in many monastic communities, the custom emerged to pray the Liturgy of the Hours in front of the exposed Blessed Sacrament.

A new development beyond the feast of Corpus Christi, namely the widespread regular worship by the laity of the Holy Eucharist outside of Mass, arose from the traditional Forty Hours Devotion which originated in the early sixteenth century in Milan, Italy, and was probably a commem-

8. In the following section I rely on the useful works of John A. Hardon, S.J., *The History of Eucharistic Adoration: Development of Doctrine in the Catholic Church* (Oak Lawn, IL: CMJ Marian Publishers, 1997) and of Benedict J. Groeschel, C.F.R. and James Monti, *In the Presence of Our Lord: The History, Theology, and Psychology of Eucharistic Devotion* (Huntington, IN: Our Sunday Visitor, 1997).

oration of the forty hours Christ's body lay in the tomb between his death and resurrection. In 1592, Pope Clement VII gave formal recognition to the devotion and decreed it to be observed in the churches of Rome. In various stages it spread throughout the Catholic Church: There were Perpetual Eucharistic Associations starting in seventeenth-century France and Men's Nocturnal Adoration societies beginning in Rome in 1810 that both spread internationally. In 1857, the Forty Hours devotion was first approved for the diocese of Baltimore, and in 1868 it was extended to all the dioceses of the United States. Most recently, the worship of the Holy Eucharist outside of Mass has been reaffirmed in the documents of liturgical reform issued subsequent to Vatican II. Analogous to the development of doctrine, we can witness in the case of Eucharistic Adoration the slow, but organic development of a particular liturgical practice. Although the historical development of this practice is much richer and complicated than the outline I have provided here, what does seem indisputable is the fact that the contemporary liturgical practice of Eucharistic adoration emerged from an early practice of reserving the consecrated elements. From there it developed through various stages into an increasingly widespread liturgical practice in the Catholic Church, a practice[9] that has been repeatedly encouraged and promoted by the magisterium.[10]

Explicit Magisterial Confirmation of Eucharistic Adoration

Because an integral component of the ongoing *traditio* of any liturgical practice in the Catholic Church is the way the Church's Magisterium theologically interprets and thus doctrinally confirms the liturgical prac-

9. In the following, I understand practice roughly along the lines that Alasdair MacIntyre introduced the concept as being a distinct, describable, and inherently meaningful matrix of actions that are ordered to and regulated by an end that is intrinsic to the practice. I extend this concept analogically to a liturgical rite in order to capture its characteristics as distinct from *poiesis* (where the activity is a means to an end extrinsic to it) and from *theoria* or contemplation (where the activity is one essentially of the intellect alone).

10. In his post-synodal apostolic exhortation *Sacramentum Caritatis* from February 22, 2007, Pope Benedict XVI explicitly states: "With the Synod Assembly . . . I heartily recommend to the Church's pastors and to the People of God the practice of eucharistic adoration, both individually and in community" (§67). More recently, on May 7, 2008, when at the end of the general audience Pope Benedict XVI greeted the sisters of the Order of Sisters of the Perpetual Adoration of the Blessed Sacrament, he renewed his call for Eucharistic adoration (www.zenit.org./article-22517?l=english).

tice, we would be in error if we were to regard the magisterial interpretation as somehow simply *extrinsic* to a proper understanding of the liturgical practice itself. The single most significant doctrinal confirmation in recent times of Eucharistic adoration was the last encyclical letter of the late Pope John Paul II from 2003, *Ecclesia de Eucharistia*. Allow me to indulge in a somewhat longer citation from this encyclical letter as §25 is utterly essential for an understanding of the doctrinal signpost that any authentic philosophical hermeneutics of the Eucharistic Adoration will need to respect:

> The *worship of the Eucharist outside of the Mass* is of inestimable value for the life of the Church. This worship is strictly linked to the celebration of the Eucharistic Sacrifice. The presence of Christ under the sacred species reserved after Mass — a presence which lasts as long as the species of bread and wine remain — derives from the celebration of the sacrifice and is directed towards communion, both sacramental and spiritual. It is the responsibility of Pastors to encourage, also by their personal witness, the practice of Eucharistic adoration, and exposition of the Blessed Sacrament in particular, as well as prayer of adoration before Christ present under the Eucharistic species.
>
> It is pleasant to spend time with him, to lie close to his breast like the Beloved Disciple (cf. Jn 13:25) and to feel the infinite love present in his heart. If in our time Christians must be distinguished above all by the "art of prayer," how can we not feel a renewed need to spend time in spiritual converse, in silent adoration, in heartfelt love before Christ present in the Most Holy Sacrament? How often, dear brothers and sisters, have I experienced this, and drawn from it strength, consolation and support!
>
> This practice, repeatedly praised and recommended by the Magisterium, is supported by the example of many saints. Particularly outstanding in this regard was Saint Alphonsus Liguori, who wrote: "Of all devotions, that of adoring Jesus in the Blessed Sacrament is the greatest after the sacraments, the one dearest to God and the one most helpful to us." The Eucharist is a priceless treasure: by not only celebrating it but also by praying before it outside of Mass we are enabled to make contact with the very wellspring of grace. A Christian community desirous of contemplating the face of Christ in the spirit which I proposed in the Apostolic Letters *Novo Millennio Ineunte* and *Rosarium Virginis Mariae* cannot fail also to develop this aspect of Eucha-

ristic worship, which prolongs and increases the fruits of our communion in the body and blood of the Lord.[11]

This whole understanding of Christ's Eucharistic presence builds upon two further fundamental aspects of the Church's doctrine. The first pertains to the meaning of the Eucharist itself:

> "The Lord Jesus on the night he was betrayed" (1 Cor 11:23) instituted the Eucharistic Sacrifice of his body and his blood. The words of the Apostle Paul bring us back to the dramatic setting in which the Eucharist was born. The Eucharist is indelibly marked by the event of the Lord's passion and death, of which it is not only a reminder but a sacramental representation. It is the sacrifice of the Cross perpetuated down the ages. . . . The Church has received the Eucharist from Christ her Lord not as one gift — however precious — among so many others, but as *the gift par excellence,* for it is the gift of himself, of his person in his sacred humanity, as well as the gift of his saving work. Nor does it remain confined to the past, since "all that Christ is — all that he did and suffered for all men — participates in the divine eternity, and so transcends all times." When the Church celebrates the Eucharist, the memorial of her Lord's death and resurrection, this central event of salvation becomes really present and "the work of our redemption is carried out."[12]

The second pertains to the particular kind of Christ's presence under the sacramental species:

> Every theological explanation which seeks some understanding of this mystery, in order to be in accord with Catholic faith, must firmly maintain that in objective reality, independently of our mind, the bread and wine have ceased to exist after the consecration, so that the adorable body and blood of the Lord Jesus from that moment on are really before us under the sacramental species of bread and wine.[13]

Arguably, the most salient aspect to be made explicit by way of a philosophical hermeneutics of the mystery of the Eucharistic sacrifice and the ensuing Eucharistic adoration is the unique presence of Christ "under the sacramental species of bread and wine."

11. Pope John Paul II, Encyclical Letter *Ecclesia de Eucharistia,* §25.
12. *Ecclesia de Eucharistia,* §11.
13. *Ecclesia de Eucharistia,* §15, citing Pope Paul VI's *Solemn Profession of Faith* from June 30, 1968.

An Instance of the Contemporary Practice of the Exposition of the Blessed Sacrament

In order to get a better sense of what is entailed in this practice, let us turn to one particular contemporary instantiation of it. Very soon after his installation in the Catholic Diocese of Raleigh, North Carolina, Bishop Michael F. Burbidge instituted a "First Friday Vocations Holy Hour" in Sacred Heart Cathedral in Raleigh. Since I have regularly taken part in this Holy Hour I shall offer a brief description of this particular instantiation of the liturgical practice of the exposition and adoration of the Blessed Sacrament. The structure of the liturgical rite is simple and straightforward: exposition, liturgy of the word, Litany of the Holy Eucharist and Lord's Prayer, benediction, and reposition.

After the entrance procession into the cathedral nave of the bishop and the clergy, the exposition of the Blessed Sacrament takes place. In a solemn act of transferal, the bishop, wearing cope[14] and humeral veil,[15] carries the Blessed Sacrament, also covered by the humeral veil, from the tabernacle to the altar and places it in the monstrance[16] on the altar while the congregation kneels. Then the bishop kneels before the altar. After incense[17] has been placed in the thurible,[18] the bishop incenses the Blessed Sacrament while the congregation sings two stanzas of the hymn "*Verbum Supernum Prodiens*" ("The Word from Heaven Now Proceeding"),[19] a hymn composed by Thomas for the office of the feast of

---

14. A cope is an ornate, cloak-like vestment that clergy wear over a white alb and a stole at Benediction and processions.

15. A humeral veil is a scarf-like liturgical garment about eight or nine feet long and two or three feet wide. It is worn over the shoulders. The presiding minister covers his hands with the ends of the veil so that it, not his hands, touches the monstrance at Benediction or during procession of the Blessed Sacrament.

16. A monstrance is a sacred vessel used for the exposition and adoration of the Blessed Sacrament.

17. Incense is granulated or powdered aromatic resin that, when sprinkled on glowing coals in a thurible (censer), becomes a fragrant cloud of smoke that symbolizes prayer rising to God.

18. See footnote 17.

19. The two stanzas sung are:

> O salutaris Hostia
> Quae coeli pandis ostium.
> Bella premunt hostilia;
> Da robur, fer auxilium.

Corpus Christi.[20] A period of silent prayer concludes the opening part of the liturgy of exposition.

A communal prayer opens the subsequent liturgy of the word, which includes a first reading from Scripture, the recitation of the responsorial psalm, and a period of silent prayer and meditation with subsequent Gospel acclamation, Gospel reading, and a homily. An extended period of silent prayer and meditation is concluded by communal intercessions that complete the liturgy of the Word.

The following major part of the rite is called the Litany of the Holy Eucharist. It comprises a litany in which Christ is addressed with many attributes that name central aspects of his life, death, and resurrection, and in which he is beseeched with the words "Lord, have mercy," "Christ, hear us," and "Christ, graciously hear us." The litany is concluded with the following prayer:

> Most merciful Father,
> You continue to draw us to Yourself
> Through the Eucharistic Mystery.
> Grant us fervent faith in this Sacrament of love,
> in which Christ the Lord Himself is contained, offered, and received.
> We make this prayer through the same Christ our Lord.

Uni trinoque Domino
Sit sempiterna gloria:
Qui vitam sine termino,
Nobis donet in patria.

O sacrifice for our salvation,
Heavenly Gates You open wide.
Our enemies press hard around us.
Give us strength; our help provide.

To the One and Triune God,
Be glory and eternal praise.
May He grant us life forever
And to our home our souls upraise.

The English translation here provided is taken from *The Aquinas Prayer Book: The Prayers and Hymns of St. Thomas Aquinas*, trans. and ed. Robert Anderson and Johann Moser (Manchester, NH: Sophia Institute Press, 2000), p. 99.

20. See "Officium de festo Corporis Christi ad mandatum Urbani Papae IV dictum Festum instituentis," in Thomas Aquinas, *Opuscula Theologica*, vol. 2 (Rome: Marietti, 1954), pp. 275-281; p. 279.

Then the Lord's Prayer follows. At its conclusion the bishop approaches the altar, genuflects, and then kneels while the congregation also kneels. As the bishop kneels, the congregation sings two stanzas of the hymn *"Pangue, Lingua, Gloriosi"* ("Acclaim, My Tongue, This Mystery")[21] (also composed by Thomas for the office of the feast of Corpus Christi),[22] and the bishop incenses the Blessed Sacrament. After the hymn the bishop rises and offers the following prayer:

> Lord Jesus Christ, you gave us the Eucharist as the memorial of your suffering and death. May our worship of this sacrament of your body and blood help us to experience the salvation you won for us and the peace of the kingdom where you live with the Father and the Holy Spirit, one God, for ever and ever. Amen.

21. The two stanzas are:

> Tantum ergo Sacramentum
> Veneremur cernui:
> Et antiquum documentum
> Novo cedat ritui:
> Praestet fides supplementum
> Sensuum defectui.

> Genitori, Genitoque
> Laus et iubilatio,
> Salus, honor, virtus quoque
> Sit et benedictio:
> Procedenti ab utroque
> Compar sit laudatio.

> So great a sacrament, therefore,
> Let us revere while kneeling down.
> Let old laws yield
> To this new rite.
> Let faith, not sense,
> Conviction ground.

> Praise and jubilation to the Father;
> Honor, virtue, blessing to the Son;
> And to the One
> Who proceeds from both
> In equal measure may praise be sung.

(The English translation here provided is taken from *The Aquinas Prayer Book*, p. 91.)
22. Thomas Aquinas, "Officium de festo Corporis Christi," pp. 275f.

After the prayer the benediction takes place. The bishop puts on the humeral veil, genuflects, covers his hands with the ends of the veil so that, once again, the veil, not his hands, touches the monstrance, then takes it and makes the sign of the cross with the monstrance over the congregation, in silence.

After the benediction the reposition of the Blessed Sacrament takes place. The bishop returns to the front of the altar, kneels, and leads the assembly in the Divine Praises[23] after which he removes the Blessed Sacrament from the monstrance, covers it with the humeral veil, and by way of a solemn transferal from the altar reposits the sacrament in the tabernacle. The bishop and the clergy bow to the altar and leave the cathedral while the congregation sings the hymn "Holy God, We Praise Thy Name."[24]

23. The Divine Praises are as follows:

> Blessed be God.
> Blessed be His Holy Name.
> Blessed be Jesus Christ, true God and true man.
> Blessed be the name of Jesus.
> Blessed be His Most Sacred Heart.
> Blessed be His Most Precious Blood.
> Blessed be Jesus in the Most Holy Sacrament of the Altar.
> Blessed be the Holy Spirit, the Paraclete.
> Blessed be the great Mother of God, Mary most holy.
> Blessed be her holy and Immaculate Conception.
> Blessed be her glorious Assumption.
> Blessed be the name of Mary, Virgin and Mother.
> Blessed be Saint Joseph, her most chaste spouse.
> Blessed be God in His angels and in His Saints.

24. This somewhat detailed description of one particular liturgical instantiation of Eucharistic adoration seems to be warranted in light of the fact that even in this ecumenical day and age most non-Catholic Christians are in grave danger of misunderstanding or misconstruing this liturgical practice. John Henry Newman made famous an egregious case of misconstrual in mid-nineteenth-century Birmingham, England. In his rightly acclaimed *Lectures on the Present Position of Catholics in England Addressed to the Brothers of the Oratory in the Summer of 1851,* he has made immemorial in the sixth lecture the observations that a "young Protestant Scripture Reader" gathered from attending a single time the liturgy of Eucharistic benediction at the Oratory chapel in Birmingham. Instead of citing the outlandish misconstrual itself — quite worthwhile to read — I will offer Newman's own brief description of the benediction of the Blessed Sacrament. For his account bears eloquent witness to the organic continuity between one particular form of the liturgical practice of Eucharistic adoration in the 1850s at the Oratory chapel in Birmingham and another, though more elaborate, instantiation of this liturgical practice at the Cathedral of Raleigh,

In the course of participating in this particular liturgical rite of Eucharistic Adoration for more than a year, I must admit it has become second-nature and is, next to the Eucharistic liturgy itself, undoubtedly the most important communal liturgical practice I am involved in. Over time, it has taught me to appreciate more deeply the Eucharist itself, and in and through it the unfathomable personal presence of Christ in his Eucharistic self-giving by way of his body and blood. Furthermore, the regular participation in this rite of Eucharistic adoration has tangibly increased my desire for sacramental communion and encouraged an ever deeper contemplation of the salvation wrought by Christ's sacrifice on the cross. Also, having been drawn ever deeper into the intentionality of this liturgical practice, I increasingly realized that it was I who was being refocused while the liturgy unfolded. Why? Because the intentionality inscribed into the liturgical practice is its utter transparency to Christ's real, substantial, and hence personal presence.

NC, in the years 2006/07: "I need hardly observe to you, my Brothers, that the Benediction of the Blessed Sacrament is one of the simplest rites of the Church. The priests enter and kneel down; one of them unlocks the Tabernacle, takes out the Blessed Sacrament, inserts it upright in a Monstrance of precious metal, and sets it in a conspicuous place above the altar, in the midst of lights, for all to see. The people then begin to sing; meanwhile the Priest twice offers incense to the King of heaven, before whom he is kneeling. Then he takes the Monstrance in his hands, and turning to the people, blesses them with the Most Holy, in the form of a cross, while the bell is sounded by one of the attendants to call attention to the ceremony. It is our Lord's solemn benediction of His people, as when He lifted up His hands over the children, or when He blessed His chosen ones when He ascended up from Mount Olivet. As sons might come before a parent before going to bed at night, so, once or twice a week the great Catholic family comes before the Eternal Father, after the bustle or toil of the day, and He smiles upon them, and sheds upon them the light of His countenance. It is a full accomplishment of what the Priest invoked upon the Israelites, 'The Lord bless thee and keep thee; the Lord show His face to thee and have mercy on thee; the Lord turn his countenance to thee and give thee peace.' Can there be a more touching rite, even in the judgment of those who do not believe in it? How many a man, not a Catholic, is moved on seeing it, to say 'Oh, that I did but believe it!' when he sees the Priest take up the Fount of Mercy, and the people bent low in adoration! It is one of the most beautiful, natural, and soothing actions of the Church — not so, however, in the judgment of our young Protestant Scripture Reader, to whom I now return." John Henry Newman, *Lectures on the Present Position of Catholics in England*, ed. Daniel M. O'Connell, S.J. (New York: The America Press, 1942), pp. 195f. If the cryptic reference to the "young Protestant Scripture Reader" does indeed arouse the reader's desire to know what he thought was going on, I can only say: "*Tolle, lege!* Pick it up and read it!" The reader will encounter a rather bizarre instance of anti-Catholic prejudice, not altogether untypical for nineteenth-century England and, I fear, not completely beyond the range of possibilities even in this ecumenical era.

Three Kinds of Divine Presence: By Way of the Divine Essence, by Way of the Mission of the Holy Spirit, and by Way of Christ's Substantial Personal Presence, Body, Soul, and Divinity

The nature of Christ's real, substantial, and personal presence presupposed in the adoration of the Blessed Sacrament can be distinguished from two other kinds of presence of Christ, two kinds of presence that indeed are both implicitly entailed in the practice of Eucharistic adoration. However, neither one of these two kinds of presence is definitive of the adoration of the reserved sacrament — though skeptics of and opponents to this kind of liturgical practice would accept at most only these two kinds of presence to obtain in it. However, the liturgical rite of the solemn exposition of the Holy Eucharist has inscribed in the very structure of its intentionality,[25] its constitutive liturgical gestures and words of adoration — especially the genuflecting, the kneeling, and the particular set of liturgical actions around the solemn exposition and reposition of the Blessed Sacrament, the prayers, and hymns — a quite unique kind of Christ's presence (one that is specifically different from the other two kinds of presence).

There is, first, the general presence of the triune God in all creatures by way of the one divine essence.[26] This kind of presence can in principle,

---

25. While the intentionality of the rite is embedded in its structure, that is, in the words of the prayers and litanies, as well as in all the gestures and liturgical actions from the side of the presiding minister and the congregation, for this intentionality to be properly effective, it depends upon the intentional submission to it by each participant in this liturgy. That is, as — and to the degree to which — the participants, by way of the act of faith, intentionally conform themselves to the liturgical rite, does the structural intentionality embedded in the rite come into effect. In short, representing the intentionality of the rite in the context of a classroom demonstration in a seminary course on liturgy or in the context of a movie or theater play does not bring per se the structural intentionality embedded in the rite into effect.

26. For a classical formulation and defense of this kind of presence of the Creator in the creature, see Thomas Aquinas, *Summa theologiae* I, q. 8, a. 1: "God is in all things; not indeed, as part of their essence, nor as an accident; but as an agent is present to that upon which it works. For an agent must be joined to that wherein it acts immediately, and touch it by its power; hence it is proved in *Physic.* vii that the thing moved and the mover must be joined together. Now since God is very being by His own essence, created being must be His proper effect; as to ignite is the proper effect of fire. Now God causes this effect in things not only when they first begin to be, but as long as they are preserved in being. . . . Therefore as long as a thing has being, God must be present to it, according to its mode of being. But being is innermost in each thing and most fundamentally inherent in all things since it is formal in respect of everything found in a thing. . . . Hence it must be that God is in all things, and innermostly."

however rarely de facto, be recognized by way of a sustained act of metaphysical contemplation, that is, without an explicit act of faith.[27] There is, second, the presence of Christ where two or three are gathered in his name, a presence arguably mediated by the mission of the Holy Spirit, who proceeds from the Father and the Son. This kind of presence is recognized by way of an explicit act of faith, that is, the intellect's assent, prompted through grace by the will, to embrace Christ's promise to be thus present. And, of course, the liturgical practice of the adoration of the Blessed Sacrament includes both of these kinds of presence. For it involves obviously the being and activity of creatures, and it is at the same time quite obviously a gathering of the faithful in Christ's name. However, while undoubtedly essential to this liturgical practice, neither kind of presence is the characteristic and defining feature of Eucharistic Adoration. Rather, the structural intentionality embedded in the specifics of the liturgical actions, prayers, and hymns "overshoots." How so? It is the solemn exposition and reposition of the Blessed Sacrament that makes it abundantly clear that the kind of divine presence giving rise to the liturgical intentionality inscribed in the matrix of the communal practice is essentially connected to the sacramental host. For the intentionality of the liturgical practice in all its components is solely focused by the Blessed Sacrament itself. I shall briefly elaborate this claim. The liturgical gestures, actions, prayers, and hymns indicate two things:

One, divine worship ("before whom every knee shall bend") of the unique personal presence of Christ is essentially connected to his Eucharistic self-gift, a presence that is not limited to or by the liturgy of Eucharistic adoration itself, but antecedes it and continues after its completion (entailed in the sacrament's exposition and reposition). Pope Benedict XVI puts the matter succinctly in *Sacramentum Caritatis:* "In the Eucharist, the Son of God comes to meet us and desires to become one with us; eucharistic adoration is simply the natural consequence of the eucharistic celebration, which is itself the Church's supreme act of adoration. . . . The act of adoration outside Mass prolongs and intensifies all that takes place during the liturgical celebration itself."[28]

Two, the Blessed Sacrament is, indeed, utterly central in this act of worship. For the Blessed Sacrament provides the proximate focus of the li-

27. For a defense of such a possibility and the severe limitations of its de facto realization, see the discussion in chapter 2 above.

28. Pope Benedict XVI, *Sacramentum Caritatis,* §66.

turgical practice. However, "focus" may not be understood along the lines our intellectual gaze usually operates.[29] For the liturgical rite does not engender a focused intellectual gaze upon the Eucharistic host as a distinct, integral "object" or "thing" that arrests the intellectual gaze, as any other small, distinctly discernible sensible object at mid-range distance might do. For such an arresting of the intellectual gaze, the Eucharistic host, as we will see later, lacks the necessary substance. Rather, precisely as "the natural consequence of the eucharistic celebration,"[30] the liturgical practice by way of faith alone produces a transportation of the intellectual gaze beyond the range of what is perceptible to the senses to Christ's substantive personal presence in his Eucharistic self-gift. The proximate focus of what is accessible to the senses, then, by holding the senses in suspense, directs the intellectual gaze to the substance of the sacrament, that is, the undiminished personal identity of Christ, body, soul, and divinity. However, the very substance of Christ, body, soul, and divinity, does not allow the intellectual gaze to arrest at some distinct point "behind" what is perceptible to the senses, but rather, the intellectual gaze is aided by the assent of faith. This then continues to draw the intellectual gaze further and further into the luminous night of an ineffable and surpassing substantial presence that the intellect, in virtue of the assent of faith, can darkly apprehend but never fully comprehend.

What kind of philosophical hermeneutics is able to make explicit the characteristic feature of this particular kind of divine presence that is definitive of Eucharistic adoration? Eucharistic adoration seems to call for a philosophical interpretation that is able to conceive of the particular kind of presence that is definitive of this liturgical practice as one essentially independent of the liturgical rite of adoration itself; that is, a kind of presence that antecedes and hence gives rise to the liturgical practice and also continues after its conclusion. Moreover, Eucharistic adoration seems to require also a philosophical interpretation that is capable of making explicit the genuine sign-character of the Blessed Sacrament, as well as the abiding personal somatic presence of Christ integral to the sacrament in such a way that even the slightest intimation of idolatry is absolutely avoided. That is, what *is* worshipped in the liturgical practice of Eucha-

29. For an astute phenomenological analysis of the intellectual gaze, for which I have great sympathy and from which I have learned considerably, see Jean-Luc Marion, *God Without Being,* trans. Thomas A. Carlson (Chicago/London: University of Chicago Press, 1991).

30. *Sacramentum Caritatis,* §66.

ristic adoration must needs be *essentially* divine, and the intention of the worshippers must needs be focused by and drawn into the abyss of Christ's abiding *personal* presence itself — body, soul, and divinity — and not be arrested by the visible features of the material object. Hence, the intellect of the worshippers must somehow behold, not what is materially constitutive of the creaturely sign, but — precisely by way of the sign — the very substance of the One who is worshipped in the liturgical practice. I would like to submit that Thomas's metaphysical way of making Christ's Eucharistic presence explicit fulfills all of these requirements.[31]

Thomas Aquinas: Metaphysical Contemplation in Service of Making Intellectually Explicit a Mystery of Faith[32]

For Thomas, sacramental conversion in the Eucharist is a mystery of faith in the strict sense. That is, it depends completely on divine revelation as unfolded by way of *sacra doctrina*. And *sacra doctrina,* according to Thomas, is constituted by nothing else than the simplicity of faith that rests on divine authority and embraces the truth as proposed in *sacra pagina,* Scripture. This fundamental understanding of revealed truth being essentially a participation in the *scientia Dei et beatorum* finds a terse expression in *Summa theologiae* III, q. 75, a. 1, the opening article of the question on sacramental conversion:

> The presence of Christ's true body and blood in this sacrament cannot be detected by sense, nor understanding, but by faith alone [*sola fide*], which rests upon Divine authority. Hence, on Luke xxii, 19: *This is My body, which shall be delivered up for you,* Cyril says: *Doubt not whether this be true; but take rather the Saviour's words with faith; for since He is the Truth, He lieth not.*[33]

31. I regard Jean-Luc Marion's profound and stimulating reflections on the Eucharist and on Eucharistic adoration in the *Hors-texte* of his *God Without Being* (pp. 161-97) as compatible with my re-reading of Thomas and the Thomist tradition. The issues of difference pertain to matters of dispute between a phenomenological approach indebted to Husserl's idealist turn and an approach indebted to what some have termed the "philosophia perennis."

32. This section draws upon arguments and analyses that I originally published in "Transubstantiation Revisited: *Sacra Doctrina,* Dogma, and Metaphysics," in *Ressourcement Thomism: Sacred Doctrine, the Sacraments, and the Moral Life,* ed. Reinhard Hütter and Matthew Levering (Washington, DC: The Catholic University of America Press, 2010), pp. 21-79.

33. *ST* III, q. 75, a. 1: "[V]erum corpus Christi et sanguinem esse in hoc sacramento,

It is deceptively simple but profoundly significant what Thomas is doing here: first, he is alluding to Christ's words of consecration according to the Gospel of Luke.[34] The dominical words themselves, taken in the *sensus literalis,* constitute the initial point of departure.[35] Second, this point of departure is itself received, since it represents the Church's own understanding of the *sensus literalis.* In order to make this crucial point plain, Thomas cites St. Cyril of Alexandria, who enjoins the readers of his own commentary on the Gospel of Luke to take Christ simply at his word, because he is the truth: "Doubt not whether this be true; but take rather the Saviour's words with faith; for since He is the Truth, He lieth not."[36] That is, Thomas lets the one authority among the Fathers who is most intimately associated with the dogma of Chalcedon make the fundamental point about Who is speaking about Himself. Third, we can observe here how Thomas displays what he calls the subalternate character of *sacra doctrina* as *scientia* in *ST* I, q. 1, a. 2:

> [S]acred doctrine is a science, because it proceeds from principles established by the light of a higher science, namely, the science of God and the blessed [*scientia Dei et beatorum*]. Hence, just as the musician accepts on authority [*tradita*] the principles taught him by the mathematician, so sacred science is established on principles revealed by God.[37]

---

non sensu deprehendi potest, sed sola fide, quae auctoritati divinae innititur. Unde super illud *Luc.* 22, [19], *Hoc est corpus meum quod pro vobis tradetur,* dicit Cyrillus: *Non dubites an hoc verum sit, sed potius suscipe verba Salvatoris in fide: cum enim sit veritas, non mentitur."*

34. "And he took bread, and when he had given thanks he broke it and gave it to them, saying, 'This is my body which is given for you. Do this in remembrance of me.' And likewise the cup after supper, saying, 'This cup which is poured out for you is the new covenant in my blood'" (Lk 22:19-20 RSV).

35. Thomas's point here is far from unreflectively naïve, as in some regrettably "premodern" sense which we see ourselves forced to transcend toward some higher, critical perspective. Rather, the Church's understanding, that is, *traditio* itself, reads this text as *Deus ipse loquitur.* Hence, when modern historical-critical exegetes are intent upon reconstructing the words of consecration as early post-Easter tradition and not as the words of the "historical" Jesus himself, their work is to be gratefully received into a deeper theological understanding of the very apostolic *paradosis* whence arose the New Testament. For this is precisely what *traditio* is all about: the reception of God's Word in the Church that is Christ's body.

36. *Patrologia Graeca,* vol. 72, p. 92.

37. ST I, q. 1, a. 2: "Et hoc modo sacra doctrina est scientia: quia procedit ex principiis notis lumine superioris scientiae, quae scilicet est scientia Dei et beatorum. Unde sicut musica credit principia tradita sibi ab arithmetico, ita doctrina sacra credit principia revelata sibi a Deo."

Consequently, in our instance, the first move of *sacra doctrina* as the subalternate *scientia* of us wayfarers short of the beatific vision is, by way of the Church's understanding — *traditio* — the reception of a truth (that is, of a communication of the *scientia Dei et beatorum*) that is not to be interpreted in light of some other more authoritative, profound, or illuminating text of Scripture itself. Rather, Christ Himself speaks, *Christus ipse locutus est.* While God, being Scripture's ultimate author,[38] surely speaks by way of and through all of Scripture, so the dominical words are exceptional, since they directly appeal to the immediate assent of faith. Remember that Thomas understands faith as adhering to the First Truth. In ST II-II, q. 5, a. 3, ad 2 he states:

> [F]aith adheres to all the articles of faith by reason of one mean, viz.,
> on account of the First Truth proposed to us in the Scriptures, according to the teaching of the Church who has the right understanding of
> them.[39]

According to the Church's right understanding of the first truth, that is, according to the *doctrina Ecclesiae,* in Luke 22:19 "the First Truth proposed to us in the Scriptures" speaks Himself, and St. Cyril's theological judgment (together with St. Hilary's and St. Ambrose's teaching as adduced in the *sed contra*) represents for Thomas paradigmatically "the teaching of the Church that has the right understanding of [the Scriptures]."

Hence, in the third part of the *Summa theologiae,* in the opening article on the question of the conversion of bread and wine into the body and blood of Christ, Thomas asserts up front that *sacra doctrina* is first and foremost the *act*[40] of faith adhering to the First Truth in the concrete instance of its self-communication as apostolically mediated and interpreted by the *doctrina Ecclesiae.* It is this divinely revealed, and doctrinally received and mediated *principium* that forms the indispensable starting point for the subsequent metaphysical contemplation. Hence, the truth of faith is emphatically *not* established by the ensuing metaphysical contem-

---

38. *ST* I, q. 1, a. 10: "[A]uctor sacrae Scripturae est Deus."

39. *ST* II-II, q. 5, a. 3, ad 2: "[O]mnibus articulis fidei inhaeret fides propter unum medium, scilicet propter veritatem primam propositam nobis in Scripturis secundum doctrinam Ecclesiae intellectis sane."

40. For *doctrina* not as a "thing" but an act, see Frederick Christian Bauerschmidt, "That the Faithful Become the Temple of God," in *Reading John with St. Thomas Aquinas,* ed. Michael Dauphinais and Matthew Levering (Washington, DC: The Catholic University of America Press, 2005), pp. 293-311.

plation; rather, having been established by the First Truth Himself as taught by the *doctrina Ecclesiae,* metaphysical contemplation *solely* makes explicit the mystery of faith. For Thomas and the Thomist tradition, the truth of faith does not depend on a successful metaphysical defense or even proof; rather the revealed truth itself elicits the metaphysical contemplation which makes explicit the truth's inherent intelligibility as a mystery of faith and contributes to a more comprehensive and penetrating intellectual reception of it.

Making Explicit: Metaphysical Contemplation

An elucidation of the metaphysical contemplation in Thomas is in order here. Referring to Thomas's commentary on the Neoplatonic *Liber de Causis,* Ralph McInerny identifies three "disarming assumptions" that capture Thomas's understanding of philosophy in a nutshell. They are:

> (1) that all philosophers are in principle engaged in the same enterprise; (2) that truths he has learned from Aristotle are simply truths, not "Aristotelian tenets"; and (3) consequently that such truths as one finds in Neoplatonism or anywhere else must be compatible with truths already known. This is the basis for saying that Thomism is not a *kind* of philosophy.[41]

Hence, it would be profoundly wrong, although not at all uncommon, to assume that Thomas submits a "theory" of the Eucharistic conversion. Rather, always proceeding conceptually from what is easier to what is more difficult to understand, Thomas analogically extends the "natural hearing," the inquiry into material being and subsequently into immaterial being as undertaken in Aristotle's *Physics* and extended in his *Metaphysics,* in order to guide the metaphysical contemplation into what remains irreducibly a mystery of faith, the *intellectus,* however, inevitably having to take departure, by analogical extension, from the world we know.[42]

---

41. Ralph McInerny, *Praeambula Fidei: Thomism and the God of the Philosophers* (Washington, DC: The Catholic University of America Press, 2006), p. 175, n. 6.

42. In its document "On the Interpretation of Dogmas," the International Theological Commission reminds us unequivocally that this very procedure is indeed of an enduring importance for the interpretation of the mysteries of faith: "It was already the First Vatican Council which taught that a deeper insight into the mysteries of faith may be possible in

Consequently, in the present intellectual context one can never recall often enough that — as John Wippel aptly put it — Thomas holds first and foremost in his theory of knowledge that "the order of thought is based upon the order of reality and reflects it. Because words in turn reflect thoughts, by attending to distinctive modes of predication we may ultimately discern different modes of being."[43] Differently put, "supreme and diverse modes of predication (as expressed in the predicaments) . . . follow from and depend upon supreme and diverse modes of being."[44] Hence, according to Thomas, we discover these supreme modes of being precisely by attending to the diverse modes of predication.[45]

The classical locus where Thomas exposits on this fundamental insight of Aristotle is in his commentary on Book III of Aristotle's *Physics*, in lecture 5 (§322):

> [Being] is divided according to the diverse modes of existing. But modes of existing are proportional to the modes of predicating. For when we predicate something of another, we say this is that. Hence the ten genera of being are called the ten predicaments. Now every predication is made in one of three ways. One way is when that which pertains to the essence is predicated of some subject, as when I say Socrates is a man, or man is animal. The predication of substance is taken in this way.[46]

---

considering them by way of analogy with natural knowledge and relating them to the ultimate goal of human beings (DS 3016)." *Origins* 20/1 (17 May 1990): 13.

43. John Wippel, *The Metaphysical Thought of Thomas Aquinas: From Finite Being to Uncreated Being* (Washington, DC: The Catholic University of America Press, 2000), p. 216.

44. Wippel, *Metaphysical Thought*, p. 211.

45. "The mode or way in which words signify does not immediately follow upon the mode of being of such things, but only as mediated by the way in which such things are understood. To put this another way, words are likenesses or signs of thoughts, and thoughts themselves are likenesses of things, as Thomas recalls from Bk I of Aristotle's *De interpretatione*" (Wippel, *Metaphysical Thought*, p. 211). That is, "Thomas follows Aristotle in singling out being as it exists outside the mind and is divided into the ten predicaments. . . . Therefore, . . . in whatever ways being is predicated, in so many ways is *esse* signified, that is, in so many ways is something signified to be" (Wippel, *Metaphysical Thought*, p. 212). For an excellent analysis of this complex matter, see also John P. O'Callaghan, *Thomist Realism and the Linguistic Turn: Toward a More Perfect Form of Existence* (Notre Dame, IN: University of Notre Dame Press, 2003).

46. Thomas Aquinas, *Commentary on Aristotle's Physics*, trans. Richard J. Blackwell, Richard J. Spath, and W. Edmund Thirlkel (Notre Dame, IN: Dumb Ox Books, 1999), p. 160 (§322). "Ad horum igitur evidentiam sciendum est quod ens dividitur in decem praedica-

The predicament "substance" connotes what subsists in itself. Differently put, of any existing thing, substance connotes nothing apart from the thing, but the thing itself. Every finite substance has need of further perfections, called accidents, which are connoted by the remaining nine predicaments of Aristotle's list. That is, substance and accident must be treated in mutual relation, since accident is a principle that complements substance and together with it, through their common existence, constitutes the individually existing thing. In short, substance is not a separable thing by itself, but a metaphysical co-principle in composition with all its attributes. Hence, substance cannot be without at least *some* accidents.

If we were to consider substance in general, this would suffice. But in Eucharistic conversion we deal with the conversion of *material* substances.[47] And because of this, we need to attend to the one accident necessarily proper to any material substance: *quantity.* Quantity is a determination of being which gives extension to a material substance, hence "dimensive" quantity. Without quantity, a material substance would have no distinguishable parts, no parts outside of parts *"partes extra partes."* Everything would "flow into each other" in the sense that there would be no spacial relationship anymore between the parts.[48] While quantity gives to material substance its dimensions, its intrinsic measure by way of the order of parts, the parts themselves are constituted and sustained by the substance itself.[49] The latter circumstance reminds us that, indeed, quantity

menta non univoce, sicut genus in species, sed secundum diversum modum essendi. Modi autem essendi proportionales sunt modis praedicandi. Praedicando enim aliquid de aliquo altero, dicimus hoc esse illud: unde et decem genera entis dicuntur decem praedicamenta. Tripliciter autem fit omnis praedicatio. Unus quidem modus est, quando de aliquo subiecto praedicatur id quod pertinet ad essentiam eius, ut cum dico *Socrates est homo,* vel *homo est animal;* et secundum hoc accipitur praedicamentum *substantiae"* (*In III Phys., lectio* 5 [§322]).

47. Immersing myself seriously in the arresting details of Thomas's demanding metaphysical contemplation of the Eucharistic conversion as a trans-substantiation in the strict metaphysical sense would go far beyond the scope of this chapter. For a penetrating analysis of the metaphysical details of transubstantiation as well as a superb defense of Thomas's position on this matter, one I completely concur with, see Stephen Brock, "St. Thomas and the Eucharistic Conversion," *The Thomist* 65, no. 4 (2001): 529-65.

48. Leo J. Elders, S.V.D., *Die Naturphilosophie des Thomas von Aquin* (Weilheim-Bierbronnen: Gustav-Siewerth-Akademie, 2004), p. 75. He is drawing his image from John of St. Thomas, *Cursus Philosophicus* I, *Log.,* p. II, q. XVI, art. 1 (Paris: Vivès, 1883), p. 466: "In sententia S. Thomae propria et formalis ratio quantitatis est extensio partium in ordine ad totum, quod est reddere partes formaliter integrantes. Unde remota quantitate, substantia non habet partes integrales formaliter in ratione partis ordinatas et distinctas."

49. John of St. Thomas, *Cursus Philosophicus* I, *Log.,* p. II, q. XVI, art. 1, p. 464: "[Q]uan-

modifies the being of substance by giving it the extension of space and hence relates intrinsically to the substance. Consequently, quantity is not something apposed into the closest proximity to substance. Rather, quantity is *of* the substance as the first of the other accidents that inhere by way of quantity in the substance. We can begin to see now the central role the predicamentals substance and quantity play in Thomas's metaphysical elucidation of the theological truth that indeed nothing less than the whole Christ is contained under this sacrament.

However, might Thomas's concentration on the predicamentals substance and quantity in the elucidation of the Eucharistic mystery not be ever so subtly reductive in that such a concentration ultimately distracts from the fact that Christ's sacramental presence is a fundamentally personal presence? Might not the focus on "substance" and "quantity" give rise to a Eucharistic "essentialism" that obscures the fact that Christ's presence is irreducibly personal?

In order to address this question we must realize first of all that the terminus of the Eucharistic conversion is the substance of Christ's body in its respective present state. At the Last Supper, Christ was present to the twelve apostles in his natural mode as the incarnate Son of the Father instituting the Eucharist and thereby marking the very beginning of "his hour," his self-oblation to the Father on the Cross for the sake of "the many." His substantial, corporeal presence in the sacrament was that of his natural body in its concrete state at the beginning of his passion. At each subsequent celebration of the Eucharist after Christ's resurrection and ascension, Christ's sacramental presence is that of his glorified bodily existence in heaven. Christ's body and blood are accompanied (*concomitari*) by all that is really associated with them in his everlasting glorified state: in virtue of Christ's human nature, his human soul, and in virtue of the hypostatic union, the divinity of the Logos. Through real concomitance, due to the integral subsistence of the risen Christ in heaven, nothing less than the whole person of Christ is in the Blessed Sacrament. Because Thomas is absolutely unequivocal on this matter, it is worth citing him at length on this crucial point:

> It is absolutely necessary to confess according to Catholic faith that the entire Christ is in this sacrament. Yet we must know that there is some-

thing of Christ in this sacrament in a twofold manner: first, as it were, by the power of the sacrament; secondly, from natural concomitance. By the power of the sacrament, there is under the species of this sacrament that into which the pre-existing substance of the bread and wine is changed, as expressed by the words of the form, which are effective in this as in the other sacraments; for instance, by the words — *This is My body,* or *This is My blood.* But from natural concomitance there is also in this sacrament that which is really united with that thing wherein the aforesaid conversion is terminated. For if any two things be really united, then wherever the one is really, there must the other also be: since things really united together are only distinguished by an operation of the mind.[50]

Since body, blood, soul, and divinity of Christ are really united and only distinguished from each other by an operation of the human mind, it would be theologically misguided from the very outset to drive a wedge — and thus create a false dichotomy — between the *substantial* and the *personal* presence of Christ in the sacrament. The presence in the sacrament of the substance of Christ's body and the substance of Christ's blood entails by way of real concomitance the real substantial presence of Christ's undiminished humanity, body and soul; and the real presence of the undiminished substance of Christ's humanity, in virtue of the hypostatic union with the Divine Word, entails the personal presence of the Logos; and the latter, by way of a mediated concomitance, indeed entails, due to the circumincession of Father, Son, and Spirit, also the personal presence of the Father and the Spirit.[51] Hence, all that is intrinsic to Christ's

50. *ST* III, q. 76, a. 1: "[O]mnino necesse est confiteri secundum fidem Catholicam quod totus Christus sit in hoc sacramento. Sciendum tamen quod aliquid Christi est in hoc sacramento dupliciter: uno modo, quasi ex vi sacramenti; alio modo, ex naturali concomitantia. Ex vi quidem sacramenti, est sub speciebus huius sacramenti id in quod directe convertitur substantia panis et vini praeexistens, prout significatur per verba formae, quae sunt effectiva in hoc sacramento sicut et in ceteris: puta cum dicitur, *Hoc est corpus meum. Hic est sanguis meus.* Ex naturali autem concomitantia est in hoc sacramento illud quod realiter est coniunctum ei in quod praedicta conversio terminatur. Si enim aliqua duo sunt realiter coniuncta, ubicumque est unum realiter, oportet et aliud esse: sola enim operatione animae discernuntur quae realiter sunt coniuncta."

51. This latter extension of concomitance is, I think, rightly held by Reginald Garrigou-Lagrange, O.P., in his *De Eucharistia accedunt De Paenitentia quaestiones dogmaticae; Commentarius in Summam theologicam S. Thomae* (Rome: Marietti, 1943), p. 148, a position that in principle we can find also in Matthias Joseph Scheeben, *The Mysteries of Christianity,* trans. Cyril Vollert, S.J. (St. Louis, MO: Herder, 1951), pp. 479-82.

personhood in virtue of the incarnation (his undiminished concrete humanity, body and soul) as well as all that is constitutive of his personhood in virtue of the divine Sonship (the subsistent Trinitarian relations) is present in the sacrament.

On the basis of the principle of real concomitance, Thomas holds that the whole Christ is contained under each species of the sacrament; however, in each case differently. Under the species of the wine, by the power of the sacrament, only the substance of Christ's blood is present, and in virtue of real concomitance, his body, soul, and divinity. Under the species of the bread, by the power of the sacrament, only the substance of his body is present, and in virtue of real concomitance his blood, soul, and divinity. Let us be mindful at this point that none of this is, of course, to be misunderstood, and hence all too quickly dismissed, as the allegedly typical way of the "scholastics" carrying matters to the extreme, but rather as a faithful and straightforwardly literal interpretation of Christ's words of consecration at the Last Supper.

The explanatory power of the predicamentals "substance" and "quantity" becomes surpassingly evident when in the third article of question 76 Thomas discusses the way in which it is to be taken that the whole Christ is entirely under every part of the species of bread and wine. Consider the second objection in order to feel the full force of the issue at stake, for this objection presses quite appropriately what the real presence of the concrete physical nature of Christ's body does indeed entail:

> [S]ince Christ's is an organic body, it has parts determinately distant; for a determinate distance of the individual parts from each other is of the very nature of an organic body, as that of eye from eye, and eye from ear. But this could not be so, if Christ were entire under every part of the species; for every part would have to be under every other part, and so where one part would be, there another part would be. It cannot be then that the entire Christ is under every part of the host or of the wine contained in the chalice.[52]

---

52. *ST* III, q. 76, a. 3, obj. 2: "[C]orpus Christi, cum sit organicum, habet partes determinate distantes: est enim de ratione organici corporis determinata distantia singularum partium ad invicem, sicut oculi ab oculo, et oculi ab aure. Sed hoc non posset esse si sub qualibet parte specierum esset totus Christus: operteret enim quod sub qualibet parte esset quaelibet pars; et ita, ubi esset una pars, esset et alia. Non ergo potest esse quod totus Christus sit sub qualibet parte hostiae vel vini contenti in calice."

In his response, Thomas properly extends his use of the principle of real concomitance. By the power of the sacrament, the substance of Christ's body is in the sacrament; by the power of real concomitance, the dimensive quantity of Christ's body is also there — the latter, as we came to understand earlier, indeed being indispensable for the proper constitution of a material substance. "Consequently, Christ's body is in this sacrament *per modum substantiae,* substantively, that is, not after the manner of dimensions, which means, not in the way in which the dimensive quantity of a body is under the dimensive quantity of a place."[53] The explanatory power of the metaphysical principle of substance and its ontological precedence in relation to all the accidents, including dimensive quantity, carries far. Let us consider Thomas's response to the second objection:

> The determinate distance of parts in an organic body is based upon its dimensive quantity; but the nature of substance precedes even dimensive quantity. And since the conversion of the substance of the bread is terminated at the substance of the body of Christ, and since according to the manner of substance the body of Christ is properly and directly in this sacrament; such distance of parts is indeed in Christ's true body, which, however, is not compared to this sacrament according to such distance, but according to the manner of its substance.[54]

In an additional step of deepening his argument, Thomas shows in which way we can understand that indeed the whole dimensive quantity of Christ's body is in the sacrament. We find the crucial axiom he applies already in the *sed contra* of article four of question 76:

> The existence of the dimensive quantity of any body cannot be separated from the existence of its substance. But in this sacrament the en-

53. *ST* III, q. 76, a. 3: "[C]orpus Christi est in hoc sacramento per modum substantiae, idest, per modum quo substantia est sub dimensionibus: non autem per modum dimensionum, idest, non per illum modum quo quantitas dimensiva alicuius corporis est sub quantitate dimensiva loci."

54. *ST* III, q. 76, a. 3, ad 2: "[I]lla determinata distantia partium in corpore organico fundatur super quantitatem dimensivam ipsius; ipsa autem natura substantiae praecedit etiam quantitatem dimensivam. Et quia conversio substantiae panis directe terminatur ad substantiam corporis Christi, secundum cuius modum proprie et directe est in hoc sacramento corpus Christi, talis distantia partium est quidem in ipso corpore Christi vero, sed non secundum hanc distantiam comparatur ad hoc sacramentum, sed secundum modum suae substantiae. . . ."

tire substance of Christ's body is present. . . . Therefore the entire dimensive quantity of Christ's body is in this sacrament.[55]

In his response, Thomas draws upon the by now familiar distinction between what is present by the power of the sacrament and what is present in virtue of real concomitance. *Vi sacramenti,* the conversion is terminated at the substance of Christ's body and clearly not at the dimensions of the body for, after all, the dimensive quantity of the bread clearly remains after the consecration. Applying the axiom of the *sed contra* that the existence of the dimensive quantity of any body cannot be separated from its substance, he then adds the following: "Nevertheless, since the substance of Christ's body is not really deprived of its dimensive quantity and its other accidents, hence it comes that by reason of real concomitance the whole dimensive quantity of Christ's body and all its other accidents are in this sacrament."[56] In the response to the first objection he puts the decisive point even more succinctly:

> Since, then, the substance of Christ's body is present on the altar by the power of this sacrament, while its dimensive quantity is there concomitantly and as it were accidentally, therefore the dimensive quantity of Christ's body is in this sacrament, not according to its proper manner (namely, that the whole is in the whole, and the individual parts in individual parts), but after the manner of substance [*per modum substantiae*], whose nature is for the whole to be in the whole, and the whole to be in every part.[57]

The presence of the dimensive quantity of Christ's body *per modum substantiae* is possible because dimensive quantity relates intrinsically to

55. *ST* III, q. 76, a. 4 sed contra: "[Q]uantitas dimensiva corporis alicuius non separatur secundum esse a substantia eius. Sed in hoc sacramento est tota substantia corporis Christi. . . . Ergo tota quantitas dimensiva corporis Christi est in hoc sacramento."

56. *ST* III, q. 76, a. 4: "Quia tamen substantia corporis Christi realiter non denudatur a sua quantitate dimensiva et ab aliis accidentibus, inde est quod, ex vi realis concomitantiae, est in hoc sacramento tota quantitas dimensiva corporis Christi, et omnia alia accidentia eius."

57. *ST* III, q. 76, a. 4, ad 1: "Quia igitur ex vi sacramenti huius est in altari substantia corporis Christi, quantitas autem dimensiva eius est ibi concomitanter et quasi per accidens, ideo quantitas dimensiva corporis Christi est in hoc sacramento, non secundum proprium modum, ut scilicet sit totum in toto et singulae partes in singulis partibus; sed per modum substantiae, cuius natura est tota in toto et tota in qualibet parte."

substance. Hence, in order to obtain after the manner of substance, dimensive quantity does not require what is the manner of dimensive quantity, namely the relation to a place. In the body of the fifth article of question 76 Thomas gives a somewhat less condensed description of dimensive quantity realized according to its proper manner: "Every body occupying a place is in the place according to the manner of dimensive quantity, namely, inasmuch as it is commensurate with the place according to its dimensive quantity."[58] And it is quite obvious that according to the proper manner of dimensive quantity it is impossible for two dimensive quantities naturally to be in the same subject at the same time. But it is not impossible at all for the dimensive quantity of the bread after the consecration to remain commensurate with the place it occupies while the dimensive quantity of Christ's body is present *per modum substantiae,* after the manner of substance.

Eventually the Thomist school had to unfold Thomas's teaching by developing a more explicit answer to the question how one can metaphysically account for dimensive quantity to subsist solely *per modum substantiae.* Unfolding the tacit entailments of Thomas's teaching became necessary in light of different philosophical conceptualities giving rise to variant theological doctrines that emerged and spread in the centuries subsequent to Thomas's death, conceptualities that in one or another way would identify substance itself with its property of quantitative extension and, in consequence, had strongly to compromise the genuine, whole presence of the dimensive quantity of Christ's body.

The late medieval school of the *via moderna* — largely indebted to the thought of William of Ockham and eventually identified by its opponents simply as the "Nominalists" *(Nominales)* — came to regard material substance to be extended per se and not by way of being informed by the absolute accident of quantity. For Ockham there obtains no real distinction between substance and quantity. Quantity, rather, has a purely nominal status; that is, quantity is a connotative term that stands for substance in its aspect of extension.[59] Consequently, Ockham has to explain how after the consecration, the substance of Christ's body becomes present without being

58. *ST* III, q. 76, a. 5: "Omne autem corpus locatum est in loco secundum modum quantitatis dimensivae, inquantum scilicet commensuratur loco secundum suam quantitatem dimensivam."

59. See Gordon Leff, *William of Ockham: The Metamorphosis of Scholastic Discourse* (Manchester: Manchester University Press; Totowa, NJ: Rowman and Littlefield, 1975), pp. 207-13.

quanta, without parts outside of parts and the consequent natural order of parts *(ordo partium).* This is his solution: Because "quantity" is a notion purely connotative to substance it can be removed without any real change in the underlying subject. And so, while the connotative notion of quantity is removed, Christ's body is nevertheless definitively present under the host and each of its parts. Hence, the natural parts of Christ's body have to inter-penetrate each other and, consequently, the natural order of parts *(ordo partium)* is dissolved. From the point of view of Thomas's teaching, the Ockhamist position fails to maintain the integrity of the dimensive quantity of Christ's body in the sacrament and consequently fails to make explicit the presence of the whole Christ in the sacrament.[60]

While substance was a key notion in René Descartes' swiftly spreading philosophy, the notion underwent a profound transmutation in his doctrine. Inspired by the clarity and certainty of mathematics, Descartes searched for a new philosophy whose foremost criterion was the clarity and distinctness of ideas. Disregarding in a not all together unproblematic way the long tradition of metaphysical inquiry on this matter, he defined substance as a thing that exists in such a way that it needs no other thing for its existence. In light of this criterion he identified two kinds of substance: one intellectual, the other material. Thought constitutes the nature of the intellectual substance, and spacial extension (length, breadth, depth) the nature of corporeal substance.[61] The consequent identification

---

60. For an extensive analysis of the excruciatingly detailed discussion Ockham provides on this matter in his philosophical and theological works, see Erwin Iserloh, *Gnade und Eucharistie in der philosophischen Theologie des Wilhelm von Ockham: Ihre Bedeutung für die Ursachen der Reformation* (Steiner: Wiesbaden, 1956), pp. 174-283, esp. pp. 186-202 for the discussion of the problem in Ockham's commentary on Lombard's *Sentences,* and pp. 202-53 for a discussion of his position in his later *De sacramento altaris.* For a discussion of Ockham's doctrine more sympathetic than Iserloh's highly — and I think rightly — critical commentary, see Gabriel Buescher, O.F.M., *The Eucharistic Teaching of William Ockham* (St. Bonaventure, NY: The Franciscan Institute; Louvain: E. Nauwelaerts, 1950), esp. pp. 65-93.

61. René Descartes, *Principles of Philosophy,* in *The Philosophical Writings of Descartes,* vol. 1, trans. John Cottingham, Robert Stoothoff, Dugald Murdoch (Cambridge: Cambridge University Press, 1985), Bk. 1, sections 48-53. Cf. esp. the following paradigmatic statements: "I recognize only two ultimate classes of things: first, intellectual or thinking things, i.e. those which pertain to mind or thinking substance; and secondly, material things, i.e. those which pertain to extended substance or body" (*Principles of Philosophy,* Bk. 1, section 48, p. 208). "A substance may indeed be known through any attribute at all; but each substance has one principal property which constitutes its nature and essence, and to which all its other properties are referred. Thus extension in length, breadth and depth constitutes the nature of corporeal substance; and thought constitutes the nature of thinking substance" (op. cit., section 53, p. 210).

in reality of substance and quantity does not come as a surprise: "There is no real difference between quantity and the extended substance; the difference is merely a conceptual one, like that between number and the thing which is numbered."[62]

Cartesian theologians, especially in France and Italy, began to apply this deceptively simple, but indeed radically changed notion of substance to the doctrine of Eucharistic conversion.[63] According to Descartes's new understanding of corporeal substance, Christ's substantial presence in the sacrament is conceived the following way: after the consecration, the dimensive quantity of the bread and the wine cannot remain (and with it none of the other accidents of bread and wine), for two corporeal substances cannot, of course, occupy the same space at the same time. According to the Cartesian theologians, what is present after the consecration is nothing but the glorious body of Christ per se. In order to veil the surpassing holiness of Christ's bodily presence and also in order not to deter the faithful from communion, God provides the sensible effects of bread and wine to the sensory organs. According to a different view defended by other Cartesian theologians, it is Christ's body that provides the sensible effects of bread and wine by taking on new surfaces similar to those of

---

62. *Principles of Philosophy*, Bk. 2, section 8, p. 226. In this particular work of Descartes, one can observe without difficulty the shift from a metaphysical consideration of the principles of reality as modes of being to the philosophical analysis of conceptions or ideas that take on the character of mental images. Such a transformation of metaphysical principles of being into univocal mental conceptions guided by the criterion of "ocular clarity" leads unavoidably to the loss of the metaphysical principle of substance itself in relationship to the accidents, and with it to a profound lack of understanding of the nature and function of predicamentals, as well as the real distinction between substance and quantity in a sensible thing. "When they make a distinction between substance and extension or quantity, either they do not understand anything by the term 'substance', or else they simply have a confused idea of the incorporeal substance, which they falsely attach to corporeal substance; and they relegate the true idea of corporeal substance to the category of extension, which, however, they term an accident. There is thus no correspondence between their verbal expression and what they grasp in their minds" (op. cit., Bk. 2, section 9, pp. 226f.).

63. For details of this intricate and theologically not at all unproblematic position, see Jean-Robert Armogathe, *Theologia cartesiana: L'explication physique de l'Eucharistie chez Descartes et dom Desgabets* (The Hague: Nijhoff, 1977); idem, "Cartesian Physics and the Eucharist in the Documents of the Holy Office and the Roman Index (1671-76)," in *Receptions of Descartes: Cartesianism and anti-Cartesianism in Early Modern Europe*, ed. Tad M. Schmaltz (London/New York: Routledge, 2005), pp. 149-70; and Tad M. Schmaltz, *Radical Cartesianism: The French Reception of Descartes* (Cambridge: Cambridge University Press, 2002), esp. pp. 34-74.

bread and wine. Furthermore, the Cartesian theologians hold that in virtue of being a corporeal substance, after the consecration Christ's body has to be locally extended. Consequently, by way of some mode of contraction or condensation it must be reduced to the circumscriptive extension of what has the visual appearance of a host or wine in a chalice.

In light of these alternative positions, one might begin to appreciate in hindsight the profundity of Thomas's teaching that the dimensive quantity of Christ is in the sacrament by way of natural concomitance after the manner of the substance. In view of the considerable metaphysical and theological problems entailed in the Nominalist and the Cartesian positions, the Thomist school engaged in a deeper metaphysical investigation. Very much by way of extrapolating Thomas's metaphysical principles, Thomist theologians inquired how it is possible and what it means for dimensive quantity to be there by way of natural concomitance after the manner of the substance. The resulting metaphysical development of Thomas's teaching comprises three central elements: (1) Because there obtains a real distinction between the principles of substance and quantity, material substance requires quantity as its absolute first accident. (2) Because local extension presupposes some distinction of parts from other parts, it is possible to distinguish between the essence of quantity, which is to have parts that are different from other parts, that is, "outside of other parts," and the specific property of quantity, which is local extension. The Thomist commentators tended to identify the former as the *ratio formalis*, or the *primary formal effect of quantity (ordo partium in toto)*, and the latter as the *secondary formal effect of quantity*, the *ordo partium in loco* or *ubi et situs*. (3) Substance as such is indivisible, and hence a substantial form or a separate substance (angel) has no capacity of local extension. Every material substance, however, has intrinsically — that is, in virtue of being a material substance — parts that are different from and hence outside of other parts, as well as a specific order among the parts, and consequently the capacity to be divided into parts and to be locally extended. While really distinct as a co-constitutive principle, in reality this essence of quantity is inseparable from a material substance. For quantity is the absolute accident of material substance. Hence, the essence of quantity obtains in virtue of its relation to substance alone, that is, it obtains always *per modum substantiae,* after the manner of substance. In its normal, locally extended existence, the manner of dimensive quantity always already presupposes the essence of quantity to obtain *per modum substantiae*, that is, the distinction of parts from other parts and the intrinsic (though not yet locally realized) order between them to obtain after the manner of substance. And hence it is not intrinsically impossible for what is ontologically a distinct (though not independent) principle of the constitution of material substances in virtue of divine first causality to subsist solely after the manner of substance.

By unfolding one aspect of Thomas's teaching in this particular way, the Thomist school was able to continue to hold (contrary to the Nominalist position) that the *whole* Christ, including his undiminished dimensive quantity, is indeed in the sacrament, and (contrary to the Cartesian position) that the Eucharistic species maintain their properly realized dimensive quantity in their local space, while Christ's body has its properly realized quantitative dimension in Christ's glorified state in heaven alone.

In summary: According to John of St. Thomas and other Thomist commentators, the primary formal effect of quantity, *ordo partium in toto,* specifies the order of distinguishable parts as a whole. This order (in which consists the essence of quantity) gives rise to a really distinct determination, the secondary formal effect, the *ordo relationis,* that is, the *ordo partium* according to their relative position or situation to other parts in space *(ubi et situs).*[64] Because the *ordo partium in toto* can be considered indeterminately, there obtains the logical separability and consequently the separability of modes of being between the primary formal effect of dimensive quantity and its secondary formal effect.

At this point, we can mark two vital results of this all too sketchy ac-

---

64. Joseph Gredt, O.S.B., *Elementa philosophiae Aristotelico-Thomisticae,* vol. 1, *Logica/Philosophia Naturalis,* 11th ed. (Freiburg: Herder, 1956): "Definitio quantitatis . . . stricte autem sumpta pro quantitate *praedicamentali* definitur: ordo partium in toto. In qua definitione 'ordo' positionem significat partium extra partes, ita ut quantitas etiam definiri possit: accidens tribuens subiecto habere partes extra partes quoad se. Ordo, in quo consistit quantitatis essentia, non est relatio ordinis, sed fundamentum huius relationis; est ordo fundamentalis, i.e., fundamentum relationis secundum prius et posterius. Quantitas igitur duo continet: *multitudinem* partium, et huius multitudinis *ordinem* secundum positionem, quatenus partes ponuntur extra partes secundum prius et posterius. . . . Quare quantitas praedicamentalis multitudini superaddit ordinem positionis secundum prius et posterius" (pp. 145-46); "THESIS X: Effectus formalis primarius quantitatis seu eius ratio formalis est ordo partium in toto, effectus formalis secundarius est ubi et situs seu ordo partium in loco. Hic effectus secundarius distinctus est realiter et separabilis a primario" (p. 252); "*Effectus formalis primarius* seu ratio formalis est constitutivum metaphysicum quantitatis. Quantitas enim utpote accidens definitur per ordinem ad subiectum, ad substantiam. Quare indicando, quid *primo* faciat in substantia formaliter (per modum causae formalis), indicatur eius essentia metaphysica" (p. 252, § 315); "ordo partium in toto potest considerari indeterminate, et tunc est *effectus formalis primarius* quantitatis" (p. 254, § 318)

count of the predicaments "substance" and "quantity" in the teaching of Thomas and the Thomist tradition. First, substance is not a mere conceptual name in the modern, nominalist sense — that is, a sheer linguistic pointer of the intellect's intentionality to some "Ding an sich." On the contrary, substances connote entities that subsist in their own existence — "unde solae substantiae proprie et vere dicuntur entia"[65] — entities that address the intellect, and are formally received by it.

Second, Thomas's teaching on material substance allows for the real distinction between the primary formal effect of quantity *(ordo partium in toto)* and its secondary formal effect *(ordo partium in loco)*. That is, even under the sacramental species of bread and wine, it is by way of the primary formal effect of quantity that the substance of Christ's body and the substance of Christ's blood are really present in their concrete particularity as *this* substance and as *that* substance. This substantial presence does, however, emphatically *not* pertain to the *ordo partium in loco (ubi et situs)*.[66] While the substance of Christ's body and blood is present without deficiency of substance (which includes the primary formal effect of quantity, the *ordo partium in toto*), no further accidents need to be realized for the substantive, real presence of Christ's body and blood to obtain. On the other hand, the Eucharistic species maintain their dimensive quantity, that is, their specific *ordo partium in loco,* as sustained by the primary formal effect of the quantity of bread and the quantity of wine. And because quantity is not identical with substance, the logical separability of the two allows for the possibility that the primary *(ordo partium in toto)* as well as the secondary *(ordo partium in loco)* formal effects of quantity are sustainable without the substance in which quantity inheres.[67] Since all the other

---

65. *ST* I, q. 90, a. 2: "Illud autem proprie dicitur esse, quod ipsum habet esse, quasi in suo esse subsistens: unde solae substantiae proprie et vere dicuntur entia. Accidens vero non habet esse, sed eo aliquid est, et hac ratione ens dicitur; sicut albedo dicitur ens, quia ea aliquid est album. Et propter hoc dicitur in VII *Metaphys.*, quod accidens dicitur 'magis entis quam ens.' Et eadem ratio est de omnibus aliis formis non subsistentibus."

66. Hence, it is crucial to remember that, when he distinguishes between substance and quantity in *ST* III, q. 76, a. 1, ad 3, Thomas is concerned with the specific entailments of the *ordo partium* in space, that is, the secondary formal effect of quantity, the *ordo partium in loco (ubi et situs)*. Because of the increasing identification between substance and quantity in later Scholasticism, the Thomist tradition had to emphasize increasingly the distinction between the primary formal effect of quantity *(ordo partium extra partes)* and the secondary formal effect of quantity, dimensive quantity.

67. *ST* III, q. 75, a. 5, ad 1: "[S]icut dicitur in libro *De causis*, effectus plus dependet a causa prima quam a causa secunda. Et ideo virtute Dei, qui est causa prima omnium, fieri

accidents inhere in substance by way of dimensive quantity, their sustainability is consequent upon the separate sustainability of dimensive quantity.[68]

What tangible difference does this distinction make? Consider the following argument advanced by Sylvester of Ferrara, the profound commentator of Thomas's *Summa contra Gentiles (ScG)* on Thomas's discussion of how the body of Christ (as a proper material substance) can be in multiple places. Here is Thomas's text from *ScG* IV, c. 64, par. 5:

> [T]he body of Christ in His own dimensions exists in one place only, but through the mediation of the dimensions of the bread passing into it its places are as many as there are places in which this sort of conversion is celebrated. For it is not divided into parts, but is entire in every single one; every consecrated bread is converted into the entire body of Christ.[69]

Advancing a succinct version of the distinction between the two effects of quantity, Sylvester of Ferrara comments thus:

> The effect of quantity is twofold. The one effect is completely intrinsic to that which has quantity [as it pertains to the *metaphysical order* of

---

potest ut remaneant posteriora, sublatis prioribus." See also John of St. Thomas, *Cursus Philosophicus* I, *Log.*, pt. II, q. XVI, a. 1; p. 463: "Caeterum oppositum hujus manifestavit nobis sacrosanctum Eucharistiae mysterium, in quo manet quantitas, quae antea erat panis, ut oculis videmus, et non manet substantia panis, ut fides docet: distinguitur ergo et separatur quantitas a re quanta. Respondent Nominales quantitatem substantiae non manere, cum ipsa enim evanuit; sed manere quantitatem qualitatum caeterorumque accidentium extensorum. Sed contra est, quia ibi sunt plura accidentia. Vel ergo unumquodque habet suam quantitatem distinctam, vel datur aliqua communis omnibus. Si datur aliqua communis omnibus, illa distinguitur etiam a substantia, quae ibi non est; ergo distinguitur quantitas a re quanta." For a detailed discussion of this particular aspect of Thomas's doctrine and of the sustainability of Thomas's teaching on the *accidentia sine subiecto remanentia*, see the instructive essay by Petrus Sedlmayr, O.S.B., "Die Lehre des hl. Thomas von den *accidentia sine subjecto remanentia* — untersucht auf ihren Einklang mit der aristotelischen Philosophie," *Divus Thomas* (F) 12 (1934): 315-26.

68. Cf. Thomas's nuanced discussion of this complex matter in *ST* III, q. 77, a. 2.

69. Translation from Thomas Aquinas, *Summa contra Gentiles. Book Four: Salvation*, trans., Charles J. O'Neil (Notre Dame, IN: University of Notre Dame Press, 1975), p. 262. ("Corpus enim Christi per suas proprias dimensiones in uno tantum loco existit: sed mediantibus dimensionibus panis in ipsum transeuntis in tot locis in quot huiusmodi conversio fuerit celebrata: non quidem divisum per partes, sed integrum in unoquoque; nam quilibet panis consecratus in integrum corpus Christi convertitur.")

the constitution of a material substance; R.H.], that is, quantification [*esse quantum*], divisibility into parts, and the order of parts as a whole. The other effect is in some manner extrinsic [as it pertains to the *physical order* of material substances relating qua quantity to other material substances; R.H.], namely insofar as quantity pertains to the thing in the outward order, that is, insofar as it corresponds to another distinguishable quantity and the parts of the one correspond to the location of the parts of the other quantity. The first effect is necessarily and per se proper to quantity. The second effect, however, only pertains to quantity if it is ordered principally and per se to a place and toward extrinsic dimensions. Consequently, in the sacrament of the altar, the quantity of Christ's body, existing under the dimensions of the bread, has the first effect. For the body of Christ is in itself divisible and has an order of parts as a whole. It does not, however, have the second effect. For the parts of Christ's body do not correspond to the dimensive parts of the bread nor to the location of these parts, but the whole is under whatsoever part. Consequently it can be said that the body of Christ is under the dimensions of the bread in a divisible as well as an indivisible way, divisible insofar as it has in and of itself divisible parts; indivisible, however, because its parts do not correspond to the parts of those dimensions, but rather the whole corresponds to whatsoever part, as is the soul as a whole in each part [of the body].[70]

Sylvester of Ferrara's commentary allows us to see with greater clarity what indeed is entailed in Thomas's own teaching. The full, undiminished iden-

---

70. My translation from *Sancti Thomae Aquinatis Doctoris Angelici Opera Omnia iussu edita Leonis XIII P.M.*, vol. 15 (Rome: Leonine Commission, 1930), p. 208: "[D]uplex est quantitatis effectus. Unus est omnino intrinsecus subiecto quanto; scilicet esse quantum, et divisibilitas in partes, atque ordo partium in toto. Alius est aliquo modo extrinsecus, inquantum scilicet convenit subiecto in ordine ad extrinsecum; scilicet condividi alteri quantitati, et partes eius partibus loci correspondere. Primum convenit quantitati necessario et per se: secundum vero sibi non convenit nisi quando habet primo et per se ordinem ad locum et ad extrinsecas dimensiones. In sacramento ergo Altaris quantitas corporis Christi, sub dimensionibus panis existens, habet primum effectum, quia ipsum corpus Christi est in seipso divisibile, et habet ordinem partium in toto: non autem secundum effectum habet, quia partes corporis Christi non correspondent partibus dimensionis panis neque partibus loci, sed totum est sub qualibet parte. Ex quo sequitur quod potest dici corpus Christi esse sub dimensionibus panis et divisibiliter et indivisibiliter; divisibiliter quidem, quia in seipso divisibilitatem partium habet; indivisibiliter autem, quia partes eius non correspondent partibus illarum dimensionum, sed totum cuilibet parti, sicut anima est tota in qualibet parte."

tity of Christ's body and blood is present under the dimensions of the Eucharistic species, yet without their proper dimensive parts spacially and hence locally realized. While the substance penetrates the whole, spaciality and locality pertain only to the dimensive parts of the Eucharistic species. Christ's surpassing personal presence in the Eucharist has its indispensable anchor in the substantial presence of his body and his blood under the Eucharistic species. For, according to Thomas, nothing less and nothing more than Christ's very humanity constitutes God's surpassingly efficacious instrument of the salvation of humanity.[71] Hence it is not only fitting, but necessary that Christ's salvific presence in the Eucharist comes about by way of his crucified humanity — the incarnate Son's utter self-giving to the Father in love, obedient to the point of death — sacramentally signified by His body and blood being separated from each other in the one Eucharistic sacrament.[72] However, as already elaborated above, since Christ's body and blood after the Eucharistic consecration are perfectly identical with Christ's body and blood in heaven, they indeed are surrounded *(concomitari)* by all that surrounds them in the person of Christ in heaven, Christ's human soul as well as His divinity. Through real concomitance, due to the integral subsistence of the risen Christ in heaven, nothing less than the whole person of Christ is in the Blessed Sacrament. Furthermore, Christ's sacrificial self-gift "for the many" constitutes the unfathomable personal relation of Christ to everyone who desires to adore and receive him under the Eucharistic species of bread and wine. In short, because the Eucharistic presence of Christ in the sacramental form of his sacrificial self-gift is really substantial, it is surpassingly personal — the abyss of God's love, given "for you."

71. For an extensive discussion of this crucial aspect of Thomas's Christology, see Theophil Tschipke, O.P., *Die Menschheit Christi als Heilsorgan der Gottheit unter besonderer Berücksichtigung der Lehre des heiligen Thomas von Aquin* (Freiburg: Herder, 1940). Cf. the recent French translation: *L'humanité du Christ comme instrument de salut de la divinité* (Fribourg: Academic Press, 2003).

72. On this utterly central element of a proper understanding of the Eucharistic sacrifice, see the arguably two most profound as well as accurate twentieth-century Eucharistic monographs *secundum mentem S. Thomae:* Abbot Vonier, O.S.B., *A Key to the Doctrine of the Eucharist* (Bethesda: Zacheus Press, 2003-2004) and Charles Cardinal Journet, *The Mass: The Presence of the Sacrifice of the Cross,* trans. Victor Szczurek, O.Praem. (South Bend, IN: St. Augustine's Press, 2008).

The Integrity of the Sacramental Sign

Lest the Thomist deployment of substance become seriously lopsided, that is, be wrongly received along the lines of a crude, non-sacramental realism, I must hasten at this point to emphasize that in Thomas's doctrine of Eucharistic conversion, the substantial presence of Christ in the sacrament does not at all occlude or thwart the abiding *sacramental* signification of the Eucharistic species. On the contrary, and contemporarily put, the Eucharistic species remain signs "all the way down." Rather than arresting the intellectual gaze upon themselves, as things with a proper substance would do, they direct the intellectual gaze beyond themselves, because faith, in assent to the dominical words, forbids the intellect to follow the path of the senses by way of the Eucharistic species to absent substances. For, as Thomas reminds us:

> [s]ubstance, as such, is not visible to the bodily eye, nor does it come under any one of the senses, nor under the imagination, but solely under the intellect, whose object is *what a thing is*. . . . And therefore, properly speaking, Christ's body, according to the mode of being which it has in this sacrament, is perceptible neither by the sense nor by the imagination, but only by the intellect, which is called the spiritual eye.[73]

Accordingly, Thomas stresses that indeed Christ's body "can be seen by a wayfarer through faith alone [*sola fide*], like other supernatural things."[74] "For," as Thomas argues, "the accidents which are discerned by the senses are truly present. But the intellect, whose proper object is substance . . . is preserved by faith from deception . . . because faith is not contrary to the senses, but concerns things which sense does not reach."[75]

Hence the character of the sacrament as a sign abides from beginning to end. It is by way of the instrumental causality inherent in sacra-

---

73. *ST* III, q. 76, a. 7: "Substantia autem, inquantum huiusmodi, non est visibilis oculo corporali, neque subiacet alicui sensui, neque imaginationi, sed soli intellectui, cuius obiectum est *quod quid est,* ut dicitur in III *de Anima.* Et ideo, proprie loquendo, corpus Christi, secundum modum essendi quem habet in hoc sacramento: neque sensu neque imaginatione perceptibile est, sed solo intellectu, qui dicitur oculus spiritualis."

74. *ST* III, q. 76, a. 7.

75. *ST* III, q. 75, a. 5, ad 2 et 3: "[I]n hoc sacramentum nulla est deceptio: sunt enim secundum rei veritatem accidentia, quae sensibus diiudicantur. Intellectus autem, cuius est proprium obiectum substantia, ut dicitur in III *de Anima,* per fidem a deceptione praeservatur."

mental signification that bread and wine constitute the irreplaceable and indispensable starting point for the sacramental conversion, and that after the consecration, the remaining sacramental species continue to carry the sacramental signification of the Eucharistic conversion.

In short, after the Eucharistic consecration, the sacramental sign — as long as it is able to signify, that is, as long as the modes of appearance of bread and wine persist — continues to signify the real substantial presence of Christ. Hence, when the Eucharistic elements are reserved, Christ's real substantial presence remains also. For the ending of the Eucharistic liturgy is without efficacious impact upon the substantial constitution of the re-served Blessed Sacrament.

By way of the genuine sign-character of the enduring Eucharistic species the adoration of the Blessed Sacrament remains intrinsically linked to the Eucharistic liturgy and by way of the latter to the whole economy of salvation as it is symbolically gathered in the Eucharistic liturgy.[76] Further, by way of Eucharistic conversion, the adoration of the Blessed Sacrament is inherently linked to Christ's abiding and lasting personal presence in the sacrament. Adoration simply means to come and give him personally and communally homage, to commune spiritually.

At this point it would be most opportune to reconsider a set of traditional distinctions well established by Thomas's time that developed in a complex process of early medieval theological discourse: *sacramentum tantum,* the sign only; *res et sacramentum,* the thing and the sign; *res tantum,* the thing only. Thomas employs these terms consistently in his sacramental theology in the *Summa theologiae.* The first, the sign only, refers to what we know as the signification, that is, the species of bread and wine. The second, the thing and the sign, refers to the body and blood of Christ substantially present at the term of the Eucharistic conversion. Now, this is called *res et sacramentum* because not only is it the *res* which is signified by the *sacramentum tantum,* but the signified thing itself, Christ's true body and blood, point beyond themselves and signify the *res tantum,* the spiritual effects of Eucharistic communion, that is, the specific sacra-

76. On the mystery of the liturgy in relationship to the economy of salvation as it is gathered in the "eternal liturgy," see Jean Corbon, O.P., *The Wellspring of Worship,* trans. Matthew J. O'Connell (San Francisco: Ignatius Press, 2005), and on the liturgy as a world of effective signs, see Cyprian Vagaggini, O.S.B., *Theologie der Liturgie,* trans. August Berz (Zurich/Cologne: Benziger, 1959). For an excellent and exhaustive study on Thomas's own interpretation of the Eucharistic liturgy, see Franck Quoëx, "Thomas d'Aquin, mystagogue: *L'expositio missae de la Somme de Théologie* (IIIᵃ, q. 83, a. 4-5)," *Revue thomiste* 105 (2005): 179-225 and 435-72.

mental grace of further incorporation into the mystical body of Christ, which is the perfect union of charity between the head and the body. Hence, rightly understood, Eucharistic adoration is nothing but a proper expression of the union of charity between Christ, the head, and the Church, his body, be it communally or individually.

Thomas's interpretation makes explicit what the Church's practice entailed long before: Christ's abiding personal presence in the consecrated sacrament transcends the boundaries of space and time of each particular Eucharistic celebration. However, Thomas's metaphysical contemplation of the Eucharistic mystery — as well as its conceptual development in the Thomist tradition — remains just that, a contemplation. The mystery is not replaced by "explanation." The metaphysical contemplation of "making explicit" is never reduced to a merely analytic, puzzle-solving "making sense of." For what is being attended to remains irreducibly a mystery. Hence a metaphysical contemplation such as the one advanced by Thomas is not a strictly probative argument for the truth of this mystery of faith, but a defensible — and possibly even the most apt — philosophical hermeneutics of the mystery. For Thomas's metaphysical meditation makes explicit what the mystery entails, offers an account for its logical possibility, and defends its coherence as a supernatural reality. The normative interpretation of the mystery of Eucharistic conversion does not rest, however, with such a metaphysical contemplation, but with *sacra doctrina,* and that in the twofold way of *"lex orandi, lex credendi,"* in the organic unity of the development of the Church's liturgy and the Church's doctrine, both normatively inscribed in and traditioned by the canon of Scripture, the former, like the saints, emerging from the bosom of the Church's life of prayer and the latter finding its proper expression in the Church's teaching, properly determined by the Church's magisterium (the *determinatio Ecclesiae*). What a metaphysical contemplation like Thomas's tends to make ontologically explicit remains conceptually rightly underdetermined by the liturgy itself, as well as by its magisterial determination. For not even the most profound metaphysical contemplation is ever able exhaustively to make explicit the *mysterium fidei.*

Coda

Hence it should not surprise us that Eucharistic Adoration finds its most beautiful expression when metaphysical contemplation gives rise to doxological adoration, when the philosopher bursts out into praise:

Adoro te devote, latens Deitas,
Quae sub his figuris vere latitas.
Tibi se cor meum totum subjicit
Quia te contemplans totum deficit.

Visus, tactus, gustus in te fallitur
Sed auditu solo tuto creditur.
Credo quidquid dixit Dei Filius.
Nil hoc verbo Veritatis verius.

Jesu, quem velatum nunc aspicio,
Oro fiat illud, quod tam sitio,
Ut te revelata cernens facie,
Visu sim beatus tuae gloriae.[77]

A Methodological Postscript: Making Explicit the Operative Understanding of Catholic Theology, Philosophy, and Liturgy

By way of a brief methodological postscript I would like to submit what I take to be the proper relationship between theology, philosophy, and the liturgy. This postscript is an attempt at clarifying some vital distinctions that are in grave danger of being disregarded in the recent interest that Anglo-American philosophers began to show in "liturgy," most widely conceived, as a topic worthy of philosophical attention and analysis. Far from exhaustive, the following observations and theses merely serve as a first *Denkanstoß*, an urgent invitation to further theological reflection.

---

77. Thomas Aquinas, "Adore te devote," in *The Aquinas Prayer Book*, pp. 68-71:

> Devoutly I adore you, hidden Deity,
> Under these appearances concealed.
> To You my heart surrenders self
> For, seeing You, all else must yield.
> Sight and touch and taste here fail;
> Hearing only can be believed.
> I trust what God's own Son has said.
> Truth from truth is best received.
> Jesus, Whom now I see enveiled,
> What I desire, when will it be?
> Beholding Your fair face revealed,
> Your glory shall I be blessed to see.

1. *"Liturgiology"*

Traditionally in Catholicism, as well as in Protestantism, the interpretation of the Christian liturgy has been the proper task of theology (and in Orthodoxy it still is — Orthodox theology at its core being nothing else than a doctrinal unfolding of and contemplation on the divine liturgy) and that meant traditionally (before the fateful Protestant, "Berlin" type divisions into subfields — a development all too happily emulated by Catholic theology in the twentieth century) the task of what now is called "dogmatic" or "systematic" theology. Only in the early twentieth century, based on certain developments in the nineteenth century, did "liturgiology" *(Liturgik/ Liturgiewissenschaft)* emerge as a distinct field of the study of Christian liturgies, a subfield that

a. unsurprisingly comprises only very few, if any, Quakers and not all too many Pentecostals, but is dominated by Roman Catholic and Anglican scholars, and then well populated by those of Lutheran, Calvinist, or Methodist convictions; and

b. operates methodologically in an eclectic way by historical, phenomenological, and anthropological approaches. I think it is fair to say that liturgiology as a distinctive, relatively recent subdiscipline of what is currently called "practical theology" finds itself still in an ongoing internal debate about the exact circumference and the inner coherence of its subject matter, the coherence of its various methodological approaches, and last but not least, the question of to what degree the descriptive, constructive, practical, and normative aspects of the discipline relate to each other.

2. *Philosophy and Christian Liturgy*

When philosophers turn to the liturgy as a topic of inquiry and analysis, we must reasonably assume that philosophy has a *sui generis* approach to the Christian liturgy, an approach *formally* distinct from that taken by theology (and/or from liturgiology). This assumption entails the need for the prior clarification of how theology and philosophy might differ *essentially* in regard to what is constitutive of them as distinct intellectual inquiries. In this book, I proceeded on the basis of the Thomist understanding that theology proper as *sacra doctrina* is formally constituted by the *scientia Dei et beatorum* as primarily conveyed by Scripture and apostolic *paradosis.* However, it seems not completely clear to me whether there presently exists or ever existed significant agreement among philosophers about the nature and task of philosophy. It might indeed just be the case that various philosophers for various reasons — most likely recognizable and laudable, but implicit, *theological* reasons (and possibly from variant, incompatible perspectives) — make the Christian liturgy a topic of intellectual inquiry — which would in that case be a tacit version of *fides quaerens intellectum.* And as long as one is not able to settle on the proper *formal* objects constitutive of theology and of philosophy as distinct modes of inquiry, these implicit theological motives and interests behind such philosophical inquiries into the Christian liturgy will, in the best of all senses, make these philosophers theologians of sorts (which, of course, is not a bad thing at all). But this circumstance simply raises in a sharper way the fundamental question of what might be the distinct contribution of a properly philosophical inquiry into the Christian liturgy.

3. Catholic Theology, Liturgy, Philosophy

Now, for the Catholic theologian — understood here in the precise sense of the vocation of the ecclesial theologian — the situation is somewhat different. For there is a relatively clear (albeit from time to time individually questioned and contested) understanding of how theology relates to Scripture, tradition, and the magisterium. The task of a fruitful philosophical investigation in relationship to the faith and its proper interpretation by theology is not absolutely prescribed but properly circumscribed in the late Pope John Paul II's encyclical letter *Fides et ratio.* What *Fides et ratio* has in mind and wants to encourage is a philosophizing in the full metaphysical range of an inquiry in principle open to the transcendent, a philosophizing that complements the faith in that it supports the *intellectus fidei;* in short, a Christian philosophizing in proper independence from the nature and task of theology proper as *sacra doctrina.*

4. A Normative Conditional

It seems to me that the only way for a Catholic theologian to envision a fruitful philosophical inquiry into the Christian liturgy is on the basis of the following conditional formulated by Ludwig Wittgenstein: "If Christianity is the truth, then all the philosophy about it is false."[78] I would like to submit that any philosopher who wants to focus on the Christian liturgy as a proper subject matter of inquiry needs to assume the truth of this conditional. In other words, as soon as philosophy is "about" the Christian liturgy in the sense that the latter must needs be "explained" in light of some comprehensive theory that allegedly conveys the presently closest approximation to the truth (let us say, "evolution"), such "philosophy about" is indeed false from the very outset. Only on the assumption that, in Wittgenstein's words, "Christianity is the truth," does it make sense for the Christian liturgy to become a possible topic of philosophical inquiry. Why? For if, on the one hand, Christianity were inherently false, philosophy would lose a proper subject matter for sustained inquiry (because the Christian liturgy would quickly be unmasked as a collective act of self-deception or as a ruse). On the other hand, if the truth of Christianity could be bracketed in the very mode and procedure of inquiry, philosophy as an inquiry *sui generis* would simply disappear, because, after all, *Religionswissenschaft* for quite some time has been studying all kinds of religious convictions, practices, rituals without any, even hypothetical commitment to whether what is studied indeed obtains in the way the religions investigated in such ways claim it to obtain.

Hence, the Catholic theologian faced with these alternatives can do at least two things meaningfully. The Catholic theologian can (1) search for and draw upon a philosophical school that (a) is inherently open to the truth-claims of Christianity; that (b) allows for a clear differentiation between the theological and the philosophical task; yet also (c) allows for a proper constructive relationship between the two. (For the Catholic theologian the search for such a philosophy is properly circumscribed most recently by the encyclical *Fides et ratio*.) Furthermore, the Catholic theologian can (2) simply observe and analyze what philosophers say about the liturgy by (a) drawing theologically upon it as helpful forms of interpretation and clarification; or (b) rejecting it theologically as illegitimately reductive; or (c) engaging it philosophically as incoherent, unconvincing, or besides the point.

---

78. Ludwig Wittgenstein, *Culture and Value* (Oxford: Blackwell, 1998), p. 89 (noted in 1949).

5. *"Liturgy": An Equivocal, Univocal, or Analogical Term?*

Next, the Catholic theologian will have to clarify the use of the notion of "liturgy." When one looks at the extant variety of Christian worship across the full spectrum of Christian communions, the unavoidable question arises whether the notion "liturgy" simply is an equivocation, or whether it can at all be applied univocally across the board, or whether the only way to use it meaningfully is in an analogical way. Consider the following: For Quakers, on the one hand, there can be a proper communal worship without formal sermon or homily, without the singing of hymns, without formal, communal prayer, without communion. For the Catholic Church, on the other hand, the Christian liturgy in the full, proper, and legitimate sense is the celebration of the Mass, presided over *in persona Christi* by a validly ordained priest, a celebration that takes place in the visible, structural unity of the Church, which finds its concrete expression in the unity of the local church with the bishop, with all bishops, and with the see of Peter. Are these latter normative aspects intrinsic to the essence of Christian liturgy in its proper integrity and plenitude — as it indeed is a "given" to the Catholic theologian? Or are these aspects merely accidental and hence extrinsic to some univocal concept of "liturgy" that could yield an essence in light of which both of the above examples could be equally grasped as particular instantiations of "liturgy" and hence critically assessed over against the shared essence of liturgy? If philosophers were to assume such, Quaker theologians and practitioners as well as Roman Catholic theologians and practitioners would rightly take umbrage at such a suffocating Hegelian embrace by a univocal concept *(Begriff),* and Wittgenstein would rightly decry such a notion as a dangerous approximation to the "philosophy about" that can only be false. For some such univocal concept of "liturgy" equally applicable to the Quaker meeting as well as the Catholic Mass would render not only the concrete, incompatible points of each particular way of worship meaningless, but also the theological axioms, underlying each, vacuous. But then, "liturgy" obviously cannot be a pure equivocation either, because clearly intelligible disagreement seems to be possible between various Christian communions about the form, scope, and content of Christian worship. And intelligible disagreements always presuppose some prior agreements (and in the wake of ecumenism, indeed, a growing convergence on a variety of matters). These prior agreements, however, cannot have their root simply in a shared act of stipulation ("Let us agree to call the following a 'liturgy'" . . .), but in an indispensable, shared point of reference: the person and work (in late modern lingo, the "identity") of Jesus Christ.

Hence, any sound philosophical inquiry into Christian liturgy will have to acknowledge the priority of certain theological norms that cannot be philosophically adjudicated, settled, or put aside without simply destroying the proper subject-matter of inquiry and consequently turning into a false "philosophy about." Moreover and more importantly, since "liturgy" does not seem to be used equivocally across its variety of instantiations, but since a univocal use of the term also does not seem to be defensible, for the Catholic theologian and philosopher, "liturgy" is unavoidably understood in an analogical way, that is, in the precise sense of the analogy by reference to a primary instance of Christian liturgy. This primary instance is nothing less than the heavenly liturgy as symbolically instantiated in the Eucharistic liturgy, the worship of "the Lamb who was slain," in which together with the angels Christ's body, the Church, participates, a body that comprises the living, the martyrs and saints in heaven, all the righteous *ab Abel,* as well as the souls in purgatory: "Worthy is the Lamb who was slain, to receive power and wealth and wisdom and might and honor and glory and blessing!" (Rev. 5:12). This heavenly liturgy shines forth from the Orthodox iconostasis, presents itself sacramentally in each celebration of the Eucharistic liturgy, and is worshipped prayerfully in the adoration of the Blessed Sacrament.[79]

6. Catholic Theology, Philosophy, and the Eucharist

If it indeed obtains, as the Catholic Church holds, that at its core and in its essence Christian liturgy is identical with the Eucharist, and if indeed it obtains that it comprises the mystery of faith per se, the following also obtains:

a. Any philosophical inquiry will need to rely upon the prior guidance of the apostolic *paradosis,* the canon of Scripture, tradition (comprising dogma and the Church's living Magisterium), and theology in order to be able to even approximate the subject matter properly instead of severely distorting or simply missing the very topic from the outset.

---

79. See Jean Corbon, O.P., *The Wellspring of Worship* (San Francisco: Ignatius Press, 2005).

b. An inquiry into a mystery of faith means that there are severe limitations to conceptual comprehension.

c. Any inquiry into the mystery of faith proper will at best be a hermeneutic of making proximately explicit what is unfathomably entailed in the mystery. However, such an inquiry can never be expected exhaustively to "make sense" of the mystery of faith — as if it were a conceptual problem or puzzle open to some eventual resolution.

d. For the Catholic theologian it is not insignificant that the Church's Magisterium has over a long time privileged a particular philosophical tradition (comprising various schools, though) of inquiry and analysis in the Church's proximate *ontological* interpretation of this mystery of faith (transubstantiation). Hence, in the reception and engagement of other philosophical approaches to and interpretations of the Eucharistic mystery, and especially of the Eucharistic conversion, the Catholic theologian will assess the best of the recent interpretive efforts submitted as analogous approximations by reference to a primary instance, this primary instance being what the Fourth Lateran Council termed as "transubstantiation" and what the Council of Trent reaffirmed to be *aptissime* expressed in the notion of "transubstantiation."

Bibliography

EDITIONS OF THOMAS AQUINAS' WORKS CITED AND CONSULTED

Theological Syntheses

Scriptum super libros Sententiarum

S. Thomae Aquinatis Opera Omnia. Vol. 1, *In Quattuor Libros Sententiarum*. Edited by R. Busa, S.J. Stuttgart-Bad Cannstatt: Frommann, 1980.

Summa contra Gentiles

Sancti Thomae Aquinatis Doctoris Angelici Opera Omnia iussu edita Leonis XIII P.M. Vols. 13-15. Rome: Leonine Commission, 1928-1930.

Summa contra Gentiles. Book 1. Edited and translated by Karl Albert and Paulus Engelhardt with cooperation by Leo Dümpelmann. Darmstadt: Wissenschaftliche Buchgesellschaft, 1974; 2nd ed., 2001.

Summa contra Gentiles. Book 2. Edited and translated by Karl Albert and Paulus Engelhardt. Darmstadt: Wissenschaftliche Buchgesellschaft, 1974; 2nd ed., 2001.

Summa contra Gentiles. Books 3.1 and 3.2. Edited and translated by Karl Allgaier. Darmstadt: Wissenschaftliche Buchgesellschaft, 1974; 2nd ed., 2001.

Summa contra Gentiles. Book 4. Edited and translated by Markus H. Wörner. Darmstadt: Wissenschaftliche Buchgesellschaft, 1974; 2nd ed., 2001.

Summa contra Gentiles. Book One: God. Translated by Anton C. Pegis. Notre Dame, IN: University of Notre Dame Press, 1975.

Summa contra Gentiles. Book Two: Creation. Translated by James F. Anderson. Notre Dame, IN: University of Notre Dame Press, 1975.

Summa contra Gentiles. Book Three: Providence. Translated by Vernon J. Bourke. Notre Dame, IN: University of Notre Dame Press, 1975.

Summa contra Gentiles. Book Four: Salvation. Translated by Charles J. O'Neil. Notre Dame, IN: University of Notre Dame Press, 1975.

Summa theologiae

Summa Theologiae. 3rd ed. Turin: Edizioni San Paolo, 1999.

Summa Theologica. Complete English Edition in Five Volumes. Translated by the Fathers of the English Dominican Province. Westminster, MD: Christian Classics, 1981.

Summa Theologica. Deutsch-Lateinische Ausgabe. Vol. 1, *ST* I, 1-13: *Gottes Dasein und Wesen.* Translation, Notes and Commentary on Questions 9-11 by Heinrich Maria Christmann, O.P. Commentary on Questions 1-8 and 12-13 by Alexander M. Siemer, O.P. Salzburg/Leipzig: Pustet, 1934.

Summa Theologica. Deutsch-Lateinische Ausgabe. Vol. 6, *ST* I, 75-89: *Wesen und Ausstattung des Menschen.* Translation, Notes, and Commentary by Petrus Wintrath, O.S.B. Salzburg/Leipzig: Pustet, 1937.

Summa Theologica. Deutsch-Lateinische Ausgabe. Vol. 10, *ST* I-II, 22-48: *Die menschlichen Leidenschaften.* Translation, Notes, and Commentary by Bernhard Ziermann, C.Ss.R. Heidelberg: Kerle; Graz/Vienna/Cologne: Styria, 1955.

Summa Theologica. Deutsch-Lateinische Ausgabe. Vol. 12, *ST* I-II, 71-89: *Die Sünde.* Translation, Notes, and Commentary by Otto Hermann Pesch. Vienna: Styria, 2004.

Summa Theologica. Deutsch-Lateinische Ausgabe. Vol. 13, *ST* I-II, 90-105: *Das Gesetz.* Translation, Notes, and Commentary by Otto Hermann Pesch. Heidelberg: Kerle; Graz/Vienna/Cologne: Styria, 1977.

Summa Theologica. Deutsch-Lateinische Ausgabe. Vol. 14, *ST* I-II, 106-14: *Der Neue Bund und die Gnade.* Translation, Notes, and Commentary by Thomas-Albert Deman, O.P. Heidelberg: Kerle; Graz/Vienna/Cologne: Styria, 1955.

Summa Theologica. Deutsch-Lateinische Ausgabe. Vol. 15, *ST* II-II, 1-16: *Glaube als Tugend.* Notes and Commentary by Fridolin Utz, O.P. Heidelberg: Kerle; Graz/Vienna/Cologne: Styria, 1950.

Summa Theologica. Deutsch-Lateinische Ausgabe. Vol. 22, *ST* 151-70: *Masshaltung (2. Teil).* Translation, Notes, and Commentary by Josef F. Groner, O.P. Graz/Vienna/Cologne: Styria, 1993.

Summa Theologica. Deutsch-Lateinische Ausgabe. Vol. 30, *ST* III, 73-83: *Das Geheimnis der Eucharistie.* Notes and Commentary by Damasus Winzen, O.S.B. Salzburg/Leipzig: Pustet, 1938.

Disputed Questions

Quaestiones disputatae De veritate

De Veritate. In: *Quaestiones Disputatae et Quaestiones Duodecim Quodlibetales.* Vols. III-IV. Turin/Rome: Marietti, 1942.

Truth. Vol. 1: Questions I-IX, translated by Robert W. Mulligan, S.J. Vol. 2: Questions X-XX, translated by James V. McGlynn, S.J. Vol. 3: Questions XXI-XXIX, translated by Robert W. Schmidt, S.J. Indianapolis/Cambridge: Hackett, 1994.

Quaestiones disputatae De potentia

De Potentia Dei. In: *Quaestiones Disputatae et Quaestiones Duodecim Quodlibetales*. Vol. I. Turin/Rome: Marietti, 1942.
On the Power of God (Quaestiones disputatae de potentia Dei). Translated by the English Dominican Fathers. London: Newman Press, 1932; Eugene, OR: Wipf & Stock, 2004.

Quaestio disputata De anima

Quaestiones de Anima: A Newly Established Edition of the Latin Text with an Introduction and Notes. Edited by James H. Robb. Toronto: Pontifical Institute of Medieval Studies, 1968.
Questions on the Soul (Quaestiones de Anima). Translated with an introduction by James H. Robb. Milwaukee: Marquette University Press, 1984.

Quaestiones disputatae De malo

The De Malo *of Thomas Aquinas*. Edited by Brian Davies; translated by Richard Regan. Oxford: Oxford University Press, 2001.
On Evil. Translated by John A. Oesterle and Jean T. Oesterle. Notre Dame, IN: University of Notre Dame Press, 1995.

Quaestiones disputatae De virtutibus

De Virtutibus in Communi. In *Quaestiones Disputatae et Quaestiones Duodecim Quodlibetales*. Vol. II, pp. 485-537. Turin/Rome: Marietti, 1942.

Quaestio disputata De spe

De Spe. In: *Quaestiones Disputatae et Quaestiones Duodecim Quodlibetales*. Vol. II, pp. 595-606. Turin/Rome: Marietti, 1942.

Commentaries on the Bible

S. Thomae Aquinatis in omnes S. Pauli Apostoli epistolas commentaria. 2 vols. Turin/Rome: Marietti, 1929.
Ad Romanos. Vol. 1, pp. 1-219.
I Ad Corinthios. Vol. 1, pp. 220-415.
II Ad Corinthios. Vol. 1, pp. 416-524.
Ad Galatas. Vol. 1, pp. 525-604.
Ad Ephesios. Vol. 2, pp. 1-81.
Ad Colossenses. Vol. 2, pp. 113-45.

I Ad Timotheum. Vol. 2, pp. 183-229.

Ad Hebraeos. Vol. 2, pp. 287-452.

Des Heiligen Thomas von Aquin Kommentar zum Römerbrief. Translated and edited by Helmut Fahsel. Freiburg: Herder, 1927.

Commentary on Saint Paul's Epistle to the Galatians. Translated by F. R. Larcher, O.P. Albany, NY: Magi Books, 1966.

Commentary on Saint Paul's Epistle to the Ephesians. Translation and Introduction by Matthew L. Lamb, O.C.S.O. Albany, NY: Magi Books, 1966.

Commentary on the Epistle to the Colossians. Translated by Fabian Larcher, O.P. Edited by Daniel A. Keating. Naples, FL: Sapientia Press, 2006.

Commentary on the Epistle to the Hebrews. Translated by Chrysostom Baer, O.Praem. South Bend, IN: St. Augustine's Press, 2006.

Commentaries on Aristotle

Sententia Libri De sensu et sensato

In Aristotelis Libros "De Sensu et Sensato" "De Memoria et Reminiscentia" Commentarium. Edited by Raimundo Spiazzi, O.P. Turin/Rome: Marietti, 1949.

Commentaries on Aristotle's "On Sense and What Is Sensed" and "On Memory and Recollection." Translated by Kevin White and Edward M. Macierowski. Washington, DC: The Catholic University of America Press, 2005.

Sententia super Physicam

In Octo Libros Physicorum Aristotelis Expositio. Edited by P. M. Maggiòlo, O.P. Turin/Rome: Marietti, 1954.

Commentary on Aristotle's Physics. Translated by Richard J. Blackwell, Richard J. Spath, and W. Edmund Thirlkel. Notre Dame, IN: Dumb Ox Books, 1999.

Sententia Libri Politicorum

In Octo Libros Politicorum Aristotelis Expositio. Edited by Raimondo M. Spiazzi. O.P. 2nd ed. Turin/Rome: Marietti, 1966.

Commentary on Aristotle's Politics. Translated by Richard J. Regan. Indianapolis: Hackett, 2007.

Sententia super Metaphysicam

In Duodecim Libros Metaphysicorum Aristotelis Expositio. Edited by Raymondo M. Spiazzi, O.P. Turin/Rome: Marietti, 1950.

Commentary on Aristotle's Metaphysics. Translated and introduced by John P. Rowan. Notre Dame, IN: Dumb Ox Books, 1995.

Treatises

De ente et essentia

De ente et essentia. In *Opuscula philosophica,* pp. 5-18. Edited by Raimundo M. Spiazzi, O.P. Turin/Rome: Marietti, 1954.

On being and essence. Translated by Armand Maurer. Toronto: Pontifical Institute of Medieval Studies, 1968.

Aquinas on Being and Essence. A Translation and Interpretation by Joseph Bobik. South Bend, IN: University of Notre Dame Press, 1965.

Über das Sein und das Wesen. (Bibliothek klassischer Texte.) Translation and commentary by Rudolf Allers. Darmstadt: Wissenschaftlich Buchgesellschaft, 1991.

De principiis naturae

De principiis naturae ad Fratrem Sylvestrum. In *Opuscula philosophica,* pp. 121-28. Edited by Raimundo Spiazzi, O.P. Turin/Rome: Marietti, 1954.

Les Principes de la réalité naturelle. Translated by Jean Madiran. Paris: Nouvelles Éditions Latines, 1963.

Aquinas on Matter and Form and the Elements. A Translation and Interpretation of the *De Principiis Naturae* and the *De Mixtione Elementorum* of St. Thomas Aquinas by Joseph Bobik. Notre Dame, IN: University of Notre Dame Press, 1998.

Die Prinzipien der Wirklichkeit. Translated by Richard Heinzmann. Stuttgart: Kohlhammer, 1999.

Compendium theologiae seu brevis compilatio theologiae ad fratrem Raynaldum

Compendium Theologiae ad fratrem Reginaldum socium suum carissimum. In *Opuscula theologica.* Vol. 1, *De re dogmatica et morali,* pp. 13-138. Edited by Raimundo A. Verardo, O.P. Turin/Rome: Marietti, 1954.

Compendium Theologiae: Grundriß der Glaubenslehre. Deutsch-Lateinisch. Translated by Hans Louis Fäh. Edited by Rudolf Tannhof. Heidelberg: Kehrle, 1963.

Compendium of Theology. Translated by Cyril Vollert, S.J. St. Louis: Herder, 1952.

Requests for Theological Analysis and Judgment

Expositio super primam et secundam Decretalem ad Archidiaconum Tudertinum

Expositio Primae Decretalis ad Archidiaconum Tudertinum. In *Opuscula theologica.* Vol. 1, *De re dogmatica et morali,* pp. 417-26. Edited by Raimundo A. Verardo, O.P. Turin/Rome: Marietti, 1954.

Liturgical Works

Officium de festo Corporis Christi ad mandatum Urbani Papae
"Officium de festo Corporis Christi ad mandatum Urbani Papae IV dictum Festum instituentis." In *Opuscula Theologica.* Vol. 2, *De re spirituali,* pp. 275-81. Edited by Raimundo M. Spiazzi, O.P. Turin/Rome: Marietti, 1954.

PAPAL, CONCILIAR, AND OTHER MAGISTERIAL (AS WELL AS MAGISTERIALLY INVITED) DOCUMENTS

Denzinger, Heinrich. *Enchiridion symbolorum definitionum et declarationum de rebus fidei et morum. Kompendium der Glaubensbekenntnisse und kirchlichen Lehrentscheidungen.* Lateinisch-Deutsch. 40th ed. Edited by Peter Hünermann. Freiburg/Basle/Vienna: Herder, 2005. (Henceforth: Denzinger-Hünermann)

Papal Documents

(All documents from Leo XIII on can be found online at http://www.vatican.va/ or http://www.papalencyclicals.net/)

Leo X. *Exsurge Domine.* 1520. (Denzinger-Hünermann, ##1451-1492)
Pius V. *Ex omnibus afflictionibus.* 1567. (Denzinger-Hünermann, ##1901-1980)
Leo XIII. Encyclical Letter *Aeterni Patris.* 1878.
Pius XII. Encyclical Letter *Mediator Dei.* 1947.
Paul VI. *Sollemnis professio fidei* ("Solemn Profession of Faith"). Pronounced at St. Peter's Basilica, 30 June 1968.
John Paul II. Encyclical Letter *Veritatis splendor.* 1993.
John Paul II. Encyclical Letter *Evangelium vitae.* 1995.
John Paul II. Encyclical Letter *Fides et ratio.* 1998.
John Paul II. Encyclical Letter *Ecclesia de Eucharistia.* 2003.
Benedict XVI. Encyclical Letter *Deus Caritas Est.* 2005.
Benedict XVI. Address to the Roman Curia, 22 December 2005.
Benedict XVI. "Faith, Reason, and the University: Memories and Reflections." Lecture given at the University of Regensburg, 12 September 2006.
Benedict XVI. Postsynodical Apostolic Exhortation *Sacramentum Caritatis.* 2007.
Benedict XVI. Encyclical Letter *Spe Salvi.* 2007.
Benedict XVI. "La Sapienza." Lecture given at the University of Rome, 17 January 2008.
Benedict XVI. Meeting with representatives from the World of Culture. Address given at the Collège des Bernardins, Paris, 12 September 2008.

Benedict XVI. *Address of His Holiness Benedict XVI on the Occasion of Christmas Greetings to the Roman Curia*, December 20, 2010.

Conciliar Documents

Acta Conciliorum Oecumenicorum. Berlin: de Gruyter, 1914ff.

Canons of the Second Council of Orange, A.D. 529: Text, with an Introduction, Translation, and Notes by F. H. Woods. Oxford: James Thornton, 1882.

Decrees of the Ecumenical Councils. Vol. 1, *Nicaea I–Lateran V*. Vol. 2, *Trent–Vatican II*. Edited by Norman P. Tanner, S.J. London: Sheed & Ward; Washington, DC: Georgetown University Press, 1990. (Henceforth: Tanner)

Lateran Council IV. Constitution *De fide catholica*. 1215. (Tanner, Vol. 1, pp. 230-31; Denzinger-Hünermann, ##800-802)

Vatican I. Dogmatic Constitution *Dei Filius*. 1870. (Tanner, Vol. 2, pp. 804-11; Denzinger-Hünermann, ##3000-3045)

Vatican II. Constitution on the Sacred Liturgy *Sacrosanctum Concilium*. 1963. (Tanner, Vol. 2, pp. 820-43; Denzinger-Hünermann, ##4001-4048)

Vatican II. Dogmatic Constitution on the Church *Lumen Gentium*. 1964. (Tanner, Vol. 2, pp. 849-900; Denzinger-Hünermann, ##4101-4179)

Vatican II. Dogmatic Constitution on Divine Revelation *Dei Verbum*. 1965. (Tanner, Vol. 2, pp. 971-81; Denzinger-Hünermann, ##4201-4235)

Vatican II. Pastoral Constitution on the Church in the World of Today *Gaudium et Spes*. 1965. (Tanner, Vol. 2, pp. 1069-1135; Denzinger-Hünermann, ##4301-4345)

Other Magisterial and Magisterially Invited Documents

Catechismus Catholicae Ecclesiae. Vatican City: Libreria Editrice Vaticana, 1997.

Catechism of the Catholic Church. Second Edition revised in accordance with the official Latin text promulgated by Pope John Paul II. Vatican City: Libreria Editrice Vaticana, 2000.

The International Theological Commission. "On the Interpretation of Dogmas." *Origins* 20/1 (17 May 1990): 1-14.

GENERAL WORKS

Adler, Mortimer J. *The Angels and Us*. New York: Macmillan, 1982.

———. *The Idea of Freedom: A Dialectical Examination of the Conceptions of Freedom*. 2 vols. New York: Doubleday, 1958-61.

Aertsen, Jan. *Medieval Philosophy and the Transcendentals: The Case of Thomas Aquinas*. Leiden: Brill, 1996.

Anderson, Robert, and Johann Moser, eds. *The Aquinas Prayer Book: The Prayers and Hymns of St. Thomas Aquinas.* Manchester, NH: Sophia Institute Press, 2000.

Anscombe, G. E. M. *Intention.* 2nd ed. Ithaca, NY: Cornell University Press, 1963.

Ariew, R. "Descartes and Scholasticism: The Intellectual Background to Descartes' Thought." In *The Cambridge Companion to Descartes,* edited by J. Cottingham, pp. 58-90. Cambridge: Cambridge University Press, 1992.

Aristotle. *The Complete Works of Aristotle: The Revised Oxford Translation.* Edited by Jonathan Barnes. 2 volumes. Princeton: Princeton University Press, 1991.

Armogathe, Jean-Robert. "Cartesian Physics and the Eucharist in the Documents of the Holy Office and the Roman Index (1671-76)." In *Receptions of Descartes: Cartesianism and Anti-Cartesianism in Early Modern Europe,* edited by Tad M. Schmalz, pp. 149-70. London/New York: Routledge, 2005.

―――. *Theologia cartesiana: L'explication physique de l'Eucharistie chez Descartes et dom Desgabets.* The Hague: Nijhoff, 1977.

Ashley, Benedict M., O.P. *The Arts of Learning and Communication: A Handbook of the Liberal Arts.* Chicago: Priory Press, 1957.

―――. "The Existence of Created Pure Spirits." In *The Ashley Reader: Redeeming Reason,* pp. 47-59. Naples, FL: Sapientia Press, 2006.

―――. *The Way toward Wisdom: An Interdisciplinary and Intercultural Introduction to Metaphysics.* Notre Dame, IN: University of Notre Dame Press, 2006.

Ashley, Benedict M., O.P., and Pierre H. Conway, O.P. *The Liberal Arts in St. Thomas Aquinas.* Washington, DC: The Thomist Press, 1959.

Augustijn, Cornelius. "Erasmus, Desiderius (1466/69-1536)." *Theologische Realenzyklopädie,* 10:1-18. Berlin: de Gruyter, 1977.

Augustin, Georg, and Klaus Krämer, eds. *Gott denken und bezeugen: Festschrift für Kardinal Walter Kasper zum 75. Geburtstag.* Freiburg: Herder, 2008.

Augustine. *The Confessions.* Translated by Maria Boulding, O.S.B. Hyde Park, NY: New City Press, 1997.

―――. *The Measure of the Soul.* Translated by Francis E. Tourscher, O.S.A. Philadelphia: Peter Reilly Co.; London: Herder, 1933.

―――. *The Teacher, The Free Choice of the Will, Grace and Free Will.* The Fathers of the Church, vol. 59. Translated by Robert P. Russell, O.S.A. Washington, DC: The Catholic University of America Press, 1968.

Balthasar, Hans Urs von. *Dare We Hope "That All Men Be Saved"? With a Short Discussion on Hell.* San Francisco: Ignatius, 1988.

―――. *Von den Aufgaben der katholischen Philosophie in der Zeit.* 2nd ed. Freiburg: Einsiedeln, 1998.

Barth, Karl. *Anselm: Fides Quaerens Intellectum. Anselm's Proof of the Existence of God in the Context of His Theological Scheme.* Translated by Ian W. Robertson. London: SCM Press, 1960.

―――. *Church Dogmatics* II/2. Edinburgh: T&T Clark, 1957.

―――. *Kirchliche Dogmatik.* Vol. I/1. 10th ed. Zurich: TVZ, 1981.

―――. *Kirchliche Dogmatik.* Vol. I/2. 7th ed. Zurich: TVZ, 1983.

Basil the Great of Caesarea. *Fontes Christiani.* Vol. 12, *De Spiritu Sancto: Über den*

Heiligen Geist. Translated by Hermann Josef Sieben, S.J. Freiburg: Herder, 1993.

―――. *On the Holy Spirit.* Translated by David Anderson. Crestwood, NY: St. Vladimir's Seminary Press, 1980.

Bauerschmidt, Frederick Christian. "That the Faithful Become the Temple of God." In *Reading John with St. Thomas Aquinas,* edited by Michael Dauphinais and Matthew Levering, pp. 293-311. Washington, DC: The Catholic University of America Press, 2005.

Beck, Heinrich. *Der Akt-Charakter des Seins.* Munich: Max Hueber, 1965.

Bernard, Ch.-A., S.J. *Théologie de l'espérance selon saint Thomas d'Aquin.* Paris: J. Vrin, 1961.

Beumer, J. B., S.J. "Gratia supponit naturam: Zur Geschichte eines theologischen Prinzips." *Gregorianum* 20 (1939): 381-406.

Bieler, Martin. *Freiheit als Gabe: Ein schöpfungstheologischer Entwurf.* Freiburg: Herder, 1991.

Böckenförde, Ernst-Wolfgang. *Staat, Gesellschaft, Freiheit: Studien zur Staatstheorie und zum Verfassungsrecht.* Frankfurt: Suhrkamp, 1976.

Bonino, Serge-Thomas, O.P., ed. *Surnaturel: A Controversy at the Heart of Twentieth-century Thomistic Thought.* Translated by Robert Williams; translation revised by Matthew Levering. Naples, FL: Sapientia Press, 2009.

―――. *Surnaturel: Une controverse au coeur du thomisme au XXe siècle. Revue thomiste.* Toulouse: École de théologie, 2001.

―――. *Un maître en théologie: Le Père Marie-Michel Labourdette, O.P. Revue thomiste* 92, no. 1 (1992): 5-428.

Bouillard, Henri, S.J. *Conversion et grâce chez S. Thomas d'Aquin.* Paris: Aubier, 1944.

Bouyer, Louis. *The Spirit and Forms of Protestantism.* Westminster, MD: Newman Press, 1956.

Braaten, Carl E., and Robert W. Jenson, eds. *Union with Christ: The New Finnish Interpretation of Luther.* Grand Rapids: Eerdmans, 1998.

Braine, David. "The Debate between Henri de Lubac and His Critics." *Nova et Vetera* (English) 6, no. 3 (2008): 543-90.

Brandom, Robert. *Making It Explicit: Reasoning, Representing, and Discursive Commitment.* Cambridge, MA: Harvard University Press, 1994.

Brennan, Robert Edward, O.P. *Thomistic Psychology: A Philosophic Analysis of the Nature of Man.* New York: Macmillan, 1941.

Brock, Stephen. "St. Thomas and the Eucharistic Conversion." *The Thomist* 65, no. 4 (2001): 529-65.

Budziszewski, J. "The Natural, the Connatural, the Unnatural." In *The Line Through the Heart: Natural Law as Fact, Theory, and Sign of Contradiction,* pp. 61-77. Wilmington, DE: ISI Books, 2009.

Buescher, Gabriel, O.F.M. *The Eucharistic Teaching of William Ockham.* St. Bonaventure, NY: The Franciscan Institute; Louvain: E. Nauwelaerts, 1950.

Bulgakov, Sergius. *The Bride of the Lamb.* Translated by Boris Jakim. Grand Rapids: Eerdmans, 2002.

Burns, J. Patout. *The Development of Augustine's Doctrine of Operative Grace.* Paris: Études Augustiniennes, 1980.

Burrell, David B., C.S.C. "Jacques Maritain and Bernard Lonergan on Divine and Human Freedom." In *The Future of Thomism,* edited by Deal W. Hudson and Dennis W. Moran, pp. 161-68. Notre Dame, IN: University of Notre Dame Press, 1992.

Butera, Gusiseppe. "On Reason's Control of the Passions in Aquinas's Theory of Temperance." *Medieval Studies* 68 (2006): 133-60.

Cates, Diana Fritz. *Aquinas on the Emotions: A Religious-Ethical Inquiry.* Washington, DC: Georgetown University Press, 2009.

Cessario, Romanus, O.P. *Christian Faith and the Theological Life.* Washington, DC: The Catholic University of America Press, 1996.

———. *The Moral Virtues and Theological Ethics.* Notre Dame, IN: University of Notre Dame Press, 1991.

———. *A Short History of Thomism.* Washington, DC: The Catholic University of America Press, 2005.

———. "Theology at Fribourg." *The Thomist* 51, no. 2 (1987): 325-366.

Chaput, Charles J., O.F.M. Cap. *Render unto Caesar: Serving the Nation by Living Our Catholic Beliefs in Political Life.* New York: Doubleday, 2008.

Chenu, Marie-Dominique, O.P. *Toward Understanding Saint Thomas.* Chicago: Regnery, 1964.

Clarke, W. Norris, S.J. *Explorations in Metaphysics: Being — God — Person.* Notre Dame, IN: University of Notre Dame Press, 1994.

———. *The One and the Many: A Contemporary Thomistic Metaphysics.* Notre Dame, IN: University of Notre Dame Press, 2001.

Clayton, Philip. *The Problem of God in Modern Thought.* Grand Rapids: Eerdmans, 2000.

Congar, Yves, O.P. "Le sens de 'l'économie' salutaire dans la 'théologie' de S. Thomas d'Aquin (Somme theologique)." In *Festgabe Joseph Lortz.* Vol. 2, *Glaube und Geschichte,* edited by Erwin Iserloh and Peter Manns, pp. 73-122. Baden-Baden: Bruno Grimm, 1958.

Conway, Pierre H., O.P. *Principles of Education: A Thomistic Approach.* Washington, DC: The Thomist Press, 1960.

Corbin, Michel. *Le chemin de la théologie chez Thomas d'Aquin.* Paris: Beauchesnes, 1974.

Corbon, Jean, O.P. *The Wellspring of Worship.* Translated by Matthew J. O'Connell. San Francisco: Ignatius Press, 2005.

Coreth, Emerich, S.J., Walter M. Neidl, and Georg Pfligersdorffer, eds. *Christliche Philosophie im katholischen Denken des 19. und 20. Jahrhunderts.* 3 vols. Graz: Styra, 1987-1990.

Cottier, Georges, O.P. *Le désir de Dieu: Sur les traces de saint Thomas.* Paris: Éditions parole et silence, 2002.

Cross, Richard. *Duns Scotus*. New York: Oxford University Press, 1999.

Cunningham, Francis L. B., O.P. *The Indwelling of the Trinity: A Historico-Doctrinal Study of the Theory of St. Thomas Aquinas*. Dubuque, IA: Priory Press, 1955.

D'Costa, Gavin. *Theology in the Public Square: Church, Academy, and Nation*. Malden, MA: Blackwell, 2005.

De Koninck, Charles. "Metaphysics and the Interpretation of Words." *Laval théologique et philosophique* 17 (1961): 22-34.

———. "The Primacy of the Common Good against the Personalists." In *The Writings of Charles De Koninck*. Vol. 2, edited and translated by Ralph McInerny, pp. 63-108. Notre Dame, IN: University of Notre Dame Press, 2008-2009.

———. *The Writings of Charles De Koninck*. Edited and translated by Ralph McInerny. 2 volumes. Notre Dame, IN: University of Notre Dame Press, 2008-2009.

Descartes, René. *Les Passions de l'âme*. Introduction by Michel Meyer and commentary by Benoît Timmermans. Paris: Librairie Générale Française, 1990.

———. *The Passions of the Soul*. In *The Philosophical Writings of Descartes*. Vol. 1, translated by John Cottingham, Robert Stoothoff, and Dugald Murdoch, pp. 325-404. Cambridge: Cambridge University Press, 1985.

———. *Principles of Philosophy*. In *The Philosophical Writings of Descartes*, vol. 1, translated by John Cottingham, Robert Stoothoff, and Dugald Murdoch. Cambridge: Cambridge University Press, 1985.

Dewan, Lawrence, O.P. "Does Being Have a Nature? (Or: Metaphysics as a Science of the Real)." In *Approaches to Metaphysics*, edited by William Sweet, pp. 23-59. Dordrecht/Boston/London: Kluwer Academic Publishers, 2004.

———. "Nature as a Topic for Metaphysical Inquiry." In *Form and Being: Studies in Thomistic Metaphysics*, pp. 205-28. Washington, DC: The Catholic University of America Press, 2006.

———. "St. Thomas and Analogy: The Logician and the Metaphysician." In *Form and Being: Studies in Thomistic Metaphysics*, pp. 81-95. Washington, DC: The Catholic University of America Press, 2006.

Dillon, Thomas E. "Commencement Day Remarks." *Communio* 35, no. 4 (2008): 671-73.

Dixon, Thomas. *From Passions to Emotions: The Creation of a Secular Psychological Category*. Cambridge: Cambridge University Press, 2003.

Djuth, Marianne. "*Initium fidei*." In *Augustine through the Ages: An Encyclopedia*, edited by Allan D. Fitzgerald, O.S.A., pp. 447-51. Grand Rapids: Eerdmans, 1999.

Dolfen, Christian. *Die Stellung des Erasmus von Rotterdam zur scholastischen Methode*. Osnabrück: Meinders & Elstermann, 1936.

Donneaud, Henry, O.P. "*Surnaturel* through the Fine-Tooth Comb of Traditional Thomism." In *Surnaturel: A Controversy at the Heart of Twentieth-century Thomistic Thought*, edited by Serge-Thomas Bonino, O.P.; translated by

Robert Williams; translation revised by Matthew Levering, pp. 41-57. Naples, FL: Sapientia Press, 2009.

Dulles, Avery Cardinal, S.J. *Magisterium: Teacher and Guardian of the Faith.* Naples, FL: Sapientia Press, 2007.

———. "Wisdom as the Source of Unity for Theology." In *Wisdom and Holiness, Science and Scholarship: Essays in Honor of Matthew L. Lamb,* edited by Michael Dauphinais and Matthew Levering, pp. 59-71. Naples, FL: Sapientia Press, 2007.

Dunne, Joseph. *Back to the Rough Ground: 'Phronesis' and 'Techne' in Modern Philosophy and in Aristotle.* Notre Dame, IN: University of Notre Dame Press, 1993.

Dupré, Louis. *Passage to Modernity: An Essay in the Hermeneutics of Nature and Culture.* New Haven, CT: Yale University Press, 1993.

Elders, Leo J., S.V.D. *Die Naturphilosophie des Thomas von Aquin.* Weilheim-Bierbronnen: Gustav-Siewerth-Akademie, 2004.

———. "St. Thomas Aquinas on Education and Instruction." *Nova et Vetera* (English) 7, no. 1 (2009): 107-24.

Erasmus von Rotterdam. *Ausgewählte Werke.* Vol. 4. Darmstadt: Wissenschaftliche Buchgesellschaft, 1969.

Fabro, Cornelio. "The Intensive Hermeneutics of Thomistic Philosophy: The Notion of Participation." Translated by B. M. Bonansea. *Review of Metaphysics* 27, no. 3 (1974): 449-91.

———. *Participation et causalité selon S. Thomas d'Aquin.* Paris: Béatrice-Nauwelaerts; Louvain: Publications Universitaires, 1961.

Farrelly, Dom M. John, O.S.B. *Predestination, Grace, and Free Will.* Westminster, MD: Newman Press, 1964.

Farthing, John L. *Thomas Aquinas and Gabriel Biel: Interpretations of St. Thomas Aquinas in German Nominalism on the Eve of the Reformation.* Durham, NC: Duke University Press, 1988.

Feingold, Lawrence. *The Natural Desire to See God According to St. Thomas Aquinas and His Interpreters.* Rome: Apollinare Studi, 2001.

———. *The Natural Desire to See God According to St. Thomas Aquinas and His Interpreters.* 2nd ed. Naples, FL: Sapientia Press, 2010.

Franks, Christopher A. *He Became Poor: The Poverty of Christ and Aquinas's Economic Teachings.* Grand Rapids: Eerdmans, 2009.

Fries, Albert, C.SS.R. "Hoffnung und Heilsgewißheit bei Thomas von Aquin." In *Studia Moralia VII: Contributiones ad problema spei,* pp. 131-236. Rome: Desclée & Socii, 1969.

Gardeil, Ambroise, O.P. *Le donné révélé et la théologie.* 2nd ed. Paris: Editions du Cerf, 1932.

———. *La structure de l'âme et l'expérience mystique.* Paris: Libraire Victor Lecoffre, 1927.

Garrigou-Lagrange, Reginald, O.P. *De Eucharistia accedunt De Paenitentia*

quaestiones dogmaticae; Commentarius in Summam theologicam S. Thomae.
Rome: Marietti, 1943.

———. *The Love of God and the Cross of Jesus.* Vol. 1. Translated by Sr. Jean Marie.
St. Louis: Herder, 1947; reprinted 1957.

———. *Le sens du mystère et le clair-obscur intellectual: Nature et surnaturel.* Paris:
Desclée de Brouwer, 1934.

———. *The Three Ages of the Interior Life.* Vol. 1. Translated by Sr. M. Timothea
Doyle, O.P. St. Louis: Herder, 1947.

Gauthier, R.-A., O.P. *Magnanimité: L'idéal de la grandeur dans la philosophie
païenne et dans la théologie chrétienne.* Paris: J. Vrin, 1951.

Geiger, L.-B., O.P. *La participation dans la philosophie de S. Thomas d'Aquin.* Paris:
J. Vrin, 1942.

Gillespie, Michael Allen. *Nihilism before Nietzsche.* Chicago: The University of Chicago Press, 1995.

———. *The Theological Origins of Modernity.* Chicago: The University of Chicago
Press, 2008.

Gilson, Étienne. *La philosophie au moyen âge.* Reprint of 2nd ed. Paris: Petite Bib-
liothèque Payot, 1976.

Gondreau, Paul. "The Passions and the Moral Life: Appreciating the Originality of
Aquinas." *The Thomist* 71, no. 3 (2007): 419-50.

———. *The Passions of Christ's Soul in the Theology of St. Thomas Aquinas.*
Beiträge zur Geschichte der Philosophie und Theologie des Mittelalters;
Neue Folge, Band 61. Münster: Aschendorff, 2002.

Gonet, Jean Baptiste, O.P. *Clypeus theologiae thomisticae contra novos ejus
impugnatores.* 6 vols. Bordeaux 1659-69; Lyons 1681; Paris 1875.

Goris, Harm. "Steering Clear of Charybdis: Some Directions for Avoiding 'Grace
Extrinsicism' in Aquinas." *Nova et Vetera* (English) 5, no. 1 (2007): 67-80.

Grane, Leif. *Contra Gabrielem: Luthers Auseinandersetzung mit Gabriel Biel in der
Disputatio Contra Scholasticam Theologiam.* Copenhagen: Gyldendal, 1962.

Gredt, Joseph, O.S.B. *Elementa Philosophiae Aristotelico-Thomisticae.* Volume 1:
Logica/Philosophia Naturalis, 11th ed. Freiburg: Herder, 1956.

Griffiths, Paul J. *Intellectual Appetite: A Theological Grammar.* Washington, DC:
The Catholic University of America Press, 2009.

Griffiths, Paul J., and Reinhard Hütter, eds. *Reason and the Reasons of Faith.* New
York: T&T Clark International, 2005.

Groeschel, Benedict J., C.F.R., and James Monti. *In the Presence of Our Lord: The
History, Theology, and Psychology of Eucharistic Devotion.* Huntington, IN:
Our Sunday Visitor, 1997.

Habermas, Jürgen. *Philosophical Discourse of Modernity: Twelve Lectures.* Translated by Frederick G. Lawrence. Cambridge, MA: MIT Press, 1987.

———. *Postmetaphysical Thinking: Philosophical Essays.* Translated by William
Mark Hohengarten. Cambridge, MA: MIT Press, 1992.

Hardon, John A., S.J. *The History of Eucharistic Adoration: Development of Doctrine
in the Catholic Church.* Oak Lawn, IL: CMJ Marian Publishers, 1997.

Hart, David Bentley. *Atheist Delusions: The Christian Revolution and Its Fashionable Enemies.* New Haven, CT: Yale University Press, 2009.

———. "The Offering of Names: Metaphysics, Nihilism, and Analogy." In *Reason and the Reasons of Faith,* edited by Paul J. Griffiths and Reinhard Hütter, pp. 255-91. New York: T&T Clark International, 2005.

Hauerwas, Stanley. "On Developing Hopeful Virtues." In *Christians Among the Virtues: Theological Conversations with Ancient and Modern Ethics,* by Stanley Hauerwas and Charles Pinches, pp. 113-28. Notre Dame, IN: University of Notre Dame Press, 1997.

———. *The State of the University: Academic Knowledges and the Knowledge of God.* Malden, MA, and Oxford: Blackwell, 2007.

Heidegger, Martin. *Nietzsche.* Pfullingen: Neske, 1961.

———. *Der Satz vom Grund.* Pfullingen: Neske, 1957.

Hibbs, Thomas S. *Dialectic and Narrative in Aquinas: An Interpretation of the "Summa Contra Gentiles."* Notre Dame, IN: University of Notre Dame Press, 1995.

Hobbes, Thomas. *Leviathan.* Edited by Edwin Curley. Indianapolis and Cambridge: Hackett, 1994.

Hochschild, Joshua. *The Semantics of Analogy: Rereading Cajetan's De Nominum Analogia.* Notre Dame, IN: University of Notre Dame Press, 2010.

Horkheimer, Max, and Theodor W. Adorno. *Dialectic of Enlightenment: Philosophical Fragments.* Edited by Gunzelin Schmid Noerr. Translated by Edmund Jephcott. Stanford, CA: Stanford University Press, 2002.

Hume, David. *A Treatise of Human Nature.* Analytical Index by L. A. Selby-Bigge. 2nd ed. With text revised and notes by P. H. Nidditch. Oxford: Clarendon Press, 1981.

Hütter, Reinhard. "The Ruins of Discontinuity." *First Things* 209 (January 2011): 37-41.

———. *Suffering Divine Things: Theology as Church Practice.* Grand Rapids: Eerdmans, 2000.

———. "Transubstantiation Revisited: *Sacra Doctrina,* Dogma, and Metaphysics." In *Ressourcement Thomism: Sacred Doctrine, the Sacraments, and the Moral Life,* edited by Reinhard Hütter and Matthew Levering, pp. 21-79. Washington, DC: The Catholic University of America Press, 2010.

Iserloh, Erwin. *Gnade und Eucharistie in der philosophischen Theologie des Wilhelm von Ockham: Ihre Bedeutung für die Ursachen der Reformation.* Wiesbaden: Steiner, 1956.

Jacob, Josef, S.V.D. *Passiones. Ihr Wesen und ihre Anteilnahme an der Vernunft nach dem hl. Thomas von Aquin.* Mödling: St. Gabriel, 1958.

Janz, Denis R. *Luther and Late Medieval Thomism: A Study in Theological Anthropology.* Waterloo: Wilfrid Laurier University Press, 1983.

Jensen, Steven. "The Error of the Passions." *The Thomist* 73, no. 3 (2009): 349-79.

Jenson, Robert W. "An Ontology of Freedom in the *De Servo arbitrio* of Luther," *Modern Theology* 10 (1994): 247-52.

————. *Systematic Theology*. Vol. 2, *The Works of God*. New York: Oxford University Press, 1999.

John of St. Thomas, O.P. *Cursus Philosophicus Thomisticus*. Vol. 1. Paris: Vivès, 1883.

————. *Cursus Theologicus*. Vol. 1. Paris: Tournai; Rome: Desclée, 1931.

————. *Cursus Theologicus*. Vol. 4. Paris: Tournai; Rome: Desclée, 1953.

Johnson, Elizabeth A. "The Right Way to Speak about God? Pannenberg on Analogy." *Theological Studies* 43, no. 2 (1982): 673-92.

Journet, Charles Cardinal. *The Mass: The Presence of the Sacrifice of the Cross*. Translated by Victor Szczurek, O.Praem. South Bend, IN: St. Augustine's Press, 2008.

Jüngel, Eberhard. *God as the Mystery of the World: On the Foundation of the Theology of the Crucified One in the Dispute between Theism and Atheism*. Translated by Darrell L. Guder. Grand Rapids: Eerdmans, 1983.

————. *Gott als Geheimnis der Welt. Zur Begründung der Theologie des Gekreuzigten im Streit zwischen Theismus und Atheismus*. 5th ed. Tübingen: Mohr Siebeck, 1986.

————. *Zum Ursprung der Analogie bei Parmenides und Heraklit*. Berlin: de Gruyter, 1964.

Kant, Immanuel: *Anthropologie in pragmatischer Hinsicht*. In *Werke in zehn Bänden*. Vol. 10, *Schriften zur Anthropologie, Geschichtsphilosophie, Politik und Pädagogik. Zweiter Teil*, edited by Wilhelm Weischedel, pp. 399-690. Darmstadt: Wissenschaftliche Buchgesellschaft, 1981.

————. *Critique of Pure Reason*. Translated by Paul Guyer and Allen W. Wood. Cambridge: Cambridge University Press, 1997.

————. *Kritik der reinen Vernunft*. Hamburg: Meiner, 1956.

————. *Kritik der Urteilskraft*. Hamburg: Meiner, 1954.

Kasper, Walter. *Das Absolute in der Geschichte. Philosophie und Theologie der Geschichte in der Spätphilosophie Schellings*. Mainz: Grünewald, 1965.

————. "Grundlinien einer Theologie der Geschichte." *Theologische Quartalschrift* 144 (1964): 129-69.

————. *Die Lehre von der Tradition in der Römischen Schule (Giovanni Perrone, Carlo Passaglia, Clemens Schrader)*. Die Überlieferung in der neueren Theologie 5. Freiburg: Herder, 1962.

————. *Die Methoden der Dogmatik — Einheit und Vielheit*. Munich: Kösel, 1967.

————. *The Methods of Dogmatic Theology*. Translated by John Drury. Glen Rock, NJ: Paulist Press, 1969.

Kerr, Fergus, O.P. *After Aquinas: Versions of Thomism*. Oxford: Blackwell, 2002.

————. *Twentieth Century Catholic Theologians: From Neo-Scholasticism to Nuptial Mysticism*. Oxford: Blackwell, 2007.

Kierkegaard, Søren. *Sickness unto Death*. Translated and edited by Howard V. Hong and Edna H. Hong. Princeton, NJ: Princeton University Press, 1980.

Klubertanz, George P., S.J. *St. Thomas Aquinas on Analogy: A Textual Analysis and Systematic Synthesis*. Chicago: Loyola University Press, 1960.

Labourdette, Marie-Michel, O.P. "Aux origins du péché de l'homme d'après saint Thomas d'Aquin." *Revue thomiste* 85, no. 3 (1985): 357-98.

———. *Cours de théologie morale.* Vol. 2, *Les Actes Humains.* Ia-IIae, 6-48. Toulouse: Typescript, n.d.

———. *Cours de théologie morale.* Vol. 9, *L'espérance (Thomas d'Aquin: Somme théologique II-II, qq. 17-22).* Toulouse: s.n., 1959-1960.

———. "Le péché originel dans la Tradition vivante de l'Église." *Revue thomiste* 84, no. 3 (1984): 357-98.

———. *Le péché originel et les origines de l'homme.* Paris: Alsatia, 1953.

———. "La vie théologale selon saint Thomas: L'object de la foi." *Revue thomiste* 58 (1958): 597-622.

Lakebrink, Bernhard. "Analektik und Dialektik: Zur Methode des Thomistischen und Hegelschen Denkens." In *Perfectio Omnium Perfectionum: Studien zur Seinskonzeption bei Thomas von Aquin und Hegel,* edited by C. Günzler et al., pp. 9-37. Vatican City: Libreria Editrice Vaticana, 1984.

LaNave, Gregory. *Through Holiness to Wisdom: The Nature of Theology according to St. Bonaventure.* Rome: Istituto storico dei Cappuccini, 2005.

———. "Why Holiness Is Necessary for Theology: Some Thomistic Distinctions." *The Thomist* 74, no. 3 (2010): 437-59.

Laporta, Jorge. *La destinée de la nature humaine selon Thomas d'Aquin.* Paris: J. Vrin, 1965.

Le Guillou, Marie-Joseph, O.P. "Surnaturel." *Revue des sciences philosophiques et théologiques* 34 (1950): 226-43.

Leff, Gordon. *William of Ockham: The Metamorphosis of Scholastic Discourse.* Manchester: Manchester University Press; Totowa, NJ: Rowman and Littlefield, 1975.

Leget, Carlos. "Martha Nussbaum and Thomas Aquinas on the Emotions." *Theological Studies* 64, no. 3 (2003): 558-81.

Levi, A., S.J. *French Moralists: The Theory of the Passions, 1585-1649.* Oxford: Clarendon Press, 1964.

Lindbeck, George A. *The Nature of Doctrine: Religion and Theology in a Postliberal Age.* 25th Anniversary Edition. Louisville: Westminster/John Knox, 2009.

———. "Participation and Existence in the Interpretation of St. Thomas Aquinas." *Franciscan Studies* 17 (1957): 1-22, 107-25.

Lombardo, Nicholas E., O.P. *The Logic of Desire: Aquinas on Emotion.* Washington, DC: The Catholic University of America Press, 2010.

Lonergan, Bernard, S.J. *Collected Works of Bernard Lonergan.* Vol. 1, *Grace and Freedom: Operative Grace in the Thought of St. Thomas Aquinas.* Edited by Frederick E. Crowe and Robert M. Doran. Toronto: University of Toronto Press, 2000.

Long, Stephen A. "Divine Providence and John 15:5." In *Reading John with St. Thomas Aquinas,* edited by Michael Dauphinais and Matthew Levering, pp. 140-52. Washington, DC: The Catholic University Press of America, 2005.

————. *Natura Pura: On the Recovery of Nature in the Doctrine of Grace.* New York: Fordham University Press, 2010.

————. "Obediential Potency, Human Knowledge, and the Natural Desire for the Vision of God." *International Philosophical Quarterly* 37, no. 1 (1997): 45-63.

————. "On the Loss, and Recovery, of Nature as a Theonomic Principle: Reflections on the Nature/Grace Controversy." In *Natura Pura: On the Recovery of Nature in the Doctrine of Grace,* pp. 10-51. New York: Fordham University Press, 2010.

————. *The Teleological Grammar of the Moral Act.* Naples, FL: Sapientia Press, 2007.

Lortz, Joseph. *The Reformation in Germany.* Vol. 1. Translated by Ronald Walls. New York: Herder, 1939, 1968.

Lubac, Henri de, S.J. *At the Service of the Church: Henri de Lubac Reflects on the Circumstances That Occasioned His Writings.* Translated by Anne Elisabeth Englund. San Francisco: Ignatius 1993.

————. *Augustinianism and Modern Theology.* Translated by Lancelot Sheppard. New York: Herder and Herder, 1969.

————. *Augustinianism and Modern Theology.* Translated by Lancelot Sheppard. New York: Crossroad, 2000.

————. *Augustinianisme et théologie moderne.* Paris: F. Aubier, 1965.

————. *Corpus Mysticum: L'Eucharistie et L'Église au Moyen Age.* Paris: Aubier-Montaigne, 1949.

————. *Corpus Mysticum: The Eucharist and the Church in the Middle Ages.* Edited by Laurence Paul Hemming and Susan Frank Parsons; translated by Gemma Simmonds, C.J., with Richard Price and Christopher Stevens. Notre Dame, IN: University of Notre Dame Press, 2006.

————. *Le mystère du surnaturel.* Paris: Aubier, 1965.

————. *The Mystery of the Supernatural.* Translated by Rosemary Sheed. New York: Herder and Herder, 1965.

————. *Surnaturel: Études historiques. Nouvelle édition avec la traducion intégrale des citations latines et grecques.* Paris: Desclée de Brouwer, 1991.

Luther, Martin. *D. Martin Luthers Werke: Kritische Gesamtausgabe.* Edited by J. F. K. Knaake et al. Weimar: Böhlau, 1883ff.

————. *Luther's Works.* Vol. 26, *Lectures on Galatians 1535, Chapters 1–4.* Edited by Jaroslav Pelikan and Walter A. Hansen. St. Louis: Concordia, 1963.

————. *Luther's Works.* Vol. 29, *Lectures on Titus, Philemon, and Hebrews.* Edited by Jaroslav Pelikan and Walter A. Hansen. St. Louis: Concordia, 1968.

Lyttkens, Hampus. *The Analogy between God and the World: An Investigation of Its Background and Interpretation of Its Use by Thomas of Aquino.* Translated by Axel Poignant. Uppsala: Almqvist and Wiksells, 1952.

MacIntyre, Alasdair. *Dependent Rational Animals: Why Human Beings Need the Virtues.* Peru, IL: Carus, 1999.

————. "The End of Education: The Fragmentation of the American University." *Commonweal* 133, no. 18 (2006): 10-14.

————. *God, Philosophy, Universities: A Selective History of the Catholic Philosophi-cal Tradition.* Lanham, MD: Rowman & Littlefield, 2009.

————. "The Intelligibility of Action." In *Rationality, Relativism, and Human Sci-ences,* edited by J. Margolis, M. Krausz, and R. M. Burian, pp. 63-80. Dordrecht: Nijhoff, 1986.

————. *Three Rival Versions of Moral Inquiry.* Notre Dame, IN: University of No-tre Dame Press, 1990.

Mahoney, Edward P., "Sense, Intellect, and Imagination in Albert, Thomas, and Siger." In *The Cambridge History of Later Medieval Philosophy,* edited by Norman Kretzmann, Anthony Kenny, Jan Pinborg, and Eleonore Stump, pp. 602-22. Cambridge: Cambridge University Press, 1982.

Mannermaa, Tuomo. *Christ Present in Faith: Luther's View of Justification.* Minne-apolis: Augsburg Fortress Press, 2005.

Manser, Gallus M., O.P. *Das Wesen des Thomismus.* 3rd enlarged ed. Freiburg: Paulusverlag, 1949.

Mansini, Guy, O.S.B. "Lonergan on the Natural Desire in the Light of Feingold." *Nova et Vetera* (English) 5, no. 1 (2007): 185-98.

Marcuse, Herbert. *One Dimensional Man: Studies in the Ideology of Advanced In-dustrial Society.* Boston: Beacon, 1966.

Marion, Jean-Luc. *God Without Being.* Translated by Thomas A. Carlson. Chicago: University of Chicago Press, 1991.

Maritain, Jacques. *Distinguish to Unite or The Degrees of Knowledge.* Translated from the 4th French ed. under the supervision of Gerald B. Phelan. New York: Charles Scribner's Sons, 1959.

————. *The Sin of the Angel: An Essay on a Re-Interpretation of Some Thomistic Po-sitions.* Translated by William L. Rossner, S.J. Westminster, MD: Newman Press, 1959.

Marshall, Bruce. "*Quod Scit Una Uetula:* Aquinas on the Nature of Theology." In *The Theology of Thomas Aquinas,* edited by Rik Van Nieuwenhove and Jo-seph P. Wawrykow, pp. 1-35. Notre Dame, IN: University of Notre Dame Press, 2005.

————. *Trinity and Truth.* Cambridge: Cambridge University Press, 2000.

McDowell, John. *Mind and World.* Cambridge, MA: Harvard University Press, 1994.

McInerny, Ralph. *Aquinas and Analogy.* Washington, DC: The Catholic University of America Press, 1996.

————. *Praeambula Fidei: Thomism and the God of the Philosophers.* Washington, DC: The Catholic University of America Press, 2006.

McSorley, Harry J., C.S.P. *Luther: Right or Wrong? An Ecumenical-Theological Study of Luther's Major Work, The Bondage of the Will.* New York: Newman Press; Minneapolis: Augsburg Press, 1969.

Merriell, Juvenal. *To the Image of the Trinity: A Study in the Development of Aqui-nas' Teaching.* Toronto: Pontifical Institute of Medieval Studies, 1990.

Milbank, John. *The Suspended Middle: Henri de Lubac and the Debate concerning the Supernatural.* Grand Rapids: Eerdmans, 2005.

Miner, Robert. *Thomas Aquinas on the Passions: A Study of Summa Theologiae 1a2ae 22-48.* Cambridge: Cambridge University Press, 2009.

Montagnes, Bernard, O.P. *La doctrine de l'analogie de l'être d'après Saint Thomas d'Aquin.* Louvain: Publications Universitaires; Paris: Béatrice-Nauwelaerts, 1963.

―――――. *The Doctrine of the Analogy of Being according to Thomas Aquinas.* Translated by E. M. Macierowski; revised and corrected by Pol Vandervelde; and edited by Andrew Tallon. Milwaukee: Marquette University Press, 2004.

Mulcahy, Matthew B., O.P. *Aquinas's Notion of Pure Nature and the Christian Integralism of Henri de Lubac and Radical Orthodoxy: Not Everything Is Grace.* New York: Peter Lang, 2011.

Muñiz, Francisco P., O.P. *The Work of Theology.* Translated by John P. Reid, O.P. Washington, DC: The Thomist Press, 1953.

Munzel, G. Felicitas. *Kant's Conception of Moral Character: The "Critical" Link of Morality, Anthropology, and Reflective Judgment.* Chicago: University of Chicago Press, 1999.

Newman, John Henry Cardinal. *The Idea of a University.* The New Edition of the Works of John Henry Newman, edited by Charles Frederick Harrold. New York: Longmans, Green and Co., 1947.

―――――. *Lectures on the Doctrine of Justification.* 1838. 3rd ed. New York: Scribner, Welford, and Armstrong, 1874.

―――――. *Lectures on the Present Position of Catholics in England.* Edited by Daniel M. O'Connell, S.J. New York: The America Press, 1942.

Nichols, Aidan, O.P. *Reason with Piety: Garrigou-Lagrange in the Service of Catholic Thought.* Naples, FL: Sapientia Press, 2008.

―――――. "Thomism and the Nouvelle Théologie." *The Thomist* 64, no. 1 (2000): 1-19.

Nicolas, Jean-Hervé, O.P. *Synthèse dogmatique: De la Trinité à la Trinité.* Fribourg: Éditions Universitaires; Paris: Éditions Beauchesne, 1985.

Nietzsche, Friedrich. "On Truth and Lies in a Nonmoral Sense." In *Philosophy and Truth: Selections from Nietzsche's Notebooks of the Early 1870's.* Translated and edited by Daniel Breazeale, pp. 79-97. Atlantic Highlands, NJ: Humanities Press, 1979.

―――――. *The Will to Power.* Translated by Walter Kaufmann and R. J. Hollingdale. New York: Vintage Books, 1968.

Oakes, Edward T., S.J. "On Milbank's *The Suspended Middle.*" *Nova et Vetera* (English) 4, no. 3 (2006): 667-96.

Oberman, Heiko A. *The Harvest of Medieval Theology: Gabriel Biel and Late Medieval Nominalism.* Grand Rapids: Baker, 2000.

O'Callaghan, John P. *Thomist Realism and the Linguistic Turn: Toward a More Perfect Form of Existence.* Notre Dame, IN: University of Notre Dame Press, 2003.

O'Connor, William. *The Eternal Quest: The Teaching of St. Thomas Aquinas on the Natural Desire for God.* New York and London: Longman, Green, and Co., 1947.

Oeing-Hanhoff, Ludger. *Ens et unum convertuntur: Stellung und Gehalt des Grundsatzes in der Philosophie des hl. Thomas von Aquin (Beiträge zur Geschichte der Philosophie und Theologie des Mittelalters,* Vol. 37/3). Münster: Aschendorff, 1953.

Osborne, Thomas M., Jr. *Love of Self and Love of God in Thirteenth-Century Ethics.* Notre Dame, IN: University of Notre Dame Press, 2005.

Palomo, Cepada, O.P. "Muñiz." In *Diccionario de Historia Eclesiástica de Espāna,* edited by Quintín Aldea Vaquero, Tomás Marín Martínez, and José Vives. Vol. 3, p. 1970. Madrid: Instituto Enrique Flórez, Consejo Superior de Investigaciones Científicas, 1972-75.

Pannenberg, Wolfhart. *Analogie und Offenbarung: Eine kritische Untersuchung zur Geschichte des Analogiebegriffes in der Lehre von der Gotteserkenntnis.* Göttingen: Vandenhoeck & Ruprecht, 2007.

―――. "Analogy and Doxology." In *Basic Questions in Theology,* volume 1. Translated by George H. Kelm, pp. 212-38. Philadelphia: Fortress, 1970.

―――. *Systematische Theologie.* Vol. 1. Göttingen: Vandenhoeck & Ruprecht, 1988.

―――. *Systematic Theology.* Translated by Geoffrey W. Bromiley. Grand Rapids: Eerdmans, 1991-1998.

―――. "Zur Bedeutung des Analogiedankens bei Karl Barth: Eine Auseinandersetzung mit Urs von Balthasar." *Theologische Literaturzeitung* 78 (1953): 17-24.

Pasnau, Robert. *Thomas Aquinas on Human Nature: A Philosophical Study of Summa theologiae 1a, 75-89.* Cambridge: Cambridge University Press, 2002.

Payne, John B. *Erasmus: His Theology of the Sacraments.* Richmond, VA: John Knox Press, 1970.

Peddicord, Richard, O.P. *The Sacred Monster of Thomism: An Introduction to the Life and Legacy of Reginald Garrigou-Lagrange, O.P.* South Bend, IN: St. Augustine Press, 2005.

Pegis, Anton C. "St. Thomas and the Unity of Man." In *Progress in Philosophy: Philosophical Studies in Honor of Rev. Doctor Charles A. Hart,* edited by James A. McWilliams, S.J., pp. 153-73. Milwaukee, WI: Bruce Publishing Co., 1955.

Pesch, Otto Hermann. *Die Deutsche Thomas-Ausgabe: Summa Theologica.* Deutsch-lateinische Ausgabe. Vol. 12, *Die Sünde.* Vienna: Styria, 2004.

―――. "Philosophie und Theologie der Freiheit bei Thomas von Aquin in quaest. Disp. 6 De malo." *Münchener Theologische Zeitschrift* 13 (1962): 1-25.

Philippe, Marie-Dominique. *Les trois sagesses: Entretiens avec Frédéric Lenoir.* Paris: Fayard, 1994.

Pieper, Josef. "Disciplining the Eyes." In *The Four Cardinal Virtues,* pp. 198-202. Notre Dame, IN: University of Notre Dame Press, 1966.

————. *On Hope*. Translated by Mary Frances McCarthy. San Francisco: Ignatius, 1986.

————. *Philosophia Negativa: Zwei Versuche über Thomas von Aquin*. Munich: Kösel, 1953.

————. *Über die Hoffnung*. Leipzig: Hegner, 1938.

Pinckaers, Servais, O.P. "La nature vertueuse de l'espérance." *Revue thomiste* 58 (1958): 405-42, 623-44.

————. "Reappropriating Aquinas's Account of the Passions." In *The Pinckaers Reader: Renewing Thomistic Moral Theology*, edited by John Berkman and Craig Steven Titus, pp. 273-87. Washington, DC: The Catholic University of America Press, 2005.

Pöggeler, Otto. *Der Denkweg Martin Heideggers*. Pfullingen: Neske, 1963.

Polanyi, Michael. *Personal Knowledge: Towards a Post-Critical Philosophy*. Chicago: University of Chicago Press, 1962.

Porter, Jean. "The Subversion of Virtue: Acquired and Infused Virtues in the *Summa Theologiae*." *Annual of the Society of Christian Ethics* 5 (1992): 19-41.

Princeton Review. *The Best 371 Colleges*. New York: Random House, 2009.

Quoëx, Franck. "Thomas d'Aquin, mystagogue: *L'expositio missae* de la *Somme de Théologie* (III^a, q. 83, a. 4-5)." *Revue thomiste* 105, no. 2 (2005): 179-225 and 435-72.

Ramírez, Santiago Maria, O.P. *De Hominis beatitudine tractatus theologicus*. Vol. 1. Matriti: Aldecoa, 1942.

————. *De Passionibus Animae in I-II Summae Theologiae Divi Thomae Expositio (QQ. XXII-XLVIII)*. Edited by Victorino Rodriguez, O.P. Madrid: Instituto de Filosofia "Luis Vives," 1973.

Ratzinger, Joseph. "Biblical Interpretation in Crisis." In *God's Word: Scripture — Tradition — Office*, pp. 91-126. San Francisco: Ignatius Press, 2008.

————. "Gratia praesupponit naturam." In *Dogma und Verkündigung*, pp. 161-81. Munich/Freiburg: Wewel, 1973.

————. *Introduction to Christianity*. Translated by J. R. Foster. London: Search Press, 1969.

————. *Jesus von Nazareth*. Freiburg: Herder, 2007.

————. *The Nature and Mission of Theology: Essays to Orient Theology in Today's Debates*. San Francisco: Ignatius, 1995.

Robillard, Hyacinthe-Marie. *De l'analogie et du concept d'être*. Montréal: Les presses de l'Université de Montréal, 1963.

Rocca, Gregory P. *Speaking the Incomprehensible God: Thomas Aquinas on the Interplay of Positive and Negative Theology*. Washington, DC: The Catholic University of America Press, 2004.

Rolnick, Philip A. *Analogical Possibilities: How Words Refer to God*. Atlanta: Scholar's Press, 1993.

Rorty, Amélie Oksenberg. "From Passions to Emotions and Sentiments." *Philosophy* 57, no. 220 (1982): 159-72.

Rupp, E. Gordon, and Philip S. Watson, eds. *Luther and Erasmus: Free Will and Salvation.* Philadelphia: Westminster Press, 1969.

Rziha, John. *Perfecting Human Actions: St. Thomas Aquinas on Human Participation in Eternal Law.* Washington, DC: The Catholic University of America Press, 2009.

Schall, James V., S.J., ed. *The Whole Truth about Man: John Paul II to University Faculties and Students.* Boston: Daughters of St. Paul, 1981.

Scheeben, Matthias Joseph. *The Mysteries of Christianity.* Translated by Cyril Vollert, S.J. St. Louis: Herder, 1951.

Schenk, Richard, O.P. "Eine Ökumene des Einspruchs. Systematische Überlegungen zum heutigen ökumenischen Prozeß aus einer römisch-katholischen Sicht." In *Die Reunionsgespräche im Niedersachsen des 17. Jahrhunderts: Royas y Spinola — Molan — Leibniz (Studien zur Kirchengeschichte Niedersachsens),* vol. 37, edited by Hans Otte and Richard Schenk, pp. 225-50. Göttingen: Vandenhoeck & Ruprecht, 1999.

————. "Factus in agonia. Zur Todesangst Christi und der Christen." In *Christus — Gottes schöpferisches Wort: Festschrift für Christoph Kardinal Schönborn,* edited by Georg Augustin, Maria Brun, Erwin Keller and Markus Schulze, pp. 401-28. Freiburg i. Br.: Herder, 2010.

Schlier, Heinrich. *Herders theologischer Kommentar zum Neuen Testament.* Vol. 6, *Der Römerbrief.* 2nd ed. Freiburg/Basel/Vienna: Herder, 1979.

Schmaltz, Tad M. *Radical Cartesianism: The French Reception of Descartes.* Cambridge: Cambridge University Press, 2002.

Schmitz, Kenneth L. *The Gift: Creation.* Milwaukee: Marquette University Press, 1982.

Schockenhoff, Eberhard. *Bonum hominis: Die anthropologischen und theologischen Grundlagen des Tugendbegriffs bei Thomas von Aquin.* Mainz: Grünewald, 1987.

Schönberger, Rolf. *Die Transformation des klassischen Seinsverständnisses: Studien zur Vorgeschichte des neuzeitlichen Seinsbegriffs im Mittelalter.* Berlin: de Gruyter, 1986.

Schulz, Walter. *Ich und Welt: Philosophie der Subjektivität.* Pfullingen: Neske, 1979.

————. *Philosophie in der veränderten Welt.* Pfullingen: Neske, 1972.

Schumacher, Bernard. *A Philosophy of Hope: Josef Pieper and the Contemporary Debate on Hope.* Translated by D. C. Schindler. New York: Fordham University Press, 2003.

Schwan, Gesine. "Das zerstörte Tabu. Ohne ein religiöses Fundament und ohne die Sehnsucht nach Wahrheit verrät die Wissenschaft ihre eigenen Ideale und verkommt zum Erfüllungsgehilfen der Wirtschaft." *Süddeutsche Zeitung,* 4 January 2003.

Seckler, Max. "Ein Tübinger Entwurf: Johann Sebastian Drey und die Theologie." In *Im Spannungsfeld von Wissenschaft und Kirche: Theologie als schöpferische Auslegung der Wirklichkeit,* pp. 178-98. Freiburg: Herder, 1980.

———. *Instinkt und Glaubenswille nach Thomas von Aquin.* Mainz: Matthias Grünewald, 1961.

Sedlmayr, Petrus, O.S.B. "Die Lehre des hl. Thomas von den *accidentia sine subjecto remanentia* — untersucht auf ihren Einklang mit der aristotelischen Philosophie," *Divus Thomas* (F) 12 (1934): 315-26.

Seils, Martin. *Der Gedanke vom Zusammenwirken Gottes und des Menschen in Luthers Theologie.* Gütersloh: Gütersloher Verlagshaus Gerd Mohn, 1962.

Senior, John. *The Restoration of Christian Culture.* Norfolk, VA: IHS Press, 2008.

Sesboüé, Bernard, S.J. "Le Surnaturel chez Henri de Lubac." *Recherches de Science Religieuse* 80 (1992): 373-408.

Sherwin, Michael S., O.P. *By Knowledge and By Love: Charity and Knowledge in the Moral Theology of St. Thomas Aquinas.* Washington, DC: The Catholic University of America Press, 2005.

———. "Christ the Teacher in St. Thomas's *Commentary on the Gospel of John.*" In *Reading John with St. Thomas Aquinas: Theological Exegesis and Speculative Theology,* ed. Michael Dauphinais and Matthew Levering, pp. 173-93. Washington, DC: The Catholic University of America Press, 2005.

———. "Infused Virtue and the Effects of Acquired Vice: A Test Case for the Thomistic Theory of Infused Cardinal Virtues." *The Thomist* 73, no. 1 (2009): 29-52.

Siewerth, Gustav: *Der Mensch und sein Leib.* Einsiedeln: Johannes Verlag, 1953.

———. *Das Schicksal der Metaphysik von Thomas zu Heidegger.* Einsiedeln: Johannes Verlag, 1959.

———. *Thomismus als Identitätssystem.* 2nd ed. Frankfurt: Schulte-Bulmke, 1961.

Sokolowski, Robert. *The God of Faith and Reason: Foundations of Christian Theology.* Notre Dame, IN: University of Notre Dame Press, 1982.

Somme, Luc-Thomas, O.P. "La résurrection des passions." *Revue thomiste* 104, no. 4 (2004): 657-66.

Spaemann, Robert. "Ende der Modernität?" In *Philosophische Essays,* pp. 232-60. Stuttgart: Reclam, 1994.

———. *Grenzen: Zur ethischen Dimension des Handelns.* Stuttgart: Klett-Cotta, 2001.

———. "Die kontroverse Natur der Philosophie." In *Philosophische Essays,* pp. 104-29. Stuttgart: Reclam, 1994.

———. *Personen: Versuche über den Unterschied zwischen "etwas" und "jemand."* Stuttgart: Klett-Cotta, 1996.

———. *Philosophische Essays. Erweiterte Ausgabe.* Stuttgart: Reclam, 1994.

Spencer, Archie J. "Causality and the *analogia entis:* Karl Barth's Rejection of the Analogy of Being Reconsidered." *Nova et Vetera* (English) 6, no. 2 (2008): 329-76.

Stallmach, Josef. "Der actus essendi und die Frage nach dem Sinn von 'Sein.'" In *Actus omnium actuum: Festschrift für Heinrich Beck zum 60. Geburtstag,* edited by Erwin Schadel, pp. 47-58. Frankfurt: Lang, 1989.

Stump, Eleonore. *Aquinas.* London: Routledge, 2003.

————. "Intellect, Will, and the Principle of Alternate Possibilities." In *Christian Theism and the Problems of Philosophy,* edited by Michael D. Beaty, pp. 254-85. Notre Dame, IN: University of Notre Dame Press, 1990.

Sweeney, Eileen C. "Restructuring Desire: Aquinas, Hobbes, and Descartes on the Passions." In *Meeting of the Minds: The Relation between Medieval and Classical Modern European Philosophy* (Acts of the International Colloquium held at Boston College June 14-16, 1996, organized by the Société Internationale pour l'Étude de la Philosophie Médiévale), edited by Stephen F. Brown, pp. 215-33. Turnhout: Brepols, 1998.

Sylvester of Ferrara, Francis, O.P. *In Libros S. Thomae de Aquino Contra gentiles commentaria.* In vols. 13-15 of *Sancti Thomae Aquinatis Opera Omnia.* Rome: Leonine Commission, 1928-1930.

Taylor, Charles. *A Secular Age.* Cambridge, MA: The Belknap Press of Harvard University Press, 2007.

te Velde, Rudi. *Aquinas on God: The "Divine Science" of the* Summa Theologiae. Aldershot, U.K., and Burlington, VT: Ashgate, 2006.

————. "Natural Reason in the *Summa contra Gentiles.*" In *Thomas Aquinas: Contemporary Philosophical Perspectives,* edited by Brian Davies, pp. 117-40. Oxford: Oxford University Press, 2002.

————. *Participation and Substantiality in Thomas Aquinas.* Leiden: Brill, 1995.

Thiselton, Anthony C. "Hebrews." In *Eerdmans Commentary on the Bible,* edited by James D. G. Dunn and John W. Rogerson, pp. 1451-82. Grand Rapids: Eerdmans, 2003.

Torrell, Jean-Pierre, O.P. *Aquinas's Summa: Background, Structure, and Reception.* Translated by Benedict M. Guevin, O.S.B. Washington, DC: The Catholic University of America Press, 2005.

————. *Saint Thomas Aquinas.* Vol. 1, *The Person and His Work.* Translated by Robert Royal. Washington, DC: The Catholic University of America Press, 1996.

————. *Saint Thomas Aquinas.* Vol. 2, *Spiritual Master.* Translated by Robert Royal. Washington, DC: The Catholic University of America Press, 2003.

Tschipke, Theophil, O.P. *L'humanité du Christ comme instrument de salut de la divinité.* Translated by Philibert Secrétan. Fribourg: Academic Press, 2003.

————. *Die Menschheit Christi als Heilsorgan der Gottheit unter besonderer Berücksichtigung der Lehre des heiligen Thomas von Aquin.* Freiburg: Herder, 1940.

Ulrich, Ferdinand. *Homo Abyssus: Das Wagnis der Seinsfrage.* 2nd ed. Edited by Martin Bieler and Florian Pitschl. Freiburg: Johannes Verlag, 1998.

Vagaggini, Cyprian, O.S.B. *Theologie der Liturgie.* Translated by August Berz. Zurich/Cologne: Benziger, 1959.

Vonier, Abbot, O.S.B. *A Key to the Doctrine of the Eucharist.* Bethesda: Zacheus Press, 2003-2004.

Wainwright, Geoffrey. "Eschatology." In *The Cambridge Companion to Hans Urs von Balthasar,* edited by Edward T. Oakes and David Moss, pp. 113-27. Cambridge: Cambridge University Press, 2004.

Wawrykow, Joseph P. *God's Grace and Human Action: "Merit" in the Theology of Thomas Aquinas*. Notre Dame, IN: University of Notre Dame Press, 1995.

Weinandy, Thomas G., O.F.M. Cap. *Does God Suffer?* Notre Dame, IN: University of Notre Dame Press, 2000.

Westphal, Merold. "Taking St. Paul Seriously: Sin as an Epistemological Category." In *Christian Philosophy*, edited by Thomas P. Flint, pp. 201-26. Notre Dame, IN: University of Notre Dame Press, 1990.

White, Graham. *Luther as Nominalist: A Study of the Logical Methods Used in Martin Luther's Disputations in the Light of Their Medieval Background*. Helsinki: Luther-Agricola-Society, 1994.

White, Kevin. "The Passions of the Soul (IaIIae, qq. 22-48)." In *The Ethics of Aquinas*, edited by Stephen J. Pope, pp. 103-15. Washington, DC: Georgetown University Press, 2002.

White, Thomas Joseph, O.P., ed. *The Analogy of Being: Invention of the Antichrist or the Wisdom of God*. Grand Rapids: Eerdmans, 2011.

———. "How Barth Got Aquinas Wrong: A Reply to Archie J. Spencer on Causality and Christocentrism." *Nova et Vetera* (English) 7, no. 1 (2009): 241-70.

———. "The 'Pure Nature' of Christology: Human Nature and *Gaudium et Spes* 22." *Nova et Vetera* (English) 8, no. 2 (2010): 283-322.

———. *Wisdom in the Face of Modernity: A Study in Thomistic Natural Theology*. Naples, FL: Sapientia Press, 2009.

Wippel, John F. *The Metaphysical Thought of Thomas Aquinas: From Finite Being to Uncreated Being*. Washington, DC: The Catholic University of America Press, 2000.

———. "Thomas Aquinas and Participation." In *Studies in Medieval Philosophy*, edited by John F. Wippel, pp. 117-58. Washington, DC: The Catholic University of America Press, 1987.

Wittgenstein, Ludwig. *Culture and Value*. Oxford: Blackwell, 1998.

Wood, Rega. "Ockham's Repudiation of Pelagianism." In *The Cambridge Companion to Ockham*, edited by Paul Vincent Spade, pp. 350-74. Cambridge: Cambridge University Press, 1999.

Young, Julian. *Heidegger's Later Philosophy*. Cambridge: Cambridge University Press, 2002.

Zenit.org. "Pope Urges More Eucharistic Adoration." May 7, 2008. http://www.zenit.org./article-22517

Credits

"Is There a Cure for Reason's Presumption and Despair?" — Why Thomas Matters Today

"Aquinas: The Directedness of Reasoning and the Metaphysics of Creation," in *Reason and the Reasons of Faith*, ed. Paul J. Griffiths and Reinhard Hütter (New York/London: T&T Clark International, 2005), 160-193. By kind permission of Continuum International Publishing Group.

"Palaeothomism?" — The Continuing Debate over the Natural Desire for the Vision of God

"*Desiderium Naturale Visionis Dei:* Some Observations about Lawrence Feingold's and John Milbank's Recent Interventions in the Debate over the Natural Desire to See God," in *Nova et Vetera: The English Edition of the International Theological Journal* 5 (2007): 81-131.

"Thomist Ressourcement" — A Rereading of Thomas on the Natural Desire for the Vision of God

"Aquinas on the Natural Desire for the Vision of God: A Relecture of *Summa contra Gentiles* III, c. 25, *après* Henri de Lubac," in *The Thomist* 73 (2009): 523-591.

"Thomas the Augustinian" — Recovering a Surpassing Synthesis of Grace and Free Will

"St. Thomas on Grace and Free Will in the *Initium Fidei:* The Surpassing Augustinian Synthesis," in *Nova et Vetera: The English Edition of the International Theological Journal* 5 (2007): 521-553.

"In Hope He Believed Against Hope" — The Unity of Faith and Hope in Paul, Thomas, and Benedict XVI

"'In hope he believed against hope' (Rom 4:18) — Faith and Hope, Two Pauline Motifs as Interpreted by Aquinas: A *Re-lecture* of Pope Benedict XVI's Encyclical Letter *Spe Salvi*," in *Nova et Vetera: The English Edition of the International Theological Journal* 7 (2009): 839-867.

"A Forgotten Truth?" — Theological Faith, Source and Guarantee of Theology's Inner Unity

"Theological Faith Enlightening Sacred Theology: Renewing Theology by Recovering Its Unity as *sacra doctrina*," in *The Thomist* 74 (2010): 369-405.

"The Wisdom of Analogy Defended" — From Effect to Cause, From Creation to God

"Attending to the Wisdom of God — From Effect to Cause, from Creation to God: A Contemporary *Relecture* of the Doctrine of the Analogy of Being according to Thomas Aquinas," in *The Analogy of Being: Wisdom of God or Invention of the Anti-Christ?*, ed. Thomas Joseph White, O.P. (Grand Rapids: Eerdmans, 2011), 209-245.

"Seeking Truth on Dry Soil and under Thornbushes" — God, the University, and the Missing Link, Wisdom

"God, the University, and the Missing Link — Wisdom: Reflections on Two Untimely Books," in *The Thomist* 73 (2009): 241-277.

"This Is My Body" — Eucharistic Adoration and Metaphysical Contemplation

"Eucharistic Adoration in the Real Personal Presence of Christ: Making Explicit the Mystery of Faith by Way of Metaphysical Contemplation," in *Nova et Vetera: The English Edition of the International Theological Journal* 7 (2009): 175-216.

Index of Names

Index of Subjects

Action, twofold, 278-80
Actus essendi, 60, 272-73, 371-72, 376-77, 381-82
Admiratio, 193n., 218, 221, 225, 233n., 240
Aeterni patris (Leo XIII), 137, 331, 397, 402, 407, 473n.
Affectivity, 9-10, 12, 81-83. *See also* Passions
 irreducible spiritual dimension, 10, 75, 80, 83, 87-88
 reductive accounts of, 9
After Virtue (MacIntyre), 76, 218, 392
Agency, 198-202, 205. *See also* Causality
 divine, 151, 153, 160, 256n., 304, 371
 divine and human as noncompetitive, 14-15, 198, 262
 human, 78, 82-83, 88n., 106, 302
Agent intellect, 48n., 158n., 210, 234, 216, 244
Analogy
 analogia entis, 349, 351n.
 analogical predication, 349-52, 356-58, 369, 373, 376-85
 of attribution, 200n., 351-53, 359, 362, 369, 379-80, 382-83
 of being, 349-51, 384
 Jüngel on, 349-53, 380
 Pannenberg on, 17, 349-51, 380-82, 384

of participation, 369-76
 transcendental, 352-54, 364, 368-69, 371, 373-74
 of two to a third, 375
Analogy and Revelation (Pannenberg), 349
Analytic philosophy, 23, 33-34, 138, 397
Angel, 8, 101, 145, 157-59, 178, 188, 193, 198-99, 201-2, 206, 208, 210-11, 213, 215, 218, 221n., 228-29, 232, 238, 292, 410, 452
Angelism, 9, 75-80, 99-100
Animalism, 9, 75-76, 79-83, 99-100
Apokatastasis, 130, 137, 139, 167, 180-81
Appetite, 52n., 54, 79, 84-85, 90, 201, 205-7. *See also* Will
 intellectual, 55-56, 77, 84-87, 92, 97, 109, 111, 122, 158, 208, 220, 229-30, 233
 irascible, 90, 123, 302
 natural, 84, 121n., 155, 170, 173-74, 178-79, 208, 219-20, 239-40
 orexis, 84
 sense, 76-77, 80-100, 111, 113n., 115, 123, 220, 301-2
Aquinas on God: The "Divine Science" of the Summa Theologiae (te Velde), 21, 195n., 201n., 224n., 352n., 377-78, 383n.

divine, 42, 195, 225, 269, 271, 281, 412
human, 14, 66, 82, 104n., 260, 262,
    270, 285
Luther's account of, 254-55
negative, 103, 105, 120
positive, 104-5
relation to grace, 14, 42, 44, 251, 258,
    261, 395, 412
Friendship, 19, 110, 151, 156, 192-93, 223,
342. *See also* Charity; Eucharist
*From Passions to Emotions: The
Creation of a Secular Psychological
Category* (Dixon), 76n., 78-79

Gaudium et Spes (Paul VI), 126, 387
Gifts of the Holy Spirit, 82, 226
God. *See also* Divine presence; Trinity
    natural desire for the vision of, 13,
        66, 131, 135, 145-48, 156, 164, 166-82,
        186, 188, 223, 225, 227-28, 230, 233,
        236-37, 239n., 244-55, 403
    natural love of, 12-13, 102, 107-10, 116,
        121-26, 134, 147, 154-56, 167-82
God as the Mystery of the World
    (Jüngel), 350-51, 383
*God, Philosophy, and Universities: A
Selective History of the Catholic
Philosophical Tradition* (MacIntyre),
389-93, 407, 415, 419
Good, the. *See Bonum communi;
Bonum universale; Summum bonum*
Grace, 12-15, 43-44, 46, 51, 59, 61-62, 66-
68, 71, 82, 99, 106, 108, 110, 113, 116,
118n., 121-23, 130, 139, 143-51, 154-57,
159-62, 164, 166-74, 176-78, 180-81,
225-26, 231-34, 240, 243, 252-55, 260-
68, 271-82, 286, 289, 293, 295, 303-4,
307, 326-27, 331, 386, 428, 436, 460
cooperative *(gratia cooperans)*, 264,
    278, 280n.
as donum ultimum, 151, 162-63, 182
gratia non tollit sed perficit naturam,
    306
habitual, 272, 274, 276-76, 289
operative *(gratia operans)*, 261, 263-
    64, 272-73, 275, 276, 279-82

perfecting nature, 252, 268, 306
prevenient, 267
relation to free will, 14, 249-51, 255,
    261-62, 282
sanctifying, 291n., 295, 306-7, 316
*Grace and Freedom: Operative Grace in
the Thought of St. Thomas Aquinas*
(Lonergan), 21, 151, 268, 270, 273-76,
279-80

Habits *(habitus)*, 85, 93, 114, 121n., 232,
282. *See also* Virtues
    infused, 15, 177, 210, 272, 274, 276-77,
        287-89, 291-92, 296-99, 304, 315,
        316, 334, 336-37, 340, 344, 418
Hermeneutics, 137, 139-40, 142, 297n.,
319, 321-23, 327, 331, 338, 342, 345, 424-
25, 428-29, 437, 460, 467
Historical-critical method, 139-40, 142,
322, 324-25, 329-30, 439n.
Holy Spirit, 52, 82, 153-55, 162-63, 226,
246, 260n., 271, 280n., 294-95, 307, 311,
314, 321n., 403, 432-36. *See also* Gifts
of the Holy Spirit
Hope, 229-30, 279, 283-86, 292-93, 296-
98, 315-16, 329, 340-41, 343, 392. *See
also* Virtues
    infused, 15, 18, 130, 173, 181, 226-27,
        229, 230-32, 240, 246, 262n., 264,
        286, 292-93, 298-300, 303-12
    ordinary, 300-302, 304-7
Human nature, 8-9, 13-14, 44, 46, 54, 77-
78, 81, 83, 87, 90, 99, 100, 106, 108, 114,
145-49, 197, 302
    Christ's, 83, 149, 159-61, 444, 446
    corruption of, 13, 100, 102, 106-8, 110-
        13, 116-18, 120-26, 131, 150, 230
    end of, 129-32, 145, 151, 153-57, 159,
        163-64, 168-79, 189, 198-99, 215, 239-
        40, 243
    fallen, 12-13, 100, 102, 106-8, 110, 113,
        115-17, 122-26, 130, 149-50, 283
    goods of, 111-18, 157
    homo infirmus, 117-18, 122-24
    homo insipiens, 217
    homo viator, 99

of the hours, 430
philosophical interpretations of, 462-64
univocally understood, 464-66
of the word, 430-31

Magisterium, 6, 130, 142-43, 178, 314, 424-25, 427-28, 460, 463, 466-67
Malo, De (Thomas Aquinas), 47, 49-50, 58-59, 144-50, 155n., 257-59, 270-71, 273-74, 279n., 281-82
Materialism, 9, 310, 414
Merit, 118n., 166, 253, 264, 268n., 272, 279, 297n. *See also* Grace
Metaphysical Thought of Thomas Aquinas, The (Wippel), 23, 44n., 269, 354, 442
Metaphysics, 23-24, 60, 133, 200, 209, 218-19, 314n., 318, 324, 337, 339, 352, 358n., 364-66, 368, 377, 384, 389, 390, 398, 401, 406, 408-10, 414, 425. *See also* First philosophy; Philosophy
of being, 15, 17, 19, 39, 60-62, 65, 67, 136n., 252, 259-60, 268-70, 274-75, 280-82
of creation, 35, 39, 44, 59-65, 67-71
crisis of, 29, 34-38, 137, 323
metaphysical contemplation, 18, 190, 193-94, 222, 240, 423, 436, 438, 440-41, 443, 460
Metaphysics, The (Aristotle), 53n., 354, 358-59, 361n., 363n., 366-67, 411-12
Meta-science. *See* Metaphysics
Methods of Dogmatic Theology, The (Kasper), 317n.
Mystery
of Christ, 19, 126, 141, 242, 271, 345, 424
of Christ's Eucharistic presence, 429, 431, 432, 444, 460, 466-67
of the faith, 161, 425, 460, 466-67
of God, 164-65, 242, 326-30, 350-51, 380
of grace and free will, 250-52, 262, 268-69, 282
of humankind, 126, 242

of the liturgy, 459, 466
metaphysical contemplation of, 425, 438-41, 460
Mystery of the Supernatural, The (de Lubac), 141, 173, 185
Mystical body of Christ, 125, 460. *See also* Catholic Church

Natural Desire to See God According to St. Thomas Aquinas and His Interpreters, The (Feingold), 134-35, 155-58, 168-79, 185
Natural science, 23, 55-56, 80, 338, 390, 392, 396, 399, 407-8, 410, 412, 414-16
Natural theology, 18, 24, 191, 218-20, 240, 336-37, 384n., 399, 401, 403
theologia perennis, 323, 331
Naturalism, 399, 414
Nature. *See also* Human nature
and grace, 12, 143, 155, 180, 182, 240, 404
pondus naturae, 184, 233
and supernature, 12, 15, 58n., 81, 84, 110, 112, 114, 119, 131-32, 135, 138, 142, 144, 147, 151-55, 403, 405, 458, 460
Necessity
necessitas consequentis in distinction from *necessitas consequentiae*, 258-62, 281
Nicomachean Ethics (Aristotle), 201, 221, 223, 303n.
Nominalism, 180, 252-53, 255, 260, 266. *See also Via moderna*
Nouvelle théologie, 132-33, 135, 138, 140, 142, 179, 183

Obediential potency, 132, 156, 176-77, 184, 237
Oikonomia. See Economy of salvation
On Free Will (Augustine, *De libero arbitrio*), 262-63
On Grace and Free Will (Augustine), 263
On the Bondage of the Will (Luther, *De servo arbitrio*), 251n., 254n., 256-58, 260, 263, 266n.